ROGET'S THESAURUS OF SYNONYMS AND ANTONYMS

ROGET'S THESAURUS
OF
SYNONYMS AND ANTONYMS

BY

PETER MARK ROGET, M.D., F.R.S.

ENLARGED BY
JOHN LEWIS ROGET, M.A.
NEW EDITION REVISED AND ENLARGED BY
SAMUEL ROMILLY ROGET, M.A.

GYAN

Published by

Gyan Publishing House
5, Ansari Road
Daryaganj, New Delhi-110002
Phone: 011-47034999, 9811692060
E-mail: books@gyanbooks.com

Distribution Network
gyanbooks.com
India, USA, Canada, UK, Australia, France

ISBN : 978-81-212-2121-4 (HB)
First Published, 1852

2nd Impression 2021

Printed at: Gyan Press, Delhi.

Roget's Thesaurus of Synonyms and Antonyms
Author: Peter Mark Roget

ROGET'S THESAURUS

OF SYNONYMS AND ANTONYMS

BY

PETER MARK ROGET, M.D., F.R.S.

ENLARGED BY

JOHN LEWIS ROGET, M.A.

NEW EDITION REVISED AND ENLARGED BY

SAMUEL ROMILLY ROGET, M.A.

PLAN OF CLASSIFICATION

Class	Section	Nos.
I. ABSTRACT RELATIONS	I. Existence	1 to 8
	II. Relation	9— 24
	III. Quantity	25— 57
	IV. Order	58— 83
	V. Number	84— 105
	VI. Time	106— 139
	VII. Change	140— 152
	VIII. Causation	153— 179
II. SPACE	I. Generally	180— 191
	II. Dimensions	192— 239
	III. Form	240— 263
	IV. Motion	264— 315
III. MATTER	I. Generally	316— 320
	II. Inorganic	321— 356
	III. Organic	357— 449
	Division	
IV. INTELLECT	(I.) Formation of Ideas	450— 515
	(II.) Communication of Ideas	516— 599
V. VOLITION	(I.) Individual	600— 736
	(II.) Intersocial	737— 819
	Section	
VI. AFFECTIONS	I. Generally	820— 826
	II. Personal	827— 887
	III. Sympathetic	888— 921
	IV. Moral	922— 975
	V. Religious	976—1000

TABULAR SYNOPSIS OF CATEGORIES

Class I. ABSTRACT RELATIONS

I. EXISTENCE

1°. Abstract	1. Existence.	2. Inexistence.
2°. Concrete	3. Substantiality.	4. Unsubstantiality.
3°. Formal	*Internal.*	*External.*
	5. Intrinsicality.	6. Extrinsicality.
4°. Modal	*Absolute.*	*Relative.*
	7. State.	8. Circumstance.

II. RELATION

1°. Absolute	9. Relation.	10. Irrelation.
	11. Consanguinity.	
	12. Correlation.	
	13. Identity.	14. Contrariety.
	15. Difference.	
2°. Continuous	16. Uniformity.	16*a*. Non-uniformity.
3°. Partial	17. Similarity.	18. Dissimilarity.
	19. Imitation.	20. Non-imitation.
	20*a*. Variation.	
	21. Copy.	22. Prototype.
4°. General	23. Agreement.	24. Disagreement.

III. QUANTITY

1°. Simple	*Absolute.*	*Relative.*
	25. Quantity.	26. Degree.
2°. Comparative	27. Equality.	28. Inequality.
	29. Mean.	
	30. Compensation.	
	By Comparison with a Standard.	
	31. Greatness.	32. Smallness.
	By Comparison with a similar Object.	
	33. Superiority.	34. Inferiority.
	Changes in Quantity.	
	35. Increase.	36. Decrease.
3°. Conjunctive	37. Addition.	38. Non-addition. Subduction.
	39. Adjunct.	40. Remainder.
		40*a*. Decrement.
	41. Mixture.	42. Simpleness.
	43. Junction.	44. Disjunction.
	45. Vinculum.	
	46. Coherence.	47. Incoherence.
	48. Combination.	49. Decomposition.

SYNOPSIS OF CATEGORIES

4°. CONCRETE	50. Whole.	51. Part.
	52. Completeness.	53. Incompleteness.
	54. Composition.	55. Exclusion.
	56. Component.	57. Extraneous.
IV. ORDER		
1°. GENERAL	58. Order.	59. Disorder.
	60. Arrangement.	61. Derangement.
2°. CONSECUTIVE	62. Precedence.	63. Sequence.
	64. Precursor.	65. Sequel.
	66. Beginning.	67. End.
	68. Middle.	
	69. Continuity.	70. Discontinuity.
	71. Term.	
3°. COLLECTIVE	72. Assemblage.	73. Non-assemblage. Dispersion.
	74. Focus.	
4°. DISTRIBUTIVE	75. Class.	
	76. Inclusion.	77. Exclusion.
	78. Generality.	79. Speciality.
5°. CATEGORICAL	80. Rule.	81. Multiformity.
	82. Conformity.	83. Unconformity.
V. NUMBER		
1°. ABSTRACT	84. Number.	
	85. Numeration.	
	86. List.	
2°. DETERMINATE	87. Unity.	88. Accompaniment.
	89. Duality.	
	90. Duplication.	91. Bisection.
	92. Triality.	
	93. Triplication.	96. Trisection.
	94. Quadruplication.	
	95. Quaternity.	97. Quadrisection.
	98. Five, &c.	99. Quinquesection, &c.
3°. INDETERMINATE	100. Plurality.	100*a*. Fraction.
		101. Zero.
	102. Multitude.	103. Fewness.
	104. Repetition.	
	105. Infinity.	
VI. TIME		
1°. ABSOLUTE	106. Time.	107. Neverness.
	Definite.	*Indefinite.*
	108. Period.	109. Course.
	108*a*. Contingent Duration.	
	110. Diuturnity.	111. Transientness.
	112. Perpetuity.	113. Instantaneity.
	114. Chronometry.	115. Anachronism.
2°. RELATIVE — 1. *to Succession*	116. Priority.	117. Posteriority.
	118. Present time.	119. Different time.
	120. Synchronism.	
	121. Futurity.	122. Preterition.
2°. RELATIVE — 2. *to a Period*	123. Newness.	124. Oldness.
	125. Morning.	126. Evening.
	127. Youth.	128. Age.
	129. Infant.	130. Veteran.
	131. Adolescence.	
2°. RELATIVE — 3. *to an Effect or purpose*	132. Earliness.	133. Lateness.
	134. Occasion.	135. Intempestivity.
3°. RECURRENT	136. Frequency.	137. Infrequency.
	138. Periodicity.	139. Irregularity.

SYNOPSIS OF CATEGORIES

VII. CHANGE

1°. SIMPLE	140. Change.	141. Permanence.
	142. Cessation.	143. Continuance.
	144. Conversion.	145. Reversion.
	146. Revolution.	
	147. Substitution.	148. Interchange.
2°. COMPLEX	149. Changeableness.	150. Stability.
	Present.	*Future.*
	151. Eventuality.	152. Destiny.

VIII. CAUSATION

1°. CONSTANCY OF SEQUENCE	153. { *Constant Antecedent.* Cause.	154. { *Constant Sequent.* Effect.
	155. { *Assignment of Cause.* Attribution.	156. { *Absence of Assignment.* Chance.
2°. CONNECTION BETWEEN CAUSE AND EFFECT	157. Power.	158. Impotence.
	Degrees of Power.	
	159. Strength.	160. Weakness.
3°. POWER IN OPERATION	161. Production.	162. Destruction.
	163. Reproduction.	
	164. Producer.	165. Destroyer.
	166. Paternity.	167. Posterity.
	168. Productiveness.	169. Unproductiveness.
	170. Agency.	
	171. Energy.	172. Inertness.
	173. Violence.	174. Moderation.
4°. INDIRECT POWER	175. Influence.	175*a*. Absence of Influence.
	176. Tendency.	
	177. Liability.	
5°. COMBINATIONS OF CAUSES	178. Concurrence.	179. Counteraction.

CLASS II. SPACE

I. SPACE IN GENERAL

1°. ABSTRACT SPACE		180*a*. Inextension.
	180. { *Indefinite.* Space.	181. { *Definite.* Region.
		182. { *Limited.* Place.
2°. RELATIVE SPACE	183. Situation.	
	184. Location.	185. Displacement.
3°. EXISTENCE IN SPACE	186. Presence.	187. Absence.
	188. Inhabitant.	189. Abode.
	190. Contents.	191. Receptacle.

II. DIMENSIONS

1°. GENERAL	192. Size.	193. Littleness.
	194. Expansion.	195. Contraction.
	196. Distance.	197. Nearness.
	198. Interval.	199. Contiguity.
2°. LINEAR	200. Length.	201. Shortness.
	202. { Breadth. Thickness.	203. { Narrowness. Thinness.
	204. Layer.	205. Filament.
	206. Height.	207. Lowness.
	208. Depth.	209. Shallowness.

SYNOPSIS OF CATEGORIES

	2°. LINEAR—*continued*	210. Summit.	211. Base.
		212. Verticality.	213. Horizontality.
		214. Pendency.	215. Support.
		216. Parallelism.	217. Obliquity.
		218. Inversion.	
		219. Crossing.	
3°. CENTRICAL	1. *General*	220. Exteriority.	221. Interiority.
		222. Centrality.	
		223. Covering.	224. Lining.
		225. Investment.	226. Divestment.
		227. Circumjacence.	228. Interjacence.
		229. Circumscription.	
		230. Outline.	
		231. Edge.	
		232. Inclosure.	
		233. Limit.	
	2. *Special*	234. Front	235. Rear.
		236. Laterality.	237. Contraposition.
		238. Dextrality.	239. Sinistrality.

III. FORM

1°. GENERAL	240. Form.	241. Amorphism.
	242. Symmetry.	243. Distortion.
2°. SPECIAL	244. Angularity.	
	245. Curvature.	246. Straightness.
	247. Circularity.	248. Convolution.
	249. Rotundity.	
3°. SUPERFICIAL	250. Convexity.	252. Concavity.
	251. Flatness.	
	253. Sharpness.	254. Bluntness.
	255. Smoothness.	256. Roughness.
	257. Notch.	
	258. Fold.	
	259. Furrow.	
	260. Opening.	261. Closure.
	262. Perforator.	263. Stopper.

IV. MOTION

1°. MOTION IN GENERAL	264. Motion.	265. Quiescence.
	266. Journey.	267. Navigation.
	268. Traveler.	269. Mariner.
	270. Transference.	
	271. Carrier.	
	272. Vehicle.	273. Ship.
2°. DEGREES OF MOTION	274. Velocity.	275. Slowness.
3°. CONJOINED WITH FORCE	276. Impulse.	277. Recoil.
4°. WITH REFERENCE TO DIRECTION	278. Direction.	279. Deviation.
	280. Precession.	281. Sequence.
	282. Progression.	283. Regression.
	284. Propulsion.	285. Traction.
	286. Approach.	287. Recession.
	288. Attraction.	289. Repulsion.
	290. Convergence.	291. Divergence.
	292. Arrival.	293. Departure.
	294. Ingress.	295. Egress.
	296. Reception.	297. Ejection.
	298. Food.	299. Excretion.
	300. Insertion.	301. Extraction.
	302. Passage.	
	303. Overstep.	304. Shortcoming.

4°. WITH REFERENCE TO DIRECTION—*cont.*...		305. Ascent.	306. Descent.
		307. Elevation.	308. Depression.
		309. Leap.	310. Plunge.
		311. Circuition.	
		312. Rotation.	313. Evolution.
		314. Oscillation.	
		315. Agitation.	

CLASS III. MATTER

I. MATTER IN GENERAL

I. MATTER IN GENERAL.......		316. Materiality.	317. Immateriality.
		318. World.	
		319. Gravity.	320. Levity.

II. INORGANIC MATTER

1°. SOLIDS.............		321. Density.	322. Rarity.
		323. Hardness.	324. Softness.
		325. Elasticity.	326. Inelasticity.
		327. Tenacity.	328. Brittleness.
		329. Texture.	
		330. Pulverulence.	
		331. Friction.	332. Lubrication.
2°. FLUIDS	1. *In General*	333. Fluidity.	334. Gaseity.
		335. Liquefaction.	336. Vaporization.
	2. *Specific*...	337. Water.	338. Air.
		339. Moisture.	340. Dryness.
		341. Ocean.	342. Land.
		343. Gulf. Lake.	344. Plain.
		345. Marsh.	346. Island.
	3. *In motion*	347. Stream.	
		348. River.	349. Wind.
		350. Conduit.	351. Air-pipe.
3°. IMPERFECT FLUIDS...		352. Semiliquidity.	353. Bubble.
		354. Pulpiness.	355. Unctuousness.
			356. Oil.
			356*a*. Resin.

III. ORGANIC MATTER

1°. VITALITY	1. *In General*....	357. Organization.	358. Inorganization.
		359. Life.	360. Death.
			361. Killing.
			362. Corpse.
			363. Interment.
	2. *Special*	364. Animality.	365. Vegetability.
		366. Animal.	367. Vegetable.
		368. Zoology.	369. Botany.
		370. Cicuration.	371. Agriculture.
		372. Mankind.	
		373. Man.	374. Woman.

SYNOPSIS OF CATEGORIES

2°. Sensation

- (1) *General* ....
  - 375. Sensibility. — 376. Insensibility.
  - 377. Pleasure. — 378. Pain.
- (2) *Special*
  - 1. *Touch* ..
    - 379. Touch.
    - 380. Sensations of Touch. — 381. Numbness.
  - 2. *Heat* ...
    - 382. Heat. — 383. Cold.
    - 384. Calefaction. — 385. Refrigeration.
    - 386. Furnace. — 387. Refrigeratory.
    - 388. Fuel.
    - 389. Thermometer.
  - 3. *Taste* ...
    - 390. Taste. — 391. Insipidity.
    - 392. Pungency.
    - 393. Condiment.
    - 394. Savouriness. — 395. Unsavouriness.
    - 396. Sweetness. — 397. Sourness.
  - 4. *Odor* ..
    - 398. Odor. — 399. Inodorousness.
    - 400. Fragrance. — 401. Fœtor.
  - 5. *Sound* ..
    - (i.) *Sound in General.*
      - 402. Sound. — 403. Silence.
      - 404. Loudness. — 405. Faintness.
    - (ii.) *Specific Sounds.*
      - 406. Snap. — 407. Roll.
      - 408. Resonance. — 408*a*. Non-resonance.
      - 409. Sibilation.
      - 410. Stridor.
      - 411. Cry. — 412. Ululation.
    - (iii.) *Musical Sounds.*
      - 413. Melody. Concord. — 414. Discord.
      - 415. Music.
      - 416. Musician.
      - 417. Musical Instruments.
    - (iv.) *Perception of Sound.*
      - 418. Hearing. — 419. Deafness.
  - 6. *Light* ...
    - (i.) *Light in General.*
      - 420. Light. — 421. Darkness.
      - 422. Dimness.
      - 423. Luminary. — 424. Shade.
      - 425. Transparency. — 426. Opacity.
      - 427. Semitransparency.
    - (ii.) *Specific Light.*
      - 428. Color. — 429. Achromatism.
      - 430. Whiteness. — 431. Blackness.
      - 432. Gray. — 433. Brown.
      - 434. Redness. — 435. Greenness.
      - 436. Yellowness. — 437. Purple.
      - 438. Blueness. — 439. Orange.
      - 440. Variegation.
    - (iii.) *Perceptions of Light.*
      - 441. Vision. — 442. Blindness.
      - 443. Dimsightedness.
      - 444. Spectator.
      - 445. Optical Instruments.
      - 446. Visibility. — 447. Invisibility.
      - 448. Appearance. — 449. Disappearance.

SYNOPSIS OF CATEGORIES

CLASS IV. INTELLECT

Division (I.). FORMATION OF IDEAS

I. OPERATIONS OF INTELLECT IN GENERAL	450. Intellect.	450*a*. Absence of Intellect.
	451. Thought.	452. Incogitancy.
	453. Idea.	454. Topic.
II. PRECURSORY CONDITIONS AND OPERATIONS	455. Curiosity.	456. Incuriosity.
	457. Attention.	458. Inattention.
	459. Care.	460. Neglect.
	461. Inquiry.	462. Answer.
	463. Experiment.	
	464. Comparison.	
	465. Discrimination.	465*a*. Indiscrimination.
	466. Measurement.	
III. MATERIALS FOR REASONING	467. Evidence.	468. Counter-evidence.
	469. Qualification.	
	Degrees of Evidence.	
	470. Possibility.	471. Impossibility.
	472. Probability.	473. Improbability.
	474. Certainty.	475. Uncertainty.
IV. REASONING PROCESSES	476. Reasoning.	477. Intuition. Sophistry.
	478. Demonstration.	479. Confutation.
V. RESULTS OF REASONING	480. Judgement.	481. Misjudgement.
	480*a*. Discovery.	
	482. Over-estimation.	483. Under-estimation.
	484. Belief.	485. Unbelief. Doubt.
	486. Credulity.	487. Incredulity.
	488. Assent.	489. Dissent.
	490. Knowledge.	491. Ignorance.
	492. Scholar.	493. Ignoramus.
	494. Truth.	495. Error.
	496. Maxim.	497. Absurdity.
	Faculties.	
	498. Intelligence. Wisdom.	499. Imbecility. Folly.
	500. Sage.	501. Fool.
	502. Sanity.	503. Insanity.
		504. Madman.
VI. EXTENSION OF THOUGHT — 1°. *To the Past*	505. Memory.	506. Oblivion.
VI. EXTENSION OF THOUGHT — 2°. *To the Future*	507. Expectation.	508. Inexpectation.
		509. Disappointment.
	510. Foresight.	
	511. Prediction.	
	512. Omen.	
	513. Oracle.	
VII. CREATIVE THOUGHT	514. Supposition.	
	515. Imagination.	

SYNOPSIS OF CATEGORIES

Division (II.). Communication of Ideas

I. Nature of Ideas Communicated

516. Meaning.	517. Unmeaningness.
518. Intelligibility.	519. Unintelligibility.
520. Equivocalness.	
521. Metaphor.	
522. Interpretation.	523. Misinterpretation.
524. Interpreter.	

II. Modes of Communication

525. Manifestation.	526. Latency.
527. Information.	528. Concealment.
529. Disclosure.	530. Ambush.
531. Publication.	
532. News.	533. Secret.
534. Messenger.	
535. Affirmation.	536. Negation.
537. Teaching.	538. Misteaching. 539. Learning.
540. Teacher.	541. Learner.
542. School.	
543. Veracity.	544. Falsehood.
	545. Deception.
	546. Untruth.
547. Dupe.	548. Deceiver.
	549. Exaggeration.

III. Means of Communication

1°. Natural Means

550. Indication.	
551. Record.	552. Obliteration.
553. Recorder.	
554. Representation.	555. Misrepresentation.
556. Painting.	
557. Sculpture.	
558. Engraving.	
559. Artist.	

2°. Conventional Means

1. Language generally

560. Language.	
561. Letter.	
562. Word.	563. Neology.
564. Nomenclature.	565. Misnomer.
566. Phrase.	
567. Grammar.	568. Solecism.
569. Style.	

Qualities of Style.

570. Perspicuity.	571. Obscurity.
572. Conciseness.	573. Diffuseness.
574. Vigour.	575. Feebleness.
576. Plainness.	577. Ornament.
578. Elegance.	579. Inelegance.

2. Spoken Language

580. Voice.	581. Aphony.
582. Speech.	583. Stammering.
584. Loquacity.	585. Taciturnity.
586. Allocution.	587. Response.
588. Interlocution.	589. Soliloquy.

3. Written Language

590. Writing.	591. Printing.
592. Correspondence.	593. Book.
594. Description.	
595. Dissertation.	
596. Compendium.	
597. Poetry.	598. Prose.
599. The Drama.	

SYNOPSIS OF CATEGORIES

CLASS V. VOLITION

Division (I.). INDIVIDUAL VOLITION

I. VOLITION IN GENERAL	1°. *Acts*	600. Will.	601. Necessity.
		602. Willingness.	603. Unwillingness.
		604. Resolution.	605. Irresolution.
		604a. Perseverance. 606. Obstinacy.	607. Tergiversation.
			608. Caprice.
		609. Choice.	609a. Absence of Choice. 610. Rejection.
		611. Predetermination.	612. Impulse.
		613. Habit.	614. Desuetude.
	2°. *Causes*	615. Motive.	615a. Absence of Motive. 616. Dissuasion.
		617. Plea.	
	3°. *Objects*	618. Good.	619. Evil.
II. PROSPECTIVE VOLITION	1°. *Conceptional*	620. Intention.	621. Chance.
		622. Pursuit.	623. Avoidance.
			624. Relinquishment.
		625. Business.	
		626. Plan.	
		627. Method.	
		628. Mid-Course.	629. Circuit.
		630. Requirement.	
	2°. *Subservience to Ends*	1. *Actual Subservience.*	
		631. Instrumentality.	
		632. Means.	
		633. Instrument.	
		634. Substitute.	
		635. Materials.	
		636. Store.	
		637. Provision.	638. Waste.
		639. Sufficiency.	
		641. Redundance.	640. Insufficiency.
		2. *Degree of Subservience.*	
		642. Importance.	643. Unimportance.
		644. Utility.	645. Inutility.
		646. Expedience.	647. Inexpedience.
		648. Goodness.	649. Badness.
		650. Perfection.	651. Imperfection.
		652. Cleanness.	653. Uncleanness.
		654. Health.	655. Disease.
		656. Salubrity.	657. Insalubrity.
		658. Improvement.	659. Deterioration.
		660. Restoration.	661. Relapse.
		662. Remedy.	663. Bane.
		3. *Contingent Subservience.*	
		664. Safety.	665. Danger.
		666. Refuge.	667. Pitfall.
		668. Warning.	
		669. Alarm.	
		670. Preservation.	
		671. Escape.	
		672. Deliverance.	

SYNOPSIS OF CATEGORIES

II. PROSPECTIVE VOLITION—*cont.*	3°. *Precursory Measures*	673. Preparation.	674. Non-preparation.
		675. Essay.	
		676. Undertaking.	
		677. Use.	678. Disuse. 679. Misuse.
III. ACTION	1°. *Simple*	680. Action.	681. Inaction.
		682. Activity.	683. Inactivity.
		684. Haste.	685. Leisure.
		686. Exertion.	687. Repose.
		688. Fatigue.	689. Refreshment.
		690. Agent.	
		691. Workshop.	
	2°. *Complex*	692. Conduct.	
		693. Direction.	
		694. Director.	
		695. Advice.	
		696. Council.	
		697. Precept.	
		698. Skill.	699. Unskilfulness.
		700. Proficient.	701. Bungler.
		702. Cunning.	703. Artlessness.
IV. ANTAGONISM	1°. *Conditional*	704. Difficulty.	705. Facility.
	2°. *Active*	706. Hindrance.	707. Aid.
		708. Opposition.	709. Co-operation.
		710. Opponent.	711. Auxiliary.
		712. Party.	
		713. Discord.	714. Concord.
		715. Defiance.	
		716. Attack.	717. Defence.
		718. Retaliation.	719. Resistance.
		720. Contention.	721. Peace.
		722. Warfare.	723. Pacification.
		724. Meditation.	
		725. Submission.	
		726. Combatant.	
		727. Arms.	
		728. Arena.	
V. RESULTS OF ACTION		729. Completion.	730. Non-completion.
		731. Success.	732. Failure.
		733. Trophy.	
		734. Prosperity.	735. Adversity.
		736. Mediocrity.	

Division (II.). INTERSOCIAL VOLITION

I. GENERAL	737. Authority.	738. Laxity.
	739. Severity.	740. Lenity.
	741. Command.	
	742. Disobedience.	743. Obedience.
	744. Compulsion.	
	745. Master.	746. Servant.
	747. Sceptre.	
	748. Freedom.	749. Subjection.
	750. Liberation.	751. Restraint.
		752. Prison.
	753. Keeper.	754. Prisoner.
	755. Commission.	756. Abrogation.
		757. Resignation.
	758. Consignee.	
	759. Deputy.	

II. Special	760. Permission.	761. Prohibition.
	762. Consent.	
	763. Offer.	764. Refusal.
	765. Request.	766. Depreciation.
	767. Petitioner.	
III. Conditional	768. Promise.	768*a*. Release.
	769. Compact.	
	770. Conditions.	
	771. Security.	
	772. Observance.	773. Non-observance.
	774. Compromise.	
IV. Possessive Relations		
1°. *Property in General*	775. Acquisition.	776. Loss.
	777. Possession.	777*a*. Exemption.
	778. Participation.	
	779. Possessor.	
	780. Property.	
	781. Retention.	782. Relinquishment.
2°. *Transfer of Property*	783. Transfer.	
	784. Giving.	785. Receiving.
	786. Apportionment.	
	787. Lending.	788. Borrowing.
	789. Taking.	790. Restitution.
	791. Stealing.	
	792. Thief.	
	793. Booty.	
3°. *Interchange of Property*	794. Barter.	
	795. Purchase.	796. Sale.
	797. Merchant.	
	798. Merchandise.	
	799. Mart.	
4°. *Monetary Relations*	800. Money.	
	801. Treasurer.	
	802. Treasury.	
	803. Wealth.	804. Poverty.
	805. Credit.	806. Debt.
	807. Payment.	808. Non-payment.
	809. Expenditure.	810. Receipt.
	811. Accounts.	
	812. Price.	813. Discount.
	814. Dearness.	815. Cheapness.
	816. Liberality.	817. Economy.
	818. Prodigality.	819. Parsimony.

Class VI. AFFECTIONS

I. AFFECTIONS GENERALLY	820. Affections.	
	821. Feeling.	
	822. Sensibility.	823. Insensibility.
	824. Excitation.	
	825. Excitability.	826. Inexcitability.

SYNOPSIS OF CATEGORIES

II. PERSONAL

1°. PASSIVE	827. Pleasure.	828. Pain.
	829. Pleasureableness.	830. Painfulness.
	831. Content.	832. Discontent. 833. Regret.
	834. Relief.	835. Aggravation.
	836. Cheerfulness.	837. Dejection.
	838. Rejoicing.	839. Lamentation.
	840. Amusement.	841. Weariness.
	842. Wit.	843. Dulness.
	844. Humorist.	
2°. DISCRIMINATIVE	845. Beauty.	846. Ugliness.
	847. Ornament.	848. Blemish.
		849. Simplicity.
	850. Taste.	851. Vulgarity.
	852. Fashion.	
		853. Ridiculousness.
		854. Fop.
		855. Affection.
		856. Ridicule.
		857. Laughing-stock.
3°. PROSPECTIVE	858. Hope.	859. Hopelessness. 860. Fear.
	861. Courage.	862. Cowardice.
	863. Rashness.	864. Caution.
	865. Desire.	867. Dislike.
	866. Indifference.	
		868. Fastidiousness.
		869. Satiety.
4°. CONTEMPLATIVE	870. Wonder.	871. Expectance.
	872. Prodigy.	
5°. EXTRINSIC	873. Repute.	874. Disrepute.
	875. Nobility.	876. Commonalty.
	877. Title.	
	878. Pride.	879. Humility.
	880. Vanity.	881. Modesty.
	882. Ostentation.	
	883. Celebration.	
	884. Boasting.	
	885. Insolence.	886. Servility.
	887. Blusterer.	

III. SYMPATHETIC

1°. SOCIAL	888. Friendship.	889. Enmity.
	890. Friend.	891. Enemy.
	892. Sociality.	893. Seclusion.
	894. Courtesy.	895. Discourtesy.
	896. Congratulation.	
	897. Love.	898. Hate.
	899. Favorite.	
		900. Resentment.
		901. Irascibility.
		901*a*. Sullenness.
	902. Endearment.	
	903. Marriage.	904. Celibacy. 905. Divorce.

2°. DIFFUSIVE	906. Benevolence.	907. Malevolence.
		908. Malediction.
		909. Threat.
	910. Philanthropy.	911. Misanthropy.
	912. Benefactor.	913. Evil doer.
3°. SPECIAL	914. Pity.	914*a*. Pitilessness.
	915. Condolence.	
4°. RETROSPECTIVE	916. Gratitude.	917. Ingratitude.
	918. Forgiveness.	919. Revenge.
		920. Jealousy.
		921. Envy.
IV. MORAL		
1°. OBLIGATIONS	922. Right.	923. Wrong.
	924. Dueness.	925. Undueness.
	926. Duty.	927. Dereliction.
		927*a*. Exemption.
2°. SENTIMENTS	928. Respect.	929. Disrespect.
		930. Contempt.
	931. Approbation.	932. Disapprobation.
	933. Flattery.	934. Detraction.
	935. Flatterer.	936. Detractor.
	937. Vindication.	938. Accusation.
3°. CONDITIONS	939. Probity.	940. Improbity.
		941. Knave.
	942. Disinterestedness.	943. Selfishness.
	944. Virtue.	945. Vice.
	946. Innocence.	947. Guilt.
	948. Good Man.	949. Bad Man.
	950. Penitence.	951. Impenitence.
	952. Atonement.	
4°. PRACTICE	953. Temperance.	954. Intemperance.
		954*a*. Sensualist.
	955. Asceticism.	
	956. Fasting.	957. Gluttony.
	958. Sobriety.	959. Drunkenness.
	960. Purity.	961. Impurity.
		962. Libertine.
5°. INSTITUTIONS	963. Legality.	964. Illegality.
	965. Jurisprudence.	
	966. Tribunal.	
	967. Judge.	
	968. Lawyer.	
	969. Lawsuit.	
	970. Acquittal.	971. Condemnation.
	973. Reward.	972. Punishment.
		974. Penalty.
		975. Scourge.
V. RELIGIOUS		
1°. SUPERHUMAN BEINGS AND REGIONS	976. Deity.	
	977. Angel.	978. Satan.
	979. Jupiter.	980. Demon.
	981. Heaven.	982. Hell.
2°. DOCTRINES	983. Theology.	
	983*a*. Orthodoxy.	984. Heterodoxy.
	985. Revelation.	986. Pseudo-revelation.
3°. SENTIMENTS	987. Piety.	988. Impiety.
		989. Irreligion.

SYNOPSIS OF CATEGORIES

4°. ACTS	990. Worship.	991. Idolatry 992. Sorcery. 993. Spell. 994. Sorcerer.
5°. INSTITUTIONS	995. Churchdom. 996. Clergy. 998. Rite. 999. Canonicals. 1000. Temple.	997. Laity.

ABBREVIATIONS, &c.

Adj.	*adj.*	Adjectives, Participles, and Words having the power of Adjectives.
Adv.	*adv.*	Adverbs and Adverbial Expressions.
Int.	*int.*	Interjections.
Phr.	*phr.*	Phrases.
V.	*v.*	Verbs.

The numbers are those of the headings, or Categories.

Words in italics within parentheses are not intended to explain the meanings of the words which precede them, but to indicate the nature of allied group of words under the numbers which follow them.

THESAURUS

OF

ENGLISH WORDS AND PHRASES

1. Existence.—N. existence, being, entity, *ens, esse,* subsistence, quiddity.

reality, realness, actuality; positiveness etc. *adj.*; fact, matter of fact, sober reality; truth etc. 494; actual existence.

presence etc. (*existence in space*) 186; coexistence etc. 120.

stubborn fact; not a -dream etc. 515; no joke.

substance, essence, prime constituent, hypostatis.

[Science of existence], ontology.

V. exist, be; have -being etc. *n.*; subsist, live, breathe, stand, obtain, be the case; occur etc. (*event*) 151; have place, rank, prevail; find oneself, pass the time, vegetate.

consist in, lie in, reside in, inhere in.

come into -existence etc. *n.*; arise etc. (*begin*) 66; come forth etc. (*appear*) 446.

become etc. (*be converted*) 144; bring into existence etc. 161; coexist, preexist, endure etc. 141.

Adj. existing etc. *v.*; existent, subsistent, under the sun; in -existence etc. *n.*; extant; afloat, on foot, current, prevalent, rife, in force, -vogue; undestroyed.

real, actual, positive, absolute; true etc. 494; substan-tial, -tive; self-existing, -ent.

well-founded, -grounded; un-ideal, -imagined; not -potential etc. 2.

Adv. actually etc. *adj.*; in -fact, – point of fact, – reality; indeed; *de* –, *ipso-facto.*

2. Nonexistence.—N. nonexistence; inexistence, -subsistence; nonentity, *nil*; negativeness etc. *adj.*; nullity; nihil-ity, -ism; *tabula rasa,* blank; abeyance; absence etc. 187; no such thing etc. 4; nothingness, oblivion, *non esse.*

annihilation; extinction etc. (*destruction*) 162.

V. not -exist etc. 1; have no -existence etc. 1; be null and void; cease to -exist etc. 1; pass away, perish; be –, become-extinct etc. *adj.*; die out; disappear etc. 449; melt away, dissolve, leave not a rack behind, leave no trace; go, be no more; die etc. 360.

annihilate, render null, nullify; abrogate etc. 756; destroy etc. 162; take away; remove etc. (*displace*) 185.

Adj. inexistent, non-existent etc. 1; negative, blank, null and void; missing, omitted; absent etc. 187; visionary etc. 515.

unreal, potential, virtual; baseless, *in nubibus*; unsubstantial etc. 4; vain.

un-born, -created, -begotten, -conceived, produced, -made.

perished, annihilated etc. *v.*; extinct, exhausted, gone, lost, departed; defunct etc. (*dead*) 360;

fabulous, ideal etc. (*imaginary*) 515; suppostitious etc. 514.

Adv. negatively, virtually, etc. *adj.*

3. Substantiality.—N. substantiality, *hypostasis*; person, thing, object, article; something, a being, an existence; creature, body, substance, flesh and blood, stuff, *substratum*; matter etc. 316; physical nature.

[Totality of existences], world etc. 318; *plenum.*

Adj. substan-tive, -tial, concrete; hypostatic; personal, bodily; tangible etc. (*material*) 316; real, corporeal, evident.

Adv. substantially etc. *adj.*; bodily, essentially.

4. Unsubstantiality.—N. un-, in-substantiality; nothingness, nihility.

nothing, naught, *nil*, nullity, zero, cipher, no one, nobody; never –, ne'er -a one; no such thing, none in the world; nothing -whatever, – at all, – on earth; not a -particle etc. (*smallness*) 32; all - talk, – moonshine, – stuff and nonsense, matter of no import.

thing of naught, man of straw, John Doe and Richard Roe; *nominis umbra,* nonentity, figurehead, lay figure; flash in the pan, *vox et praeterea nihil.*

shadow; phantasm, phantom etc. (*fallacy of vision*) 443; dream etc. (*imagination*) 515; *ignis fatuus* etc. (*luminary*) 423; 'such stuff as dreams are made of;' air, thin air; bubble etc. 353; 'baseless fabric of a vision;' mockery.

hollowness, blank; vacuity, void etc. (*absence*) 187.

inanity, fool's paradise, fatuity, stupidity, emptiness of mind.

V. vanish, evaporate, fade, sink, fly –, die –, melt- away, dissolve, disappear etc. 449; become extinct, become invisible.

Adj. unsubstantial; fleeting; base-, ground-less; ungrounded; without –, having no- foundation.

visionary etc. (*imaginary*) 515; immaterial etc. 317; spectral etc. 980; dreamy; shadowy; ethereal, airy, imponderable, tenuous, vague.

vacant, vacuous; empty etc. 187; eviscerated; blank, hollow; nominal; null; inane.

Phr. there's nothing in it.

5. Intrinsicality.—**N.** intrinsicality, inbeing, inherence, inhesion, immanence; subjectiveness; *ego*; essence; essentialness etc. *adj.*; essential part, essential stuff, substance, quintessence, incarnation, quiddity, gist, pith, core, kernel, marrow, sap, lifeblood, backbone, heart, soul, life, flower; important part etc. (*importance*) 642.
principle, nature, constitution, character, ethos, type, quality, crasis, *diathesis*.
habit; temper, -ament; spirit, humor, grain, disposition, streak, tendency etc. 176.
endowment, capacity; capability etc. (*power*) 157; moods, declensions, features, aspects; peculiarities etc. (*specialty*) 79; idiosyncrasy; idiocrasy; diagnostics.
V. be –, run- in the blood; be born so; be - intrinsic etc. *adj.*
Adj. derived from within, subjective; idiocratic, idiosyncratic, intrin-sic, -sical; fundamental, cardinal, normal, inherent, essential, natural; in-nate, -born, -bred, -dwelling, -grained; -wrought; radical, incarnate, thoroughbred, hereditary, inherited, immanent; congen-ital, -ite; connate, running in the blood; coeval with birth, genetic, ingenerate, -genite; indigenous; in the -grain etc. *n.*; bred in the bone, instinctive; inward, internal etc. 221; to the manner born; virtual.
characteristic etc. (*special*) 79, (*indicative*) 550; invariable, incurable, ineradicable, fixed, settled, constant, unchanging.
Adv. intrinsically etc. *adj.*; at bottom, in the main, in effect, essentially, practically, virtually, substantially, *au fond*; fairly.

6. Extrinsicality.—**N.** extrinsicality, objectiveness, *non ego;* extraneousness etc. 57; accident; letter of the law.
Adj. derived from without; objective; extrinsic, -sical; extraneous etc. (*foreign*) 57; modal, adventitious, additional, supervenient, fortuitous; a-, ad-scititious; incidental, casual, accidental, unessential, non-essential, accessory.
implanted, ingrafted; instilled, inculcated.
outward etc. (*external*) 220.
Adv. extrinsically etc. *adj.*

7. State.—**N.** state, condition, category, estate, lot, case, trim, mood, pickle, plight etc. 704; temper; aspect etc. (*appearance*) 448.
constitution, habitude, *diathesis;* frame, fabric etc. 329; stamp, set, fit, mold.
mode, modality, schesis; fettle; form etc. (*shape*) 240.
tone, tenor, turn; trim, guise, fashion, light, complexion, style, character.
V. be in –, possess –, enjoy –, labor under- a -state etc. *n.;* be on a footing, do, fare; come to pass.
Adj. conditional, modal, formal; structural, organic.
Adv. conditionally etc. *adj.;* as -the matter stands, – things are; such being the case etc. 8.

8. Circumstance.—**N.** circumstance, situation, phase, position, posture, attitude, place, point; terms; *régime;* footing, standing, status.
occasion, juncture, conjuncture; contingency etc. (*event*) 151.
predicament; emergen-ce, -cy; exigency, crisis, pinch, pass, push; turning point; crossroads.
bearings, how the land lies.
Adj. circumstantial; given, conditional, provisional; critical; modal; contingent, incidental; adventitious etc. (*extrinsic*) 6.
Adv. in the circumstances etc. *n.*, under the conditions etc. 7; thus, in such wise.
accordingly; that –, such- being the case; that being so, since, seeing that.
as matters stand; as -things, – times- go.
conditionally, provided, if, in case; if -so, – so be, – it be so; if it so -happen, – turn out; in the event of; in such a -contingency, – case, – event; provisionally, unless, without.
according to -circumstances, – the occasion; as it may -happen, – turn out, – be; as the -case may be, – wind blows; *pro re natâ.*

9. Relation.—**N.** relation, bearing, reference, connection, apposition, interconnection, concern, cognation; applicability, appositeness; correlation etc. 12; analogy; similarity etc. 17; affinity, intimacy, friendship; homology, alliance, homogeneity, association, rapport; approximation etc. (*nearness*) 197; filiation etc. (*consanguinity*) 11; interest; relevancy etc. 23; relationship, relative position; relativity; interrelation etc. 12.
comparison etc. 464; ratio, proportion.
link, tie, bond, bond of union.
V. be-related etc. *adj.;* have a relation etc. *n.;* relate –, refer- to; bear upon, regard, concern, touch, affect, have to do with; pertain –, belong –, appertain- to; have respect to; answer to; interest.
bring -into relation with, – to bear upon; connect, associate, draw a parallel; link etc. 43.
Adj. relative; correlative etc. 12; cognate; relating to etc. *v.;* relative to, in relation with, referable *or* referrible to; belonging to etc. *v.;* appurtenant to, in common with.
related, connected; implicated, associated, affiliated, akin, allied to; collateral, cognate, congenial, kindred, affinitive, *en rapport*, in touch with.
approxima-tive, -ting; approaching; proportion-al, -ate, -able; allusive, comparable.
in the same -category etc. 75; like etc. 17; relevant etc. (*apt*) 23.
Adv. relatively etc. *adj.;* pertinently etc. 23.
thereof; as -to, – for, – respects, – re-gards; about; concerning etc. *v.;* anent; relating –, as relates- to; with -relation, – reference, – respect, – regard-to; in respect of; while speaking –, *à propos*-of; in connection with; by the -way, – by; whereas; for –, in -as much as; in point of, as far as; on the -part, – score- of; *quoad hoc; pro re natâ;* under the -head etc. (*class*) 75- of; in the matter of, *in re.*
Phr. 'thereby hangs a tale.'

10. Irrelation. [Want, or absence of relation.]—**N.** irrelation, dissociation; inapplicability; inconnection; multifariousness; disconnection etc. (*disjunction*) 44; inconsequence, independence; incommensurability; irreconcilableness etc. (*disagreement*) 24; heterogeneity;

unconformity etc. 83; irrelevancy, impertinence, *nihil ad rem;* intrusion etc. 24.

V. have no -relation etc. 9 to, — bearing upon, — concern etc. 9 with, — business with; not -concern etc. 9; have -nothing to do with, — no business there; intrude, etc. 24.

bring —, drag —, haul —, lug- in head and shoulders.

Adj. irrelative, irrespective, unrelated, irrelated; arbitrary; independent, unallied; un-, dis-connected; adrift, isolated, insular; extraneous, strange, alien, foreign, outlandish, exotic.

not comparable, incommensurable, heterogeneous; unconformable etc. 83.

irrelevant; rambling etc. 279; inapplicable; not -pertinent, — to the purpose; impertinent, inapposite, beside the mark, *à propos de bottes;* away from —, foreign to —, beside- the -purpose, — question, — transaction, — point; misplaced etc. (*intrusive*) 24.

remote, far fetched, out of the way, forced, neither here nor there, quite another thing; detached, segregated, segregate.

multifarious; discordant etc. 24.

incidental, parenthetical, *obiter dictum,* episodic.

Adv. parenthetically etc. *adj.;* by the -way, — by; *en passant,* incidentally; irrespecitively etc. *adj.;* without reference, — regard- to; in the abstract etc. 87; *a se.*

11. Consanguinity. [Relations of kindred.]—**N.** consanguinity, relationship, kindred, blood; parentage etc. (*paternity*) 166; filiation, affiliation; lineage, agnation, connection, cognation, alliance; family -connection, — tie; ties of blood; blood relationship; nepotism.

kins-man, -folk; people; kith and kin; relation, -tive; connection; sib; next of kin; uncle, aunt, nephew, niece; cousin, -german; first —, second- cousin; cousin -once, — twice etc.- removed; near —, distant-relation; brother, sister, one's own flesh and blood.

family, patriarch, matriarch; fraternity; brother-, sister-, cousin-hood.

race, stock, generation; sept etc. 166 ; stirps, side; strain; breed, clan, tribe.

V. be -related etc. *adj.* — to; claim -relationship etc. *n.*- with.

Adj. related, akin, consanguineous, matrilinear, patrilineal, of the blood, family, allied, collateral; cog-, ag-, con-nate; kindred; affiliated, affine; fraternal, avuncular.

intimately —, nearly —, closely —, remotely —, distantly- related, — allied; german.

12. Correlation. [Double or reciprocal relation.]—**N.** reciprocalness etc. *adj.;* recipro-city, -cality, -cation; mutuality, correlation, correspondence, interdependence; interchange etc. 148; exchange, barter; interrelation, interconnection; alternation, see-saw.

V. reciprocate, alternate; interchange etc. 148; exchange; counterchange; interact, correspond, mutualize, give and take.

Adj. reciprocal, mutual, commutual, correlative; alternate; interchangeable; international; correspondent, complementary, analogous.

Adv. *mutatis mutandis; vice versâ;* each other; by turns etc. 148; reciprocally etc. *adj.;* to and fro etc. 314.

13. Identity.—**N.** identity, sameness, oneness, ditto, homogeneity; unity, coincidence, coalescence: convertibility; equality etc. 27; selfness, self, oneself; identification.

monotony, tautology etc. (*repetition*) 104.

synonym.

fac-simile etc. (*copy*) 21; *alter ego* etc. (*similar*) 17; *ipsissima verba* etc. (*exactness*) 494; same; self —, very —, one and the same; very —, actual-thing, no other.

V. be -identical etc. *adj.;* match, coincide, coalesce.

treat as —, render--the same , —identical; identify; recognize the identity of.

Adj. identical; self, ilk; the -same etc. *n.;* self same; synonymous; one and the same.

coincid-, coalesc-ent, -ing; indistinguishable; one; equivalent etc. (*equal*) 27; much -the same, — of a muchness; unaltered.

Adv. identically etc. *adj.;* on all fours; ibid-, -em.

14. Contrariety. [Non-coincidence.]—**N.** contrariety, contrast, foil, antithesis, oppositeness; counterpole; contradiction; antagonism etc. (*opposition*) 708; counteraction etc. 179.

inversion etc. 218; the -opposite, — reverse, — inverse, — converse, — antipodes, — other extreme etc. 237.

antonym.

V. be -contrary etc. *adj.;* contrast with, oppose; differ *toto coelo.*

invert, reverse, turn the tables etc. 218.

contra-dict, -vene; antagonize etc. 708.

Adj. contrar-y, -ious, -iant; opposite, counter, dead against; ad-, con-, reverse; opposed, antithetical, contrasted, antipodean, antagonistic, opposing; conflicting, inconsistent, contradictory, at cross purposes; negative; hostile etc. 708.

differing *toto coelo;* diametrically opposite; as opposite as -black and white, — light and darkness, — fire and water, — the poles, as different as chalk from cheese; 'Hyperion to a satyr;' quite the -contrary, — reverse; no such thing, just the other way, *tout au contraire.*

Adv. contrarily etc. *adj.; contra, contrariwise, per contra,* on the contrary, nay rather; topsy-turvy; *vice versâ;* on the other hand etc. (*in compensation*) 30.

15. Difference.—**N.** difference, unlikeness; heterogeneity; vari-ance, -ation, -ety; diversity, dissimilarity etc. 18; disagreement etc. 24; disparity etc. (*inequality*) 28; distinction, contradistinction; distinctness; discrepancy, divergence, contrast etc. 18; nonconformity, incompatibility, antithesis.

discord etc. 713.

modification, moods and tenses.

nice —, fine —, delicate —, subtle- distinction; shade of difference, *nuance;* discrimination etc. 465; *differentia.*

different thing, something else, variant, apple

off another tree, horse of another color, another pair of shoes; this that or the other.

V. be -different etc. *adj.;* differ, vary, ablude, mismatch, contrast; diverge –, depart –, deviate- -from; divaricate; differ *-toto coelo, — longo intervallo.*

disagree etc. 713.

vary, modify etc. (*change*) 140.

discriminate etc. 465.

Adj. differing etc. *v.;* different, diverse, divided, heterogeneous; distinguishable; varied, modified; divergent, incongruous, diversified, various; discrepant, dissentient, differential; divers, all manner of; variform etc. 81; discordant etc. 713.

other, another, not the same; unequal etc. 28; unmatched; widely apart.

distinctive, characteristic; discriminative; distinghishing.

Adv. differently etc. *adj.*

Phr. *il y a fagots et fagots; tot nomines tot sententiae;* one man's meat is another man's poison.

16. Uniformity.—N. uniformity; homogeneity, -ousness; continuity, stability, consistency; connatural-ity, -ness; homology; accordance; conformity etc. 82; agreement etc. 23.

regularity, constancy, even tenor, routine; monotony, evenness, sameness, dead level; steadiness, equability, unity.

V. be -uniform etc. *adj.;* accord with etc. 23; run through.

become -uniform etc. *adj.;* conform to etc. 82.

render uniform etc. *adj.;* assimilate, level, smooth, dress.

Adj. uniform; homo-geneous, -logous; of a piece, consistent, steady; connatural; monotonous, changeless, dreary, even, invariable, equable, level, regular, stereotyped, unchanged, unvarying; methodical etc. 60; habitual etc. 613.

Adv. uniformly etc. *adj.;* uniformly with etc. (*conformably*) 82; in harmony with etc. (*agreeing*) 23; in a -rut, — groove.

always, ever etc. 112; invariably, without exception, never otherwise; by clock-work; endlessly etc. 112.

Phr. *ab uno disce omnes.*

16a. Non-uniformity. [Absence or want of uniformity.]—**N.** diversity, irregularity, unevenness; multiformity etc. 81; unconformity etc. 83; roughness etc. 256; heterogeneity, heteromorphism.

Adj. diversified, varied, irregular, uneven, rough etc. 256; multifarious; multiform etc. 81; of various kinds; all -manner, — sorts, — kinds- of.

Adv. in all manner of ways, here there and everywhere.

17. Similarity.—N. similarity, resemblance, likeness, similitude, semblance; affinity, approximation, parallelism; parity; agreement etc. 23; ana-logy, -logicalness; correspondence, equality etc.

connatural-ness, -ity; brotherhood, family likeness.

alliteration, rhyme, pun.

repetition etc. 104; sameness etc. (*identity*) 13; uniformity etc. 16.

analogue; the like; match, *pendant,* fellow, companion, pair, mate, twin, double, counterpart, brother, sister; one's second self, *alter ego,* chip of the old block, *par nobile fratrum, Arcades ambo,* birds of a feather, *et hoc genus omne.*

parallel; simile; type etc. (*metaphor*) 521; image etc. (*representation*) 554; photograph; close –, striking –, speaking –, faithful etc *adj.* — likeness, — resemblance.

V. be -similar etc. *adj.;* look like, resemble, bear resemblance, favor; savor –, smack- of; approximate; parallel, match, rhyme with; take after; imitate etc. 19; run in pairs.

Adj. similar; resembling etc. *v.;* like, alike; twin.

analog-ous, -ical; parallel, of a piece; such as, so.

connatural, congeneric, allied to; corresponding, cognate; akin to etc. (*consanguineous*) 11.

approximate, much the same, near, close, something like, such like; a show of; mock, *pseudo,* simulating, representing.

exact etc. (*true*) 494; lifelike, faithful, realistic; true to -nature, — the life; the -very image — picture- of; for all the world like, *comme deux gouttes d'eau;* as like as -two peas, — it can stare; *instar omnium,* case in the same mold, ridiculously like.

Adv. as if, so to speak; as –, as if- it were; *quasi,* just as, *veluti in speculum.*

18. Dissimilarity.—N. dissimil-arity, -itude; unlikeness, diversity, disparity, dissemblance; divergence, inequality, difference etc. 15; novelty; variation, variety, originality, disguise.

V. be -unlike etc. *adj.;* vary etc. (*differ*) 15; bear no resemblance to, differ *toto coelo.*

render -unlike etc. *adj.;* vary etc. (*diversify*) 140.

Adj. dissimilar, unlike, disparate; of a different kind etc. (*class*) 75; unmatched, unique; new, novel; unprecedented etc. 83; original.

nothing of the kind; no such –, quite another- thing; far from it, other than, cast in a different mold, *tertium quid,* as like a dock as a daisy, 'very like a whale;' as different as -chalk from cheese, — Macedon and Monmouth; *lucus a non lucendo.*

diversified etc. 16*a.*

Adv. otherwise, *alias.*

19. Imitation.—N. imitation; copying etc. *v.;* transcription; repetition, mimeograph, mimeotype, duplication, reduplication; quotation; reproduction.

mockery, mimicry, mime, simulation, personation; representation etc. 554; semblance, pretence; copy etc. 21; assimilation.

paraphrase, parody etc. 21.

plagiarism; forgery etc. (*falsehood*) 544.

imitator; echo, cuckoo, parrot, ape, monkey, mocking-bird, mimic, impersonator, copyist.

V. imitate, copy, mirror, reflect, reproduce, repeat, borrow; do like, echo, re-echo, catch; transcribe; match, parallel.

mock, take off, mimic, ape, simulate, personate, impersonate; forge; act etc. (*drama*) 599; represent etc. 554; counterfeit, duplicate; portray, parody, travesty, caricature, burlesque.

follow —, tread- in the- -steps, — footsteps, — wake- of; pattern after, take pattern by; follow - suit, — the example of; walk in the shoes of, take a leaf out of another's book, strike in with; take —, model -after; emulate.

Adj. imitated etc. *v.*; mock, mimic; counterfeit, false, pseudo; modelled after, molded on, paraphrastic; literal; imitative, apish; second-hand; imitable; sham etc. 545.

Adv. literally, to the letter, strictly, precisely, *verbatim, literatim, sic, totidem verbis*, word for word, *mot à mot*.

Phr. like master like man.

20. Non-Imitation.—**N.** no imitation, genuineness, originality; creativeness.

Adj. unimitated, uncopied; unmatched, unparalleled; inimitable etc. 33; *unique*, original, primordial, primary, pristine, underived, first-hand, archetypal, prototypal.

20a. Variation.—**N.** variation; alteration etc. (*change*) 140. modification, moods and tenses; modulation.

divergency etc. 291; deviation etc. 279; aberration; innovation.

V. vary etc. (*change*) 140; deviate etc. 279; diverge etc. 291.

Adj. varied etc. *v.*; modified; dissimilar etc. 18; diversified etc. 16*a*.

21. Copy. [Result of imitation.]—**N.** copy, facsimile, counterpart, *effigies*, effigy, symbol, image, form, likeness, similitude, semblance, resemblance, cast, electrotype, stereotype, tracing, ectype; imitation etc. 19; model, representation, adumbration, study; counterfeit presentment, portrait etc. (*representment*) 554.

duplicate; transcript, -ion; reflex, -ion; shadow, echo; chip of the old block; reprint, reproduction, casting, engraving, replica; transfer; second edition etc. (*repetition*) 104; *réchauffé* apograph, fair copy; revise.

parody, caricature, cartoon, burlesque, travesty, paraphrase.

servile -copy, — imitation; counterfeit etc. (*deception*) 545; *pasticcio*.

Adj. faithful; lifelike etc. (*similar*) 17.

22. Prototype. [Thing copied.]—**N.** prototype, original, model, pattern, founding, precedent, standard, scantling, type, arche-, anti-type; protoplast, copy-book, module, exemplar, example, ensample, specimen; paradigm; guide; templet; lay-figure.

text, copy, manuscript, MS., design; fugleman, keynote.

die, mold; matrix, engraving, last, plasm; pro-, proto-plasm; mint; seal, punch, *intaglio*, negative, stamp.

V. be —, set- an example; set a copy; standardize.

23. Agreement.—**N.** agreement; ac-cord, -cordance; unison, harmony, concord etc. 714; concordance, concert, understanding, convention, *entente -cordiale, consortium*, consensus of opinion, pact, mutual understanding, unanimity.

conformity etc. 82; conformance; uniformity etc. 16; consonance, consentaneousness, consistency; congruity, -ence; keeping; congeniality; correspondence, concinnity, parallelism, apposition, union.

fitness, aptness etc. *adj.*; relevancy; pertinence, -cy; sortance; case in point; aptitude, propriety, applicability, admissibility, commensurability, compatibility, suitability; cognation etc (*relation*) 9.

adaptation, adjustment, arrangement, graduation, accommodation; reconcil-iation -ement; assimilation; attunement.

consent etc. (*assent*) 448; concurrence etc. 178; co-operation etc. 709.

right man in the right place, very thing; quite —, just- the thing.

V. be -accordant etc. *adj.*; agree, accord, harmonize; correspond, tally, respond; meet, suit, fit, befit, do, adapt itself to; fall in —, chime in —, square —, quadrate —, consort —, comport- with; dovetail, assimilate; fit like a glove; fit to a -tittle, — T; match etc. 17; become one.

consent etc. (*assent*) 488.

render -accordant etc. *adj.*; fit, suit, adapt, accommodate; graduate; adjust etc. (*render equal*) 27; dress, regulate, readjust; accord, harmonize, reconcile; fadge, dovetail, square.

Adj. agreeing, suiting etc. *v.*; in accord, accordant, concordant, consonant, congruous, consentaneous, correspondent, corresponding, homologous, congenial; becoming; harmonious, reconcilable, conformable; in -accordance, — harminy, — keeping, — unison, etc. *n.*;-with; at one with, of one mind, of a piece; consistent, compatible, proportionate, answerable; commensurate; on all fours.

apt, apposite, pertinent, pat; to the -point, — purpose; happy, felicitous, germane, *ad rem*, in point, bearing upon, applicable, relevant, admissible.

fit, adapted, *in loco, à propos*, appropriate, seasonable, sortable, suitable, idoneous, deft; meet etc. (*expedient*) 646.

at home, in one's proper element.

Adv. *à propos of*; pertinently etc. *adj.*; *pro rata*.

Phr. *rem acu tetigisti*, the cap fits.

24. Disagreement.—**N.** disagreement, discord, -cordance; disunion, dissonance, dissidence, discrepancy; unconformity etc. 83; incongru-ity, -ence; discongruity, *mésalliance, oxymoron*; jarring etc. *v.*; clash, collision, dissension etc. 713; conflict etc. (*opposition*) 708; controversy etc. 720; falling out, wrangle, argument.

disparity, mismatch, misfit, disproportion; disproportionateness etc. *adj.*; variance, divergence, repugnance.

unfitness etc. *adj.*; inaptitude, impropriety; inapplicability etc. *adj.*; inconsistency, inconcinnity; irrelevancy etc. (*irrelation*) 10.

misjoin-ing, -der; syncretism, intrusion, interference; *concordia discors*.

fish out of water.

V. disagree; clash, quarrel, jar etc. (*discord*) 713; interfere, intrude, come amiss; not concern etc. 10; mismatch; *hymano capiti cervicem jungere equinam*.

Adj. disagreeing etc. *v.;* discordant, discrepant; at -variance, — war; hostile, antagonistic, repugnant, factious, contradictory, dissentious, incompatible, irreconcilable, inconsistent with; unconformable, exceptional etc. 83; intrusive, incongruous; disproportionate, -ed; unharmonious; unconsonant; divergent, repugnant to.

inapt, unapt, inappropriate, inept, infelicitous, improper; unsuit-ed, -able; inapplicable; un-fit, -fitting, -befitting; unbecoming; ill-timed, ill-adapted, unseasonable, *mal à propos*, inadmissible; inapposite etc. (*irrelevant*) 10.

uncongenial; ill-assorted, -sorted, -matched; mis-matched, -mated, -joined, -placed; unaccommodating, irreducible, uncommensurable, unsympathetic.

out of -character, — keeping, — proportion, — joint, — tune, — place, — season, — its element; at -odds, — variance with.

Adv. in -defiance, — contempt, — spite-of; discordantly etc. *adj.; à tort et à travers*.

25. Quantity. [Absolute quantity.]—**N.** quantity, magnitude; size etc. (*dimensions*) 192; amplitude, mass, amount, *quantum*, measure, measurement, substance, strength.

[Science of quantity.] Mathematics, Mathesis.

[Definite or finite quantity] arm-, hand-, mouth-, spoon-, thimble-, capful; stock, batch, lot, dose, ration, quotum, quota, pittance, driblet, part, portion etc. 51.

Adj. quantitative, some, any, more or less.

Adv. to the tune of.

26. Degree. [Relative quantity.]—**N.** degree, grade, extent, measure, proportion, amount, ratio, stint, standard, height, pitch; reach, amplitude, range, scope, size, caliber; gradation, shade; tenor, compass; sphere, station, rank, standing; rate, way, sort.

point, mark, step, stage etc. (*term*) 71; intensity, strength etc. (*greatness*) 31.

V. compare, graduate, calibrate, measure.

Adj. comparative; gradual, shading off, gradational; within the bounds etc. (*limit*), 233.

Adv. by degrees, gradually, inasmuch, *pro tanto*; how-ever, -soever; step by step, bit by bit, little by little, inch by inch, drop by drop, gradatim; by -inches, — slow degrees, — little and little; in some -degree, — measure; to some extent; just a bit.

27. Equality. [Sameness of quantity or degree.]—**N.** equality, parity, co-extension, symmetry, balance, poise; evenness, monotony, level.

equivalence; equi-pollence, -poise, -librium, -ponderance; par, quits; not a pin to choose; distinction without a difference, six of one and half a dozen of the other; identity etc. 13; similarity etc. 17; isotropism; coequality.

equalization, equation, equilibration, coordination, adjustment, readjustment.

drawn -game, -battle, draw, stalemate; neck and neck race; tie, dead heat.

match, peer, compeer, equal, mate, fellow, brother; equivalent.

V. be -equal etc. *adj.;* equal, match, reach, keep pace with, run abreast; come —, amount —, come upto; be —, lie- on a level with; balance; cope with; come to the same thing; level off.

render -equal etc. *adj.;* equalize, level, dress, balance, equate, handicap, give points, trim, adjust, poise; fit, accommodate; adapt etc. (*render accordant*) 23; strike a balance; establish —, restore- equality, — equilibrium; readjust; stretch on the bed of Procrustes.

Adj. equal, even, level, monotonous, coequal, symmetrical, coordinate; on a -par, — level, — footing- with; up to the mark; equiparent.

equivalent, tantamount; quits; homologous; synonymous etc. 522; resolvable into, convertible, much at one, as broad as long, neither more nor less; much the same —, the same thing —, as good- as; all -one, — the same; equi-pollent, -ponderant, -ponderous, -balanced; equalized etc. *v.;* drawn; half and half; isochronous; isoperimetrical.

Adv. equally etc. *adj.; pari passu, ad eundem, caeteris paribus; in equilibrio;* to all intents and purposes.

Phr. it -comes, -adds up, — amounts- to the same thing.

28. Inequality. [Difference of quantity or degree.]—**N.** inequality; dis-, im-parity; odds; difference etc. 15; ill-balanced; unevenness; inclination of the balance, partiality; shortcoming; casting —make- weight; superiority etc. 33; inferiority etc. 34.

V. be -unequal etc. *adj.;* countervail; have —, give- the advantage; turn the scale; kick the beam; topple, -over; over-match etc. 33; not come up to etc. 34.

Adj. unequal, uneven, disparate, partial; un-, over-balanced; top-heavy, lop-sided.

Adv. *haud passibus aequis*.

29. Mean.—**N.** mean, medium, intermedium, average, run of the mill, normal, balance; mediocrity, generality, rule, ordinary -run, -ruck; golden mean etc. (*mid-course*) 628; middle etc. 68; compromise etc. 774; neutrality; middle point, middle course.

V. split the difference; take the -average etc. *n.;* reduce to a -mean etc. *n.;* strike a balance, pair off.

Adj. mean, intermediate; medial; middle etc. 68; average, normal, standard, neutral; middling, moderate.

médiocre, middle-class; *bourgeois*, commonplace etc. (*unimportant*) 643.

Adv. on an average, in the long run; taking -one with another, — all things together, — it for all in all; *communibus annis*, in round numbers.

30. Compensation.—**N.** compensation, equation; commutation; indemnification; compromise etc. 774; neutralization, nullification; counteraction etc. 179; reaction; measure for measure; retaliation etc. 718; equalization etc. 27; redemption, recoupment, recompense.

set-off, offset; make- casting-weight; counterpoise, equipoise, ballast; indemnity, reparation etc. 790; equivalent, *quid pro quo;* bribe, hush-money, tribute etc. 784; amends etc. (*atonement*) 952; counterclaim, counterbalance, equiponderance, countervail, cross demand.

V. make -amends, — compensation; compensate, -pense; indemnify; counter-act, -vail, -poise; equiponderate; balance; out-, over-, counterbalance; set off, offset, cancel; hedge, square, give and take; make up -for, — lee way; cover, fill up, neutralize, nullify; equalize etc. 27; make good; redeem etc. (*atone*) 952; recoup, pay etc. 973.

Adj. compensat-ing, -ory; amendatory, reparative, countervailing etc. *v.;* in the opposite scale; equivalent etc. (*equal*) 27.

Adv. in -return, — consideration; but, however, yet, still, notwithstanding; neverthe-, nathless; although, though; al-, how-beit; in spite of, despite; mauger; at -all events, — any rate; be that as it may, for all that, even so, on the other hand, at the same time, *quoad minus, quand même,* however that may be; after all, — is said and done; taking one thing with another etc. (*average*) 29.

31. Greatness.—N. greatness etc. *adj.;* magnitude; size etc. (*dimensions*) 192; multitude etc. (*number*) 102; immensity, enormity, infinity etc. 105; might, strength, intensity, fulness; importance etc. 642; fame etc. 873.

great quantity, quantity, deal, power, sight, pot, volume, world; mass, heap etc. (*assemblage*) 72; stock etc. (*store*) 636; peck, bushel, load, cargo; cart —, wagon —, car —, truck —, ship-load; flood, spring tide; abundance etc. (*sufficiency*) 639.

principal —, chief —, main —, greater —, major —, best —, essential- part; bulk, mass etc. (*whole*) 50.

V. be -great etc. *adj.;* run high, soar, loom up, tower, bulk large, transcend; rise —, carry- to a great height; know no bounds; scale, overtop, ascend.

enlarge etc. (*increase*) 35, (*expand*) 194.

Adj. great; greater etc. 33; large, considerable, fair, above par; big, massive, huge etc. (*large in size*) 192, ample; abundant etc. (*enough*) 639; Herculean etc. 159; full, intense, strong, sound, passing, heavy, plenary, deep, high; signal, at its height, in the zenith.

world-wide, wide-spread, extensive; wholesale; many etc. 102.

goodly, noble, precious, mighty; sad, grave, serious; far gone, arrant, downright; utter, -most; crass, gross, arch, profound, intense, consummate; rank, unmitigated, red-hot, desperate; glaring, flagrant, stark staring; thorough-paced, -going; roaring, thumping, thundering, strapping, whacking; extraordinary; important etc. 642; unsurpassed etc. (*supreme*) 33; complete etc. 52.

vast, immense, enormous, extreme; inordinate, excessive, extravagant, exorbitant, outrageous, preposterous, unconscionable, swinging, monstrous, over-grown; towering, stupendous, prodigious, astonishing, incredible; terrific, frightful; marvelous etc. (*wonder*) 870; grand.

unlimited etc. (*infinite*) 105; unapproachable, unutterable, indescribable, ineffable, unspeakable, inexpressible, beyond expression, fabulous.

un-diminished, -abated, -reduced, -restricted.

absolute, positive, stark, decided, unequivocal, essential, perfect, finished.

remarkable, of mark, marked, pointed, veriest; noticeable, uncommon, noteworthy, eminent etc. 873.

Adv. [in a positive degree] truly etc. (*truth*) 494; decidedly, unequivocally, purely, absolutely, seriously, essentially, fundamentally, radically, downright, in all conscience; for the most part, in the main.

[in a complete degree] entirely etc. (*completely*) 52; abundantly, etc. (*sufficiently*) 639; widely, far and wide.

[in a great or high degree] greatly etc. *adj.;* much, muckle, well, indeed, very, very much, a deal, no end of, most not a little; pretty, — well; enough, in a great measure, passing richly; to a -large, — great, — gigantic- extent; on a large scale; so; never —, ever- so; ever so much; by wholesale; mightily, mighty, powerfully; with a witness, *ultra,* in the extreme, extremely, exceedingly, intensely, exquisitely, acutely, indefinitely, immeasurably; beyond -compare, — comparison, — measure, — all bounds; incalculably, infinitely.

[in a supreme degree] pre-eminently, superlatively etc. (*superiority*) 33.

[in a too great degree] immoderately, unduly, monstrously, grossly, preposterously, inordinately, exorbitantly, excessively, enormously, out of all proportion, with a vengeance.

[in a marked degree] particularly, remarkably, singularly, curiously, uncommonly, unusually, peculiarly, notably, signally, strikingly, pointedly, mainly, chiefly; famously, egregiously, prominently, glaringly, emphatically, strangely, wonderfully, amazingly, surprisingly, astonishingly, incredibly, marvelously, awfully, stupendously.

[in an exceptional degree] peculiarly etc. (*unconformity*) 83.

[in a violent degree] furiously etc. (*violence*) 173; severely, desperately, tremendously, extravagantly, confoundedly, deucedly, devilishly, with a vengeance; *à —, à toute- outrance.*

[in a painful degree] painfully, sadly, grossly, sorely, bitterly, piteously, grievously, miserably, cruelly, woefully, lamentably, shockingly, frightfully, dreadfully, fearfully, terribly, horribly, distressingly, balefully.

32. Smallness.—N. smallness etc. *adj.;* littleness etc. (*small size*) 193; tenuity; paucity; fewness etc. (*small number*) 103; meanness, insignificance etc. (*unimportance*) 643; mediocrity, moderation.

small quantity, *modicum, minimum;* vanishing point; material point, electron, atom, particle, molecule, corpuscle, point, dab, fleck, speck, dot, mote, jot, iota, ace; *minutiae,* details; look, thought, idea, *soupçon,* whit, tittle, shade, shadow; spark, *scintilla,* gleam; touch, cast; grain, scruple, granule, globule, minim, sup, sip, sop, spice, drop, droplet, sprinkling, dash, smack, tinge, tincture; inch, patch, scantling, dole; scrap, shred, tag, splinter, rag, tatter, cantlet, flitter, gobbet, mite, bit, morsel, crumb, seed, fritter, shive; snip, -pet; snick, snack, snatch, slip, scrag; chip, -ping; shiver, sliver, driblet, clipping, paring, shaving, hair.

nutshell; thimble-, spoon-, hand-, cap-, mouthful; fragment; fraction etc. (*part*)51; drop in the ocean, drop in the bucket.

animalcule etc. 193.

trifle etc. (*unimportant thing*) 643; mere —, next to- nothing; hardly anything; just enough to swear by; the shadow of a shade.

finiteness, finite quantity.

V. be -shall etc. *adj.*; lie in a nutshell.

diminish etc. (*decrease*) 36, (*contract*) 195.

Adj. small, little, tiny, weeny; diminutive etc. (*small in size*) 193; minute; minikin, fine, inconsiderable, dribbling, paltry etc. (*unimportant*) 643; faint etc. (*weak*) 160; slender, light, slight, scanty, scant, limited; meager etc. (*insufficient*) 640; sparing; few etc. 103; low, so-so, middling, tolerable, no great shakes; below —, under-par, — the mark; at a low ebb; half-way; moderate, modest; tender, subtle; petty, shallow, skin-deep.

inappreciable, evanescent, infinite-simal, homeopathic, very small, atomic, molecular, ultra-, -microscopic.

petty, shallow etc. 499.

mere, simple, sheer, stark, bare; near run.

Adv. [in a small degree] to a small extent, on a small scale; a -little, — wee, — tiny bit; slightly etc. *adj.*; imperceptibly; miserably, wretchedly; insufficiently etc. 640; imperfectly; faintly etc. 160; passably, pretty well, well enough.

[in a certain or limited degree] partially, in part; in —, to a certain degree; to a certain extent; comparatively; some, rather; in some -degree, -measure; some-thing, -what; simply, only, purely, merely; at —, at the- -least, — most; ever so little, as little as may be, *tant soit peu*, in ever so small a degree; thus far, *pro tanto;* within bounds, in a manner, after a fashion.

almost, nearly, well nigh, short of, not quite, all but; near —, close- upon; *peu s'en faut*, near the mark; within an -ace, — inch- of; on the brink of; scarcely, hardly, barely, only just, no more than.

[in an uncertain degree] about, therabouts, somewhere about, nearly, say; be the same - more, — little more- or less.

[in no degree] no- ways, — wise; not -at all, — in the least, — a bit, — a bit of it, — a whit, — a jot, — a shadow; in no -wise, — respect; by no - means, — manner of means; on no account, at no hand.

33. Superiority.—N. superiority, supremacy, majority; greatness etc. 31; advantage, odds, pull; preponderance, -ation; predominance, vantage ground, coign of vantage, prevalence, partiality; personal superiority; sovereignty etc. 737; nobility etc. (*rank*) 875; Triton among the minnows, ***primus inter pares, nulli secundus***, superman; captain etc. 475.

supremacy, pre-eminence; primacy, lead, *maximum;* record; climax, crest, top; culmination etc. (*summit*) 210; transcendence; *ne plus ultra;* lion's share, Benjamin's mess; excess; bisque, surplus etc. (*remainder*) 40, (*redundance*) 641.

V. be -superior etc. *adj.;* exceed, excel, transcend; out-do, -balance, -weigh, -rival, -Herod, outrank, pass, surpass, surmount, get ahead of; over-top, -ride, -pass, -balance, -weigh, -match; top, o'er-top, cap, beat, win out, cut out; beat hollow; outstrip etc. 303; eclipse, throw into the shade, take the shine out of, put one's nose out of joint; have the -upper hand, — whip hand of, — advantage; turn the scale, play first fiddle etc. (*importance*) 642; preponderate, predominate, prevail; precede, take .precedence, come first; come to a head, culminate; beat etc. all others, bear the palm; break the record, take the cake.

become —, render- -larger, etc. (*increase*) 35, (*expand*) 194.

Adj. superior, greater, major, higher; exceeding etc. *v.*; great etc. 31; distinguished, *ultra;* vaulting; more than a match for.

supreme, greatest, maximal, maximum, utmost, paramount, pre-eminent, foremost, crowning; first-rate etc. (important) 642, (*excellent*) 648; unrivalled; peer-, match-less; none such, second to none, *sans pareil;* un-paragoned, -paralleled, -equalled, -approached, -surpassed; superlative, inimitable, *facile princeps*, incomparable, sovereign, without parallel, *nulli secundus, ne plus ultra;* beyond -compare, — comparison; culminating etc. (*topmost*) 210; transcendent, -ental; *plus royaliste que le Roi.*

increased etc. (*added to*) 35; enlarged etc. (*expanded*) 194.

Adv. beyond, more, over; over —, above- the mark; above par; upwards —, in advance- of; over and above; at the top of the scale, on the crest, at it height.

[in a superior or supreme degree] eminently, egregiously, pre-eminently, surpassing, prominently, superlatively, supremely, above all, of all things, the most, to crown all, *par excellence*, principally, especially, particularly, peculiarly, *a fortiori*, even, yea, still more.

Phr. 'we shall not look upon his like again.'

34. Inferiority.—N. inferiority, minority, subordinancy; shortcoming, deficiency; handicap; *minimum;* smallness etc. 32; imperfection, shabbiness.

[personal inferiority] commonalty etc. 876; subordinate, substitute, sub.

V. be -inferior etc. *adj.;* fall —, come- short of; not -pass, — come up to; want.

become —, render- smaller etc. (decrease) 36, (*contract*) 195; hide its diminished head, retire into the shade, yield the palm, play second fiddle, take a back seat; bow.

Adj. inferior, smaller; small etc. 32; minor, less, lesser, deficient, minus, lower, subordinate, secondary; second-rate etc. (*imperfect*) 651; sub, subaltern; thrown into the shade; weighed in the balance and found wanting; not fit to hold a candle to.

least, smallest etc. (*see* little, small etc. 193); lowest.

diminished etc. (*decreased*) 36; reduced etc. (*contracted*) 195; unimportant etc. 643.

Adv. less; under —, below- -the mark, — par; at -the bottom of the scale, — a low ebb, — a disadvantage; short of, under.

35. Increase.—**N.** increase; augmentation, addition, enlargement, extension; dilatation etc. (*expansion*) 194; multiplication; increment, accretion; accession etc. 37; production etc. 161; development, growth; aggrandizement, aggravation, intensification; rise; ascent etc. 305; anabasis; ex-aggeration, -acerbation; spread etc. (*dispersion*) 73; flood-, spring-, -tide; gain, produce, profit etc. 618; booty, plunder etc. 793.

V. increase, augment, add to, enlarge; dilate etc. (*expand*) 194; grow, wax, mount, swell, get ahead, gain strength; advance; run —, shoot- up; rise; ascend etc. 305; sprout etc. 194.

aggrandize; raise; exalt; deepen, heighten; lengthen; thicken; strengthen; intensify, enhance, inflate, magnify, double, redouble; multiply; aggravate, exaggerate; ex-asperate, -acerbate; add fuel to the flame, *oleum addere camino*, superadd etc. (*add*) 37; spread etc. (*disperse*) 73.

Adj. increased etc. *v.*; on the increase, undiminished, additional etc. (*added*) 37; increasing etc. *v.*; growing, crescent, intensive, cumulative.

Adv. *crescendo*, increasingly.

Phr. *vires acquirit eundo*.

36. Non-Increase. Decrease.—**N.** decrease, diminution, lessening etc. *v.*; subtraction etc. 38; reduction, abatement, declension; shrinkage etc. (*contraction*) 195; coarctation; abridgment etc. (*shortening*) 201; extenuation.

subsidence, catabasis, wane, ebb-, neap-tide, decline; descent etc. 306; decrement, reflux, depreciation; erosion, wear and tear, deterioration etc. 659; anticlimax; mitigation etc. (*moderation*) 174.

V. decrease, diminish, lessen; abridge etc. (*shorten*) 201; shrink etc. (*contract*) 195; drop —, fall —, tail- off; fall away, waste, wear, erode; wane, ebb, decline; descent etc. 306; subside; deliquesce, melt —, die -away; retire into the shade, hide its diminished head, fall to a low ebb, run low, languish, decay, crumble, consume away.

bate, abate, dequantitate; discount; depreciate; extenuate, lower, weaken, attenuate, fritter away; mitigate etc.(*moderate*) 174; belittle, minimize; dwarf, throw into the shade; keep down, reduce etc. 195; shorten etc. 201; subtract etc. 38.

Adj. unincreased etc. (*see* increase etc. 35); decreased etc. *v.*; decreasing etc. *v.*; on the -wane etc. *n.*; deliquescent.

Adv. *diminuendo, decrescendo*, decreasingly.

37. Addition.—**N.** addition, annexation, adjection; junction etc. 43; super-position, -addition, -junction, -fetation; accession, reinforcement; increase etc. 35; increment, supplement; accompaniment etc. 88; interposition etc. 228; insertion etc. 300; summation etc. 85; adjunct etc. 39.

V. add, annex, adject, affix, attach, superadd, subjoin, superpose; clap —, saddle- on; tack to, postfix, append, tag; ingraft; saddle with; sprinkle; introduce etc. (*interpose*) 228; insert etc. 300.

become added, accrue; ad-, supervene; add up etc. 85.

reinforce, strengthen, swell the ranks of; augment etc. 35.

Adj. added etc. *v.*; additional; supplement, -al, -ary; suppletory, subjunctive; adjec-, adsci-, ascititious; additive, extra, spare, further, fresh, more, new, ulterior, other, auxiliary, supernumerary, accessory.

Adv. in addition, more, plus, extra; and, also, likewise, too, furthermore, further, item; and -also, — eke; else, besides, to boot, *et cetera*; etc.; and so -on, — forth; into the bargain, *cum multis aliis*, over and above, moreover.

with, withal; including, inclusive, as well as, not to mention, let alone; together —, along —, coupled —, in conjunction- with; conjointly; jointly etc. 43.

38. Non-Addition. Subduction.—**N.** sub-traction, -duction; deduction, retrenchment; removal; ab-, sub-lation; abstraction etc. (*taking*) 789; garbling etc. *v.*; mutilation, detruncation; amputation, severance; abs-, ex-, re-cision; curtailment etc. 201; minuend, subtrahend; decrease etc. 36; abrasion.

V. sub-tract, -duct; rebate, de-duct, — duce; bate, retrench; remove, withdraw; take — from, — away; detract.

garble, mutilate, amputate, sever, detruncate; cut -off, — away, — out; expurgate; abscind, excise; pare, thin, prune, decimate; abrade, scrape, file; geld, castrate, emasculate, unman, spay, caponize; eliminate.

diminish etc. 36; curtail etc. (*shorten*) 201; deprive of etc. (*take*) 789; weaken.

Adj. subtracted etc. *v.*; subtractive.

tailless, acaudal.

Adv. in -deduction etc. *n.*; less; short of; minus, without, except, excepting, with the exception of, barring, bar, save, exclusive of, save and except, with a reservation.

39. Adjunct. [Thing added.]—**N.** adjunct, addit-ion, -ament; *additum*, affix, appendage, annex; augment, -ation; increment, reinforcement, supernumerary, accessory, item; garnish, sauce; accompaniment etc. 88; adjective, *addendum*, accession, complement, supplement; continuation; extension, subscript, tag, appendix, postscript, interlineation, interpolation, insertion.

rider, codicil, off-shoot, episode, side issue, corollary; piece; flap, lapel, label, tab, strip, fold, lappet, apron, skirt, embroidery, trappings, *cortège*; tail, suffix etc. (*sequel*) 65; wing.

Adj. additional etc. 37.

Adv. in addition etc. 37.

40. Remainder. [Thing remaining.]—**N.** remainder, residue; remains, *remanet*, remnant, rest, relic, relict; leavings, heel-tap, odds and ends, cheese-parings, candle ends, orts; *residuum*; dottle, dregs, etc. (*dirt*) 653; refuse etc. (*useless*) 645; stubble, result, educt; fag-end, stub; ruins, wreck, skeleton, stump; *alluvium*.

surplus, overplus, excess; balance, complement; superfluity etc. (*redundance*) 641; survival, -ance; afterglow.

V. remain; be -left etc. *adj.*; exceed, survive; leave.

Adj. remaining, left; left -behind, — over;

residu-al, -ary; over, odd; unconsumed, sedimentary; surviving; net; exceeding, over and above; outlying, -standing; cast off etc. 782; superfluous etc. (*redundant*) 641.

V. remain; be -left; left -behind, — over; redidual, -ary; over, odd; unconsumed, sedimentary; surviving; net; exceeding, over and above; outlying, -standing; cast off etc. 782; superfluous etc. (*redundant*) 641.

40a. Decrement. [Thing deducted.]—**N.** decrement, discount, rebate, defect, loss, deduction, eduction, tare; drawback; waste, wastage; reprise.

41. Mixture. [Forming a whole without coherence.]—**N.** mix-, admix-, commix-ture, -tion, mingling; commixion, immixture, interfusion, intermixture, alloyage, matrimony; junction etc. 43; combination etc. 48; entanglement, interlacing; miscegenation, interbreeding.

impregnation; in-, dif-, suf-, transfusion; infiltration; seasoning, sprinkling, interlarding; interpolation etc. 228; adulteration, sophistication.

[Thing mixed] tinge, tincture, touch, dash, smack, sprinkling, spice, seasoning, infusion, *soupçon*.

[Compound resulting from mixture] alloy, brass, bronze, pewter etc.; amalgam, *magma*, blend, half-and-half, *mélange*, *tertium*, *quid*, miscellany, *ambigu*, medley, mess, hash, hotchpotch, hodgepodge, *pasticcio*, patchwork, odds and ends, all sorts; jumble etc. (*disorder*) 59; salad, sauce, mash, *omnium gatherum*, gallimaufry, ragout, *olla podrida*, *olio*, salmagundi, *potpourri*, Noah's ark; texture, mingled yarn; mosaic etc. (*variegation*) 440.

half-blood, -caste, -breed, Eurasian; mulatto; terc-, quart-, quinteron etc.; quad-, octo-roon; *griffo*, *zambo*; cross, hybrid, mongrel etc. 83.

V. mix; join etc. 43; combine etc. 48; com-, im-, inter-mix; mix up with, mingle; com-, inter-, bemingle; shuffle etc. (*derange*) 61; pound together; hash —, stir- up; knead, brew; impregnate with; interlard etc. (*interpolate*) 228; intertwine, -weave etc. 219; associate with, miscegenate, interbreed.

be mixed etc.; get among, be entangled with.

instil, imbue; in-, suf-, trans-fuse; infiltrate, dash, tinge, tincture, season, sprinkle, besprinkle, attemper, medicate, blend, cross; alloy, amalgamate, compound, adulterate, sophisticate, infect.

Adj. mixed etc. *v.*; implex, composite, half-and-half, linsey-wolsey, hybrid, mongrel, heterogeneous; motley etc. (*variegated*) 440; miscellaneous, promiscuous, indiscriminate; miscible.

Adv. among, amongst, amid, amidst, with; in the midst of, in the crowd.

42. Simpleness [Freedom from mixture.]—**N.** simpleness etc. *adj.*; purity, homogeneity.

elimination; sifting etc. *v.*; purification etc. (*cleanness*) 652.

V. render -simple etc. *adj.*; simplify.

sift, winnow, bolt, eliminate; narrow down; get rid of, exclude etc. 55; clear; purify etc. (*clean*) 652; disentangle etc. (*disjoin*) 44.

Adj. simple, uniform, of a piece, homogeneous, single, pure, clear, sheer, neat; Attic.

un-mixed, -mingled, -blended, -combined, -compounded; elementary, undecomposed; un-adulterated, -sophisticated, -alloyed, -tinged, -fortified; pure and simple.

free —, exempt- from; exclusive.

Adv. simply etc. *adj.*; only.

43. Junction.—**N.** junction; joining etc. *v.*; joinder, union; con-nection, -junction, -jugation, compendency, annex-ion, -ation, -ment; coalition; astriction, attachment, compagination, vincture, ligation, alligation; accouplement; marriage etc. (*wedlock*) 903; infibulation, inosculation, symphysis, anastomosis, confluence, communication, concatenation; concurrence, meeting, reunion; assemblage etc. 72.

copulation, coition, intercourse.

joint, joining, juncture, chiasma, pivot, hinge, articulation, commissure, seam, suture, gusset, stitch, splice; link etc. 45; miter, mortise.

closeness, tightness etc. *adj.*; coherence etc. 46; combination etc. 48.

V. join, unite; con-join, -nect; associate; put —, lay —, clap —, hang —, lump —, hold —, piece —, tack —, fix —, bind up- together; embody, re-embody; roll into one.

attach, fix, affix, saddle on, fasten, bind, secure, clinch, twist, make -fast etc. *adj.*; tie, pinion, string, strap, sew, lace, stitch, tack, paste, knit, button, buckle, hitch, lash, truss, bandage, braid, splice, swathe, gird, tether, moor, picket, harness, chain; fetter etc. (*restrain*) 751; lock, latch, belay, brace, hook, grapple, leash, couple, accouple, link, yoke, bracket; marry etc. (*wed*) 903; bridge over, span.

pin, nail, bolt, hasp, clasp, clamp, screw, rivet; impact, solder, braze, cement, set; weld —, fuse- together; wedge, rabbet, mortise, miter, jam, dovetail, enchase; graft, ingraft, inosculate; en-, in-twine; inter-link, -lace, -twine, -twist, -weave; entangle; twine round, belay; tighten; trice —, screw-up.

be -joined etc.; hang —, hold- together; cohere etc. 46.

Adj. joined etc. *v.*; joint; con-joint, -junct; corporate, compact; hand in hand.

firm, fast, close, tight, taut, taught, tense, secure, set, intervolved; in-separable, -dissoluble, -secable, -severable.

Adv. jointly etc. *adj.*; in conjunction with etc. (*in addition to*) 37; fast, firmly etc. *adj.*; intimately.

44. Disjunction.—**N.** dis-junction, -connection, -unity, -union, -association, -engagement, -sociation; discontinuity etc. 70; inconnection; abstraction, -edness; isolation; insul-arity, -ation; oasis; separateness etc. *adj.*; severalty; *disjecta membra*; dispersion etc. 73; apportionment etc. 786.

separation; parting etc. *v.*; detachment, segregation; divorce, sejunction, seposition, diduction, diremption, discerption; elision; *caesura*, division, subdivision, break, fracture, rupture; compartition; dis-memberment, -integration, -location; luxation; sever-, dis-severance; scission; re-, ab-scission; circumcision;

lacer-, dilacer-ation; dis-, ab-ruption; avulsion, divulsion; section, resection, cleavage; fission; separability; separatism.

fissure, breach, rent, split, rift, crack, slit, slot, incision.

dissection, anatomy; decomposition etc. 49; cutting instrument etc. (*sharpness*) 253; saw.

V. be -disjoined etc.; come –, fall- -off, – to pieces; peel off; get loose.

dis-join, -connect, -engage, -unite, -sociate, -pair; divorce, part, dispart, detach, uncouple, separate, cut off, rescind, segregate; set –, keep- apart; insulate, isolate; throw out of gear; cut adrift; loose; un-loose, -do, -bind, -tie, -hitch, -chain, -lock etc. (*fix*) 43, -pack, -ravel; disentangle; set free etc. (*liberate*) 750.

sunder, divide, subdivide, sectionalize, sever, dissever, abscind; cut; segment; in-cide, -cise; circumcise; saw, snip, nib, nip, cleave, rive, rend, slit, split, splinter, chip, crack, snap, break, tear, burst; rend etc. -asunder, – in twain; wrench, rupture, shatter, shiver, cranch, crunch, craunch, chop; rip up; hack, hew, slash; whittle; haggle, hackle, discind, lacerate, scamble, mangle, gash, hash, slice.

cut up, carve, quarter, dissect, anatomize; take –, pull –, pick –, tear- to pieces; tear to tatters, – piecemeal; divellicate; skin etc. 226; dis-integrate, -member, -branch, -band; disperse etc. 73; dis-locate, -joint; break up; mince; comminute etc. (*pulverize*) 330; distribute, apportion etc. 786.

part, – company; separate, leave; alienate, estrange.

Adj. disjoined etc. *v.;* discontinuous etc. 70; bipartite, multipartite, abstract; digitate; disjunctive; isolated etc. *v.;* insular, separate, disparate, discrete, apart, asunder, far between, loose, free; unattached, -annexed, -associated, -connected; distinct; adrift, straggling; rift, reft, cleft, split.

[capable of being divided] scissile, partible, divisible, separable, severable, detachable.

Adv. separately etc. *adj.;* one by one, severally, apart; adrift, asunder, in twain; in the abstract, abstractedly.

45. Vinculum. [Connecting medium.]—**N.** vinculum, link, *nexus*; connec-tive, -tion; junction etc. 43; bond of union, copula, intermedium, hyphen; bracket; bridge, stepping-stone, isthmus.

bond, tendon, tendril; fiber; cord, -age; riband, ribbon, rope, guy, cable, line, halser, hawser, painter, moorings, wire, chain; string etc. (*filament*) 205.

fastening, tie; liga-ment, -ture; strap; bowline, halliard, tackle, lanyard, rigging, shrouds; standing –, running- rigging; traces, harness; yoke; band, -age; brace, roller, fillet; inkle; with, withe, withy; thong, braid; girder, tie-beam; girt, cinch, girth, girdle, cestus, garter, braces, suspenders, halter, noose, lasso, lariat, surcingle, knot, hitch, running knot, frog.

pin, corking pin, nail, brad, tack, skewer, staple, cleat, clamp; cramp, screw, button, buckle, clasp, hasp, hinge; hank, catch, latch, bolt, ring, latchet, pawl, tag; tooth; stud; hook, – and eye; morse, lock, holdfast, padlock, rivet; anchor, grappling-iron, drawbar, coupler, drawhead, coupling, treenail, trennel, stake, pale, pile, post, bollard.

cement, glue, gum, paste, size, wafer, solder, lute, putty, bird-lime, mortar, stucco, plaster, grout.

shackle, rein etc. (*means of restraint*) 752; suspender etc. 214; prop etc. (*support*) 215.

V. bridge over, span; connect etc. 43; hang etc. 214.

46. Coherence.—**N.** co-, ad-herence, -hesion, -hesiveness; concretion, accretion; con-, agglutination, -glomeration; aggregation; consolidation, set, cementation; sticking, soldering etc. *v.;* connection.

tenacity, toughness; stickiness etc. 352; insepara-bility, -bleness; hur, remora.

conglomerate, concrete etc. (*density*) 321.

V. cohere, adhere, stick, cling, cleave, hold, take hold of, hold fast, close with, embrace, clasp, hug; grow –, hang-together; twine round etc. (*join*) 43.

stick like -a leech, – wax; stick close; cling like -ivy, – a bur; adhere like -a remora, – Dejanira's shirt.

glue; ag-, con-glutinate; cement, lute, paste, gum; solder, weld; cake, coagulate, consolidate etc. (*solidify*) 321; agglomerate.

Adj. co-, ad-hesive, -hering etc. *v.;* tenacious, tough; sticky etc. 352.

united, unseparated, sessile, inseparable, inextricable, infrangible; compact etc. (*dense*) 321.

47. Incoherence. [Want of adhesion, non-adhesion, immiscibility.]—**N.** non-adhesion; immiscibility; incoherence; looseness etc. *adj.;* laxity; relaxation; loosening etc. *v.*; freedom; disjunction etc. 44; rope of sand.

V. make -loose etc. *adj.;* loosen, slacken, relax; un-glue etc. 46; detach etc. (*disjoin*) 44.

Adj. non-adhesive, immiscible; incoherent, detached, loose, slack, baggy, lax, relaxed, flapping, streaming; dishevelled; segregated, like grains of sand; un-consolidated etc. 321; -combined etc. 48; non-cohesive.

48. Combination.—**N.** combination; mixture etc. 41; alloy; junction etc. 43; union, unification, synthesis, incorporation, amalgamation, embodiment, coalescence, crasis, fusion, blend, blending, absorption, centralization, federation.

compound, amalgam, composition, *tertium quid;* resultant, impregnation.

V. combine, unite, incorporate, alloy, intertwine etc. 41; amalgamate, embody, absorb, re-embody, blend, merge, fuse, melt into one, consolidate, coalesce, centralize, impregnate; put –, lump- together; federate, associate; fraternize; cement a union, marry, wed, couple, pair, ally.

Adj. combined etc. *v.;* conjunctive, conjugate, conjoint, allied, confederate; impregnated with, ingrained, inoculated.

49. Decomposition.—**N.** decomposition, analysis, diaeresis dissection, resolution, catalysis, electrolysis, hydrolysis, photolysis, dissolution; dispersion etc. 73; disjunction etc. 44;

putrescence, caries, necrosis, corruption etc. (*uncleanness*) 653.

V. decom-pose, -pound; analyze, disembody, dissolve; resolve –, separate- into its elements; electrolyze; dissect, decentralize, break up; disintegrate; disperse etc. 73; unravel etc. (*unroll*) 313; crumble into dust; decay etc. *n.;* deteriorate etc. 659.

Adj. decomposed etc. *v.;* catalytic, analytical.

50. Whole. [Principal part.]—**N.** whole, totality, integrity; totalness etc. *adj.;* entirety, *ensemble*, collectiveness; unity etc. 87; completeness etc. 52; indivisibility, indiscerptibility; integration, embodiment; integer, integral.

all, the whole, total, aggregate, one and all, gross amount, sum, sum-total, *tout ensemble*, length and breadth of, Alpha and Omega, 'be all and end all,' lock, stock and barrel.

bulk, mass, lump, tissue, staple, body, torso, *compages;* truck, bole, hull, hulk, skeleton; greater –, major –, best –, principal –, main-part; essential part etc. (*importance*) 642; lion's share, Benjamin's mess; the long and the short; nearly –, almost- all.

V. form –, constitute- a whole; integrate, embody, amass; aggregate etc. (*assemble*) 72; amount to, come to.

Adj. whole, total, integral, entire; complete etc. 52; one, individual.

un-broken, -cut, -divided, -severed, -clipped, -cropped, -shorn; seamless; undiminished; undemolished, -dissolved, -destroyed, -bruised.

in-divisible, -dissoluble, -dissolvable, -discerptible.

wholesale, sweeping, comprehensive.

Adv. wholly, altogether; totally etc. (*completely*) 52; entirely, all, all in all, considering all things, in a body, collectively, all put together; in the -aggregate, – lump; – mass, – gross, – main, – long run; *en masse*, on the whole, as a whole, bodily, *en bloc, in extenso*, throughout, every inch; substantially.

51. Part.—**N.** part, portion; dose; item, particular; aught, any; division, ward; subdivision, section; chapter, verse; article, clause, count, paragraph, passage; phrase; number, volume, book, fascicule; sector, segment; fraction, fragment; cantle, -t; frustum; detachment, parcel, unit, class etc. 75.

piece, lump, bit; cut, -ting; chip, chunk, collop, slice, scale, shard; lamina etc. 204; moiety; small part; morsel, scrap, crumb; particle etc. (*smallness*) 32; instalment, dividend; share etc. (*allotment*) 786.

débris, odds and ends, oddments, *detritus; excerpta;* member, limb, lobe, lobule, arm, wing, scion, branch, bough, joint, link, offshoot, ramification, twig, stipule, tendril, bush, spray, sprig; runner; leaf, -let; stump; constituent, ingredient, component part etc. 56.

compartment; department etc. (*class*) 75; county etc. (*region*) 181.

V. part, divide, break etc. (*disjoin*) 44; partition etc. (*apportion*) 786.

Adj. fractional, fragmentary; sectional, aliquot; divided etc. *v.;* in compartments, multifid, incomplete, partial, divided etc. 44.

Adv. partly, in part, partially; piecemeal, part by part; by -instalments, – snatches, – inches, – driblets; bit by bit, inch by inch, foot by foot, drop by drop; in -detail, – lots.

52. Completeness.—**N.** completeness etc. *adj.;* completion etc. 729; integration; integrality.

entirety; universality; totality; perfection etc. 650; solid-ity, -arity; unity; all; *ne plus ultra*, ideal, limit.

complement, supplement, make-weight; filling up etc. *v.*

impletion; satur-ation, -ity; high water; high –, flood –, spring- tide; fill, load, bumper, bellyful; brimmer; sufficiency etc. 639.

V. be -complete etc. *adj.*; come to a head.

render -complete etc. *adj.*; complete etc. (*accomplish*) 729; fill, charge, load, replenish; make-up, – good; piece –, eke- out; supply deficiencies; fill -up, – in, – to the brim, – the measure of; saturate etc. 869.

go the whole -hog, – length, go all lengths.

Adj. complete, entire; whole etc. 50; perfect etc. 650; full, good, absolute, thorough, plenary; solid, undivided; with all its parts.

exhaustive, radical, sweeping, thorough-going; dead.

regular, consummate, unmitigated, sheer, unqualified, unconditional, free; abundant etc. (*sufficient*) 639.

brimming; brim-, top-ful; chock –, choke-full; as full as- an egg is of meat, – a vetch, – a tick; saturated, crammed; replete etc. (*redundant*) 641; fraught, laden; full-laden, -fraught, -charged; heavy laden.

completing etc. *v.;* supplement-al, -ary; ascititious.

Adv. completely etc. *adj.;* altogether, outright, wholly, totally, *in toto*, quite; over head and ears; effectually, for good and all, nicely, fully, through thick and thin, head and shoulders; neck and -heel, – crop; all out; in -all respects, – every respect; at all points, out and out, to all intents and purposes; *toto coelo;* utterly, clean, – as a whistle; to the -full, – utmost, – backbone; hollow, stark; heart and soul, root and branch; down to the ground.

to the top of one's bent, as far as possible, *à outrance*.

throughout; from -first to last, – beginning to end, – end to end, – one end to the other, – Dan to Beersheba, – head to foot, – head to heels, – top to toe, – top to bottom; *de fond en comble; à fond, a capite ad calcem, ab ovo usque ad mala*, fore and aft; every -whit, – inch; *cap-à-pie*, to the end of the chapter; up to the -brim, – ears, – eyes; as ... as can be.

on all accounts; *sous tous les rapports;* with a -vengeance, – witness.

53. Incompleteness.—**N.** incompleteness etc. *adj.;* deficiency, short -measure, – wieght; shortcoming etc. 304; insufficiency etc. 640; imperfection etc. 651; immaturity etc. (*nonpreparation*) 674; half measures.

[part wanting] defect, deficit, shortage, ullage, defalcation, omission, *caret;* interval etc. 198; break etc. (*discontinuity*) 70; non-completion etc. 730; missing link.

V. be -incomplete etc. *adj.;* fall short of etc. 304; lack etc. (*be insufficient*) 640; neglect etc. 460.

Adj. incomplete; imperfect etc. 651; unfinished; uncompleted etc. (*see* complete etc. 729); defective, deficient, wanting; failing; in -default, — arrear; short, — of; hollow, meagre, lame, half-and-half, perfunctory, sketchy; crude etc. (*unprepared*) 674.

mutilated, garbled, mangled, docked, lopped, truncated; bobtailed, cropped, bobbed, shingled.

in -progress, — hand; going on, proceeding.

Adv. incompletely etc. *adj.;* by halves.

Phr. *caetera desunt; caret.*

54. Composition.—**N.** composition, constitution, crasis, synthesis; make-up; combination etc. 48; inclusion, admission, comprehension, reception; embodiment, formation, conformation, production.

compilation etc. 72. (*musical*) composition etc. 415; painting etc. 556; writing etc. 590; typography etc. 591.

V. be -composed, — made, — formed, — made up- of; consist of, be resolved into.

include etc. (*in a class*) 76; subsume; synthesize; contain, hold, comprehend, take in, admit, embrace, embody; involve; implicate, drag into.

compose, constitute, form, make; make —, fill —, build- up; weave, construct, fabricate; compile; write, draw; set up (*printing*); enter into the composition of etc. (*be a component*) 56.

Adj. containing, constituting etc. *v.*

55. Exclusion.—**N.** exclusion, non-admission, omission, exception, rejection, repudiation; exile etc. (*seclusion*) 893, preclusion, lock out, ostracism, prohibition; disbarment, expulsion, ban.

separation, segregation, seposition, elimination, coffer-dam.

V. be excluded from etc.

exclude, bar, ban; leave —, shut —, thrust —, bar- out; reject, repudiate, spurn, blackball; ostracize, boycott; lay —, put —, set-apart, — aside; relegate, segregate; throw overboard; strike -off, — out; neglect etc. 460; banish etc. (*seclude*) 893; separate etc. (*disjoin*) 44.

pass over, omit; garble; eliminate, weed, winnow.

Adj. excluding etc. *v.;* exclusive.

excluded etc. *v.;* unrecounted, not included in; inadmissible; preventive, interdictive.

Adv. exclusive of, barring, except; with the exception of; save, bating.

56. Component.—**N.** component; component —, integral —, integrant-part; element, constituent, ingredient, leaven; part and parcel; contents; appurtenance; feature; member etc. (*part*) 51; personnel.

V. enter into, — the composition of; be a - component etc. *n.;* be —, form- part of; merge —, be merged- in; be implicated in; share in etc. (*participate*) 778; belong —, appertain- to.

form, make, constitute, compose.

Adj. forming etc. *v.;* inclusive; inherent etc. 5.

57. Extraneousness.—**N.** extraneousness etc. *adj.;* extrinsicality etc. 6; exteriority etc. 220; alienism.

foreign -body, — substance, — element; alien, stranger, intruder, interloper, foreigner, tramontane, *novus homo*, new comer, immi-, emi-grant; creole, Afrikander; outsider, outlander, tenderfoot.

Adj. extraneous, foreign, alien, ulterior; exterior, external, outside, outlandish; oversea; tra-, ultra-montane.

excluded etc. 55; inadmissible; exceptional.

Adv. in foreign -parts, — lands; abroad, beyond seas, overseas.

58. Order.—**N.** order, regularity etc. 80; uniformity, symmetry, *lucidus ordo;* harmony, music of the spheres.

gradation, progression; series etc. (*continuity*) 69.

subordination; course, even tenor, routine; method, disposition, arrangement, array, system, economy, discipline; orderliness etc. *adj.*

rank, place etc. (*term*) 71.

V. be —, become- in order etc. *adj.;* form, fall in, draw up; arrange —, range —, place- itself; adjust; fall into —, take- -one's place, — rank; rally round; arrange etc. 60.

Adj. orderly, regular; in -order, — trim, — apple-pie order, according to Cocker, — its proper place, neat, neat as a pin, tidy, *en règle*, well regulated, correct, methodical, uniform, symmetrical, ship-shape, business-like, systematic; habitual; unconfused etc. (*see* confuse etc. 61) arranged etc. 60.

Adv. in order; methodically etc. *adj.;* in -turn, — its turn; step by step; by regular -steps, — gradations, — stages, — intervals; *seriatim*, systematically, by clockwork, *gradatim;* at stated periods etc. (*periodically*) 138.

59. Disorder. [Absence, or want of Order, etc.]—**N.** disorder; derangement etc. 61; irregularity; anomaly etc. (*unconformity*) 83; anar-chy, -chism; want of method; dishevelment, untidiness etc. *adj.;* disunion; discord etc. 24.

confusion, confusedness etc. *adj.;* disarray, jumble, mix-up, huddle, litter, lumber; *cahotage;* farrago; mess, muss, mash, muddle, hash; hotchpotch; *imbroglio*, chaos, *omnium gatherum*, medley; mere -mixture etc. 41; fortuitous concourse of atoms, *disjecta membra, rudis indigestaque moles.*

complexity; complexness etc. *adj.;* com-, implication; intri-cacy, -cation; perplexity; network, maze, labyrinth, wilderness, jungle; involution, ravelling, entanglement; coil etc. (*convolution*) 248; sleave, tangled skein, knot, Gordian know, kink, web; wheels within wheels.

turmoil; ferment, etc. (*agitation*) 315; to do, trouble, pudder, pother, row, disturbance, convulsion, tumult, pandemonium, uproar, riot, rumpus, stour, scramble, *fracas*, embroilment, *mêleé*, spill and pelt, rough and tumble; whirlwind etc. 349; bear garden, Babel, Saturnalia, Donnybrook Fair, confusion worse confounded, most admired disorder, *concordia discors;* Bedlam —, hell- broke loose; bull in a china shop;

all the fat in the fire, *diable à quatre*, Devil to pay; pretty kettle of fish; pretty piece of -work, — business.

slattern, slut, sloven; draggle-tail.

V. be -disorderly etc. *adj.*; ferment, play at cross purposes.

put out of order; derange etc. 61; ravel etc. 219; ruffle, rumple; bungle, botch.

Adj. disorderly, orderless; out of -order; — place, — gear, — whack; irregular, desultory; anomalous etc. (*unconformable*) 83; acephalous, disorganized, straggling; un-, im-methodical; unsymmetric; unsystematic; untidy, slovenly, bedraggled, messy; dislocated; out of sorts; promiscuous, indiscriminate; chaotic, anarchical, lawless; unarranged etc. 60; confused, tumultuous, turbulent, tempestuous; deranged etc. 61; topsy turvy etc. (*inverted*) 218; shapeless etc. 241; disjointed, out of joint.

com-plex, -plexed; intricate, complicated, perplexed, involved, ravelled, entangled, knotted, tangled, inextricable; irreducible.

troublous; riotous etc. (*violent*) 173.

Adv. irregularly etc. *adj.*; by fits and -snatches, — starts; pell-mell; higgledy-piggledy; helter-skelter, harum-scarum; in a ferment; at -sixes and sevens, — cross purposes; upside down etc. 218.

Phr. the cart before the horse, chaos is come again.

60. Arrangement. [Reduction to Order.]—**N.** arrangement; plan etc. 626; preparation etc. 673; dispos-al, -ition; col-, al-location; disbribution; sorting etc. *v.*; assortment, allotment; grouping; apportionment, *taxis*, taxonomy, *syn-taxis*, graduation, organization, grading; re-organization, rationalization.

analysis, classification, division, digestion; systematism.

[Result of arrangement] order, orderliness, form, array; digest, synopsis etc. (compendi-um) 596; *syntagma*, table, atlas; register etc. (*record*) 551; score etc. 415; cosmos, organism, architecture.

[Instrument for sorting] sieve etc. 260; file, card index.

V. reduce to —, bring into- order; introduce order into; rally.

arrange, dispose, place, form; put —, set —, place- in order; straighten up, tidy up; set out, collocate, allocate, pack, marshal, range, size, rank, array, group, parcel out, allot, space, distribute, deal; cast —, assign- the parts; dispose of, assign places to; assort, sort; sift, riddle; put —, set- -to rights, — into shape, — in trim, — in array.

class, -ify; divide; file, string together, thread; register etc. (*record*) 551; list, catalogue, tabulate, index, alphabeticize, graduate, digest, grade, codify; orchestrate, score.

methodize, regulate, systematize, standardize, co-ordinate, organize, settle, fix.

unravel, disentangle, ravel, card; disembroil.

Adj. arranged etc. *v.*; embattled, in battle array; cut and dried; methodical, orderly, regular, systematic, tabular.

61. Derangement. [Subversion of Order; bringing into disorder.]—**N.** derangement etc. *v.*; disorder etc. 59; evection, discomposure, disturbance; dis-, de-organization; involvement; dislocation; perturbation, interruption; shuffling etc. *v.*; inversion etc. 218; corrugation etc. (*fold*) 258; insanity etc. 503.

V. derange; dis-, mis-arrange; dis-, mis-place; mislay, discompose, disorder, de-, dis-organize; embroil, unsettle, disturb, confuse, trouble, perturb, jumble, tumble; huddle, shuffle, muddle, toss, hustle, fumble, riot; bring —, put —, throw- into -disorder etc. 59; break the ranks, disconcert, convulse; break in upon.

unhinge, dislocate, put out of joint, throw out of gear.

turn topsy-turvy etc. (*invert*) 218; bedevil; complicate, involve, perplex, confound; im-, embrangle; tangle, en-tangle, ravel, tousle, dishevel, ruffle, rumple etc. (*fold*) 258; dement.

litter, scatter; mix etc. 41.

Adj. deranged etc. *v.*; syncre-tic, -tistic.

62. Precedence.—**N.** precedence; coming before etc. *v.*; the lead, *le pas*; superiority etc. 33; importance etc. 642; anteced-ence, -ency; anteriority etc. (*front*) 234; precursor etc. 64; priority etc. 116; precession etc. 280; anteposition, preference.

V. precede; come -before, — first; forerun, head, lead, take the lead; lead the -way, — dance; introduce, usher in; have the *pas*; set the fashion etc. (*influence*) 175; lead off, kick off, open the ball; take —, have- precedence; outrank; have the start etc. (*get before*) 280.

place before; prefix; premise, prelude, preface.

Adj. preceding etc. *v.*; pre-, antecedent; anterior, prior etc. 116; before; former, foregoing; before-, above-mentioned; aforesaid, said; precurs-ory, -ive; prevenient, preliminary, prefatory, introductory; prelus-ive, -ory; proemial, preparatory.

Adv. before; in advance etc. (*precession*) 280.

Phr. *seniores priores.*

63. Sequence.—**N.** sequence, coming after; going after etc. (*following*) 281; consecution, succession; posteriority etc. 117.

continuation; prolongation, order of succussion; successiveness; Elijah's mantle.

secondariness; subordinancy etc. (*inferiority*) 34.

V. succeed; come -after, — on, — next; follow, ensue, step into the shoes of; alternate.

place after, suffix, append.

Adj. succeeding etc. *v.*; sequent; sub-, consequent; sequacious, proximate, next; consecutive etc. (*continuity*) 69; alternate, amoebaean.

latter; posterior etc. 117.

Adv. after, subsequently; behind etc. (*rear*) 235.

64. Precursor.—**N.** precursor, antecedent, precedent, predecessor; forerunner, van-courier, *avant-coureur*, pioneer, prodrome, *prodromos*, outrider; leader, bell-wether; herald, harbinger; dawn.

prelude, preamble, preface, prologue, foreword, *avant-propos*, *protasis*, prolusion, proem, *prolepsis*, *prolegomena*, prefix, introduction;

lead, heading, frontispiece, groundwork; preparation etc. 673; overture, voluntary, *exordium*, symphony, *ritornello;* premises.

prefigurement etc. 511; omen etc. 512.

Adj. precursory; prelu-sive, -sory, -dious; proemial, introductory, prefatory, prodromous, inaugural, preliminary; precedent etc. (*prior*) 116.

65. Sequel.—N. sequel, suffix, successor; tail, *queue*, train, wake, trail, rear; retinue, suite; appendix, postscript, subscript; epilogue; conclusion; peroration; codicil; continuation, *sequela;* appendage etc. 39; tail —, heel-piece; tag, more last words; *colophon*.

follower, after-glow, -growth, -crop, -taste, -math.

after-part, -piece, -course, -thought, -game; *arrière penseé*, second thoughts.

66. Beginning.—N. beginning, commencement, opening, outset, incipience, inception, inchoation; introduction etc. (*precursor*) 64; *alpha;* initial; foundation; inauguration, *début, le premier pas*, embarcation, rising of the curtain; zero hour; exordium, curtain raiser; maiden speech; prelude; outbreak, onset, brunt; initiative, move, first move; gambit, narrow —, thin- end of the wedge; fresh start, new departure; forefront.

origin etc. (*cause*) 153; source, rise; bud, germ etc. 153; egg, rudiment; genesis, birth, nativity, cradle, infancy, incunabula; start, starting-point etc. 293; dawn etc. (*morning*) 125.

title-page; head, -ing, caption; van etc. (*front*) 234.

en-trance, -try; inlet, orifice, mouth, chops, lips, porch, portal, portico, *propylon*, door; gate, -way; postern, wicket, threshold, vestibule; skirts, border etc. (*edge*) 231; tee.

first -stage, blush, — glance, — impression, — sight.

rudiments, elements, outlines, *principia*, grammar, *protasis;* alphabet, ABC.

V. begin, commence, inchoate, rise, arise, originate, institute, conceive, initiate, open, dawn, set in, take its rise, enter upon, start; enter; set out etc. (*depart*) 293; embark in.

usher in; lead -off, — the way; take the -lead, — initiative; inaugurate, head; stand -at the head, — first, — for; lay the foundations etc. (*prepare*) 673; found etc. (*cause*) 153; set -up, — on foot, — agoing, — abroach, — the ball in motion; apply the match to a train; launch, broach; open -up, — the door to; set -about, — to work; make a -beginning, — start; handsel; take the first step, lay the first stone, cut the first turf; break -ground, — the ice, — cover; pass —, cross- the Rubicon; open -fire, — the ball; ventilate, air; undertake etc. 676.

come into -existence, — the world; make one's *début*, take birth; burst forth, break out; spring —, crop- up.

begin -at the beginning, — *ab ovo*, — again, — *de novo;* start afresh, make a fresh start, shuffle the cards, resume, recommence.

Adj. beginning etc. *v.;* initi-al, -atory, -ative; inceptive, introductory, incipient; proemial, inaugural; incho-ate, -ative; embryonic, rudimental; primogenial; primeval etc. (*old*) 124; rudimentary, aboriginal; natal, nascent.

first, foremost, front, leading, head; maiden. begun etc. *v.;* just -begun etc. *v.*

Adv. at —, in- the beginning etc. *n.;* first, in the first place, *imprimis*, first and foremost; *in limine;* in -the bud, — embryo, — its infancy; from -the beginning, — its birth; *ab -initio*, — *ovo*, — *incunabilis*, primarily, originally.

67. End.—N. end, close, termination; desinence, conclusion, *finis, finale*, period, term, *terminus*, last, *omega;* extreme, -tremity; gable —, butt —, fagend; tip, nib, point; tail etc. (*rear*) 235; verge etc. (*edge*) 231; tag, epilogue, peroration; *bonne bouche*, bitter end, tail end; terminal; *apodosis;* appendix.

consummation, *dénouement;* finish etc. (*completion*) 729; fate; doom, -sday; crack of doom, day of Judgment, fall of the curtain, wind-up; goal, destination; limit, stoppage, end all, determination; expiration, expiry; death etc. 360; end of all things; finality; eschatology.

break up, *commencement de la fin*, last stage, turning point; *coup de grâce*, death-blow; knock-out.

V. end, close, finish, terminate, conclude, be all over; expire; die etc. 360; come —, draw- to a -close etc. *n.;* have run its course; run out, pass away.

bring to an -end etc. *n.;* put an end to, make an end of; determine; get through; achieve etc. (*complete*) 729; stop etc. (*make to cease*) 142; shut up shop.

Adj. ending etc. *v.;* final, terminal, definitive, conclusive; crowning etc. (*completing*) 729; last, ultimate; hindermost; rear etc. 235; caudal.

contermin-ate, -ous, -able.

ended etc. *v.;* at an end; settled, decided, over, played out, set at rest.

penultimate; last but -one, — two, etc.

unbegun, uncommenced; fresh.

Adv. finally etc. *adj.;* in fine; at the last; once for all.

68. Middle.—N. middle, midst, mediety; mean etc. 29; medium, middle term; center etc. 222; mid-course etc. 628; *mezzo termine; juste milieu* etc. 628; half-way house, nave, navel, omphalos; nucle-us, -olus.

equidistance, bisection, half-distance; equator, diaphragm, midriff; interjacence etc. 228.

Adj. middle, medial, mesial, mean, mid; middle-, mid-most; middling; mediate; intermediate etc. (*interjacent*) 228; equidistant; central etc. 222; mediterranean, equatorial.

Adv. in the middle; in the thick; mid-, half-way; midships, *in medias res*.

69. Continuity. [Uninterrupted sequence.]—**N.** continuity; consecu-tion,, -tiveness etc. *adj.;* succession, round, suite, progression, series, train, chain; cat-, concatenation; catena; scale; gradation, course, constant flow, perpetuity.

procession, column; retinue, *cortège*, cavalcade, rank and file, line of battle, array.

pedigree, genealogy, lineage, race etc. 166.

rank, file, line, row, range, tier, string, thread, team; suit; colonnade.

V. follow in —, form- a series etc. *n.;* fall in.

arrange in a -series etc. *n.*; string together, catenate, file, thread, graduate, tabulate.

Adj. continu-ous, -ed; consecutive; progressive, gradual; serial, successive; immediate, unbroken, entire; linear; in a -line, — row etc. *n.*; uninter-rupted, -mitting; unremitting; perennial, evergreen; constant.

Adv. continuously etc. *adj.*; *seriatim*; in a -line etc. *n.*; in -succession, — turn; running, gradually, step by step, *gradatim*, at a stretch; in -file, — column, — single file, — Indian file.

70. Discontinuity. [Interrupted sequence.]—**N.** discontinuity; disjunction etc. 44; anacoluthon; interruption, break, fracture, flaw, fault, split, crack, cut; gap etc. (*interval*) 198; solution of continuity, *caesura*; broken thread; parenthesis, episode; rhapsody, patchwork; intermission; alternation etc. (*periodicity*) 138; dropping fire.

V. be -discontinuous etc. *adj.*; alternate, intermit.

discontinue, pause, interrupt; intervene; break, — in upon; interpose etc. 228; break —, snap- the thread; disconnect etc. (*disjoin*) 44.

Adj. discontinuous, unsuccessive, broken, interrupted, *décousu*; dis-, un-connected, discrete, disjunctive; fitful etc. (*irregular*) 139; spasmodic, desultory, intermit-ting etc. *v.*; -tent; alternate; recurrent etc. (*periodic*) 138; few and far between.

Adv. at intervals; by -snatches, — jerks, — skips, — catches, — fits and starts; skippingly, *per saltum; longo intervallo*.

71. Term.—**N.** term, rank, station, stage, step; degree etc. 26; scale, remove, grade, link, peg, round —, rung- of the ladder, *status*, position, place, point, mark, *pas*, period, pitch; stand, -ing; footing, range.

V. hold —, occupy —, fall into- a place etc. *n.*

72. Assemblage.—**N.** assemblage; col-lection, location, -ligation; compilation, levy, gathering, ingathering, mobilization, meet, foregathering, muster, *attroupement*; con-course, -flux, -gregation, -tesseration, -vergence etc. 290; meeting, *levée, réunion*, drawing room, at home; conversazione etc. (*social gathering*) 892; assembly, congress, eisteddfod; conven-tion, -ticle; gemote; conclave, etc. (*council*) 696; posse, *posse comitatus;* Noah's ark.

miscellany, *collectanea*, symposium; museum, menagerie, etc. (*store*) 636.

crowd, throng, multitude; flood, rush, deluge; rout, rabble, mob, press, crush, *cohue*, jam, horde, body, tribe; crew, gang, knot, squad, band, party; swarm, shoal, school, covey, flock, herd, drove, kennel; array, bevy, galaxy; *corps*, company, troop, *troupe;* army, force, regiment, etc. (*combatants*) 726; host etc. (*multitude*) 102; populousness.

clan, brotherhood, association etc. (*party*) 712.

volley, shower, storm, cloud.

group, cluster, Pleiades, clump, pencil; set, batch, lot, pack; budget, *dossier*, assortment, bunch; parcel; pack-et, -age; bundle, *fasciculus*, fascine, bale; ser-on, oon; faggot, wisp, truss, tuft; shock, rick, fardel, stack, sheaf, swath, gavel, haycock, stook.

accumulation etc. (*store*) 636; congeries, heap, lump, pile, *rouleau*, tissue, mass, pyramid; drift; snow-ball, -drift; acervation, cumulation; amassment, glom-, agglom-eration; conglobation; conglomeration, -ate; coacervation, coagmentation, aggregation, concentration, congestion, *omnium gatherum, spicilegium*, black hole of Calcutta; quantity etc. (*greatness*) 31.

collector, gatherer; whip, -per in.

V. [be or come together] assemble, collect, muster; meet, unite, join, rejoin; cluster, flock, swarm, surge, stream, herd, crowd, throng, associate; con-gregate, -glomerate, -centrate; center round, *rendezvous*, resort; come —, flock —, get —, pig- together; forgather; huddle; reassemble.

[get or bring together] assemble, muster, mobilize; bring —, get —, put —, draw —, scrape —, lump- together; col-lect, -locate, -ligate; get —, whip- in; gather; hold a meeting; con-vene, -voke, -vocate; rake up, dredge; heap, mass, pile; pack, put up, truss, cram; acervate; ag-glomerate, -gregate; compile; group, aggroup, concentrate, unite; collect —, bring- into a focus; amass, accumulate etc. (*store*) 636; collect in a drag-net; heap Ossa upon Pelion.

Adj. assembled etc. *v.*; closely packed, dense, serried, crowded to suffocation, teeming, swarming, populous; as thick as hops; all of a heap, fasciculated; cumulative.

Phr. the plot thickens.

73. Non-assemblage. Dispersion.—**N.** dispersion; disjunction etc. 44; divergence etc. 291; scattering etc. *v.*; dissemination, broadcasting, diffusion, dissipation, distribution; apportionment etc. 786; spread, respersion, circumfusion, interspersion, spargefaction.

waifs and estrays, flotsam and jetsam, *disjecta membra*.

V. disperse, scatter, sow, disseminate, radiate, diffuse, shed, spread, ted, bestrew, overspread, dispense, disband, disembody, demobilize, dismember, distribute; apportion etc. 786; blow off, let out, dispel, cast forth, draught off; strew, straw, strow; spirtle, cast, sprinkle, shatter; issue, deal out, retail, utter; re-, inter-sperse; set abroach, circumfuse.

turn —, cast- adrift; scatter to the winds; sow broadcast.

spread like wildfire, disperse themselves.

Adj. unassembled etc. (*see* assemble etc. 72); dispersed etc. *v.*; sparse, dispread, broadcast, sporadic, widespread; far-flung; epidemic etc. (*general*) 78; adrift, stray; dishevelled, streaming.

Adv. *sparsim*, here and there, *passim*.

74. Focus. [Place of meeting.]—**N.** focus; point of- convergence etc. 290; corradiation; center etc. 222; gathering-place, resort; haunt; retreat; *venue, rendezvous;* rallying point, head-quarters, home, club; *dépôt* etc. (*store*) 636; tryst, trysting-place; place of -meeting, — resort, — assignation; *point de —, lieu de- réunion;* issue.

V. bring to- a point, — a focus, — an issue; focus.

75. Class.—**N.** class, category, *categorema, head*, order, section; division, subdivision; department, province, domain, sphere.

kind, sort, genus, species, variety, branch, family, race, tribe, caste, sept, clan, breed; *clique, coterie;* type, kit, sect, set; assortment; feather, kidney; suit; range; gender, sex, kin.

manner, description, denomination, persuasion, connection, designation, character, stamp; predicament; conviction etc. 484.

similarity etc. 17.

76. Inclusion. [Comprehension under, or reference to a class.]—**N.** inclusion, admission, incorporation, comprehension, reception.

composition etc. (*inclusion in a compound*) 54.

V. be -included in etc.; come –, fall –, range- under; belong –, pertain- to; range with; merge in.

include, compromise, comprehend, contain, admit, embrace, receive; enclose etc. (*circumscribe*) 229; incorporate, cover, embody, encircle.

reckon –, enumerate –, number- among; refer to; place –, arrange-under, – with; take into account.

Adj. includ-ed; -ing etc. *v.;* inclusive; comprehensive, all-embracing; congen-er, -erous; of the same -class etc. 75.

Phr. *et hoc genus omne*, etc.; *et caetera.*

77. Exclusion.*—**N.** exclusion etc. 55.

* The same set of words is used to express *Exclusion from a class* and *Exclusion from a compound*. Reference is therefore made to the former at 55. This identity does not occur with regard to *Inclusion*, which therefore constitutes a separate category.

78. Generality.—**N.** general-ity, -ization; universality; catholic-ity, -ism; miscel-lany, -laneousness; drag-net.

every-one, -body; all hands, all the world and his wife; any body, N or M, all sorts; *tout le monde*.

prevalence, run.

V. be -general etc. *adj.;* prevail, obtain, be going about, stalk abroad.

render -general etc. *adj.;* generalize; spread, broadcast.

Adj. general, usual, current, generic, collective; broad, comprehensive, sweeping; encyclopedical, panoramic, widespread etc. (*dispersed*) 73.

universal; catho-lic, -lical; common, worldwide; e-cumenical; transcendental; prevalent, prevailing, rife, epidemic, besetting; all over, covered with.

every, all; indeterminate, indefinite, unspecified, impersonal.

customary etc. (*habitual*) 613.

Adv. what-ever, -soever; to a man, one and all, without exception.

generally etc. *adj.;* always, for better for worse; in general, generally speaking; speaking generally; for the most part; in the long run etc. (*on an average*) 29.

79. Speciality.—**N.** speciality, *spécialité;* individ-uality, -uity; particularity, peculairity; idiocrasy etc. (*tendency*) 176; personality, characteristic, mannerism, idiosyncrasy, attribute specificness etc. *adj.;* singularity etc. (*unconformity*) 83; reading, version, lection; state; *trait;* distinctive feature; technicality; *differentia.*

particulars, details, minutiae, items, counts.

I, self, I myself, *ego*; my-, him-, her-, it-self.

V. specify, particularize, individualize, realize, specialize, designate, differentiate, determine, define, denote, indicate, itemize, detail.

descend to particulars, enter into detail, come to the point.

Adj. special, particular, individual, specific, proper, personal, intimate, original, private, respective, definite, concrete, determinate, especial, certain, esoteric, endemic, partial, party, peculiar, marked, appropriate, several, characteristic, diagnistic, exact, exclusive; singular etc. (*exceptional*) 83; idiomatic; typical, representative, distinctive.

this, that; yon, -der.

Adv. specially etc. *adj.;* in particular, *in propriâ personâ; ad hominem*; for my part.

each, apiece, one by one; severally, respectively, each to each; *seriatim*, in detail, bit by bit; *pro hac vice, – re natâ.*

namely, that is to say, *videlicet*, viz.; to wit.

80. Rule.—**N.** regularity, uniformity etc. 16; clock-work precision; punctuality etc. (*exactness*) 494; routine etc. (*custom*) 613; formula; system; rut; canon, convention, maxim; rule etc. (*form, regulation*) 697; key-note, standard, model; precedent etc. (*prototype*) 22; conformity etc. 82.

nature, principle; law; order of things; normal –, natural –, ordinary –, model- -state, – condition; standing -dish, – order; normality; Procrustean law; law of the Medes and Persians; hard and fast rule.

Adj. regular, uniform, symmetrical, constant, steady; according to rule etc. (*conformable*) 82; customary etc. 613; orderly etc. 58.

81. Multiformity.—**N.** multi-, omniformity; variety, diversity; multifariousness etc. *adj.*

Adj. multi-form, -fold, -farious, -generous; multiplex, variform, manifold, many-sided, multiplicate; omni-form, -genous, -farious; polymorphic; protean; heterogeneous, motley, mosaic; epicene, indiscriminate, desultory, irregular, diversified, different, divers; all manner of; of -every description, – all sorts and kinds; *et hoc genus omne;* and what not? *de omnibus rebus et quibusdam aliis.*

82. Conformity.—**N.** conform-ity, -ance; observance.

naturalization; conventionality etc. (*custom*) 613; agreement etc. 23.

example, instance, specimen, sample, quotation; exemplification, illustration, case in point; object lesson.

conventionalist, formalist, Philistine.

pattern etc. (*prototype*) 22.

V. conform to, – rule; accommodate –, adapt- oneself to; rub off corners.

be -regular etc. *adj.;* move in a groove; follow —, observe —, go by —, bend to —, obey- -rules, — precedents; comply —, tally —, chime in —, fall in-with; be -guided, — regulated- by; fall into a -custom, — usage; follow the -fashion, — multitude; pass muster, do as others do, ***hurler aves les loups;*** do at Rome as the Romans do; go —, swim- with the -stream, — current, — tide; tread the beaten track etc. (*habit*) 613; rubber-stamp; keep one in countenance.

exemplify, illustrate, cite, quote, put a case; produce an- instance etc. *n.*

Adj. conformable to rule, adaptable, compliant, consistent, agreeable; regular etc. 80; according to -regulation, — rule, — Cocker; ***en règle, selon les règles,*** well regulated, orderly; symmetric etc. 242.

conventional commonplace etc. (*customary*) 613; of -daily, — every day- occurrence; in the natural order of things; ordinary, common, — or garden, prosaic, habitual, usual.

in the order of the day; naturalized.

typical, normal, formal; canonical, orthodox, sound, strict, rigid, positive, uncompromising, Procrustean; point device.

secundum artem, ship-shape, technical.

exemplary, illustrative, in point.

Adv. conformably etc. *adj.;* by rule; agreeably to; in -conformity, — accordance, — keeping-with; according to: consistently with; as usual, ***ad instar, instar omnium; more -solito, — majorum.***

for the sake of conformity; of —, as a matter of- course; ***pro formâ,*** for form's sake, by the card; according to plan.

invariably etc. (*uniformly*) 16.

for -example, — instance: ***exempli gratiâ; e.g.; inter alia.***

Phr. ***cela va sans dire, ex pede Herculem, noscitur a sociis.***

83. Unconformity.—N. non-conformity etc. 82; un-, dis-conformity; unconventionality, informality, abnormity, anomaly; anomalousness etc. *adj.;* exception, peculiarity, etc. 79; infraction —, breach —, violation —, infringement- of -law, — custom, — usage; eccentricity, ***bizarrerie,*** oddity, ***je ne sais quoi,*** monstrosity, rarity; freak of Nature.

individuality, idiosyncrasy, singularity, oritinality, mannerism.

aberration; irregularity; variety; singularity; exemption; salvo etc. (*qualification*) 469.

nonconformist; nondescript, character, original, nonsuch, monster, prodigy, wonder, miracle, curiosity, missing link, flying fish, black swan, ***lusus naturae, rara avis,*** queer fish; mongrel; half-caste, -blood, -breed; ***métis,*** cross breed, hybrid, mule, mulatto, sacatra, marabou; ***tertium quid,*** hermaphrodite, gynander, androgyn.

phoenix, chimera, hydra, sphinx, minotaur; griff-in, -on; centaur; hippogriff, -centaur; sagittary; kraken; cockatrice, wyvern, roc, liver, dragon, sea-serpent; mermaid; unicorn; Cyclops, 'men whose heads do grown beneath their shoulders:. Teratolgy.

fish out of water; neither -one thing nor another, — fish flesh nor fowl nor good red herring; one in a -way, — thousand; out-cast, -law; Ishmael, pariah; oasis.

V. be -unconformable etc. *adj.;* leave the beaten -track, — path; infringe —, break —, violate- a -law, — habit, — usage, — custom; drive a coach and six through; stretch a point; have no business there; baffle —, beggar- all description.

Adj. unconformable, exceptional; abnorm-al, -ous; anomal-ous, -istic; out of -order, — place, — keeping, — tune, — one's element; irregular, arbitrary; lawless, informal, aberrant, stray, wandering, wanton; peculiar, exclusive, unnatural, eccentric, crotchety, egregious; out of the -beaten track, — common, — common run, — pale of; misplaced; funny.

un-usual, -accustomed, -customary, -wonted, -common; rare, singular, ***unique,*** curious, odd, extraordinary, strange, monstrous; wonderful etc. 870; unexpected, unaccountable; ***outré,*** out of the way, remarkable, noteworthy; queer, quaint, nondescript, none such, ***sui generis;*** original, unconventional, Bohemian, unfashionable; un-described, -precedented, -paralleled, -exampled, -heard of, -familiar; fantastic, newfangled, grotesque, ***bizarre;*** outlandish, exotic, ***tombé de nues,*** preternatural; denaturalized.

heterogeneious, heteroclite, amorphous, mongrel, amphibious, epicene, half-blood, hybrid; androgyn-ous, -al; unsymmetric etc. 243.

qualified etc. 469.

Adv. unconformably etc. *adj.;* except, unless, save, barring, beside, without, save and except, let alone.

however, yet, but.

Int. what -on earth! — in the world!

Phr. never was -seen, — heard, — known- the like.

84. Number.—N. number, symbol, numeral, figure, cipher, digit, integer; counter; round number; formula; function; series.

sum, total, aggregate, difference, complement, subtrahend; product; multipli-cand, -er, -cator; coefficient, multiple; dividend, divisor, factor, quotient, sub-multiple, fraction; mixed number; numerator, denominator; decimal, circulating decimal, repetend; common measure, aliquot part; reciprocal; prime number; totitive, totient.

permutation, combination, variation; election.

ratio, proportion; progression; arithmetical —, geometrical —, harmonical- progression; percentage.

figurate —, pyramidal —, polygonal- numbers.

power, root, exponent, index, logarithm, antilogarithm; modulus.

differential, integral, fluxion, fluent.

Adj. numeral, complementary, divisible, aliquot, reciprocal, prime, fractional, decimal, figurate, incommensurable.

proportional, exponential, logarithmic, logometric, differential, fluxional, integral.

positive, negative; rational, irrational; surd, radical, real, imaginary, impossible.

85. Numeration.—N. numeration, numbering etc. *v.;* pagination; tale, tally, recension, enumeration, summation, reckoning, computation, supputation; calcu-lation, -lus; algorithm, rhabdology, dactylonomy; measurement etc. 466; statistics.

arithmetic, analysis, algebra, fluxions; differential —, integral —, infinitesimal-calculus; calculus of differences.

[Statistics] dead reckoning, muster, poll, census, capitation, roll-call, recapitulation; account, etc. (*list*) 86.

[Operations] notation, addition, subtraction, multiplication, division, proportion, rule of three, practice, equations, extraction of roots, reduction, involution, evolution, approximation, interpolation, differentiation, integration.

[Instruments] abacus, swan-pan, logometer, sliding —, slide- rule, tallies, Napier's bones, calculating —, adding- machine, difference engine; cash register.

arithmetician, calculator, abacist; mathematician, actuary, statistician, surveyor, geodesist.

V. number, count, tell; call —, run- over, take an account of, enumerate, call the roll, muster, poll, recite, recapitulate; sum; sum —, cast- up; tell off, score, cipher, compute, calculate, set a price, reckon, — up, estimate; suppute, add, subtract, multiply, divide, extract roots.

check, prove, demonstrate, balance, audit, overhaul, take stock; affix numbers to, page, foliate, paginate.

amount —, come- to.

Adj. numer-al, -ical; arithmetical, analytic, algebraic, statistical, numerable, computable, calculable; commensur-able, -ate; incommensur-able, -ate.

86. List.—**N.** list, catalogue, enumeration, inventory, schedule; register etc. (*record*) 551; account; bill, — of costs, syllabus; terrier, tally, file; almanac, calendar, index, table, atlas, contents, card index, rota, ticket; book, ledger; synopsis, *catalogue raisonné; tableau*, scroll, manifest, invoice, bill of lading; prospectus, *programme;* bill of fare, *menu, carte;* score, census, statistics, returns; Red —, Blue —, Domesday- book; *cadaster;* directory, gazetteer, dictionary, glossary, lexicon, thesaurus, gradus.

roll; check —, chequer —, bead- roll, — of honor; muster -roll, — book; roster, panel; cartulary, diptych.

V. list, enrol, schedule, register etc. *n.;* indent, post, docket; matriculate.

Adj. cadastral, listed etc. *v.*

87. Unity.—**N.** unity; oneness etc. *adj.;* individuality; solitude etc. (*seclusion*) 893; isolation etc. (*disjunction*) 44; unification etc. 48.

one, unit, ace; item; individual; solo, none else, no other, naught beside.

V. be -one, — alone etc. *adj.;* dine with Duke Humphrey.

isolate etc. (*disjoin*) 44.

render one; unite etc. (*join*) 43, (*combine*) 48.

Adj. one, sole, single, solitary, only- begotten; individual, apart, alone; kithless.

un-accompanied, -attended; *solus*, single-handed; singular, odd, unique, unrepeated, azygous, first and last; isolated etc. (*disjoined*) 44; insular; unitary.

lone; lone-ly, -some; desolate, dreary.

in-secable, -severable, -discerptible; compact, irresolvable.

Adv. singly etc. *adj.;* alone, by itself, *per se*, only, apart, in the singular number, in the abstract; one -by one, — at a time; simply; one and a half, *sesqui-*.

Phr. *natura il fece, e poi roppe la stampa.*

88. Accompaniment.—**N.** accompaniment; appurtenance, adjunct etc. 39; context.

coexistence, concomitance, company, association, companionship; part-, copart-nership; coefficiency.

concomitant, accessory, coefficient; companion, attendant, fellow, associate, consort, spouse, colleague, *fidus Achates;* part-, co-partner; satellite, hanger on, shadow; excort, *entourage*, suite, *cortège;* convoy, follower etc. 65; attribute.

V. accompany, coexist, attend, convoy, chaperon; hang —, wait- on; go hand in hand with; synchronize etc. 120; bear —, keep- company; row in the same boat; bring in its train, associate —, couple- with.

Adj. accompanying etc. *v.;* concomitant, fellow, twin, joint; associated —, coupled- with; accessory, attendant, *obbligato*.

Adv. with, withal; together —, along —, in company- with; hand in hand, side by side; cheek by -jowl, — jole; arm in arm; there-, here-with; and etc. (*addition*) 37.

together, in a body, collectively.

89. Duality.—**N.** dual-ity, -ism; duplicity; biplicity, -formity; span, polarity.

two, deuce, couple, couplet, doublet, brace, pair, cheeks, twins, Castor and Pollus, *gemini*, Siamese twins; fellows; yoke, conjugation, dyad, distich.

V. [unite in pairs] pair, couple, bracket, yoke; conduplicate, mate.

Adj. two, twain; dual, -istic; binary, binomial; twin, biparous; dyadic; conduplicate; duplex etc. 90; *tête-à-tête;* paired; dihedral.

coupled etc. *v.;* conjugate.

both, — the one and the other.

90. Duplication.—**N.** duplication, doubling etc. *v.;* gemi-, ingemi-nation; reduplication; iteration etc. (*repetition*) 104; renewal.

V. double; re-double, -duplicate; geminate; repeat etc. 104; renew etc. 660; duplicate, copy etc. 21.

Adj. double; doubled etc. *v.;* bicameral, bicapital, bi-fold, -form, -lateral, -farious, -facial; two-fold, -sided, -headed, -edged etc.; duplex; double-faced; twin, duplicate, ingeminate; second; dual etc. 29.

Adv. twice, once more; over again etc. (*repeatedly*) 104; as much again; twofold.

secondly, in the second place, again.

91. Bisection. [Division into two parts.]—**N.** bi-section, -partition; di-, subdi-chotomy; halving etc. *v.;* dimidiation; *hendiadis*.

bifurcation, forking, branching, furcation, ramification, divarication; fork, prong; fold.

half, moiety.

V. bisect, halve, divide, split, cut in two, cleave, dimidiate, dichotomize, divaricate.

go halves, divide with.

separate, fork, bifurcate; branch -off, – out; ramify.

Adj. bisected etc. *v.*; cloven, cleft; bipartite, biconjugate, bicuspid, bifid; bifur-cous, -cate, -cated; semi-, demi- hemi-.

92. Triality.—**N.** triality, trinity,* triplicity.

three, triad, triplet, trey, trio, ternion, trinomial, leash; tierce; triennium; trefoil, triangle, trident, tripod, triumvirate, *troika*.

third power, cube.

Adj. three; tri-form, -nal, -nomial; tertiary; triune.

**Trinity* is hardly ever used except in a theological sense: *see* Deity 976.

93. Triplication.—**N.** tripli-cation, -city; trebleness, trine, trilogy.

V. treble, triple, triplicate, cube.

Adj. treble, triple; tern, -ary; triplex, triplicate, threefold, trilogistic; third; trinal; trihedral.

Adv. three -times, – fold; thrice, in the third place, thirdly; trebly etc. *adj.*

94. Trisection. [Division into three parts.]—**N.** tri-section, -partition, -chotomy; third, – part.

V. trisect, divide into three parts, trifurcate.

Adj. trifid; trisected etc. *v.*; tripartite, -chotomous, -sulcate.

95. Quaternity.—**N.** quaternity, four, tetrad, quartet, quaternion, square, quadrature, quarter, quadruplet; quadrilateral, quadrangle, quatrefoil; *quadriga*.

V. reduce to a square, square.

Adj. four; quat-ernary, -ernal; quadratic; quartile, quartic, tetractic, tetrad, tetrahedral; quadrennial; quadrivalent.

96. Quadruplication.—**N.** quadruplication.

V. multiply by four, quadruplicate, biquadrate.

Adj. fourfold; quad-ruple, -ruplicate, -rible; quadruplex; fourth.

Adv. four times; in the fourth place, fourthly.

97. Quadrisection. [Division into four parts.]—**N.** quadri-section, -partition; quartering etc. *v.*; fourth; quart, -er, -ern; farthing (*i.e.* fourthing); quarto.

V. quarter, divide into four parts, quadrisect.

Adj. quartered etc. *v.*; quadri-fid, -partite.

98. Five, etc.—**N.** five, cinque, quint, quincunx, quintuplet, quintet, pentagon, pentameter, Pentateuch; six, half-a-dozen; sextet, hexagon, hexameter; seven, Heptarchy; eight, octet, octagon, octave; nine, three times three; ten, decade; eleven; twelve, dozen; thirteen; long –, baker's-dozen.

twenty, score; twenty-four, four and twenty, two dozen; twenty-five, five and twenty, quarter of a hundred; forty, two score; fifty, half a hundred; sixty, three score, sexagenarian; seventy, three score and ten, septuagenarian; eighty, four score, octogenarian; ninety, four score and ten, nonagenarian.

hundred, centenary, hecatomb, century; hundredweight, cwt.; one hundred and forty-four, gross; bicentenary, tercentenary etc.

thousand, chiliad; myriad, millennium, ten thousand; lac, lakh, one hundred thousand, plum; million; thousand million, *milliard*.

billion, trillion etc.

V. centuriate.

Adj. five, quinary, quintuple; fifth; senary, sextuple; sixth; seventh; octuple; eighth; ninefold, ninth; tenfold, decimal, denary, decuple, tenth; eleventh; duo-denary, -denal; twelfth; in one's 'teens, thirteenth.

vices-, viges-imal; twentieth; twenty-fourth etc. *n.*

cent-uple, -uplicate, -ennial, -enary, -urial; secular, hundredth; thousandth; millenary etc.

99. Quinquesection, etc.—**N.** division by -five etc. 98; quinquesection etc.; fifth etc.; decimation.

V. decimate, quinquesect.

Adj. quinque-fid, -partite; quinquarticular; octifid; decimal, tenth, tithe, teind; duodecimal, twelfth; sexagesimal, -genary; hundredth, centesimal; millesimal etc.

100. Plurality. [More than one.]—**N.** plurality; a -number, – certain number; one or two, two or three etc.; a few, several; multitude etc. 102.

Adj. plural, more than one, upwards of, some, certain; not -alone etc. 87.

Adv. *et cetera, etc.*, etc.

Phr. *non deficit alter.*

100a. Fraction [Less than one.]—**N.** fraction, fractional part, fragment; part etc. 51.

Adj. fractional, fragmentary, partial.

101. Zero.—**N.** zero, nothing, naught, nought, duck's egg, goose egg; cipher, none, nobody; not a soul; *âme qui vive*; absence etc. 187; unsubstantiality etc. 4.

Adj. not -one, – any.

102. Multitude.—**N.** multitude; numerousness etc. *adj.*; numer-osity, -ality; multiplicity; profusion etc. (*plenty*) 639; legion, host; great –, large –, round –, enormous- number; a quantity, numbers, array, sight, army, sea, galaxy; scores, peck, bushel, school, shoal, swarm, draft, bevy, cloud, flock, herd, drove, flight, covey, hive, brood, litter, farrow, fry, nest; mob, crowd etc. (*assemblage*) 72; lots, loads, heaps; all the world and his wife.

[Increase of number] greater number, majority; multiplication, multiple.

V. be -numerous etc. *adj.*; swarm –, teem –, crawl –, creep -with; crowd, swarm, come thick upon; outnumber, multiply; people; swarm like -locusts, — bees.

Adj. many, several, sundry, divers, various,

not a few; a -hundred, — thousand, — myriad, — million, — thousand and one; some -ten or a dozen, — forty or fifty etc.; half a -dozen, — hundred etc.; very —, full —, ever so- many; numer-ous, -ose; profuse, in profusion; manifold, multiplied, multitudinous, multiferous, multiple, multinomial, teeming, crawling, populous, peopled, crowded, thick, studded; galore.

thick coming, many more, more than one can tell, a world of; no end -of, — to; *cum multis aliis*; thick as -hops, — hail; plenty as blackberries; numerous as the -stars in the firmament, — sands on the sea-shore, — hairs on the head; and -what not, — heaven knows what; endless etc. (*infinite*) 105.

Phr. their name is 'Legion.'

103. Fewness.—N. fewness etc. *adj.*; paucity, small number; small quantity etc. 32; scarcity, sparsity; rarity; infrequency etc. 137; handful; maniple; minority, exiguity.

[Diminution of number] reduction; weeding etc. *v.*; elimination, sarculation, decimation.

V. be -few etc. *adj.*

render -few etc. *adj.*; reduce, diminish the number, weed; eliminate, thin, decimate.

Adj. few; scarce; scant, -y; thin, rare, thinly scattered, few and far between; exiguous; infrequent etc. 137; *rari nantes*; hardly —, scarcely-any; to be counted on one's fingers; reduced etc. *v.*; unrepeated.

Adv. here and there.

104. Repetition.—N. repetition, iteration, reiteration, duplication, ding-dong, alliteration; *epistrophe;* harping, recurrence, succession, run; batto-, tauto-logy; monotony, tautophony; rhythm etc. 138; pleonasm, redundancy, diffuseness.

chimes, repetend, echo, *ritornello,* burden of a song, *refrain;* rehearsal; encore; *réchauffé, rifacimento,* recapitulation.

cuckoo etc. (*imitation*) 19; reverberation etc. 408; drumming etc. (*roll*) 407; renewal etc. (*restoration*) 660.

twice-told tale; old -story, — song, chestnut; second —, new edition; reprint, new impression; return game, return match, reappearance, reproduction; periodicity etc. 138.

V. repeat, iterate, reiterate, reproduce, parrot, echo, re-echo, drum, harp upon, battologize, hammer, redouble.

recur, revert, return, reappear; renew etc. (*restore*) 660.

rehearse; do —, say- over again; ring the changes on; harp on the same string; din —, drum- in the ear; conjugate in all its moods, tenses and inflexions, begin again, go over the same ground, go the same round, never hear the last of; resume, return to, recapitulate, reword.

Adj. repeated etc. *v.*; repetition-al, -ary; recurrent, -ring; ever recurring, thick coming; frequent, incessant, redundant, pleonastic, tautological.

monotonous, harping, iterative; mocking, chiming; retold; aforesaid, -named; abovementioned, said; habitual etc. 613; another.

Adv. repeatedly, often, again, afresh, anew, over again, once more; ditto, *encore, de novo, bis, da capo.*

again and again; over and over, — again; many times over; time- and again, — after time; year after year; day by day etc.; many —, several —, a number of- times; many —, full many- a time; times out of number, year in and year out, morning, noon and night; frequently etc. 136.

Phr. *ecce iterum Crispinus, toujours perdrix,* cut and come again; 'tomorrow and tomorrow.'

105. Infinity.—N. infini-ty, -tude, -teness etc. *adj.;* perpetuity etc. 112.

V. be -infinite etc. *adj.;* know —, have- no -limits, — bounds; go on for ever.

Adj. infinite, immense; number-, count-, sum-, measure-less; innumer-, immeasur-, incalcul-, illimit-, intermin-, unfathom-, unapproach-able; exhaustless, inexhaustible, indefinite; without -number, — measure, — limit, — end; incomprehensible; limit-, end-, bound-, termless; un-told, -numbered, -measured, -bounded, -limited; illimited; perpetual etc. 112.

Adv. infinitely etc. *adj.; ad infinitum.*

106. Time.—N. time, duration; period, term, stage, space, span, spell, season; the whole -time, — period; course etc. 109.

intermediate, time, while, *interim,* interval, bit, pendency; inter-vention, -mission, -mittence, -regnum, -lude; respite.

era, epoch, eon, cycle; time of life, age, year, date; decade etc. (*period*) 108; moment, etc. (*instant*) 113; reign etc. 737.

glass —, ravages —, whirligig —, noiseless foot- of time; scythe.

V. continue, last, endure, go on, hold out, remain, stay, persist, abide, run; intervene; elapse etc. 109.

take —, take up —, fill —, occupy- time.

pass —, pass away —, spend —, while away —, consume —, talk against —, kill- time; tide over; use —, employ- time; tarry etc. 110; seize an opportunity etc. 134; waste time etc. (*be inactive*) 683.

Adj. continuing etc. *v.;* on foot; permanent etc. (*durable*) 110.

Adv. while, whilst, during, pending; during the -time, — interval; in the course of; for the time being, day by day; in the time of, when; meantime, -while; in the -meantime, — *interim; ad interim, pendente lite; de die in diem;* from -day to day, — hour to hour etc.; hourly, always; for a -time, — season; till, until, up to, yet; the whole —, all the- time; all along; throughout etc. (*completely*) 52; for good etc. (*diuturnity*) 110.

here-, there-, where-upon; then; *anno, — Domini;* A.D.; *ante Christum;* A.C.; before Christ; B.C.; *anno urbis conditae;* A.U.C.; *anno regni,* A.R.; once upon a time, one fine morning.

Phr. time -runs, — runs against; *tempus fugit.*

107. Neverness.—N. 'neverness;' absence of time, no time; *dies non;* Tib's eve; Greek Kalends.

Adv. never; at no -time, — period; on no occasion, never in all one's born days, nevermore, *sine die.*

108. Period. [Definite duration, or portion of time.]—**N.** period; second, minute, hour, day, week, sennight, octave, month, moon, quarter, semester, year, *lustrum, quinquennium,* decade, *decennium,* indiction, lifetime, generation, epoch, era, cycle.

century, age, *millennium; annus magnus.*

Adj. horary; hourly, annual etc. (*periodical*) 138.

108a. Contingent Duration.—Adv. during - pleasure, — good behavior; *quamdiu se bene gesserit.*

109. Course. [Indefinite duration.]—**N.** course —, progress —, process —, succession —, lapse —, flow —, flux —, effluxion, stream —, tract —, current —, sweep —, tide —, march —, step —, flight- of time; duration etc. 106.

[Indefinite time] aorist.

V. elapse, lapse, flow, run, proceed, advance, pass; roll —, wear —, press —, drag- on; flit, fly, slip, slide, glide, crawl; run -its course.

out; expire; go —, pass- by; be -past etc. 122.

Adj. elapsing etc. *v.;* aoristic; progressive, transient etc. 111.

Adv. in due -time, — season; in -course, — process, — the fulness- of time; in time.

Phr. *labitur et labetur; truditur dies die; fugaces labuntur anni;* 'tomorrow and tomorrow and tomorrow creeps in this petty pace from day to day.'

110. Diuturnity. [Long duration.]—**N.** diuturnity; a -long —, length of -time; an age, a century, an eternity, aeons; slowness etc. 275; perpetuity etc. 112; blue moon.

dura-bleness, -bility; persistence, lastingness etc. *adj.;* continuance, assiduity, endurance, standing; permanence etc. (*stability*) 150; survi-val, -vance; longevity etc. (*age*) 128; distance of time.

protraction —, prolongation —, extension- of time; delay etc. (*lateness*) 133.

V. last, endure, stand, remain, abide, continue, brave a thousand years.

tarry etc. (*be late*) 133; drag -on, — its slow length along, — a lengthening chain; protract, prolong; spin —, eke —, draw —, lengthen- out; temporize; gain —, make —, talk against- time.

out-last, -live; survive; live to fight again.

Adj. durable; perdurable; lasting etc. *v.;* of long -duration, — standing; permanent, chronic, long-standing; intransi-ent, -tive; intransmutable, persistent; life-, live-long; longeval, long-lived, macrobiotic, diuturnal, sempervirent, evergreen, perennial; unin-, ter-, unremitting; perpetual etc. 112.

lingering, protracted, prolonged, spun out etc. *v.;* long-pending, -winded; slow etc. 275.

Adv. long; for -a long time, — an age, — ages, — ever so long, — many a long day; long ago etc. (*in a past time*) 122; *longo intervallo.*

all the -day long, — year round; the livelong day, as the day is long, morning, noon and night; hour after hour, day after day, etc.; for good; permanently etc. *adj.*

111. Transientness. [Short duration.]—**N.** transientness etc. *adj.*; evanescence, impermanence, fugacity, transitoriness, volatility, caducity, mortality, span; flash in the pan, nine days' wonder, bubble, May-fly; spurt; temporary arrangement, interregnum.

velocity etc. 274; suddenness etc. 113; changeableness etc. 149.

V. be -transient etc. *adj.;* flit, pass away, fly, gallop, vanish, fade, fleet, melt away, evaporate; pass away like a -cloud, — summer cloud, — shadow, — dream.

Adj. transi-ent, -tory, -tive; passing, evanescent, fleeting; flying etc. *v.;* fug-acious, -itive; shifting, slippery; spasmodic.

tempor-al, -ary; provis-ional, -ory; cursory, short-lived, ephemeral, deciduous; perishable, mortal, precarious; impermanent.

brief, quick, brisk; cometary, meteoric, extemporaneous, summary; pressed for time etc. (*haste*) 684; sudden, momentary etc. (*instantaneous*) 113.

Adv. temporarily etc. *adj.; pro tempore;* for - the moment, — a time; awhile, *en passant, in transitu;* in a short time; soon etc. (*early*) 132; briefly etc. *adj.;* at short notice; on the -point, — eve -of; *in articulo;* between cup and lip.

Phr. one's days are numbered; the time is up; her to-day and gone tomorrow; *non semper erit aestas; eheu! fugaces labuntur anni; sic transit gloria mundi.*

112. Perpetuity. [Endless duration.]—**N.** perpetuity, eternity, timelessness; everness, aye, sempiternity, immortality, athanasia; everlastingness etc. *adj.;* perpetuation; infinite duration.

V. last —, endure —, go on- for ever; have no end.

eternize, eternify, perpetuate, immortalize.

Adj. perpetual, eternal, eterne; everlasting, - living, -flowing; continual, constant, sempiternal; co-eternal; endless, unending; ceaseless, incessant, uninterrupted, indesinent, unceasing; interminable, having no end; unfading, evergreen, amaranthine; neverending, -dying, -fading; deathless, immortal, undying, imperishable.

Adv. perpetually etc. *adj.;* always, ever, evermore, aye; for -ever, — aye, — evermore, — ever and a day, —, ever and ever; in all ages, from age to age; without end; world —, time- without end; *in saecula saeculorum;* to the -end of time, — crack of doom, — 'last syllable of recorded time;' till doomsday; constantly etc. (*very frequently*) 136.

Phr. *esto perpetuum; labitur et labetur in omne volubilis aevum.*

113. Instantaneity. [Point of time.]—**N.** instantane-ity, -ousness; sudden-, abrupt-ness.

moment, instant, second, minute; twinkling, trice, flash, breath, crack, jiffy, *coup,* burst, flash of lightning, stroke of time.

epoch, time; time of -day, — *night;* hour, minute; very -minute etc., — time, — hours; present —, right —, true —, exact —, correct-time.

V. be -instantaneous etc. *adj.;* twinkle, flash.

Adj. instantaneous, momentary, extempore, sudden, instant, abrupt; subitaneous, hasty; quick as- thought,* — lightning, — a flash; rapid as electricity.

Adv. instantaneously etc. *adj.*; in – in less than- no time; *presto, subito, instanter,* suddenly, at a stroke, like- a shot, – greased lightning; in a trice, in a moment etc. *n.*; eftsoons, in the twinkling of - ar eye, – a bed post; at one jump, in the same breath, *per saltum, uno saltu*; at –, all at- once; in one's tracks; plump, slap; 'at one fell swoop;' at the same -instant etc. *n.*; immediately etc. (*early*) 132; *ex tempore,* on the -spot, – spur of the moment, – dot; just then; slap- dash etc. (*haste*) 684; before you could -turn round, – say -knife, – Jack Robinson.

Phr. touch and go; no sooner said than done.
*See note on 264.

114. Chronometry. [Estimation, measurement, and record of time.]—**N.** chrono-, horo-metry, -logy; date, epoch; style, era.

almanac, calendar, ephemeris; register, -try; chronicle, annals, journal, diary, chronogram.

[Instruments for the measurement of time] clock, watch; chrono-meter, -scope, -graph; repeater, alarum; time-keeper, -piece; dial, sun-dial, *gnomon, pendule,* horologe, pendulum, hourglass, water clock, clepsydra.

mean –, Greenwich –, solar –, sidereal –, local –, summer- time; daylight saving.

chrono-grapher, -loger, -logist; annalist.

V. fix –, mark- the time; date, register, chronicle; measure –, beat –, mark- time; bear date.

Adj. chrono-logical, -metrical, -grammatical; isochronal.

Adv. o'clock; *a.m., p.m.*

115. Anachronism. [False estimate of time.]—**N.** ana-, meta-, para-, prochronism; *prolepsis,* misdate; anticipation, antichronism.

disregard –, neglect –, oblivion- of time.

intempestivity etc. 135.

V. mis-, ante-, post-, over-date, anticipate; take no note of time.

Adj. misdated etc. *v.*; undated; overdue; out of date; anachronous etc. *n.*

116. Priority.—**N.** priority, antecedence, anteriority, pre-existence, precedence etc. 62; precession etc. 280; precursor etc. 64; the past etc. 122; premises.

V. precede, come before; forerun; antecede, go before etc. (*lead*) 280; pre-exist; dawn: premise, presage etc. 511.

be -beforehand etc. (*be early*) 132; steal a march upon, anticipate, forestall; have –, gain- the start.

Adj. prior, previous; preced-ing, -ent; anterior, antecedent; pre-existing, -existent; foresighted; former, foregoing; afore –, before-, above-mentioned; aforesaid, said; introductory etc. (*precursory*) 64; pre-war.

Adv. before, prior to; earlier; previously etc. *adj.*; afore, ere, theretofore, erewhile, ere –, before- -then, – now; erewhile, already, yet, beforehand; aforetime; on the eve of, in anticipation.

117. Posteriority.—**N.** posteriority; succession, sequence; following etc. 281; subsequence, supervention; futurity etc. 121; successor; sequel etc. 65; remainder, reversion.

V. follow etc. 281 –, come –, go- after; ensue, result; succeed, supervene; step into the shoes of.

Adj. subsequent, posterior, following, after, later, succeeding, postliminious, postnate; successive etc. 63; postdiluvial, -an; *puisné;* posthumous; post-war, future etc. 121.

Adv. subsequently, after, afterwards, since, later; at a -subsequent, – later- period; next, in the sequel, close upon, thereafter, thereupon, upon which, eftsoons; from that -time, – moment; after a -while, –time; in process of time.

postcenal, postcibal, postprandial, after-dinner.

118. The Present Time.—**N.** the present -time, – day, – moment, – juncture, – occasion; the times, existing time, time being; twentieth century; nonce, crisis, epoch, day, hour.

age, time of life.

Adj. present, actual, instant, current, latest, existing, that is.

Adv. at this -time, – moment etc. 113; at the -present time etc. *n.*; now, at present.

at this time of day, to-day, now-adays; already; even –, but –, just-now; on the present occasion; for the -time being, – nonce; *pro hâc vice;* on the -nail, – spot; on the spur of the -moment, – occasion.

until now; to -this, – the present day.

119. Different Time. [Time different from the present.]—**N.** different –, other- time.

[Indefinite time] aorist.

Adj. aoristic.

Adv. at that –, at which- -time, – moment, – instant; then, on that occasion, upon.

when; when-ever, -soever; upon which, on which occasion; at -another, – a different, – some other, – any - time; at various times; some –, one- -of these days, – fine morning, – day; sooner or later; some time or other; once upon a time, once.

120. Synchronism.—**N.** synchronism; coexistence, coincidence; simultaneousness etc. *adj.*; concurrence, concomitance, unity of time, interim.

[Having equal times] isochronism, syntony.

contemporary, coetanian.

V. coexist, concur, accompany, go hand in hand, keep pace with; synchronize, isochronize.

Adj. synchron-ous, -al, -ical, -istical; simultaneous, coexisting, coincident, concomitant, concurrent; coev-al, -ous; contempora-ry, -neous; coetaneous; coterminous, coeternal; isochronous.

Adv. at the same time; simultaneously etc. *adj.*; together, in concert, during the same time; in the same breath; *pari passu;* in the interim.

at the -very moment etc. 113; just as, as soon as; meanwhile etc. (*while*) 106.

121. Futurity. [Prospective time.]—**N.** futurity, -ition; future, hereafter, time to come; approaching –, coming –, after- -time, – age, – days, – hours, – years, – ages, – life;

morrow, to-morrow, by and by; millennium. doomsday, day of judgment, crack of doom, remote future.

approach of time, advent, time drawing on, womb of time; destiny etc. 152; eventuality.

heritage, heirs, posterity, descendants.

prospect etc. (*expectation*) 507; foresight etc. 510.

V. look forwards; anticipate etc. (*expect*) 507, (*foresee*) 510; forestall etc. (*be early*) 132.

come –, draw- on; draw near; approach, await, threaten; impend etc. (*be destined*) 152.

Adj. future, to come; coming etc. (*impending*) 152; next, near; near –, close- at hand; eventual, ulterior; expectant, prospective, in prospect etc. (*expectation*) 507.

Adv. prospectively, hereafter, on the knees of the gods, in future; to-morrow, the day after to-morrow; in -course, – process, – the fulness- of time; eventually, ultimately, sooner or later; *proximo; paulo post futurum;* in after time; one of these days; after a -time, – while.

from this time; hence-forth, -forwards; thence; thence-forth, -forward; whereupon, upon which.

soon etc. (*early*) 132; on the -eve, – point, – brink- of; about to; close upon.

122. Preterition. [Retrospective time.]—**N.** preterition, priority etc. 116; the past, past time; days –, times- -of yore, – of old, – past, – gone by; bygone days, good old days; old –, ancient –, former -times; fore time; yesterdays; the olden –, good old- time; auld lang syne; eld.

antiquity, antiqueness, *status quo;* time immemorial; distance of time; remote -age, – time; ancient history; remote past; rust of antiquity; ancientness.

pale-ontology, -ography, -ology; palaetiology,* archaeology; archaism, antiquarianism, mediaevalism, pre- Raphaelitism; retrospection, looking back, memory etc. 505.

laudator temporis acti; mediaevalist, pre-Raphaelite; antiqu-ary, -arian; archaeologist etc.; Oldbuck, Dryasdust.

ancestry etc. (*paternity*) 166.

V. be -past etc. *adj.;* have -expired etc. *adj.;* – run its course, – had its day; pass; pass –, go- - by, – away, – off; lapse, blow over.

look –, trace –, cast the eyes- back; exhume.

Adj. past, gone, gone by, over, passed away, bygone, foregone; elapsed, lapsed, preterlapsed, expired, no more, run out, blown over, that has been, whilom, extinct, never to return, exploded, forgotten, irrecoverable; obsolete etc. (*old*) 124; extinct as the dodo.

former, pristine, *quondam, ci-devant,* late; ancestral.

foregoing; last, latter; recent, overnight; past, preterite, preter-perfect, -pluperfect, past perfect.

looking back etc. *v.;* retro-spective, -active; archaelogical etc. *n.*

Adv. formerly; of -old, –yore; erst, whilom, erewhile, time was, ago, over; in -the olden time etc. *n.;* anciently, long -ago, – since; a long - while, – time- ago; years –, ages-ago; some time -ago, – since, – back.

yesterday, the day before yesterday; last -year, – season, – month etc.; *ultimo,* lately etc. (*newly*) 123.

retrospectively; ere –, before –, till- now; hitherto, heretofore; no longer; once, – upon a time; from time immemorial; in the memory of man; time out of mind; already, yet, up to this time; *ex post facto.*

Phr. time was; the time -has, – hath- been.

**Whewell.*

123. Newness.—**N.** newness etc. *adj.;* neologism, neoterism; novelty, recency; immaturity; youth etc. 127; gloss of novelty.

innovation; renovation etc. (*restoration*) 660.

modernist, neologist, neoteric.

modernism, modernity; mushroom; latest fashion, *dernier cri.*

upstart, *parvenu, nouveau riche.*

V. renew etc. (*restore*) 660; modernize.

Adj. new, novel, recent, fresh, green; young etc. 127; evergreen; raw, immature; virgin; untried, -handseled, -used, -trodden, -beaten; fledgling.

late, modern, neoteric; new-born, -fashioned, -fangled, -fledged; of yesterday; just out, brand –, span-new, up to date, topical; vernal, renovated; innovatory.

fresh as -a rose, – a daisy, – paint; spick and span.

Adv. newly etc. *adj.;* afresh, anew, lately, just now, only yesterday, the other day; latterly, of late.

not long –, a short time- ago.

124. Oldness.—**N.** oldness etc. *adj.*; age, antiquity; cobwebs of antiquity.

maturity, ripeness; decline, decay; senility etc. 128.

seniority, eldership, primogeniture.

archaism etc. (*the past*) 122; thing –, relic- of the past; megatherium.

tradition, prescription, custom, folklore, immemorial usage, common law.

V. be -old etc. *adj.;* have -had, – seen- its day; become -old etc. *adj.;* age, fade.

Adj. old, olden, ancient, antique; of long standing, time-honored, venerable; eld-er, -est; first-born.

prime; prim-itive, -eval, -igenous; primordi-al, -nate; aboriginal etc. (*beginning*) 66; diluvian, antediluvian; pre-historic; patriarchal, preadamite; paleocrystic; fossil, paleozoic, preglacial, ante-mundane; archaic, classic, mediaeval, pre-Raphaelite, ancestral, black-letter.

immemorial, traditional, prescriptive, customary, whereof the memory of man runneth not to the contrary; inveterate, rooted.

antiquated, of other times, rococo, of the old school, after-age, obsolete; fusty, moth-eaten; out of -date, – fashion; stale, old-fashioned, behind the -age, – times; exploded; gone out, – by; *passé,* outworn, run out; disused; senile etc. 128; time-worn; crumbling etc. (*deteriorated*) 659; second-hand.

old as -the hills, – Methuselah, – Adam, – history.

Adv. since the -world was made, – year one, – days of Methuselah.

125. Morning. [Noon.]—**N.** morning, morn, matins, forenoon, *a.m.*, prime, dawn, daybreak, daylight, sun-up, peep –, break- of day; aurora,

Eos; first blush —, prime- of the morning; twilight, crepuscule, sunrise, cockcrow.
spring; vernal equinox.
noon; mid-, noon-day; noontide, meridian, prime.
summer, midsummer; summer solstice.
Adj. matin, matutinal; vernal, aestival.
Adv. at -sunrise etc. *n.*; with the lark, when the morning dawns.

126. Evening. [Midnight.]—**N.** evening, eve; decline —, fall —, close- of day; eventide, evensong, vespers; candlelight; nightfall, curfew, dusk, twilight, blind man's holiday; eleventh hour; sun-set, -down; going down of the sun, cock-shut, dewy eve, gloaming, bed-time.
afternoon, *post meridiem, p.m.*
autumn; fall, — of the leaf; autumnal equinox, Indian summer, harvest-time.
midnight; dead —, witching time- of night; winter, — solstice.
Adj. vespertine, autumnal, nocturnal, wintry, brumal, hiemal.

127. Youth.—**N.** youth; juven- -ility, -escence; juniority; infancy; baby-, child-, boy-, girl-, youth-hood; *incunabula;* minority, immaturity, nonage, teens, tender age, bloom.
cradle, nursery, leading-strings, pupilage, puberty, *pucelage.*
prime —, flower —, spring-tide —, seedtime —, golden season - of life; heyday of youth, school days; rising generation, younger generation.
Adj. young, youthful, juvenile, green, callow, budding, sappy, *puisné,* beardless, unfledged, unripe, under age, in one's teens; *in statu pupillari;* younger, junior.

128. Age.—**N.** age; oldness etc. *adj.;* old —, advanced- age; sen-ility, -escence; years, anility, grey hairs, climacteric, grand climacteric, declining years, decrepitude, hoary age, caducity, superannuation; second childhood, -ishness; dotage; vale of years, decline of life, 'sear and yellow leaf;' three-score years and ten; green old age, ripe old age; longevity; time of life.
seniority, eldership; elders etc. (*veteran*) 130; firstling; *doyen,* dean, father; primogeniture; nostology.
V. be -aged etc. *adj.;* grow —, get- old etc. *adj.;* age; decline, wane.
Adj. aged; old etc. 124; elderly, senile; matronly, anile; in years; ripe, mellow, run to seed, declining, waning, past one's prime; grey, -headed; hoar, -y; venerable, time-worn, antiquated, *passé,* effete, doddering, decrepit, superannuated; advanced in -life, — years; stricken in years; wrinkled, marked with the crow's foot; having one foot in the grave; doting etc. (*imbecile*) 499.
old-, eld-er, -est; senior; first-born.
turned of, years old; of a certain age, no chicken, old as Methuselah; gerontic; ancestral; patriarchal etc. (*ancient*) 124.

129. Infant.—**N.** infant, babe, baby; nurse-, suck-, year-, wean-ling; *papoose, bambino.*
child, bairn, little- one, — tot, — mite, chick, brat, chit, pickaninny, kid, urchin; bant-, brat-ling; elf.
youth, boy, lad, slip, sprig, stripling, youngster, cub, unlicked cub, younker, callant, whipster, whipper-snapper, schoolboy, hobbledehoy, hopeful, cadet, minor, master.
scion; sap-, seed-ling; tendril, olive branch, nestling, chicken, duckling; larva, caterpillar, chrysalis, cocoon; tadpole, whelp, cub, pullet, fry, callow; codlin, -g; *foetus,* calf, colt, pup, foal, kitten; lamb, -kin.
girl; lass, -ie; wench, miss, damsel, *demoiselle,* damozel; maid, -en; virgin; nymph; colleen; minx, baggage, school-girl; tomboy, flapper, hoyden.
Adj. infant-ine, -ile; puerile; boy-, girl-, child-, baby-, kitten-ish; baby; new-born, unfledged, new-fledged, callow.
in -the cradle, — swaddling clothes, — long clothes, — arms, — leading strings; at the breast; in one's teens; young etc. 127.

130. Veteran.—**N.** veteran, old man, seer, patriarch, greybeard, dugout, grand-father, -sire; grandam, beldam; gaffer, gammer; hag, crone; pantaloon; sexage-, octoge-, nonage-, cente-narian; old stager; dotard etc. 501.
preadamite, Methuselah, Nestor, Rip van Winkle, old Parr; elders; forefathers etc. (*paternity*) 166.

131. Adolescence.—**N.** adolescence, pubescence, majority; adultness etc. *adj.;* manhood, virility, maturity; flower of age; prime —, meridian- of life.
man etc. 373; woman etc. 374; adult, no chicken.
V. come -of age, — to man's estate, — to years of discretion; attain majority, assume the *toga virilis;* have -cut one's eye-teeth, — sown one's wild oats, settle down.
Adj. adolescent, pubescent, of age; of -full, — ripe- age; out of one's teens, grown up, mature, full- blown, — grown, in one's prime, in full bloom, manly, virile, adult; womanly, matronly; marriageable, nubile.

132. Earliness.—**N.** earliness etc. *adj.;* morning etc. 125.
punctuality; promptitude etc. (*activity*) 682; haste etc. (*velocity*) 274; suddenness etc. (*instantaneity*) 113.
prematurity, precocity, precipitation, anticipation; prevenience, a stitch in time.
V. be -early etc. *adj.;* — beforehand etc. *adv.;* keep time, take time by the forelock, anticipate, forestall; have —, gain- the start; steal a march upon; gain time, draw on futurity; bespeak, secure, engage, pre-engage.
accelerate; expedite etc. (*quicken*) 274; make haste etc. (*hurry*) 684.
Adj. early, prime, timely, in time, punctual, forward; prompt etc. (*active*) 682; summary.
premature, precipitate, precocious; prevenient, anticipatory; rathe.
sudden etc. (*instantaneous*) 113; unexpected etc. 508; impending, imminent; near, — at hand; immediate.

Adv. early, soon, anon, betimes, rathe; eft, -soons; ere —, before- long; punctually etc. *adj.;* to the minute; in time; in -good, — military, — pudding, — due- time; time enough.

beforehand; prematurely etc. *adj.;* precipitately etc. (*hastily*) 684; too soon; before -its, — one's- time; in anticipation; unexpectedly etc. 508.

suddenly etc. (*instantaneously*) 113; before one can say 'Jack Robinson,' at short notice, extempore; on the spur of the -moment, — occasion; at once; on the -spot, — instant; at sight; off —, out of- hand; *à vue d'oeil;* straight, -way, -forth; forthwith, incontinently, summarily, instanter, immediately, briefly, shortly, quickly, speedily, apace, before the ink is dry, almost immediately, presently, at the first opportunity, in no long time, by and by, in a while, directly.

Phr. touch and go, no sooner said than done.

133. Lateness.—**N.** lateness etc. *adj.;* tardiness etc. (*slowness*) 275.

de-lay, -lation; cunctation, procrastination; detention; deferring etc. *v.;* filibuster, postponement, adjournment, prorogation, retardation, respite, reprieve, stay; protraction, prolongation, moratorium; contango; demurrage; remand; Fabian policy, *médecine expectante,* chancery suit; leeway; high time.

V. be -late etc. *adj.;* tarry, wait, stay, bide, take time; dawdle etc. (*be inactive*) 683; linger, loiter, saunter, lag behind; bide —, take- one's time; hang -about, — around, — back, — in the balance; gain time; hang fire; stand —, lie-over.

put off, defer, delay, lay over, suspend; shift —, stave- off; waive, retard, remand, postpone, adjourn; procrastinate; dally; prolong, protract; spin —, draw —, lengthen- out; prorogue; keep back; tide over; push —, drive- to the last; let the matter stand over; reserve etc. (*store*) 636; temporize; consult one's pillow, sleep upon it.

shelve, table, lay on the table.

lose an opportunity etc. 135; be kept waiting, dance attendance; kick —, cool- one's heels; *faire antichambre;* wait impatiently; await etc. (*expect*) 507; sit up, — at night.

Adj. late, tardy, slow, behindhand, belated, postliminious, posthumous, backward, unpunctual; dilatory etc. (*slow*), overdue 275; delayed etc. *v.;* in abeyance.

Adv. late; late-, back-ward; late in the day; at -sunset, — the eleventh hour, — length, — last, — long; ultimately; after —, behind- time; too late; too late for etc. 135.

slowly, leisurely, deliberately, at one's leisure; *ex post facto; sine die.*

Phr. *nonum prematur in annum.*

134. Occasion.—**N.** occasion, opportunity, opening, room, scope, field; suitable —, proper- -time, — season; high time; opportuneness etc. *adj.;* tempestivity.

crisis, turn, juncture, emergency, conjuncture; turning point; given time.

nick of time; golden —, well-timed —, fine —, favorable- opportunity; clear stage, fair field; *mollia tempora; fata Morgana;* spare time etc. (*leisure*) 685.

V. seize etc. (*take*) 789 —, use etc. 677 —, give etc. 784- an -opportunity, — occasion; improve the occasion.

suit the occasion etc. (*be expedient*) 646.

strike the iron while it is hot, *battre le fer sur l'enclume,* make hay while the sun shines, take time by the forelock, *prendre la balle au bond.*

Adj. opportune, timely, well-timed, timeous, timeful, seasonable.

providential, lucky, fortunate, happy, favorable, propitious, auspicious, critical; suitable etc. 23; *obiter dicta.*

Adv. opportunely etc. *adj.* ; in -proper, — due- -time, — course, — season; for the nonce; in the -nick, — fulness- of time; all in good time; just in time, at the eleventh hour, now or never.

by the -way, — by; *en passant, à propos; pro re natâ, — hac vice; par parenthèse,* parenthetically, by way of parenthesis; while -speaking of, — on this subject; *ex tempore;* on the spur of the -moment, — occasion; on the spot etc. (*early*) 132.

Phr. *carpe diem; occasionem cognosce;* one's hour is come, the time is up; that reminds me.

135. Intempestivity.—**N.** intempestivity; unseasonableness; unsuitable —, improper-time; unreasonableness etc. *adj.;* evil hour; *contretemps;* intrusion; anachronism etc. 115.

V. be -ill timed etc. *adj.;* mistime, intrude, come amiss, break in upon; have other fish to fry; be -busy, — engaged, — tied up, — occupied.

lose —, throw away —, waste —, neglect etc. 460- an opportunity; allow —, suffer- the -opportunity, — occasion- to -pass, — slip, — go by, — escape, — lapse; waste time etc. (*be inactive*) 683; let slip through the fingers, lock the stable door when the steed is stolen.

Adj. ill-, mis-timed; untimely, intrusive, unseasonable; out of -date, — season; inopportune, timeless, untoward, *mal à propos,* unlucky, inauspicious, unpropitious, unfortunate, unfavorable; unsuited etc. 24; inexpedient etc. 647.

unpunctual etc. (*late*) 133; too late for; premature etc. (*early*) 132; too soon for; wise after the event.

Adv. inopportunely etc. *adj.;* as ill luck would have it, in an evil hour, the time having gone by, a day after the fair.

Phr. after meat mustard, after death the doctor.

136. Frequency.—**N.** frequency, oftness; repetition, etc. 104.

V. recur etc. 104; do nothing but; keep, — on.

Adj. frequent, many times, not rare, thickcoming, incessant, perpetual, continual, constant, recurrent, repeated etc. 104; habitual etc. 613; hourly, etc. 138.

Adv. often, often to be met with, oft; oft-, often-times; frequently; repeatedly etc. 104; unseldom, not unfrequently; in -quick, — rapid- succession; many a time and oft; daily, hourly etc.; every -day, — hour, — moment etc.

perpetually, continually, constantly, incessantly, without ceasing, at all times, daily and hourly, night and day, day and night, day after day, morning, noon and night, ever and anon.

most often; commonly etc. (*habitually*) 613.

sometimes, occasionally, at times, now and then, from time to time, there being times when, *toties quoties*, often enough, again and again etc. 104.

137. Infrequency.—N. infrequency, infrequence, rareness, rarity; fewness etc. 103; seldomness, uncommonness.

V. be -rare etc. *adj.*

Adj. un-, in-frequent; uncommon, sporadic, rare, — as a blue diamond; few etc. 103; scarce; almost unheard of, unprecedented, which has not occurred within the memory of the oldest inhabitant, not within one's previous experience.

Adv. seldom, rarely, scarcely, hardly; not often, unfrequently, infrequently, unoften; scarcely —, hardly- ever; once in a blue moon.

once; once -for all, — in a way; *pro hac vice;* like angels' visits, few and far between.

138. Regularity of recurrence. **Periodicity.—N.** periodicity, intermittence; beat; oscillation etc. 314; pulse, pulsation; rhythm; alternation, -nateness, -nativeness, -nity.

bout, round, revolution, rotation, turn.

anniversary, birthday, jubilee, centenary, bi-, ter-centenary.

[Regularity of return] rota, cycle, period, stated time, routine; days of the week; Sunday, Monday etc.; months of the year; January etc.; feast, fast, saint's day etc.; Christmas, Easter, New Year's Day etc. 998; quarter-, Lady-, Midsummer-, Michaelmas-day; May Day, the King's Birthday; leap year, seasons.

punctuality, regularity, steadiness.

V. recur in regular -order, — succession; return, revolve, rotate; come -again, — in its turn; come round, — again; beat, pulsate; alternate; intermit.

Adj. periodic, -al; serial, recurrent, cyclic-, -al, rhythmic-, -al, even; recurring etc. *V.;* inter-, remittent; alternate, every other.

hourly; diurnal, daily; quotidian, tertian, weekly; hebdomad-al, -ary; bi-weekly, fortnightly; monthly, menstrual, catamenial; yearly, annual; biennial, triennial, etc.; bissextile; centennial, secular; paschal, lenten, etc.

regular, steady, punctual, constant, methodical, regular as clockwork.

Adv. periodically etc. *adj.;* at -regular intervals, — stated times; at -fixed, — established-periods; punctually etc. *adj.; de die in diem;* from day to day, day by day.

by turns, in -turn, — rotation; alternately, every other day, off and on, ride and tie, round and round.

139. Irregularity of recurrence.—**N.** irregularity, uncertainty, unpunctuality; fitfulness etc. *adj.*

Adj. irregular, uneven, uncertain, unpunctual, capricious, erratic, desultory, fitful, flickering; rambling, rhapsodical; spasmodic, unsystematic, unequal, variable, halting.

Adv. irregularly etc. *adj.;* by fits and starts etc. (*discontinuously*) 70.

140. Change. [Difference at different times.]—**N.** change, alteration, mutation, permutation, variation, modification, modulation, inflexion, mood, qualification, innovation, *metastasis*, deviation, shift, turn; diversion; break.

transformation, transfiguration; metamorphosis; metabolism; transmutation; transsubstantiation; metagenesis, transanimation, transmigration, metempsychosis; version, metathesis, transmogrification; catalysis; *avatar*; alterative.

conversion etc. (*gradual change*) 144; revolution etc. (*sudden or radical change*) 146; inversion etc. (*reversal*) 218; displacement etc. 185; transference etc. 270.

changeableness etc. 149; tergiversation etc. (*change of mind*) 607.

V. change, alter, vary, wax and wane; modulate, diversify, qualify, tamper with; turn, shift, veer, jibe, tack, chop, shuffle, swerve, dodge, warp, deviate, turn aside, evert, intervert; pass to, take a turn, turn the corner, resume.

work a change, modify, vamp, revamp, superinduce; trans-form, —mute, -ume, -figure etc. *n.;* metamorphose, ring the changes; convert, resolve; revolutionize; chop and change; patch, re-shape.

innovate, introduce new blood, shuffle the cards, spin the wheel; give a -turn, — color- to; influence, turn the scale; shift the scene, turn over a new leaf.

recast etc. 146; reverse etc. 218; disturb etc. 61; convert into etc. 144.

Adj. changed etc. *v.;* new-fangled; changeable etc. 149; transitional; modifiable; alterative.

Adv. *mutatis mutandis.*

Int. *quantum mutatus!*

Phr. 'a change came o'er the spirit of my dream;' *nous avons changé tout cela; tempora mutantur et nos mutamur in illis; non sum qualis eram.*

141. Permanence. [Absence of change.]—**N.** stability etc. 150; quiescence etc. 265; obstinacy etc. 606.

permanence, -cy, persistence, fixity, fixity of purpose, endurance, durability; standing, *status quo;* maintenance, preservation, conservation; conservatism; *laissez-faire;* law of the Medes and Persians; standing dish.

V. let -alone, — be; persist, remain, stay, tarry, rest; hold, — on; last, endure, bide, abide, aby, dwell, maintain, keep; stand, — still, — fast; subsist, live, outlive, survive; hold —, keep- one's ground, — footing; hold good.

Adj. stable etc. 150; persisting etc. *v.;* permanent; established, fixed; durable; unchanged etc. (change etc. 140); unrenewed; intact, inviolate; persistent; monotonous, uncheckered; unfailing.

un-destroyed, -repealed, -suppressed; conservative, *qualis ab incepto;* prescriptive etc. (*old*) 124; stationary etc. 265.

Adv. *in statu quo;* for good, finally; at a stand, -still; *uti possidetis;* without a shadow of turning.

Phr. as you were!; *j'y suis j'y reste; esto perpetua; nolumus leges Angliae mutari;* let sleeping dogs lie.

142. Cessation. [Change from action to

rest.]—**N.** cessation, discontinuance, desistance, desinence.

inter-, re-mission; sus-pense, -pension, interruption, hitch; hartal; stop; stopping etc. *v.;* closure, stoppage, halt; arrival etc. 292.

pause, rest, lull, respite, truce, armistice, drop; interregnum, abeyance.

closure etc. 261.

dead -stop, — stand, — lock; checkmate; comma, colon, semicolon, period, full stop; end etc. 67; death etc. 360; *caesura.*

V. cease, discontinue, desist, stay; break —, leave- off; hold, stop, pull up, stall, stop short, check; stick, deadlock, hand fire; halt; pause, rest.

have done with, give over, surcease, shut up shop; give up etc. (*relinquish*) 624.

hold —, stay- one's hand; rest on one's oars, repose on one's laurels.

come to a -stand, — standstill, — dead lock, — full stop; arrive etc. 292; go out, die away, peter out; wear -away, — off; pass away etc. (*be past*) 122; be at an end.

intromit, interrupt, suspend, interpel; inter-, re-mit; put -an end, — a stop, — a period- to; bring to a stand, -still; stop, cut out, cut short, arrest, avast; stem the -tide, — torrent; pull the check string; switch off.

Int. halt! hold! stop! enough! avast! have done! a truce to! soft! leave off! shut up! give over! chuck it!

143. Continuance in action.—**N.** continu-ance, -ation; run; extension, prolongation; maintenance, perpetuation; persistence etc. (*perseverance*) 604a; repetition etc. 104.

V. continue, persist; go —, jog —, keep —, carry —, run — hold- on; abide, keep, pursue, stick to; endure; take —, maintain- its course; keep up.

sustain, uphold, hold up, keep on foot; follow up, perpetuate. prolong; maintain; preserve etc. 604*a*; harp upon etc. (*repeat*) 104.

keep -going, — alive, — at it, — the pot boiling, — the ball rolling, — up the ball; plod-, plug-along; slog on; die in harness; hold on —, pursue-the even tenor of one's way.

let be; *stare super antiquas vias; quieta non movere;* let things take their course.

Adj. continuing etc. *v.;* uninterrupted, unintermitting, unremitting, unvarying, unshifting; unreversed, unstopped, unrevoked, unvaried; sustained; undying etc. (*perpetual*) 112; inconvertible.

follow-up.

Int. carry on! right away!

Phr. *vestigia nulla retrorsum, labitur et labetur.*

144. Conversion. [Gradual change to something different.]—**N.** conversion, reduction, transmutation, transformation, development, resolution, assimilation; assumption; naturalization.

chemistry, alchemy; progress, growth, lapse, flux.

passage; transit, -ion; transmigration, shifting etc. *v.;* conjugation; convertibility.

crucible, alembic, caldron, retort, test tube etc.

convert, neophyte, proselyte, pervert, renegade, deserter, apostate, turncoat.

V. be converted into; become, get, wax; come —, turn- -to, — into; turn out, lapse, shift; run —, fall —, pass —, slide —, glide —, grow —, ripen —, open —, resolve itself —, settle —, merge- into; melt, grow, come round to, mature, mellow; assume the -form, — shape, — state, — nature, — character- of; illapse; assume a new phase, undergo a change.

convert —, resolve- into; make, render; mold, form etc. 240; remodel, new model, refound, reform, reorganize; assimilate —, bring —, reduce- to; transform.

Adj. converted into etc. *v.;* convertible, resolvable into; transitional; naturalized.

Adv. gradually etc. (*slowly*) 275; *in transitu* etc. (*transference*) 270.

145. Reversion.—**N.** reversion, return; revulsion; reaction.

turning point, turn of the tide; *status quo ante bellum;* calm before a storm.

alternation etc. (*periodicity*) 138; inversion etc. 219; recoil etc. 277; regression etc. 283; restoration etc. 660; relapse etc. 661; vicinism, atavism, throwback.

V. revert, turn back, return; relapse etc. 661; recoil etc. 277; retreat etc. 283; restore etc. 660; undo, unmake; turn the -tide, — scale; escheat.

Adj. reverting etc. *v.;* revulsive, reactionary.

Adv. *à rebours,* wrong side out.

146. Revolution. [Sudden or violent change.]—**N.** revolution, *bouleversement,* subversion. break up; destruction etc. 162; sudden —, radical —, sweeping —, organic- change; clean sweep, *coup d'état,* overthrow, *débâcle;* counter-revolution, rebellion etc. 742.

transilience, jump, leap, plunge, jerk, start; explosion; spasm, convulsion, throe, revulsion; storm, earthquake, eruption, upheaval, cataclysm.

legerdemain etc. (*trick*) 545.

V. revolutionize; new model, remodel, recast; strike out something new, break with the past; change the face of, unsex; revert etc. 742.

Adj. unrecognizable.

Revolutionary, Bolshevik etc. 742.

147. Substitution. [Change of one thing for another.]—**N.** substitution, subrogation, commutation; supplanting etc. *v.;* supersession, metonymy etc. (*figure of speech*) 521.

[Thing substituted.] substitute, *succedaneum,* make-shift, temporary expedient, shift, *pis aller,* stop-gap, jury-mast, *locum tenens,* warming-pan, dummy, goat, scape-goat; double; changeling; *quid pro quo,* alternative; remount; representative etc. (*deputy*) 759; palimpsest.

price, purchase-money, consideration, equivalent.

V. substitute, put in the place of, change for; make way for, give place to; supply —, take- the place of; supplant, supersede, replace, cut out, serve as a substitute; step into —, stand in- the shoes of; make a shift —, put up- with; borrow of Peter to pay Paul; commute, redeem, compound for.

Adj. substituted etc. *v.;* vicarious, subdititious; substitutional.

Adv. instead; in -place, — lieu, — the stead, — the room- of; *faute de mieux*.

148. Interchange. [Double or mutual change.]—**N.** inter-, ex-change; com-, per-, intermutation; reciprocation, transposal, transposition, shuffling; reciprocity, castling [at chess]; hocus-pocus.

interchange-ableness, -ability.

barter etc. 794; tit for tat etc. (*retaliation*) 718; cross fire, battledore and shuttlecock; *quid pro quo*.

V. inter-, ex-, counter-change; bandy, transpose, shuffle, change hands, swap, trade, permute, reciprocate, commute; give and take, return the compliment; play at -puss in the corner, — battledore and shuttlecock; retaliate etc. 718; barter etc. 794.

Adj. interchanged etc. *v.;* reciprocal, mutual, commutative, interchanged etc. *v.;* interchangeable, intercurrent.

Adv. in exchange, *vice versâ*, *mutatis mutandis*, backwards and forwards, by turns, turn and turn about, turn about; each —, every one- in his turn.

149. Changeableness.—**N.** changeableness etc. *adj.*; mutability, inconstancy; versatility, mobility; instability, unstable equilibrium; vacillation etc. (*irresolution*) 605; fluctuation, vicissitude; alternation etc. (*oscillation*) 314.

restlessness etc. *adj.;* fidgets, disquiet; dis-, inquietude; unrest; agitation etc. 315.

moon, Proteus, chameleon, kaleidoscope, quicksilver, shifting sands, weathercock, harlequin, Cynthia of the minute, April showers; wheel of Fortune; transientness etc. 111.

V. fluctuate, vary, waver, flounder, flicker, flitter, flit, flutter, shift, shuffle, shake, totter, tremble, vacillate, wamble, turn and turn about, ring the changes; sway —, shift- to and fro; change and change about; oscillate etc. 314; vibrate —, oscillate- between two extremes; alternate; have as many phases as the moon.

Adj. change-able, -ful; changing etc. 140; mutable, variable, checkered, ever changing, kaleidoscopic, prote-an, -iform; versatile.

unstaid, inconstant; un-steady, -stable, -fixed, -settled; fluctuating etc. *v.;* restless; mercurial; agitated etc. 315; erratic, fickle; irresolute etc. 605; capricious etc. 608; touch-and-go; inconsonant, fitful, spasmodic; vibratory; afloat; alternating; alterable, plastic, mobile; fleeting, transient etc. 111.

Adv. see-saw etc. (*oscillation*) 314; off and on.

150. Stability.—**N.** stability; immutability etc. *adj.;* unchangeableness etc. *adj.;* constancy; stable equilibrium, immobility, soundness, vitality, stabiliment, stabilization, stiffness, ankylosis, solidity, *aplomb*.

establishment, fixture; rock, pillar, tower, foundation, leopard's spots, Ethiopian's skin, law of the Medes and Persians.

stabilimeter, stabilizator.

permanence etc. 141; obstinacy etc. 606.

V. be -firm etc. *adj.;* stick fast; stand —, keep —, remain- firm; weather the storm.

settle, establish, stablish, ascertain, fix, set, stabilitate, stabilize; retain, stet, keep hold; make -good, — sure; fasten etc. (*join*) 43; set on its legs, float; perpetuate.

settle down; strike —, take- root; take up one's abode etc. 184; build one's house on a rock.

Adj. unchangeable, immutable; unalter-ed, -able; not to be changed, constant; permanent etc. 141; invariable, undeviating; stable, durable; perennial etc. (*diuturnal*) 110.

fixed, steadfast, firm, fast, steady, balanced; confirmed, valid, fiducial, immovable, irremovable, riveted, rooted; settled, established etc. *v.;* vested; incontrovertible, stereotyped, indeclinable.

tethered, anchored, moored, at anchor, on a rock, firm as a rock; firmly -seated, — established etc. *v.;* deep-rooted, ineradicable; inveterate; obstinate etc. 606.

transfixed, stuck fast, aground, high and dry, stranded.

indefeasible, irretrievable, intransmutable, incommutable, irresoluble, irrevocable, irreversible, reverseless, inextinguishable, irreducible; indissol-uble, -vable; indestructible, undying, imperishable, indelible, indeciduous; insusceptible, — of change.

Int. *stet*.

151. Eventuality.—**N.** eventuality, event, occurrence, incident, affair, transaction, proceeding, fact; matter of —, naked- fact; phenomenon; advent.

business, concern; circumstance, particular, casualty, happening, accident, adventure, passage, crisis, pass, emergency, contingency, consequence etc. 154.

the world, life, things, doings, affairs, matters; things —, affairs- in general; the times, state of affairs, order of the day; course —, tide —, stream —, current —, run —, march- of -things, — events; ups and downs of life; chapter of accidents etc. (*chance*) 156; situation etc. (*circumstances*) 8.

V. happen, occur; take -place, — effect; come, become of; come -off, — about, — round, — into existence, — forth, — to pass, — on; pass, present itself; fall; fall —, turn- out; run, be on foot, fall in; be-fall, -tide, -chance; prove, eventuate, draw on; turn —, crop —, spring —, cast- up; super-, sur-vene; issue, emanate, arrive, ensue, arise, start, hold, take its course; pass off etc. (*be past*) 122.

meet with; experience; fall to the lot of; be one's -chance, — fortune, — lot; find; encounter, undergo; pass —, go- through; endure etc. (*feel*) 821.

Adj. happening etc. *v.;* going on, doing, current; in the wind, afloat; on -foot, — the *tapis;* at issue, in question; incidental.

eventful, momentous, signal; stirring, bustling, full of incident.

Adv. eventually, ultimately, in -the event of, — case; in the course of things; in the -natural, — ordinary- course of things; as -things, — times- go; as the world -goes, — wags; as the -tree falls, — cat jumps; as it may -turn out, — happen.

Phr. the plot thickens.

152. Destiny.—**N.** destiny etc. (*necessity*) 601; hereafter, future —, post- existence; future state, next world, world to come, after life; futurity etc. 121; everlasting -life, — death; prospect etc. (*expectation*) 507.

V. impend; hang —, lie —, hover- over; threaten, loom, await, come on, approach, stare one in the face; fore-, pre-ordain; predestine, doom, foredoom, foreshadow, have in store for.

Adj. impending etc. *v.*; destined; about to -be, — happen; coming, in store, to come, going to happen, instant, at hand, near; near —, close- at hand; overhanging, hanging over one's head, imminent; brewing, preparing, forthcoming; in the wind, on the cards, in reserve; that -will, — is to-be; in prospect etc. (*expected*) 507; looming in the -distance, — horizon, — future; unborn, in embryo; in the womb of -time; — futurity; on the knees of the gods; pregnant etc. (*producing*) 161.

Adv. in -time, — the long run; all in good time; eventually etc. 151; whatever may happen etc. (*certainly*) 474; as -chance etc. 156- would have it.

153. Cause. [Constant antecedent.]—**N.** cause, origin, source, principle, element; occasioner, prime mover, engine, turbine, motor, *primum mobile; vera causa*; author etc. (*producer*) 164; main-spring, agent; dynamo, generator, battery (electric); leaven; groundwork, foundation etc. (*support*) 215.

spring, fountain, well, font; fountain —, spring- head; *fons et origo*, genesis; descent etc. (*paternity*) 166; remote cause; influence.

pivot, hinge, turning-point, lever; key, kernel, core; proximate cause, *causa causans;* last straw that breaks the camel's back.

ground; reason, — why; why and wherefore, rationale, occasion, derivation; final cause etc. (*intention*) 620; *le dessous des cartes;* undercurrents.

rudiment, egg, germ, embryo, fetus, bud, root, *radix*, radical, etymon, nucleus, seed, stem, stalk, stock, *stirps*, trunk, tap-root; latent organism.

nest, cradle, nursery, womb, *nidus*, birth-, breeding-place, hot-bed.

caus-ality, -ation; origination; production etc. 161.

V. be the -cause etc. *n.*- of; originate; give - origin, — rise, — occasion- to; cause, occasion, sow the seeds of, kindle, suscitate; bring -on, — to pass, — about; produce; create etc. 161; set - up, — afloat, — on foot; found, broach, institute, lay the foundation of, inaugurate; lie at the root of.

procure, induce, draw down, open the door to, superinduce, evoke, entail, operate; elicit, provoke.

conduce to etc. (*tend to*) 176; contribute; promote; have a -hand in, — finger in- the pie; determine, decide, turn the scale, give the casting vote; have a common origin; derive its origin etc. (*effect*) 154.

Adj. caused etc. *v.*; causal, original; prim-ary, -itive, -ordial; aboriginal; radical; inceptive, embry-onic, -otic; *in -embryo, — ovo;* seminal, germinal; formative, productive etc. 168; at the bottom of; connate, having a common origin.

Adv. because etc. 155; behind the scenes.

154. Effect. [Constant sequent.]—**N.** effect, consequence, sequela; derivative, -tion; result; result-ant, -ance; upshot, issue, *dénouement;* outcome; termination, end etc. 67; development, outgrowth, fruit, crop, harvest, product, bud, blossom, florescence, ear.

production, produce, product, finished product, work, handiwork, fabric, performance; creature, creation; offspring, -shoot; first-fruits, -lings; *prémices*.

V. be the -effect etc. *n.*- of; be -due, — owing-to; originate -in, — from; rise —, arise —, take its rise —, spring —, proceed —, emanate —, come —, grow —, bud —, sprout —, germinate —, issue —, flow —, result —, follow —, derive its origin —, accrue- from; come -to, — of, — out of; depend —, hand —, hinge —, turn- upon.

take the consequences, sow the wind and reap the whirlwind.

Adj. owing to; resulting from etc. *v.*; resultant; derivable from; due to; caused etc. by, 153; dependent upon; derived —, evolved- from; derivative; hereditary.

Adv. of course, it follows that, naturally, consequently; as a —, in- consequence; through all, all along of, necessarily, eventually.

Phr. *cela va sans dire*, thereby hangs a tale.

155. Attribution. [Assignment of cause.]—**N.** attribution, theory, etiology, ascription, reference to, rationale; accounting for etc. *v.*; imputation, derivation from.

fil-, affil-iation; pedigree etc. (*paternity*) 166.

explanation etc. (*interpretation*) 522; reason why etc. (*cause*) 153.

V. attribute —, ascribe —, impute —, refer —, lay —, point —, trace —, bring home- to; put —, set- down- to; charge —, ground- on; invest with, assign as cause, charge with, blame, lay at the door of, father upon; saddle with; affiliate; account for, derive from, point out the -reason etc. 153; theorize; tell how it comes; put the saddle on the right horse.

Adj. attributed etc. *v.*; attributable etc. *v.*; refer-able, -rible; due to, derivable from; owing to etc. (*effect*) 154; putative.

Adv. hence, thence, therefore, for, since, on account of, because, owing to; on that account; from -this, — that- cause; thanks to, forasmuch as; whence, *propter hoc*.

why? wherefore? whence? how -comes, — is, — happens- it? how does it happen?

in -some, — some such- way; somehow, — or other.

Phr. that is why; *hinc illae lachrymae; cherchez la femme*.

156. Chance.† [Absence of assignable cause.]—**N.** chance, indetermination, accident, fortune, hazard, hap, haphazard, chance-medley, random, luck, *raccroc*, casualty, fortuity, contingence, coincidence, adventure, hit; fate etc. (*necessity*) 601; equal chance; lottery, raffle, tombola, sweepstake; toss up etc. 621; turn of the -table, — cards; hazard of the die, chapter of accidents; cast —, throw- of the dice; heads or tails, wheel of Fortune, whirligig of chance; *sortes*; — *Virgilianae*.

probability, possibility, contingency, odds, long odds, run of luck; main- chance.

theory of -probabilities, – chances; book-*making*; assurance; speculation, gamble, gaming etc. 621.

V. chance, hap, turn up; fall to one's lot; be one's -fate etc. 601; stumble on, light –, blunder –, hit- upon; take one's chance etc. 621.

Adj. casual, fortuitous, accidental, haphazard, random, stray, adventitious, adventive, causeless, incidental, contingent, uncaused, undetermined, indeterminate; possible etc. 470; unintentional etc. 621.

Adv. by -chance, – accident; casually; perchance etc. (*possibly*) 470; for aught one knows; as -good, – bad, – ill-luck etc. *n.*- would have it; as it may -be, – chance, – turn up, – happen; as the case may be.

†The word *Chance* has two distinct meanings: the first, the absence of assignable *cause*, as above; and the second, the absence of *design*—for the latter see 621.

157. Power.—**N.** power; poten-cy, -tiality; puissance, might, force; energy etc. 171; dint; right -hand, – arm; ascendency, sway, control; pre-potency, -pollence; almightiness, omnipotence; authority etc. 737; strength etc. 159.

ability; ableness etc. *adj.;* competency; efficiency, -cacy; validity, cogency; enablement; vantage ground; influence etc. 175; horse power; dynamometer.

pressure; elasticity; gravity; attraction, repulsion; *vis -inertiae, – mortua, – viva;* friction, suction.

electricity, magnetism, galvanism, voltaic electricity, voltaism, electro-magnetism, electrostatics, electrification; electric – current, – power; potential –, dynamic –, kinetic –, electrical –, chemical –, atomic- energe; electric field, circuit, charge, discharge, shock, polarity, pole; amperage, voltage, wattage, resistance, conduction, induction, electrification, electrolysis.

electronics, radionics, electron physics, electrophysics, avionics, radiometry, photoelectronics; electron, negatron, positron, photoelectron, thermion, barytron; electronic effect; electron emission; electron –, cathode –, anode –, positive – ray; electron – current, – flow – stream, – beam, – volt; electronic circuit; conductance; electron tube, tube, vacuum tube, photoelectric tube, call; transistor.

capability, capacity; *quid valeant humeri quid ferre recusent;* faculty, quality, attribute, endowment, virtue, gift, property, qualification, susceptibility.

V. be -powerful etc. *adj.;* gain -power etc. *n.*

belong –, pertain- to; lie –, be- in one's power; can.

electrify, generate, magnetize.

give –, confer –, exercise- power etc. *n.;* empower, enable, invest; in-, en-due; endow, arm; strengthen etc. 159; compel etc. 744.

Adj. powerful, puissant; potent, -ial; capable, able; equal –, up- to; cogent, valid; effect-ive, -ual; efficient, efficacious, adequate, competent; multi-, pleni-, omni-, armi- potent; mighty, ascendent; almighty.

electric, electrical, electronic etc.

forcible etc. *adj.* (*energetic*) 171; influential etc. 175; productive etc. 168.

Adv. powerfully etc. *adj.;* by -virtue, – dint-of.

158. Impotence.—**N.** impotence; in-, dis-ability; disablement, impuissance, imbecility, caducity; incapa-city, -bility; inapt-, inept-itude; indocility; invalidity, inefficiency, incompetence, disqualification.

telum imbelle, brutum fulmen, blank cartridge, flash in the pan, *vox et praeterea nihil,* dead letter, bit of waste paper, dummy; scrap of paper.

inefficacy etc. (*inutility*) 645; failure etc. 732.

helplessness etc. *adj.;* prostration, paralysis, palsy, ataxia, apoplexy, syncope, sideration, *deliquium*, collapse, exhaustion, softening of the brain, emasculation, inanition, senility etc. 128; castrato, eunuch.

cripple, old woman, muff, molly-coddle, milksop.

V. be -impotent etc. *adj.;* *not have a leg to* stand on.

vouloir -rompre l'anguille au genou, – prendre la lune avec les dents.

collapse, faint, swoon, fall into a swoon, drop; go by the board; end in smoke etc. (*fail*) 732.

render -powerless etc. *adj.;* deprive of power; decontrol; dis-able, -enable; disarm, incapacitate, disqualify, unfit, invalidate, undermine, deaden, cramp, tie the hands; double up, prostrate, paralyze, muzzle, cripple, becripple, maim, lame, hamstring, draw the teeth of; throttle, strangle, *garrotte;* ratten, silence, sprain, clip the wings of, render *hors de combat*, spike the guns; take the wind out of one's sails, scotch the snake, put a spoke in one's wheel; break the -neck, – back; un-hinge, -fit; put out of gear.

unman, unnerve, devitalize, attenuate, enervate; emasculate, spay, caponize, castrate, geld; effeminize.

shatter, exhaust; weaken etc. 160.

Adj. powerless, impotent, unable, incapable, incompetent; ineff-icient, -ective; inept; un-fit, -fitted; un-, dis-qualified; unendowed; in-, un-apt; crippled, decrepit; disabled etc. *v.;* armless.

harmless, unarmed, weaponless, defenceless, *sine ictu*, unfortified, indefensible, vincible, pregnable, untenable.

para-lytic, -lyzed; palsied, imbecile; nerve-, sinew-, marrow-, pith-, lust-less; *emasculate, disjointed*, out of -joint, – gear; un-nerved, -hinged; water-logged, on one's beam ends, rudderless; laid on one's back; done up, dead beat, exhausted, shattered, demoralized; gravelled etc. (*in difficulty*) 704; helpless, unfriended, fatherless; without a leg to stand on, *hors de combat*, laid on the shelf.

null and void, nugatory, imoperative, good for nothing; dud; invertebrate; ineffectual etc. (*failing*) 732; inadequate etc. 640; inefficacious etc. (*useless*) 645.

159. Strength. (Degree of power.)—**N.** strength; power etc. 157; energy etc. 171; vigor, force; main –, physical –, brute- force; spring, elasticity, tone, tension, tonicity.

stoutness etc. *adj.;* lustihood, stamina, nerve,

muscle, sinew, thews and sinews, *physique;* pith, -iness; virility, vitality.

athlet-ics, -icism; gymnastics, feats of strength.

adamant, steel, iron, oak, heart of oak; iron grip; grit, bone.

athlete, gymnast, tumbler, acrobat; Atlas, Hercules, Antaeus, Samson, Cyclops, Goliath, Titan; tower of strength; giant refreshed.

strengthening etc. *v.;* invigoration, refreshment, refocillation.

[Science of forces] dynamics, statics.

V. be -strong etc. *adj.*, — stronger; overmatch.

render -strong etc. *adj.;* give -strength etc. *n.;* strengthen, invigorate, brace, nerve, fortify, buttress, sustain, harden, case-harden, steel; gird; screw —, wind —, set- up; gird —, brace- up one's loins; recruit, set on one's legs; vivify; refresh etc. 689; refect; reinforce etc. (*restore*) 660.

Adj. strong, mighty, vigorous, forcible, hard, adamantine, stout, robust, sturdy, hardy, powerful, potent, puissant, valid.

resistless, irresistible, invincible, proof against, impregnable, unconquerable, indomitable, inextinguishable, unquenchable; incontestable; more than a match for; over-powering, -whelming; all-powerful; sovereign.

able-bodied; athletic, gymnastic; Herculean, Cyclopean, Atlantean; muscular, husky, brawny, wiry, well-knit, broad-shouldered, sinewy, strapping, stalwart, gigantic.

man-ly, -like, -ful; masculine, male, virile, in the prime of manhood.

un-weakened, -allayed, -withered, -shaken, -worn, -exhausted; in full -force, — swing; in the plenitude of power.

stubborn, thick-ribbed, made of iron, deep-rooted; strong as -a lion, — a horse, — brandy; sound as a roach; in -fine, — high- feather; in fine fettle; like a giant refreshed.

Adv. strongly etc. *adj.*; by -force etc. *n.*; by main force etc. (*by compulsion*) 744.

Phr. 'our withers are unwrung.'

160. Weakness.—**N.** weakness etc. *adj.;* debility, atony, relaxation, languor, enervation; impotence etc. 158; infirmity; effeminancy, feminality; fragility, flaccidity; inactivity etc. 683.

declension —, loss —, failure- of strength; delicacy, invalidation, decrepitude, asthenia, adynamy, cachexy, *cachexia,* anemia, bloodlessness, sprain, strain.

reed, thread, rope of sand, broken reed, house -of cards, — built on sand.

soft-, weak-ling; infant etc. 129; youth etc. 127.

V. be -weak etc. *adj.;* drop, crumble, give way, totter, tremble, shake, halt, limp, fade, languish, decline, flag, fail, have one foot in the grave.

render -weak etc. *adj.;* weaken, enfeeble, debilitate, shake, deprive of strength, relax, enervate; un-brace, -nerve; cripple, unman, etc. (*render powerless*) 158; cramp, reduce, sprain, strain, blunt the edge of; dilute, impoverish; decimate; extenuate; reduce -in strength, — the strength of; invalidate; *mettre de l'eau dans son vin.*

Adj. weak, feeble, debile; impotent etc. 158; relaxed, unnerved etc. *v.;* sap-, strength-, powerless; weakly, unstrung, flaccid, adynamic, asthenic; nervous.

soft, effeminate, feminate, womanish.

frail, fragile, shattery, frangible, brittle etc. 328; flimsy, unsubstantial, gimcrack, gingerbread; rickety, cranky; creachy; drooping, tottering etc. *v.;* broken, lame, halt, game, withered, shattered, shaken, crazy, shaky, tumble-down; palsied etc. 158; decrepit; C3.

lanquid, poor, poorly, infirm; faint, -ish; sickly etc. (*disease*) 655; dull, slack, evanid, spent, short-winded, effete; weatherbeaten; decayed, rotten, worn, seedy, languishing, wasted, washy, wishy-washy, laid low, pulled down, the worse for wear.

un-strengthened etc. 159, -supported, -aided, -assisted; aidless, defenceless etc. 158.

on its last legs; weak as a -child, — baby, — chicken, — cat, — rat; weak as -water, — water gruel, — gingerbread, — milk and water; colorless etc. 429.

Phr. *non sum qualis eram.*

161. Production.—**N.** production, creation, construction, formation, fabrication, manufacture; building, architecture, erection, edification; coinage; organization; *nisus formativus;* putting togeher etc. *v.;* establishment; workmanship, performance; achievement etc. (*completion*) 729; effect etc. 154.

flowering, fructification fruition.

bringing forth etc. *v.;* parturition, birth, birth-throe, child-birth, delivery, confinement, *accouchement,* travail, labour, midwifery, obstetrics; geniture; gestation etc. (*maturation*) 673; evolution, development, growth; genesis, fertilization, breeding, conception, germination, generation, *epigenesis,* pro-creation, -generation, -pagation; fecundation, impregnation; spontaneous generation; *arche-genesis, -biosis; bio-, abio-, homo-, xeno-genesis.*

authorship, publication; works, *oeuvre, opus.*

edifice, building, structure, fabric, erection, pile, tower, flower, fruit.

V. produce, perform, operate, do, make, gar, form, construct, fabricate, frame, contrive, manufacture; weave, forge, coin, carve, chisel; build, raise, edify, rear, erect, put together; set —, run- up; establish, constitute, compose, organize, institute, get up; achieve, accomplish etc. (*complete*) 729.

flower, sprout, blossom, burgeon, bear fruit, fructify, spawn, teem, ean, yean, farrow, drop, calf, pup, whelp, kitten, kindle; bear, lay, bring forth, give birth to, lie in, be brought to bed of, evolve, pullulate, usher into the world.

make productive etc. 168; create; beget, conceive, get, generate, fecundate, impregnate; procreate, -generate, -pagate; engender; bring —, call- into -being, — existence; breed, hatch, develop, bring up.

induce, superinduce; suscitate; cause etc. 153; acquire etc. 775.

Adj. produc-ed, -ing etc. *v.;* productive of; prolific etc. 168; creative; formative; gen-etic, -ial, -ital; fertile, pregnant; *enceinte,* big —, fraught-with; with child, in the family way, teeming, parturient, in the straw, brought to bed of; puerper-al, -ous.

architectonic; constructive.

162. Destruction. [Non-production.]—**N.** destruction; waste, dissolution, breaking up; di-, dis-ruption; consumption; disorganization.

fall, downfall, ruin, perdition, crash, smash, havoc, *délabrement, débâcle;* break -down, – up; prostration; desolation, *bouleversement*, wreck, crack-up, crash, wrack, shipwreck, cataclysm; Caudine Forks, Sedan.

extinction, annihilation; destruction of life etc. 361; knock-out, knock-down blow; doom, crack of doom.

destroying etc. *v.*; demo-lition, -lishment; biblioclasm; overthrow, subversion, suppression; abolition etc. (*abrogation*) 756; sacrifice; ravage, devastation, *sabotage, razzia*; incendiarism; revolution etc. 146; extirpation etc. (*extraction*) 301; *commencement de la fin,* road to ruin; dilapidation etc. (*deterioration*) 659.

V. be -destroyed etc.; perish; fall, – to the ground; tumble, topple; go –, fall- to pieces; break up; crumble, – to dust; go to -the dogs, – the wall, – smash, – shivers, – wreck, – pot, – wrack and ruin; go -by the board, – all to smash, – to pieces, – under; be all -over, – up- with; totter to its fall.

destroy; do –, make- away with; nullify; annul etc. 756; sacrifice, demolish; tear up; over-turn, -throw, -whelm; upset, subvert, put an end to; seal the doom of, do for, dish, undo; break -, cut- up; break –, cut –, pull –, mow –, blow –, beat- down; suppress, quash, put down; cut short, take off, blot out; dispel, dissipate, dissolve; consume.

smash, – to smithereens, quell, squash, squelch, crumple up, shatter, shiver; batter; tear –, crush –, cut –, shake –, pull –, pick- to pieces; nip; tear to -rags, – tatters; crush –, knock- to atoms; pulverize; ruin; strike out; throw –, knock- -down, – over; lay by the heels; fell, sink, swamp, scuttle, wreck, crash, shipwreck, engulf, submerge; lay in -ashes, – ruins; sweep away, erase, expunge, strike out, delete, efface, raze; level, – with the -ground, – dust.

deal destruction, lay waste, ravage, gut; disorganize; dismantle etc. (*render useless*) 645; devour, swallow up, desolate, devastate, sap, mine, blast, confound; exterminate, extinguish, quench, annihilate; snuff –, put –, stamp –, trample- out; lay –, trample- in the dust; prostrate; tread –, crush –, trample- under foot; lay the axe to the root of; make -short work, – a clean sweep, – mincemeat- of; cut up root and branch; fling –, scatter- to the winds; throw overboard; strike at the root of, sap the foundations of, spring a mine, blow up; ravage with fire and sword; cast to the dogs; eradicate etc. 301.

Adj. destroyed etc. *v.;* perishing etc. *v.;* trembling –, nodding –, tottering- to its fall; in course of destruction etc. *n.;* extinct.

destructive, subversive, ruinous, incendiary, deletory; destroying etc. *v.*; suicidal; deadly etc. (*killing*) 361.

Adv. with -crushing effect, – a sledge-hammer.

Phr. *delenda est Carthago.*

163. Reproduction.—**N.** reproduction, renovation; restoration etc. 660; renewal; new edition, reprint etc. 21; revival, regeneration, palingenesia, revivification; apotheosis; resuscitation, reanimation, resurrection, resurgence, reappearance, atavism; Phoenix; reincarnation.

generation etc. (*production*) 161; multiplication.

V. reproduce; restore etc. 660; revive, renovate, renew, regenerate, revivify, resuscitate, reanimate, refashion, stir the embers, put into the crucible; multiply, repeat, resurge.

crop up, spring up like mushrooms.

Adj. reproduced etc. *v.;* renascent, reappearing; reproductive; resurgent; progenitive; Hydra-headed.

164. Producer.—**N.** producer, creator, deviser, designer, originator, inventor, author, founder, generator, *mover, architect;* grower, constructor, maker etc. (*agent*) 690.

165. Destroyer.—**N.** destroyer etc. (destroy etc. 162); cankerworm etc. (*bane*) 663; iconoclast; assassin etc. (*killer*) 361; executioner etc. (*punish*) 975; Hun, Vandal, nihilist, anarchist.

166. Paternity.—**N.** paternity; parentage; fatherhood; consanguinity etc. 11.

parent, father, sire, dad, daddy, papa, governor, *pater, paterfamilias, abba;* genitor, progenitor, procreator, begetter; ancestor; grandsire, -father; great-grandfather.

house, stem, truck, tree, stock, *stirps*, pedigree, lineage, line, family, tribe, sept, race, clan; genealogy, descent, extraction, birth, ancestry; forefathers, forbears, patriarchs.

motherhood, maternity; mother, dam, mamma, *materfamilias;* grand-mother; matriarch.

Adj. paternal, parental; maternal; family, ancestral, linear, matrilinear, patrilineal, patriarchal.

167. Posterity.—**N.** posterity, progeny, breed, issue, offspring, brood, litter, seed, farrow, spawn, spat; family, children, grandchildren, heirs; great-grandchild.

child, son, daughter; kid; infant etc. 129; bantling, scion; shoot, sprout, olive branch, sprit, branch; off-shoot, -set; ramification; descendant; heir, -ess; heir -apparent, – presumptive; chip of the old block; heredity; rising generation.

straight descent, sonship, line, lineage, filiation, promogeniture.

Adj. filial.

168. Productiveness.—**N.** productiveness etc. *adj.;* fecundity, fertility, luxuriance, uberty.

pregnancy, pullulation, fructification, multiplication, propagation, procreation; superfetation.

milch cow, rabbit, hydra, warren, seed-plot, land flowing with milk and honey; second crop, after-crop, -growth, -math; fertilization.

V. make -productive etc. *adj.;* fructify; procreate, generate, fertilize, spermatize, impregnate; fecund-ate, -ify; teem, pullulate, multiply; produce etc. 161; conceive.

Adj. productive, prolific; teem-ing, -ful; fertile, fruitful, frugiferous, fruit-bearing; fructiferous; fecund, luxuriant; pregnant, uberous.

procre-ant, -ative; generative, life-giving, spermatic; originative; multiparous; omnific; propagable.

parturient etc. (*producing*) 161; profitable etc. (*useful*) 644.

169. Unproductiveness.—N. unproductiveness etc. *adj.;* infertility, steril; ity, infecundity; impotence etc. 158- unprofitableness etc. (*inutility*) 645.

waste, desert, Sahara, wild, wilderness, howling wilderness.

V. be -unproductive etc. *adj.;* hang fire, flash in the pan, come to nothing.

Adj. unproductive, inoperative, barren, addle, unfertile, unprolific, arid, sterile, unfruitful, acarpous, infecund; *sine prole;* fallow; teem-, issue-, fruitless; unprofitable etc. (*useless*) 645; null and void, of no effect.

170. Agency.—N. agency, operation, force, working, strain, function, office, maintenance, exercise, work, swing, play; inter-working, -action, procuration, procurement.

causation etc. 153; instrumentality etc. 631; influence etc. 175; action etc. (*voluntary*) 680; *modus operandi* etc. 627.

quickening –, maintaining- power; home stroke.

V. be -in action etc. *adj.;* operate, work; act, – upon; perform, play, support, sustain, strain, maintain, take effect, quicken, strike.

come –, bring- into -operation, – play; have -play, – free play; bring to bear upon.

Adj. operative, efficient, efficacious, practical, effectual.

at work, on foot; acting etc. (*doing*) 680; in -operation, – force, – action, – play, – exercise; acted –, wrought- upon.

Adv. by the -agency etc. *n.*- of; through etc. (*instrumentality*) 631; by means of etc. 632.

171. Physical Energy.—N. energy, physical energy, force; keenness etc. *adj.;* intensity, vigor, strength, elasticity; go; pep, live wire, high pressure; backbone, mettle, fire, vim.

acri-mony, -tude, -dity; causticity, virulence, poignancy; harshness etc. *adj.;* severity, edge, point; pungency etc. 392.

cantharides; Spanish fly; seasoning etc. (*condiment*) 393, stimulant, excitant.

activity, agitation, effervescence; ferment, -ation; ebullition, splutter, perturbation, stir, bustle; voluntary energy etc. 682; quicksilver.

resolution etc. (*mental energy*) 604; exertion etc. (*effort*) 686; excitation etc. (*mental*) 824.

V. give -energy etc. *n.;* energize, stimulate, kindle, excite, activate, exert; sharpen, pep up, intensify; inflame etc. (*render violent*) 173; wind up etc. (*strengthen*) 159.

strike, – into, – hard, – home; make an impression.

Adj. strong, energetic, forcible, active; strenuous, forceful, mettlesome, enterprising, go ahead; intense, deep-dyed, severe, keen, vivid, sharp, acute, incisive, trenchant, brisk, vigorous, live.

rousing, irritating; poignant; virulent, caustic, corrosive, mordant, harsh, stringent; double-edged, – shotted, – distilled; drastic, escharotic; racy etc. (*pungent*) 392; sarcastic etc. 932.

potent etc. (*powerful*) 157; radio-active.

Adv. strongly etc. *adj.; fortiter in re;* with telling effect.

Phr. the steam is up; *vires acquirit eundo.*

172. Physical Inertness.—N. inertness, dulness etc. *adj.;* inertia, *vis inertiae*, inertion, inactivity, torpor, languor; dormancy, quiescence etc. 265; latency, inaction, passivity.

mental inertness; sloth etc. (*inactivity*) 683; inexcitability etc. 826; irresolution etc. 605; obstinacy etc. 606; permanence etc. 141.

V. be -inert etc. *adj.;* hang fire, smoulder.

Adj. inert, inactive, passive, pacific; torpid etc. 683; sluggish, stagnant, dull, heavy, flat, slack, tame, slow, blunt; lifeless, dead, uninfluential.

latent, dormant, smouldering, unexerted.

Adv. inactively etc. *adj.;* in -suspense, -abeyance.

173. Violence.—N. violence, -inclemency, vehemence, might, impetuosity; boisterousness etc.; *adj.;* effervescence, ebullition; turbulence, bluster; uproar, riot, row, rumpus, *le diable à quatre*, devil to pay, all the fat in the fire.

severity etc. 739; ferocity, rage, berserk, fury; exacerbation, exasperation, malignity; fit, paroxysm, orgasm; force, brute force; outrage; *coup de main;* strain, shock, shog; spasm, convulsion, throe; hysterics, passion etc. (*state of excitability*) 825.

out-break, -burst; burst, bounce, dissilience, discharge, volley, explosion, blow up, blast, detonation, rush, eruption, displosion, torrent.

turmoil etc. (*disorder*) 59; ferment etc. (*agitation*) 315; storm, tempest, rough weather; squall etc. (*wind*) 349; earthquake, volcano, thunderstorm.

fury, dragon, demon, tiger, beldame, Tisiphone, Megaera, Alecto, madcap, wild beast; fire-eater etc. (*blusterer*) 887.

V. be -violent etc. *adj.*; run high; ferment, effervesce; romp, rampage; run -wild, – riot; break the peace; rush, tear; rush head-long, -foremost; run amuck, raise a storm, make a riot; make –, kick up- a row, – a fuss; bluster, rage, roar, riot, storm; boil, – over; fume, foam, come in like a lion, wreak, bear down, ride roughshod, out-Herod Herod; spread like wildfire.

break –, fly –, burst- out; bounce, shock, strain; break-, pry-, force-, prize- open.

render -violent etc. *adj.;* sharpen, stir up, quicken, excite, incite, urge, lash, stimulate; irritate, inflame, exacerbate, kindle, suscitate, foment; accelerate, aggravate, exasperate, convulse, infuriate, madden, lash into fury; fan –, add fuel to- the flame; *oleum addere camino.*

explode, go off, displode, fly, detonate, thunder, blow up, flash, flare, erupt, burst; let - off, — fly; discharge, detonize, fulminate.

Adj. violent, vehement, forcible; warm; acute, sharp; rough, rude, ungentle, bluff, boisterous, wild, vicious; brusque, abrupt, waspish; impetuous; rampant.

turbulent; disorderly; blustering, raging etc. *v.;* troublous, riotous; tumultu-ary, -ous; obstreperous, uproarious; extravagant; unmitigated; ravening, tameless; frenzied etc. (*insane*) 503; desperate etc. (*rash*) 863; infuriate, towering, furious, outrageous, frantic, hysteric, in hysterics.

fiery, flaming, scorching, hot, red-hot, ebullient.

savage, fierce, ferocious, fierce as a tiger.

excited etc. *v.;* un-quelled, -quenched, -extinguished, -repressed, -bridled, -ruly; headstrong; un-governable, -appeasable, -mitigable; un-, in-controllable; insup-, irre-pressible.

spasmodic, convulsive, explosive; detonating etc. *v.;* volcanic, meteoric; stormy etc. (*wind*) 349.

Adv. violently etc. *adj.;* amain; by -storm, — force, — main force; with might and main; tooth and nail, *vi et armis*, at the point of the -sword, — bayonet; at one fell swoop; with a high hand, through thick and thin; in desperation, with a vengeance; *à —, à touteoutrance;* head-long, -foremost, -first; like a bull at a gate.

174. Moderation.—**N.** moderation; lenity etc. 740; temperance, temperateness, gentleness etc. *adj.;* sobriety; quiet; mental calmness etc. (*inexcitability*) 826.

moderating etc. *v.;* relaxation, remission, mitigation etc. 834; tranquilization, alleviation, assuagement, appeasement, contemporation, pacification.

measure, *juste milieu*, golden mean etc. 29.

moderator; lullaby, sedative, lenitive, demulcent, rose-water, balm, soothing syrup, poppy, opiate, anodyne, milk, opium, laudanum, 'poppy or mandragora;' wet blanket; palliative, calmative.

V. be -moderate etc. *adj.;* keep within -bounds, — compass; sober —, settle- down; keep the pease, remit, relent; take in sail.

moderate, soften, mitigate, temper, accoy; at-, con-temper; mollify, lenify, dull, take off the edge, blunt, obtund, sheathe, subdue, chasten; sober —, tone —, smooth- down; censor, blue-pencil, weaken etc. 160; lessen etc. (*decrease*) 36; check; palliate.

tranquilize, assuage, appease, dulcify, swage, lull, soothe, compose, still, calm, cool, quiet, hush, quell, sober, pacify, tame, damp, lay, allay, rebate, slacken, smooth, alleviate, rock to sleep, deaden, smother; throw -cold water on, — a wet blanket over; slake; curb etc. (*restrain*) 751; tame etc. (*subjugate*) 749; smooth over; pour oil on the -waves, — troubled waters; pour balm into, *mettre de l'eau dans son vin*.

go out like a lamb, 'roar you as gently as any sucking dove.'

Adj. moderate; lenient etc. 740; gentle, mild; cool, sober, temperate, reasonable, measured; tempered etc. *v.;* calm, unruffled, quiet, tranquil, still; slow, smooth, untroubled; tame; peaceful, -able; pacific, halcyon.

un-exciting, -irritating; soft, bland, oily, demulcent, lenitive, anodyne; hypnotic etc. 683; sedative; assuaging.

mild as mother's milk; milk and water; gentle as a lamb.

Adv. moderately etc. *adj.;* gingerly; *piano;* under easy sail, at half speed; within -bounds, — compass; in reason.

Phr. *est modus in rebus.*

175. Influence.—**N.** influence; importance etc. 642; weight, pressure, preponderance, prevalence, sway, pull; predomi-nance, -nancy; ascendency; control, dominance, reign; authority etc. 737; capability etc. (*power*) 157; interest; spell, magic, magnetism.

footing; purchase etc. (*support*) 215; play, leverage, vantage ground.

tower of strength, host in himself; protection, patronage, auspices.

V. have -influence etc. *n.;* be -influential etc. *adj.;* carry weight, actuate, sway, bias, weigh, tell; have a hold upon, magnetize, bear upon, gain a footing, work upon; take -root, — hold; strike root in.

run through, pervade, prevail, dominate, predominate, subject; out-, over-weigh; over-ride, -bear, — come; gain head; rage; be -rife etc. *adj.;* spread like wildfire; have —, get —, gain- -the upper hand, — full play.

be -recognized, — listened to; make one's voice heard, gain a hearing; play a -part, — leading part- in; lead, control, rule, master; get the mastery over; make one's influence felt, cut ice with; take the lead, pull the strings; turn —, throw one's weight into- the scale; set the fashion, lead the dance.

Adj. influential; important etc. 642; weighty; prevailing etc. *v.;* prevalent, rife, rampant; dominant, regnant, predominant, in the ascendant, hegemonical; authoritative, recognized, telling, with authority.

Adv. with telling effect.

175a. Absence of Influence.—**N.** impotence etc. 158; inertness etc. 172; irrelevancy etc. 10.

V. have no -influence etc. 175.

Adj. uninfluential; unconduc-ing, -ive, -ting to; powerless etc. 158; irrelevant etc. 10.

176. Tendency.—**N.** tendency; apt-ness, -*itude*; proneness, proclivity, bent, turn, tone, bias, set, warp, leaning to, predisposition, inclination, conatus, propensity, susceptibility; liability etc. 177; quality, nature, temperament; characteristic, idio-crasy, -syncrasy; cast, vein, grain; humor, mood; drift etc. (*direction*) 278; conduciveness, -ducement; applicability etc. (*utility*) 644; subservience etc. (*instrumentality*) 631.

V. tend, contribute, conduce, lead, dispose, incline, verge, bend to, warp, turn, trend, affect, carry, redound to, bid fair to, gravitate towards; promote etc. (*aid*) 707.

Adj. tending etc. *v.;* conducive, working towards, in a fair way to, calculated to; liable etc. 177; subservient etc. (*instrumental*) 631; useful etc. 644; subsidiary etc. (*helping*) 707.

Adv. for, whither.

177. Liability.—**N.** lia-bility, -bleness; possibility, contingency; suscepti-vity, -bility.

V. be -liable etc. *adj.*; incur, lay oneself open to; run the —, stand a- chance; lie under, expose oneself to, open a door to.

Adj. liable, subject; in danger etc. 665; open —, exposed —, obnoxious- to; answerable, responsible, accountable, amenable; unexempt from; apt to; dependent on; incident to.

contingent, incidental, possible, on the cards, within range of, at the mercy of.

178. Concurrence.—**N.** concurrence, co-operation, coagency; coincidence, consilience; union; agreement etc. 23; consent etc. (*assent*) 488; alliance; concert etc. 709; partnership etc. 712; collaboration, conformity.

V. con-cur, -duce, -spire, -tribute; agree, unite, harmonize; hang —, pull- together etc. (*co-operate*) 709; help to etc. (*aid*) 707.

keep pace with, run parallel to; go —, go along —, go hand in hand- with.

Adj. concurring etc. *v.*; concurrent, conformable, joint, co-operative, concordant, coincident, concomitant, harmonious; in alliance with, banded together, of one mind, at one with; parallel.

Adv. with one consent.

179. Counteraction.—**N.** counteraction, opposition; contrariety etc. 14; antagonism, polarity; clashing etc. *v.*; collision, interference, resistance, renitency, friction; reaction; retroaction; repercussion etc. (*recoil*) 277; counterblast; neutralization etc. (*compensation*) 30; *vis inertiae*; check etc. (*hindrance*) 706.

voluntary -opposition etc. 708. — resistance etc. 719; repression etc. (*restraint*) 751.

V. counteract; run counter, clash, cross; interfere —, conflict- with; jostle; go —, run —, beat —, militate- against; stultify; antagonize, frustrate, oppose etc. 708; withstand etc. (*resist*) 719; hinder etc. 706; repress etc. (*restrain*) 751; react etc. (*recoil*) 277.

undo, neutralize, cancel; counterpoise etc. (*compensate*) 30; overpoise.

Adj. counteracting etc. *v.*; antagonistic, conflicting, retroactive, renitent, reactionary; contrary etc. 14.

Adv. although etc. 30; in spite of etc. 708; *malgré*; against.

180. Space. [Indefinite space.]—**N.** space, extension, extent, superficial extent, expanse, stretch; capacity, volume, room, accommodation, scope, range, latitude, field, way, expansion, compass, sweep, play, swing, spread.

dimension, fourth dimension; relativity, geometry.

spare —, elbow —, house- room; stowage, roomage, margin; opening, sphere, arena; lee-, sea-, head-way.

open —, free- space; wide open spaces, void etc. (*absence*) 187; waste; wild-, wilder-ness; up-, bottom-, moor -land; *campagna, veldt*, prairie, steppe.

abyss etc. (*interval*) 198; unlimited space; infinity etc. 105; world, wide world; ubiquity etc. (*presence*) 186; length and breadth of the land.

proportions, acreage; acres, — roods and perches; square -inches, — yards etc.

V. reach, extend, stretch, sweep, spread, range, cover, thrust out, reach forth.

Adj. spacious, roomy, extensive, expansive, capacious, ample; wide-spread, vast, world-wide, uncircumscribed; boundless etc. (*infinite*) 105; shore-, track-, path-less; large etc. 192.

spatial, dimensional, proportional; two-, three-, four-dimensional; stereoscopic.

Adv. extensively etc. *adj.*; wherever; everywhere; far and -near, — wide; right and left, all over, all the world over; throughout the -world, — length and breadth of the land; under the sun, in every quarter; in all -quarters, — lands; here, there and everywhere; from -pole to pole, — China to Peru, — Indus to the pole, — Dan to Beersheba, — end to end; on the face of the earth, in the wide world, from all points of the compass; to the -four winds, — uttermost parts of the earth.

180a. Inextension.—**N.** in-, non-extension; point; atom etc. (*smallness*) 32; pinprick; limitation etc. 229.

181. Region. [Definite space.]—**N.** region, sphere, sphere of influence, corridor, ground, soil, area, realm, hemisphere, quarter district, beat, orb, orbit, zone, belt, circuit, circle; pale etc. (*limit*) 233; com-, department; domain, tract, territory, terrain, country, canton, county, shire, province, *arrondissement*, diocese, parish, township, borough, constituency, *commune*, ward, wapentake, hundred, riding, lathe, garth, soke, tithing, bailiwick; empire, kingdom, principality, duchy, grand —, arch- duchy, palatinate, republic, commonwealth, dominion, colony, state, island.

arena, precincts, *enceinte*, walk, march; patch, plot, enclosure, etc. 232; close, *enclave*, field, court; street etc. (*abode*) 189.

clime, climate, zone, meridian, latitude.

Adj. territorial, local, parochial, provincial, insular.

182. Place. [Limited space.]—**N.** place, lieu, spot, point, dot; niche, nook, etc. (*corner*) 244; hole; pigeonhole etc. (*receptacle*) 191; compartment; premises, precinct, station, confine; area, court, yard, quadrangle, square, compound; abode etc. 189; locality etc. (*situation*) 183.

ins and outs; every hole and corner.

Adv. somewhere, in some place, wherever it may be, here and there, in various places, *passim*.

183. Situation.—N. situation, position, locality, *locale, status,* latitude and longitude; footing, standing, standpoint, post; stage, aspect, attitude, posture, *pose.*

place, site, base, station, seat, *venue,* whereabouts, environment, neighborhood; bearings etc. (*direction*) 278; spot etc. (*limited space*) 182.

top-, ge-, chor-ography; map etc. 554.

V. be -situated, — situate; lie; have its seat in.

Adj. situ-ate, -ated; local, topical, topographical etc. *n.*

Adv. *in -situ, — loco;* here and there, *passim;* here-, there-, whereabouts; in place, here, there.

in —, amidst- such and such- -surroundings, — *environs, — entourage.*

184. Location.—N. loca-tion, -lization; lodgement; de-, re-position; stow-, pack-age; collocation; packing, lading; establishment, settlement, installation; fixation; insertion etc. 300.

anchorage, roadstead, mooring, mooring mast, encampment, camp, bivouac.

plantation, colony, settlement, cantonment, encampment, reservation; colonization, domestication, situation; habitation etc. (*abode*) 189; cohabitation; 'a local habitation and a name;' indenization, naturalization.

V. place, situate, locate, localize, make a place for, put, lay, set, seat, station, lodge, quarter, post, install; storehouse, stow; extablish, fix, pin, root; graft; plant etc. (*insert*) 300; shelve, pitch, camp, lay down, deposit, reposit; cradle; moor, tether, picket; pack, tuck in; embed; vest, invest in.

billet on, quarter upon, saddle with; load, lade, freight; pocket, put up, bag.

inhabit etc. (*be present*) 186; domesticate, colonize, populate, people; take —, strike-root; anchor; cast —, come to an- anchor; sit —, settle-down; settle; take up one's -abode, — quarters; plant —, establish —, locate- oneself; squat, perch, hive, *se nicher,* bivouac, burrow, get a footing; encamp, pitch one's tent; put up -at, — one's horses at; keep house.

indenizen, naturalize, adopt.

put back, replace etc. (*restore*) 660.

Adj. placed etc. *v.;* situate, posited, ensconced, embedded, embosomed, rooted; domesticated; vested in unremoved; settled, stationed, established.

moored etc. *v.;* at anchor.

185. Displacement.—N. displacement, elocation, transposition.

ejectment etc. 297; exile etc. (*banishment*) 893; removal etc. (*transference*) 270; unshipment.

misplacement, dislocation etc. 61; fish out of water.

V. dis-place, -plant, -lodge, -nest, -establish; misplace, unseat, disturb; exile etc. (*seclude*) 893; ablegate, set aside, remove; take —, cart- away; take —, draft- off; lade etc. 184, unship.

unload, empty etc. (*eject*) 297; transfer etc. 270; dispel.

vacate; depart etc. 293.

Adj. displaced etc. *v.;* un-placed, -housed, -harbored, -established, -settled; house-, homeless; out of -place, — a situation.

misplaced, out of its element.

186. Presence.—N. presence; occupancy, -ation; attendance; whereness.

permeation, pervasion; diffusion etc. (*dispersion*) 73.

ubi-ety, -quity, -quitariness; omnipresence.

bystander etc. (*spectator*) 444.

V. exist in space, be -present etc. *adj.;* assist at; make one -of, — at; look on, attend, remain; find —, present- oneself; show one's face; fall in the way of, occur in a place; lie, stand; occupy.

people; inhabit, dwell, reside, stay, sojourn, live, room, abide, bunk, lodge, nestle, roost, perch; take up one's abode etc. (*be located*) 184; tenant, occupy.

resort to, frequent, haunt; revisit.

fill, pervade, permeate; be -diffused, — disseminated- through; over-spread, -run; run through; meet one at every turn.

Adj. present; occupying, inhabiting etc. *v.;* moored etc. 184; residential, resi-ant, -dent, -dentiary; domiciled.

ubiquit-ous, -ary; omnipresent.

peopled, populous, full of people, inhabited.

Adv. here; there, where, everywhere, aboard, on board, at home, afield; on the spot; here, there and everywhere etc. (*space*) 180; in presence of, before; under the -eyes, —nose- of; in the face of; *in propriâ personâ.*

187. Absence. [Nullibiety.]**—N.** absence; inexistence etc. 2; non-residence, absenteeism; non-attendance, *alibi.*

emptiness etc. *adj.;* void, *vacuum;* vac-uity, -ancy; *tabula rasa;* exemption; *hiatus* etc. (*interval*) 198; no man's land.

truant, absentee.

nobody; nobody -present, — on earth; no one; not a soul; *âme qui vive.*

V. be -absent etc. *adj.;* keep -away, — out of the way; play truant, absent oneself, stay away.

withdraw, make oneself scarce, vacate; go away, slip out, slip away, retreat etc. 293.

Adj. absent, not present, away, nonresident, gone, from home; missing; lost; wanted, wanting; omitted; nowhere to be found; inexistent etc. 2.

empty, void; blank, vac-ant, -uous; untenanted, -occupied, -inhabited; tenantless; desert, -ed; devoid; un-, uninhabitable.

exempt from, not having.

Adv. without, *minus,* nowhere; elsewhere; neither here nor there; in default of; *sans;* behind one's back.

Phr. the bird has flown, *non est inventus.*

188. Inhabitant.—N. inhabitant; habitant, resident, -iary; dweller, in-dweller; occup-ier, -ant, farmer, planter; householder, *lodger,* boarder, paying guest; inmate, tenant, renter, incumbent, sojourner, *locum tenens,* commorant; settler, squatter, backwoodsman, colonist; islander; denizen, citizen; burgher, oppidan, cockney, cit, townsman, burgess; villager; cottager, -tier, -ter; compatriot.

native, indigene, aboriginal, aborigines, autochthones; Briton, Englishman, John Bull; new comer etc. (*stranger*) 57.

garrison, crew; population; people etc. (*mankind*) 372; colony, settlement; household.

V. inhabit etc. (*be present*) 186; indenizen etc. (*locate oneself*) 184.

Adj. indigenous; enchorial; national, nat-ive, -al; autochthonous; British, English; colonial; domestic, domiciliated, -ed; naturalized, vernacular, domesticated; domiciliary.

in the occupation of; garrisoned –, occupied-by.

189. Abode. [Place of habitation, or resort.]—**N.** abode, dwelling, lodging, -s; diggings, domicile, residence, address, habitation, where one's lot is cast, local habitation, berth, seat, lap, sojourn, housing, quarters, headquarters, resiance, tabernacle, throne, ark.

home, fatherland, mother country, country etc. 181; home-stead, -stall; fireside, chimney corner; hearth, – stone; household gods, *lares et penates*, roof, household, housing, *dulce domum*, paternal domicile; native -soil, – land, blighty.

nest, *nidus*, snuggery; arbor, bower etc. 191; lair, den, cave, hole, hidingplace, cell, *sanctum sanctorum*, aerie, eyry, rookery, hive; *habitat*, haunt, covert, resort, retreat, perch, roost; nidification.

bivouac, camp, encampment, cantonment, castrametation; barrack, casemate, casern.

tent etc. (*covering*) 223; building etc. (*construction*) 161; chamber etc. (*receptacle*) 191.

tenement, messuage, farm, farmhouse, grange, *hacienda*.

cot, cabin, log cabin, shack, hut, *châlet*, croft, shed, booth, stall, hovel, bothy, shanty, igloo, tepee, wigwam; pen etc. (*inclosure*) 232; barn, bawn; kennel, sty, dog-hole, cote, coop, hutch, byre; cowhouse, -shed; stable, dove-cote, shippen.

house, mansion, place, villa, cottage, box, lodge, hermitage, *rus in urbe*, folly, rotunda, tower, *château*, castle, pavilion, hotel, court, manor-house, capital messuage, hall, palace, alcazar; country seat; kiosk, bungalow; temple etc. 1000; home of rest, alms-, poor-, work-house, asylum; boarding-, lodging-house; flat, maisonette, duplex, penthouse, suite of rooms, apartments, rooms, room building etc. 161; Mansion House, town hall, Capitol.

assembly-room, auditorium, coliseum, meeting-house, pump-room, spa, health resort, watering-place; club; theatre etc. 840; drill hall, gymnasium, church etc. 1000; Houses of Parliament etc. 696; school etc. 542; inn; hostel, -ry; hotel, tavern, caravansary, khan, hospice; public-, ale-, pot-, mug-house; gin-palace, gin mill; coffee-, eating-house; canteen, *restaurant*, *rotisserie*, cafeteria, grill-room, *buffet*, *café*, *estaminet*, *posada*, *bodega*; bar; saloon, speakeasy, shebeen.

hamlet, village, thorp, dorp, ham, kraal; borough, burgh, town, county-seat, – town, city, capital, metropolis; suburb, quarter, parish etc. 181; ghetto; province, country.

street, place, terrace, parade, esplanade, promenade, pier, embankment, road, villas, row, walk, lane, alley, court, quadrangle, quad, wynd, close, yard, passage, rents, mansions, buildings, mews.

square, polygon, circus, crescent, mall, *piazza*, arcade, colonnade, peristyle, cloister; gardens, grove, residences; block of buildings, market-place, *place*.

anchorage, roadstead, roads; dock, basin, wharf, quay, port, harbor; dry-, graving-, floating-dock.

garden, park, pleasure-ground, pleasance, demesne.

V. take up one's abode etc. (*locate oneself*) 184; inhabit etc. (*be present*) 186.

Adj. urban, oppidan, metropolitan; suburban; provincial, rural, rustic; countrified; regional, parochial, domestic; cosmopolitan; palatial.

190. Contents. [Things contained.]—**N.** contents; cargo, lading, freight, shipment, load, bale, burden; cart-, ship-load; cup –, basket –, etc. (*receptacle*) 191 - of; inside etc. 221; stuffing, ullage.

V. load, lade, ship, charge, fill, stuff.

191. Receptacle.—**N.** receptacle, container; inclosure etc. 232; recipient, receiver, reservatory.

compartment; cell, -ule; follicle; hole, corner, niche, recess, nook; crypt, stall, pigeon-hole, cove, oriel; cave etc. (*concavity*) 252.

capsule, vesicle, cyst, pod, calyx, *cancelli*, utricle, bladder, udder.

stomach, paunch, *venter*, abdomen, ventricle, crop, craw, ingluvies, maw, gizzard, bread-basket, belly, little Mary; mouth.

pocket, pouch, fob, sheath, scabbard, socket, bag, vanity bag, compact, sac, sack, saccule, despatch –, attaché-, tachy- case, wallet, scrip, card-, note-, case, billfold, poke, knit, knap-, haver-, ruck-sack, sachel, satchel, reticule, budget, net; ditty-, -box, -bag, kitbag; portfolio; saddlebags, holster; quiver etc. (*magazine*) 636.

chest, box, coffer, caddy, case, casket, pyx, pix, *caisson*, desk, *bureau*, reliquary, shrine; trunk, portmanteau, band-box, *valise*, suitcase, hand-, traveling-, overnight-, Gladstone-, carpet-bag, brief case; boot, imperial; *vache*; cage, manger, rack.

vessel, vase, bushel, barrel; canister, jar; pottle, basket, punnet, pannier, buck-basket, hopper, maund, creel, cran, crate, cradle, bassinet, wisket, whisket, *jardinière*, *corbeille*, hamper, wastepaper basket, dosser, dorser, tray, hod, scuttle, utensil, spittoon, cuspidor.

[For liquids] cistern etc. (*store*) 636; vat, caldron, barrel, cask, puncheon, keg, rundlet, tun, butt, firkin, hogshead, kilderkin, carboy, amphora, ampulla, bottle, jar, leather bottle, decanter, ewer, cruse, carafe, crock, kit, canteen, flagon; demijohn; flask, -et; stoup, noggin, vial, phial, ampoule, cruet, caster; gourd; urn, *épergne*, salver, *patella*, *tazza*, *patera*; pig-, big-gin; tea-, coffee-pot, percolator, *samovar*; tyg, nipperkin, pocket-pistol; tub, bucket, pail, skeel, pot, tankard, jug, pitcher, toby, mug, pipkin; gal-, gall-ipot, pannikin; matrass, receiver, retort, alembic, bolthead, can, kettle; bowl, basin, jorum, punch-bowl, cup, goblet, chalice, tumbler, glass, wineglass, rummer, beaker, tass, horn, saucepan, skillet, posnet, tureen, terrine, *casserole*, sauce-, gravy-boat.

plate, platter, paten, dish, vegetable –, *entrée*-dish, trencher, calabash, porringer, potager, saucer, pan, crucible.

shovel, trowel, spoon; table-, dessert-, tea-, egg-,

salt-spoon; spatula, ladle; dipper; baler; watch-glass, thimble.

closet, commode, cupboard, cellaret, *chiffonnière*, locker, bin, bunker, *buffet*, press, safe, sideboard, drawer, chest of drawers, till, *scrutoire*, *secrétaire*, *escritoire*, davenport, book-case, cabinet, canterbury; corner cupboard, wardrobe.

chamber, apartment, room, cabin; office, court, hall, atrium; suite of rooms, flat, story; saloon, *salon*, parlor; presence-chamber; sitting-, drawing-, reception-, state-, living-, work-room; gallery, cabinet, closet, cubicle; pew, box; *boudoir*; *adytum*, *sanctum*; bed-room, dormitory, dressing-room; refectory, dining-room, *salle-à-manger*; nursery, schoolroom; library, study; *studio*; billiard-, bath-, smoking-room; den, canteen, mess, officers' mess; gun-, ward-, mess-room.

attic, loft, garret, cockloft, clerestory; cellar, vault, hold, cockpit; *entre-sol*; mezzanine floor; ground-floor, *rez-de-chaussée*; basement, kitchen, cook-house, galley, pantry, scullery, offices; store-room etc. (*depository*) 636; lumber-room; dust-hole, -bin; dairy, laundry, coachhouse; *garage*; *hangar*; out-, pent-house; lean-to.

portico, porch, piazza, verandah, lobby, court, hall, vestibule, corridor, passage; ante-room, chamber; lounge; *foyer*, *loggia*.

conservatory, green-house, glass-house, vinery, bower, arbor, summer-house, alcove, grotto, hermitage, pergola.

lodging etc. (*abode*) 189; bed etc. (*support*) 215; carriage etc. (*vehicle*) 272.

Adj. capsular; saccu-lar, -lated; recipient; ventricular, cystic, vascular, vesicular, cellular, camerated, locular, multilocular, poly-gastric; marsupial; siliqu-ose, -ous.

192. Size.—N. size, magnitude, dimension, bulk, volume; largeness etc. *adj.*; greatness etc. (*of quantity*) 31; expanse etc (*space*) 180; amplitude, mass; proportions.

capacity; ton-, tun-nage; caliber, scantling.

turgidity etc. (*expansion*) 194; corpulence, obesity; plumpness, etc. *adj.*; *embonpoint*, corporation, flesh and blood, lustihood.

hugeness etc. *adj.*; enormity, immensity, monstrosity.

giant, Brobdingnagian, Antaeus, Goliath, Gog and Magog, Gargantua, monster, mammoth, Cyclops; whale, porpoise, behemoth, leviathan, elephant, hippopotamus; colossus; tun, lump, bulk, block, loaf, mass, clod, nugget, bushel, thumper, whopper, spanker, strapper; Triton among the minnows.

mountain, mound; heap etc. (*assemblage*) 72. largest portion etc. 50; full-, life-size.

V. ve- large etc. *adj.*; become -large etc. (*expand*) 194.

Adj. large, big; great etc. (*in quantity*) 31; considerable, bulky, voluminous, ample, massive, massy; capacious, comprehensive; spacious etc. 180; mighty, towering, fine, magnificent.

corpulent, stout, fat, plump, squab, full, lusty, strapping, bouncing; portly, burly, well-fed, full-grown; stalwart, brawny, fleshy; goodly; in good -case, – condition; in condition; chopping, jolly; chub-, chubby-faced.

lubberly, hulky, unwieldy, lumpish, gaunt, spanking, whacking, whopping, thumping, thundering, hulking; overgrown; puffy etc. (*swollen*) 194.

huge, immense, enormous, mighty; vast, -y; amplitudinous, stupendous; monst-er, -rous; gigantic, elephantine; giant, -like; colossal, Cyclopean, Brobdingnagian, Garguantuan, Titanic; infinite etc. 105.

large as life; plump as a dumpling, – partridge; fat as -a pig, – a quail, – butter, – brawn, – bacon.

193. Littleness.—N. littleness etc. *adj.*; smallness etc. (*of quantity*) 32; exiguity, inextension; parvi-tude, -ty; duodecimo; Elzevir edition, epitome, microcosm; rudiment; vanishing point; thinness etc. 203.

dwarf, pigmy, atomy, Liliputian, midget, chit, pigwidgeon, urchin, elf; doll, puppet; Tom Thumb, Hop-o'-my thumb, Humpty-dumpty; man-, mannikin; *homunculus*, dapperling, fingerling, dandiprat, cock-sparrow, scalawag.

animalcule, monad, mite, insect, emmet, fly, midge, gnat, shrimp, minnow, worm, maggot, entozoon; *bacillus*, microbe, micro-organism, *bacteria*; *infusoria*; microbe; grub; tit, tomtit, runt, mouse, small fry; millet-, mustard-seed; barleycorn; pebble, grain of sand; mole-hill, button, bubble.

point; atom etc. (*small quantity*) 32; fragment etc. (*small part*) 51; powder etc. 330; point of a pin, mathematical point; *minutiae* etc. (*unimportance*) 643.

micro-graphy, -meter, -scope; vernier; scale.

V. be -little etc. *adj.*; lie in a nutshell; become small etc. (*decrease*) 36, (*contract*) 195.

Adj. little; small etc. (*in quantity*) 32; minute, diminutive, microscopic; inconsiderable etc. (*unimportant*) 643; exiguous, puny, tiny, wee, petty, minikin, miniature, pigmy, elfin; under sized; dwarf, -ed, -ish; spare, stunted, limited; cramp, -ed; pollard, Liliputian, dapper, pocket; port-ative, -able; duodecimo; dumpy, squat; compact, handy; short etc. 201.

impalpable, intangible, evanescent, imperceptible, invisible, inappreciable, infinitesimal, homeopathic; atomic, corpuscular, molecular; rudiment-ary, -al; embryonic.

weazen, scant, scraggy, scrubby; thin etc. (*narrow*) 203; granular etc. (*powdery*) 330; shrunk etc. 195.

Adv. in a -small compass, – nutshell; on a small scale.

194. Expansion.—N. expansion; increase etc. 35 -of size; enlargement, extension, augmentation; ampli-fication, -ation; aggrandizement, spread, increment, growth, development, pullulation, swell, dilation, dilatation, rarefaction; turg-escence, -idness, -idity; obesity etc. (*size*) 192; dropsy, tumefaction, intumescence, swelling, tumor, *diastole*, distension; puff-ing, -iness; inflation; pandiculation.

dilatability, expansibility.

germination, growth, upgrowth; accretion etc. 35.

over-growth, -distension; hypertrophy, tympany.

bulb etc. (*convexity*) 250; plumper; superiority of size.

V. become -larger etc. (large etc. 192); expand, widen, enlarge, extend, grow, increase, incrassate, swell, gather; fill out; deploy, take open order, dilate, stretch, spread; mantle, was; grow –, spring- up; bud, bourgeon, shoot, sprout, germinate, put forth, vegetate, pullulate, open, burst forth, flower, blow etc. 734; gain –, gather- flesh; outgrow; spread like wildfire, overrun.

be larger than; surpass etc. (*be superior*) 33.

render -larger etc. (large etc. 192); expand, spread, extend, aggrandize, distend, develop, amplify, spread out, widen, magnify, rarefy, inflate, puff, puff out, blow up, stuff, pad, cram; exaggerate; fatten.

Adj. expanded etc. *v.*; larger etc. (large etc. 192); swollen; expansive; wide-open, -spread; fan-shaped; flabelliform; overgrown, exaggerated, bloated, fat, turgid, tumid, hypertrophied, dropsical; pot-, swag-bellied; edematous, obese, puffy, pursy, blowzy, distended; patulous; bulbous etc. (*convex*) 250; full-blown, -grown, -formed; big etc. 192.

195. Contraction.—N. contraction, reduction, diminution; decrease etc. 36- of size; defalcation, decrement; lessening, shrinkage; collapse, emaciation, attenuation, tabefaction, consumption, marasmus, atrophy; systole, neck, hourglass.

condensation, compression, constraint, compactness; compendium etc. 596; squeezing etc. *v.*; strangulation; corrugation; astringency, constringency; astringents, sclerotics; contractility, compressibility; coarctation.

inferiority in size.

V. become -small, – smaller; lessen, decrease etc. 36; grow less, dwindle, shrink, contract, narrow, shrivel, collapse, wither, lose flesh, wizen, fall away, waste, wane, ebb; decat etc. (*deteriorate*) 659.

be smaller than, fall short of; not come up to etc. (*be inferior*) 34.

render smaller, lessen, diminish, contract, draw in, shrink, shrivel, narrow, coarctate; constrict, constringe; condense, compress, boil down, deflate, exhaust, empty; squeeze, corrugate, crush, crumple up, warp, purse up, pack, stow; pinch, tighten, strangle; cramp; dwarf, bedwarf; shorten etc. 201; circumscribe etc. 229; restrain etc. 751; fold etc. 258.

pare, reduce, attenuate, rub down, scrape, file, grind, chip, shave, shear.

Adj. contracting etc. *v.*; astringent; shrunk, contracted etc. *v.*; strangulated, tabid, wizened, stunted, tabescent; marasmic; waning etc. *v.*: neap; compact; shriveled, preshrunk.

unexpanded etc. (expand etc. 194); inswept; contractile; compressible; smaller etc. small etc. 193).

196. Distance.—N. distance; space etc. 180; remoteness, farness; far- cry to; longinquity, elongation; offing, background; removedness; parallax; reach, span, stride; drift.

out-post, -skirt; horizon, sky-line; aphelion; foreign parts, *ultima Thule*, *ne plus ultra*, antipodes; long range, giant's stride.

dispersion etc. 73.

V. be -distant etc. *adj.*; extend –, stretch –, reach –, spread –, go –, get –, stretch away- to; range, outrange, outreach.

remain at a distance; keep –, stand- -away, – off, – aloof, – clear of.

Adj. distant; far -off, away; remote, telescopic, distal, wide of; stretching to etc. *v.*; yon, -der; ulterior; trans-marine, -pontine, -atlantic, -pacific, -continental, -polar, -equatorial, -alpine; tramontane; ultra-montane, -mundane; hyperborean, antihodean; inaccessible, out of the way; unapproached, -able; incontiguous.

Adv. far -off, – away; afar, -off; off; away; a -long, – great, – good- way off; wide away, aloof; wide –, clear- of; out of -the way, – reach; abroad, yonder, farther, further, beyond; *outre mer*, over the border, far and wide, over the hills and far away; from pole to pole etc. (*over great space*) 180; to the -uttermost parts, – ends- of the earth; out of -hearing, – range, nobody knows where, *à perte de vue*, out of the sphere of, wide of the mark; a far cry to.

apart, asunder; wide -apart, – asunder; *longo intervallo*; at arm's length.

197. Nearness.—N. nearness etc. *adj.*; proximity, propinquity; vicinity, -age; neighborhood, adjacency; contiguity etc. 199.

short -distance, – step, – cut; earshot, close quarters, brief span; stone's throw; bow –, gun –, pistol- shot; hair's breadth, span; close-up.

purlieus, neighborhood, vicinage, *environs*, *alentours*, suburbs, confines, *banlieue*, borderland; whereabouts.

bystander; neighbor, borderer.

approach etc. 286; convergence etc. 290; perihelion.

V. be -near etc. *adj.*; adjoin, hang about, trench on; border-, verge upon; stand by, approximate, tread on the heels of, cling to, clasp, hug; cuddle, huddle; hang about the skirts of, hover over; burn; abut.

bring –, draw- -near etc. 286; converge etc. 290; crowd etc. 72; place -side by side etc. *adv.*

Adj. near, nigh; close-, near- at hand; close, neighboring, propinquent, bordering upon; adjacent, adjoining, limitrophe; proxim-ate, -al; at hand, handy; near the mark, near run; home, intimate.

Adv. near, nigh; hard –, fast- by; close -to, upon, – up; at the point of; next door to; within -reach, – call, – hearing, – earshot, – range; within an ace of; but a step, not far from, at no great distance; on the -verge, – brink, – skirts- of; in the -environs etc. *n.*; at one's -door, – feet, – elbow, – finger's end, – side; on the tip of one's tongue; under one's nose; within a -stone's throw etc. *n.*; in -sight, – presence- of; at close quarters; cheek by -jole, – jowl; beside, alongside, side by side, *tête-à-tête*; in juxtaposition etc. (*touching*) 199; yard-arm to yard-arm; at the heels of; on the confines of, at the threshold, bordering upon, verging to; in the way.

about; here-, there-abouts; rougly, in round

numbers; approxim- -ately, – atively; as good as, well nigh.

198. Interval.—N. interval, interspace; separation etc. 44; break gap, opening; hole etc. 260; chasm, *hiatus*, caesura; inter-ruption,-regnum; interstice, *lacuna*, cleft, mesh, crevice, chink, rime, creek, cranny, crack, chap, slit, slot, fissure, scissure, rift, flaw, breach, fracture, rent, gash, cut, leak, dike, ha-ha.

gorge, defile, ravine, canon, *crevasse*, abyss, abysm; gulf; inlet, frith, strait, gully, gulch, nullah; pass; notch; furrow etc. 259; yawning gulf; *hiatus - maxime, — valde- deflendus*; parenthesis etc. (*interjacence*) 228; void etc. (*absence*) 187; incompleteness etc. 530.

V. gape etc. (*open*) 260; part, remove.

Adj. with an interval, far between; separated, spaced, split.

Adv. at intervals etc. (*discontinuously*) 70; *longo intervallo.*

199. Contiguity.—N. contiguity, contact, proximity, apposition, juxtaposition, touching etc. *v.*; abutment, osculation; meeting, appulse, appulsion, *rencontre*, rencounter, syzygy, coincidence, conjunction, coexistence; adhesion etc. 46.

border-land; frontier etc. (*limit*) 233; tangent.

V. be -contiguous etc. *adj.*; join, adjoin, abut on, march with, border; tick, graze, touch, meet, osculate, kiss, come in contact; coincide; coexist; adhere etc. 46.

Adj. contiguous; touching etc. *v.*; in -contact etc. *n.*, conterminous, end to end, osculatory; pertingent; tangential.

hand to hand; close to etc. (*near*) 197; with no - interval etc. 198.

200. Length.—N. length, longitude, span, extent, mileage.

line, bar, rule, stripe, streak, spoke, radius.

lengthening etc. *v.*; pro-longation, -duction, -traction; ten-sion, -sure; extension.

[Measures of length] line, nail, inch, hand, palm, foot, cubit, yard, ell, fathom, rod, pole, perch, furlong, mile, league; chain, meter, kilo-, centi-, milli- etc meter.

pedometer, perambulator, odometer, odograph, speedometer, cyclometer, log, telemeter, range finder; scale etc. (*measurement*) 466.

V. be -long etc. *adj.*; stretch out, sprawl; extend —, reach —, stretch -to; make a long arm, 'drag its slow length along.'

render -long etc. *adj.*; lengthen, extend, elongate; stretch; pro-long, -duce, -tract; let —, pay —, draw —, spin- out; drawl.

enfilade, look along, view in perspective.

Adj. long, -some; lengthy, lank, wiredrawn, outstretched; stretched, drawn out, lengthened etc. *v.*; sesquipedalian etc. (*words*) 577; interminable, no end of.

line-ar, -al; longitudinal, oblong.

as long as -my arm, —to-day and to-morrow; unshortened etc. (shorten etc. 201).

Adv. lengthwise, at length, longitudinally, endlong, along; *tandem*; in a line etc. (*continuously*) 69; in perspective.

from -end to end; —stem to stern, —head to foot, —the crown of the head to the sole of the foot, —top to toe, —head to heels; fore and aft.

201. Shortness.—N. shortness etc. *adj.*; brevity; littleness etc. 193; a span.

shortening etc. *v.*; abbrevia-tion, -ture; abridgment, concision, retrenchment, curtailment, decurtation; reduction etc. (*contraction*) 195; epitome etc. (*compendium*) 596.

abridger, abstractor, epitomiser.

elision, ellipsis; conciseness etc. (*in style*) 572.

V. be -short etc. *adj.*; render -short etc. *adj.*; shorten, curtail, abridge, abbreviate, take in, reduce; compress etc. (*contract*) 195; epitomize etc. 596.

retrench, cut short, obtruncate; scrimp, cut, chop up, hack, hew; cut —, pare- *down; clip, snip, dock*, lop, prune; shear, shave, mow, reap, crop; snub; truncate, pollard, stunt, nip, nip in the bud, check the growth of; [in drawing] foreshorten.

Adj. short, brief, curt; compendious, compact; stubby, scrimp; shorn, stubbed; stumpy, thickset, podgy, stocky, pug; squab, -by; squat, dumpy; little etc. 193; curtailed of its fair proportions; short by; oblate; concise etc. 572; summary.

Adv. shortly etc. *adj.*; in short etc. (*concisely*) *572.*

202. Breadth. Thickness.—N. breadth, width, latitude, amplitude; diameter, bore, calibre, radius; superficial extent etc. (*space*) 180.

thickness, crassitude; corpulence etc. (*size*) 192; dilatation etc. (*expansion*) 194.

V. be -broad etc. *adj.*; become —, render- -broad etc. *adj.*; expand etc. 194; thicken, widen.

Adj. broad, wide, ample, extended; discous; fan-like; out-spread, -stretched; wide as a church-door.

thick, dumpy, squab, squat, thickset, tubby; thick as a rope, stubby etc. 201.

203. Narrowness. Thinness.—N. narrowness etc. *adj.*; closeness, exility; exiguity etc. (*little*) 193.

line; hair's —, finger's -breadth; strip, streak, vein.

thinness etc. *adj.*; tenuity; emaciation, slenderness, macilency, *marcor.*

shaving, slip etc. (*filament*) 205; threadpaper, skeleton, shadow, scrag, anatomy, spindle-shanks, barebones, lantern jaws, mere skin and bone.

middle construction, stricture, neck, waist, isthmus, wasp, hour-glass; ridge, *ghaut*, pass; ravine etc. 198.

narrowing, coarctation, angustation, tapering; contraction etc. 195.

V. be-narrow etc. *adj.*; narrow, taper, diminish, contract etc. 195; render -narrow etc. *adj.*

Adj. narrow, close; slender, thin, fine; *svelte;* thread-like etc. (*filament*) 205; finespun, taper, slim, gracile, slight, slight-made; scant, -y; spare, delicate, incapacious; contracted etc. 195; unexpanded etc. (expand etc. 194); slender as a thread, capillary.

emaciated, lean, meager, gaunt, macilent; lank, -y; weedy, skinny, scrawny, scraggy; starv-ed, -eling; attenuated, shrivelled; wizened, pinched, peaky, skeletal, spindling, spindle- -legged, -shanked; extenuated, tabid, marcid, bare-bone, raw-boned; herring-gutted; worn to a shadow, lean as a rake; thin as a -lath,—whipping post,—wafer; hatchet-faced; lantern-jawed.

204. Layer.—N. layer, stratum, course, bed, zone, *substratum*, floor, flag, stage, story, tier, slab, escarpment, table, tablet, panel, plaque; board, plank; trencher, platter.

plate; lam-ina, -ella; sheet, flake, foil, wafer, scale, coat, peel, pellicle, ply, thickness, membrane, film, leaf, slice, shive, cut, rasher, shaving, integument etc. (*covering*) 223.

V. slice, shave, pare, peel; plate, coat, veneer; cover etc. 223.

Adj. lamell-ar, -ated, -iform; laminated, -iferous; micaceous; schist-ose, -ous; scaly; filmy, membranous, flaky, squamous; folia-ted, -ceous; stratified, -form; tabular, discoid, spathic.

205. Filament.—N. filament, line; fiber, fibril; funicle, vein, hair, capillament, *cilium*, tendril, gossamer; hair-stroke; harl.

wire, string, thread, packthread, cotton, sewing-silk, twine, twist, whip-cord, cord, rope, cable, yarn, hemp, oakum, jute, wool, worsted.

strip, shred, slip, spill, list, band, fillet, *fascia*, ribbon, riband, tape, roll, lath, slat, strake, splinter, shiver, shaving.

beard etc. (*roughness*) 256; ramification; strand.

Adj. fil-amentous, -aceous, -iform; fibr-ous, -illous; thread-like, wiry, stringy, ropy; capill-ary, -iform; funicular, wire-drawn; anguilliform; flagelliform; hairy etc. (*rough*) 256; ligulate.

206. Height.—N. height, altitude, elevation, ceiling; eminence, pitch; loftiness etc. *adj.*; sublimity.

tallness etc. *adj.*; stature, procerity; prominence etc. 250.

colossus etc. (*size*) 192; giant, grenadier, giraffe.

mount, -ain; hill, butte, monticle, fell, knap; cape; head-, fore-land; promontory; ridge, hog's back, dune; rising —, vantage- ground; down; moor, -land; Alp; up-, table-, high-lands; heights etc. (*summit*) 210; knoll, hummock, hillock, barrow, mound, mole, *kopje*; steeps, bluff, cliff, craig, tor, peak, pike, clough; escarpment, edge, ledge, brae; dizzy height.

tower, pillar, column, pylon, obelisk, monument, steeple, spire, minaret, *campanile*, belfry, turret, roof, dome, cupola, pagoda, pyramid; sky scraper; Eiffel tower.

pole, pikestaff, maypole, flagstaff; mast, top—, topgallant- mast.

ceiling etc. (*covering*) 223.

high water; high—, flood—, spring-tide.

altimetry etc. (*angle*) 244; altimeter, height-finder, hypsometer, barograph.

V. be -high etc. *adj.*; tower, soar, command; hover; cap, culminate; overhang, hang over, impend, beetle; bestride, ride, mount; perch, surmount; cover etc. 233; overtop etc. (*be superior*) 33; stand on tiptoe.

become -high etc. *adj.*; grow, — higher, — taller; upgrow; rise etc. (*ascend*) 305.

render -high etc. *adj.*; heighten etc. (*elevate*) 307.

Adj. high, elevated, eminent, exalted, lofty, supernal; tall; gigantic etc. (*big*) 192; Patagonian; towering, beetling, soaring, hanging [gardens]; elevated etc. 307; upper; highest etc. (*topmost*) 210; monticulous, perching, hill-dwelling.

up-, moor-land; hilly, mountainous, alpine, subalpine, heaven-kissing; cloud-topt, -capt, -touching; aerial.

overhanging etc. *v.*; incumbent, overlying; super-incumbent, -natant, -imposed; prominent etc. 250.

tall as a -maypole, —poplar,—steeple; lanky etc. (*thin*) 203.

Adv. on high, high up, aloft, up, above, aloof, overhead; up—, above- stairs; in the clouds; on -tiptoe, —stilts,—the shoulders of; over head and ears; breast high.

over, upwards; from top to bottom etc. (*completely*) 52.

207. Lowness.—N. lowness etc. *adj.*; debasement, depression; prostration etc. (*horizontal*) 213; depression etc. (*concave*) 252.

molehill; lowlands; bottomlands; basement-ground-floor; *rez de chaussée* etc. 211; hold; feet, heels.

low water; low—, ebb—, neap—, spring- tide.

V. be -low etc. *adj.*; lie -low, —flat; underlie; crouch, slouch, wallow, grovel; lower etc. (*depress*) 308.

Adj. low, neap, debased; nether, -most; flat, level with the ground; lying low etc. *v.*; crouched, subjacent, squat, prostrate etc. (*horizontal*) 213.

Adv. under; be-, under-neath; below; down, -wards; adown, at the foot of; under-foot, -ground; down—, below-stairs; at a low ebb; below par.

208. Depth.—N. depth; deepness etc. *adj.*; profundity, depression etc. (*concavity*) 252.

hollow, pit, shaft, well, crater, abyss; gulf etc. 198; bowels of the earth, bottomless pit, hell.

soundings, sonar, depth of water, water, draught, submersion; plummet, sound, probe; sounding -rod, — line, — machine; lead; submarine, diving bell, bathysphere; diver.

V. be -deep etc. *adj.*; render -deep etc. *adj.*; deepen.

plunge etc. 310; sound, heave the lead, take soundings; dig etc. (*excavate*) 252.

Adj. deep, -seated; profound, sunk, buried; submerged etc. 310; sub-aqueous, -marine, -terranean, -terrene; underground.

bottom-, sound-, fathom-less; unfathom-ed, -able; abysmal; deep as a well, deep-sea.

knee-, ankle-deep.

Adv. beyond—, out of- one's depth; over head and ears, over one's head.

209. Shallowness.—N. shallowness etc. *adj.*; shoals; mere scratch; veneer, gloss, pinprick.

Adj. shallow, superficial; skin—, ankle—, knee-deep; just enough to wet one's feet; shoal, -y.
V. shallow, shoal, skim— over, —the surface, touch on.

210. Summit.—N. summit, -y; top, vertex, apex, zenith, pinnacle, acme, acropolis, culmination, meridian, utmost height, *ne plus ultra,* height, pitch, maximum, climax, apogee; culminating —, crowning —, turning- point; turn of the tide, fountain head; water-shed, -parting; sky, pole.

tip, -top; crest, crow's nest, cap, truck, peak, nib; end etc. 67; crown, brow; head, nob, noddle, pate, skull, cranium.

high places, heights.

top-, top-gallant mast, sky scraper; quarter —, hurricane- deck.

architrave, frieze, cornice, coping, coping-stone, zoophorus, capital, headpiece, capstone, epistyle, sconce, pediment, entablature; tympanum; ceiling etc. (*covering*) 223.

attic, loft, garret, house-top, upper story, roof, topping, icing, frosting.

V. culminate, cap, crown, top; overtop etc. (*be superior to*) 33.

Adj. highest etc. (high etc. 206); top; top-, upper-most; tip-top; culminating etc. *v.*; meridi-an, -onal; capital, head, polar, supreme, supernal, top-gallant.

Adv. a-top, at the top of — the tree, — the heap.

211. Base.—N. base, -ment; plinth, dado, wainscot, baseboard; foundation etc. (*support*) 215; substructure, *sub · stratum,* sump, ground, earth, pavement, floor, paving, flag, carpet, ground-floor, deck; footing, groundwork, basis; hold, bilge, orlop deck.

bottom, nadir, foot, sole, toe, hoof, keel, kelson, root.

Adj. bottom; under-, nether-most; fundamental; founded —, based —, grounded —, built- on.

212. Verticality.—N. verticality; erectness etc. *adj.*; perpendicularity; right angle, normal; azimuth circle.

wall, palisade, precipice, cliff, steep, bluff.

elevation, erection; square, plumb-line, plummet.

V. be -vertical etc. *adj.*; stand -up, — on end, — erect, — upright; stick —, cock-up.

render -vertical etc. *adj.*; set —, stick —, raise —, cock- up; erect, rear, raise, pitch, raise on its legs.

Adj. vertical, upright, erect, perpendicular, normal, plumb, straight, bolt upright; rampant; straight —, standing- up etc. *v.*; rectangular, orthogonal.

Adv. vertically etc. *adj.*; up, on end; up —, right- on end; *à plomb*, endwise; on one's legs; at right angles.

213. Horizontality.—N. horizontality; flatness; level, plane; stratum etc. 204; dead -level, — flat; level plane.

recumbency; lying down etc. *v.*; reclination, decumbence; de-, discumbency; proneness etc. *adj.*; accubation, supination, resupination, prostration; azimuth.

plain, floor, platform, bowling-green; cricket-ground; court; gridiron; base-ball diamond; hockey rink; tennis-, croquet-ground, — lawn; billiard table; terrace, estrade, esplanade, *parterre*, table-land, *plateau*, ledge.

spirit-, level; T-square.

V. be -horizontal etc. *adj.*; lie, recline, couch; lie -down, — flat, — prostrate; sprawl, loll; sit down.

render -horizontal etc. *adj.*; lay, — down, — out; level, flatten, even, raze, equalize, smooth, align; prostrate, knock down, floor, fell, ground.

Adj. horizontal, level, even, plane; flat etc. 251; flat as a -billiard table, — bowling green; alluvial; calm, — as a mill-pond; smooth, —as glass.

re-, de-, pro-, ac-cumbent; lying etc. *v.*; prone, supine, couchant, jacent, *prostrate*.

Adv. horizontally etc. *adj.*; on -one's back, —all fours, — its beam ends.

214. Pendency.—N. pend-, dependency; suspension, hanging etc. *v.*

pendant, drop, tippet, tassel, lobe, tail, train, flap, lappet, skirt, pig-tail, queue, pendulum, hanger, suspender, supporter.

peg, knob, button, hook, nail, stud, ring, staple, tenterhook; davit; fastening etc. 45; spar, horse.

chande-, gase-, electro-lier.

V. be -pendent etc. *adj.*; hang, depend, swing, dangle, droop, sag; swag; daggle, flap, trail, flow.

suspend, hang, sling, hook up, hitch, fasten to, append.

Adj. pend-ent, -ulous; pensile; hanging etc. *v.*; dependent; suspended etc. *v.*; lowering, overhanging, beetling, decumbent; loose, flowing.

having a -peduncle etc. *n.*; pedunculate, tailed, caudate.

215. Support.—N. support, backing, ground, foundation, base, basis; *terra firma*; bearing, fulcrum, *point d'appui*, caudex, purchase, footing, hold, *-locus standi*; landing, — stage, — place; stage, platform; block; rest, resting-place; ground-work, *substratum*, sustentation, subvention; floor etc. (*basement*) 211.

supporter; aid etc. 707; prop, stand, anvil, fulciment; hod, stay, shore, skid, rib, sprag, truss, bandage; sleeper; stirrup, stilts, shoe, sole, heel, splint, lap; bar, rod, boom, sprit, outrigger.

staff, stick, crutch, alpenstock, bourdon; *bâton*, maulstick, colstaff, cowlstaff, staddle; stalk, ped-icel, -icle, — uncle.

post, pillar, shaft, column, pilaster; pediment, pedestal; plinth, shank, leg, socle, zocle; buttress, jamb, mullion, abutment; pile, baluster, banister, stanchion, king post; balustrade.

frame, -work, body, *chassis*, *fuselage*; scaffold, skeleton, beam, rafter, girder, lintel, joist, cantilever, travis, trave, corner-stone, summer, transom; rung, round, step, sill.

columella, back-bone; key-stone; axle, -tree; axis; arch, ogive, mainstay.

trunnion, pivot, rowlock; peg etc. (*pendency*)

214; tie-beam etc. (*fastening*) 45; thole pin.

board, ledge, shelf, hob, bracket, trevet, trivet, arbor, rack, hatrack; mantel, -piece, -shelf; slab, console; counter, dresser; flange, corbel; table, trestle, teapoy; shoulder; perch; horse; easel, desk; retable, predella.

seat, throne, dais; divan, musnud; chair, bench, form, stool, camp-stool, sofa, settee, davenport, stall, miserere, arm —, easy —, elbow —, rocking-chair; couch, day bed, *fauteuil*, woolsack, ottoman, settle, squab, bench, box, dicky; saddle, pannel, pillion; side —, pack- saddle; pommel.

bed, berth, pallet, tester, crib, cot, bassinet, hammock, shakedown, camp bed, bunk, truckle-bed, cradle, litter, stretcher, bedstead; four-poster, French bed; bedding, mattress, *paillasse;* pillow, bolster; mat, rug, cushion.

stool, footstool, hassock, faldstool, *prie-dieu*; tabouret; tripod.

Atlas, Persides, Atlantes, Caryatides, Hercules.

V. be -supported etc.; lie —, sit —, recline —, lean —, loll —, rest —, stand —, step —, repose —, abut —, beat —, be based etc.- on; have at one's back; be-stride, -straddle.

support, bear, carry, hold, sustain, shoulder; hold —, back —, bolster —, shore- up; up-hold, -bear; prop; under-prop,-pin, -set; bandage, etc. 43; brace, truss; cradle, pillow.

give —, furnish —, afford —, supply —, lend- -support, — foundations; bottom, found, base, ground, embed.

maintain, keep on foot; aid etc. 707.

Adj. support-ing, -ed, etc.*v.*; atlantean, columellar; sustentative, fundamental, basal.

Adv. astride on, astraddle; pick-a-back.

216. Parallelism.—N. parallelism; coextension, concentricity, collimation.

V. be —, lie- parallel to; collimate; equate, match.

Adj. parallel; coextensive, collateral, concentric, concurrent, abreast, aligned.

Adv. alongside, abreast etc. (*laterally*) 236.

217. Obliquity.—N. obliquity, inclination, skew, slope, slant; crookedness etc. *adj.*; slopeness; leaning etc. *v.*; bevel, bezel, ramp, tilt; bias, list, twist, warp, swag, cant, lurch; distortion etc. 243; bend etc. (*curve*) 245; tower of Pisa.

acclivity, rise, ascent, grade, gradient, *glacis*, rising ground, hill, bank, declivity, downhill, dip, fall, devexity; gentle —, rapid- slope; easy -ascent, — descent; shelving beach; *talus; montagne Russe; facilis descensus Averni.*

steepness etc. *adj.*; cliff, precipice etc. (*vertical*) 212; escarpment, scarp.

[Measure of inclination]clinometer, theodolite, level, sextant, quadrant, protractor; angle, sine, cosine, tangent etc. hypothenuse.

diagonal; zigzag, chevron.

V. be -oblique etc. *adj.*; slope, slant, lean, incline, shelve, stoop, decline, descent, bend, heel, careen, sag, swag, seel, slouch, cant, sidle.

render -oblique etc. *adj.*; sway, bias; slope, slant; incline, bend, crook; cant, tilt; distort etc. 243.

Adj. oblique, inclined; sloping etc. *v.*; tilted etc. *v.*; recumbent, clinal, skew, askew, slant, aslant, bias, plagiedral, indirect, wry, awry, ajee, crooked; knock-kneed etc. (*distorted*) 243; bevel, out of the perpendicular.

uphill, rising, ascending, acclivous; downhill, falling, descending; declining, declivous, devex, anticlinal; steep, abrupt, precipitous, breakneck.

diagonal; trans-verse, -versal; athwart, antiparallel; curved etc. 245.

Adv. obliquely etc. *adj.*; on —, all on- one side; askew, askant, askance, aslope, asquint, edgewise, at an angle; side-long, -ways; slope-, slant-wise; by a side wind.

218. Inversion.—N. in-, e-, sub-, re-, retro-, intro-version; contraposition etc. 237; contrariety etc. 14; reversal; turn of the tide.

overturn; upset, capsize; somer-sault, -set; summerset; *culbute*; revulsion; *pirouette.*

transposition, transposal, anastrophy, *metastasis, hyperbaton, anastrophe, hysteron--proteron,* hypallage, *synchysis, tmesis,* parenthesis; *metathesis*; palindrome; Spoonerism.

pronation and supination.

V. be -inverted etc.; turn —, go —, wheel- -round, — about, — to the right about; turn —, go —, tilt —, topple-over; capsize, turn turtle.

in-, sub-, retro-, intro-vert; reverse; up-, overturn, -set; turn -topsy turvy etc. *adj.*; *culbuter*; transpose, put the cart before the horse, turn the tables.

Adj. inverted etc. *v.*; wrong side -out, — up; inside out, upside down; bottom —, keel- upwards; supine, on one's head, topsy turvy, *sens dessus sens dessous.*

inverse; reverse etc. (*contrary*) 14; opposite etc. 237.

topheavy, unstable.

Adv. inversely etc.*adj.*; hirdie-girdie; heels over head, head over heels.

219. Crossing.—N. crossing etc. *v.*; intersection, — lacement, — twinement, -digitation; decussation, transversion; convolution etc. 248.

reticulation, meshwork, network; inosculation, anastomosis, inter-texture, mortise.

net, *plexux*, web, mesh, twill, skein, sleeve, felt, lace; wicker; mat, -ting; plait, trellis, wattle, lattice, grating, *grille*, gridiron, tracery, fretwork, filigree, reticle; tissue, netting, mokes.

cross, crucifix, rood, crisscross, crux; chain, wreath, braid, cat's cradle,knot; entanglement etc. (*disorder*) 59.

[woven fabrics] cloth, linen, muslin, cambric, drill, homespun, tweed, broadcloth etc.

V. cross, decussate; inter-sect, -lace, -twine, -twist, -weave, -digitate, -link.

twine, entwine, weave, inweave, twist, wreathe; anastomose, inosculate, dovetail, splice, link.

mat, plait, plat, braid, felt, twill; tangle, entangle, ravel; net, knot; dishevel, raddle.

Adj. crossing etc.*v.*; crossed, matted etc. *v.*; transverse.

cross, cruciform, crucial; reti-form, -cular, -culated; areolar, cancellated, mullioned, latticed, grated, barred, streaked; textile, secant, plexal; interfretted.

Adv. across, thwart, athwart, transversely, crosswise.

220. Exteriority.—N. exteriority; outside, exterior; surface, superficies; skin etc. (*covering*) 223; *superstratum*; disk, disc; face, facet, external, the open.

excentricity; circumjacence etc. 227.

V. be -exterior etc. *adj.*; lie around etc. 227.

place -exteriorly, — outwardly, — outside; put —, turn- out.

Adj. exter-ior, -nal; extraneous, outer, -most; out-ward, -lying, -side, -door; round about etc. 227; extramural.

superficial, skin-deep; frontal, discoid.

extraregarding; eccentric; outstanding; extrinsic etc. 6.

Adv. externally etc. *adj.*; out, without, over, outwards, *ab extra*, out of doors; *extra muros.*

in the open air; *sub -Jovè, — dio; à la belle étoile, al fresco.*

221. Interiority.—N. interiority; inside, -land, interior, endocrine; interspace, subsoil, *substratum*.

contents etc. 190; substance, pith, marrow; backbone etc. (*center*) 222; heart, bosom, breast, abdomen; vitals, viscera, entrails, bowels, belly, intestines, guts, chitterlings, womb, lap; gland, cell; internal organs, *penetralia*, recesses, innermost recesses; cave etc. (*concavity*) 252.

inhabitant etc. 188.

V. be -inside etc. *adj.*, — within etc. *adv.*

place —, keep- within; enclose etc. (*circumscribe*) 229; intern; embed etc. (*insert*) 300.

Adj. inter-ior, -nal; inner, inside, intimate, inward, intraregarding; in-, inner-most; deep-seated; visceral, intestine, -tinal; inland; subcutaneous; interstitial etc. (*interjacent*) 228; inwrought etc. (*intrinsic*) 5; enclosed etc. *v.*

home, domestic, indoor, intramural, vernacular; endemic.

Adv. internally etc. *adj.*; inwards, within, in, inly; here-, there-, where-in; *ab intra*, withinside; in —, within- doors; at home, in the bosom of one's family.

222. Centrality.—N. centrality, centricalness, center; middle etc. 68; focus etc. 74.

core, kernel; nucleus, nucleolus; heart, pole, axis, pivot, fulcrum, bull's eye; hub, nave, navel; *umbilicus*, spine, backbone, marrow, pith; hot-bed; concentration etc. (*convergence*) 290; centralization; symmetry.

center of -gravity, — pressure, — percussion, — oscillation, — buoyancy etc. metacenter.

V. be -central etc. *adj.*; converge etc. 290.

render central, centralize, concentrate; bring to a focus.

Adj. centr-al, -ical; middle etc. 68; axial, pivotal, focal, umbilical, concentric; middlemost, nuclear, centric, centraidal; spinal, vertebral.

Adv. middle; midst; centrally etc. *adj.*

223. Covering.—N. covering, cover; canopy, tilt, awning, baldachin, tent, marquee, *tente d'abri*, umbrella, parasol, sunshade; veil (*shade*) 424; shield etc. (*defense*) 717; hall.

roof, dome, cupola, mansard roof; ceiling; thatch, tile; pan-, pen-tile; tiling, shingles, slates, slating, leads; shed etc. (*abode*) 189.

top, lid, covercle, door, *operculum*, eyelid, blind, curtain.

bandage, plaster, lint, wrapping, dossil, finger stall.

coverlet, counterpane, sheet, quilt, comforter, eiderdown; tarpaulin, blanket, rug, drugget, linoleum, oilcloth; housing.

in-, tegument; skin, pellicle, fleece, fell, fur, ermine, miniver, sable, sealskin etc.; fabrikoid; leather, morocco, calf, pigskin, elk, kid, cowhide etc.; shagreen, hide; pelt, -ry; cuticle, *dermis*, scarf-skin, *epidermis*.

clothing etc. 225; mask etc. (*concealment*) 530.

peel, crust, bark, rind, *cortex*, husk, shell, coat.

capsule; ferrule; sheath, -ing; pod, cod; casing, case, theca; *elytron; involucrum;* wrapp-ing, -er, cellophane; envelope, vesicle; dermatology, conchology.

armor, -plate, armoring; veneer, facing; pavement; scale etc. (*layer*) 204; coating, paint, stain; varnish etc. (*resin*) 356*a*; anointing etc. *v.*; inunction; incrustation, superposition, obduction, ground, enamel, whitewash, plaster, stucco, rough cast, pebble dash, compo; rendering; cerement; ointment etc. (*grease*) 356.

V. cover; super-pose, -impose; over-lay, -spread; wrap etc. 225; incase; face, case, veneer, pave, paper; tip, cap, bind, revet.

coat, paint, varnish, pay, incrust, stucco, cement, dab, plaster, tar; wash; be-, smear; be-, daub; anoint, do over; gild, plate, electroplate, japan, laquer, lacker, enamel, whitewash; lay it on thick.

over-lie, -arch; conceal etc. 528.

Adj. covering etc. *v.*; cutaneous, dermal, cortical, cuticular, tegumentary, skinny, scaly, squamous; covered etc. *v.*; imbricated, loricated, armor-plated, iron-clad; under cover, hooded, cloaked, cowled.

224. Lining.—N. lining, inner coating; coating etc. (*covering*) 223; stalactite, -agmite.

filling, stuffing, wadding, padding, bushing.

wainscot, *parietes*, wall brattice.

V. line, stuff, incrust, wad, pad, fill.

Adj. lined etc. *v.*

225. Investment.—N. investment; covering etc. 223; dress, clothing, raiment, drapery, costume, attire, guise, toilet, *toilette*, trim; habiliment; vesture, -ment; garment, garb, palliament, apparel, wardrobe, wearing apparel, clothes, things.

array; tailoring, millinery; best bib and tucker; finery etc. (*ornament*) 847; full dress etc. (*show*) 882; garniture; theatrical properties.

outfit, equipment, *trousseau*; uniform, khaki, regimentals; academicals, canonicals etc. 999; livery, gear, harness, turn out, accoutrement, caparison, suit, rigging, trappings, traps, slops, togs, toggery; masquerade.

dishabille, morning dress, lounge suit, tea-gown, *kimono*, *négligé*, dressing-gown, *peignoir*, wrapper, undress; shooting-coat; smoking jacket, mufti; rags, tatters, old clothes; mourning, weeds; duds; slippers.

robe, tunic, dolman, *paletot*, habit, gown, coat, coatee, frock, blouse, *pelisse*, middy, sagum, *toga*, smock-frock; frock-, dress-, morning-, tail- coat; dress-suit, — clothes, swallow-tail coat, dinner-, Eton-jacket.

cloak, pall; mantle, mantlet, mantua, shawl, *pelisse*, veil, yashmak; cape, tippet, kirtle, plaid, muffler, comforter, Balaclava helmet, haik, huke, chlamys, mantilla, tabard, housing, horse-cloth, burnous, *roquelaure*, *houppelande*; sur-, top-, over-, great-coat; *surtout*, spencer, cardigan, sweater, blazer; mackintosh, waterproof, slicker, raincoat, oilskin, trench coat, ulster, monkey-, pea-, pilot-jacket, redingote; wraprascal, poncho, cardinal, pelerine, talma.

jacket, jumper, vest, jerkin, waistcoat, doublet, *camisole*, gabardine; stays, *corsage*, corset, corselet, bodice; stomacher; skirt, petticoat, slip, farthingale, kilt, jupe, crinoline, bustle, hobble skirt, *panier*, apron, pinafore; loin cloth.

trousers; breeches, trews, pantaloons, unmentionables, inexpressibles, overalls, pajamas, smalls, small-clothes; tights, pants, shorts, drawers; knickerbockers, knickers, plus fours, bloomers, divided skirt; phil-, fill-ibeg.

head-dress, -gear; cap, *béret*, tam o' shanter, glengarry, topee, sombrero; hat; cocked —, high —, tall —, top —, silk —, opera —, crush - hat, *gibus*, beaver, castor, bonnet, tile, wideawake, billy-cock; bowler; soft felt —, straw —, leghorn- hat, panama; toque; wimple; night-, mob-, skull-cap, biretta; hood, cowl, coif; capote, calach; scull-cap; kerchief, snood; head, *coiffure*; crown etc. (*circle*) 247; *chignon*, pelt, wig, front, peruke, periwig; caftan, turban, fez, *tarboosh*, taj, shako, csako, busby; *képi*, forage cap, bearskin; helmet etc. 717; mask, domino.

body clothes; linen; shirt, sark, smock, shift, *chemise*, *lingerie*; night-gown, -shirt; bed-gown, *sac de nuit*; jersey, guernsey; underclothing, -waistcoat.

neck-erchief, -cloth; tie, ruff, collar, cravat, stock, handkerchief, bandana, scarf; bib, tucker; dicky; boa; girdle etc. (*circle*) 247; cummerbund.

shoe, pump, brogue, boot, slipper, sandal, galoche, galoshes, arctics, rubber boots, overshoes, patten, clog, sabot; high-low; Blucher —, Wellington —, Hessian —, jack —, top- boot; Balmoral; legging, puttee, buskin, greave, galligaskin, moccasin, *gamache*, gambado, gaiter, spatter-dash, spat, antigropeles; stocking, hose, gaskins, trunk-hose, sock, hosiery.

glove, gauntlet, mitten, cuff, muffettee, wristband, sleeve.

swaddling cloth, baby-linen, *layette*; pocket-handkerchief.

shroud, etc. 363.

clothier, tailor, milliner, *costumier*, sempstress, seamstress, snip; dress-, habit-, breeches-, shoemaker; cordwainer, cobbler, Crispin, hosier, hatter; draper, linendraper, haberdasher, mercer.

V. invest; cover etc. 223; envelop, lap, involve; in-, en-wrap; wrap; fold —, wrap —, lap —, muffle-up; overlap; sheathe, swathe, swaddle, roll up in, shroud, circumvest.

vest, clothe, array, dress, dight, drape, robe, enrobe, attire, tire, garb, habilitate, apparel, accouter, rig, fit out; bedizen, deck etc. (*ornament*) 847; perk; equip, harness, caparison; dress up, wear; don; put —, huddle —, slip- on; mantle.

Adj. invested etc. *v.*; habited; dight, -ed; clad, *costumé*, shod, *chaussé*; *en grande tenue* etc. (*show*) 882.

sartorial.

226. Divestment.—N. divestment; taking off, stripping, removal etc. *v.*

nudity; bareness etc. *adj.*; undress; dishabille etc. 225, altogether; nu-, denu-dation; decortication, depilation, excoriation, desquamation; molting; exfoliation.

baldness, alopecia, acomia.

V. divest; uncover etc. (*cover* etc. 223); denude, bare, strip; undress, unclothe, disrobe etc. (dress, enrobe, etc. 225); uncoif; dismantle; uncase; put —, take —, cast- off; shed, doff; husk, peel, pare, decorticate, desquamate; excoriate, skin, scalp, flay, bark, expose, lay open; exfoliate, molt, mew; cast the skin.

Adj. divested etc. *v.*; bare, naked, nude; undressed, -draped, -clad, -clothed, -appareled; exposed; in dishabille; *décolleté*; bald, threadbare, ragged, callow, roofless.

in -a state of nature, — nature's garb, — buff, — native buff, — birthday suit; *in puris naturalibus*; with nothing on, stark naked; bald as a coot, bare as the back of one's hand; out at elbows; barefoot; bareback; leaf-, nap-, hairless, shaved, clean shaven, tonsured, beardless, bald-headed, acomous.

227. Circumjacence.—N. circumjacence, -ambience; environment, encompassment; atmosphere, medium; surroundings, *entourage*.

outpost; border etc. (*edge*) 231; girdle etc. (*circumference*) 230; outskirts, *boulevards*, suburbs, purlieus, precincts, *faubourgs*, *environs*, *banlieue*, neighborhood, vicinity.

V. lie -around etc. *adv.*; surround, beset, compass, encompass, environ, inclose, enclose, encircle, circle, embrace, circumvent, lap, gird; begird, girdle, engird; skirt, twine round; hem in etc. (*circumscribe*) 229; besiege, invest, blockade.

Adj. circum-jacent, -ambient, -fluent; ambient; surrounding etc. *v.*; circumferential, suburban.

Adv. around, about; without; on -every side, — all sides; right and left, all round, round about; in the neighborhood.

228. Interjacence.—N. inter-jacence, -currence, -venience, -location, -digitation, -penetration; permeation.

inter-jection, -polation, -lineation, -spersion, -calation; embolism.

inter-vention, -ference, -position; in-, ob-trusion; insinuation; insertion etc. 300; dovetailing; infiltration; intromission.

intermedi-um, -ary; go-between, agent, middleman, medium, bodkin, intruder, interloper; parenthesis, episode; fly-leaf.

partition, *septum*, diaphragm, mid-riff; party-wall, panel, vail, bulkhead, brattice, *cloison*; half-way house.

V. lie —, come —, get- between; intervene, slide in, interpenetrate, permeate.

put between, introduce, intromit, import; throw —, wedge —, edge —, jam —, worm —, foist —, run —, plough —, work- in; interpose, -ject, -calate, -polate, -line, -leave, -sperse, -weave, -lard, -digitate; let in, dovetail, splice, mortise; insinuate, smuggle; infiltrate, ingrain.

interfere, put in an oar, thrust one's nose in; intrude, obtrude; have a finger in the pie; introduce the thin end of the wedge; thrust in etc. (*insert*) 300.

Adj. inter-jacent, -current, -venient, -vening etc. *v.*, -mediate, -mediary, -calary, -sitital, -costal, -mural, -planetary, -stellar; embolismal.

parenthetical, episodic; mediterranean; intrusive; embosomed; merged, mean, middle, medium, median.

Adv. between, betwixt; 'twixt; among, -st; amid, st; 'mid, -st; in the thick of; betwixt and between; sandwich-wise; parenthetically, *obiter dictum*.

229. Circumscription.—N. circumscription, limitation, inclosure; confinement etc. (*restraint*) 751; circumvallation, encincture; envelope etc. 232.

V. circumscribe, limit, bound, confine, restrict, enclose; surround etc. 227; compass about; imprision etc. (*restrain*) 751; hedge —, wall —, rail-in; fence —, hedge- round; embar; picket, corral.

enfold, bury, incase, pack up, enshrine, inclasp; wrap up etc. (*invest*) 225; embosom.

Adj. circumscribed etc. *v.*; begirt, lapt; circumambient; buried —, immersed- in; embosomed, in the bosom of, imbedded, encysted, mewed up; imprisoned etc. 751; land-locked, in a ring fence.

230. Outline.—N. outline, circumference; perimeter, -phery; ambit, circuit, lines, *tournure*, *contour*, profile, *silhouette*, lineaments; bounds, coastline.

zone, belt, girth, band, baldric, zodiac, girdle, tire, cingle, clasp, girt; *cordon* etc. (*inclosure*) 232; circlet etc. 247.

V. outline, delineate, *silhouette*, circumscribe etc. 229; profile, block out.

Adj. outlined etc. *v.*; circumferential, perimetric, peripheral.

231. Edge.—N. edge, verge, brink, brow, brim, margin, border, confines, skirt, rim, felloe, felly, flange, side, mouth; jaws, chops, chaps, *fauces*; lip, muzzle.

threshold, door, porch; portal etc. (*opening*) 260; coast, shore, strand, beach, bank, wharf, quay, dock.

frame, fringe, flounce, frill, list, trimming, edging, skirting, hem, selvedge, welt; furbelow, valance, exergue.

Adj. border, marginal, skirting; labial; labiated, marginated.

232. Inclosure.—N. inclosure, enclosure, envelope; package, box, crate, case etc. (*receptacle*) 191; wrapper; girdle etc. 230.

pen, fold, croft, sty; pen-, in-, sheep--fold; paddock, pound, corral, kraal; yard, compound; net, seine net.

wall; hedge, -row; *espalier*; fence etc. (*defence*) 717; pale, paling, balustrade, rail, railing, gunwale; quickset hedge, park paling, circumvallation, *enciente*, ring fence.

barrier, barricade; gate; -way; door, hatch, *cordon*; prison etc. 752.

dike, dyke, ditch, fosse, moat, trench.

V. inclose; circumscribe etc. 229.

233. Limit.—N. limit, boundary, bounds, confine, *enclave*, term, bourn, verge, kerb-stone, curbstone, but, pale; termin-ation, -us; stint, frontier, precinct, marches.

boundary line, landmark; line of -demarcation, — circumvallation; pillars of Hercules; Rubicon, turning-point; *ne plus ultra*; sluice, flood-gate.

V. limit, bound, confine, define, circumscribe, demarcate, delimit, encompass.

Adj. definite; contermin-ate, -able, terminable, limitable; terminal, frontier, border, bordering, boundary.

Adv. thus far, — and no further.

234. Front.—N. front; fore, — part; foreground; forefront, face, disk, disc, frontage, *façade*, *proscenium*, facia, frontispiece; priority, anteriority; obverse [of a medal].

fore —, front- rank, first line; van, -guard; advanced guard; outpost, scout.

brow, forehead, visage, physiognomy, phiz, features, countenance, map, mug; rostrum, beak, bow, stem, prow, prore, jib, bowsprit; forecastle.

pioneer etc. (*precursor*) 64; metoposcopy.

V. be —, stand- in front etc. *adj.*; front, face, confront, breast, brave; bend forwards; come to the -front, — fore.

Adj. fore, forward, anterior, front, frontal, head-on, leading, first, primary.

Adv. before; in -front, — the van, — advance; ahead, right ahead; fore-, head-most; in the foreground; before one's -face, — eyes; face to face, *vis-à-vis*.

235. Rear.—N. rear, back, posterior-ity; rear -rank, — guard; background, *hinterland*.

occiput, nape, scruff, chine; heels; tail, rump, croup, buttock, posteriors, bottom, seat, backside, scut, breech, *dorsum*, loin; dorsal —, lumbar-region; hind quarters.

stern poop, after-part, counter; postern, heel-, tail-piece, crupper.

wake; train etc. (*sequence*) 281.

reverse; other side of the shield.

V. be -behind etc. *adv.*, fall astern; bend backwards; bring up the rear; follow etc. 622; tail, shadow.

Adj. back, rear; hind, -er, -most, -ermost; postern, -erior; dorsal, after; caudal, lumbar; mizzen."

Adv. behind; in the -rear, — ruck, — background; behind one's back; at the -heels, – tail, – back- of; back to back.

after, -most, aft, abaft, astern, stern- most, aback, rear-, hind-, back-ward.

236. Laterality.—N. laterality; side, flank, beam, quarter, lee; hand; cheek, jowl, jole, wing; profile; temple, *parietes*, loin, haunch, hip.

gable, -end; broadside; lee side.

points of the compass; East, Orient, Levant; West, occident; orientation.

V. be -on one side etc. *adv.*; flank, outflank; sidle; skirt, border.

Adj. lateral, sidelong; collateral; parietal, flanking, skirting; flanked; sideling.

many-sided; multi-, bi-, tri-, quadri- lateral.

East-ern, -ward, -erly; orient, -al, auroral, Levantine; West-ern, -ward, -erly; occidental, Hesperian; equatorial.

Adv. side-ways, -long; broadside on; on one side, abreast, abeam, alongside, beside, aside; by, – the side of; side by side; cheek by jowl etc. (*near*) 197; to -windward, – leeward; laterally etc. *adj.*; right and left; on her beam ends.

237. Contraposition.—N. contraposition, opposition; polarity; inversion etc. 218; opposite side; antithesis; reverse, inverse; counterpart; antipodes; opposite poles, North and South.

V. be -opposite etc. *adj.*; subtend.

Adj. opposite; reverse, inverse; antipodal, subcontrary; fronting, facing, diametrically opposite.

Northern, Septentrional, Boreal, arctic; Southern, Austral, antarctic, polar.

Adv. over, – the way, – against; against; face to face, vis-à-vis; as poles asunder.

238. Dextrality.—N. dextrality; right, – hand; dexter, offside, starboard.

Adj. dextral, right-handed; ambidextral; dexterous, dextrorsal etc.

239. Sinistrality.—N. sinistrality; left, – hand; *sinister*, nearside, larboard, port.

Adj. sinistral, sinister, sinistrorsal etc., left-handed, sinistromanual, sinistrous.

240. Form.—N. form, figure, shape, physique; con-formation, -figuration; make, formation, frame, construction, design, cut, set, build, trim, cut of one's jib; stamp, type, cast, mold; fashion; contour etc. (*outline*) 230, structure etc. 329.

feature, lineament, outline, turn; phase etc. (*aspect*) 448; posture, attitude, *pose*.

[Science of form] morphology.

[Similarity of form] isomorphism.

forming etc. *v.*; form-, figur-, efform- ation; sculpture.

V. form, shape, figure, fashion, efform, carve, cut, chisel, hew, cast; rough-hew, -cast; sketch; block –, hammer- out; trim; lick –, put- into shape; model, knead, work up into, set, mold, sculpture; cast, stamp; built etc. (*construct*) 161.

Adj. formed etc. *v.*

[Receiving form] plastic, fictile, full- fashioned etc.

[Giving form] plasmic, etc.

[Similar in form] isomorphous etc.

241. Amorphism. [Absence of form.]—**N.** amorphism, informity, uncouthness; unlicked cub, rough diamond; *rudis indigestaque moles*; disorder etc. 59; deformity etc. 243.

disfigure-, deface-ment, deformation; mutilation.

V. [Destroy form] deface, disfigure, deform, mutilate, truncate; derange etc. 61.

Adj. shapeless, amorphous, malformed, formless; un-formed, -hewn, -fashioned, -shapen; rough, rude, Gothic, barbarous, rugged, in the rough; misshapen etc. 243.

242. Symmetry. [Regularity of form.]—**N.** symmetry, shapeliness, finish; beauty etc. 845; proportion, eurythmy, eurythmic, uniformity, parallelism; bi-, tri-, multi-lateral symmetry; centrality etc. 222.

arborescence, branching, ramification.

Adj. symmetrical, shapely, well set, finished; beautiful etc. 845; classic, chaste, severe.

regular, uniform, balanced; equal etc. 27; parallel, coextensive.

arbor-escent, -iform; dendr-iform, -oid; branching; ramous, ramose.

243. Distortion. [Irregularity of form.]—**N.** dis-, de-, con-tortion; knot, mop, warp, buckle, screw, twist; crookedness etc. (*obliquity*) 217; grimmace; deformity; mal-, malcon-formation; monstrosity, misproportion, want of symmetry, *anamorphosis*; ugliness etc. 846; teratology.

V. distort, contort, twist, warp etc. *n.*; wrest, writhe, make faces, deform, misshape.

Adj. distorted etc. *v.*; out of shape, irregular, unsymmetric, awry, wry, askew, crooked, sinuous; anamorphous; not -true, – straight; on one side, crump, deformed; mis-shapen, -begotten; mis-, ill-proportioned; ill-made; grotesque, crooked as a ram's horn; hump-, hunch-, bunch-, crook-backed; bandy; bandy-, bow-legged; bow-, knock-kneed; splay-, club-footed; taliped; round-shouldered; snub-nosed; curtailed of one's fair proportions; scalene, stumpy etc. (*short*) 201; gaunt etc. (*thin*) 203; bloated etc. 194.

Adv. all manner of ways.

244. Angularity.—N. angular-ity, -ness; aduncity; angle, cusp, bend; fold etc. 258; notch etc. 257; fork, bifurcation.

elbow, knee, knuckle, ankle, groin, crotch, crane, fluke, scythe, sickle, zigzag, kimbo.

corner, nook, recess, niche, oriel.

right angle etc. (*perpendicular*) 212; obliquity etc. 217; angle of 45 degrees, miter; acute –, obtuse –, salient –, re-entrant –, spherical –, solid –, dihedral- angle.

angular -measurement, — elevation, — distance, — velocity; trigon-, goni-ometry; altimetry; clin-, graph-, goni-ometer; theodolite; transit circle; sextant, quadrant; dichotomy.

triangle, trigon, wedge; rectangle, square, lozenge, diamond; rhomb, -us; quadr-angle, -ilateral; parallelogram; quadrature; poly-, penta-, hexa-, hepta-, octa-, deca-gon.

Platonic bodies; cube, rhomboid; tetra-, penta-, hexa-, octa-, dodeca-, icosa-hedron; prism, pyramid; parallelopiped.

V. bend, fork, bifurcate, crinkle, divaricate, branch, ramify.

Adj. angular, bent, crooked, aduncous, uncinated, aquiline, jagged, serrated; falc-iform, -ated; furcular, furcated, forked, bifurcate, crotched; zigzag; dovetailed; knock-kneed, crinkled, akimbo, kimbo, geniculated; oblique etc. 217.

fusiform, wedge-shaped, cuneiform; tri-angular, -gonal, -lateral; quadr-angular, -ilateral; rectangular, square, foursquare, multilateral; polygonal etc. *n.*; cubical, rhomboidal, pyramidal.

245. Curvature.—N. curv-ature, -ity, -ation; incurv-ity, -ation; bend; flex- ure, -ion; conflexure; crook, hook, bought, bending; de-, inflexion; arcuation, devexity, turn; deviation, *détour*, sweep; curl, -ing; bough; recurv-ity, -ation; sinuosity etc. 248; aduncity.

curve, arc, arch, arcade, vault, dome, bow, crescent, *meniscus*, half-moon, lunule, horse-shoe, loop, crane-neck; para-, hyper-bola; catenary, festoon; conch-, cardi-oid; caustic, instep; tracery.

V. be -curved etc. *adj.*; sweep, swag, sag; deviate etc. 279; turn; re-enter.

render -curved etc. *adj.*; bend, curve, incurvate; de-, in-flect, crook; turn, round, arch, arcuate, arch over, loop the loop, concamerate; bow, coil, curl, recurve, frizzle.

Adj. curved etc. *v.*; curvi-form, -lineal, -linear, devex, devious; recurv-ed, -ous; *retroussé*; crump; bowed etc. *v.*; vaulted; hooked; falc-iform, -ated; semicircular, crescentic; lun-iform, -ular; semilunar, meniscal; conchoidal; cord-iform, -ated; cardioid; heart-, bell-, pear-, fig shaped; reniform; lenti-form, -cular; bow-legged etc. (*distorted*) 243; oblique etc. 217; circular etc. 247.

246. Straightness.—N. straightness, rectilinearity, directness; inflexibility etc. (*stiffness*) 323; straight —, right —, direct-, bee- line; short cut.

V. be -straight etc. *adj*; have no turning; not -incline, — bend, — turn, — deviate- to either side; go straight; steer for etc. (*direction*) 278.

render straight, straighten, rectify; set —, put- straight; un-bend, -fold, -curl etc. 248, -ravel etc. 219, -wrap.

Adj. straight; rectiline-ar, -al; direct, even, right, true, in a line; unbent etc. *v.*; un-deviating, -turned, -distorted, -swerving; straight as an arrow etc. (*direct*) 278; inflexible etc. 323.

247. Circularity. [Simple circularity.]—**N.** circularity, roundness; rotundity etc. 249.

circle, circlet, ring, washer, areola, hoop, roundlet, *annulus*, annulet, bracelet, armlet, armilla; ringlet; eye, loop, wheel; cycle, orb, orbit, rundle, zone, belt, *cordon*, band; sash, girdle, cestus, cincture, baldric, fillet, *fascia*, wreath, garland; crown, corona, coronet, chaplet, snood, necklace, collar; noose, lasso, lariat.

ellipse, oval, ovule; ellipsoid, cycloid; epicycloid, -cycle; semi-circle; quadrant, sextant, sector.

V. make -round etc. *adj.*; round.

go round; encircle etc. 227; describe -a circle etc. 311.

Adj. round, rounded, circular, annular, orbicular; oval, ovate; elliptic, -al; ovoid, egg-shaped; pear-shaped etc. 245; cycloidal etc. *n.*; spherical etc. 249.

248. Convolution. [Complex circularity.]—**N.** winding etc. *v.*; con-, in-, circum-volution; wave, undulation, tortuosity, anfractuosity; sinu-osity, -ation, sinuousness; meandering, circuit, circumbendibus, twist, twirl, windings and turnings, *ambages*; torsion; inosculation; reticulation etc. (*crossing*) 219.

coil, roll, curl, buckle, spire, spiral, helix, corkscrew, worm, volute, whorl, rundle; tendril; scollop, scallop, escalop; kink.

serpent, snake, eel, maze, labyrinth.

V. be -convoluted etc. *adj.*; wind, twine, turn and twist, twirl; wave, undulate, meander; inosculate; entwine, intwine; twist, coil, roll; wrinkle, curl, crisp, twill; frizz, -le; crimp, crape, indent, scollop, scallop; wring, intort; contort; wreathe etc. (*cross*) 219.

Adj. convoluted; winding, twisted etc. *v.*; tortile, tortive; wavy; und-ated, -ulatory; circling, snaky, snake-like, serpentine; serpent-, anguill-, verm-iform, vermicular; mazy, tortuous, anfractuous, sinuous, flexuous, wavy, sigmoidal.

involved, intricate, complicated, perplexed; labyrinth-ic, -ian, -ine; circuitous; peristaltic; daedalian, curly.

wreathy, frizzly, *crêpé*, buckled; ravelled etc. (*in disorder*) 59.

spiral, coiled, helical, turbinated.

Adv. in and out, round and round.

249. Rotundity.—N. rotundity; roundness etc. *adj.*; cyclindricity; spher-icity, -oidity; globosity.

cylin-der, -droid; barrel, drum; roll, -er; *rouleau*, column, rolling-pin, rundle; chimney-pot, drain-pipe.

cone, conoid; pear-, egg-, bell-shape.

sphere, globe, orb, orbit, ball, boulder, bowlder; spher-, ellips-, ge-, glob-oid, oblong —, oblate-spheroid; drop, spherule, globule, vesicle, bulb, bullet, pellet, *pelote*, clew, pill, marble, pea, knob, pommel, knot.

V. render -spherical etc. *adj.*; form into a sphere, sphere, roll into a ball; give -rotundity etc. *n.*; round.

Adj. rotund; round etc. (*circular*) 247; cylindric, -ical, -oid; columnar, lumbriciform; conic, -al; spher-ical, -oidal; glob-ular, -ated, -ous, -ose; egg-, bell-, pear-shaped; ov-oid, -iform; gibbous; campaniform, -ulate, -iliform; fungiform, bead-like, moniliform, pyriform, bulbous; *teres atque rotundus*; round as -an orange, — an apple, — a ball, — a billiard ball, — a cannon ball.

250. Convexity.—N. convexity, prominence, projection, swelling, gibbosity, bilge, bulge, protuberance, protrusion; excrescency, camber.

intumescence; tumor; tubercle, -osity; excrescence; hump, hunch, bunch, gnarl.

tooth, knob, elbow, process, *apophysis*, condyle, bulb, node, nodule, nodosity, tongue, *dorsum*, boss, embossment, bump, clump; sugar-loaf etc. (*sharpness*) 253; bow; mamelon.

pimple, wen, wheal, *papula*, postule, pock, proud flesh, growth, goiter, *sarcoma*, caruncle, corn, bunion, wart, furnuncle, polypus, adenoid, fungus, fungosity, *exostosis*, bleb, blister, blain; boil etc. (*disease*) 655; bubble, blob.

papilla, nipple, teat, pap, breast, dug, mammilla; proboscis, .ose, neb, beak, snout, nozzle, snozzle; Adam's apple; belly, paunch, corporation; withers, back, shoulder, lip, flange.

peg, button, stud, ridge, rib, jutty, trunnion, snag.

cupola, dome, bee-hive; arch, balcony, eaves; pilaster.

relief, relievo, *cameo*; *basso-*, *mezzo-*, *altorilievo*; low-, bas-, high-relief.

hill etc. (*height*) 206; cape, promontory, mull; fore-, head-land; point of land, naze, ness, mole, jetty, hummock, ledge, spur.

V. be -prominent etc. *adj.*; project, bulge, protrude, bag, belly, pout, bouge, bunch; jut —, stand —, stick —, poke- out; stick —, bristle —, start —, cock —, shoot- up; swell —, hang —, bend-over; beetle.

render -prominent etc. *adj.*; raise 307; emboss, chase.

Adj. convex, prominent, protuberant, underhung, undershot; projecting etc. *v.*; bossed, bossy, nodular, bunchy; clav-ate, -ated; hummocky, *moutonné*, mammiform; papul-ous, -ose; hemispheric, bulbous; bowed, arched; bold; bellied; tuber-ous, -culous; tumorous; cornute, knobby, odontoid; lenti-form, -cular; gibbous.

salient, in relief, raised, *repoussé*; bloated etc. (*expanded*) 194.

251. Flatness.—N. flatness etc. *adj.*; smoothness etc. 255.

plane; level etc. 213; plate, platter, table, tablet, slab.

V. render flat, flatten, squash; level etc. 213.

Adj. flat, plane, even, flush, scutiform, discoid; level etc. (*horizontal*) 213; smooth; flat as -a pancake, — a fluke, — a flounder, — a board, — my hand.

252. Concavity.—N. concavity, depression, dip; hollow, -ness; indentation, *intaglio*, cavity, antrum, dent, dint, dimple, follicle, pit, *sinus*, *alveolus*, *lacuna*; excavation, trench, shaft, sap, mine, tunnel, burrow; trough etc. (*furrow*) 259; honeycomb.

cup, basin, crater, punch-bowl; cell etc. (*receptacle*) 191; socket, faucet.

valley, vale, dale, dell, gap, dingle, combe, bottom, slade, strath, glade, grove, glen, cave, cavern, cove; grot, -to; alcove, *cul-de-sac*, blind alley; gully etc. 198; arch etc. (*curve*) 245; bay etc. (*of the sea*) 343.

excavator, sapper, miner.

V. be -concave etc. *adj.*; retire, cave in.

render -concave etc. *adj.*; depress, hollow; scoop, — out; gouge, dig, delve, excavate, dent, dint, mine, sap, undermine, burrow, tunnel, stave in.

Adj. depressed etc. *v.*; concave, hollow, stove in; dished; spoon-like; retiring; retreating; cavernous; porous etc. (*with holes*) 260; cellular, spongy, spongious; honeycombed, alveolar; infundibul-ar, -iform; funnel-, bell-shaped; campaniform, capsular; vaulted, arched.

253. Sharpness.—N. sharpness etc. *adj.*: acuity, acumination; spinosity.

point, spike, spine, *spiculum*, tine; needle, pin; tack, nail; prick, -le; spur, rowel, barb; spit, cusp; horn, antler; snag; tag; thorn, bristle.

nib, tooth, incisor, tusk; spoke, cog, ratchet.

crag, crest *arête*, cone, peak, sugar-loaf, pike, *aiguille*; spire, pyramid, steeple.

beard, *chevaux de frise*, porcupine, hedgehog, brier, bramble, thistle; comb, awn, bur.

wedge; knife-, cutting- edge; blade, edge-tool, cutlery, knife, penknife, whittle, razor; scalpel, bistoury, lancet; chisel; ploughshare, coulter; hatchet, axe, pick-axe, mattock, pick, adze, bill; billhook, cleaver, cutter; skiver; scythe, sickle, scissors, shears; sword etc. (*arms*) 727; bodkin etc. (*perforator*) 262.

sharpener, hone, strop; grind-, whet-stone; steel, emery.

V. be -sharp etc. *adj.*; taper to a point; bristle with.

render -sharp etc. *adj.*; sharpen, point, aculeate, acuminate, whet, barb, spiculate, set, strop, grind.

cut etc. (*sunder*) 44.

Adj. sharp, keen; acute; aci-cular, -form; aculeated, -minated; pointed; tapering; conical, pyramidal; mucron-ate, -ated; spindle-, needle-shaped; spiked, spiky, ensiform, peaked, salient, cusp-ed; -idate, -idated; corn-ute, -uted, -iculate; prickly; spiny, spinous; thorny, bristling, muricated, pectinated, studded, thistly, briery; craggy etc. (*rough*) 256; snaggy; digitated, two-edged, fusiform; denti-form, -culated; toothed; odontoid; star-like; stell-ated, -iform; arrow-headed; arrowy, barbed, spurred, sagittal; spear-shaped, hastate; horned; conical.

cutting; sharp-, knife-edged; sharp —, keen- as a razor; sharp as a needle; sharpened etc. *v.*; set.

254. Bluntness.—N. bluntness etc. *adj.*; abruptness, dullness.

V. be —, render- blunt etc. *adj.*; obtund, dull; take off the -point, — edge; turn.

Adj. blunt, obtuse, dull, bluff.

255. Smoothness.—N. smoothness etc. *adj.*; polish, gloss; lubric-ity, -ation.

down, velvet, silk, satin; slide; bowling green etc. (*level*) 213; glass, ice; asphalt, pavement, flags.

roller, steam-roller; iron, flat-iron, tailor's goose; sand-, emery-paper; burnisher, turpentine and bees-wax.

V. smooth, -en; plane; file; mow, shave; level, roll; macadamize; polish, burnish, planish, levigate, calender, glaze; iron, hot-press, mangle; lubricate etc. (*oil*) 332.

Adj. smooth; polished etc. *v.*; even; level etc. 213; plane etc. (*flat*) 251; sleek, glossy; silken, silky; lanate, downy, velvety; glabrous, slippery, glassy, lubricous, oily, soft; unwrinkled; smooth as -glass, — ice, — velvet, — oil; slippery as an eel; wooly etc. (*feathery*) 256.

256. Roughness.—N. roughness etc. *adj.*; tooth, grain, texture, ripple; asperity, rugosity, salebrosity, corrugation, nodosity; arborescence etc. 242.

brush, hair, beard, shag, mane, whisker, mutton-chops, *moustache*, *mustachio*, imperial, Van Dyke, tress, lock, curl, ringlet, *fimbriae*, *cilia*, *villi*; eye-lashes, eye-brows, love-lock.

plum-age, -osity; plume, *panache*, crest; feather, tuft, tussock, fringe, toupee.

wool, velvet, plush, nap, pile, floss, fluff, fur, down; byssus, moss, bur.

V. be -rough etc. *adj.*; go against the grain.

render -rough etc. *adj.*; roughen, rough cast, knurl; ruffle, crisp, crumple, crinkle, corrugate, engrail; set on edge, stroke —, rub- the wrong way, rumple.

Adj. rough, uneven; scabrous, knotted; nodular; rug-ged, -ose, -ous; asperous, crisp, salebrous, gnarled, unpolished, unsmooth, rough-hewn; knurled, cross-grained, crag-gy, -ged; crankling, scraggy, jagged, unkempt, prickly etc. (*sharp*) 253; arborescent etc. 242; leafy, well-wooded; feathery; plum-ose, -igerous; tufted, fimbriated, hairy, bristly, ciliated, filamentous, hirsute; crin-ose, -ite; bushy, hispid, villous, pappous, bearded, pilous, shaggy, shagged; fringed, befringed; set-ous, -ose, -aceous; 'like quills upon the fretful porcupine;' rough as a -nutmeg grater, — bear.

downy, velvety, flocculent, wolly; lan-ate, -ated; lanugin-ous, ose; tomentous.

Adv. against the grain, in the rough, on edge.

257. Notch.—N. notch, dent, nick, cut; indent, -ation; serration; dimple.

embrasure, battlement, machicolation; saw, tooth, crenelle, scallop, scollop, vandyke.

V. notch, nick, cut, pink, mill, score, dent, indent, jag, scarify, scotch, crimp, scollop, crenulate, vandyke.

Adj. notched etc. *v.*; crenate, -d; dentate, -d; denticulate, -d; toothed, palmated, serrated.

258. Fold.—N. fold, plicature, pleat, plait, ply, crease; tuck, gather; flexion, flexure, joint, elbow, doubling, duplicature, wrinkle, rimple, crinkle, crankle, crumple, rumple, rivel, ruck, ruffle, dog's ear, corrugation, frounce, flounce, lapel; pucker, crow's feet.

V. fold, double, plicate, pleat, plait, crease, wrinkle, crinkle, crankle, curl, smock, cockle up, crocker, rimple, rumple, frizzle, frounce, rivel, twill, corrugate, ruffle, crimple, crumple, pucker; turn —, double- -down, — under; tuck, ruck, hem, gather.

Adj. folded etc. *v.*

259. Furrow.—N. furrow, groove, rut, *sulcus*, scratch, streak, *striae*, crack, score, incision, slit; chamfer, fluting.

channel, gutter, trench, ditch, dike, dyke, moat, fosse, trough, kennel; ravine etc. (*interval*) 198.

V. furrow etc. *n.*; flute, groove, carve, corrugate, plough; incise, chase, enchase, grave, engrave, etch, bite in, cross-hatch.

Adj. furrowed etc. *v.*; ribbed, straited, sulcated, fluted, canaliculated; bisculc-ous, -ate; trisulcate; corduroy.

260. Opening.—N. hole, foramen; puncture, blow-out, perforation; pin-, key-, loop-, port-, peep-, mouse-, pigeon-hole; eye, — of a needle; eyelet; slot.

opening; apert-ure, -ness; hiation, yawning, oscitancy, dehiscence, patefaction, pandiculation; gap, chasm etc. (*interval*) 198.

embrasure, window, casement, light; sky-, fan-light; lattice; bay-, bow-window; oriel; dormer, lantern.

out-, in-let; vent, vomitory; *embouchure*; orifice, mouth, sucker, muzzle, throat, gullet, placket, weasand, wizen, nozzle, *esophagus*.

portal, porch, gate, ostiary, postern, wicket, trap-door, hatch, door; arcade; gate-, door-, hatch-, gang-way; lych-gate.

way, path etc. 627; thoroughfare; channel, passage, tube, pipe; waterpipe etc. 350; air-pipe etc. 351; vessel, tubule, canal, gut, fistula; adjutage, ajutage; chimney, smoke stack, flue, tap, funnel, gully, tunnel, main; mine, pit, adit, shaft; gallery.

alley, aisle, glade, lane, vista.

bore, caliber; pore; blind orifice.

por-ousness, -osity; sieve, cullender, colander; grater, shredder, cribble, riddle, screen; honeycomb.

apertion, perforation; piercing etc. *v.*; terebration, empalement, pertusion, puncture, acupuncture, penetration.

opener, corkscrew, can opener, key, master-key, *passe-partout*.

V. open, ope, gape, dehisce, yawn, bilge; fly open.

perforate, pierce, empierce, tap, bore, drill; mine etc. (*scoop out*) 252; tunnel; trans-pierce, -fix; enfilade, impale, spike, spear, gore, spit, stab, pink, puncture, lance, trepan, trephine, stick, prick, riddle, punch; stave in.

cut a passage through; make -way, — room- for.

un-cover, -close, -rip; lay —, cut —, rip —, throw- open.

Adj. open; perforated etc. *v.*; perforate; wide open, agape, ajar; un-closed, -stopped; oscitant, gaping, yawning; patent.

tubular, cannular, fistulous; per-vious, -meable; foraminous; vesi-, vas-cular; porous, follicular,

cribriform, honeycombed, infundibular, riddled; tubul-ous, -ated, piped.
opening etc. *v.*; aperient.
Int. *open sesame!*

261. Closure.—N. closure, occlusion, blockade; shutting up etc. *v.*; obstruction etc. (*hindrance*) 706; gag; embolism; contraction etc. 195; infarction; con-, ob-stipation; blind -alley, — corner; *cul-de-sac*, *caecum*; imperforation, -viousness etc. *adj.*; -meability; stopper etc. 263; *operculum*.

V. close, occlude, plug; block —, stop —, fill —, bung —, cork —, button —, stuff —, shut —, dam-up, obturate; blockade; obstruct etc. (*hinder*) 706; bar, bolt, stop, seal, plumb; choke, throttle; ram down, tamp, dam, cram; trap, clinch; put to —, shut- the door; batten down the hatches.

Adj. closed etc. *v.*; shut, operculated; unopened.
unpierced, imporous, caecal; imperforate, -vious, -meable; impenetrable; un-, im-passable; invious; path-, way-less; untrodden.
unventilated; air-, water-tight; hermetically sealed; tight, snug.

262. Perforator.—N. perforator, piercer, borer, auger, gimlet, stylet, drill, wimble, awl, bradawl, scoop, terrier, corkscrew, dibble, trocar, trepan, trephine, probe, bodkin, needle, stiletto, broach, reamer, rimer, warder, lancet; punch, -eon; spikebit, gouge; spear etc. (*weapon*) 727.

263. Stopper.—N. stopper, stopple; plug, cork, bung, spike, spill, stop-cock, tap; rammer; ram, -rod; piston; stopgap; wadding, stuffing, padding, stopping, dossil, pledget, tompion, tourniquet, obturator; wad.
cover etc. 223; valve, slide valve; vent-peg, spigot.
janitor, door —, gate- keeper, porter, commissionaire, *concierge*, warder, beadle, Cerberus, usher, guard, sentry, sentinel; ostiary.

264. Motion. [Successive change of place.*]—**N.** motion, movement, move; motivity, motility, going etc. *v.*; unrest.
stream, current, flow, flux, run, course, stir; conduction, evolution; kinematics.
step, rate, pace, tread, stride, gait, clip, port, footfall, cadence, carriage, velocity, angular velocity; progress, locomotion; journey etc. 266; voyage etc. 267; transit etc. 270.
restlessness etc. (*changeableness*) 149; mobility; movableness, motive power; laws of motion; mobilization.

V. be -in motion etc. *adj.*; move, go, hie, gang, budge, stir, pass, flit; hover -round, — about; shift, slide, slither, glide; roll, — on; flow, stream, run, drift, sweep along; wander etc. (*deviate*) 279; walk etc. 266; change —, shift- one's -place, — quarters; dodge; keep -going, — moving.
put —, set- in motion; move; impel etc. 276; propel etc. 284; render movable, mobilize.

Adj. moving etc. *v.*; in motion; motile, transitional; motory, motive; shifting, movable, mobile, mercurial, unquiet; restless etc. (*changeable*) 149; nomadic etc. 266; erratic etc. 279.

Adv. under way; on the -move, — wing, — tramp, — march.

*A thing cannot be said to *move* from one place to another, unless it passes in succession through every intermediate place; hence motion is only such a change of place as is *successive*. 'Rapid, swift, etc., as thought' are therefore incorrect expressions.

265. Quiescence.—N. rest; stillness etc. *adj.*; quiescence; stag-nation, -nancy; fixity, immobility, catalepsy; indisturbance; quietism.
quiet, tranquillity, calm; repose etc. 687; peace; dead calm, anticyclone; statue-like repose; silence etc. 403; not a -breath of air, — mouse stirring; sleep etc. (*inactivity*) 683.
pause, lull etc. (*cessation*) 142; stand, — still; standing still etc. *v.*; lock; dead -lock, — stop, — stand; full stop; fix; embargo.
resting-place; bivouac; home etc. (*abode*) 189; pillow etc. (*support*) 215; haven etc. (*refuge*) 666; goal etc. (*arrival*) 292.

V. be -quiescent etc. *adj.*; stand —, lie- still; keep quiet, repose, hold the breath.
remain, stay; stand, lie to, ride at anchor, remain *in situ*, mark time, tarry; bring —, heave —, lay- to; pull —, draw- up; hold, halt; stop, — short; rest, pause, anchor; cast —, come to an- anchor; rest on one's oars; repose on one's laurels, take breath; stop etc. (*discontinue*) 142.
stagnate, vegetate; *quieta non movere*; let -alone, — well alone; abide, rest and be thankful; keep within doors, stay at home, go to bed.
dwell etc. (*be present*) 186; settle etc. (*be located*) 184; alight etc. (*arrive*) 292.
stick, — fast; stand, — like a post; not stir a -peg, — step; be at a -stand etc. *n.*
quell, becalm, hush, stay, lull to sleep, lay an embargo on; put the brake on.

Adj. quiescent, still; motion-, move-less; fixed; stationary; at -rest, — a stand, — a stand-still, — anchor; stock-still; immotile; standing still etc. *v.*; sedentary, untravelled, stay-at-home; becalmed, stagnant, quiet; un-moved, -disturbed, -ruffled; calm, restful; cataleptic; immovable etc. (*stable*) 150; sleeping etc. (*inactive*) 683; silent etc. 403; still as -a statue; — a post, — a mouse, — death.

Adv. at a stand etc. *adj.*; *tout court*; at the halt.

Int. stop! stay! avast! halt! hold, — hard! whoa!

Phr. *requiescat in pace*.

266. Journey. [Locomotion by land.]—**N.** travel; traveling etc. *v.*; wayfaring, campaigning.
journey, excursion, expedition, tour, trip, grand tour, circuit, peregrination, discursion, ramble, pilgrimage, *trek*, course, ambulation, march, walk, hike, promenade, constitutional, stroll, saunter, tramp, jog-trot, turn, stalk, perambulation; noctambulation; somnambulism, sleep walking; outing, ride, drive, airing, jaunt.
equitation, horsemanship, riding, *manège*, ride and tie.

roving, vagrancy, pererration; marching and countermarching; nomadism; vagabond-ism, -age; gadding; flit, -ting; migration; e-, im-, de-, inter- migration.

plan, itinerary, guide; hand-, road- book; Baedeker, Murray, Bradshaw, time table.

procession, parade, cavalcade, caravan, file, *cortège*, column.

[Organs and instruments of locomotion] vehicle etc. 272; locomotive etc. 271; legs, feet, pegs, pins, trotters.

traveler etc. 268.

V. travel, journey, course; tour; take —, go- a journey, take —, go out for- -a walk etc. *n.*; have a run; take the air.

flit, take wing; migrate, emigrate, *trek*; rove, prowl, roam, range, patrol, pace up and down, traverse; scour —, traverse- the country; peragrate; per-, circum-ambulate; nomadize, wander, ramble, stroll, saunter, hover, go one's rounds, straggle; gad; — about; expatiate.

walk, march, step, tread, pace, plod, wend; promenade; trudge, tramp; stalk, stride, straddle, strut, foot it, stump, bundle, bowl along, toddle; paddle; tread —, follow —, pursue- a path.

take horse, ride, drive, trot, amble, canter, prance, fisk, frisk, *caracoler*; gallop etc. (*move quickly*) 274; motor, cycle, taxi; go by -car, — train, — tram, — bus, — plane.

peg —, jog —, wag —, shuffle- on; stir one's stumps; bend one's -steps, — course; make —, find —, wend —, pick —, thread —, plough- one's way; coast, slide, glide, skim, skate, ski; march in procession, file off, defile.

go —, repair —, resort —, hie —, betake oneself- to.

Adj. traveling etc. *v.*; ambulatory, itinerant, peripatetic, perambulatory, roving, rambling, gadding, discursive, vagrant, migratory, nomadic; circumforane-an, -ous; somnambular, nocti-, mundi- vagant; locomotive, automotive, self-moving.

way-faring, -worn; travel-stained.

Adv. on -foot, — horseback, — Shanks's mare; by the Marrowbone stage; *in transitu* etc. 270; *en route* etc. 282.

Int. come along!

267. Navigation. [Locomotion by water, or air.]—**N.** navigation; aquatics; boating, cruising, yachting; ship etc. 273; oar, scull, sweep, punt pole, paddle, — wheel, screw, propeller, stern wheel, sail, canvas.

natation, swimming; fin, flipper, fish's tail.

aeronautics, aviation, flying, winging, cruising, gliding, ballooning; blind —, instrument — flying; avigation, take-off.

flight, trip, run; solo —, nolo (pilotless) —, supersonic —, test — flight; air -lift, -drop; shuttle, reconnaisence, mission, dry run (coll.), search mission, combat flight, sortie, air raid, bombing mission; air — support, — cover, — umbrella; formation flying, maneuvers, aerobatics, stunt flying (coll.), diving, rolling, barrel roll, spin, tail spin, loop, buzzing.

landing, instrument —, crash — landing.

angle, center, axis, stability, load, pressure, torsion, torque, thrust, propulsion, jet propulsion, pitch, lift, dray, yaw, resistance, drift, flow, wash.

course, heading, altitude; air -route, -lane.

voyage, sail, cruise, passage, circumnavigation, *periplus*; head-, stern-, lee-way.

astro-, cosmo- nautics; space —, interplanetary — travel; space — exploration, — flight.

mariner, aeronaut etc. 269.

V. sail; put to sea etc. (*depart*) 293; take ship, get under way; spread -sail, — canvas; gather way, have way on; make —, carry- sail; plough the - waves, — deep, — main, — ocean; walk the waters.

navigate, warp, luff, scud, boom, kedge; drift, course, cruise, coast; hug the -shore, — land; circumnavigate.

ply the oar, row, paddle, pull, scull, punt, steam.

swim, float; buffet the waves, ride the storm, skim, *effleurer*, dive, wade.

fly, pilot, copilot, astronavigate, solo, take off, taxi, ascend, climb, stunt, spin, loop, roll, dive, buzz, land, descend, level off, bail out, parachute.

Adj. sailing etc. *v.*; seafaring, nautical, maritime, naval; sea-going, coasting; afloat; navigable, aquatic, *natatory*.

volitant, volant, aerostatic, aerial, aeronautic; alar, alate, pennate.

Adv. under -way, — sail, — canvas, — steam; on the wing.

268. Traveler.—**N.** traveler, wayfarer, voyager, itinerant, passenger.

tourist, excursionist, globe-trotter; explorer, adventurer, mountaineer, Alpine Club; peregrinator, wanderer, rover, straggler, rambler; bird of passage; gad-about, -ling; vagrant, scatterling, landloper, waifs and estrays, wastrel, stray; loafer; tramp, -er, hobo, beachcomber, vagabond, nomad, Bohemian, gipsy, Arab, Wandering Jew, Hadji, pilgrim, palmer; peripatetic; somnambulist; sleep walker, noctambulist; emigrant, fugitive, refugee, *émigré*.

runner, courier, King's messenger; Mercury, Iris, Ariel, comet.

pedestrian, walker, foot-passenger; cyclist; wheelman.

rider, horseman, equestrian, cavalier, jockey, rough rider, trainer, breaker, huntsman.

driver, coachman, whip, Jehu, charioteer, postilion, post-boy, carter, wagoner, drayman, truckman; cab-man, -driver; *voiturier*, *vetturino*, *condottiere*; engine-driver; stoker, fireman, guard, brakeman, conductor; chauffeur, automobilist, motorist, motor —, truck —, taxi- driver.

269. Mariner.—**N.** sailor, mariner, navigator, argonaut; sea-man, -farer, -faring man; yachtsman; tar, jack tar, salt, gob, sea-dog, shellback, able seaman, A.B.; man-of-war's man, bluejacket, marine, jolly; midshipman, middy, reefer; captain, commander, master mariner, skipper, mate; ship-, boat-, ferry-, water-, lighter-, barge-, longshore- man, hoveller; bargee, gondolier; oar-, -sman; rower; boat-, cock-swain; coxswain; steersman, helmsman, pilot; crew; lascar.

aerial navigator, navigator; aero-, astro-, cosmonaut; balloonist, Icarus, aviator, pilot, flyer, copilot, spaceman; fighter —, bomber — pilot; bombardier, gunner; meteorologist; stewardess, aviatrix, aviatress; ground crew, aeromechanic, aeronautical engineer; parachutist, paratrooper.

270. Transference.—N. transfer, -ence; trans-, e-location; displacement; *meta-stasis*, *-thesis*; removal; re-, a-motion; relegation; de-, asportation; extradition, conveyance, draft; carrying, carriage; convection, -duction, -tagion, infection; transfusion; transfer etc. (*of property*) 783.

transit, transition; passage, ferry, gestation; portage, porterage, carting, cartage; shoveling etc. *v.*; vect-ion, -ure, -itation; shipment, freight, wafture; trans-mission, -port, -portation, -umption, -plantation, -lation; shift-, dodg-ing; dispersion etc. 73; transposition etc. (*interchange*) 148; traction etc. 285.

[Thing transferred] drift, alluvium, detritus, *moraine*; gift, legacy, bequest, lease; freight, mails, cargo, luggage, baggage, goods.

V. trans-fer, -mit, -port, -place, -plant; convey, assign, carry, bear; fetch and carry; carry —, ferry-over; hand, pass, forward; shift; conduct, convoy, bring, fetch, reach.

send, delegate, consign, mail post, relegate, turn over to, pass the buck, deliver; ship, embark; waft; switch, shunt; transpose etc. (*interchange*) 148; displace etc. 185; throw etc. 284; drag etc. 285.

shovel, lade, dip, ladle, bale, decant, draft off, transfuse.

Adj. transferred etc. *v.*; drifted; movable, portable, -ative; conductive; contagious, infectious.

transferable, assignable, conveyable, devisable, negotiable, transmissible.

Adv. from -hand to hand, — pillar to post.

on —, by- the way; on the -road, — wing; as one goes; *in transitu*, *en route*, *chemin faisant*, *en passant*, in mid-progress.

271. Carrier.—N. carrier, porter, red cap, bearer, messenger, postman, tranter, conveyer; stevedore; coolie; conductor, locomotive, tractor, caterpillar tractor, motor.

beast of burden, cattle, horse steed, nag, palfrey, Arab, blood horse, thorough-bred, galloway, charger, courser, racer, hunter, jument, pony, filly, colt, foal, barb, roan, jade, hack, *bidet*, pad, cob, tit, punch, roadster, goer; race-, pack-, draft-, cart-, dray-, post-horse, mount; Shetland pony, sheltie; garran; jennet, genet, bayard, mare, stallion, gelding; stud.

Pegasus, Bucephalus, Rozinante.

ass, donkey, jackass, mule, hinny; sumpter -horse, — mule; reindeer; camel, dromedary, mehari, llama, elephant; carrier pigeon.

carriage etc. (*vehicle*) 272; ship etc. 273.

Adj. equine, asinine.

272. Vehicle.—N. vehicle, conveyance, carriage, car, caravan, van, furniture van, pantechnicon; wagon, wain, dray, cart, lorry.

carriole; sledge, sled, sleigh, bob-sleigh, toboggan, *luge*, truck, tram; limber, tumbrel, pontoon; barrow; wheel-, hand- -barrow, — cart, trolley; perambulator; Bath —, wheel —, sedan-chair, jinriksha, rickshaw; ekka; chaise; palankeen, -quin; litter, horse-litter, brancard, crate, hurdle, stretcher, ambulance; velocipede, hobby-horse, coaster, scooter, go-cart; cycle; bi-, tri-, quadri-cycle; tandem, safety; skate, roller —, ice — skate; sled, sleigh; ski, snow-shoe.

equipage, turn-out; coach, chariot; *quadriga*, chaise, phaëton, break, brake, mail-phaëton, wagonette, drag, curricle, tilbury, whisky, landau, *barouche*, victoria, brougham, clarence, calash, *calèche*, britzska, *araba*, kibitka; berlin; sulky, *désobligeant*, sociable, *vis-à-vis*, *dormeuse*; jaunting —, outside- car; *tarantass*; runabout; shay.

post-chaise; diligence, stage; stage —, mail —, hackney —, glass- coach; stage-wagon; car, omnibus, bus, fly, *cabriolet*, cab, hansom, shofle, fourwheeler, growler, *droshki*, drosky.

dog-cart, trap, gig, whitechapel, buggy, four-in-hand, unicorn, random, tandem; shandredhan, *char-à-banc*.

automobile, motor-, auto-, touring-, racing-, cycle-, side-, steam-, electric- car; motor — cycle, — bike; motorized vehicle; bus, mini-bus; buggy, crate, tub, flivver, jalopy, wreck, clunker, dog, heap (all slang); coupe, coup, sedan, convertible, hard-top; camper, trailer, mobile home; limosine, landaulette, cabriolet, *coupé*, *voiturette*, runabout, electromobile, taxi, -cab.

train; passenger —, express —, freight —, subway —, special —, corridor —, parliamentary —, luggage —, goods- train, *train de luxe*; 1st-, 2nd-, 3rd- class- -train, — carriage, — compartment; Pullman —, sleeping-, club-, observation-, dining-, restaurant-car; mail-, luggage-, brake-van, coach, car, carriage; rolling stock; horse-box, cattle- truck.

273. Ship.—N. ship, vessel, sail; craft, bottom. navy, marine, fleet, flotilla, squadron; shipping.

man of war etc. (*combatant*) 726; transport, tender, store-ship; merchant ship, merchantman; packet, liner; whaler, slaver, collier, coaster, tanker, freighter, freight steamer, cargo boat, lighter; fishing-, pilot- boat; trawler, drifter; cable ship; hulk; yacht; floating palace, ocean greyhound.

ship, bark, barque, brig, snow, hermaphrodite brig; brigantine, barquentine; schooner; topsail —, fore and aft —, three masted- schooner; *chasse-marée*; sloop, cutter, corvette, clipper, foist, yawl, dandy, ketch, smack, lugger, barge, hoy, cat-, -boat, buss; sail-er, -ing vessel, wind jammer; steamer, -boat, -ship; mail—, paddle —, screw —, stern-wheel- steamer; tug; train-ferry; line of steamers etc.

boat, pinnace, launch, motor-boat, picket-boat; hydroplane; life-, long-, jolly-, bum-, fly-, cock-, ferry-, canal- boat, dory, dugout, galliot; shallop, gig, funny, skiff, dingy, scow, cockleshell, wherry, coble, punt, cog, lerret; eight-, four-, pair- oar; randan; out- rigger; float, raft, pontoon; prame, ice-yacht.

state barge, bucentaur.

catamaran, coracle, gondola, carvel, caravel; felucca, caique, canoe; trireme; galley, — foist; bilander, dogger, hooker, howker; argosy, carack; galliass, galleon; galliot, polacca, polacre, corsair, tartane, junk, lorcha, praam, proa, prahu, saick, sampan, xebec, dhow; dahabeah; nuggar, cayak, piroque; trireme.

submarine, submersible.

aircraft (*combatant*) etc. 726; flying machine, air mail, aero-, air-, mono-, bi-, tri-, hydro aeroplane, plane, cabin —, transport —, propeller — plane; *avion*, flying boat, glider; helicopter, rotor —, gyro-plane, whirlybird, autogyro, gyrodine; sea-, hydro-plane; amphibian; jet, — plane; turbo-, ram-, pulse-, subsonic —, supersonic —, strato- jet; rocket — plane, — ship.; space ship; war-, combat — plane; kamikaze, fleet, armada; trainer, fliight simulator; aerostat, dirigible, blimp (coll.), zeppelin; parachute, chute (coll.); kite.

rocket, flying —, ballistic —, guided — missile; projectile; rocket —, robot —, buzz-bomb; multistage —, step —, test — rocket; booster; satellite; flying saucer, unidentified flying object. (UFO).

nacelle, car, gondola, aileron; hangar, airport, landing field, airdrome; catwalk, controls, rudder, tail.

Adj. marine, maritime, naval, nautical, seafaring, sea-, ocean-going, sea-worthy.

aerial, aeronautical, air-worthy, flying etc. *n.*

Adv. afloat, aboard; on -board, — ship board, — board ship.

274. Velocity.—N. velocity, speed, celerity; swiftness etc. *adj.*; rapidity, eagle speed; expedition etc. (*activity*) 682; pernicity; acceleration; haste etc. 684.

spurt, rush, dash, race, steeplechase; smart —, lively —, swift etc. *adj.* —, rattling —, spanking —, strapping- -rate, — pace; round pace; flying, flight.

gallop, canter, trot, round trot, run, scamper; hand —, full- gallop; swoop.

lightning, light, electricity, wind; cannon-ball, rocket, arrow, dart, quicksilver; telegraph, express train; torrent; swallow flight.

eagle, antelope, courser, race-horse, gazelle, greyhound, hare, doe, squirrel.

Mercury, Ariel, Camilla, Harlequin.

[Measurement of velocity.] speedometer, log, -line, tachometer.

air speed, speed of sound, sonic —, subsonic —, supersonic —, ultrasonic —, hypersonic —, transonic — speed.

V. move quickly, trip, fisk; speed, hie, hasten, sprint, spurt, post, spank, scuttle; scud, -dle, scurry; scour, — the plain; scamper, sprint, dash, run, — like mad; fly, race, run a race, cut away, cut and run, shoot, tear, whisk, whiz, sweep, skim, brush; cut —, bowl- along; rush etc. (*be violent*) 173; dash -on, — off, — forward; bolt; trot, gallop, bound, flit, spring, dart, boom; march in -quick, — double-time; ride hard; et over the ground, scorch.

hurry etc. (*hasten*) 684; accelerate, put on; quicken; quicken —, mend- one's pace; clap spurs to one's horse; make-haste, — rapid strides, — forced marches, — the best of one's way; put one's best leg foremost, stir one's stumps, wing one's way, set off at a score; carry —, crowd- sail; go off like a shot, go ahead, gain ground; outstrip the wind, fly on the wings of the wind.

keep -up, — pace- with; outstrip etc. 303.

Adj. fast, speedy, swift, rapid, quick, fleet; nimble, agile, expeditious; express; active etc. 682; flying, galloping etc. *v.*; light- nimble-footed; winged; eagle-winged, mercurial, electric telegraphic; light-legged; light of heel; swift as -an arrow etc. *n.*; quick as -lightning etc. *n.*, — thought.*

Adv. swiftly etc. *adj.*; with -speed etc. *n.*; apace; at -a great rate, — full speed, — railway speed; full -drive, — gallop; post-haste, in full sail, tantivy; trippingly; instantaneously etc. 113; like a shot.

under press of -sale, — canvas, — sail and steam; *velis et remis*, on eagle's wing, in double quick time; with -rapid, — giant- strides; *à pas de géant*; in seven league boots; whip and spur; *ventre à terre*; as fast as one's -legs, — heels- will carry one; as fast on one can lay feet to the ground, at the top of one's speed; by leaps and bounds; with haste etc. 684; in- high — gear, — speed.

Phr. *vires acquirit eundo.*

*See note on *274.*

275. Slowness.—N. slowness etc. *adj.*; languor etc. (*inactivity*) 683; drawl; creeping etc. *v.*, lentor.

retardation; slackening etc. *v.*; delay etc. (*lateness*) 133; claudication.

jog-, dog-trot, walk; mincing steps; slow -march, — time.

slow -goer, — coach, — back; lingerer, loiterer, sluggard, tortoise, snail; dawdle etc. (*inactive*) 683.

V. move -slowly, etc. *adv.*; creep, crawl, lag, slug, walk, drawl, linger, loiter, saunter; plod, trudge, stump along, lumber; trail; drag; dawdle etc. (*be inactive*) 683; grovel, worm one's way, steal along; jog —, rub —, bundle- on; toddle, waddle, wabble, slug; traipse, slouch, shuffle, halt, hobble, limp, claudicate, shamble; flag, falter, totter, stagger; mince, step short; march in -slow time, — funeral procession; take one's time; hang fire etc. (*be late*) 133.

retard, relax; slacken, check, moderate, rein in, curb; reef; strike —, shorten —, take in- sail; put on the drag, apply the brake; clip the wings; reduce the speed, decelerate; slacken -speed, — one's pace, lose ground; back -water, — pedal, put the engines astern, throttle down.

Adj. slow, slack; tardy; dilatory etc. (*inactive*) 683; gentle, easy; leisurely; deliberate, gradual; insensible, imperceptible; languid, sluggish, apathetic, phlegmatic, slow-paced, tardigrade, snail-like; creeping etc. *v.*

Adv. slowly etc. *adj.*; leisurely; *piano*, *adagio*; *largo*, *larghetto*; at half speed, under easy sail; at a -foot's, — snail's, — funeral- pace; slower than molasses in January; in slow time; with -mincing steps, — clipped wings; *haud passibus aequis*; in- low —, gear, — speed.

gradually etc. *adj.*; *gradatim*; by -degrees, — slow degrees, — inches, — little and little; step by step; inch by inch, bit by bit, little by little, *seriatim*; consecutively.

276. Impulse.—N. impulse, impulsion, impetus; momentum; push, pulsion, thrust, shove, jog, jolt, brunt, booming, boost, throw; explosion etc. (*violence*) 173; propulsion etc. 284, jet propulsion; firing, launching, projection, trajection.

percussion, concussion, collision, occursion, clash, encounter, cannon, *carambole*, appulse, shock, crash, bump; impact; *élan*; charge etc. (*attack*) 716; beating etc. (*punishment*) 972.

blow, dint, stroke, knock, tap, rap, slap, smack, pat, dab; fillip; slam, bang; hit, whack, thwack, clout; cuff etc. 972; squash, dowse, whap, swap, punch, thump, swipe, jab, pelt, kick, punce, calcitration; *ruade*; arietation; cut, thrust, lunge, yerk.

hammer, sledge-hammer, mall, maul, mallet, flail; ram, -mer; battering-ram, monkey, pile-driver, punch, bat, tamper, tamping iron; cudgel etc. (*weapon*) 727; axe etc. (*sharp*) 253.

[Science of mechanical forces] mechanics, dynamics etc.

V. give an -impetus etc. *n.*; impel, push; start, give a start to, set going; drive, urge, boom; thrust, prod, foin; cant; elbow, shoulder, jostle, justle, hustle, hurtle, shove, jog, jolt, bean, encounter; run –, bump –, butt- against; knock –, run- one's head against; impinge.

fire, launch, project, traject, propel, 284.

strike, knock, hit, bash, tap, rap, bat, slap, flap, dab, pat, thump, beat, bang, slam, dash; punch, thwack, whack; hit –, strike- hard; swap, batter, dowse, baste; pelt, patter, skelter, buffet, belabor, tamp; fetch one a blow, swat; poke at, pink, lunge, yerk; kick, calcitrate; butt; strike at etc. (*attack*) 716; whip etc. (*punish*) 972; propel etc. 284.

come –, enter- into collision; collide; foul; fall –, run- foul of.

throw etc.

Adj. impelling etc. *v.*; im-pulsive, -pellent; booming; dynamic, -al; impelled etc. *v.*

277. Recoil.—N. recoil; re-, retro-action; revulsion; rebound, *ricochet*; re-percussion, -calcitration; kick, *contre-coup*; springing back etc. *v.*; elasticity etc. 325; reflexion, reflex, reflux; reverberation etc. (*resonance*) 408; rebuff, repulse; return.

ducks and drakes; boomerang; spring; reactionist, reactionary.

V. recoil, resile, react; spring –, fly –, bound-back; rebound, reverberate, repercuss, recalcitrate, echo, *ricochet*.

Adj. recoiling etc. *v.*; re-fluent, -percussive, -calcitrant, -actionary; retroactive.

Adv. on the -recoil etc. *n.*

278. Direction.—N. direction, bearing, course, set, drift, tenor; tendency etc. 176; incidence; bending, trending etc. *v.*; dip, tack, aim, collimation; steer-ing, -age.

point of the compass, cardinal –, half –, quarter- points; North, East, South, West; N by E, ENE, NE by N, NE etc; rhumb, azimuth, line of collimation.

line, path, road, range, quarter, line of march; alignment; straight shot, bee-line.

course, bearing, heading, altitude, air -route, -lane, angle, center, axis, torsion, torque, pitch, lift, drift, flow, wash.

V. tend –, bend –, point- towards; conduct –, go- to; point -to, – at; bend, trend, verge, incline, dip, determine.

steer –, make- -for, – towards; aim –, level- at; take aim; keep –, hold- a course; be bound for; bend one's steps towards; direct –, steer –, bend –, shape- one's course; align –, align- one's march; go straight, – to the point; march -on, – on a point.

ascertain one's -direction etc. *n.*; *s'orienter*, see which way the wind blows; box the compass.

Adj. directed etc. *v.*, – towards; pointing towards etc. *v.*; bound for; aligned –, with; direct, straight; un-deviating, -swerving; straightforward; North, -ern, -erly, etc. *n.*

directable etc. *v.*

Adv. towards; on the -road, – high road- to; versus, to; hither, thither, whither; directly; straight, – forwards, – as an arrow; point blank; in a -direct, – straight- line -to, – for, – with; in a line with; full tilt at, as the crow flies.

before –, near –, close to –, against- the wind; windwards, in the wind's eye.

through, *via*, by way of; in all -directions, – manner of ways; *quaqua-versum*, from the four winds.

279. Deviation.—N. deviation; swerving etc. *v.*; obliquation, warp, refraction; flection, flexion; sweep; de-flection, -flexure; declination.

diversion, digression, departure from, aberration, drift, sheer; divergence etc. 291; zigzag; *détour* etc. (*circuit*) 629.

[Desultory motion] wandering etc. *v.*; vagrancy, evagation; by-paths and crooked ways.

[Motion sideways, oblique motion] sidling etc. *v.*; *échelon*, leeway; knight's move (at chess).

V. alter one's course, deviate, depart from, turn, trend; bend, curve, etc. 245; swerve, heel, bear off.

intervert; deflect; divert, – from its course; put on a new scent, shift, shunt, switch, wear, draw aside, crook, warp, short circuit.

stray, straggle; sidle, edge; diverge etc. 291; tralineate, digress, divagate, wander; wind, twist, meander, meander around Robin Hood's barn; veer, tack, sheer; turn -aside, – a corner, – away from; wheel, steer clear of; ramble, rove, drift; go -astray, – adrift; yaw, dodge; step aside, ease off, make way for, shy.

fly off at a tangent; glance off; turn, wheel –, face- about; turn –, face- to the right about; wabble etc. (*oscillate*) 314; go out of one's way etc. (*perform a circuit*) 629; lose one's way.

Adj. deviating etc. *v.*; aberrant, errant; ex-, dis-cursive; devious, desultory, loose; rambling; stray, erratic, vagrant, undirected; circuitous, indirect, zigzag; crab-like.

Adv. astray from, round about, wide of the mark; to the right about; all manner of ways; circuitously etc. 629.

obliquely, sideling, like the move of the knight on a chessboard.

280. Precession. [Going before.]**—N.** precession, leading, heading; precedence etc. 62; priority etc. 116; the lead, *le pas*; van etc. (*front*) 234; precursor etc. 64.

V. go -before, – ahead, – in the van, – in advance; precede, forerun; usher in, introduce, herald, head, take the lead; lead, – the way, – the dance; get –, have- the start; steal a march; get -before, – ahead, – in front of; outstrip etc. 303; take precedence etc. (*first in order*) 62.

Adj. foremost, first, leading etc. *v.*

Adv. in advance, before, ahead, in the van; fore-head-most; in front.

Phr. *seniores priores.*

281. Sequence. [Going after.]—**N.** sequence, run; coming after etc. (*order*) 63; (*time*) 117; following; pursuit etc. 622.

follower, attendant, satellite, shadow, dangler, train.

V. follow; pursue etc. 622; go –, fly- after.

attend, beset, dance attendance on, dog, be-dog; tread -in the steps of, – close upon; be –, go –, follow- in the -wake, – trail, – rear- of; trail, follow as a shadow, hang on the skirts of; tread –, follow- on the heels of, tag after.

lag, get behind.

Adj. following etc. *v.*

Adv. behind; in the -rear etc. 235, – train of, wake of; after etc. (*order*) 63, (*time*) 117.

282. Progression. [Motion forwards; progressive motion.]—**N.** progress, -ion, -iveness; advancing etc. *v.*; advance, -ment; ongoing; flood-tide, headway; march etc. 266; rise; improvement etc. 658.

V. advance; proceed, progress; get -on, – along, – over the ground; gain ground; jog –, rub –, wag- on; go with the stream; keep –, hold on- one's course; go –, move –, come –, get –, pass –, push –, press- -on, – forward, – forwards, – ahead; press onwards, step forward; make –, work –, carve –, push –, force –, edge –, elbow- one's way; make -progress, – head, – way, – headway, – advances, – strides, – -rapid strides etc. (*velocity*) 274; go –, shoot- ahead; distance; make up leeway.

Adj. advancing etc. *v.*; pro-gressive, -fluent; advanced.

Adv. forward, onward; forth, on ahead, under way, ***en route*** for, on -one's way, – the way, – the road, – the high road- to; in -progress, – mid progress; ***in transitu*** etc. 270.

Phr. ***vestigia nulla retrorsum.***

283. Regression. [Motion backwards.]—**N.** regress, -ion; retro-cession, -gression, -gradation, -action; ***reculade***; retreat, withdrawal, retirement, remigration; recession etc. (*motion from*) 287; recess; crab-like motion.

re-fluence, -flux; backwater, regurgitation, ebb, return; resilience; reflexion (*recoil*) 277; ***volte-face***.

counter -motion, – movement, – march; veering, tergiversation, recidivation, backsliding, fall, relapse; deterioration etc. 659.

turning point etc. (*reversion*) 145.

V. re-cede, -grade, -turn, -vert, -treat, -tire; retro-grade, -cede; back, – down, – out, crawl; withdraw; rebound etc. 277; go –, come –, turn –, hark –, draw –, fall –, get –, put –, run- back; lose ground; fall –, drop- astern; back water, put about; veer, – round; double, wheel, counter-march; ebb, regurgitate; *jib*, shrink, shy.

turn -tail, – round, – upon one's heel, – one's back upon; retrace one's steps, dance the back step; sound –, beat- a retreat; go home.

Adj. receding etc. *v.*; retro-grade, -gressive; regressive, -fluent, -flex, -cidivous, -silient; crab-like; reactionary etc. 277; counter-clockwise.

Adv. back, -wards; reflexively, to the right about; ***à reculons, à rebours.***

Phr. ***revenons à nos moutons***, as you were.

284. Propulsion. [Motion given to an object situated in front.]—**N.** pro-pulsion, -jection; ***vis a tergo***; push etc. (*impulse*) 276; e-, jaculation; ejection etc. 297; throw, fling, toss, shot, discharge, shy.

[Science of propulsion] steam –, gas –, diesel –, jet –, rocket – propulsion, gunnery, ballistics, archery.

missile, projectile, ball, *discus*, javelin, hammer, quoit, brickbat, shot, bullet; arrow, shaft, gun etc. (*arms*) 727.

shooter, shot; gunner, gun-layer; archer, toxophilite; bow-, rifle-, marks- man; good –, crack- shot; sharpshooter etc. (*combatant*) 726.

V. propel, project, throw, fling, cast, pitch, chuck, toss, jerk, heave, shy, hurl; flirt, fillip.

dart, lance, tilt; e-, jaculate; fulminate, bolt, drive, sling, pitchfork.

send; send –, let –, fire- off; discharge, shoot; launch, send forth, let fly; dash.

put –, set- in motion; set agoing, start; give -a start, – an impulse- to; push, impel etc. 276; trundle etc. (*set in rotation*) 312; expel etc. 297.

carry one off one's legs; put to flight.

Adj. propelled etc. *v.*; propelling etc. *v.*; propulsive, -jectile.

285. Traction. [Motion given to an object situated behind.]—**N.** traction; drawing etc. *v.*; draft, pull, tug, haul; rake; 'a long pull, a strong pull and a pull all together;' towage, haulage.

V. draw, pull, haul, lug, rake, drag, draggle, tug, tow, trail, trawl, train; take in tow.

wrench, jerk, twitch.

Adj. drawing etc. *v.*; tractive, tractile; ductile, pulling, hauling, tugging, towing.

286. Approach. Motion towards.]—**N.** approach, approximation, appropinquation; access; appulse; afflux, -ion; advent etc. (*approach of time*) 121; pursuit etc. 622; convergence etc. 290.

V. approach, approximate; near; get –, go –, draw- near; come, – near, – to close quarters; move –, set in- towards; drift; make up to; gain upon; pursue etc. 622; tread on the heels of; bear up; make the land; hug the -shore, – land.

Adj. approaching etc. *v.*; approximative; convergent; affluent; impending, imminent etc. (*destined*) 152.

Adv. on the road.

Int. come hither! approach! here! come! come near!

287. Recession. [Motion from.]—**N.** recession, retirement, withdrawal; retreat; retrocession etc. 283; departure etc. 293; recoil etc. 277; flight etc. (*avoidance*) 623.

V. recede, go, move from, retire, ebb, withdraw, shrink; come –, move –, go –, get –, drift- away; depart etc. 293; retreat etc. 283; move –, stand –, sheer- off; swerve from; fall back, stand aside; run away etc. (*avoid*) 623.

remove, shunt, side track, switch off.

Adj. receding etc. *v.*

288. Attraction. [Motion towards, actively.]—**N.** attract-ion, -iveness; pull; drawing to, pulling towards, adduction, magnetism, gravity, attraction of gravitation; lure, bait, decoy.

lode-stone, -star; magnet, siderite, magnetite.

V. attract; draw –, pull –, drag- towards; adduce.

lure, bait, decoy.

Adj. attracting etc. *v.*; attrahent, attractive, adducent, adductive, alluring.

289. Repulsion. [Motion from, actively.]—**N.** repulsion; driving from etc. *v.*; repulse; abduction.

V. repel; push –, drive – etc. 276; from; chase, dispel; retrude; abduce, abduct; send away, repulse, dismiss.

keep at arm's length, turn one's back upon, give the cold shoulder; send packing; send -off, – away- with a flea in one's ear, – about one's business.

Adj. repelling etc. *v.*; repellant, repulsive; abducent, abductive.

290. Convergence. [Motion nearer to.]—**N.** con-vergence, -fluence, -course, -flux, -gress, -currence, -centration; appulse, meeting; corradiation.

assemblage etc. 72; resort etc. (*focus*) 74; asymptote.

V. converge, concur; come together, unite, meet, fall in with; close -with, – in upon; center -round, – in; enter in; pour in.

gather together, unite, concentrate, bring into a focus.

Adj. converging etc. *v.*; con-vergent, -fluent, -current; centripetal; asymptotical.

291. Divergence. [Motion further off.]—**N.** diverg-ence, -ency; divarication, ramification, radiation; separation etc. (*disjunction*) 44; dispersion etc. 73; deviation etc. 279; aberration, declination.

V. diverge, divaricate, radiate; ramify; branch –, glance –, file- off; fly off, – at a tangent; spread, scatter, disperse etc. 73; deviate etc. 279; part etc. (*separate*) 44; splay apart.

Adj. diverging etc. *v.*; divergent, radiant, centrifugal; aberrant.

292. Arrival. [Terminal motion at.]—**N.** arrival, advent; landing; de-, disem-barkation; reception, welcome, *vin d'honneur*.

home, goal, bourn; landing-place, -stage; resting –, stopping -place; destination, harbor, haven, port; terminal, terminus, railway station, depot, airport; halt, halting -place, – ground; anchorage etc. (*refuge*) 666.

return, recursion, remigration; meeting; ren-, encounter.

completion etc. 729.

V. arrive; get to, come to; come; reach, attain; come up, – with, – to; overtake; make, fetch; complete etc. 729; join, rejoin.

light, alight, dismount; land, go ashore; debark, disembark; put -in, – into; visit, cast anchor, pitch one's tent; sit down etc. (*be located*) 184; get to one's journey's end; make the land; be in at the death; come –, get- -back, – home; return; come in etc. (*ingress*) 294; make one's appearance etc. (*appear*) 446; drop in; detrain; outspan.

come to hand; come -at, – across; hit; come –, light –, pop –, bounce –, plump –, burst –, pitch- upon; meet; en- ren-counter; come in contact.

Adj. arriving etc. *v.*; homewardbound; terminal.

Adv. here, hither.

Int. welcome! hail! all hail! good- day, – morrow; greetings! hullo! well!

293. Departure. [Initial motion from.]—**N.** departure, decession, decampment; embarkation; take-off; outset, start; removal; exit etc. (*egress*) 295; exodus, Hejira, flight.

leave-taking, *congé*, valediction, valedictory, adieu, farewell, good-bye, stirrup-cup.

starting -point, – post; point –, place- of -departure, – embarkation; port of embarkation.

V. depart; go, – away; take one's departure, set out; set –, march –, put –, start –, be –, move –, get –, whip –, pack –, go –, take oneself- off; start, issue, march out, debouch; go –, sally- forth; sally, set forward; be gone.

leave a place, quit, vacate, evacuate, abandon; go off the stage, make ones' exit; retire, withdraw, remove; go -one's way, – along, – from home; take -flight, – wing; spring, fly, flit, wing one's flight; fly –, whip- away; take off, hop off; embark; go -on board, – aboard; set sail; put –, go- to sea; sail, take ship; hoist blue Peter; get under way, weigh anchor; strike tents, break camp, decamp; walk one's chalks, make tracks, cut one's stick; cut and run; take leave; say –, bid- -good-bye etc. *n.*; disappear etc. 449; abscond etc. (*avoid*) 623; entrain, embus, emplane; saddle –, harness –, hitch- up; inspan.

Adj. departing etc. *v.*; valedictory; outward bound.

Adv. whence, hence, thence; with a foot in the stirrup; on the -wing, – move.

Int. begone! etc. (*ejection*) 297; to horse! all aboard! farewell! adieu! good-bye, – day! *au revoir! auf wiedersehen!* fare you well! so long! God -bless you, – speed! *bon vayage!*

294. Ingress. [Motion into.]—**N.** ingress; entrance, entry; introgression; influx; intrusion, inroad, incursion, invasion, irruption; pene-, interpene- tration; illapse, import, importation, infiltration; immigration; admission etc. (*reception*) 296; insinuation etc. (*interjacence*) 228; insertion etc. 300.

inlet; way in; mouth, door etc. (*opening*) 260; path etc. (*way*) 627; conduit etc. 350; immigrant, visitor, incomer, newcomer, colonist.

V. have the *entrée*; enter; go –, come –, pour –, flow –, creep –, slip –, pop –, break –, burst- -into, – in; set foot on; burst –, break-in upon; invade, intrude, butt in, horn in, crash; insinuate itself; inter-, penetrate; infiltrate; find one's way –, wriggle –, worm oneself- into.

give entrance to etc. (*receive*) 296; insert etc. 300.

Adj. incoming, ingressive etc. *n.*; inward bound.
Adv. inward.

295. Egress. [Motion out of.]—**N.** egress, exit, issue; emer-sion, -gence; disemboguement; out-break, -burst; e-, pro-ruption; emanation; evacuation; ex, trans-udation; extravasation, perspiration, sweating, leakage, percolation, distillation, oozing; gush etc. (*water in motion*) 348; outpour, -ing; effluence, effusion; efflux, -ion; drain; dribbling etc. *v.*; defluxion; drainage; outcome, -put; discharge etc. (*excretion*) 299.
export; expatriation; e-, re-migration; *débouche*; exodus etc. (*departure*) 293; emigrant, migrant, *émigré*, colonist.
outlet, vent, spout, tap, sluice, floodgate; pore; vomitory, out-gate, sally-port; way out; mouth, door etc. (*opening*) 260; path etc. (*way*) 627; conduit etc. 350; air-pipe etc. 351.
V. emerge, emanate, issue; go –, come –, move –, pass –, pour –, flow- out of; pass off, evacuate; migrate.
ex-, trans-ude; leak; run, – out, – through; per-, trans-colate; seep; strain, distil; perspire, sweat, drain, ooze; filter, filtrate; dribble, gush, spout, flow out; well, – out; pour, trickle etc. (*water in motion*) 348; effuse, extravasate, disembogue, discharge itself, debouch; come –, break-forth; burst- out, – through; find vent, escape etc. 671.
Adj. effused etc. *v.*; outgoing, outward bound.
Adv. outward.

296. Reception. [Motion into, actively.]—**N.** reception; admission, admittance, *entrée*, importation; initiation; intro-duction, -mission, -ception; immission, ingestion, imbibition, absorption, ingurgitation, inhalation, suction, sucking; eating, drinking etc. (*food*) 298; insertion etc. 300; interjection etc. 228.
V. give -entrance to, – admittance to, – the *entrée*; intro-duce, -mit; usher, admit, receive, import, initiate, bring in, open the door to, throw open, ingest, absorb, imbibe, inhale, infiltrate; let –, take –, suck- in; re-admit, -sorb, -absorb; snuff up; swallow, ingurgitate; enfull, engorge, gulp; eat, drink etc. (*food*) 298.
Adj. admit-ting etc. *v.*, -ted etc. *v.*; admissible; absorbent; introductory, introceptive, intromittent, initiatory.

297. Ejection. [Motion out of, actively.]—**N.** ejection, emission, effusion, rejection, expulsion, eviction, extrusion, trajection; discharge.
egestion, evacuation, vomition, disgorgement, voidance, eruption, eruptiveness; ruc-, eruc-tation, blood-letting, venesection, phlebotomy, paracentesis; tapping, drainage; clear-ance, -age, voidance; vomiting, excretion etc. 299.
deportation; banishment etc. (*punishment*) 972; rogue's march; relegation, extradition; dislodgment.
V. give -exit, – vent- to; let –, give –, pour –, send- out; des-, dis-patch; exhale, excern, excrete, disembogue, secrete, secern; extravasate, shed, void, evacuate, egest, emit; open the -sluices, – floodgates; turn on the tap; extrude, detrude; effuse, spend, expend; pour forth; squirt, spirt, spill, slop; perspire etc. (*exude*) 295; breathe, blow etc. (*wind*) 349.
tap, draw off; bale –, lade- out; let blood, broach.
eject, reject; expel, discard; cut, send to Coventry, boycott, ostracize; *chasser*; banish etc. (*punish*) 972; throw etc. 284 -out, – up, – off, – away, – aside; push etc. 276 -out, – off, – away, – aside; shovel –, sweep- -out, – away; brush –, whisk –, turn –, send- -off, – away; discharge; send –, turn –, cast- adrift; turn –, bundle- out; throw overboard; give the sack to; send -packing, – about one's business, – to the right about; strike off the roll etc. (*abrogate*) 756; turn out- neck and heels, – head and shoulders, – neck and crop; pack off; send away with a flea in the ear; send to Jericho; bow out, show the door to, dismiss, fire, sack.
turn out of -doors, – house and home; evict, oust; exorcise, un-house, -kennel; dislodge; un-, dis-people; depopulate; relegate, deport.
empty; drain, – to the dregs; sweep off; clear, – off, – out, – away; such, draw off, extract; clean out, make a clean sweep of, clear decks, purge.
em-, dis-, disem-bowel; eviscerate, gut; unearth, root -out, – up; averruncate; weed –, get out; eliminate, get rid of, do away with, shake off; exenterate.
vomit, spew, puke, keck, retch; belch, – out, eruct, eructate; cast –, bring- up; disgorge; expectorate, salivate, clear the throat, hawk, spit, sputter, splutter, slobber, drool, drivel, slaver, slabber.
unpack, unlade, unload, unship; break bulk.
be let out; ooze etc. (*emerge*) 295.
Adj. emitt-ing, -ed etc. *v.*
begone! get you gone! get –, go- away, – along, – along with you! go your way! away, – with! off with you! go, – about your business! be off! avaunt! aroynt! get out!

298. Food. [Eating.]—**N.** eating etc. *v.*; deglutition, gulp, epulation, mastication, manducation, rumination, gastronomy, gastrology; panto-, hippo-, ichthyo-phagy etc.; gluttony etc. 957; carnivorousness, vegetarianism.
mouth, jaws, mandible, mazard, chops.
drinking etc. *v.*; potation, draught, libation; carousal etc. (*amusement*) 840; drunkenness etc. 959.
food, *pabulum*; aliment, nourishment, nutriment; susten-ance, -tation; nurture, subsistence, provender, feed, fodder, provision, ration, keep, commons, board; commissariat etc. (*provision*) 637; prey, forage, pasture, pasturage; fare, cheer; diet, -ary; regimen; belly timber, staff of life; bread, -and cheese; proteins, carbohydrates, vitamines.
comestibles, eatables, victuals, edibles, *ingesta*; grub, prog, tack, hard tack, meat; bread, -stuffs; cereals; viands, cates, delicacy, dainty, creature comforts, contents of the larder, flesh-pots; festal board; ambrosia; good -cheer, – living.
hors-d'oeuvre; soup, pottage, *potage*, broth,

bouillon*, *consommé*, *purée*, *borsch*,** stock, skilly, gumbo; fish, – cakes, – pie; joint, ***rôti*, *pièce de résistance*, *relevé, hash, ***réchauffé***, stew, ***ragoût***, fricassee, mince, ***salim*, *goulash*, *bouillabaisse*, *remove*, *entrée*, *croquette*, *rissole***, sausage, curry, bubble and squeak; haggis, collops, giblets; poultry, game etc.; biscuit, bun, scone, rusk, pancake, pie, pastry, pasty, patty, ***patisseria***, tart, turnover, ***vol-au-vent*, *soufflé***, dumpling, pudding, duff, ***compote***, fritters, cake, napoleon, ***blancmange***, custard, jelly, jam, sweets etc. 396; ***entremet***; oatmeal, porridge, hasty pudding, gruel; eggs, omelet, cheese, matzoon, savory; vegetable, salad, ***mayonnaise***, fruit; sauce, condiment etc. 393; kickshaws.

table, ***cuisine***, bill of fare, ***menu*, *table d'hôte***, ordinary, ***à la carte***; cover.

meal, repast, feed, spread; mess; dish, plate, course, side dish; regale; regale-, refresh-, entertain-ment; refection, collation, picnic, feast, banquet, junket; breakfast; lunch, -eon, ***déjeuner***, bever, tiffin, tea, dinner, supper, snack, whet, bait, dessert; pot-luck, ***table d'hôte*, *déjeuner à la fourchette***; hearty –, square –, substantial –, full- - meal; blow out; light refreshment; pemmican.

mouthful, bolus, gobbet, tit-bit, morsel, sop, sippet.

drink, beverage, liquor, broth, soup; potion, dram, draft, drench, swill; nip, peg, sip, sup, gulp.

wine, champagne, spirits, ***liqueur*** beer, porter, stout, ale, malt liquor, julep, Sir John Barleycorn, stingo, heavy wet, bitter, lager- beer, cider; grog, toddy, flip, purl, punch, negus, cup, bishop, posset, wassail; bitters, ***apéritif***, high-ball, cocktail; whisky, rum, absinthe; gin etc. (***intoxicating liquor***) 959; coffee, chocolate, cocoa, tea, ***maté***, the cup that cheers but not inebriates.

eating-house etc. 189.

V. eat, feed, fare, devour, swallow, take; gulp, bolt, snap; fall to; despatch, dispatch; discuss; take –, get –, gulp-down; lay –, tuck- in; lick, pick, peck; gormandize etc. 957; bite, champ, munch, cranch, craunch, crunch, chew, masticate, nibble, gnaw, mumble.

live on; feed –, batten –, fatten –, feast- upon; browse, graze, crop, regale; carouse etc. (***make merry***) 840; eat heartily, do justice to, play a good knife and fork, banquet.

break -bread, – one's fast; breakfast; lunch, dine, take tea, sup.

drink, – in, – up, – one's fill; quaff, sip, sup; suck, – up; lap; swig; swill, tipple etc. (***be drunken***) 959; empty one's glass, drain the cup; toss -off, – one's glass; wash down, crack a bottle, wet one's whistle.

cater, purvey etc. 637.

Adj. eatable, edible, esculent, comestible, alimentary; cereal, cibarious; dietetic; culinary; nutri-tive, -tious; succulent; drinkable, pot-able, -ulent; bibulous.

omn-, carn-, herb-, frug-, gran-, gramin-, phytivorous; ichthyophagous.

prandial.

299. Excretion.—N. excretion, discharge, emanation; ejection etc. 297; exhalation, exudation, extrusion, secretion, effusion, extravasation, ***ecchymosis***, evacuation, cacation, defecation, dysentery, dejection, ***feces***, excrement; perspiration, sweat; sub-, exud-ation; ***diaphoresis***; sewage.

saliva, spittle, rheum; ptyalism, salivation, catarrh, distemper; diarrhea; ***ejecta*, *egesta*, *sputum*, *sputa***; ***excreta***; lava; ***exuviae*** etc. (***uncleanness***) 653.

hemorrhage, bleeding; catamenia, menses; outpouring etc. (***egress***) 295; leucorrhea.

V. excrete etc. (***eject***) 297; emanate etc. (***come out***) 295.

Adj. excretory, fecal, secretory; ejective, eliminant.

300. Insertion. [Forcible ingress.]—**N.** insertion, implantation, intercalation, embolism, introduction; interpolation, insinuation etc. (***intervention***) 228; planting etc. *v.*; injection, inoculation, importation, infusion; forcible -ingress etc. 294; immersion; submersion, -gence; dip, plunge; bath etc. (***water***) 337; interment etc. 363.

V. insert; intro-duce, -mit; put –, run- into; import; inject; interject etc. 228; infuse, instil, inoculate, impregnate, imbue, imbrue.

graft, ingraft, bud, plant, implant; dovetail.

obtrude; thrust –, stick –, ram –, stuff –, tuck –, press –, drive –, pop –, whip –, drop –, put- in; impact; empierce etc. (***make a hole***) 260.

embed; immerse, immerge, merge; bathe, soak etc. (***water***) 337; dip, plunge etc. 310.

bury etc. (***inter***) 363.

insert etc. -itself; plunge ***in medias res***.

Adj. inserted etc. *v.*

301. Extraction. [Forcible egress.]—**N.** extraction; extracting etc. *v.*; removal, elimination, extrication, eradication, evolution.

evulsion, avulsion; wrench; expression, squeezing; extirpation, extermination; ejection etc. 297; export etc. (***egress***) 295; distillation.

extractor, corkscrew, forceps, pliers.

V. extract, draw, pit; take –, draw –, pull –, tear –, pluck –, pick –, get- out; wring from, wrench; extort; root –, weed –, grub –, rake-up, – out; eradicate; pull –, pluck- up by the roots; averruncate; unroot; uproot, pull up, extirpate, dredge.

remove; educe, elicit; evolve, extricate; eliminate etc. (***eject***) 297; eviscerate etc. 297.

express, squeeze –, press- out; distil.

Adj. extracted etc. *v.*

302. Passage. [Motion through.]—**N.** passage, transmission; permeation; pene-, interpene-tration; transudation, infiltration; ***osmosis***, osmose, endos-, exos-mose; intercurrence; ingress etc. 294; egress etc. 295; path etc. 627; conduit etc. 350; opening etc. 260; journey etc. 266; voyage etc. 267.

V. pass, – through; perforate etc. (***hole***) 260; penetrate, permeate, thread, thrid, enfilade; go -through, – across; go –, pass- over; cut across; ford, cross; pass and repass, work; make –, thread –, worm –, force- one's way; make –, force- a passage; cut one's way through; find its -way, –

vent; transmit, make way, clear the course; traverse, go over the ground.

Adj. passing etc. *v.*; intercurrent; osmotic etc. *n.*

Adv. *en passant* etc. (*transit*) 270.

303. Overstep. [Motion beyond.]—**N.** transcursion, -ilience, -gression; infraction, intrusion; trespass; encroach-, infringe-ment; extravagation, transcendence; redundance etc. 641; ingress etc. 294.

V. transgress, surpass, pass; go- beyond, – by; show in –, come to the- front; shoot ahead of; steal a march –, gain- upon.

over-step, -pass, -reach, -go, -ride- -leap, -jump, -skip, -lap, -shoot the mark; out-strip, -leap, -jump, -go, -step, -run, -ride, -rival, -do; beat, – hollow; distance; leave in the -lurch, – rear; go one better, throw into the shade; exceed, transcend, surmount; soar etc. (*rise*) 305.

encroach, intrude, trespass, infringe, invade, trench upon, intrench on; strain; stretch –, strain- a point; pass the Rubicon.

Adj. surpassing etc. *v.*

Adv. beyond the mark, ahead.

304. Shortcoming. [Motion short of.]—**N.** shortcoming, failure; delinquency; falling short etc. *v.*; de-fault, -falcation; leeway; labor in vain, no go.

incompleteness etc. 53; imperfection etc. 651; insufficiency etc. 640; noncompletion etc. 730; failure etc. 732.

V. come –, fall –, stop- -short, – short of; not reach; want; keep within -bounds, – the mark, – compass.

break down, stick in the mud, collapse, come to nothing; fall -through, – to the ground, – down; cave in, end in smoke, fizzle out, miss the mark, fail; lose ground; miss stays, slump.

Adj. unreached; deficient; short, – of; *minus*; out of depth; perfunctory etc. (*neglect*) 460.

Adv. within -the mark, – compass, – bounds; behindhand; *re infectâ*; to no purpose; far from it.

Phr. the bubble burst.

305. Ascent. [Motion upwards.]—**N.** ascent, ascension; rising etc. *v.*; rise, upgrowth; leap etc. 309; acclivity, hill etc. 217; stair, stairs, stair-case, -way, flight of -steps, – stairs; ladder, companion, – way; lift, elevator etc. 307.

rocket, lark; sky-rocket, -lark; Alpine Club.

V. ascend, rise, mount, arise, uprise; go –, get –, work one's way –, start –, spring –, shoot- up; zoom; aspire.

climb, clamber, ramp, scramble, swarm, *escalade*, surmount; scale, – the heights.

tower, soar, hover, spire, plane, swim, float, surge; leap etc. 309.

Adj. rising etc. *v.*; scandent, buoyant; supernatant, -fluitant; excelsior.

Adv. uphill.

306. Descent. [Motion downwards.]—**N.** descent, descension, declension, declination; fall; falling etc. *v.*; drop, cadence; subsidence, lapse; come-down, downfall, tumble, slip, tilt, trip, lurch; cropper, *culbute*; titubation, stumble; fate of Icarus; dive, nose-dive, *volpané*.

avalanche, *débâcle*, landslip, slide.

V. descend; go –, drop –, come-down; fall, gravitate, drop, slip, slide, glissade, dive, plunge, settle; decline, slump, set, sink, droop; come down a peg.

dismount, alight, light, get down; swoop; stoop etc. 308; fall prostrate, precipitate oneself; let fall etc. 308.

tumble, trip, stumble, titubate, lurch, pitch, swag, topple; topple –, tumble- -down, – over; tilt, sprawl, plump down, come a cropper.

Adj. descending etc. *v.*; descendent, declivitous; downcast; decur-rent, sive; labent, deciduous; nodding to its fall.

Adv. down, -hill, -wards.

307. Elevation.—N. elevation; raising etc. *v.*; erection, lift; sublevation, upheaval; sublimation, exaltation; prominence etc. (*convexity*) 250.

lever etc. 633; crane, derrick, windlass, capstan, winch, dredger, lift, elevator, escalator, dumb waiter.

V. heighten, elevate, raise, lift, erect; set –, stick –, perch –, perk –, tilt- up; rear, hoist, heave; up-lift, -raise, -rear, -bear, -cast, -hoist, -heave; buoy, weigh, mount, give a lift; exalt, sublimate; place –, set- on a pedestal.

take –, drag –, fish- up; dredge.

stand –, rise –, get –, jump- up; spring to one's feet; hold -oneself, – one's head- up; draw oneself up to his full height.

Adj. elevated etc. *v.*; standing up; stilted, attollent, rampant.

Adv. on -stilts, – the shoulders of, – one's legs, – one's hind legs.

308. Depression.—N. lowering etc. *v.*; depression; dip etc. (*concavity*) 252; abasement; detrusion; reduction.

over-throw, -set, -turn; upset; prostration, subversion, precipitation.

bow; courtesy, curtsy; genuflexion, *kowtow*, obeisance, *salaam*.

V. depress, lower; let –, take- -down, – down a peg; cast; let -drop, – fall; sink, debase, bring low, abase, slash, reduce, detrude, pitch, precipitate.

over-throw, -turn, -set; upset, subvert, prostrate, level, fell; cast –, take –, throw –, fling –, dash –, pull –, cut –, knock –, hew- down; raze, – to the ground; humiliate, trample in the dust, pull about one's ears.

sit, – down; couch, squat, crouch, stoop, bend, bow, courtsey, curtsy; bob, duck, dip, genuflect, kneel; *kowtow*, *salaam*, make obeisance, prostrate oneself; bend, bow- the -head, – knee; incline the head; bow down; cower; recline etc. (*be horizontal*) 213.

Adj. depressed etc. *v.*; at a low ebb; prostrate etc. (*horizontal*) 213; detrusive.

309. Leap.—N. leap, jump, hop, spring, bound, vault, saltation.

dance, caper, gambol; curvet, caracole; *gambade*, *-bado*; capriole, demivolt; buck, — jump; hop, skip and jump.

kangaroo, jerboa, chamois, goat, frog, grasshopper, flea.

V. leap; jump -up, — over the moon; hop, spring, bound, vault, ramp, cut capers, gambol, trip, skip, dance, caper, curvet, *caracole*; foot it, bob, bounce, flounce, start, frisk etc. (*amusement*) 840; jump about etc. (*agitation*) 315; trip it on the light fantastic toe, dance oneself off one's legs.

Adj. leaping etc. *v.*; saltatory, frisky.

Adv. on the light fantastic toe.

310. Plunge.—**N.** plunge, dip, dive, header; ducking etc. *v.*; submergence, immersion, diver.

V. plunge, dip, souse, duck; dive, plump; take a -plunge, — header, make a plunge; bathe etc. (*water*) 337

sub-merge, -merse; immerse, douse, sink, engulf, send to -the bottom, — Davy Jones' locker.

get out of one's depth; go -to the bottom, — down like a stone; founder, welter, wallow.

311. Circuition. [Curvilinear motion.]—**N.** circuition, circulation; turn, curvet; excursion; circum-vention, -navigation, -ambulation; north-west passage; ambit, gyre, lap, circuit etc. 629.

turning etc. *v.*; wrench; evolution; coil, helix, spiral; corkscrew.

V. turn, bend, wheel; go —, put- about; heel; go —, turn -round, — to the right about; turn on one's heel; make —, describe- a -circle, — complete circle; encircle; go —, pass- through -180°, — 360°.

circum-navigate, -aviate, -ambulate, -vent; put a girdle round the earth, go the round, make the round of.

turn —, round- a corner; double a point.

wind, circulate, meander; whisk, twirl; twist etc. (*convolution*) 248; make a *détour* etc. (*circuit*) 629.

Adj. turning etc. *v.*; circuitous; circumforaneous, -fluent; devious, roundabout, circumambient, -flex, -navigable.

Adv. round about.

312. Rotation. [Motion in a continued circle.]—**N.** rotation, revolution, gyration, circulation, roll; circum-rotation, -volution, -gyration; volutation, circination, turbination, *pirouette*, convolution.

verticity; whir, whirl, swirl, eddy, vortex, whirlpool, gurge; cyclone, tornado; surge; *vertigo*, dizzy round; Maelstrom, Charybdis; Ixion; wheel of Fortune.

wheel, screw, propeller, whirligig, rolling stone, windmill; top, teetotum, merry-go-round; roller; cog-, fly-wheel, spit; jack; caster.

axis, axle, spindle, spool, pivot, pin, hinge, pole, swivel, gimbals, arbor, bobbin, mandrel, shaft.

[Science of rotatory motion] trochilics, gyrostatics.

V. rotate; roll, — along; revolve, spin; turn, — round; circumvolve; circulate; gyre, gyrate, wheel, whirl, swirl, twirl, trundle, troll, bowl; slew round.

roll up, furl; wallow, welter; box the compass; spin like a -top, — teetotum.

Adj. rotating etc. *v.*; rota-tory, -ry; circumrotatory, trochilic, vertiginous, gyratory; vortic-al, -ose.

Adv. head over heels, round and round, like a horse in a mill.

313. Evolution. [Motion in a reverse circle.]—**N.** evolution, unfolding, development; eversion etc. (*inversion*) 218.

V. evolve; un-fold, -roll, -wind, -coil, -twist, -furl, -twine, -ravel; disentangle; develop.

Adj. evolving etc. *v.*; evolved etc. *v.*

314. Oscillation. [Reciprocating motion, motion to and fro.]—**N.** oscillation; vibration, libration; motion of a pendulum; nutation; undulation; pulsation; pulse; throb; seismic disturbance.

alternation; coming and going etc. *v.*; ebb and flow, flux and reflux, ups and downs; wave, vibratiuncle, swing, beat, shake, wag, see-saw, dance, lurch, dodge; fluctuation; vacillation etc. (*irresolution*) 605.

seismometer, vibroscope, seismograph.

V. oscillate; vi-, li-brate; alternate, undulate, wave; sway, rock, swing; pulsate, beat; wag, -gle; nod, bob, courtesy, curtsy; tick; play; chatter, wamble, wabble; teeter, dangle, swag.

fluctuate, dance, curvet, reel, quake; quiver, quaver, shake, flicker; wriggle; roll, toss, pitch; flounder, stagger, totter, waddle; move —, bob- up and down etc. *adv.*; pass and repass, ebb and flow, come and go, shuttle; vacillate etc. 605.

brandish, shake, flourish.

Adj. oscillating etc. *v.*; oscill-, undul-, puls-, libr-atory; vibrat-ory, -ile; pendulous, shutterwise, seismic.

Adv. to and fro, up and down, backwards and forwards, see-saw, zigzag, wibble-wabble, in and out, from side to side, like buckets in a well.

315. Agitation. [Irregular motion.]—**N.** agitation, stir, tremor, shake, ripple, jog, jolt, jerk, shock, succession, trepidation, quiver, quaver, dance; jactit-ation, -ance; shuffling etc. *v.*; twitter, flicker, flutter.

disquiet, perturbation, commotion, turmoil, turbulence; tumult, -uation; hubbub, rout, bustle, fuss, racket, *subsultus*, staggers, megrims, epilepsy, fits, twitching, vellication, St. Vitus' dance.

spasm, throe, throb, palpitation, convulsion, paroxysm; tetanus.

disturbance etc. (*disorder*) 59; restlessness etc. (*changeableness*) 149.

ferment, -ation; ebullition, effervescence, hurly burly, *cahotage*; tempest, storm, ground swell, heavy sea, whirlpool, vortex etc. 312; whirlwhind etc. (*wind*) 349.

V. be -agitated etc.; shake; tremble, — like an aspen leaf; quiver, quaver, quake, shiver, twitter, twire, dither, dodder; twitch, writhe, toss, shuffle, tumble, stagger, bob, reel, sway; wag, -gle, wiggle; wriggle, — like an eel; squirm; dance, stumble, shamble, flounder, totter, flounce, flop, curvet, prance.

throb, pulsate, beat, palpitate, go pit-a-pat; flutter, flitter, flicker, bicker; bustle.

ferment, effervesce, foam; boil, – over; bubble, – up; simmer.

toss –, jump- about; jump like a parched pea; shake like an aspen leaf; shake to its -center, – foundations; be the sport of the winds and waves; reel to and fro like a drunken man; move –, drive- from post to pillar and from pillar to post; keep between hawk and buzzard.

agitate, shake, convulse, toss, tumble, bandy, wield, brandish, flap, flourish, whisk, jerk, hitch, jolt; jog, -gle; hostle, buffet, hustle, disturb, stir, shake up, churn, jounce, wallop, whip, vellicate.

Adj. shaking etc. *v.*; agitated, tremulous; de-, sub-sultory; shambling; giddy-paced, saltatory, convulsive, jerky, unquiet, restless, all of a twitter.

Adv. by fits and starts; subsultorily etc. *adj.*: *per saltum*; hop, skip and jump; in -convulsions, – fits, pit-a-pat.

316. Materiality.—N. material-ity, -ness; materialization; corpor-eity, -ality; substantiality, material existence, incarnation, flesh and blood, *plenum*; physical condition.

matter, body, substance, brute matter, stuff, element, principle, protoplasm, plasma, *parenchyma*, material, *substratum*, hyle, *corpus*, *pabulum*; frame.

object, article, thing, something; still life; stocks and stones; materials etc. 635.

[Science of matter] physics; somatology, -ics; natural –, experimental- philosophy; physical science, *philosophie positive*, materialism, hylism; applied –, micro-, molecular –, nuclear – physics.

atomics, atomic science, nucleonics, quantum mechanics, radiology.

atom, radical, tracer, isotope, pleiad; atomic – nucleus, – cluster; nuclear particle, neutron, protron, shell, valence electron.

materialist, physicist, atomic scientist, radiologist.

V. materialize, incorporate, incarnate, substantiate, embody.

atomize, split –, smash – the atom; radio-activate.

Adj. material, bodily; corpor-eal, -al; physical; somat-ic, -oscopic; sensible, tangible, ponderable, palpable, substantial; fleshly, incarnate.

physical, bio-, electro-, geo-physical; atomic, nuclear, thermonuclear, radio-active.

objective, impersonal, neuter, unspiritual, materialistic.

317. Immateriality.—N. immaterial-ity, -ness; incorporeity, dematerialization, unsubstantiality, spirituality; inextension; astral plane.

personality; I, myself, me; *ego*, spirit etc. (*soul*) 450; astral body; immaterialism; spiritual-ism, -ist; subliminal –, subconscious- self.

V. disembody, spiritualize, dematerialize.

Adj. immateri-al, -ate; incorpor-eal, -al; asomatous, unextended; un-, dis-embodied; extramundane, supersensible, unearthly; pneumatoscopic; spiritual etc. (*psychical*) 450; aery.

personal, subjective.

318. World.—N. world, creation, nature, universe; earth, globe, wide world; *cosmos*; terraqueous globe, sphere; macro-, mega-cosm; music of the spheres; strato-, tropo-sphere.

heavens, sky, welkin, empyrean; starry -heaven, – host; firmament; vault –, canopy- of heaven; celestial spaces.

heavenly bodies, stars, luminaries, nebulae; galaxy, milky way, galactic circle, *via lactea.*

sun, orb of day, Apollo, Phoebus; photo-, chromo-sphere; solar system; planet, -oid, asteroid; comet; satellite; moon, orb of night, Diana, Luna; aerolite, meteor; falling –, shooting-star; meteorite.

constellation, zodiac, signs of the zodiac, Charles's wain, Great Bear, Southern Cross, Orion's belt, Cassiopeia's chair, Pleiades etc.

colures, equator, ecliptic, orbit.

[Science of heavenly bodies] astronomy; uranography, -logy; cosmo-logy, -graphy, -gony; *eidouranion*, orrery; geography; geodesy etc. (*measurement*) 466; star-gazing, -gazer; astronomer; cosmogonist, geodesist, geographer; observatory.

Adj. cosmic, cosmical, mundane; terr-estrial, -estrious, -aqueous, -ene, -eous; telluric, earthly, geotic, geodetic, cosmogonal, under the sun; sublunary, -astral.

solar, heliacal; lunar; celestial, heavenly, empyreal, sphery; starry, stellar; sider-eal, -al; astral; nebular.

Adv. in all creation, on the face of the globe, here below, under the sun.

319. Gravity.—N. gravi-ty, -tation; weight; heaviness etc. *adj.*; specific gravity; ponderosity, pressure, load; bur-den, -then; ballast, counterpoise; lump –, mass –, weight- of.

lead, millstone, mountain, Ossa on Pelion.

weighing, ponderation, trutination; weights; avoirdupois –, troy –, apothecaries'- weight; grain, scruple, drachm, ounce, pound, lb., load, stone, hundredweight, cwt., ton, quintal, carat, pennyweight, tod, gram, kilogram etc.

[Weighing instrument] balance, scales, steelyard, beam, weighbridge, spring balance, weighing machine.

[Science of gravity] statics.

V. be -heavy etc. *adj.*; gravitate, weigh, press, cumber, load.

[Measure the weight of] weigh, poise.

Adj. weighty; weighing etc. *v.*; heavy, – as lead; ponder-ous, -able; lump-ish, -y; cumber-, burden-some; cumbrous, unwieldy, massive.

in-, superin-cumbent.

320. Levity.—N. levity; lightness etc. *adj.*; imponderability, imponderables, buoyancy, volatility.

feather, dust, mote, down, thistledown, flue, cobweb, gossamer, straw, cork, bubble; float, bouy; ether, air.

leaven, ferment, barm, yeast, enzyme.

V. be -light etc. *adj.*; float, swim, be buoyed up.

render -light etc. *adj.*; lighten, levitate; leaven.

Adj. light, subtile, subtle, airy; imponder-ous, -able; astatic, weightless, ethereal, sublimated; uncompressed, volatile; buoyant, floating etc. *v.*; barmy, frothy; portable.

light as -a feather, – thistle down, – air.

fermenting etc. *n.*

321. Density.—**N.** density, solidity; solidness etc. *adj.*; impenetra-, impermea-bility; incompressibility; imporosity; cohesion etc. 46; constipation, consistence, spissitude.

specific gravity; hydro-, areo-meter.

condensation; solid-ation, -ification; consolidation; concretion, caseation, coagulation; petrifaction etc. (*hardening*) 323; crystallization, precipitation; deposit, precipitate, silt; inspissation; thickening etc. *v.*

indivisibility, indiscerptibility, indissolvableness.

solid body, mass, block, knot, lump; con-cretion, -crete, -glomerate; cake, clot, stone, curd, coagulum, grume; bone, gristle, cartilage.

V. be -dense etc. *adj.*; become –, render- solid etc. *adj.*; solid-ify, -ate; concrete, set, take a set, consolidate, congeal, coagulate; curd, -le; fix, clot, cake, candy, precipitate, deposit, cohere, crystallize; petrify etc. (*harden*) 323.

condense, thicken, inspissate, incrassate; compress, squeeze, ram down, constipate.

Adj. dense, solid, solidified etc. *v.*; cohe-rent, -sive etc. 46; compact, close, serried, thickset; substantial, massive, lumpish; impenetrable, impermeable, imporous; incompressible; constipated; concrete etc. (*hard*) 323; knot-ted, -ty; gnarled; crystal-line, -lizable; thick, grumous, stuffy.

un-dissolved, -melted, -liquified, -thawed.

in-divisible, -discerptible, -frangible, -dissolvable, -dissoluble, -soluble, -fusible.

322. Rarity.—**N.** rarity; tenuity; absence of -solidity etc. 321; subtility; sponginess, compressibility.

rarefaction, expansion, dilatation, inflation, subtilization.

ether etc. (*gas*) 334.

V. rarefy, expand, dilate, subtilize, attenuate, thin.

Adj. rare, subtile, thin, fine, tenuous, compressible, flimsy, slight; light etc. 320; cavernous, spongy etc. (*hollow*) 252.

rarefied etc. *v.*; unsubstantial; uncom-pact, -pressed.

323. Hardness.—**N.** hardness etc. *adj.*; rigidity, renitence, inflexibility, temper, callosity, durity.

induration, petrifaction; lapid-ification, -escence; vitri-, ossi-, corni-fication; crystallization.

stone, pebble, flint, marble, rock, fossil, crag, crystal, quartz, granite, adamant; bone, cartilage; heart of oak, block, board, deal board; iron, steel; cast –, wrought- iron; nail; brick, concrete; cement.

V. render -hard etc. *adj.*; harden, stiffen, indurate, petrify, temper, ossify, vitrify.

Adj. hard, rigid, stubborn, stiff, firm; starch, -ed; stark, unbending, unlimber, unyielding; inflexible, tense; indurate, -d; gritty, proof.

adamant-ine, -ean; concrete, stony, rocky, lithic, granitic, vitreous; crystalline; horny, corneous; bony; oss-eous, -ific; cartilaginous; hard as a -stone etc. *n.*; stiff as -buckram, – a poker.

324. Softness.—**N.** softness, pliableness etc. *adj.*; flexibility; pli-ancy, -ability; sequacity, malleability; flabbiness; duct-, tract-ility; extend-, extensibility; plasticity; inelasticity; flaccidity, laxity.

clay, wax, butter, dough, pudding; cushion, pillow, feather-bed, pad, down, padding, wadding.

mollification; softening etc. *v.*

V. render -soft etc. *adj.*; soften, mollify, mellow, relax, temper; mash, knead, squash, *massage*.

bend, yield, relent, relax, give.

Adj. soft, tender, supple; pli-ant, -able; flexible, -ile; lithe, -some; lissom, limber, plastic; ductile; tract-ile, -able; malleable, extensile, sequacious, inelastic, mollient.

yielding etc. *v.*; flabby, limp, flimsy.

flaccid, flocculent, downy; spongy, edematous, medullary, doughy, argillaceous, mellow.

soft as -butter, – down, – silk; yielding as wax; tender as a chicken.

325. Elasticity.—**N.** elasticity, springiness, spring, resilience, renitency, buoyancy.

india-rubber, caoutchouc, gutta-percha, whalebone, gum elastic.

V. be -elastic etc. *adj.*; spring back etc. (*recoil*) 227.

Adj. elastic, tensile, springy, ductile, resilient, renitent, buoyant.

326. Inelasticity.—**N.** want of –, absence of- elasticity etc. 325; inelasticity etc. (*softness*) 324.

Adj. inelastic etc. (*soft*) 324.

327. Tenacity.—**N.** tenacity, toughness, strength; cohesion etc. 46; sequacity; stubbornness etc. (*obstinacy*) 606; viscidity etc. 352.

leather; gristle, cartilage.

V. be -tenacious etc. *adj.*; resist fracture.

Adj. tenacious, tough, cohesive, adhesive, strong, resisting, sequacious, stringy, gristly, cartilaginous, leathery, coriaceous, tough as whit-leather; stubborn etc. (*obstinate*) 606.

328. Brittleness.—**N.** brittleness etc. *adj.*; frag-, friab-, frangib-, fiss-ility; frailty; house of -cards, – glass.

V. be -brittle etc. *adj.*; live in a glass house.

break, crack, snap, split, shiver, splinter, crumble, break short, burst, fly, give way; fall to pieces; crumble -to, – into- dust.

Adj. breakable, brittle, frangible, fragile, frail, friable, delicate, gimcrack, shivery, fissile; splitting etc. *v.*; lacerable, splintery, crisp, crimp, short, brittle as glass.

329. Texture. [Structure.]—**N.** structure, organization, anatomy, frame, mold, fabric, construction; frame-work, carcass, architecture; stratification, cleavage.

substance, stuff, *compages*, *parenchyma*; constitution, staple, organism.

[Science of structures] organ-, oste-, my- splanchn-, neur-, angi-, aden-ology; angi-, aden-ography.

texture; inter-, con-texture; tissue, grain, web, surface; warp and -woof, – weft; tooth, nap etc. (*roughness*) 256; fineness –, coarseness- of grain.

[Science of textures] histology.

Adj. structural, organic; anatomic, -al.

text-ural, -ile; fine-, coarse-grained; fine, delicate, subtile, gossamery, filmy; coarse; homespun; linsey-woolsey.

330. Pulverulence. [State of powder.]—**N.** pulverulence; sandiness etc. *adj.*; efflorescence; friability.

powder, dust, sand, shingle; sawdust; grit; attrition; meal, bran, flour, *farina*, spore, sporule; crumb, seed, grain; particle etc. (*smallness*) 32; thermion; limature, filings, *débris*, *detritus*, scobs, magistery, fine powder; *flocculi*.

smoke; cloud of -dust, – sand, – smoke; puff –, volume -of smoke; sand –, dust- storm.

[Reduction to powder] pulverization, comminution, attenuation, granulation, disintegration, subaction, contusion, trituration, levigation, abrasion, detrition, multure; limation; filing etc. *v.*

[Instruments for pulverization] mill, millstone, grater, rasp, file, pestle and mortar, nutmeg grater, teeth, molar, grinder, chopper, grindstone, kern, quern, muller.

V. come to dust; be -disintegrated, – reduced to powder etc.

reduce –, grind- to powder; pulverize, comminute, granulate, triturate, levigate; scrape, file, abrade, rub down, grind, grate, rasp, pound, bray, bruise; con-tuse, -tund; beat, crush, cranch, craunch, crunch, muller, scranch, crumble, disintegrate; attenuate etc. 195.

Adj. powdery, pulverulent, granular, mealy, floury, farinaceous, branny, furfuraceous, flocculent, dusty, sandy, sabulous; aren-ose, -arious, -aceous; gritty; efflorescent, impalpable.

pulverizable; friable, crumbly, shivery; pulverized etc. *v.*; attrite; in pieces.

331. Friction.—**N.** friction, attrition; rubbing etc. *v.*; erasure; con-frication, -trition; affriction, abrasion, arrosion, limature, frication, rub; elbow-grease; rosin; *massage*.

V. rub, scratch, abrade, scrape, scrub, fray, rasp, graze, curry, scour, polish, rub out, erase, gnaw; file, grind etc. (*reduce to powder*) 330; *massage*.

set one's teeth on edge; rosin.

Adj. anatriptic, abrasive.

332. Lubrication. [Absence of friction. Prevention of friction.]—**N.** smoothness etc. 255; unctuousness etc. 355.

lubri-cation, -fication; anointment; oiling etc. *v.*

synovia; lubricant, graphite, glycerine, oil etc. 356; saliva; lather.

V. lubri-cate, -citate; oil, grease, lather, soap; wax.

Adj. lubricated etc. *v.*

333. Fluidity.—**N.** fluidity, liquidity; liquidness etc. *adj.*; gaseity etc. 334; liquefaction etc. 334.

fluid, inelastic fluid; liquid, liquor; lymph, humor, juice, sap, serum, blood, serosity, gravy, rheum, ichor, sanies.

solu-bility, -bleness.

[Science of liquids] hydro-logy, -statics, -dynamics, hydraulics, etc.

V. be -fluid etc. *adj.*; flow etc. (*water in motion*) 348; liquefy etc. 335.

Adj. liquid, fluid, serous, juicy, succulent, sappy; fluent etc. (*flowing*) 348.

liquefied etc. 335; uncongealed; soluble, hydrostatic etc. *n.*

334. Gaseity.—**N.** gaseity, gaseousness, vapourousness etc. *adj.*; flatulence, -lency; volatility, aeration, gasification.

elastic fluid, gas, air, vapor, ether, steam, fume, reek, *effluvium*, *flatus*; cloud etc. 353.

[Science of elastic fluids] pneumat-ics, -ostatics; aero-statics, -dynamics etc.

gas-, gaso-meter.

V. gassify, aerate, aerify; emit vapor etc. 336.

Adj. gaseous, aeriform, ethereal, aerial, airy, vaporous, volatile, evaporable; flatulent; aerostatic etc. *n.*

335. Liquefaction.—**N.** liquefaction; liquescen-ce, -cy, deliquescence; melting etc. (*heat*) 384; colliqu-ation, -efaction; thaw; de-, liquation; lixiviation, dissolution.

solution, apozem, lixivium, infusion, decoction, flux.

solvent, diluent, menstruum, alkahest, *aqua fortis*.

V. render -liquid etc 333; liquefy, run, deliquesce; melt etc. (*heat*) 384; solve; dissolve, resolve; liquate; hold in solution; leach, lixiviate.

Adj. lique-fied etc. *v.*, -scent, -fiable; deliquescent, soluble, colliquative; solvent.

336. Vaporization.—**N.** vapor-, volatilization; gasification; e-, vaporation; distillation, cohobation, sublimation, exhalation; volatility.

vaporizer, still, retort, spray, atomizer; fumigation, steaming.

V. render -gaseous etc. 334; vaporize, volatilize; distil, sublime; evaporate, exhale, smoke, transpire, emit vapor, fume, reek, steam, fumigate.

Adj. volatilized etc. *v.*; reeking etc. *v.*; volatile; evaporable, vaporizable.

337. Water.—N. water; serum, serosity; lymph; rheum; diluent.
dilution, maceration, lotion; washing etc. *v.*; im-, mersion; humectation, infiltration, spargefaction, affusion, irrigation, *douche*, balneation, bath.
deluge etc. (*water in motion*) 348; high water, flood-, spring-tide.
V. be -watery etc. *adj.*; reek.
add water, water, wet; moisten etc. 339; dilute, dip, immerse; merge; im-, sub-merge; plunge, souse, duck, drown; soak, steep, macerate, pickle, wash, sprinkle, sparge, lave, bathe, affuse, splash, swash, douse, slosh, drench; dabble, slop, slobber, irrigate, inundate, deluge; syringe, inject, gargle; infiltrate, percolate.
Adj. watery, aqueous, aquatic, lymphatic; balneal, diluent; drenching etc. *v.*; diluted etc. *v.*; weak; wet etc. (*moist*) 339.
Phr. the waters are out.

338. Air.—N. air etc. (*gas*) 334; common –, atmospheric- air; atmosphere, stratosphere, isothermal layer, troposphere, Heaviside layer.
open, – air; sky, welkin; blue, – sky; cloud etc. 353.
weather, climate, rise and fall of the barometer, isobar.
[Science of air] pneumatics, aero-logy, -scopy, -graphy; meteorology, climatology; eudio-, baro-, aero-meter; aneroid, baro-graph, -scope; weather-gauge, -glass, -cock.
exposure to the -air, – weather; ventilation; aero-station; -nautics; -naut etc. 265 and 269.
V. air, ventilate; fan etc. (*wind*) 349.
Adj. containing air, flatulent, effervescent; windy etc. 349.
atmospheric, airy; aeri-al, -form; pneumatic; meteorological; weather-wise.
Adv. in the open air, out of doors, *à la belle étoile*, *al fresco*; *sub -Jove*, *– dio*.

339. Moisture.—N. moisture; moistness etc. *adj.*; hum-idity, -ectation; madefaction, dew; *serein*; marsh etc. 345; Hygromet-ry, -er.
V. moisten, wet; humect, -ate; sponge, damp, dampen, bedew; imbue, imbrue, infiltrate, saturate; seethe, sop; soak, drench etc. (*water*) 337.
be -moist etc. *adj.*; not have a dry thread; perspire etc. (*exude*) 295.
Adj. moist, damp; watery etc. 337; undried, humid, wet, dank, muggy, dewy; roric; roscid; juicy.
wringing wet; wet -through, – to the skin; saturated etc. *v.*
swashy, soggy, dabbled; reeking, seething, dripping, soaking, soft, sodden, sloppy, muddy; swampy etc. (*marshy*) 345; irriguous.

340. Dryness.—N. dryness etc. *adj.*; siccity, aridity, drought, ebb-, neap-tide, low water.
drying, ex-, de-siccation; evaporation; dehydration; arefaction, dephlegmation, drainage.
drier, desiccator.
V. be -dry etc. *adj.*; render -dry etc. *adj.*; dry; dry –, soak- up; sponge, swab, wipe; ex-, desiccate, dehydrate, anhydrate; drain, parch.
be fine, hold up.
Adj. dry, anhydrous, arid, waterless; dried etc. *v.*; undamped; juice-, sap- less; sear; husky; rainless, without rain, fine; dry as -a bone, – dust, – a stick, – a mummy, – a biscuit; disiccated; dehydrated; water-proof, -tight.

341. Ocean.—N. sea, ocean, main, deep, brine, salt water, waters, waves, billows, high seas, offing, great waters, watery waste, 'vasty deep,' briny ocean, herring pond, steamer track, the seven seas; wave, tide etc. (*water in motion*) 348.
hydrograph-y, -er, oceanography; Neptune, Thetis, Triton, Naiad, Nereid; sea-nymph, Siren, mer-maid, -man; trident, dolphin.
Adj. oceanic; mar-ine, -itime; pleagic, -ian; sea-going, -worthy; hydrographic.
Adv. at –, on- sea; afloat, on the high seas.

342. Land.—N. land, earth, ground, dry land, *terra firma*.
continent, mainland, peninsula, delta; tongue –, neck- of land; isthmus; oasis; promontory etc. (*projection*) 250; highland etc. (*height*) 206.
coast, shore, scar, strand, beach; bank, lea; seaboard, -side, -shore, -bank, -coast, -beach; rock-, iron- bound coast; loom of the land; derelict; innings; *alluvium*, alluvion.
soil, glebe, clay, loam, marl, clodge, chalk, gravel, mold, subsoil, clod, clot; rock, crag, cliff.
acres; real estate etc. (*property*) 780; landsman, land-lubber, farmer.
geography etc. 318; agriculture etc. 371.
V. land, come to land; set foot on -the soil, – dry land; come –, go- ashore.
Adj. earthy; continental, midland; littoral, riparian, ripuarian; alluvial; terrene etc. (*world*) 318; landed, predial, territorial.
Adv. ashore; on -shore, – land.

343. Gulf. Lake.—N. land covered with water, gulf, gulph, bay, inlet, bight, estuary, arm of the sea, fiord, armlet; frith, firth, ostiary, mouth; lagune, lagoon; indraught; cove, creek; natural harbor; roads; strait, narrows; Euripus; sound, belt, gut, kyles.
lake, loch, lough, mere, tarn, plash, broad, pond, pool, lin, puddle, well, artesian well, tank, sump; standing –, dead –, sheet of- water; fish –, mill-pond; race; ditch, dike, dyke, dam; reservoir etc. (*store*) 636.
Adj. lacustrine; land locked.

344. Plain.—N. plain, table land, mesa, face of the country; open –, champaign-country; basin, downs, waste, weary waste, desert, tundra, wild, steppe, pampas, savanna, prairie, champaign, heath, common, wold, veld; moor, -land, uplands, fell; bush; *plateau* etc. (*level*) 213; *campagna*.
meadow, mead, haugh, pasturage, park, field,

lawn, green, plat, plot, grass-plat, greensward, sward, grass, turf, sod, heather; lea, ley, lay; grounds.

Adj. campestrian, champaign, alluvial.

345. Marsh.—N. marsh, swamp, morass, marish, moss, fen, bog, quagmire, slough, sump, wash; mud, squash, slush.

Adj. marsh, -y; swampy, boggy, plashy, poachy, quaggy, soft; muddy, sloppy, squashy, spongy; paludal; moor-ish, -y; fenny.

346. Island.—N. island, isle, islet, eyot, ait, holm, reef, atoll, breaker; archipelago; islander.

Adj. insular, sea-girt.

347. Stream. [Fluid in motion.]—**N.** stream etc. (*of water*) 348, (*of air*) 349.

V. flow etc. 348; blow etc. 349.

348. River. [Water in motion.]—**N.** running water.

jet, spirt, squirt, spout, splash, swash, rush, gush, *jet d'eau*; sluice, chute.

water-spout, -fall; fall, cascade, force, foss; lin, -n, ghyll, Niagara; cata-ract, -dupe, -clysm; *débâcle*, inundation, deluge.

rain, -fall; *serein*; shower, scud; downpour, cloud burst; driving –, pouring –, drenching-rain; hyeto-logy, -graphy; rainy season, monsoon; predominance of Aquarius, reigh of St. Swithin; mizzle, drizzle, *stilliciduim*, plash; dropping etc. *v.*

stream, course, flux, flow, profluence; effluence etc. (*egress*) 295; defluxion; flowing etc. *v.*; current, tide, race.

spring; fount, -ain; rill, rivulet, gill, gullet, rillet; stream-, brook-let; runnel, sike, burn, beck, brook, stream, river; reach; tributary.

body of water, torrent, rapids, flush, flood, swash, spate; spring –, high –, full-tide; bore; eagre, *hugre*; fresh, -et; undertow, indraught, reflux, undercurrent, eddy, vortex, gurge, whirlpool, Maelstrom, regurgitation, overflow; confluence, corrivation.

wave, billow, surge, swell, ripple; roller, ground swell, surf, breaker, white horses; comber, beach-comber; rough –, heavy –, cross –, long –, short –, chopping –, choppy- sea, choppiness; tidal wave.

[Science of fluids in motion] Hydrodynamics; Hydraul-ics etc.; raingauge etc.

water-bearer, – carrier, Aquarius.

irrigation etc. (*water*) 337; pump; watering-pot, – cart; hydrant, standpipe, hose, sprinkler, drencher; fire engine, squirt, syringe.

V. flow, run; meander; gush, pour, spout, roll, jet, well, issue; drop, drip, dribble, plash, squirt, spurt, spirtle, trill, trickle, distil, percolate; stream, overflow, inundate, deluge, flow over, splash, swash; guggle, murmur, babble, bubble, purl, gurgle, sputter, regurgitate; ooze, flow out etc. (*egress*) 295.

rain, – hard, – in torrents, – cats and dogs, – pitchforks; come down in sheets; pour with rain, drizzle, mizzle, spit, sprinkle, set in.

flow –, fall –, open –, drain- into; discharge itself, desembogue.

[Cause a flow] pour; pour out etc. (*discharge*) 297; shower down; irrigate, drench etc. (*wet*) 337; spill, splash.

[Stop a flow] stanch; dam, -up etc. (*close*) 261; obstruct etc. 706.

Adj. fluent; dif-, pro-, af-fluent; tidal; flowing etc. *v.*; meand-ering, -ry, -rous; fluvi-al, -atile; streamy, showery, rainy, drizzly, drizzling, pluvial, pluviose, stillicidous.

349. Wind. [Air in motion.]—**N.** wind, draught, *flatus*, *afflatus*, air; breath, – of air; puff, whiff, zephyr; blow, drift; *aura*; stream, current; under-current.

gust, blast, breeze, squall, gale, half a gale, storm, tempest, hurricane, whirlwind, tornado, samiel, cyclone, typhoon; simoon; harmattan, monsoon, trade wind, sirocco, *mistral*, *bise*, *föhn*, tramontane, levanter; capful of wind; fresh –, stiff- breeze; keen blast; blizzard.

windiness etc. *adj.*; ventosity; rough –, dirty –, ugly –, stress of- weather; dirty-, windy-, mackerel- sky; mare's tail; thick –, black –, white- squall.

anemography, aerodynamics; windgauge, anemometer, weather-cock, vane.

suf-, insuf-, per-, in-, af-flation; blowing, fanning etc. *v.*; ventilation.

sneezing etc. *v.*; sternutation; hic-cup, -cough; catching of the breath; breathing etc.

Eolus, Eurus, Boreas, Zephyr, cave of Eolus.

air-pump, lungs, bellows, blow-pipe, fan, blower; pulmotor, ventilator, punkah, aspirator, exhauster, ejector.

V. blow, waft; blow -hard, – great guns, – a hurricane etc. *n.*; whistle, roar, howl, ring in the shrouds; stream, issue

respire, breathe, in-, ex-hale, puff; whif, -fle; gasp, wheeze; snuff, -le; sniff, -le; sneeze, cough, belch.

fan, ventilate; in-, per-flate; blow –, pump- up.

Adj. blowing etc. *v.*; windy, airy, aeolian, flatulent; breezy, gusty, squally; stormy, tempestuous, blustering; boisterous etc. (*violent*) 173.

pulmon-ic, -ary.

350. Conduit. [Channel for the passage of water.]—**N.** conduit, channel, duct, watercourse, race; head –, tail- race; adit, aqueduct, canal, trough, flume, gutter, pantile; dike, canyon, ravine, gorge, hollow, main, gully, moat, ditch, drain, sewer, culvert, *cloaca*, sough, kennel, siphon, *piscina*; pipe etc. (*tube*) 260; funnel; tunnel etc. (*passage*) 627; water –, waste- pipe; emunctory, gully-hole, artery, aorta, vein, blood vessel; lymphatic; throat, alimentary canal, intestine; pore, spout, scupper; ad-, a-jutage; hose; gar-, gurgoyle; penstock, weir; flood-, water-gate; sluice, lock, valve; rose; waterworks.

Adj. vascular etc. (*with holes*) 260.

351. Air-pipe. [Channel for the passage of air.]—**N.** air-pipe, – shaft, – way, – passage, –

tube; shaft, flue, chimney, funnel, vent, blow-hole, nostril, nozzle, throat, weasand, *trachea*; *bronchus*, *-ia*; larynx, tonsils, wind-pipe, spiracle; ventiduct, -lator; louvre, Venetian blinds; blow-pipe etc. (*wind*) 349; pipe etc. (*tube*) 260.

352. Semiliquidity.—N. semiliquidity; stickiness etc. *adj.*; visc-idity, -osity; gumm-, glûtin-, muc-osity; spiss-, crass-itude; lentor; adhesiveness etc. (*cohesion*) 46.

inspiss-, incrass-ation; thickening, coagulation.

jelly, aspic, mucilage, gelatin, isinglass; colloid, mucus, phlegm; pituite, lava; glair, starch, gluten, albumen, milk, cream, protein; syrup, treacle; gum, size, glue, paste; wax, bee's-wax; emulsoid, emulsion, soup; squash, mud, slush, slime, ooze; moisture etc. 339; marsh etc. 345.

V. inspiss-, incrass-ate; coagulate, gelatinize, gelatinify, gel, jell, emulsify, thicken; mash, squash, churn, beat up.

Adj. semi-fluid, -liquid; half-melted, -frozen; milky, muddy etc. *n.*; lact-eal, -ean, -eous, -escent, -iferous; emulsive, curdled, thick, succulent, uliginous.

gelat-, album-, mucilag-, glut-inous; gelatine, mastic, amylaceous, ropy, clammy, clotted; vis-cid, -cous; sticky, tacky; slab, -by; lentous, pituitous; mu-cid, -culent, -cous.

353. Bubble. [Mixture of air and water.] [Cloud.]—**N.** bubble; foam, froth, head, fume, spume, lather, suds, spray, surf, yeast, barm, spindrift.

cloud, vapor, fog, mist, haze, steam; scud, rack, *nimbus*; *cumulus*, woolpack, *cirrus*, *stratus*; *cirro-*, *cumulo-stratus*; *cirro-cumulus*; mackerel sky, mare's tail, dirty sky.

[Science of clouds] nephelognosy, nephology.

effervescence, fermentation; bubbling etc. *v.*

nebula; cloudiness etc. (*opacity*) 426; nebulosity etc. (*dimness*) 422.

V. bubble, boil, foam, froth, spume, mantle, sparkle, guggle, gurgle; effervesce, ferment, fizzle; aerate; cloud, overcast, befog.

Adj. bubbling etc. *v.*; frothy, nappy, effervescent, sparkling, *mousseux*, up, fizzy, with a head on.

cloudy etc. *n.*; vaporous, nebulous, overcast; nubiferous, nephological; foggy, brumous.

354. Pulpiness.—N. pulpiness etc. *adj.*; pulp, paste, dough, sponge, curd, pap, rob, jam, pudding, mush, fool, poultice, grume.

Adj. pulpy etc. *n.*; pultaceous, grumous.

V. pulp, pulpify, mash.

355. Unctuousness.—N. unctuousness etc. *adj.*; unctuosity, lubricity; ointment etc. (*oil*) 356; anointment; lubrication etc. 332.

V. oil etc. (*lubricate*) 332.

Adj. unctuous, oily, oleaginous, adipose, sebaceous; fat, -ty; greasy; waxy, butyraceous, soapy, saponaceous, pinguid, lardaceous; slippery.

356. Oil.—N. oil, fat, butter, cream, grease, tallow, suet, lard, dripping, margarine, oleomargarine, exunge, blubber; glycerine, stearine, elaine, oleagine; soap; soft soap, wax, cerement; paraffin, spermaceti, adipocere; petroleum, mineral –, rock –, crystal- oil, kerosene, vegetable –, colza –, olive –, linseed –, cotton seed –, rape –, nut –, fusel- oil; animal –, neat's foot –, signal –, train- oil; ointment, unguent, liniment, salve, pomade, pomatum, brilliantine, spike –, nard.

356a. Resin.—N. resin, rosin, colophony; gum; lac, shellac, sealing-wax; amber, -gris; bitumen, pitch, tar, asphalt, -e, -um; varnish, copal, mastic, magilp, lacquer, japan.

V. varnish etc. (*overlay*) 223.

Adj. resinous, bituminous, pitchy, tarry.

357. Organization.—N. organized -world, – nature; living –, animated- nature; living beings; organic remains, organism; fossils; animal and vegetable kingdom, *fauna* and *flora*, biota.

prot-oplasm, -ein; albumen; structure etc. 329; organ-ization, -ism.

[Science of living beings] biology; natural history,* organic –, bio-chemistry, anatomy, physiology, embryology, morphology, evolution, Darwinism, Lamarkism, zoology etc. 368; botany etc. 369; naturalist, biologist etc.

Adj. organ-ic, -ized.

*The term *Natural History* is also used as relating to all the objects in Nature whether organic or inorganic, and including therefore *Mineralogy*, *Geology*, *Meteorology*, etc.

358. Inorganization.—N. mineral -world, – kingdom; unorganized –, inorganic –, brute –, inanimate- matter.

[Science of the mineral kingdom] mineralogy; geo-logy, -gnosy, -scopy; metall-urgy, -ography; lithology; orycto-logy, -graphy.

V. turn to dust, pulverize.

Adj. in-organic, -animate; unorganized; azoic; mineral.

359. Life.—N. life; vi-tality, -ability; animation; vital -spark, – flame, – force.

respiration, wind; breath -of life, – of one's nostrils; life-blood; Archeus; existence etc. 1.

vivification, vitalization; revivification etc. 163; Prometheus; life to come etc. (*destiny*) 152.

[Science of life] physiology, etiology, embryology, biology; animal economy.

nourishment, staff of life etc. (*food*) 298.

V. be -alive etc. *adj.*; live, breathe, respire; subsist etc. (*exist*) 1; walk the earth; strut and fret one's hour upon a stage; be spared.

see the light, be born, come into the world; fetch –, draw- -breath, – the breath of life; quicken; revive; come to, – life.

give birth to etc. (*produce*) 161; bring to life, put into life, vitalize; vivi-fy, -ficate; reamimate etc. (*restore*) 660; keep -alive, – body and soul together, – the wolf from the door; support life.

have nine lives like a cat.

Adj. living, alive; in -life, – the flesh, – the land of the living; on this side of the grave, above ground, breathing, quick, animated, viable; lively etc. (*active*) 682; alive and kicking; tenacious of life.

vital; vivi-fying; -fied etc. *v.*; Promethean.

Adv. *vivendi causâ.*

360. Death.—N. death, dying etc. *v.*; de-cease, -mise; dissolution, departure, *obit*, release, rest, *quietus*, fall; loss, bereavement.

end etc. 67 –, cessation etc. 142 –, loss –, extinction –, ebb- of -life etc. 359.

death-warrant, -watch, -rattle, -bed; stroke –, agonies –, shades –, valley of the shadow –, jaws –, hand- of death; last -breath, – gasp, – agonies; dying -day, – breath, – agonies; swan song, *chant du cygne*; *rigor mortis*; Stygian shore; crossing the bar, the great adventure.

King -of terrors, – Death; Death, Angel of Death; mortality; doom etc. (*necessity*) 601.

euthanasia; happy release; break up of the system; natural -death, – decay; sudden –, violent- death; untimely end, watery grave; suffocation, *asphyxia*; heart failure; fatal disease etc. (*disease*) 655; death-blow etc. (*killing*) 361.

necrology, bills of mortality, obituary; death-song etc. (*lamentation*) 839.

V. die, expire, perish; meet one's -death, – end; pass away, be taken; yield –, resign- one's breath; resign one's -being, – life; end one's -days, – life, – earthly career; breathe one's last; cease to -live, – breathe; depart this life; be -no more etc. *adj.*; go –, drop –, pop -off; lose –, lay down –, relinquish –, surrender- one's life; drop –, sink- into the grave; close one's eyes; fall –, drop- dead, – down dead; break one's neck; give –, yield- up the ghost; be all over with one.

pay the debt to nature, shuffle off this mortal coil, take one's last sleep; go the way of all flesh; join the -greater number, – majority, – choir invisible, to life immortal awake; come –, turn- to dust; cross the Stygian ferry; go to -one's long account, – one's last home, – Davy Jones's locker, – the wall; receive one's death warrant, make one's will, die a natural death, go out like the snuff of a candle; come to an untimely end; catch one's death; go off the hooks, kick the bucket, pet out; go West; hop the twig, turn up one's toes; die a violent death etc. (*be killed*) 361; make the supreme sacrifice.

Adj. dead, lifeless; deceased, demised, departed, defunct; late, gone, no more; ex-, in-animate; out of the world, taken off, released; departed this life etc. *v.*; dead and gone; bereft of life, stone dead, dead as -a door nail, – a door post, – mutton, – a herring, – nits; launched into eternity, gathered to one's fathers, numbered with the dead, gone to a better land, behind the veil, beyond the grave, – mortal ken.

dying etc. *v.*; mori-bund, -ent, Acherontic; hippocratic; *in -articulo*, – *extremis*; in the -jaws, – agony- of death; going, – off; *aux abois*; on one's -last legs, – death bed; at -the point of death, – death's door, – the last gasp; near one's end, given over, booked, fey; with one foot in –, tottering on the brink of- the grave.

still-born; mortuary; deadly etc. (*killing*) 361.

Adv. *post -obit*, – *mortem*.

Phr. life -ebbs, – fails, – hangs by a thread; one's -days are numbered, – hour is come, – race is run, – doom is sealed; Death -knocks at the door, – stares one in the face; the breath is out of the body; the grave closes over one; *sic itur ad astra*.

361. Killing. [Destruction of life; violent death.]—**N.** killing etc. *v.*; homicide, manslaughter, murder, assassination, trucidation, occision; lynching, effusion of blood; blood, -shed; gore, slaughter, carnage, butchery; *battue*, gladiatorial combat.

massacre; *fussillade*, *noyade*, *pogrom*; thuggism; racketeering.

death blow, finishing stroke, *coup de grâce*, *quietus*; execution etc. (*capital punishment*) 972; judicial murder; martyrdom.

butcher, slayer, murderer, Cain, assassin, cutthroat, garrotter, *bravo*, thug, racketeer, gunman, mobster, gangster, Moloch, *matador*, *sabreur*; *guet-à-pens*; gallows, executioner etc. (*punishment*) 975; man-eater.

regicide, parricide, fratricide, infanticide, aborticide etc.

suicide, *felo de se*, *suttee*, *hara kiri*, Juggernaut; immolation, holocaust.

suffocation, strangulation, *garrotte*; hanging etc. *v.*

deadly weapon etc. (*arms*) 727; Aceldama; the potter's field, the field of blood.

fatal accident, violent death, casualty.

[Destruction of animals] slaughtering; phthiozoics;* sport, -ting; the chase, venery; hunting, coursing, shooting, fishing; pig-sticking; sports-, hunts-, fisher-man; hunter, Nimrod; slaughterer, knacker, slaughter-house, shambles, *abattoir*.

V. kill, put to death, slay, shed blood; murder, assassinate, butcher, slaughter; victimize, immolate; massacre; take away –, deprive of- life; make away with, put an end to; despatch, dispatch; burke settle, do, – to death, – for.

strangle, garrotte, hang, lynch, throttle, choke, stifle, suffocate, stop the breath, smother, asphyxiate, drown.

saber; cut -down, – to pieces, – the throat; jugulate; stab, run through the body, bayonet; put to the -sword, – edge of the sword.

shoot, – dead; blow one's brains out; brain, knock on the head; stone, lapidate; give –, deal- a death blow; give a -*quietus*, – *coup de grâce*.

behead, bowstring etc. (*execute*) 972.

hunt, shoot etc. *n.*

cut off, nip in the bud, launch into eternity, send to one's last account, bump off, rub out, sign one's death warrant, strike the death knell of.

give no quarter, pour out blood like water; decimate; run amuck, wade knee-deep –, imbrue one's hands- in blood.

die a violent death, welter in one's blood; dash –, blow- out one's brains; commit suicide; kill –, -make away with –, put an end to- oneself.

Adj. killing etc. *v.*; murd-, slaught-erous; sanguin-ary, -olent; blood-stained, -thirsty;

homicidal, red-handed; bloody, -minded; ensanguined, gory, sanguineous.

mortal fatal, lethal; dead-, death-ly; mort-, lethiferous; unhealthy etc. 657; internecine; suicidal.

sporting; piscator-ial, -y.

Adv. in at the death.

*Bentham, 'Chrestomathia.'

362. Corpse.—N. corpse, corse, carcass, bones, skeleton, dry-bones; defunct, relics, *relinquiae*, remains, mortal remains, dust, ashes, earth, clay; mummy; carrion; food for- worms, – fishes; tenement of clay, this mortal coil.

shade, ghost, *manes*, apparition etc. 980.

organic remains, fossils.

Adj. cadaverous, corpse-like; unburied etc. 363.

363. Interment.—N. interment, burial, inhumation, sepulture, entombment; in-, humation; obs-, ex-equies; funeral, wake, pyre, funeral pile; cremation.

funeral -rite, – solemnity; knell, passing bell, tolling; dirge etc. (*lamentation*) 839; cypress; *obit*, dead march, muffled drum; coroner, mortician, undertaker, mute, mourner, professional mourner, pallbearer; elegy; funeral -oration, – sermon; epitaph.

grave clothes, shroud; winding-sheet, cere-cloth; cerement.

coffin, shell, sarcophagus, urn, pall, bier, hearse, catafalque, cinerary urn.

grave, pit, sepulcher, tomb, vault, crypt, catacomb, mausoleum, *Golgotha*, house of death, narrow house, long home; cemetery, necropolis, boneyard; burial-place, -ground; grave-, churchyard; God's acre; mortuary, tope, cromlech, dolmen, menhir, barrow, tumulus, cairn; ossuary; bone-, charnel-, dead-house; *Morgue*; lich-gate; crematorium.

sexton, grave-digger.

monument, memorial, cenotaph, shrine; grave-, head-, tomb-stone; *memento mori*; hatchment, stone, cross.

exhumation, disinterment; necropsy, autopsy, *post mortem* examination.

V. inter, bury, lay in –, consign to- the -grave, – tomb; en-, in-tomb; inhume; lay out, prepare for burial, embalm, mummify; conduct a funeral, hold services; toll the knell; put to bed with a shovel.

exhume, disinter, unearth.

Adj. buried etc. *v.*; burial; fune-real, -brial; mortuary, sepulchral, cinerary; elegiac; necroscopic.

Adv. *in memoriam*; *post-obit*, *-mortem*; beneath –, under- the sod.

Phr. *hic jacet, ci-git, requiescat in pace.*

364. Animality.—N. animal life; anima-tion, -lity, -lization; breath.

flesh, – and blood; corporeal nature; *physique*; strength etc. 159.

V. animalize, incorporate.

Adj. fleshly, incarnate, carnal, corporeal, human.

365. Vegetability.—N. vegetable life; vegeta-tion, -bility; herbage.

V. vegetate, germinate, sprout, shoot; cultivate.

Adj. vegetable etc. 367; rank, lush.

366. Animal.*—N. animal, – kingdom; *fauna*; brute creation.

beast, brute, creature, created being; creeping –, living- thing; dumb -animal, – creature.

flocks and herds, live stock; domestic –, wild-animals; game, *ferae naturae*; beasts of the fields, fowls of the air, denizens of the day.

vertebrate, bi-, quadru-ped, mammal, marsupial, bird, reptile, batrachian, amphibian, fish, crustacean, shell fish, articulate, mollusc, worm, insect, zoophyte; protozoon, animalcule etc. 193.

horse etc. (*beast of burden*) 271; cattle, kine, ox; bull, -ock; steer, stot; cow, milch-cow, calf, heifer, shorthorn; sheep; lamb, -kin; ewe –, pet-lamb; ewe, ram, tup; pig, swine, boar, hog, shoat, sow; tag, teg, wether.

dog, bitch, hound; pup, -py; whelp, cur, mutt, mongrel; house-, watch-, sheep-, shepherd's, sporting-, fancy-, lap-, toy-, bull-, badger-dog; mastiff; blood-, grey-, stag-, deer-, fox-, otter-, hound; harrier, beagle, spaniel, pointer, setter, retriever; Newfoundland; water -dog, – spaniel; pug, poodle; dachshund; Pinscher; turnspit; terrier; fox –, Skye- terrier; Dandie Dinmont; colley.

cat; puss,-y; kitten; grimalkin; gib-, tom-cat; mouser; fox, Reynard, vixen, stag, deer, hart, buck, doe, roe, antelope.

bird; poultry, fowl, cock, hen, chicken, chanticleer, partlet, rooster, dunghill cock, barn-door fowl; feathered -tribes, – songster; singing –, dicky- bird; canary; finch; auk, dodo, moa, roc, phoenix.

snake, serpent, viper, adder; newt, eft; asp, vermin.

Adj. animal, zoological.

equine, bovine, vaccine, canine, feline; fishy; piscator-y, -ial; molluscous, vermicular.

*Extended lists of names of specific varieties of animals, vegetables, etc., are beyond the scope of this work.

367. Vegetable.*—N. vegetable, – kingdom; *flora*, verdure.

plant; tree, shrub, bush; creeper; vine; herb, -age; grass.

annual; per-, bi-, tri-ennial; exotic.

timber; primeval –, virgin- forest; wood, -lands; hurst; frith, holt, weald, park, chase, greenwood, brake, grove, copse, coppice, *bocage*, *tope*, clump of trees, thicket, spinet, spinney; under-, brushwood; boscage, scrub; the oak and the ash and the bonny ivy tree.

bush, jungle, prairie; heath, -er; fern, bracken, furze, gorse, whin, broom; grass, turf, grassland, greensward, green, lawn, meadow; pas-ture, -turage; turbary; sedge, rush, weed; fungus, mushroom, toadstool; lichen, moss, conferva, mold; seaweed etc.; growth, crop.

foliage, leafage, branch, bough, ramage; spray etc. 51; leaf, frond, flag, petal, shoot, tendril.

flower, blossom, bud, bloom, bine; flowering plant; tree, sapling, pollard; timber-, fruit-tree; palm-, gum-tree; pulse, legume.

Adj. veget-able, -ous; herb-aceous, -al; botanic; sylvan, silvan; arbor- ary, -eous, -escent, -ical; dendritic, dendriform; woody, grassy; ver-dant, -durous; floral, mossy; lign-ous, -eous; wooden, leguminous; end-, ex-ogenous.

*Extended lists of names of specific varieties of animals, vegetables, etc., are beyond the scope of this work.

368. Zoology. [The science of animals.]—**N.** zoo-logy, -nomy, -graphy, -tomy; anatomy; comparative anatomy; animal —, comparative-physiology; morphology.

anthrop-, ornith-, ichthy-, herpet-, ophi-, malac-, helminth-, entom-, oryct-, paleont-ology; ichthy-etc. -otomy; taxidermy.

zo- etc. -ologist.

Adj. zoological etc. *n.*

369. Botany. [The science of plants.]—**N.** botany; phyto-graphy, -logy, -tomy; vegetable physiology, herborization, dendr-, myc-, fung-, algology; flora, pomona; botanist etc.; botanic garden etc. (*garden*) 371; *hortus siccus, herbarium*, herbal.

herb-ist, -arist, -alist, -orist, -arian etc.

V. botanize, herborize.

Adj. botanical etc. *n.*

370. Cicuration. [The economy or management of animals.]—**N.** taming etc. *v.*; cicuration, zoohygiantics; domestication, -ity; *manège*; veterinary art; breeding, pisciculture, apiculture etc.

menagery, vivarium, zoological garden, zoo; bear-pit; aviary, apiary, hive; aquarium, fishery, fish hatchery; duck-, fish-pond; stud-farm; stock farm, dairy,

[Destruction of animals] phthisozoics etc. (*killing*) 361.

neat-, cow-, shep-herd, shepherdess; grazier; drover, cowboy, cowkeeper; trainer, breeder, groom, ostler etc. 746; veterinary surgeon, vet, horse doctor; farrier; keeper; game keeper.

cage etc. (*prison*) 752; hen-coop, bird-cage, cauf; sheep-fold etc. (*inclosure*) 232.

V. tame, domesticate, acclimatize, breed, tend, break in, train, corral, round up; cage, bridle etc. (*restrain*) 751; . le etc. 266.

drive, yoke, harness, hitch; groom, curry-comb; milk; shear; hatch; incubate.

Adj. pastoral, bucolic; tame, domestic, domesticated, broken in, gentle, docile.

371. Agriculture. [The economy or management of plants.]—**N.** agriculture, cultivation, husbandry, farming; georgics, geoponics; tillage, tilth, agronomy, gardening, spade husbandry, vintage; hort-, arbor-, silv-, citr-, vit-, flor-iculture; intensive culture; landscape gardening; forestry, afforestation.

husbandman, horticulturist, citriculturist, gardener, florist; agricult-or, -urist; yeoman, farmer, cultivator, tiller of the soil, ploughman, sower, reaper; woodcutter, backwoodsman, forester; vine grower, vintager; Boer; Triptolemus.

field, meadow, garden; botanic —, winter —, ornamental —, flower —, kitchen —, truck —, market —, hop- garden; nursery; green-, hot-, glass-house; conservatory, cucumber frame, *cloche*, bed, border, seed-plot; grass-plat, lawn; park etc. (*pleasure ground*) 840; *partere*, shrubbery, plantation, avenue, *arboretum*, pinery, *pinetum*, orchard, vineyard, vinery; orangery; farm etc. (*abode*) 189.

V. cultivate; till, — the soil; farm, garden; sow, plant; reap, mow, cut; manure, dress the ground, dig, delve, dibble, hoe, plough, plow, harrow, rake, weed, lop and top, force, transplant, thin out, bed out, prune, graft.

Adj. agr-icultural, -airan, -estic.

arable; predial, rural, rustic, country, bucolic, Boeotian; horticultural.

372. Mankind.—**N.** man, -kind; human -race, — species, — nature; humanity, mortality, flesh, generation.

[Science of man] anthropo-logy, -graphy, -sophy; ethno-logy, -graphy; humanitarianism.

human being; person, -age; individual, creature, fellow creature, mortal, body, somebody, one; such a —, someone; soul, living soul; earthling; party, head, hand; *dramatis personae*.

people, persons, folk, public, *society*, *world*; community, — at large; general public; nation, -ality; state, realm; common-weal, -wealth; republic, body politic; million etc. (*commonalty*) 876; population etc. (*inhabitant*) 188.

cosmopolite; lords of the creation; ourselves.

Adj. human, mortal, personal, individual, national, civic, public, cosmopolitan; anthropoid.

373. Man.—**N.** man, male, he; manhood etc. (*adolescence*) 131; gentleman, sir, master; yeoman, wight, swain, fellow, guy, blade, *beau*, chap, gaffer, good man; husband etc. (*married man*) 903; Mr., mister, *monsieur, sahib, Herr, señor, signor*; boy etc. (*youth*) 129; Adonis.

[Male animal] cock, drake, gander, dog, boar, stag, hart, buck, horse, entire horse, stallion; gib-, tom-cat; he-, Billy-goat; ram, tup; bull, -ock; capon, ox, gelding; steer, stot.

Adj. male, he, masculine; manly, virile; un-womanly, -feminine.

374. Woman.—**N.** woman, she, female, petticoat, skirt, moll, broad.

feminality, feminity, muliebrity; womanhood etc. (*adolescence*) 131; feminism; gynecology, gyniatrics, gynics.

womankind; the -sex, — fair; fair —, softer- sex; weaker vessel; the distaff side.

dame, madam, *madame*, mistress, Mrs., lady, *mem-sahib, Frau, señora, signora, donna, belle*, matron, dowager, goody, gammer; good -woman, — wife; squaw; wife etc. (*marriage*) 903; matron-age, -hood.

Venus, nymph, wench, *grisette*; little bit of fluff; girl etc. (*youth*) 129.

inamorata (love) etc. 897; courtesan etc. 962.

spinster, old maid, virgin, bachelor girl, new woman, amazon.

[Female animal] hen, slut, bitch, sow, doe, roe, mare; she-, Nanny-goat; ewe, cow; lioness, tigress; vixen.

gynecaeum, harem, *seraglio*, *zenana*, *purdah*.

Adj. female, she; feminine, womanly, ladylike, matronly, maidenly; womanish, effeminate, unmanly, gynecic.

375. Physical Sensibility.—N. sensibility; sensitiveness etc. *adj.*; physical sensibility, feeling, perceptivity, anaphylaxis, susceptibility, esthetics; moral sensibility etc. 882.

sensation, impression, effect; consciousness etc. (*knowledge*) 490.

external senses.

V. be -sensible etc. *adj.* -of; feel, perceive.

render, -sensible etc. *adj.*; excite, stir, sharpen, cultivate, tutor.

cause sensation, impress; excite –, produce- an impression.

Adj. sens-ible, -itive, -uous; esthetic, perceptive, sentient; conscious etc. (*aware*) 490; impressionable, responsive, alive to.

acute, sharp, keen, vivid, lively, impressive, thin-skinned.

Adv. to the quick.

376. Physical Insensibility.—N. insensibility, physical insensibility; obtuseness etc. *adj.*; palsy, paralysis, *anesthesia*, *analgesia*, *narcosis*, *hypnosis*, twilight sleep, stupor, coma, trance, catalepsy; sleep etc. (*inactivity*) 683; moral insensibility etc. 823; numbness etc. 381.

anesthetic agent, general –, local- anesthetic, opium, ether, chloroform, cocaine, novocaine, chloral; nitrous oxide, laughing gas; refrigeration.

V. be -insensible etc. *adj.*; have a -thick skin, – rhinoceros hide.

render -insensible etc. *adj.*; blunt, pall, obtund, benumb, deaden, paralyze; anesthetize, drug, dope; put under the influence of -chloroform etc. *n.*; hypnotize; stupefy, stun, narcotize.

Adj. insensible, unfeeling, senseless, comatose, dazed, impercipient, callous, thick-skinned, pachydermatous; hard, -ened; case-hardened; proof; obtuse, dull; anesthetic; paralytic, palsied, numb, dead.

377. Physical Pleasure.—N. pleasure; physical –, sensual –, sensuous- pleasure; bodily enjoyment, animal gratification, sensuality; hedonism, luxuriousness etc. *adj.*; dissipation, round of pleasure; titillation, *gusto*, creature comforts, comfort, ease; pillow etc. (*support*) 215; luxury, lap of luxury; purple and fine linen; bed of -down, – roses; velvet, clover; cup of Circe etc. (*intemperance*) 954.

treat; diversion, divertisement, entertainment; refreshment, regale; feast; *délice*; dainty etc. 394; *bonne bouche*.

source of pleasure etc. 829; happiness etc. (*mental enjoyment*) 827.

V. feel –, experience –, receive- pleasure; enjoy, relish; luxuriate –, revel –, riot –, bask –, swim –, wallow- in; feast on; gloat -over, – on; smack the lips.

live -on the fat of the land, – in comfort etc. *adv.*; bask in the sunshine, *faire ses choux gras*.

give pleasure etc. 829.

Adj. enjoying etc. *v.*; luxurious, voluptuous, sensual, hedonistic, comfortable, cosy, snug, in comfort, at ease.

agreeable etc. 829; grateful, refreshing, comforting, cordial, genial; sensuous; palatable etc. 394; sweet etc. (*sugar*) 396; fragrant etc. 400; melodious etc. 413; lovely etc. (*beautiful*) 845.

Adv. in -comfort etc. *n.*; on -a bed of roses etc. *n.*; at one's ease.

378. Physical Pain.—N. pain; suffering, -ance; bodily – physical -pain, – suffering; mental suffering etc. 828; dolor, ache; aching etc. *v.*; smart; shoot, -ing; twinge, twitch, gripe, head-, ear-, toothache; *migraine*, neuralgia, neuritis, lumbago, gout, sciatica; hurt, cut; sore, -ness; discomfort, *malaise*; *tic douloureux*.

spasm, cramp; nightmare, *ephialtes*; crick, stitch, kink; thrill, convulsion, throe; throb etc. (*agitation*) 315; pang.

sharp –, piercing –, throbbing –, shooting –, gnawing –, burning- pain; anguish, agony.

torment, torture; rack; cruci-ation, -fixion; martyrdom; martyr, toad under a harrow, vivisection.

V. feel –, experience –, suffer –, undergo- pain etc. *n.*; suffer, ache, smart, bleed; tingle, shoot; twinge, twitch, lancinate; writhe, wince, make a wry face; sit on -thorns, – pins and needles.

give –, inflict- pain; pain, hurt, chafe, sting, bite, gnaw, gripe, stab, grind; pinch, tweak; grate, gall, fret, prick, pierce, wring, convulse; torment, torture; rack, agonize; crucify; excruciate; break on the wheel, put to the rack; flag etc. (*punish*) 972; grate on the ear etc. (*harsh sound*) 410.

Adj. in -pain etc. *n.*; – a state of pain; pained etc. *v.*

painful; aching etc. *v.*; biting, poignant; sore, raw, tender, with exposed nerve.

379. Touch. [Sensation of pressure.] **—N.** touch; tact, -ion, -ility; feeling, palp-ation, -ability; manipulation; brush, tick, graze, contact etc. 199.

[Organ of touch] hand, finger, fore-finger, thumb, paw, feeler, *antenna*.

V. touch, feel, handle, finger, thumb, paw, fumble, grope, grabble; twiddle, tweedle; pass –, run- the fingers over, massage, rub, knead; palpate, stroke, manipulate, wield; throw out a feeler.

Adj. tact-ual, -ile; tangible, palpable; lambent.

380. Sensations of Touch.—N. itching etc. *v.*; titillation, formication, *aura*.

V. itch, tingle, creep, thrill, sting; prick, -le; tickle, titillate.

Adj. itching etc. *v.*

381. Numbness. [Insensibility to touch.] **—N.**

numbness etc. (*physical insensibility*) 376; pins and needles.

local anesthetic, cocaine novocaine etc.; morphia.

V. benumb etc. 376; freeze, dull, deaden.

Adj. numb; benumbed etc. *v.*; intangible, impalpable.

382. Heat.—N. heat, caloric; temperature, warmth, fervor, calidity; incal-, incand-, recal-, decal-escence; glow, flush, blush; fever, hectic.

phlogiston; fire, spark, scintillation, flash, flame, blaze; arc; bonfire; firework, pyrotechny; wild-fire; sheet of fire, lambent flame; devouring element; conflagration.

summer, dog-days, canicule; baking etc. 384 –, white –, tropical –, Afric –, Bengal –, summer –, blood- heat; heat wave, sirocco, simoon; broiling sun; isolation; warming etc. 384.

sun etc. (*luminary*) 423; fire worshipper etc. 991; furnace etc. 386.

geyser, hot spring, volcano.

: Science of heat. pyrology; thermology, -otics; thermometer etc. 389.

V. be -hot etc. *adj.*; glow, incandesce, flush, sweat, swelter, bask, smoke, reek, stew, simmer, seethe, boil, burn, singe, scorch, scald, grill, broil, blaze, flame; smoulder; parch, fume, pant.

heat etc. (*make hot*) 384; thaw, fuse, melt, give.

Adj. hot, heated, warm, mild, genial, tepid, lukewarm, unfrozen; therm-al, -ic; calorific; ferv-ent, -id; ardent; aglow.

sunny, torrid, tropical, estival, canicular; close, sultry, stifling, stuffy, suffocating, oppressive; reeking etc. *v.*; baking etc. 384.

red –, white –, smoking –, bruning etc. *v.* –, piping- hot; like -a furnace, – an oven; hot as -fire, – pepper; hot enough to roast an ox.

fiery; incand-, incal-escent; candent, ebullient, glowing, smoking; on fire; blazing etc. *v.*; in - flames, – a blaze; alight, afire, ablaze; unquenched, -extinguished; smouldering; in a -heat, – glow, – fever, – perspiration, – sweat; sudorific; swelter-ing, -ed; blood-hot, -warm; warm as -a toast, – wool; recalescent, thermogenic, pyrotechnic, feverish, febrile, inflamed.

volcanic, plutonic, igneous; isother-mal, -mic, -al.

Phr. Not a breath of air.

383. Cold.—N. cold, -ness etc. *adj.*; frigidity, gelidity, algidity, inclemency, *fresco*..

winter; depth of –, hard- winter; Siberia, Nova Zembla; Ant-, arctic, North –, South- Pole.

ice; snow, – flake, – crystal – drift; sleet; hail, -stone; rime, frost; hoar –, white –, hard –, sharp- frost; icicle, thick-ribbed ice; fall of snow, snow storm, heavy fall, *avalanche*; ice-berg, -floe; floe, berg; *glacier*; *nevée*, *serac*.

[Sensation of cold] chilliness etc. *adj.*; chill shivering etc. *v.*; goose- skin, -flesh; *rigor*, horripilation, chattering of teeth; frostbite, chilblain.

V. be -cold etc. *adj.*; shiver, starve, quake, shake, tremble, shudder, didder, quiver; perish with cold; chill etc. (*render cold*) 385.

Adj. cold, cool; chill, -y; gelid, frigid, algid; fresh, keen, bleak, raw, inclement, bitter, biting, niveous, cutting, nipping, piercing, pinching; clay-cold; starved etc. (*made cold*) 385; shivering etc. *v.*; aguish, *transi de froid*; frost- bitten, -bound, -nipped.

cold as -a stone, – marble, – lead, – iron, – a frog, – charity, – Christmas; cool as -a cucumber, – custard.

icy, glacial, frosty, freezing, wintry, brumal, hibernal, boreal, arctic, antarctic, polar, Siberian, hyemal; hyperbore-an, -al; ice-bound; frozen out.

un-warmed, -thawed, -heated; isocheimal, -chimenal.

Adv. coldly, bitterly etc. *adj.*; *à pierre fendre*.

384. Calefaction.—N. increase of temperature; heating etc. *v.*; cale-, tepe-, torre-faction; melting, fusion; liquefaction etc. 335; burning etc. *v.*; kindling, combustion; in-, ac-censión; con-, cremation; scorification; cauter-y, -ization; ustulation, calcination; in-, cineration; cupellation; carbonization.

ignition, inflammation, adustion, *flagration; de-*, con-flagration; empyrosis, incendiarism; arson; *auto da fé*; suttee.

boiling etc. *v.*; coction, ebullition, estuation, elixation, decoction.

furnace etc. 386; blanket, flannel, fur, muffler, wrap; wadding etc. (*lining*) 224; clothing etc. 225.

match etc. (*fuel*) 388; incendiary, pryomaniac; *pétroleur, pétroleuse*; cauterant, caustic, lunar caustic, apozem, moxa.

sunstroke, *coup de soliel*; insolation, sunburn.

pottery, ceramics, crockery, porcelain, china; earthen-, stone-ware; pot, mug, *terra-cotta*, brick, clinker; cinder, ash, *scoriae*; embers, dress, slag, products of combustion, coke, carbon, charcoal.

inflamma-, combusti-bility.

[Transmission of heat] diathermancy, transcalency, diathermy.

V. heat, warm, chafe, stive, foment; make -hot etc. 382; sun oneself, bask in the sun.

fire; set -fire to, – on fire; kindle, enkindle, light, ignite, strike a light; apply the -match, – torch- to; re-kindle, -lume; fan –, add fuel to- the flame; poke –, stir –, blow- the fire; make a bonfire of; burn at the stake.

melt, thaw, fuse; liquefy etc. 335.

burn, inflame, roast, toast, fry, grill, singe, parch, bake, torrefy, scorch; brand, cauterize, sear, burn in; corrode, char, carbonize, calcine, incinerate; smelt, cupel, scorify; reduce to ashes; burn to a cinder; commit –, consign- to the flames.

boil, digest, stew, cook, seethe, scald, parboil, simmer; do to rags.

take –, catch- fire; blaze etc. (*flame*) 382.

Adj. heated etc. *v.*; molten, sodden; réchauffé; heating etc. *v.*

inflammable, burnable, inflammatory, combustible; diatherm-al, -anous; burnt etc. *v.*; volcanic.

386. Refrigeration.—N. refrigeration, infrigidation, reduction of temperature; cooling etc. *v.*; con-gelation, -glaciation; ice etc. 383; solidification etc. (*density*) 321; refrigerator etc. 387.

extincteur; fire, – engine, – extinguisher, – annihilator, – brigade, – man; sprinkler, hose, hydrant, standpipe.

incombusti-bility, -bleness etc. *adj.*

V. cool, fan, refrigerate, refresh, ice; congeal, freeze, glaciate; benumb, starve, pinch, chill, petrify, chill to the marrow, nip, cut, pierce, bite, make one's teeth chatter; damp, slack; quench; put –, stamp- out; extinguish.

go –, burn- out.

Adj. cooled etc. *v.*; frozen out; cooling etc. *v.*; frigorific.

incombustible; un-, unin-flammable; fire-proof.

386. Furnace.—N. furnace, blast furnace, fire-box, stove, incinerator, destructor, crematorium, crematory, kiln, oven, oast-house; hot-, bake-, wash-house; laundry; conservatory; hearth, focus; athanor, hypocaust, reverberatory; volcano; forge, fiery furnace; *tuyère*, brasier, salamander, heater, warming-pan, foot-warmer, hot-water bottle; radiator; boiler, geyser, caldron, seething caldron, pot; urn, kettle; chafing-dish; retort, crucible, alembic, still; saggar.

fire-place, -dog, -irons; hearth, ingle, grate, range, kitchener; kitchen range; oil-, gas-, electric, -cooker, -stove; fireless cooker; fire; galley; ca-, cam-boose; poker, tongs, shovel, hob, trivet; and-, grid-iron; frying-, stew-pan etc.

hot –, Turkish –, Russian –, vapor –, shower –, warm- bath; *calidarium*, *tepidarium*, *sudatorium*, sudatory; *hammam*.

387. Refrigerator.—N. refrigerator, -y; *frigidarium*; cold storage; refrigerating-plant, – machine; ice-house, -pail, -bag, -chest, -pack; cooler, damper; wine-cooler, freezing mixture.

388. Fuel.—N. fuel, firing, combustible, coal, wallsend, anthracite, bituminous coal, slack, culm, cannel coal, lignite, briquette, coke, carbon, charcoal; turf, peat, fire-wood, bobbing, faggot, log, yule log, ember, cinder etc. (*products of combustion*) 384; kindling wood, tinder, touch-wood; fumigator, sulphur, brimstone; incense; port-fire; fire-barrel, -ball, -brand.

fuel oil, gas, gasoline, electricity.

brand, torch, fuse; wick; spill, match, safety match, light, lucifer, congreve, vesuvian, vesta, fusee, locofoco; linstock; illuminant.

candle etc. (*luminary*) 423; oil etc. (*grease*) 356; petrol, gasoline, methylated –, spirit; gas, acetylene.

Adj. carbonaceous; combustible, inflammable.

V. stoke, fire, feed, add fuel to the flames.

389. Thermometer.—N. thermo-meter, -scope, -stat, -pile, differential thermometer; pyro-, calorimeter; radio micrometer etc.

390. Taste.—N. taste, flavor, gust, *gusto*, relish, savor; sapor, sapidity; twang, smack, smatch; after-taste, tang.

tasting; de-, gustation.

palate, tongue, tooth, stomach.

V. taste, savor, smatch, smack, flavor, twang; tickle the palate etc. (*savory*) 394; smack the lips.

Adj. sapid, saporific; gusta-ble, -tory; strong; flavored, spiced, savory; palatable etc. 394.

391. Insipidity.—N. insipidity; tastlessness etc. *adj.*

V. be -tasteless etc. *adj.*

Adj. void of -taste etc. 390; insipid; jejune; taste-, gust-, savor-less; ingustible, mawkish, milk and water, weak, stale, flat, vapid, *fade*, wishy-washy, mild; untasted.

392. Pungency.—N. pungency, piquancy, poignancy, *haut-goût*, strong taste, twang, race, tang.

sharpness etc. *adj.*; acrimony, acridity; roughness etc. (*sour*) 397; unsavoriness etc. 395.

niter, saltpeter; mustard, cayenne, caviar; seasoning etc. (*condiment*) 393; brine.

dram, cordial, nip, pick-me-up, bracer, potion.

nicotine, tobacco, snuff, quid; segar; cigar, -ette, gasper, fag; cheroot; weed; fragrant –, Indian-weed; pipe, clay pipe, churchwarden, brier, meerschaum, hookah, hubble-bubble.

V. be -pungent etc. *adj.*; bite the tongue.

render -pungent etc. *adj.*; season, spice, salt, pepper, pickle, brine, devil, curry.

smoke, chew, take snuff.

Adj. pungent, strong; high-, full-flavored; high-tasted, -seasoned; gamy; sharp, stinging, rough, *piquant*, racy; biting, mordant; spicy; seasoned etc. *v.*; hot, – as pepper; peppery, vellicating, escharotic, meracious; acrid, acrimonious, bitter; rough etc. (*sour*) 397; unsavory etc. 395.

salt, saline, brackish, briny; salt as -brine, – a herring, – Lot's wife.

393. Condiment.—N. condiment, flavoring, salt, mustard, pepper, cayenne, curry, seasoning, sauce, spice, cinnamon, chillies, relish, *sauce piquante*, caviare, pot-herbs, onion, garlic, pickle, chutney, nutmeg etc.

V. season etc. (*render pungent*) 392.

394. Savoriness.—N. savoriness etc. *adj.*; relish, zest.

tit-bit, dainty, delicacy, ambrosia, nectar, *bonne bouche*; game, turtle, venison.

V. taste good, be -savory etc. *adj.*; tickle the palate, – appetite; flatter the palate.

render -palatable etc. *adj.*

relish, like, smack the lips.

Adj. savory, well-tasted, to one's taste, tasty, good, palatable, nice, dainty, delectable; tooth-ful, -some; gustful, appetizing, lickerish, delicate, delicious, exquisite, rich, luscious, ambrosial.

Adv. *per amusare la bocca.*

Phr. *cela se laisse manger.*

395. Unsavoriness.—N. unsavoriness etc. *adj.*; amaritude; acri-mony, -tude; roughness etc. (*sour*) 397; acerbity, austerity; gall and worm-wood, rue, quassia, aloes; sickener.

V. be -unpalatable etc. *adj.*; sicken, disgust, nauseate, pall, turn the stomach.

Adj. un-savory, -palatable, -sweet; ill-flavored, un-appetizing, -eatable, inedible; bitter, – as gall; acrid, acrimonious; rough.

offensive, repulsive, nasty; sickening etc. *v.*; nauseous; loath-, ful-some; unpleasant etc. 830.

396. Sweetness.—N. sweetness, dulcitude, saccharinity.

sugar, cane-, beet-sugar; saccharine, glucose, syrup, treacle, molasses, honey, manna; confection, -ary; sweets, grocery, conserve, preserve, *confiture*, jam, marmalade, julep; sugar-candy, -plum; licorice, liquorice, plum, lollipop, *bon bon*, *jujube*, comfit, sweetmeat, caramel, toffee, butterscotch.

nectar; hydromel, mead, metheglin, honeysuckle, *liqueur*, sweet wine.

pastry, pie, tart, puff, pudding, cake.

dulc-ification, -oration.

V. be sweet etc. *adj.*

render -sweet etc. *adj.*; sugar, saccharize, sweeten; edulcorate; dulc-orate, -ify; candy; mull.

Adj. sweet, sugary; sacchar-ine, -iferous; dulcet, honied, candied, luscious, nectarious, melliferous; sweetened etc. *v.*

sweet as -a nut, – sugar, – honey.

397. Sourness.—N. sourness etc. *adj.*; acid, -ity; acetous fermentation; acerbity.

vinegar, verjuice, crab, alum.

V. be –, turn- -sour etc. *adj.*; set the teeth on edge.

render -sour etc. *adj.*; acid-ify, -ulate.

Adj. sour; acid, -ulous, -ulated; acerb; tart, crabbed; acet-ous, -ose; sour as vinegar, sourish, acescent, sub-acid; styptic, hard, rough; unripe, green.

398. Odor.—N. odor, smell, odorament, scent, effluvium; eman-, exhal-ation; fume, essence, trail, nidor, redolence.

sense of smell; scent; act of -smelling etc. *v.*

V. have an -odor etc. *n.*; smell, – of, – strong of; exhale; give out a -smell etc. *n.*; scent.

smell, scent; snuff, – up; sniff, nose, inhale.

Adj. odor-ous, -iferous; smelling, strong-scented; redolent, graveolent, nidorous, pungent.

[Relating to the sense of smell] olfactory, quick-scented..

399. Inodorousness.—N. inodorousness; absence –, want- of smell.

V. be -inodorous etc. *adj.*; not smell.

deodorize.

Adj. inodor-ous, -ate; scentless; without –, wanting- smell etc. 398.

deodoriz-ed, -ing.

400. Fragrance.—N. fragrance, aroma, redolence, perfume, *bouquet*; sweet smell, aromatic perfume.

perfumery; incense; musk, frankincense; pastil, -le; myrrh, perfumes of Arabia, chypre; otto, ottar, attar; bergamot, balm, civet, *pot-pourri*, pulvil; nosegay, *boutonnière*; scent, -bag; *sachet*, scent-bottle, smelling bottle, *vinaigrette*; toilet water, *eau de Cologne*; thurible, censer, thurification.

perfumer; incense bearer.

V. be -fragrant etc. *adj.*; have a -perfume etc. *n.*; smell sweet, scent, perfume, thurify, embalm.

Adj. fragrant, aromatic, redolent, spicy, balmy, scented; sweet-smelling, -scented; perfum-ed, -atory; thuriferous; fragrant as a rose, muscadine, ambrosial.

401. Fetor.—N. fetor, fetidness; bad etc. *adj.*; -smell, – odor; stench, stink; mephitis, foul –, mal- odor; *empyreuma*; mustiness etc. *adj.*; rancidity; foulness etc. (*uncleanness*) 653.

stoat, polecat, skunk; asafetida; fungus, garlic; stink-pot, -bomb.

V. have a -bad smell etc. *n.*; smell; stink, – in the nostrils, – like a polecat; smell -strong etc. *adj.*; – offensively.

Adj. fetid; strong-smelling; high, bad, strong, fulsome, offensive, noisome, rank, rancid, reasty, tainted, musty, fusty, frouzy; olid, -ous; nidorous; smelling, stinking; putrid etc. 653; suffocating, mephitic; empyreumatic.

402. Sound.—N. sound, noise, strain; accent, twang, intonation, tone, tune; cadence; sonority, sonorousness etc. *adj.*; audibility; resonance etc. 408; voice etc. 580.

[Science of sound] acou-, acu-stics; catacoustics; cataphonics; phon-ics, -etics, -ology, -ography; diacoustics, -phonics.

telephone, phonograph etc. 418.

V. produce sound; sound, make a noise; give out –, emit- sound; phonetize, phonate; resound etc. 408.

Adj. sounding; soniferous; sonorific; resonant, audible, acoustic, auditory, distinct; stertorous; phonic, sonant; phonetic.

403. Silence.—N. silence; stillness etc. (*quiet*) 265; peace, hush, lull, rest; muteness etc. 581; solemn –, awful –, dead –, deathlike-silence.

V. be -silent etc. *adj.*; hold one's tongue etc. (*not speak*) 585.

render -silent etc. *adj.*; silence, still, hush; stifle, muffle, gag, stop; muzzle, put to silence etc. (*render mute*) 581.

Adj. silent; still, -y; calm, quiet; noise-, sound-, speech-less; hushed etc. *v.*; mute etc. 581; aphonic.

soft, solemn, awful, deathlike, silent as the grave; inaudible etc. (*faint*) 405.

Adv. silently etc. *adj.*; *sub silentio*; in perfect silence.

Int. hush! 'sh! silence! soft! whist! tush! chut! tut! *pax!* mum's the word! hold your tongue! shut up! be silent! be quiet! stop that noise! hold your row! dry up! peace, be still!

Phr. one might hear a -feather, – pin- drop.

404. Loudness.—N. loudness, power; loud noise, din; clang, -or; clatter, noise, bombilation, roar, uproar, racket, static, grinders, hubbub, *fracas*, *charivari*, trumpet blast, blare, flourish of trumpets, fanfare, *tintamarre*, peal, swell, blast, alarum, boom; resonance etc. 408.

vociferation; pandemonium, hullaballoo etc. 411; lungs; Stentor; megaphone; siren.

artillery, cannon, gunfire, shellburst, bomb; thunder.

V. be -loud etc. *adj.*; peal, swell, clang, boom, thunder, fulminate, roar; resound etc. 408; speak up, shout etc. (*vociferate*) 411; bellow etc. (*cry as an animal*) 412; give tongue.

rend the -air, – skies; fill the air; din –, ring –, thunder- in the ear; pierce –, split –, rend- the-ears, – head; deafen, stun; *faire le diable a quatre*; make one's windows shake; awaken –, startle- the echoes; make the welkin ring.

Adj. loud, sonorous; high-, big- sounding; blatant; deep, full, powerful, noisy, clangorous, multisonous, *fortisimo*; thundering, deafening etc. *v.*; trumpet-tongued; ear-splitting, -rending, -deafening; piercing; obstreperous, rackety, uproarious; enough to wake the -dead, – seven sleepers.

shrill etc. 410; clamorous etc. (*vociferous*) 411; stentor-ian, -ophonic.

Adv. loudly etc. *adj.*; aloud; at the top of one's voice, lustily, in full cry.

Phr. the air rings with.

405. Faintness.—N. faintness etc. *adj.*; faint sound, whisper, breath; under-tone, -breath; murmur, hum, rustle, buzz, purr; plash; sough, moan, sigh, susurration; tinkle; 'still small voice.'

hoarseness etc. *adj.*; raucity.

silencer, soft pedal, damper, mute, *sourdine*.

V. whisper, breathe, murmur, purl, hum, gurgle, ripple, babble, flow; tinkle; mutter etc. (*speak imperfectly*) 583.

steal on the ear; melt in –, float on- the air. muffle, mute, deaden, damp, stifle.

Adj. inaudible; scarcely –, just- audible; low, dull; stifled, muffled; hoarse, husky; gentle, soft, faint; floating; purling, flowing etc. *v.*; whispered etc. *v.*; liquid; soothing; dulcet etc. (*melodious*) 413.

Adv. in a whisper, with bated breath, *sotto voce*, between the teeth, aside; *pian-o*, *-issimo*; *à la sourdine*; *con sourdine*; out of earshot, inaudibly etc. *adj.*

406. Snap. [Sudden and violent sounds.]—**N.** snap etc. *v.*; rapping etc. *v.*; de-, crepitation; smack, clap, report; thud; burst, explosion, discharge, detonation, blow-out, back-fire, firing, salvo, volley, pistol-shot.

squib, cracker, gun, rifle, pop-gun.

V. rap, snap, tap, knock; click; clash; crack, -le; crash; pop; slam, bang, clap, thump, plump; toot; back-fire, explode, burst on the ear.

Adj. rapping etc. *v.*

Int. crash! bang!

407. Roll. [Repeated and protracted sounds.]—**N.** roll etc. *v.*; drumming etc. *v.*; tattoo; ding-dong; tantara; rataplan; whirr; rat-a-tat; rub-a-dub; pit-a-pat; quaver, clutter, *charivari*, racket; cuckoo; repetition etc. 104; peal of bells, devil's tattoo; reverberation etc. 408.

drumfire, barrage.

machine gun.

V. roll, drum, rumble, rattle, clatter, rustle, roar, drone, patter, clack.

hum, trill, shake; chime, peal, toll; tick, beat. drum –, din- in the ear.

Adj. rolling etc. *v.*; monotonous etc. (*repeated*), 104; like a bee in a bottle.

408. Resonance.—N. resonance; ring etc. *v.*; ringing etc. *v.*; tintinnabulation; reflection, reverberation, clangor.

low –, base –, bass –, flat –, grave –, deep –, pedal- note; bass; *basso*, – *profondo*; bari-, bary-tone; *contralto*.

V. re-sound, -verberate, -echo; ring, ding, sing, jingle, gingle, chink, clink; tink, -le; chime; gurgle etc. 405; plash, guggle, echo, ring in the ear.

Adj. resounding etc. *v.*; resonant, tinnient; tintinnabulary; deep-toned, -sounding, -mouthed; hollow, sepulchral; gruff etc. (*harsh*) 410.

408a. Non-resonance.—N. thud, thump, dead sound; non-resonance; muffled drums, cracked bell; silencer, damper; mute, *sourdine*.

V. sound dead; stop –, damp- the -sound, – reverberations; deaden, muffle.

Adj. non-resonant, dead, muted, muffled.

409. Sibilation. [Hissing sounds.]—**N.** sibilation; hiss etc. *v.*; sternutation; high note etc. 410.

goose, serpent, snake.

V. hiss, buzz, whiz, rustle; fizz, -le, sizzle, swish; wheeze, whistle, snuffle; squash; sneeze.

Adj. sibilant; hissing etc. *v.*; wheezy.

410. Stridor. [Harsh sounds.]—**N.** creak etc. *v.*; creaking etc. *v.*; discord etc. 414; stridor; harshness, roughness, sharpness etc. *adj.*, cacophony.

acute –, high- note; *soprano*, treble, tenor, *alto*, falsetto, *voce di testa*; shriek, cry etc. 411.

piccolo, fife, penny -whistle, – trumpet.

V. creak, grate, jar, burr, pipe, twang, jangle, clank, clink; scream etc. (*cry*) 411; yelp etc. (*animal sound*) 412; buzz etc. (*hiss*) 409.

set the teeth on edge, *écorcher les orielles*; pierce –, split- the -ears, – head; offend –, grate upon –, jar upon- the ear.

Adj. creaking etc. *v.*; strident, stridulous, harsh,

coarse, hoarse, horrisonous, raucous, metallic, rough, gruff, grum, sepulchral.

sharp, high, acute, shrill, high-pitched; trumpet-toned; piercing, ear-piercing; cracked; discordant etc. 414; cacophonous.

411. Cry.—N. cry etc. *v.*; voice etc. (*human*) 580; bark etc. (*animal*) 412.

vociferation, outcry, hullaballoo, chorus, clamor, hue and cry, plaint; lungs; stentor.

V. cry, roar, shout, bawl, brawl, halloo, halloa, hail, hoop, whoop, yell, bellow, howl, scream, screech, screak, shriek, shrill, squeak, squeal, squall, whine, whinny, pule, pipe, yaup.

cheer, hurrah; hoot; grumble, maon, groan.

snore, snort; grunt etc. (*animal sounds*) 412.

vociferate; raise –, lift up- the voice; call –, sing –, cry- out; exclaim; rend the air; thunder –, shout- at the -top of one's voice, – pitch of one's breath; *s'égosiller*; strain the -throat, – voice, – lungs; give a -cry etc.

Adj. crying etc. *v.*; clam-ant, -orous; vociferous; stentorian etc. (*loud*) 404; open-mouthed.

412. Ululation. [Animal sounds.]—**N.** cry etc. *v.*; crying etc. *v.*; ululation, latration, belling; reboation; call, note; bark, howl, yelp; twittering, woodnote; insect cry, fritinancy, drone; screech; cuckoo.

V. cry, ululate, howl, roar, bellow, blare, rebellow, bark, yelp; bay, – the moon; yap, growl, yarr, yawl, snarl, howl; grunt, -le; snort, squeak; neigh, bray; mew, mewl; purr, caterwaul, pule; bleat, low, moo; troat, croak, crow, screech, caw, coo, gobble, quack, cackle, gaggle, guggle; chuck, -le; cluck; clack; cheep, chirp, chirrup, twitter, sing, cuckoo; pout, wail, hum, buzz; hiss, blatter; hoot.

Adj. crying etc. *v.*; blatant, latrant, re-, mugient; deep-, full-mouthed.

Adv. in full cry.

413. Melody. Concord.—N. melody, rhythym, measure; rhyme etc. (*poetry*) 597.

pitch, *timbre*, intonation, tone, overtone.

scale, gamut; diapason; diatonic –, chromatic –, enharmonic- scale; key, clef, chords.

modulation, temperament, syncope, syncopation, preparation, suspension, resolution.

staff, stave, line, space, brace; bar, rest; *appogiato, -tura*; *acciaccatura*, shake, *arpeggio*.

note, musical note, notes of a sclae; sharp, flat, natural; high note etc. (*shrillness*) 410; low note etc. 408; interval; semitone; second, third, fourth etc.; diatessaron.

breve, semibreve, minim, crotchet, quaver; semi-, demisemi- quaver; sustained note, drone, burden.

tonic; key-, leading-, fundamental-, note; supertonic, mediant, dominant; sub-mediant, -dominant, organ-, pedal-point; octave, tetrachord; major –, minor- -mode, – scale, – key; Doric mode, passage, phrase.

concord, harmony; unison, -ance; chime, homophony; euphon-y, -ism; tonality; consonance; concent; part.

orchestration; harmonization, – phrasing.

[Science of harmony] harmon-y, -ics; thorough-, fundamental- bass; counterpoint; faburden.

piece of music etc. 415; composer, harmonist, contrapuntist.

V. be -harmonious etc. *adj.*; harmonize, chime, symphonize, transpose; put in tune, tune, accord, string; score, arrange, orchestrate..

Adj. harmoni-ous, -cal; in -concord etc. *n.*, – tune, – concert; unisonant, concentual, symphonizing, isotonic, homophonous, assonant, consonant.

measured, rhythmical, diatonic, chromatic, enharmonic.

melodious, musical; tuneful, tunable; sweet, dulcet, canorous; mell-ow, -ifluous; soft; clear, – as a bell; silvery; euphon-ious, -ic, -ical; symphonious; enchanting etc. (*pleasure-giving*) 829; fine-, full-, silver-toned.

Adv. harmoniously etc. *adj.*

414. Discord.—N. discord, -ance; dissonance, cacaphony, caterwauling; harshness etc. 410; consecutive fifths.

[Confused sounds] Babel, pandemonium; Dutch –, cat's- concert; marrow-bones and cleavers.

V. be -discordant etc. *adj.* ; jar etc. (*sound harshly*) 410.

Adj. discordant; dis-, ab-sonant; *out of tune*, tuneless; un-musical, -tunable; un-, im-melodious; un-, in-harmonious; sing-song; cacophonous; jarring, harsh etc. 410.

415. Music.—N. music, classical –, modern –, descriptive- music; concert, recital; strain, tune, air, *motif*; melody etc. 413; *aria*, *arietta*; piece of music, *sonata*; *rond-o, -eau*; *pastorale*, *cavatina*, roulade, *fantasia*, *toccata*, *concerto*, overture, symphony, symphonic poem, tone poem, prelude, voluntary, *intermezzo*, variations, *cadenza*; cadence; fugue, canon, serenade, *nocturne*, *notturno*, rhapsody, romance, *aubade*, dithyramb; opera, operetta; oratorio; composition, movement, stave.

instrumental music; full-, orchestral- score; minstrelsy, tweedledum and tweedledee, band, orchestra etc. 416; concerted piece, *potpourri*, medley, *capriccio*, incidental music; improvisation; peal.

vocal music, vocalism; chaunt, chant; psalm, -ody; hymn; song etc. (*poem*) 597; canticle, canzonet, *cantata*, *bravura*, *coloratura*; lay, ballad, ditty, carol, barcarolle, pastoral, recitative, *recitativo*, *solfeggio*, tonic sol-fa.

Lydian measures; slow -music, – movement; *adagio* etc. *adv.*; minuet; siren strains, soft music, lullaby; *berceuse*, cradle song, dump; dirge etc. (*lament*) 839; pibroch; martial music, march, funeral-, dead- march; dance music; waltz etc. (*dance*) 840; rag-time, syncopation, jazz.

solo, duet, *duo*, *trio*; quartet; quintet, sextet, sep-, tet; part song, descant, glee, madrigal, catch, round, chorus, *chorale*; antiphon, -y; accompaniment, second –, alto –, tenor –, bass-part; score, thorough bass; counterpoint.

composer etc. 413; musician etc. 416.
V. compose, perform etc. 416; attune.
Adj. musical; instrumental, orchestral, vocal, choral, lyric, operatic; harmonious etc. 413.
Adv. *adagio*; *largo*, *larghetto*, *andan-te*, *-tino*; *alla capella*; *maestoso*, *moderato*; *allegr-o*, *-etto*; *spiritoso*, *vivace*, *veloce*; *prest-o*, *-issimo*; *pian-o*, *-issimo*, *fort-e*, *-issimo*, *sforzando*; *con brio*; *capriccioso*; *scherz-o*, *-ando*; *legato*, *sostenuto*, *staccato*, *crescendo*, diminuendo, *rallentando*, *affettuoso*, *arioso*; *parlante*, *cantabile*; *obbligato*; *pizzacato*, *tremolo*, *vibrato*.

416. Musician. [Performance of Music.]—**N.** musician, *artiste*, *virtuoso*, performer, player, minstrel; bard etc. (*poet*) 597; instrumental-, organ-, accompan-, pian-, violin-, flaut-, harp-ist; harper, fiddler, fifer, trumpeter, piper, drummer; catgut scraper.
band, orchestra, waits.
vocal-, melod-ist; singer, warbler; songst-, chaunt-er, -ress; *diva*, *cantatrice*, coloratura, soprano, mezzo-soprano, alto, contralto, tenor, baritone, bass, *basso*, *-profundo*.
choir, quire, chorister; chorus, – singer; choral society, festival, *eisteddfod*.
nightingale, philomel, thrush; siren; Orpheus, Apollo, the Muses, Erato, Euterpe, Terpsichore; tuneful -nine, – quire.
composer etc. 413.
performance, virtuosity, execution, touch, expression, solmization.
V. play, pipe, strike –, tune-up, sweep the chords, tickle –, paw- the ivories, vamp, tweedle, fiddle; strike the lyre, beat the drum; blow –, sound –, wind- the horn; grind the organ; touch the -guitar etc. (*instruments*) 417; thrum, strum, twang, drum, beat –, keep- time, conduct.
execute, perform; accompany; sing –, play- a second; compose, write music, set to music, arrange, harmonize, orchestrate.
sing, chaunt, chant, hum, warble, carol, chirp, chirrup, lilt, purl, quaver, trill, shake, twitter, whistle; sol-fa; intone.
have -an ear for music, – a musical ear, – a correct ear, – absolute pitch.
Adj. playing etc. *v.*; musical, lyric.
Adv. *adagio*, *andante* etc. (*music*) 415.

417. Musical Instruments.—**N.** musical instruments; band; string-, brass-, drum and fife-, military-, bugle-, German-, dance-, jazz-band; orchestra, string quartet; orchestration, orchestrelle.
[Stringed instruments] mono-, poly-chord; harp, lyre, lute, archlute, thearbo; mandol-a, -in, -ine; guitar; *ukulele*; psaltery, zither; bandore, cither, -n; gittern, rebeck, *bandurria*, banjo, zither banjo, *balalaika*, *samisen*; plectrum.
viol, -in, Cremona, Stradivarius; fiddle; kit; *vielle*, *viola*, – *d'amore*, – *di gamba*; tenor, *violoncello*, cello; bass, bass-, bass-viol; double-bass, *contrabasso*, *violone*, hurdy-gurdy; strings, catgut; bow, fiddlestick.
piano, -forte; grand –, concert grand –, baby –, upright –, cottage- piano; pianino, pianette; harpsi-, clavi-, clari-, mani-chord; *clavier*, spinet, virginals; dulcimer, *cymbalo*; Eolian harp; piano-organ, -player, electric piano, player-piano, pianola.
[Wind instruments] organ, church –, pipe –, American- organ; harmoni-um, -phon; accordion, seraphina, concertina; melodeon; barrel- organ; humming top.
flute, fife, piccolo, flageolet, penny-whistle, reed instrument; clari-net, -onet; bass clarionet; saxophone; basset horn, *corno di bassetto*; musette, shawm, oboe, hautboy, *cor Anglais*, *corno Inglese*, bassoon, double bassoon, *contrafagotto*; bag-, union-pipes; ocarina, Pandean pipes; calliope; sirene, pipe, pitch-pipe; sourdet; whistle, catcall.
horn, bugle, key bugle, cornet, *cornet-à-pistons*, cornopean, clarion, trumpet, trombone, ophicleide, serpent; English-, French-, bugle-, sax-, flugel-, alt-, helicon-, post-horn; sackbut, euphonium, bombardon, tuba, bass tuba.
[Vibrating surfaces] cymbal, bell, gong, peal of bells, *carillon*; tambour, -ine; drum, tom-tom, tabor, -ret, -ourine, -orin; *sistrum*, *grand caisse*, bass-, big-, side-, kettle-drum; *tympani*; war drums; tymbal, timbrel, castanet, bones; musical-glasses, -stones; harmonica, sounding– board, rattle; gramophone, phonograph.
[Vibrating bars] reed, tuning-fork, triangle, Jew's harp, musical box, harmonicon, xylophone, marimba, *celeste*.
sord-ine, -et; *sourd-ine*, *-et*; mute.

418. Hearing. [Sense of sound.]—**N.** hearing etc. *v.*; audition, auscultation; eavesdropping; audibility; acoustics etc. 402.
acute –, nice –, delicate –, quick –, sharp –, correct –, musical -ear; ear for music.
ear, auricle, lug, acoustic organs, auditory apparatus, ear-drum, tympanum; ear-, speaking-trumpet, megaphone; telephone, radiophone, stethoscope, phonograph, gramophone, microphone.
hearer, auditor, listener, eavesdropper; audi-tory, -ence.
V. hear, overhear; hark, -en; list, -en; give –, lend –, bend- an ear; give attention; catch a sound, prick up one's ears; give -a hearing, – audience -to.
hang upon the lips of, be all ear, listen with both ears, monitor.
become audible; meet –, fall upon –, catch –, reach- the ear; be heard; ring in the ear etc. (*resound*) 408.
Adj. hearing etc. *v.*; auditory, auricular, aural, auditive, acoustic.
Adv. *arrectis auribis*.
Int. hark, – ye! hear! list, -en! *Oyez!* attention! lend me your ears!

419. Deafness.—**N.** deafness, hardness of hearing, surdity; inaudibility.
V. be -deaf etc. *adj.*; have no ear; shut –, stop –, close- one's ears; turn a deaf ear to.
render deaf, stun, deafen.
Adj. deaf, earless, surd; hard –, dull- of hearing; deaf-mute, stunned, deafened; stone deaf; deaf as -a post, – an adder, – a beetle, – a trunk-maker.
inaudible etc. 405; out of hearing.

420. Light.—**N.** light, ray, beam, stream, gleam, streak, pencil; sun-, moon-beam; dawn, aurora.

day; sunshine; light of -day, – heaven; sun etc. (*luminary*) 432, day-, broad day-, noontide- light; noon-tide, -day; glare.

glow etc. *v.*; afterglow, sunset; glimmering etc. *v.*; glint; play –, flood- of light; phosphorescence.

flush, halo, glory, nimbus, aureole, *aureola.*

spark, *scintilla*; *facula*; sparkling etc. *v.*; emication, scintillation, flash, blaze, coruscation, fulguration; flame etc. (*fire*) 382; lightning, *ignis fatuus*, etc. (*luminary*) 423, radio-activity.

luster, sheen, shimmer, reflection; gloss, tinsel, spangle, brightness, brilliancy, splendor; ef-, re-fulgence; ful-gor, -gidity; dazzlement, resplendence, transplendency; luminousness etc. *adj.*; luminosity; lucidity; renitency; radi-ance, -ation; irradiation, illumination, phosphorescence, luminescence.

radiation, radiant heat, infra-red rays, visible radiation, ultra-violet –, actinic- rays, actinism; X –, Roentgen- rays; phot-, heli-ography; optical instruments etc. 445.

[Science of light] optics; photo-logy, -metry; di-, cat-optrics.

[Distribution of light] *chiaroscuro*, *clair-obscur*, clear obscure, breadth, light and shade, black and white, tonality, half-tone, mezzotint.

reflection, refraction, dispersion, double refraction, polarization, diffraction, interference.

illuminant etc. 423.

V. shine, glow, glitter, phosphoresce; glis-ter, -ten; twinkle, gleam; flare, – up; glare, beam, shimmer, glimmer, flicker, sparkle, scintillate, coruscate, flash, fulgurate, blaze; be -bright etc. *adj.*; reflect light, daze, dazzle, bedazzle, raidate, shoot out beams.

clear up, brighten.

lighten, enlighten; light, – up; irradiate, shine upon; give –, hang out- a light; cast –, throw –, shed- -luster, – light- upon; illum-e, -ine, -inate, relume, strike a light; kindle etc. (*set fire to*) 384.

Adj. shining etc. *v.*; lumin-ous, -iferous; luc-id, -ent, -ulent, -ific, -iferous; illuminating, light, -some; bright, vivid, splendent, nitid, lustrous, shiny, brilliant, beamy, scintillant, radiant, lambent; sheen, -y; glossy, burnished, glassy, sunny, orient, meridian; noon-day, -tide; cloudless, clear; unclouded, -obscured.

garish; re-, tran-splendent; re-, effulgent; ful-gid, -gent; relucent, splendid, blazing, in a blaze, ablaze, rutilant, meteoric, phosphorescent; aglow.

bright as silver; light –, bright- as -day, – noonday, – the sun at noonday.

optical, actinic; photo-genic, -graphic; heliographic, radioactive.

421. Darkness.—**N.** darkness etc. *adj.*; blackness etc. (*dark color*) 431; obscurity, gloom, murk; dusk etc. (*dimness*) 422;, tenebrosity, umbrageousness.

Cimmerian –, Stygian –, Egyptian- darkness; night; midnight; dead of –, witching time of- night; blind man's holiday; darkness -visible; – that can be felt; palpable, obscure; Erebus.

shade, shadow, umbra, penumbra; sciagraphy; *silhouette*; radiograph, skiagraph.

obscuration; ad-, ob-umbration; obtenebration, offuscation, caligation; extinction; eclipse, total eclipse; gathering of the clouds.

shading; distribution of shade; *chiaroscuro* etc. (*light*) 420.

noctivagation, noctograph, noctuary.

obscurantist.

V. be -dark etc. *adj.*

darken, obscure, shade; dim; tone down, lower; over-cast, -shadow; cloud, eclipse; ob-, of-fuscate; ob-, ad-umbrate, cast into the shade; be-cloud, -dim, -darken; cast –, throw –, spread- a -shade, – shadow, – gloom.

extinguish; put –, blow –, snuff- out; doubt.

Adj. dark, -some, -ling; obscure, tenebrous, tenebrious, sombrous, pitch dark, pitchy, caliginous; black etc. (*in color*) 431.

sunless, lightless etc. (*see* sun, light etc. 423); somber, dusky; unilluminated etc. (*see* illuminate etc. 420); nocturnal; dingy, lurid, gloomy; murk-y, -some; shady, umbrageous; overcast etc. (*dim*) 422; cloudy etc. (*opaque*) 426; darkened etc. *v.*

dark as -pitch, – a pit, – Erebus.

benighted; noctivag-ant, -ous.

Adv. in the -dark, – shade; at night.

422. Dimness.—**N.** dimness etc. *adj.*; darkness etc. 421; paleness etc. (*light color*) 429.

half-light, *demi-jour*; partial -shadow, – eclipse; shadow of a shade; glimmer, -ing; *nebulosity*; *cloud* etc. 353; eclipse.

aurora, dusk, twilight, gloaming, blind man's holiday, shades of evening, crepuscule, cockshut time; break of day, daybreak, dawn.

moon-light, -beam, -shine; star- owl's-, candle-, rush-, fire-light; farthing candle.

V. be –, grow- -dim etc. *adj.*; flicker, twinkle, glimmer; loom, lower; fade; darken; pale, – its ineffectual fire.

render -dim etc. *adj.*; dim, bedim, obscure.

Adj. dim, dull, lack-luster, dingy, darkish, shorn of its beams; dark 421.

faint, shadowed forth; glassy; bleary; cloudy; misty etc. (*opaque*) 426; muggy, fuliginous; nebul-ous, -ar; obnubilated, overcast, crepuscular, twilight, muddy, lurid, leaden, dun, dirty; looming etc. *v.*

pale etc. (*colorless*) 429; confused etc. (*invisible*) 447.

423. Luminary. [Source of light.]—**N.** luminary; light etc. 420; flame etc. (*fire*) 382.

spark, *scintilla*; phosphorescence.

sun, orb of day, day star, Phoebus, Apollo, Helios, Phaethon, Hyperion, Ra, Aurora; star, orb, meteor; falling –, shooting- star; blazing –, dog-star; Sirius, canicula, Aldebaran; morning star, Lucifer, Phosphor, evening star; Hesperus, Venus, planet, moon etc. 318; constellation, galaxy; northern light, *aurora -borealis*, – *australis*, zodiacal light; mock sun, parhelion.

lightning; fork –, sheet –, summer- lightning, St. Elmo's fire; phosphorus; *ignis fatuus*; Jack o' – Friar's- lantern; Will o' the wisp, fire-drake, *Fata Morgana.*

glow-worm, fire-fly.

radium, luminous paint.

[Artificial light] gas; gas –, lime –, electric –, head –, search –, spot –, flash –, flood –, footlight; lamp, oil –, gas –, arc –, incandescent-lamp; flare; lant-ern, -horn; dark lantern, bull's eye, projector; candle, ***bougie***, tallow –, wax-candle; dip, farthing dip; taper, rush-light; oil etc. (*grease*) 356; wick, burner; Argand, moderator, duplex; torch, *flambeau*, link, brand; cresset; gase-, chande-, electro-lier; candelabrum, *girandole*, sconce, luster, candle-stick.

firework, fizgig; pyrotechnics; Roman candle, Very light, star shell, parachute light; rocket, lighthouse etc. (*signal*) 550.

V. illuminate etc. (*light*) 420.

Adj. self-luminous, incandescent; phosphor-ic, -escent; luminescent, fluorescent, radiant etc. (*light*) 420.

424. Shade.—**N.** shade; awning etc. (*cover*) 223; parasol, sunshade, umbrella; screen, curtain, shutter, blind, gauze, veil, mantle, mask; cloud, mist, gathering of clouds; smoke screen; smoked glasses, colored spectacles; blinkers, blinders.

umbrage, glade; shadow etc. 421.

V. draw a curtain; put up –, close- a shutter; veil etc. *v.*; cast a shadow etc. (*darken*) 421; screen, obstruct the view.

Adj. shady, umbrageous, bowery.

425. Transparency.—**N.** transparen-ce, -cy; translucen-ce, -cy; diaphaneity; luc-, pelluc-, limpidity.

transparent medium, glass, crystal, mica; lymph, water.

v. be -transparent etc. *adj.*; transmit light.

Adj. transparent, pellucid, lucid, diaphanous; trans-, tra-lucent; limpid, clear, serene, crystalline, clear as crystal, vitreous, transpicuous, glassy, hyaline.

426. Opacity.—**N.** opacity; opaqueness etc. *adj.*

film; cloud etc. 353.

V. be -opaque etc. *adj.*; obstruct the passage of light; ob-, of-fuscate.

Adj. opaque, impervious to light.

dim etc. 422; turbid, thick, muddy, opacous, obfuscated, fuliginous, cloudy, hazy, foggy, vaporous, nubiferous, muggy.

smoky, fumid, murky, dirty.

427. Semitransparency.—**N.** semitransparency, opalescence, milkiness, pearliness; gauze, muslin; film; mist etc. (*cloud*) 353; frosted glass.

Adj. semi-transparent, -pellucid, -diaphanous, -opacous, -opaque; opal-escent, -ine; pearly, milky, frosted, mat; misty.

428. Color.—**N.** color, hue, tint, tinge, dye, complexion, shade, tincture, cast, livery, coloration, chromatism, glow, flush; tone, key.

pure –, positive –, primary –, primitive –, complementary- color; three primaries; spectrum, chromatic dispersion; broken –, secondary –, tertiary- color.

local color, coloring, keeping, tone, value, aerial perspective.

[Science of color] chromatics, spectrum analysis; prism, spectroscope.

pigment, coloring matter, paint, dye, wash, distemper, stain; medium; mordant; oil-paint etc. (*painting*) 556.

V. color, dye, tinge, stain, tint, tinct, tone, paint, wash, ingrain, grain, illuminate, emblazon, imbue; paint etc. (*fine art*) 556; daub.

Adj. colored etc. *v.*; colorific, tingent, tinctorial; chormatic, prismatic; full-, high-, deep-colored; doubly-dyed; polychromatic.

bright, vivid, intense, deep; fresh, unfaded; rich, gorgeous; highly colored; gay; variegated etc. 440.

gaudy, florid; garish; showy, flaunting, flashy; raw, crude; glaring, flaring; discordant, inharmonious.

mellow, harmonious, pearly, sweet, delicate, tender, refined.

429. Achromatism. [Absence of color.]—**N.** achromatism; de-, dis-coloration; pall-or, -idity; paleness etc. *adj.*; etoilation; neutral tint, monochrome, black-and-white.

V. lose -color etc. 428; fade, fly, go; become -colorless etc. *adj.*; turn pale, pale, whiten.

deprive of color, decolorize, bleach, tarnish, achromatize, blanch, etiolate, wash out, tone down.

Adj. uncolored etc. (*see* color etc. 428); colorless, achromatic, hueless, pale, pallid; pale-, tallow-faced; faint, dull, cold, muddy, leaden, dun, wan, sallow, dead, dingy, ashy, ashen, ghastly, cadaverous, glassy, lack-luster; discolored etc. *v.*

light-colored, fair, *blond*; white etc. 430.

pale as -death, – ashes, – a witch, – a ghost, – a corpse.

430. Whiteness.—**N.** whiteness etc. *adj.*; argent.

albification, albescence, albinism, etiolation.

snow, paper, chalk, milk, lily, ivory, silver, alabaster; white lead, chinese –, flake –, ivory –, zinc- white, white-wash, -ning, whiting.

V. be -white etc. *adj.*

render -white etc. *adj.*; whiten- bleach, blanch, etiolate, whitewash, silver, frost.

Adj. white; milky, milk-, snow-white; snowy, niveous, candid, chalky; hoar, -y; frosted, silvery; argent, -ine; canescent.

whitish, creamy, pearly, ivory, fair, *blond*, ash-blond, platinum blond; blanched etc. *v.*; high in tone, light.

white as -a sheet, – driven snow, – a lily, – silver; like -ivory etc. *n.*

431. Blackness.—**N.** blackness etc. *adj.*; darkness etc. (*want of light*) 421; swarthness, lividity, dark color, tone, color; *chiaroscuro* etc. 420.

nigrification, infuscation, denigration.

jet, ink, ebony, coal, pitch, soot, smudge, charcoal, sloe, raven, crow; black.

[Pigments] lamp –, ivory –, blue-black; writing –, printing –, printer's –, Indian- ink.

V. be -black etc. *adj.*

render -black etc. *adj.*; blacken, infuscate, denigrate; blot, -ch; smutch; smirch; darken etc. 421.

Adj. black, sable, swarthy, somber, dark, inky, ebon, atramentous, jetty; coal-, jet-black; fuliginous, pitchy, sooty, swart, dusky, dingy, murky, low-toned, low in tone; of the deepest dye.

black as -jet etc. *n.*, – my hat, – a shoe, – a tinker's pot, – November, – thunder, – midnight; nocturnal etc. (*dark*) 421; nigrescent; gray etc. 432; obscure etc. 421.

Adv. in mourning.

432. Gray.—N. gray etc. *adj.*; neutral tint, silver, pepper and salt, *chiaroscuro*, *grisaille*, grayness.

[Pigments] Payne's gray; black etc. 431.

Adj. gray, grey; steel –, iron- gray, dun, drab, dingy, leaden, livid, somber, sad, pearly; silver, -y, -ed; ash-en, -y; ciner-eous, -itious; grizzl-y, -ed; dove-, slate-, stone-, mouse-, ash-colored; mole; cool.

433. Brown.—N. brown etc. *adj.*

[Pigments] bister, ocher, sepia, Vandyke brown.

Adj. brown, adust, bay, dapple, auburn, chestnut, nutbrown, cinnamon, hazel, fawn, puce, *écru*, russet, tawny, fuscous, chocolate, maroon, foxy, tan, brunette, whitey-brown; snuff-, liver-colored; brown as -a berry, – mahogany; reddish brown; copper-, rust- colored; henna, bronze, khaki; russet, roan, sorrel.

sub-burnt; tanned etc. *v.*

V. render -brown etc. *adj.*; tan, embrown, bronze.

434. Redness.—N. red, scarlet, vermilion, cardinal, Post Office, red, carmine, crimson, pink, lake, *cerise*, cherry red, maroon, carnation, *couleur de rose*, *rose du Barry*; magenta, damask; flesh -color, – tint; color; fresh –, high- color; warmth; gules.

ruby, garnet, carbuncle; rose; rust, iron-mold.

[Dyes and pigments] cinnabar, cochineal; fuchsine; ruddle, madder, redlead; light –, Venetian- red; red ink, annotto.

redness etc. *adj.*; rub-escence, -icundity, -ification; erubescence, blush.

V. be –, become- -red etc. *adj.*; blush, flush, color up, mantle, redden.

render- red etc. *adj.*; redden, rouge; rub-ify, -ricate; incarnadine; ruddle.

Adj. red etc. *n.*; -dish; rufous, ruddy, florid, incarnadine, sanguine, bloody, gory; ros-y, -eate; blowz-y, -ed; brunt; rubi-cund, -form; lurid, stammel, blood-red; russet, murrey, carroty, sorrel, lateritious.

rose-, ruby-, cherry-, claret-, wine-, plum-, flame-, flesh-, peach-, salmon-, brick-, brickdust-colored, reddish brown etc. 433.

red as -fire, – blood, – scarlet, – a turkeycock, – a lobster; warm, hot; foxy.

435. Greenness.—N. green etc. *adj.*; blue and yellow; vert.

emerald, verd antique, verdigris, malachite, beryl, aquamarine, reseda.

[Pigments] *terre verte*, verditer, bice, chlorophyl.

greenness, verdure, verdancy; viridity, -escence.

Adj. green, verdant; glaucous, olive; porraceous; green as grass.

emerald –, pea –, grass –, apple –, sea –, olive –, bottle –, leaf- green.

greenish; vir-ent, -escent.

436. Yellowness.—N. yellow etc. *adj.*; or.

[Pigments] gamboge; cadmium –, chrome –, Indian –, lemon- yellow; orpiment, yellow ocher, Claude tint, aureolin.

crocus, saffron, topaz, gold.

jaundice; London fog; yellowness etc. *adj.*

Adj. yellow, aureate, gold, golden, gilt, gilded, flavous, citrine, fallow; fulv-ous, -id; sallow, luteous, fawny, creamy, sandy; xanth-ic, -ous; jaundiced.

gold-, citron-, saffron-, lemon-, sulphur-, amber-, straw-, primrose-, cream-colored; flazen, yellowish, buff.

yellow as a -quince, – guinea, – crow's foot.

437. Purple.—N. purple etc. *adj.*; blue and red, bishop's purple; aniline dyes, gridelin, amethyst; purpure.

livid-ness, -ity.

V. empurple.

Adj. purple, violet, plum-colored, lavender, lilac, puce, *mauve*; livid.

438. Blueness.—N. blue etc. *adj.*; garter-blue; watchet.

[Pigments] ultramarine, smalt, cobalt, cyanogen; Prussian –, syenite- blue; bice, indigo, woad.

lapis lazuli, sapphire, turquoise.

blue-, bluish-ness; bloom

Adj. blue, azure, cerulean; sky-blue, -colored, -dyed; navy-blue, aquamarine, electric blue, royal blue, cyanic; bluish; atmospheric, retiring; cold.

439. Orange.—N. orange, red and yellow; gold; or; flame etc. color, *adj.*

[Pigments] ochre, Mars orange, cadmium.

V. gild, warm.

Adj. orange; ocherous; orange-, gold-, flame-, copper-, brass-, apricot-colored; warm, hot, glowing.

440. Variegation.—N. variegation; di-, tri-chromism; iridescence, irisation, play of colors, polychrome, maculation, spottiness, striae.

spectrum, rainbow, iris, tulip, peacock, chameleon, butterfly, tortoiseshell; mackerel, — sky; zebra, leopard, mother-of-pearl, nacre, opal, marble, batik.

check, plaid, tartan, patchwork; mar-, parquetry; mosiac, *tesserae*, tesselation, chess-board, checkers, chequers; harlequin; Joseph's coat; tricolor; patches, bands, stripes, spots etc of color.

V. be -variegated etc. *adj.*; variegate, stripe, streak, checker, chequer; be-, speckle, fleck; be-, sprinkle; stipple, maculate, dot, bespot; tattoo, inlay, tesselate, damascene; embroider, braid, quilt.

Adj. variegated etc. *v.*; many-colored, -hued; divers-, parti-colored; di-, poly-chromatic; bi-, tri-, versi-color; of all -the colors of the rainbow, — manner of colors; kaleidoscopic.

iridescent; opal-ine, -escent; prismatic, nacreous, pearly, shot, *gorge de pigeon*, *chatoyant*, irisated.

pied, piebald, skewbald; motley; mottled, marbled; pepper and salt, paned, dappled, clouded, cymophanous.

mosiac, tesselated, chequered, plaid; tortoiseshell etc. *n.*

spott-ed, -y; punctuated, powdered; speckled etc. *v.*; freckled, fleabitten, studded; fleck-ed, -ered; striated, barred, veined; brind-ed, -led; tabby; watered; grizzled; listed; embroidered etc. *v.*; daedal.

441. Vision.—N. vision, sight, optics, eye-sight.

view, look, espial, glance, ken, *coup d'oeil*; glimpse, peep, glint; gaze, stare, leer; perlustration, contemplation; conspect-ion, -uity; regard, survey; in-, intro-spection; *reconnaissance*, speculation, watch, espionage, *espionnage*, autopsy; ocular - inspection, — demonstration; sight-seeing.

macrography, micrography.

point of view; view-, stand- point; gazebo, loophole, *belvedere*, watchtower.

field of view; theater, amphitheater, arena, vista, horizon; commanding —, bird's eye —, panoramic- view; periscope.

visual organ, organ of vision; eye; naked —, unassisted- eye; eye-ball, retina, pupil, iris, cornea, white; optics, orbs; saucer —, goggle —, gooseberry-eyes.

short sight etc. 443; clear —, sharp —, quick —, eagle —, piercing-, —, penetrating- -sight, — glance, — eye; perspicacity, discernment; catopsis.

eagle, hawk; cat, lynx; Argus.

evil eye; basilisk, cockatrice.

spectacles, telescope etc. 445.

V. see, behold, discern, perceive, have in sight, descry, sight, make out, discover, distinguish, recognize, spy, espy, ken; get —, have —, catch- a - sight, — glimpse- of; command of view of; witness, contemplate, speculate; cast —, set- the eyes on; be a -spectator etc. 444- of; look on etc. (*be present*) 186; see sights etc. (*curiosity*) 445; see at a glance etc. (*intelligence*) 498.

look, view, eye; lift up the eyes, open one's eye; look -at, — on, — upon, — over, — about one, — round; survey, scan, inspect; run the eye -over, — through; reconnoiter, glance -round, — on, — over; turn —, bend- one's looks upon; direct the eyes to, turn the eyes on, cast a glance, make eyes at.

observe etc. (*attend to*) 457; watch etc. (*care*) 459; see with one's own eyes; watch for etc. (*expect*) 507; peek, peep, peer, pry, take a peep; play at bo-peep.

look -full in the face, — hard at, — intently; strain one's eyes; fix —, rivet- the eyes upon; stare, gaze; pore over, gloat -over, — on; leer, ogle, glare; goggle; cock the eye, squint, gloat, look askance; give the glad eye.

Adj. seeing etc. *v.*; visual, ocular, -al; ophthalmic.

far-, clear-sighted etc. *n.*; eagle-, hawk-, lynx-, keen-, Argus-eyed.

visible etc. 446.

Adv. visibly etc. 446; in sight of, with one's eyes open.

at -sight, — first sight, — a glance, — the first blush; *primâ facie*.

Int. look! etc. (*attention*) 457.

Phr. the scales falling from one's eyes.

442. Blindness.—N. blindness, anopsia, cecity, excecation, *amaurosis*, cataract, ablepsy, prestriction; dim-sightedness etc. 443.

V. be -blind etc. *adj.*; not see; lose sight of; have the eyes bandaged; grope in the dark.

not look; close —, shut —, turn away —, avert- the eyes; look another way; wink etc. (*limited vision*) 443; shut the eyes —, be blind- to; wink —, blink- at.

render -blind etc. *adj.*; blind, -fold; hoodwink, dazzle; put one's eyes out; throw dust into one's eyes; *jeter de la poudre aux yeux*; screen from sight etc. (*hide*) 528.

Adj. blind; eye-, sight-, vision-less; dark; stone-, sand-, stark-blind; undiscerning; dim-sighted etc. 443.

blind as -a bat, — a buzzard, — a beetle, — a mole, — an owl; wall-eyed.

blinded etc. *v.*

Adv. blind-ly, -fold; darkly.

443. Dim-sightedness. [Imperfect vision.] [Fallacies of vision.]—**N.** dim —, dull —, half —, short —, near —, long —, double —, astigmatic —, failing- sight; dim etc -sightedness; snow blindness; purblindness, lippitude; my-, presby-opia; confusion of vision; astigmatism; nystagmus; color-blindness, dichromism, chromato-pseudo-blepsis, Daltonism; nyctalopy; *strabismus*, strabism, squint, cast in the eye, swivel eye, goggle eyes; obliquity of vision.

winking etc. *v.*; nictitation; blinkard, albino.

dizziness, swimming, scotomy; cataract; ophthalmia.

[Limitation of vision] eye shade, blinker, blinder; screen etc. (*hider*) 530.

[Fallacies of vision] *deceptio visûs*; refraction, distortion, illustion, false light, *anamorphosis*, virtual image, *spectrum*, *mirage*, looming, phasma; phant-asm, -asma, -om; vision; specter, apparition, ghost; *ignis fatuus* etc. (*luminary*) 423; specter of the Brocken; magic mirror; magic lantern etc. (*show*) 448; mirror, lens etc. (*instrument*) 445.

V. be -dim-sighted etc. *n.*; see double; have a -mote in the eye, – mist before the eyes, – film over the eyes; see through a -prism, – glass darkly; wink, blink, nictitate; squint; look ask-ant, -ance; screw up the eyes, glare, glower.

dazzle, glare, blur, swim, loom.

Adj. dim-sighted etc. *n.*; my-, presby-opic; astigmatic; moon-, mope-, blear-, goggle-, gooseberry-, one-eyed; blind of one eye, monoculous; half-, pur-, color-blind; dichromatic.

blind as a bat etc. (*blind*) 442; winking etc. *v.*

—

444. Spectator.—N. spectator, beholder, observer, inspector, viewer, looker-on, onlooker, witness, eye-witness, bystander, passer by; sight-seer.

spy, scout; sentinel etc. (*warning*) 668.

v. witness, behold etc. (*see*) 441; look on etc. (*be present*) 186.

445. Optical Instruments.—N. optical instruments; lens, meniscus, magnifier, reading –, burning- glass; micro-, mega-, teino-scope; spectacles, glasses, barnacles, goggles, giglamps, eyeglass, *pince-nez*, monocle; periscopic lens; telescope, glass, lorgnette, binocular; spy-, opera-, field-glass, periscope, range finder.

mirror, reflector, speculum; looking-, pier-, cheval-, hand-glass.

prism; camera, *camera-lucida*, *-obscura*; projector, stereopticon, magic lantern etc. (*show*) 448; chro-, thau-matrope; stereo-, pseudo-, poly-, kaleido-scope.

photo-, opto-, erio-, actino-, luci-, radio-, spectro-meter; polari-, polemo-, spectro-scope, diffraction grating.

optics, optician, optometry, optometrist; microscop-y, -ist; photometry, photography; photographer.

446. Visibility.—N. visibility, perceptibility; conspicuousness, distinctness etc. *adj.*; conspicuity; appearance etc. 448; exposure; manifestation etc. 525; ocular -proof, – evidence, – demonstration; field of view etc. (*vision*) 441.

V. be –, become- -visible etc. *adj.*; appear, emerge, open to the view; meet –, catch- the eye; present –, show –, manifest –, produce –, discover –, reveal –, expose –, betray- itself; stand -forth, – out; show; arise; peep –, peer –, crop- out; start –, spring –, show –, turn –, crop- up; glimmer, glitter, glow, loom; glare; burst forth, scintillate; burst upon the -view, – sight; heave in sight; come -in sight, – into view, – out, – forth, – forward; see the light of day; break through the clouds; make its appearance, show its face, materialize, appear to one's eyes, come upon the stage, enter; float before the eyes, speak for itself. etc. (*manifest*) 525; attract the attention etc. 457; reappear; live in a glass house.

expose to view etc. 525.

Adj. visible, perceptible, perceivable, discernible, apparent; in -view, – full view, – sight; exposed to view, *en évidence*; unclouded.

obvious etc. (*manifest*) 525; plain, clear, distinct, definite; well-defined, -marked; in focus; recognizable, palpable, autoptical; glaring, staring, conspicuous; stereoscopic; in -bold, – strong, – high- relief.

periscopic, panoramic.

before –, under- one's eyes; before one, *à vue d'oeil*, in one's eye, *oculis subjecta fidelibus.*

Adv. visibly etc. *adj.*; in sight of; before one's eyes etc. *adj.*; *veluti in speculum.*

447. Invisibility.—N. invisibility, nonappearance, imperceptibility; indistinctness etc. *adj.*; mystery, delitescence.

concealment etc. 528; latency etc. 526.

V. be -invisible etc. *adj.*; be hidden etc. (*hide*) 528; lurk etc. (*lie hidden*) 526; escape notice.

render -invisible etc. *adj.*; conceal etc. 528; put out of sight.

not see etc. (*be blind*) 442; lose sight of.

Adj. invisible, imperceptible; un-, in-discernible; un-, non-apparent; out of –, not in- sight; *à perte de vue*; behind the -scenes, – curtain; view-, sightless; in-, un-conspicuous; unseen etc. (*see* see etc. 441); covert etc. (*latent*) 526; eclipsed, under an eclipse.

dim etc. (*faint*) 422; mysterious, dark, obscure, confused; indistin-ct, -guishable; shadowy, indefinite, undefined; ill-defined, -marked; blurred, fuzzy, out of focus; misty etc. (*opaque*) 426; veiled etc. (*concealed*) 528; delitescent.

448. Appearance.—N. appearance, phenomenon, sight, spectacle, show, premonstration, scene, species, view, *coup d'oeil*; look-out, out-look, prospect, vista, perspective, bird's-eye view, scenery, landscape, picture, *tableau*; display, exposure, *mise en scène*; scenery, *décor*; rising of the curtain.

phant-asm, -om etc. (*fallacy of vision*) 443.

pageant, *spectacle*; peep-, raree-, gallanty-show; *ombres chinoises*; projector, optical –, magic-lantern, phantasmagoria, dissolving views; cinema, -tograph; bio-scope, -graph; moving pictures, movies, film, screen etc.; pan-, di-, cosm-, georama; *coup –, jeu- de théâtre*; pageantry etc. (*ostentation*) 882; insignia etc. (*indication*) 550.

aspect, phase, *phasis*, seeming; shape etc. (*form*) 240; guise, look, complexion, color, image, mien, air, cast, carriage, port, demeanor; presence, expression, first blush, face of the thing; point of view, light.

lineament, feature, trait, lines; out-line, -side; contour, *silhouette*, face, countenance, physiognomy, visage, phiz, mug, cast of countenance, profile, *tournure*, cut of one's jib, metoposcopy; outside etc. 220.

V. appear; be –, become- visible etc. 446; seem, look, show; present –, wear –, carry –, have –, bear –, exhibit –, take –, take on –, assume- the -appearance, – semblance- of; look like; cut a figure, figure; present to the view; show etc. (*make manifest*) 525.

Adj. apparent, seeming, ostensible; on view.

Adv. apparently; to all -seeming, – appearance; ostensibly, seemingly, as it seems, on the face of it, *primâ facie*; at the first blush, at first sight; in the eyes of; to the eye.

449. Disappearance.—N. disappearance, evanescence, eclipse, occultation.

departure etc. 293; exit, vanishing point; dissolving views.

V. disappear, vanish, dissolve, fade, melt away, pass, go, avaunt; be -gone etc. *adj.*; leave -no trace, — 'not a rack behind;' go off the stage etc. (*depart*) 293; suffer —, undergo- an eclipse; be lost to —, retire from- -sight, — view.

lose sight of.

efface etc. 552.

Adj. disappearing etc. *v.*; evanescent; missing, lost; lost to -sight, — view; gone; *spurlos versenkt.*

Int. vanish! disappear! avaunt! etc. (*ejection*) 297.

450. Intellect.—N. intellect, mind, understanding, reason, thinking principle; rationality; cogitative —, cognitive —, intellectual- faculties; faculties, senses, consciousness, observation, percipience, apperception, mentality, intelligence, intellection, intuition, association of ideas, instinct, flair, conception, judgment, wits, parts, capacity, intellectuality, reasoning power, brains, genius; wit etc. 498; ability etc. (*skill*) 698; wisdom etc. 498.

soul, spirit, ghost, inner man, heart, breast, bosom, *penetralia mentis, divina particula aurae,* heart's core; ego, psyche, pneuma, subconsciousness, subconscious, subliminal self; dual personality.

organ —, seat- of thought; *sensorium*, sensory, brain, gray matter; head, -piece; pate, noddle, skull, scull, *pericranium*, *cerebrum*, *cranium*, brain-pan, -box; sconce, upper story.

[Science of mind] metaphysics; psychics, psycho-logy, -metry, -genesis, -analysis, -physics, psychi-atry, -cal research, thought reading etc. 992; ideology; mental —, moral- philosophy; philosophy of the mind; pneumat-, phren-ology; no —, craniology, -scopy.

ideal-ity, -ism; transcendental-, spiritual-ism; immateriality etc. 317.

metaphysician, psychologist etc.

V. note, notice, mark; take -notice, — cognizance- of; be -aware, — conscious- of; realize; appreciate; ruminate etc. (*think*) 451; fancy etc. (*imagine*) 515; conceive, reason, understand.

Adj. [Relating to intellect] intellectual, mental, rational, subjective, metaphysical, nooscopic, spiritual; ghostly; psych-ical, -ological; cerebral.

immaterial etc. 317; endowed with reason.

Adv. *in petto.*

450a. Absence or want **of Intellect.—N.** absence —, want- of -intellect etc. 450; imbecility etc. 499; brutality; brute -instinct, — force.

Adj. unendowed with reason.

451. Thought.—N. thought; exercitation —, exercise- of the intellect; reflection, cogitation, consideration, meditation, study, lucubration, speculation, deliberation, pondering; head-, brain-work; cerebration; mentation, deep reflection; close study, application etc. (*attention*) 457.

abstract thought, abstraction, contemplation, musing; brown study etc. (*inattention*) 458; reverie, Platonism; depth of thought, workings of the mind, thoughts, inmost thoughts; self-counsel, communing, -consultation.

association —, succession —, flow —, train —, current- of -thought, — ideas.

after —, mature- thought; reconsideration, second thoughts; retrospection etc. (*memory*) 505; excogitation; examination etc. (*inquiry*) 461; invention etc. (*imagination*) 515.

thoughtfulness etc. *adj.*

V. think, reflect, reason, cogitate, excogitate, consider, deliberate; bestow -thought, — consideration- upon; speculate, contemplate, meditate, ponder, muse, dream, ruminate; brood —, con- over; animadvert, study; bend—, apply- the mind etc. (*attend*) 457; digest, discuss, hammer at, weigh, perpend; realize, appreciate; fancy etc. (*imagine*) 515; trow.

take into consideration; take counsel etc. (*be advised*) 695; commune with —, bethink- oneself; collect one's thoughts; revolve —, turn over —, run over- in the mind; chew the cud —, sleep- upon; take counsel of —, advise with- one's pillow.

rack —, ransack —, crack —, beat —, cudgel- one's brains; set one's -brain, — wits- to work.

harbor —, entertain —, cherish —, nurture- an idea etc. 453; take into one's head; bear in mind; reconsider.

occur; present —, suggest- itself; come —, get- into one's head; strike one, flit across the view, come uppermost, run in one's head; enter —, pass in —, cross —, flash on —, flash across —, float in —, fasten itself on —, be uppermost in —, occupy- the mind; have in one's mind.

make an impression; sink —, penetrate- into the mind; engross the thoughts.

Adj. thinking etc. *v.*; thoughtful, pensive, meditative, reflective, cogitative, museful, wistful, contemplative, speculative, deliberative, studious, sedate, introspective, Platonic, philosophical.

lost —, engrossed —, rapt —, absorbed- in thought etc. (*inattentive*) 458; deep musing etc. (*intent*) 457.

in the mind, under consideration, in contemplation.

Adv. all things considered; taking everything into account.

Phr. the mind being on the stretch; the -mind, — head- -turning, — running- upon.

452. Incogitancy. [Absence or want of thought.]—**N.** incogitancy, vacancy, inunderstanding; inanity, fatuity etc. 499; thoughtlessness etc. (*inattention*) 458.

V. not -think etc. 451; not think of; dismiss from the -mind, — thoughts etc. 451.

indulge in reverie etc. (*be inattentive*) 458.

put away thought; unbend —, relax —, divert- the mind.

Adj. vacant, unintellectual, unideal, unoccupied, unthinking, inconsiderate, thoughtless; absent etc. (*inattentive*) 458; diverted; irrational etc. 499; narrow-minded etc. 481.

un-thought of, -dreamt of, -considered; off one's mind; incogitable, not to be thought of, inconceivable.

453. Idea. [Object of thought.]—**N.** idea, notion, conception, thought, apprehension, impression, perception, image, sentiment, reflection, observation, consideration; abstract idea, principle; archetype.

view etc. (*opinion*) 484; theory etc. 514; conceit, fancy; phantasy etc. (*imagination*) 515.

point of view etc. (*aspect*) 448; field of view.

454. Topic. [Subject of thought.]—**N.** subject of —, material for- thought; food for the mind, mental *pabulum*.

subject, -matter; matter, theme, topic, what it is about, *thesis*, text, business, affair, matter in hand, argument; motion, resolution; head, chapter; case, point; proposition, theorem; field of inquiry; moot point, problem, etc. (*question*) 461.

V. float —, pass- in the mind etc. 451.

Adj. thought of; uppermost in the mind; *in petto*.

Adv. under -discussion, — consideration, — advisement; in -question, — the mind; on -foot, — the carpet, — the *tapis*; before the house, relative to etc. 9.

455. Curiosity. [The desire of knowledge.]—**N.** interest, thirst for knowledge; curi-osity, -ousness; inquiring mind; inquisitiveness.

sight-seer, quidnunc, newsmonger, Paul Pry, peeping Tom, eavesdropper; gossip etc. (*news*) 532; questioner, *enfant terrible*.

V. be -curious etc. *adj.*; take an interest in, stare, gape; prick up the ears, see sights, lionize; pry, speer; dig up.

Adj. curious, inquisitive, burning with curiosity, overcurious, nosey; inquiring etc. 461; prying; inquisitorial; agape etc. (*expectant*) 507; attentive etc. 457.

Phr. what's the matter? what next?

456. Incuriosity. [Absence of curiosity.]—**N.** incuriosity, incuriousness etc. *adj.*; *insouciance* etc. 866; indifference, apathy.

V. be -incurious etc. *adj.*; have no -curiosity etc. 455; take no interest in etc. 823; mind one's own business.

Adj. incurious, uninquisitive, uninterested, indifferent, bored; impassive etc. 823.

457. Attention.—**N.** attention; mindfulness etc. *adj.*; intent-ness, -iveness; thought etc. 451; adverten-ce, -cy; observ-ance, -ation; consideration, reflection, perpension; heed; particularity; notice, regard etc. *v.*; circumspection etc. (*care*) 459; study, scrutiny, once-over; in-, intro-spection; revision, -al.

active —, diligent —, exclusive —, minute —, close —, intense —, deep —, profound —, abstract —, labored —, deliberate- -thought, — attention, — application, — study.

minuteness, attention to detail etc. 459.

absorption of mind etc. (*abstraction*) 458.

indication, calling attention to etc. *v.*

V. be -attentive etc. *adj.*; attend, advert to, observe, look, see, view, remark, notice, regard, take notice, mark; give —, pay- -attention, — heedto; listen in, incline —, lend- an ear to; trouble one's head about; give a thought —, animadvert- to; occupy oneself with; contemplate etc (*think of*) 451; look -at, — to, — after, — into, — over; see to; turn —, bend —, apply —, direct —, give- the -mind, — eye, — attention- to; have -an eye to, — in one's eye; bear in mind; take into -account, — consideration; keep in -sight, — view; have regard to, heed, mind, take cognizance of, be engaged in, entertain, recognize; make —, take- note of; note.

examine cursorily; glance -at, — upon, — over; cast —, pass- the eyes over; run over, turn over the leaves, dip into, perstringe; skim etc. (*neglect*) 460; take a cursory view of.

examine, — closely, — intently; scan, scrutinize, consider; give —, bend- one's mind to; overhaul, revise, pore over; inspect, review, pass under review; take stock of; fix —, rivet —, focus —, devote- the - eye, — mind, — thoughts, — attention- on *or* to; hear —, think- out; mind *one's business*.

revert —, hark back- to; watch etc. (*expect*) 507, (*take care of*) 459; hearken —, listen- to; prick up the ears; have —, keep- the eyes open; come to the point.

meet with attention; fall under one's -notice, — observation; be -under consideration etc. (*topic*) 454.

catch —, strike- the eye; attract notice; catch —, awaken —, wake —, invite —, solicit —, attract —, claim —, excite —, engage —, occupy —, strike —, arrest —, fix —, engross —, absorb —, rivet-the-attention, — mind, — thoughts; be -present to, — uppermost in- the mind.

bring under one's notice; point -out, — to, — at, — the finger at; lay the finger on, indigitate, indicate; direct —, call- attention to; show; put a -mark etc. (*sign*) 550- upon; call soldiers to 'attention;' bring forward etc. (*make manifest*) 525.

Adj. attentive, mindful, heedful, observant, regardful; alive —, awake- to, alert; observing etc. *v.*; taken up —, occupied- with; engaged —, engrossed —, interested —, wrapped- in; absorbed, rapt; breathless; pre-occupied etc. (*inattentive*) 458; watchful etc. (*careful*) 459; intent on, open-eyed, breathless, undistracted, upon the stretch; on the watch etc. (*expectant*) 507.

steadfast.

Int. see! look, — here, — out, — alive, — you, — to it! mark! lo! behold! soho! hark, — ye! mind ! halloo! observe! lo and behold! attention! *nota bene*; N.B.; *.†; I'd have you to know; notice! take notice! O yes! *Oyez!*

Phr. this is —, these are- to give notice.

458. Inattention.—**N.** in-attention, consideration; inconsiderateness etc. *adj.*; oversight; inadverten-ce, -cy; non-observance, disregard.

supineness etc. (*inactivity*) 683; *étourderie*; want of thought; heedlessness etc. (*neglect*) 460; *insouciance* etc. (*indifference*) 866.

abstraction; absence —, absorption- of mind; preoccupation, distraction, reverie, brown study, deep musing, fit of abstraction, woolgathering.

V. be -inattentive etc. *adj*.; overlook, disregard; pass by etc. (*neglect*) 460; not -observe etc. 457; think little of.

close —, shut- one's eyes to; wink at; pay no attention to; dismiss —, discard —, discharge- from one's -thoughts, — mind; drop the subject, think no more of; set —, turn —, put- aside; turn -away from, — one's attention from, — a deaf ear to, — one's back upon.

abstract oneself, dream, indulge in reverie.

escape -notice, — attention; come in at one ear and go out at the other; forget etc. (*have no remembrance*) 506.

call off —, draw off —, call away —, divert —, distract- the -attention, — thoughts, — mind; put out of one's head; dis-concert, -compose; put out, confuse, perplex, bewilder, fluster, muddle, dazzle; throw a sop to Cerberus.

Adj. inattentive; un-observant, -mindful, -heeding, -*discerning*; inadvertent; mind-, regard-, respect-less; listless etc. (*indifferent*) 866; blind, deaf; flighty, hand over head; cur-, percur-sory; giddy-, scatter-, hare-brained; unreflecting, *écervelé*, inconsiderate, off-hand, thoughtless, dizzy, muzzy, brainsick; giddy, — as a goose; wild, harum-scarum, ranipole, high-flying; heed-, careless etc. (*neglectful*) 460.

absent, absent-minded, abstracted, *distrait*; lost; lost —, wrapped- in thought, woolgathering; rapt, in the clouds, bemused; dreaming —, musing- on other things; pre-occupied; engrossed etc. (*attentive*) 457; in a -reverie etc. *n*.; off one's guard etc. (*inexpectant*) 508; napping; dreamy.

disconcerted, put out etc. *v*.; rattled.

Adv. inattentively, inadvertently etc. *adj*.; *per incuriam, sub silentio*.

Int. stand -at ease, — easy!

Phr. the attention wanders; one's wits gone a -woolgathering, — bird's nesting; it never entered into one's head; the mind running on other things; one's thoughts being elsewhere; had it been a bear it would have bitten you.

459. Care. [Vigilance.]—**N.** care, solicitude, heed; heedfulness etc. *adj*.; scruple etc. (*conscientiousness*) 939.

watchfulness etc. *adj*.; vigilance, *surveillance*, eyes of Argus, watch, vigil, look out, watch and ward, *l'oeil du maître*.

alertness etc. (*activity*) 682; attention etc. 457; prudence etc., circumspection etc. (*caution*) 864; forethought etc. 510; precaution etc. (*preparation*) 673; tidiness etc. (*order*) 58, (*cleanliness*) 652; accuracy etc. (*exactness*) 494; minuteness, attention to detail; meticulousness, nicety, circumstantiality.

V. be -careful etc. *adj*.; reck; take care etc. (*be cautious*) 864; pay attention to etc. 457; take care of; look —, see- -to, — after; keep -an eye, — a sharp eye- upon; keep -watch, — watch and ward; mount guard, set watch, watch; keep in -sight, — view; chaperon, play gooseberry; mind, — one's business.

look -sharp, — about one; look with one's own eyes; keep a -good, — sharp- look-out; have all one's -wits, — eyes- about one; watch for etc. (*expect*) 507; stand to; keep one's eyes —, have the eyes —, sleep with one eye- open.

take precautions etc. 673; protect etc. (*render safe*) 664.

do one's best etc. 682; mind one's Ps and Qs, speak by the card, pick one's steps.

Adj. care-, regard-, heed-ful; taking care etc. *v*.; particular; prudent etc. (*cautious*) 864; considerate; thoughtful etc. (*deliberative*) 451; provident etc. (*prepared*) 673; alert etc. (*active*) 682; sure-footed.

guarded, on one's guard; on the *qui vive*, — alert, — watch, — look-out; awake, broad awake, vigilant; watch-, wake-, wist-ful; Argus-, lynx-eyed; wide awake etc. (*intelligent*) 498; on the watch for etc. (*expectant*) 507.

tidy etc. (*orderly*) 58, (*clean*) 652; accurate etc. (*exact*) 494; scrupulous etc. (*conscientious*) 939; *cavendo tutus* etc. (*safe*) 664.

Adv. carefully etc. *adj*.; with care, gingerly.

Phr. *quis custodiet ipsos custodes?*

460. Neglect.—N. neglect; carelessness etc. *adj*.; trifling etc. *v*.; negligence; omission, laches, default; remissness, slackness, procrastination; supineness etc. (*inactivity*) 683; inattention etc. 458; *nonchalance* etc. (*insensibility*) 823; imprudence, recklessness etc. 863; slovenliness etc. (*disorder*) 59; (*dirt*) 653; improvidence etc. 674; non-completion etc. 730; inexactness etc. (*error*) 495.

paraleipsis [in rhetoric].

trifler, slacker, waster, waiter on Providence; Micawber.

V. be -negligent etc. *adj*.; take no care of etc. (take care of etc. 459); neglect; let -slip, — go; lay —, set —, cast —, put- aside; keep —, leave- out of sight; lose sight of.

overlook, disregard; pass -over, — by; let pass; blink; wink —, connive- at; gloss over; take no -note, — notice, — thought, — account- of; pay no regard to; *laisser aller*; allow to lie on the table.

scamp; trifle, fribble; do by halves; skimp; cut; slight etc. (*despise*) 930; play —, trifle- with; slur; skim, — the surface; *effleurer*; take a cursory view of etc. 457.

slur —, slip —, skip —, jump- over; pretermit, miss, skip, jump, omit, give the go-by to, push aside, throw into the background, shelve, sink; ignore, shut one's eyes to, refuse to hear, turn a deaf ear to; leave out of one's calculation; not -attend to etc. 457, — mind; not trouble -oneself, — one's head- -with, — about; forget etc. 506; be caught napping etc. (*not expect*) 508; leave a loose thread; let the grass grow under one's feet.

render -neglectful etc. *adj*.; put —, throw- off one's guard.

Adj. neglecting etc. *v*.; unmindful, negligent, neglectful; heedless, careless, thoughtless; perfunctory, remiss, slack.

inconsiderate; un-, in-circumspect; off one's guard; un-wary, -watchful, -guarded; offhand.

supine etc. (*inactive*) 683; inattentive etc 458; *insouciant* etc. (*indifferent*) 823; imprudent, reckless etc. 863; slovenly etc. (*disorderly*) 59, (*dirty*) 653; inexact etc. (*erroneous*) 495; improvident etc. 674.

neglected etc. *v*.; un-heeded, -cared for, -

perceived, -seen, -observed, -noticed, -noted, -marked, -attended to, -thought of, -regarded, -remarked, -missed; shunted, shelved.

un-examined, -studied, -searched, -scanned, -weighed, -sifted, -explored.

Adv. negligently etc. *adj.*; hand over head, anyhow; in an unguarded moment etc. (*unexpectedly*) 508; *per incuriam*.

Int. never mind, no matter, let it pass; it will be all the same a hundred years hence.

461. Inquiry. [Subject of Inquiry. Question.]—**N.** inquiry; request etc. 765; search, research, quest; pursuit etc. 622.

examination, review, scrutiny, investigation, indagation; per-quisition, -scrutation, -vestigation; inqu-est, -isition; exploration; *exploitation*, ventilation.

sifting; calculation, analysis, dissection, resolution, induction; Baconian method.

strict —, close —, searching —, exhaustive- inquiry; narrow —, strict- search; study etc. (*consideration*) 451.

scire facias, *ad referendum*; trial.

questioning etc. *v.*; interroga-tion, -tory; third degree; interpellation; challenge, examination, cross-examination, catechism; feeler, Socratic method, zetetic philosophy; leading question; discussion etc. (*reasoning*) 476; questionnaire, questionary.

reconnoitering, *reconnaissance*; prying etc. *v.*; espionage, *espionnage*; domiciliary visit, peep behind the curtain; lantern of Diogenes.

question, query, problem, *desideratum*, point to be solved, porism; subject —, field- of -inquiry, — controversy; point —, matter- in dispute; moot-point; issue, question at issue; bone of contention etc. (*discord*) 713; plain —, fair —, open- question; enigma etc. (*secret*) 533; knotty point etc. (*difficulty*) 704; *quod-libet*; threshold of an inquiry.

inquirer, investigator, experimenter, inquisitor, inspector, querist, examiner, catechist; scrut-ator, -ineer; analyst; quidnunc etc. (*curiosity*) 455.

V. make -inquiry etc. *n.*; inquire, seek, search, frisk, speer, look -for, — about for, — out for; scan, reconnoiter, explore, sound, rummage, ransack, pry, peer, look round; look —, go- over, — through; spy, over-haul.

scratch the head, slap the forehead.

look —, peer —, pry- into every hole and corner; look behind the scenes; trace up; hunt —, fish —, dig —, ferret- out; unearth; leave no stone unturned.

seek a -clue, — clew; hunt, track, trail, shadow, mouse, dodge, trace; follow the -trail, — scent; pursue etc. 622; beat up one's quarters; fish for; feel for etc. (*experiment*) 463.

investigate; take up —, institute —, pursue —, follow up —, conduct —, carry on —, prosecute- -an inquiry etc. *n.*; look -at, — into; pre-examine; discuss, canvass, agitate.

examine, study, consider, calculate; dip —, dive —, delve —, go deep- into; make sure of, probe, sound, fathom; probe to the -bottom, — quick; scrutinize, analyze, anatomize, dissect, parse, resolve, sift, winnow; view —, try- in all its phases; thresh out.

bring in question, subject to examination; put to the proof etc. (*experiment*) 463; audit, tax, pass in review; take into consideration etc. (*think over*) 451; take counsel etc. 695.

ask, question, demand; put —, pop —, propose —, propound —, moot —, start —, raise —, stir —, suggest —, put forth —, ventilate —, grapple with —, go into- a question.

put to the question, interrogate, catechize, pump, grill; cross-question, -examine; dodge; require an answer; pick —, suck- the brains of; feel the pulse.

be -in question etc. *adj.*; undergo examination.

Adj. inquiry etc. *v.*; inquisitive etc. (*curious*) 455; requisit-ive, -ory; catechetical, inquisitorial, analytic; in -search, — quest- of; on the look-out for, interrogative, zetetic; all-searching.

un-determined, -tried, -decided; in -question, — dispute, — issue, — course of inquiry; under -discussion, — consideration, — investigation etc. *n.*, *sub judice*, moot, proposed; doubtful etc. (*uncertain*) 475.

Adv. what? why? wherefore? whence? whither? where? *quaere?* how -comes, — happens, — is- it? what is the reason? what's -the matter, — up, in the wind? what on earth? when? who?

462. Answer.—**N.** answer, response, reply, replication, *riposte*, rejoinder, surrejoinder, rebutter, surrebutter, counter-evidence etc. 468, counter-charge, defence, plea; retort, repartee; contradiction etc. 536; rescript, -ion; antiphon, -y; acknowledgment; password; echo.

discovery etc. 480*a*; solution etc. (*explanation*) 522; rationale etc. (*cause*) 153; clue etc. (*indication*) 550.

Oedipus; oracle, etc. 513; return etc. (*record*) 551.

V. answer, respond, reply, rebut, retort, rejoin; give —, return for- answer; acknowledge, echo.

explain etc. (*interpret*) 522; solve etc. (*unriddle*) 522; discover etc. 480*a*; fathom, hunt out etc. (*inquire*) 461; satisfy, set at rest, determine.

Adj. answering etc. *v.*; respon-sive, -dent; oracular; antiphonal; conclusive.

Adv. because etc. (*cause*) 153; on the -scent, — right scent.

Int. *eureka!*

463. Experiment.—**N.** experiment; essay etc. (*attempt*) 675; research etc. (*investigation*) 461; trial, tentative method, *tâtonnement*.

verification, probation, *experimentum crucis*, proof, criterion, diagnostic test, tryout, crucial test, acid test.

crucible, reagent, check, touchstone, pix; assay, ordeal; ring.

empiricism, rule of thumb.

feeler; pilot —, messenger- balloon, *ballon d'essai*; pilot engine; scout; straw to show the wind.

speculation, random shot, leap in the dark.

analy-zer, -st; adventurer, explorer, sourdough, prospector; experiment-er, -ist, -alist; assayer.

V. experiment; essay etc. (*endeavor*) 675; try, assay, sample; make -an experiment, — trial of; give a trial to; put upon —, subject to- trial; experiment upon; rehearse; put —, bring —, submitto the -test, — proof; prove, verify, test, touch, practise upon, try one's strength.

grope; feel —, grope- -for, — one's way; fumble; *tâtonner, aller à tâtons*; put —, throw- out a feeler; send up a pilot balloon; see how the -land lies, — wind blows; consult the barometer; feel the pulse; fish —, bob- for; cast —, beat- about for; angle, trawl, cast one's net, beat the bushes.

venture, try one's fortune etc. (*adventure*) 675; explore etc. (*inquire*) 461.

Adj. experimental; probat-ive, ory, -ionary; analytic, docimastic; tentative; empirical; speculative, tentive.

under probation, on one's trial, on trial, on approval.

464. Comparison.—N. comparison, collation, contrast; identification.

sim-ile, -ilitude; allegory etc. (*metaphor*) 521.

V. compare -to, — with; collate, confront; place side by side etc. (*near*) 197; set —, pit- against one another; contrast balance.

identify, draw a parallel, parallel.

compare notes; institute a comparison; *parva componere magnis*.

Adj. comparative, relative; metaphorical etc. 521.

compared with etc. *v.*; comparable.

Adv. relatively etc. (*relation*) 9; as compared with etc. *v.*

465. Discrimination.—N. discrimination, distinction, differentiation, diagnosis, diorism; nice perception; perception —, appreciation- of difference; acuteness; estimation etc. 466; nicety, refinement; taste etc. 850; *critique*, judgement, tact; insight, discernment etc. (*intelligence*) 498; *nuances*.

V. discriminate, distinguish, differentiate, severalize; separate; draw the line, sift; separate —, winnow- the chaff from the wheat; split hairs.

estimate etc. (*measure*) 466; know -which is which, — one's stuff, — one's way about, — what is what, — 'a hawk from a handsaw.'

take into -account, — consideration; give —, allow- due weight to; weigh carefully.

Adj. discriminating etc. *v.*; dioristic, discriminative, critical, distinctive; nice.

Phr. *il y a fagots et fagots*; *rem acu tetigisti*.

465a. Indiscrimination.—N. indiscrimination; promiscuity; indistinctness, -ion; uncertainty etc. (*doubt*) 475; obtuseness.

V. not -indiscriminate etc. 465; overlook etc. (*neglect*) 460- a distinction; con-found, -fuse, jumble; swallow whole.

Adj. indiscriminate, undiscriminating, promiscuous; undistinguish-ed, -able, -ing; unmeasured.

466. Measurement.—N. measurement, admeasurement, mensuration, survey, valuation, appraisment, assessment, assize; estim-ate, -ation; dead reckoning; reckoning etc. (*numeration*) 85; gauging etc. *v.*

metrology, weights and measures, compound arithmetic.

measure, yard measure, standard, rule, foot-rule, chain, tape, staff, compass, callipers; dividers; gage, gauge, planimeter; meter, line, rod, check.

volt, kilowatt, ampere, candle power; horse power; axle load; foot pound.

flood —, high water- mark; Plimsoll mark; index etc. 550.

scale; gradu-ation, -ated scale; nonius; vernier etc. (*minuteness*) 193; pedo (*length*)- 200, sounding line etc. (*depth*) 208, thermo (*heat* etc. 398)-, baro (*air* etc. 338)-, dynamo (*power*)- 276, anemo (*wind* 349)-, gonio (*angle* 244)- meter; landmark etc. (*limit*) 233; balance etc. (*weight*) 310; optical instruments etc. 445.

co-ordinates, ordinate and abscissa, polar coordinates, latitude and longitude, declination and right ascension, altitude and azimuth.

geo-, stereo-, hypso-metry; metage; surveying, land surveying; geo-desy, -detics, -desia; ortho-, alti-metry; *cadastre*.

astrolabe, armillary sphere.

land, -surveyor; geometer, topographer, cartographer, hydrographer.

V. measure, meter, mete; value, assess, rate, appraise, estimate, form as estimate, set a value on; appreciate; standardize.

span, pace, step; apply the -compass etc. *n.*; gauge, plumb, probe, calliper, sound, fathom etc. 208; heave the -log, — lead; weigh etc. 319; survey.

take an average etc. 29; graduate.

Adj. measuring etc. *v.*; metric, -al; measurable; geodetical, cadastral, topographical.

467. Evidence. [on one side]**—N.** evidence; facts, premises, *data*, *praecognita*, grounds.

indication etc. 550; criterion etc. (*test*) 463.

testi-mony, -fication; attestation; deposition etc. (*affirmation*) 535; examination.

admission etc. (*assent*) 488; authority, warrant, credential, diploma, voucher, certificate, docket; record etc. 551; document, muniments; *pièce justificative*; deed, warranty etc. (*security*) 771; signature, seal etc. (*identification*) 550; exhibit, citation, reference.

witness, indicator; eye-, ear-witness; deponent; sponsor.

oral —, documentary —, hearsay —, external —, extrinsic —, internal —, intrinsic —, circumstantial —, cumulative —, *ex parte* —, presumptive —, collateral —, constructive- evidence; proof etc. (*demonstration*) 478; evidence in chief; finger prints, dactylogram.

secondary evidence; confirmation, corroboration, adminicle, support; ratification etc. (*assent*) 488; authentication, verification; compurgation, wager of law, comprobation.

citation, reference.

V. be -evidence etc. *n.*; evince, show, betoken, tell of; indicate etc. (*denote*) 550; imply, involve, argue, bespeak, breathe.

have —, carry- weight; tell, speak volumes; speak for itself etc. (*manifest*) 525.

rest —, depend- upon; repose on.

bear -witness etc. *n.*; give -evidence etc. *n.*; testify, depose, witness, vouch for; sign, seal, undersign, set one's hand and seal, sign and seal, deliver as one's act and deed, certify, attest; acknowledge etc. (*assent*) 488.

make absolute, confirm, ratify, corroborate, endorse, countersign, support, bear out, vindicate, uphold, warrant.

adduce, attest, cite, quote; refer —, appeal- to; call, — to witness; bring -forward, — into court; allege, plead; produce —, confront- witnesses; collect —, bring together —, rake up- evidence.

have —, make out- a case; establish, circumstantiate, authenticate, substantiate, verify, make good, quote chapter and verse; bring -home to, — to book.

Adj. showing etc. *v.*; evidential, indica-tive, -tory; deducible etc. 478; grounded —, founded —, based- on; first hand, authentic, verifiable; corroborative, confirmatory; significant, conclusive.

Adv. by inference; according to, witness, *a fortiori*; still -more, — less; *raison de plus*; in corroboration etc. *n.* of; *valeat quantum*; under -seal, — one's hand and seal.

468. Counter-evidence. [Evidence on the other side, on the other hand.]—**N.** counter-evidence; evidence on the other -side, — hand; disproof; refutation etc. 479; negation etc. 536; conflicting evidence.

plea etc. 617; vindication etc. 937; counter-protest; *tu quoque* argument; other side —, reverse- of the shield.

V. countervail, oppose; run counter; rebut etc. (*refute*) 479; subvert etc. (*destroy*) 162; check, weaken; contravene; contradict etc. (*deny*) 536; tell another story, turn the -tables, — scale; alter the case; cut both ways, prove a negative.

audire alteram partem.

Adj. countervailing etc. *v.*; contradictory, in rebuttal.

un-attested, -authenticated, -supported by evidence; suppositious, trumped up.

Adv. *per contra*, conversely, on the other hand.

469. Qualification.—N. qualification, limitation, modification, coloring.

allowance, grains of allowance, consideration, extenuating circumstances.

condition, proviso, exception; exemption; salvo, saving clause; discount etc. 813.

V. qualify, limit, modify, affect, temper, leaven, give a color to, introduce new conditions.

allow —, make allowance- for; admit exceptions, take into account.

take exception, object.

Adj. qualifying etc. *v.*; conditional; extenuatory; exceptional etc. (*unconformable*) 83.

hypothetical etc. (*supposed*) 514; contingent etc. (*uncertain*) 475.

Adv. provided, — always; if, unless, but, yet; according as; conditionally, admitting, supposing; on the supposition of etc. (*theoretically*) 514; with the understanding, even, although, though, for all that, after all, at all events.

with grains of allowance, *cum grano salis*; *exceptis excipiendis*; wind and weather permitting; if possible etc. 470.

subject to; with this -proviso etc. *n.*

470. Possibility.—N. possibility, potentiality; what -may be, — is possible etc. *adj.*; compatibility etc. (*agreement*) 23.

practicability, feasibility; practicableness etc. *adj.*

contingency, chance etc. 156.

V. be -possible etc. *adj.*; stand a chance, have a leg to stand on; admit of, bear.

render -possible etc. *adj.*; put in the way of.

Adj. possible; on the -cards, — dice; *in posse*, within the bounds of possibility, conceivable, credible, imaginable; compatible etc. 23.

practicable, feasible, workable, performable, achievable; within -reach, — measurable distance; accessible, superable, surmountable; at-, obtainable; contingent etc. (*doubtful*) 475.

Adv. possibly, by possibility; perhaps, -chance, -adventure; may be, *haply*, *mayhap*.

if possible, wind and weather permitting, God willing, *Deo volente*, D.V.

471. Impossibility.—N. impossibility etc. *adj.*; what -cannot, — can never- be; sour grapes; infeasibility, impracticability; hopelessness etc. 859.

V. be -impossible etc. *adj.*; have no chance whatever.

attempt impossibilities; square the circle; discover the -philosopher's stone — elixir of life, — secret of perpetual motion; wash a blackamoor white; skin a flint; make -a silk purse out of a sow's ear, — bricks without straw; have nothing to go upon; weave a rope of sand, build castles in the air, *prendre la lune avec les dents*, extract sunbeams from cucumbers, set the Thames on fire, milk a he-goat into a sieve, catch a weasel asleep, *rompre l'anguille au genou*, be in two places at once.

Adj. impossible; not -possible etc. 470; absurd, contrary to reason; unlikely, at variance with facts; unreasonable etc. 477; incredible etc. 485; beyond the bounds of -reason, — possibility; from which reason recoils; visionary; inconceivable etc. (*improbable*) 473; prodigious etc. (*wonderful*) 870; un-, in-imaginable, unthinkable, not a Chinaman's chance.

impracticable, unachievable; un-, in-feasible; insuperable; un-, in-surmountable; unat-, unobtainable; out of -reach, — the question; not to be -had, — thought of; beyond control; desperate etc. (*hopeless*) 859; incompatible etc. 24; inaccessible, uncomeatable, impassable, impervious, innavigable, inextricable.

out of —, beyond- one's -power, — depth, — reach, — grasp; too much for; *ultra crepidam*.

Phr. the grapes are sour; *non possumus*; *non nostrum tantas componere lites*.

472. Probability.—N. probability, likelihood; likeliness etc. *adj.*

vraisemblance, verisimilitude, plausibility;

color, semblance, show of; presumption; presumptive —, circumstantial- evidence; credibility.

reasonable —, fair —, good —, favorable- -chance, — prospect; prospect, well-grounded hope; chance etc. 156.

V. be -probable etc. *adj.*; give —, lend- color to; point to; imply etc. (***evidence***) 467; bid fair etc. (***promise***) 511; stand fair for; stand —, run- a good chance.

presume, infer, suppose, take for granted.

think likely, dare say, flatter oneself; expect etc. 507; count upon etc. (***believe***) 484.

Adj. probable, likely, hopeful, to be expected, in a fair way.

plausible, specious, ostensible, colorable, ***ben trovato***, well-founded, reasonable, credible, easy of belief, presumable, presumptive, apparent.

Adv. probably etc. *adj.*; belike; in all -probability, — likelihood; very —, most- likely; as likely as not; like enough; ten etc. to one; apparently, seemingly, according to every reasonable expectation; ***primâ facie***; to all appearance etc. (***to the eye***) 448.

Phr. the -chances, — odds- are; appearances —, chances- are in favor of; there is reason to -believe, — think, — expect; I dare say; all Lombard Street to a China orange.

473. Improbability.—N. improbability, unlikelihood; unfavorable —, bad —, little —, small —, poor —, scarcely any —, no —, not a ghost of a- chance; bare possibility; long odds; incredibility etc. 485.

V. be -improbable etc. *adj.*; have a -small chance etc. *n.*

Adj. improbable, unlikely, contrary to all reasonable expectation, implausible.

rare etc. (***infrequent***) 137; unheard of, inconceivable; un-, in-imaginable; incredible etc. 485; more than doubtful.

Int. not likely! no fear!

Phr. the chances are against.

474. Certainty.—N. certainty; necessity etc. 601; certitude, certainness, surety, assurance, sureness; dead —, moral- certainty; infallibleness etc. *adj.*; infallibility, reliability.

gospel, scripture, church, pope, court of final appeal; ***res judicata, ultimatum***.

positiveness; dogmat-ism, -ist, -izer; ***doctrinaire***, know-all, bigot, -ry; opinionist, Sir Oracle; ***ipse dixit***; zealot.

fact; positive —, matter of- fact; ***fait accompli***.

V. be -certain etc. *adj.*; stand to reason.

render -certain etc. *adj.*; in-, en-, as-sure; clinch, make sure; determine, decide, set at rest, 'make assurance double sure;' know etc. (***believe***) 484; dismiss all doubt.

dogmatize, lay down the law.

Adj. certain, sure; assured etc. *v.*; solid, well-founded.

unqualified, absolute, positive, determinate, definite, clear, unequivocal, categorical, unmistakable, decisive, decided, ascertained.

inevitable, unavoidable, ineluctable, avoidless.

unerring, infallible; unchangeable etc. 150; to be depended on, trustworthy, reliable, bound.

un-impeachable, -deniable, -questionable; indisputable, -contestable, -controvertible, -defeasible, -dubitable; irrefutable etc. (***proven***) 478; conclusive, without power of appeal, final.

indubious; without —, beyond a —, without a shade or shadow or- -doubt — question; past dispute; beyond all -question, — dispute; undoubted, -contested, -questioned, -disputed; question-, dount-less.

bigoted, fanatical, dogmatic, opinionat-ed, -ive, ***doctrinaire***.

authoritative, authentic; official.

sure as -fate, — death and taxes, — a gun.

evident, self-evident, axiomatic; clear, — as day, — as the sun at noonday; obvious.

Adv. certainly etc. *adj.*; for certain, certes, sure, no doubt, doubtless, and no mistake, ***flagrante delicto***, sure enough, to be sure, of course, as a matter of course, ***à coup sur***, to a certainty, undoubtedly; in truth etc. (***truly***) 494; at -any rate, — all events; without fail; ***coûte que coûte***; whatever may happen, if the worst come to the worst; come —, happen- what -may, — will; sink or swim; rain or shine.

Phr. ***cela va sans dire***; there is -no question, — not a shadow of doubt; the die is cast etc. (***necessity***) 601.

475. Uncertainty.—N. uncertainty, incertitude, doubt; doubtfulness etc. *adj.*; dubi-ety, -tation, -tancy, -ousness.

hesitation, suspense; perplexity, embarrassment, dilemma, quandary, Morton's fork, bewilderment; timidity etc. (***fear***) 860; indecision, vacillation etc. 605; ***diaporesis***, indetermination.

vagueness etc. *adj.*; haze, fog; obscurity etc. (***darkness***) 421; ambiguity etc. (***double meaning***) 520; contingency, double contingency, possibility upon a possibility; conjecture; open question etc. (***question***) 461; ***onus probandi***; blind bargain, pig in a poke, leap in the dark, something or other; needle in a bottle of hay; roving commission.

fallibility, unreliability, untrustworthiness, precariousness.

V. be -uncertain etc. *adj.*; wonder whether.

lose the -clue, — clew, — scent; miss one's way.

not know -what to make of etc. (***unintelligibility***) 519, — which way to turn, — whether one stands on one's head or one's heels; float in a sea of doubt, hesitate, flounder; lose -oneself, — one's head, — one's way, wander aimlessly; muddle one's brains.

render -uncertain etc. *adj.*; put out, pose, puzzle, perplex, embarrass; confuse, -found; bewilder, mystify, bother, nonplus, addle the wits, throw off the scent; ***ambiguas in vulgus spargere voces***; keep in suspense.

doubt etc. (***disbelieve***) 485; hang —, tremble- in the balance; depend.

Adj. uncertain; casual; random etc. (***aimless***) 621; changeable etc. 149.

doubtful, dubious; indecisive; unsettled, -decided, -determined; in suspense, open to discussion; controvertible; in question etc. (***inquiry***) 461; insecure, unstable.

vague; in-determinate, -definite; ambiguous, equivocal; undefin-ed, -able; confused etc. (*indistinct*) 447; mystic, mysterious, veiled, obscure, cryptic, oracular.

perplexing etc. *v.*; enigmatic, paradoxical; apocryphal, problematical, hypothetical; experimental etc. 463.

fallible, questionable, precarious, slippery, ticklish, debatable, disputable; un-reliable, -trustworthy.

contingent, — on, dependent on; subject to; dependent on circumstances; occasional; provisional.

unauth-entic, -enticated, -oritative; unascertained, -confirmed; undemonstrated; un-told, -counted.

in a -state of uncertainty, — cloud, — maze; ignorant etc. 491; on the horns of a dilemma; afraid to say; out of one's reckoning, astray, adrift; as -sea, — fault, — a loss, — one's wit's end, — a *nonplus*; puzzled etc. *v.*; lost abroad, *désorienté*; dis-tracted, -traught.

Adv. *pendente lite*; *sub spe rati*.

Phr. Heaven knows; who can tell? who shall decide when doctors disagree?

476. Reasoning.—N. reasoning; ratio-cination, -nalism; dialectics, induction, generalization.

discussion, comment; ventilation; inquiry etc. 461.

argumentation, controversy, debate; polemics, wrangling; contention etc. 720; logomachy; disputation, -ceptation; paper war.

art of reasoning, logic.

process —, train —, chain- of reasoning; de-, induction; systhesis, analysis.

argument; case, plea, *plaidoyer*, opening; *lemma*, proposition, terms, premises, postulate, *data*, starting point, principle; inference etc. (*judgment*) 480.

pro-, syllogism; enthymeme, sorites, dilemma, *perilepsis*, *a priori* reasoning, *reductio ad absurdum*, horns of a dilemma, *argumentum ad hominem*, comprehensive argument.

reasoner, logician, dialectician; disputant; controver-sialist, -tist; wrangler, arguer, debater, polemic, casuist, rationalist; scientist.

logical sequence; good case; correct —, just —, sound —, valid —, cogent —, logical —, forcible —, persuasive —, persuasory —, consectary —, conclusive etc. 478 —, subtle- reasoning; force of argument; strong -point, — argument.

arguments, reasons, pros and cons.

V. reason, argue, discuss, debate, dispute, wrangle; bandy -words, — arguments; chop logic; hold —, carry on- an argument; controvert etc. (*deny*) 536; canvass; comment —, moralize-upon; consider etc. (*examine*) 461.

open a -discussion, — case; join —, be at- issue; moot; come to the point; stir —, agitate —, ventilate —, torture- a question; try conclusions; take up a -side, — case.

contend, take one's stand upon, insist, lay stress on; infer etc. 480.

follow from etc. (*demonstration*) 478.

Adj. rational; reasoning etc. *v.*; rationalistic; argumentative, controversial, dialectic, polemical; discurs-ory, -ive; disputations.

debatable, controvertible.

logical; in-, de-ductive; synthetic, analytic; relevant etc. 23.

Adv. for, because, hence, whence, seeing that, since, sith, then, thence, so; for -that, — this, — which- reason; for-, inasmuch as; whereas, *ex concesso*, considering, in consideration of; there-, where-fore; consequently, *ergo*, thus, accordingly; *a fortiori*.

in -conclusion, — fine; finally, after all, *au bout du compte*, on the whole, taking one thing with another.

rationally etc. *adj*.

477. Sophistry. [The absence of reasoning.] **Intuition.** [False or vicious reasoning; show of reason.]**—N.** intuition, instinct, association; presentiment; rule of thumb.

sophistry, paralogy, perversion, casuistry, jesuitry, equivocation, evasion, mental reservation; chicane, -ry; quiddit, quiddity; mystification; special pleading; speciousness etc. *adj.*; nonsense etc. 497; word-, tongue-fence.

false —, vicious- reasoning; *petitio principii*, *ignoratio elenchi*; *post hoc ergo propter hoc*; *non sequitur*, *ignotum per ignotius*.

misjudgment etc. 481; false teaching etc. 538.

sophism, solecism, paralogism; quibble, quirk, *elenchus*, elench, fallacy, *quodlibet*, subterfuge, subtlety, quillet; inconsistency, antilogy; 'a mockery, a delusion and a snare;' claptrap, mere words; 'lame and impotent conclusion.'

meshes —, cobwebs- of sophistry; flaw in an argument; weak point, bad case.

over-refinement; hair-splitting etc. *v.*

sophist, casuist, paralogist.

V. judge -intuitively, — by intuition; hazard a proposition, talk at random.

reason -ill, — falsely etc. *adj.*; paralogize; misjudge etc. 481.

pervert, quibble; equivocate, mystify, evade, elude; gloss over, varnish; misteach etc. 538; mislead etc. (*error*) 495; cavil, refine, subtilize, split hairs; misrepresent etc. (*lie*) 544.

beg the question, reason in a circle, cut blocks with a razor, beat about the bush, play fast and loose, blow hot and cold, prove that black is white and white black, travel out of the record, *parler à tort et à travers*, put oneself out of court, not have a leg to stand on.

Adj. intuitive, instinctive, impulsive; independent of —, anterior to- reason; gratuitous; hazarded; unconnected.

unreasonable, illogical, false, unsound, invalid; unwarranted, not following; inconsequent, -ial; inconsistent, incongruous; abson-ous, -ant; unscientific; untenable, inconclusive, incorrect; fall-acious; -ible; groundless, unproved.

deceptive, sophistical, sophisticated, casuistical, jesuitical; illus-ive, -ory; specious, hollow, plausible, *ad captandum*, evasive; irrelevant etc. 10.

weak, feeble, poor, flimsy, loose, vague, irrational; nonsensical etc. (*absurd*) 497; foolish etc. (*imbecile*) 499; frivolous, pettifogging, quibbling; finespun, over-refined.

at the end of one's tether, *au bout de son latin*.

Adv. intuitively etc. *adj.*; by intuition; illogically etc. *adj.*

Phr. *non constat*; that goes for nothing.

478. Demonstration.—**N.** demonstration, proof; conclusiveness etc. *adj.*; *apodixis*, probation, comprobation.

logic of facts etc. (*evidence*) 467; *experimentum curcis* etc. (*test*) 463; argument etc. 476; irrefragability.

V. demonstrate, prove, establish, make good; show; evince etc. (*be evidence of*) 467; verify etc. 467; settle the question, reduce to demonstration, set the question at rest.

make out, — a case; prove one's point, have the best of the argument; draw a conclusion etc. (*judge*) 480.

follow, — of course; stand to reason; hold -good, — water.

Adj. demonstra-ting etc. *v.*, -tive, -ble; probative, unanswerable, conclusive; apodictic, -al; irre-sistible, -futable, -fragable, undeniable.

categorical, decisive, crucial.

demonstrated etc. *v.*; proven; unconfuted, -answered, -refuted; evident etc. 474.

deducible, consequential, consectary, inferential, following.

Adv. of course, in consequence, consequently, as a matter of course.

Phr. *probatum est*; there is nothing more to be said, Q.E.D., it must follow.

479. Confutation.—**N.** con-, re-futation; answer, complete answer; disproof, conviction, redargution, invalidation; expos-ure, -ition; clincher; retort; *reductio ad absurdum*; knock down —, *tu quoque*- argument.

V. con-, re-fute; parry, negative, disprove, redargue, expose, show the fallacy of, rebut, defeat; demolish etc. (*destroy*) 162; over-throw, -turn; scatter to the winds, explode, invalidate; silence; put —, reduce- to silence; clinch -an argument, — a question; give one a set down, stop the mouth, shut up; have, — on the hip; get the better of; confound, convince.

not leave a leg to stand on, cut the ground from under one's feet.

be confuted etc.; fail; expose —, show- one's weak point.

Adj. confut-ing, -ed etc. *v.*; capable of refutation; re-, con-futable.

condemned -on one's own showing, — out of one's own mouth.

Phr. the argument falls to the ground, *cadit quaestio*, it does not hold water, '*suo sibi gladio hunc jugulo.*'

480. Judgment. [Conclusion.]—**N.** result, conclusion, upshot; deduction, inference, ergotism, illation; corollary, porism; moral.

estimation, valuation, appreciation, judication; di-, ad-judication; arbitr- ament, -ement, -ation; assessment, ponderation.

award, estimate; review, criticism, *critique*, notice, report.

decision, determination, judgment, finding, verdict, sentence, decree, — nisi, — absolute, — interlocutory; dictum; *res judicata*.

plébiscite, referendum, voice, casting vote; vote etc. (*choice*) 609; opinion etc. (*belief*) 484; good judgment etc. (*wisdom*) 498.

judge, jurist, umpire; arbi-ter, -trator; assessor, referee; censor, reviewer, critic; *connoisseur*; commentator etc. 524; inspector, inspecting officer.

V. judge, conclude; come to —, draw —, arrive at- a conclusion; ascertain, determine, make up one's mind.

deduce, derive, gather, collect, draw an inference, make a deduction, weet, ween.

form an estimate, estimate, size up, appreciate, value, count, assess, rate, rank, account; regard, consider, think of; look upon etc. (*believe*) 484.

settle; pass —, give- an opinion; decide, try, pronounce, rule; pass -judgment, — sentence; sentence, doom; find; give —, deliver- judgment; adjud-ge, -icate; arbitrate, award, report; bring in a verdict; make absolute, set a question ar rest; confirm etc. (*assent*) 488.

comment, criticize; review, pass under review etc (*examine*) 457; investigate etc. (*inquire*) 461.

hold the scales, sit in judgment; try —, hear- a cause.

Adj. judging etc. *v.*; judicious etc. (*wise*) 498; determinate, conclusive, censorious, critical etc. 932.

Adv. on the whole, all things considered.

480a. Discovery. [Result of search or inquiry.]—**N.** discovery, invention, detection, disenchantment, disclosure, find, ascertainment, revelation.

trover etc. 775.

V. discover, find, determine, evolve; fix upon; find —, trace —, make —, hunt —, fish —, worm —, ferret —, root-out; fathom; bring —, draw-out; educe, elicit, bring to light, invent; dig —, grub —, fish- up; unearth, disinter.

solve, resolve; un-riddle, -ravel, -lock; pick —, open- the lock; find a -clue, — clew- to; interpret etc. 522; disclose etc. 529.

trace, get at; hit it, have it; lay one's -finger, — hands- upon; spot; get —, arrive- at the -turth etc. 494; put the saddle on the right horse, hit the right nail on the head.

be near the truth, burn; smoke, scent, sniff, smell a rat.

open the eyes to; see -through, — daylight, — in its true colors, — the cloven foot; detect; catch, — tripping.

pitch —, fall —, light —, hit —, stumble —, pop- upon; come across; meet —, fall in- with.

recognize, realize, verify, make certain of, identify.

Int. *eureka!*

481. Misjudgment.—**N.** misjudgment, obliquity of —, warped- judgment; mis-calculation, -computation, -conception etc. (*error*) 495; hasty conclusion.

prejud-gment, -ication, -ice; foregone conclusion; pre-notion, -vention, -conception, -dilection, -possession, -apprehension, -sumption, -sentiment; fixed —, preconceived- idea; *idée fixe*; *mentis gratissimus error*; fool's paradise.

esprit de corps, party spirit, race —, class-prejudice, partisanship, clannishness, *prestige*.

bias, warp, twist; hobby, fad, whim, craze, quirk, crotchet, partiality, infatuation, blind side, mote in the eye.

one-sided —, partial —, narrow —, confined —, superficial- -views, — ideas,— conceptions, — notions; narrow mind; bigotry etc. (*obstinacy*) 606; *odium theologicum*; pedantry; hypercriticism. *doctrinaire* etc. (*positive*) 474.

V. mis-judge, -estimate, -think, -conjecture, -conceive etc. (*error*) 495; fly in the face of facts; mis-calculate, -reckon, -compute.

overestimate etc. 482; underestimate etc. 483.

pre-, fore-judge; pre-suppose, -sume, -judicate; dogmatize; have a -bias etc. *n.*; have only one idea; *jurare in verba magistri*, run away with the notion; jump —, rush- to a conclusion; look only at one side of the shield; view -with jaundiced eye, — through distorting spectacles; not see beyond one's nose; *dare pondus fumo*; get the wrong sow by the ear etc. (*blunder*) 699.

give a -bias, — twist; bias, warp, twist; prejudice, -possess.

Adj. misjudging etc. *v.*; ill-judging, wrong-headed; prejudiced, prejudicial, etc. *v.*; jaundiced; short-sighted, pur-blind; partial, one-sided, superficial.

narrow-minded; confined, insular, provincial, parochial, illiberal, intolerant, narrow, besotted, infatuated, fanatical, cracked, warped, *entêté*, positive, dogmatic, dictatorial; conceited; opin-, opini-ative; opinion-ed, -ate, -ative, -ated; self-opinioned, wedded to an opinion, *opiniâtre*; bigoted etc. (*obstinate*) 606; crotchety, fussy, impracticable; unreason-able, -ing; stupid etc. 499; credulous etc. 486.

misjudged etc. *v.*

Adv. *ex parte*.

Phr. nothing like leather; the wish the father to the thought.

482. Overestimation.—N. overestimation etc. *v.*; exaggeration etc. 549; vanity etc. 880; optim-, pessim-ism, -ist; megalomania.

much -cry and little wool, — ado about nothing; storm in a teacup; fine talking, rodomontade, gush, hot air, gas, bombast.

egotism etc. 880; boasting etc. 884.

V. over-estimate, -rate, -value, -prize, -weigh, -reckon, -strain, -praise; estimate too highly, attach too much importance to, make mountains of molehills, catch at straws; strain, magnify; exaggerate etc. 549; set too high a value upon; think —, make- -much, — too much- of; outreckon.

extol, — to the skies; make the -most, — best, — worst- of, eulogize, panegyrize, gush, puff, boost; make two bites of a cherry.

have too high an opinion of oneself etc. (*vanity*) 880.

Adj. overestimated etc. *v.*; oversensitive etc. (*sensibility*) 822; inflated, puffed up, exaggerated etc. 549.

Phr. all his geese are swans; *parturiunt montes*.

483. Underestimation.—N. underestimation; depreciation etc. (*detraction*) 934; pessim-ism, -ist; undervaluing etc. *v.*; modesty etc. 881.

V. under-rate, -estimate, -value, -reckon; depreciate; disparage etc. (*detract*) 934; not do justice to; mis-, dis-prize; ridicule etc. 856; slight etc. (*despise*) 930; neglect etc. 460; slur over, under-state.

make -light, — little, — nothing, — no account- of; minimize, belittle, run down, think nothing of; set -no store by, — at naught; shake off as dewdrops from the lion's mane.

Adj. depreciat-ing, -ed, -ive, -ory, etc. *v.*; unappreciated, -valued, -prized; pejorative.

484. Belief.—N. belief; credence; credit; assurance; faith, trust, troth, confidence, presumption, sanguine expectation etc. (*hope*) 858; dependence on, reliance on.

persuasion, conviction, convincement, plerophory, self-conviction; certainty etc. 474; opinion, mind, view; conception, thinking; impression etc. (*idea*) 453; surmise etc. 514; conclusion etc. (*judgment*) 480.

tenet, dogma, principle, way of thinking; popular belief etc. (*assent*) 488.

firm —, implicit —, settled —, fixed —, rooted —, deep-rooted —, staunch —, unshaken —, steadfast —, inveterate —, calm —, sober —, dispassionate —, impartial —, well-founded- -belief, — opinion etc.; *uberrima fides*.

system of opinions, school, doctrine, articles, canons; declaration —, profession- of faith; tenets, *credenda*, creed; thirty-nine articles etc. (*orthodoxy*) 983*a*; catechism; assent etc. 488; *propaganda* etc. (*teaching*) 537.

credibility etc. (*probability*) 472.

V. believe, credit; give -faith, — credit, — credence- to; see, realize; assume, receive; set down —, take- for; have —, take- it; consider, esteem, presume.

count —, depend —, calculate —, pin one's faith —, reckon —, lean —, build —, rely —, rest- upon; lay one's account for; make sure of.

make oneself easy -about, — on that score; take on -trust, — credit; take for -granted, — gospel; allow —, attach- some weight to.

know, — for certain; have —, make- no doubt; doubt not; be — rest- -assured etc. *adj.*; persuade —, assure —, satisfy- oneself; make up one's mind.

give one credit for; confide —, believe —, put one's trust- in; place —, repose- implicit confidence in; take -one's word for, — at one's word; place reliance on, rely upon, swear by, regard to.

think, hold; take, — it; opine, be of opinion, conceive, trow, ween, fancy, apprehend; have —, hold —, possess —, entertain —, adopt —, imbibe —, embrace —, get hold of —, hazard —, foster —, nurture —, cherish- -a belief, — an opinion etc. *n.*

view —, consider —, take —, hold —, conceive —, regard —, esteem —, deem —, look upon —, account —, set down- as; surmise etc. 514.

get —, take- it into one's head; come round to an opinion; swallow etc. (*credulity*) 486.

cause to -be believed etc. *v.*; satisfy, persuade, have the ear of, gain the confidence of, assure; convince, -vict, -vert; put across, sell; wean, bring round; bring —, put —, win- over; indoctrinate etc. (*teach*) 537; cram down the throat; produce —, carry- conviction; bring —, drive- home to.

go down, find credence, pass current; be -received etc. *v.*, — current etc. *adj.*; possess —, take hold of —, take possession of- the mind.

Adj. believing etc. *v.*; certain, sure, assured, positive, cocksure, satisfied, confident, unhesitating, convinced, secure.

under the impression; impressed —, imbued —, penetrated- with.

confiding, trustful, suspectless; unsusp-ecting, -icious; void of suspicion; credulous etc. 486; wedded to.

believed etc. *v.*; accredited, putative; unsuspected.

worthy of —, deserving of —, commanding- -belief, — *confidence*; credible, reliable, trusted, trustworthy, to be depended on, undoubted; satisfactory; probable etc. 472; fiduci-al, -ary; persuasive, impressive.

relating to belief, doctrinal.

Adv. in the -opinion, — eyes- of; *me judice*; me-seems, -thinks; to the best of one's belief; I -dare say, — doubt not, — have no doubt, — am sure; in my opinion; sure enough etc. (*certainty*) 474; depend —, rely- upon it; be —, rest- assured; I'll warrant you etc. (*affirmation*) 535.

485. Unbelief. Doubt.—N. un-, dis-, mis-belief; discredit, miscreance; infidelity etc. (*irreligion*) 989; dissent etc. 489; change of -opinion etc. 484; retraction etc. 607.

doubt etc. (*uncertainty*) 475; skepticism, misgiving, demur; dis-, mis-trust; misdoubt, suspicion, jealousy, scruple, qualm; *onus probandi*.

incredib-ility, -leness; incredulity; unbeliever etc. 487.

V. dis-believe, -credit; not -believe etc. 484; misbelieve; refuse to admit etc. (*dissent*) 489; refuse to believe etc. (*incredulity*) 487.

doubt; be -doubtful etc. (*uncertain*) 475; doubt the truth of; be -skeptical as to etc. *adj.*; diffide; dis-, mis-trust; suspect, smoke, scent, smell a rat; have —, harbor —, entertain- -doubts, — suspicions; have one's doubts.

demur, stick at, pause, hesitate, scruple, waver, stop and consider.

hang in -suspense, — doubt.

throw doubt upon, raise a question; bring —, call- in question; question, challenge, query; dispute; deny etc. 536; cavil; cause —, raise —, start —, suggest —, awake- a -doubt, — suspicion; ergotize.

startle, stagger; shake —, stagger- one's faith, — belief.

Adj. unbelieving; incredulous —, skeptical- as to; distrustful —, shy —, suspicious- of; doubting etc. *v.*

doubtful etc. (*uncertain*) 475; disputable; unworthy —, undeserving- of -belief etc. 484; questionable; sus-pect, -picious; open to -suspicion, — doubt; staggering, hard to believe, incredible, not to be believed, inconceivable.

fallible etc. (*uncertain*) 475; undemonstrable; controvertible etc. (*untrue*) 495.

Adv. *cum grano salis.*

Phr. *fronti nulla fides*; *nimium ne crede colori*; '*timeo Danaos et dona ferentes*;' *credat Judaeus Apella*; let those believe who may.

486. Credulity.—N. credul-ity, -ousness etc. *adj.*; gull-, cull-ibility; gross credulity, infatuation; self-delusion, -deception; blind reasoning; superstition; one's blind side; bigotry etc. (*obstinacy*) 606; hyper-orthodoxy etc. 984; misjudgment etc. 481.

credulous person etc. (*dupe*) 547.

V. be -credulous etc. *adj.*; *jurare in verba magistri*; follow implicitly; swallow, — whole, gulp down; take on trust; take for -granted, — gospel; run away with -a notion, — an idea; jump —, rush- to a conclusion; think the moon is made of green cheese; take —, grasp- the shadow for the substance; catch at straws.

impose upon etc. (*deceive*) 545.

Adj. credulous, gullible; easily -deceived etc. 545; simple, green, soft, childish, silly, stupid; over-credulous, -confident; infatuated, superstitious; confiding etc. (*believing*) 484.

Phr. the wish the father to the thought; *credo quia impossibile.*

487. Incredulity.—N. incredul-ous-ness, -ity; skepticism, pyrrhonism; want of faith etc. (*irreligion*) 989.

suspiciousness etc. *adj.*; scrupulosity; suspicion etc. (*unbelief*) 485; dissent etc. 489.

unbeliever, skeptic, aporetic; atheist, agnostic, infidel, disbeliever, misbeliever, pyrrhonist etc. 989; heretic etc. (*heterodox*) 984.

v. be -incredulous etc. *adj.*; distrust etc. (*disbelieve*) 485; refuse to believe; shut one's -eyes, — ears- to; turn a deaf ear to; hold aloof; ignore; *nullis jurare in verba magistri.*

Adj. incredulous, skeptical, unbelieving, inconvincible; hard —, shy- of belief; suspicious, scrupulous, distrustful, heterodox etc. 984.

488. Assent.—N. assent, -ment; acquiescence, admission; nod; ac-, con-cord, -cordance; agreement etc. 23; affirm-ance, -ation; recognition, acknowledgment, avowal; confession, — of faith.

unanimity, common consent, *consensus*, acclamation, chorus, *vox populi*; popular —, current- -belief, — opinion; public opinion; concurrence etc. (*of causes*) 178; co-operation etc. (*voluntary*) 709.

ratification, confirmation, corroboration, approval, acceptance, *visa*; indorsement etc. (*record*) 551.

consent etc. (*compliance*) 762.

affirmant, consenter, covenantor, subscriber, endorser, upholder.

V. assent; give —, yield —, nod- assent; acquiesce; agree etc. 23; receive, accept, accede, accord, concur, lend oneself to, consent, coincide, reciprocate, go with; be -at one with etc. *adj.*; go along —, chime in —, strike in —, close- with; echo, enter into one's views, agree in opinion; vote —, give one's voice- for; recognize; subscribe —, conform —, defer- to; say -yes, — ditto, — amen; — aye- to.

acknowledge, own, admit, allow, avow, confess; concede etc. (*yield*) 762; come round to; abide by; permit etc. 760.

come to —, arrive at- -an understanding, — terms, — an agreement.

con-, af-firm; ratify, approve, endorse, countersign; visa; corroborate etc. 467.

go —, swim- with the stream, float with the current; be in the fashion, join in the chorus; be in every mouth.

Adj. assenting etc. *v.*; of one -accord, — mind; of the same mind, at one with, agreed, acquiescent, content; willing etc. 602.

un-contradicted, -challenged, -questioned, -controverted.

carried —, agreed- -*nem. con.* etc. *adv.*; unanimous; agreed on all hands, carried by acclamation.

affirmative etc. 535.

Adv. yes, yea, ay, aye, true; good; well; very -well, — true; well and good; granted; *placet*; even —, just- so; to be sure, surely, 'thou hast said;' truly, exactly, precisely, that's just it, indeed, certainly, certes, *ex concesso*; of course, unquestionably, assuredly, no doubt, doubtless, undoubtedly.

be it so; so -be it, — let it be, so mote it be; amen; with all my heart; willingly etc. 602.

with one -consent, — voice, — accord; unanimously, *unâ voce*, by common consent, in chorus, to a man, *nem. con.*; *nemine -contradicente*, — *dissentiente*; without a dissentient voice; as one man, one and all, on all hands.

489. Dissent.—N. dissent; discordance etc. (*disagreement*) 24; difference —, diversity- of opinion.

non-conformity etc. (*heterodoxy*) 984; protestantism, recusancy, schism; disaffection; secession etc. 624; recantation etc. 607.

dissension etc. (*discord*) 713; discontent etc. 832; cavilling.

protest; contradiction etc. (*denial*) 536; non-compliance etc. (*rejection*) 764; disapprobation etc. 932; hartal.

dissent-ient, -er; non-juror, -content; recusant, sectary, schismatic, protestant, non-conformist, separatist, non-co-operator, conscientious objector, passive resister.

V. dissent, demur; call in question etc. (*doubt*) 485; differ in opinion, disagree; say -no etc. 536; refuse -assent, — to admit; cavil, protest, raise one's voice against, make bold to differ; repudiate; contradict etc. (*deny*) 536; agree to differ.

have no notion of, differ *toto caelo*; revolt -at, — from the idea.

shake the head, shrug the shoulders; look -askance, — askant.

secede; recant etc. 607.

Adj. dissenting etc. *v.*; negative etc. 536; dissident, -entient; unconsenting etc. (*refusing*) 764; non-content, -juring; protestant, recusant; unconvinced, -verted.

unavowed, unacknowledged; out of the question.

discontented etc. 832; unwilling etc. 603; extorted.

sectarian, denominational, schismatic, heterodox, intolerant.

Adv. no etc. 536; at -variance, — issue- with; under protest; *non placet*.

Int. God forbid! not for the world; not on your life; I beg to differ; I'll be hanged if; never tell me; your humble servant, pardon me; tell that to the marines.

Phr. many men many minds; *quot homines tot sententiae*; *tant s'en faut*; *il s'en faut bien*.

490. Knowledge.—N. knowledge; cogn-izance, -ition, -oscence; acquaintance, experience, ken, privity, insight, familiarity; com-, ap-prehension; recognition; appreciation etc. (*judgment*) 480; intuition; consci-ence, -ousness; preception, precognition; acroamatics.

light, enlightenment; glimpse, inkling; side light; glimmer, -ing; dawn; scent, suspicion; impression etc. (*idea*) 453; discovery etc. 480*a*.

system —, body- of knowledge; science, philosophy, pansophy; theory, Etiology; circle of the sciences; pandect, doctrine, body of doctrine; cy-, ency-clopedia; school etc. (*system of opinions*) 484.

tree of knowledge; republic of letters etc. (*language*) 560.

erudition, learning, lore, scholarship, reading, letters; literature; booklearning, bookishness; biblio-mania, -latry; information, general information; store of -knowledge etc.; education etc. (*teaching*) 537; culture, attainments; acquirements, -sitions; accomplishments, proficiency; practical knowledge etc. (*skill*) 698; higher education, liberal education; dilettantism; rudiments etc. (*beginning*) 66.

deep —, profound —, solid —, accurate —, acroatic —, acroamatic —, vast —, extensive —, encyclopedical- -knowledge, — learning; omniscience, pantology.

march of intellect; progress —, advance- of -science, — learning; schoolmaster abroad.

V. know, ken, scan, wot; wot —, be aware etc. *adj.*- of; ween, weet, trow, have, possess.

conceive; ap-, com-prehend; take, realize, understand, appreciate; fathom, make out; recognize, discern, perceive, see, get a sight of, experience.

know full well; have —, possess- some knowledge of; be -*au courant* etc. *adj.*; have -in one's head, — at one's fingers' ends; know by -heart, — rote; be master of; *connaître le dessous des cartes*, know what's what etc. 698.

see one's way; learn, discover etc. 480*a*.

come to one's knowledge etc. (*information*) 527.

Adj. knowing etc. *v.*; cognitive; acroamatic.

aware —, cognizant —, conscious- of; acquainted —, made acquainted- with; privy —, no stranger- to; *au -fait*, — *courant*; in the secret; up —, alive- to; sensible of; behind the -scenes, — curtain; let into; apprized —, informed- of; undeceived.

proficient —, versed —, read —, forward —,

strong —, at home- in; conversant —, familiar- with.

erudite, instructed, learned, lettered, educated; high-brow; well-conned, -informed, -read, -grounded, -educated; enlightened, shrewd, insightful, *savant*, blue, bookish, scholastic, solid, profound, deep-read, book-learned; accomplished etc. (*skilful*) 698; omniscient; self-taught, -educated.

known etc. *v.*; ascertained, well-known, recognized, received, notorious, noted; proverbial; familiar, — as household words, to every schoolboy; hackneyed, trite, commonplace.

knowable, cogn-oscible, -izable.

Adv. to —, to the best of- one's knowledge.

Phr. one's eyes being opened etc. (*disclosure*) 529.

491. Ignorance.—N. ignorance, nescience, *tabula rasa*, crass ignorance, *ignorance crasse*; unacquaintance; unconsciousness etc. *adj.*; dark-, blind-ness; incomprehension, inexperience, simplicity.

unknown quantities, *x*, *y*, *z*.

sealed book, *terra incognita*, virgin soil, unexplored ground; dark ages.

[Imperfect knowledge] smattering, superficiality, half-learning, sciolism, glimmering; bewilderment etc. (*uncertainty*) 475; incapacity.

[Affectation of knowledge] pedantry; charlatanry, -ism.

V. be -ignorant etc. *adj.*; not -know etc. 490; know -not, — not what, — nothing of; have no -idea, — notion, — conception; not have the remotest idea; not know chalk from cheese.

ignore, be blind to; keep in ignorance etc. (*conceal*) 528.

see through a glass darkly; have a -film over the eyes, — glimmering etc. *n.*; wonder whether; not know what to make of etc. (*unintelligibility*) 519; not pretend —, not take upon oneself- to say.

Adj. ignorant, nescient; un-knowing, -aware, -acquainted, -apprized, -witting, -weeting, -conscious; wit-, weet-less; a stranger to; unconversant.

un-informed, -cultivated, -versed, -instructed, -taught, -initiated, -tutored, -schooled, -guided, -enlightened; Philistine; behind the age.

shallow, superficial, green, rude, empty, half-learned, illiterate; un-read, -informed, -educated, -learned, -lettered, -bookish; empty-headed; lowbrow; pedantic.

in the dark; be-nighted, -lated; blind-ed, -fold; hoodwinked; misinformed; *au bout de son latin*, at the end of his tether; at fault; at sea etc. (*uncertain*) 475; caught tripping.

un-known, -apprehended, -explained, -ascertained, -investigated, -explored, -heard of, -perceived; concealed etc. 528; novel.

Adv. ignorantly etc. *adj.*; unawares; for -anything, — aught- one knows; not that one knows.

Int. God —, Heaven —, the Lord —, nobody-knows.

Phr. a little learning is a dangerous thing.

492. Scholar.—N. scholar, *connoissuer*, *savant*, pundit, schoolman, professor, graduate, wrangler, moonshee; academ-ician, -ist; fellow, don, post graduate, advanced student; master —, bachelor- of arts; doctor, licentiate, gownsman; philo-sopher, -math; scientist, clerk; soph, -ist, -ister; linguist, classicist; glosso-, etymo-, philologist; philologer; lexico-, glosso-grapher; scholiast, commentator, annotator, grammarian; *littérateur*, *literati*, *dilettanti*, *illuminati*; Mezzofanti, admirable Crichton, Maecenas.

book-worm, *helluo librorum*, biblio-phile, -maniac; blue-stocking, *bas-bleu*; big-wig, learned Theban.

learned —, literary- man; *homo multarum literarum*; man of -learning, — letters, — education; high-brow, intelligentsia.

antiquar-ian, -y; archeologist; sage etc. (*wise man*) 500.

pendant, *doctrinaire*; pedagogue, Dr. Pangloss; pantologist.

teacher etc. 540; schoolboy etc. (*learner*) 541.

Adj. learned etc. 490; brought up at the feet of Gamaliel.

493. Ignoramus.—N. ignoramus, illiterate, moron, dunce, numskull; wooden spoon; no scholar.

sciolist, smatterer, dabbler, half-scholar; *charlatan*; wiseacre.

novice, griffin; greenhorn etc. (*dupe*) 547; tyro etc. (*learner*) 541.

lubber etc. (*bungler*) *701; fool etc. 501; pedant etc. 492.*

Adj. bookless, shallow, simple, dense, dumb, thick, dull, ignorant etc. 491.

494. Truth. [Object of knowledge.]**—N.** fact, reality etc. (*existence*) 1; plain matter of fact; nature etc. (*principle*) 5; truth, verity; gospel; orthodoxy etc. 983*a*; authenticity; veracity etc. 543.

accuracy, exactitude; exact-, precise-ness etc. *adj.*; precision, delicacy; rigor, mathematical precision, punctuality; clockwork precision etc. (*regularity*) 80.

orthology; *ipsissima verba*; letter of the law, realism.

plain —, honest —, sober —, naked —, unalloyed —, unqualified —, stern —, exact —, intrinsic- truth; *nuda veritas*; the very thing; not an -illusion etc. 495; real Simon Pure; unvarnished tale; the truth, the whole truth and nothing but the truth; just the thing.

V. be -true etc. *adj.*, — the case; stand the test; have the true ring; hold -good, — true, — water; conform to rule.

render —, prove- -true etc. *adj.*; substantiate etc. (*evidence*) 467.

get at the truth etc. (*discover*) 480*a*.

Adj. real, actual etc. (*existing*) 1; veritable, true; certain etc. 474; substantially —, categorically-true etc; true -to the letter; — to life, — to scale, — the facts, — as gospel; unimpeachable; veracious etc. 543; unre-, uncon-futed; un-ideal -imagined; realistic.

exact, accurate, definite, precise, well defined, just, right, correct, strict, severe; close etc. (*similar*) 17; literal; rigid, rigorous; scrupulous etc. (*con-*

scientious) 939; religiously exact, punctual, mathematical, scientific; faithful, constant, unerring; curious, particular, punctilious, meticulous, nice, delicate, fine.

genuine, authentic, legitimate, pukka; orthodox etc. 983*a*; official, *ex officio*.

pure, natural, sound, sterling; un-sophisticated, -adulterated, -varnished, -colored; in its true colors.

well-grounded, -founded; solid, substantial, tangible, valid; undis-torted, -guised; un-affected, -exaggerated, -romantic, -flattering.

Adv. truly etc.*adj.*; verily, indeed, in reality; as a matter of fact; beyond -doubt, – question; with truth etc. (*veracity*) 543; certainly etc. (*certain*) 474; actually etc. (*existence*) 1; in effect etc. (*intrinsically*) 5.

exactly etc. *adj.* ; *ad amussim*; *verbatim*, – *et literatim*; word for word, literally, *literatim*, *totidem verbis*, *sic*, to the letter, chapter and verse, *ipsissimis verbis*; *ad unguem*; to an inch; to a -nicety, – hair, – tittle, – turn, – T; *au pied de la lettre*; neither more nor less; in -every respect, – all respects; *sous tous les rapports*; at -any rate, – all events; strictly speaking.

Phr. the -truth, – fact- is; *rem acu tetigisti*.

495. Error.—N. error, fallacy; misconception, -apprehension, -understanding; inexactness etc. *adj.*; laxity; misconstruction etc. (*misinterpretation*) 523; miscomputation etc. (*misjudgment*) 481; *non-sequitur* etc. 477; misstatement, -report; anachronism; malapropism.

mistake; miss, fault, blunder, boner, bloomer, howler, *quid pro quo*, cross purposes, oversight, misprint, *erratum*, *corrigendum*, slip, blot, flaw, loose thread; trip, stumble etc. (*failure*) 732, botchery etc. (*want of skill*) 699; slip of the -tongue, – pen; *lapsus -linguae*, – *calami*, clerical error; bull etc. (*absurdity*) 497.

Il-, de-lusion; false impression, – idea; bubble; self-deceit, -deception; warped notion; mists of error; superstition, exploded notion.

heresy etc. (*heterodoxy*) 984; hallucination etc. (*insanity*) 503; false light etc. (*fallacy of vision*) 443; dream etc. (*fancy*) 515; fable etc. (*untruth*) 546; bias etc. (*misjudgment*) 481; misleading etc. *v.*

V. be -erroneous etc. *adj.*

cause error; mis-lead, -guide; lead -astray, – into error; beguile, misinform etc. (*misteach*) 538; delude; give a false -impression, – idea; falsify, garble, misstate; deceive etc. 545; lie etc. 544.

err; be -in error etc. *adj.*; – mistaken etc. *v.*; be deceived etc. (*duped*) 547; mistake, receive a false impression, deceive oneself; fall into –, lie under –, labor under- -an error etc. *n.*; be in the wrong, blunder; mis-apprehend, -conceive, -understand, -reckon, -count, -calculate etc. (*misjudge*) 481.

play –, be- at cross purposes etc. (*misinterpret*) 523.

trip, stumble; lose oneself etc. (*uncertainty*) 475; go astray; fail etc. 732; take the wrong sow by the ear etc. (*mismanage*) 699; put the saddle on the wrong horse; reckon without one's host; take the shadow for the substance etc. (*credulity*) 486; dream etc. (*imagine*) 515.

Adj. erroneous, untrue, false, devoid of truth, fallacious, faulty, apocryphal, unreal, ungrounded, groundless; unsubstantial etc. 4; heretical etc. (*heterodox*) 984; unsound; illogical etc. 477; wrong.

in-, un-exact; in-accurate, -correct; indefinite etc. (*uncertain*) 475.

illus-ive, -ory; delusive; mock; ideal etc. (*imaginary*) 515; spurious etc. 545; deceitful etc. 544; perverted.

controvertible, unsustain-able, -ed; unauthenticated, untrustworthy.

exploded, refuted, discarded.

in –, under an- error etc. *n.*; mistaken etc. *v.*; tripping etc. *v.*; out, – in one's reckoning; aberrant; beside –, wide of the- -mark, – truth; astray etc. (*at fault*) 475; on -a false, – the wrong-scent; in the wrong box; at cross purposes, all in the wrong, all abroad, at sea.

Adv. more or less.

496. Maxim.—N. maxim, aphorism; apo-, apoph-thegm; *dictum*, saying, gnome, adage, saw, proverb, epigram; sentence, *mot*, motto, word, by-word, precept, moral, phylactery, *protasis*, brocard.

axiom, postulate, theorem, *scholium*, truism.

reflection etc. (*idea*) 453; conclusion etc. (*judgment*) 480; golden rule etc. (*precept*) 697; principle, *principia*; profession of faith etc. (*belief*) 484; formula.

wise –, sage –, received –, admitted –, recognized- maxim etc.; true –, common –, hackneyed –, trite –, commonplace- saying etc.

Adj. aphoristic, proverbial, phylacteric; axiomatic, gnomic.

Adv. as -the saying is, – they say.

497. Absurdity.—N. absurd-ity, -ness etc. *adj.*; imbecility etc. 499; alogy, nonsense, paradox, inconsistency; stultiloqu-y, -ence, futility.

blunder, muddle, bull; Irish-, Hibernic-ism; slip-slop; anti climax; bathos; sophism etc. 477.

farce, burlesque, *galimatias*, *amphigouri*, rhapsody; farrago etc. (*disorder*) 59; extravagance, romance; sciomachy.

joke, catch, sell, pun, verbal quibble, macaronic.

jargon, fustian, twaddle etc. (*no meaning*) 517; exaggeration etc. 549; moonshine, stuff; mare's nest.

vagary, tomfoolery, mummery, monkey trick, practical joke, *boutade*, *escapade*.

V. play the fool etc. 499; stultify, blunder, muddle; joke; talk nonsense, *parler à tort et à travers*; *battre la campagne*; be -absurd etc. *adj.*

Adj. absurd, nonsensical, preposterous, egregious, senseless, farcical, inconsistent, ridiculous, extravagant, quibbling, futile; macaronic, punning, paradoxical.

foolish etc. 499; sophistical etc. 477; unmeaning etc. 517; without rhyme or reason; fantastic.

Int. fiddle-de-dee! pish! pish and tush! pho! stuff and nonsense! rubbish! !rot! bosh! in the name of the Prophet—figs!

Phr. *credat Judaeus Apella*; tell it to the marines.

498. Intelligence. Wisdom.—N. intelligence, capacity, comprehension, understanding, intellect etc. 450; nous, parts, sagacity, mother wit, wit, *esprit*, gumption, quick parts, grasp of intellect; acuteness etc. *adj.*; acumen, subtlety, penetration; perspica-cy, -city; discernment; long-headedness, due sense of, good judgment; discrimination etc. 465; craftiness, cunning etc. 702; refinement etc. (*taste*) 850.

head, brains, gray matter, headpiece, upper story, long head; eagle -eye, – glance; eye of a -lynx, – hawk.

wisdom, sapience, sense; good –, common –, plain –, horse- sense; clear thinking; rationality, reason; reasonableness etc. *adj.*; judgment; solidity, depth, profundity, caliber; enlarged views; reach –, compass- of thought; enlargement of mind.

genius, inspiration, *geist*, fire of genius, heaven-born genius, soul; talent etc. (*aptitude*) 698.

[Wisdom in action] prudence etc. 864; vigilance etc. 459; tact etc. 698; foresight etc. 510; sobriety, self-possession, *aplomb*, ballast, mental -poise, – balance.

a bright thought, inspiration, brainwave, not a bad idea.

V. be -intelligent etc. *adj.*; have all one's wits about one; understand etc. (*intelligible*) 518; catch –, take in- an idea; take a -joke, – hint.

see -through, – at a glance, – with half an eye, – far into, – through a millstone; penetrate; discern etc. (*descry*) 441; foresee etc. 510.

discriminate etc. 465; know what's what etc. 698; listen to reason.

Adj. [Applied to persons] intelligent, quick of apprehension, keen, acute, alive, brainy, awake, bright, quick, sharp; quick-, keen-, clear-, sharp- -eyed, -sighted, -witted; wide awake; canny, shrewd, astute; clear-headed; far-sighted etc. 510; discerning, perspicacious, penetrating, piercing; argute nimble-, needle-witted; sharp as a needle; alive to etc. (*cognizant*) 490; clever etc. (*apt*) 698; arch etc. (*cunning*) 702; *pas si bête*; acute etc. 682.

wise, sage, sapient, sagacious, reasonable, rational, sound, in one's right mind, sensible, *abnormis sapiens*, judicious, strong-minded.

un-prejudiced, -biassed, -bigoted, -prepossessed; un-dazzled, -perplexed; of unwarped judgment, impartial, equitable, fair, broad-minded.

cool; cool-, long-, hard-, strong-headed; long-sighted, calculating, thoughtful, reflecting; solid, deep, profound.

oracular; heaven-directed, -born.

prudent etc. (*cautious*) 864; sober, staid, solid; considerate, politic, wise in one's generation; watchful etc. 459; provident etc. (*prepared*) 673; in advance of one's age; wise as -a serpent, – Solomon, – Solon.

[Applied to actions] wise, sensible, reasonable, judicious; well-judged, -advised; prudent, politic; expedient etc. 646.

499. Imbecility. Folly.—N. want of -intelligence etc. 498, – intellect etc. 450; shallow-, silli-, foolish-ness etc. *adj.*; imbecility, incapacity, vacancy of mind, poverty of intellect, clouded perception, poor head, apartments to let; stup-, stolidity; hebetude, dull understanding, meanest capacity; short-sightedness; incompetence etc. (*unskilfulness*) 699.

one's weak side; bias etc. 481; infatuation etc. (*insanity*) 503.

simplicity, puerility, babyhood; dotage, anility, second childishness, senile dementia, fatuity; idiocy, -tism; driveling.

folly, frivolity, desipience, irrationality, trifling, ineptitude, nugacity, inconsistency, lip-wisdom, conceit; sophistry etc. 477; giddiness etc. (*inattention*) 458; eccentricity etc. 503; extravagance etc. (*absurdity*) 497; rashness etc. 863.

act of folly etc. 699.

V. be -imbecile etc. *adj.*; have no -brains, – sense etc. 498.

trifle, drivel, *radoter*, dote; ramble etc. (*madness*) 503; play the -fool, – monkey, – goat, take leave of one's senses; not see an inch beyond one's nose; stultify oneself etc. 699; talk nonsense etc. 497.

Adj. [Applied to persons] un-intelligent, -intellectual, -reasoning; mind-, wit-, reason-, brain-less; having no -head etc. 498; not -bright etc. 498; inapprehensible.

weak-, addle-, puzzle-, blunder-, muddle-, muddy-, pig-, beetle-, maggotty-, gross-headed; beef-, fat- -witted, -headed.

weak, feeble-minded; dull-, shallow-, rattle-, lack-brained; half-, nit-, short-, dull-, blunt-witted; shallow-, clod-, addle-pated; dim-, short-sighted; thick-skulled; weak in the upper story.

shallow, *borné*, weak, wanting, soft, nutty, sappy, spoony; dull, – as a beetle; stupid, heavy, insulse, obtuse, blunt, stolid, doltish, asinine; inapt etc. 699; prosaic etc. 843.

child-ish, -like; infant-ine, -ile; baby-, bab-ish; puerile; anile; simple etc. (*credulous*) 486.

fatuous, idiotic, imbecile, moronic, driveling; blatant, babbling; vacant; sottish; bewildered etc. 475.

blockish, unteachable; Boeot-ian, -ic; bovine; un-gifted, -discerning, -enlightened, -wise, -philosophical; apish.

foolish, silly, senseless, irrational, insensate, nonsensical, inept; maudlin.

narrow-minded etc. 481; bigoted etc. (*obstinate*) 606; giddy etc. (*thoughtless*) 458; rash etc. 863; eccentric etc. (*crazed*) 503.

[Applied to actions] foolish, unwise, indiscreet, injudicious, improper, unreasonable, without reason, ridiculous, silly, stupid, asinine; ill-imagined, -advised, -judged, -devised; inconsistent, irrational, unphilosophical; extravagant etc. (*nonsensical*) 497; sleeveless, idle; useless etc. 645; inexpedient etc. 647; frivolous etc. (*trivial*) 643; absurd etc. 497.

Phr. *Davis sum non Oedipus.*

500. Sage.—N. sage, wise man; pundit; master -mind, – spirit of the age; longhead, thinker, philosopher.

authority, oracle, mentor, luminary, shining light, *esprit fort*, *magnus Apollo*, Solon, Solomon, Nestor, Magi, 'second Daniel.'

man of learning etc. 492; expert etc. 700; wizard etc. 994.

[Ironically] wiseacre, bigwig.

Adj. wise, learned; authoritative, oracular; erudite etc. 490; venerable, reverenced, revered, *emeritus*.

501. Fool.—N. fool, idiot, tomfool, wiseacre, simpleton, Simple Simon, nit-wit, witling, dizzard, donkey, ass; ninny, -hammer; moron, dolt, booby, Tom Noddy, looby, hoddy-doddy, noddy, nonny, noodle, nizy, owl; goose, -cap; *imbécile*; gaby, *radoteur*, nincompoop, *badaud*, zany; trifler, babbler; pretty fellow; natural, *niais*.

child, baby, infant, innocent, milksop, sop.

oaf, lout, loon, lown, dullard, doodle, calf, colt, buzzard, block, put, stick, stock, numps, tony.

bull-, dunder-, addle-, block-, dull-, logger-, jolt-, jolter-, beetle-, gross-, thick-, giddy-head; num-, thick- skull; lack-, shallow-brain; half-, lack-wit; dunder-pate; fat-head, poor stick.

sawney, gowk; clod, -hopper; clod-, clot-poll, -pate; bull-calf; men of Boeotia, wise men of Gotham.

un sot à triple étage, sot; jobbernowl, changeling, mooncalf, *gobemouche*.

dotard, driveller; old -fogey, – woman; crone, grandmother.

greenhorn etc. (*dupe*) 547; dunce etc. (*ignoramus*) 493; lubber etc. (*bungler*) 701; madman etc. 504.

one who -will not set the Thames on fire, – did not invent gunpowder; *qui n'a pas inventé la poudre*; no conjuror.

502. Sanity.—N. sanity; soundness etc. *adj.*; rationality, normality, sobriety, lucidity, lucid interval; senses, sober senses, sound mind, *mens sana*.

V. be -sane etc. *adj.*; retain one's senses, – reason.

become -sane etc. *adj.*; come to one's senses, sober down.

render -sane etc. *adj.*; bring to one's senses, sober.

Adj. sane, rational, reasonable, *compos mentis*, of sound mind; sound, -minded.

self-possessed; sober, -minded.

in one's -sober senses, – right mind; in possession of one's faculties.

Adv. sanely etc. *adj.*

503. Insanity.—N. disordered -reason, – intellect; diseased –, unsound –, abnormal- mind; derangement, unsoundness.

insanity, lunacy; madness etc. *adj.*; mania, *rabies*, *furor*, mental aliénation, paranoia, aberration; *amentia*, dementation, -tia, -cy; *dementia praecox*; *morosis*, idiocy, phrenitis, frenzy, raving, incoherence, wandering, delirium, calenture of the brain, delusion, hallucination; lycanthropy, brain storm, *delirium tremens*, D.T.'s.

vertigo, dizziness, swimming; sunstroke, *coup de soleil*, siriasis.

fanatisism, infatuation, craze; oddity, eccentricity, twist, monomania; klepto-, dipso-mania; hypochondriasis etc. (*low spirits*) 837; *melancholia*, hysteria.

screw –, tile –, slate- loose; bee in one's bonnet, rats in the upper story.

dotage etc. (*imbecility*) 499.

V. be –, become- -insane etc. *adj.*; lose one's senses, – reason, – faculties, – wits; go –, run- mad, run amuck; rave, dote, ramble, wander; drivel etc. (*be imbecile*) 499; have a -screw loose etc. *n.*, – devil; *avoir le diable au corps*; lose one's head etc. (*be uncertain*) 475.

derange, render –, drive- -mad etc. *adj.*; madden, dementate, addle the wits, derange the head, infatuate, befool; turn -the brain, – one's head.

Adj. insane, mad, lunatic; crazy, crazed, *aliéné*, *non compos mentis*; not right, cracked, touched; bereft of reason; unhinged, deranged, unsettled in one's mind; insensate, reasonless, beside oneself, demented, daft; phren-, fren-zied, -etic; possessed, – with a devil; far gone, maddened, moonstruck; shatterpated; barmy; mad-, scatter-, shatter-, crack-brained, off one's head; bug-house, *loco*.

maniacal; manic, manic-depressive; delirious, light-headed, incoherent, rambling, doting, wandering; frantic, raving, stark staring mad, amok, amuck.

corybantic, dithyrambic; rabid, giddy, vertiginous, dizzy, wild, haggard, mazed; flighty; distracted, -aught; bewildered etc. (*uncertain*) 475.

mad as a -March hare, – hatter; of -unsound mind etc. *n.* touched –, wrong –, not right- in one's -head, – mind, – wits, – upper story; out of one's -mind, – senses, – wits; not in one's right mind.

fanatical, infatuated, odd, eccentric; hypp-ed, -ish.

imbecile, silly etc. 499.

Adv. like one possessed.

Phr. the mind having lost its balance; the reason under a cloud; *tête -exaltée, -montée*.

504. Madman—N. madman, lunatic, maniac, bedlamite, candidate for Bedlam, raver, madcap; energumen; paranoiac; auto-, mono-, pyro-, megalo-, dipso-, klepto-maniac; hypochondriac etc. (low spirit) 837.

dreamer etc. 515; rhapsodist, seer, high-flier, enthusiast, crank, eccentric, nut, fanatic, *fanatico*; *exalté*; knight errant, Don Quixote.

idiot etc. 501.

505. Memory.—N. memory, remembrance; reten-tion, -tiveness; tenacity; *veteris vestigia flammae*; tablets of the memory; readiness.

reminiscence, recognition, recurrence, recollection, rememoration; retrospect, -ion; after-thought.

suggestion etc. (*information*) 527; prompting etc. *v.*; hint, reminder, token of remembrance, *memento*, *souvenir*, keepsake, relic, *memorandum*; remembrancer, flapper; memorial etc. (*record*) 551; commemoration etc. (*celebration*) 883.

things to be remembered, *memorabilia*.

art of –, artificial- memory; *memoria technica*; mnemo-nics, -technics; phrenotypics; Mnemosyne; memorandum-, note-, engagement-, prompt-book.

retentive –, tenacious –, green –, trustworthy –, capacious –, faithful –, correct –, exact –, ready –, prompt- memory.

V. remember, mind; retain the -memory, – remembrance- of; keep in view.

have –, hold –, bear –, carry –, keep –, retain- in *or* in the -thoughts, – mind, – memory, – remembrance; be in –, live in –, remain in –, dwell in –, haunt –, impress- one's -memory, – thoughts, – mind.

sink in the mind; run in the head; not be able to get it out of one's head; be deeply impressed with; rankle etc. (*revenge*) 919.

recur to the mind; flash -on the mind, – across the memory.

recognize, recollect, bethink oneself, recall, call up, conjure up, retrace; look –, trace- -back, – backwards; think –, look back- upon; review; call –, recall –, bring- to mind; remembrance; carry one's thoughts back; rake up the past.

suggest etc. (*inform*) 527; prompt; put –, keep- in mind; remind; fan the embers; call –, summon –, rip- up; renew; ***infandum renovare dolorem***; task –, tax –, jog –, flap –, refresh –, rub up –, awaken- the memory; pull by the sleeve; bring back the memory, put in remembrance, memorialize.

get –, have –, learn –, know –, say –, repeat- by -heart, – rote; drive –, get- into -one's head; say one's lesson; repeat, – as a parrot; have at one's finger's ends.

commit to memory; memorize; con, – over; fix –, rivet –, imprint –, impress –, stamp –, grave –, engrave –, store –, treasure up –, bottle up –, embalm –, enshrine- in the memory; load –, store –, stuff –, burden- the memory with.

redeem from oblivion; keep the memory -alive, – green; ***tangere ulcus***; keep up the memory of; commemorate etc. (***celebrate***) 883.

make a note of etc. (***record***) 551.

Adj. remember-ing, -ed etc. *v.*; mindful, reminiscential; retained in the memory etc. *v.*; pent up in one's memory; fresh; green, – in remembrance, still vivid; unforgotten, present to the mind; within one's -memory etc. *n.*; indelible; not to be forgotten, unforgettable, enduring; uppermost in one's thoughts; memorable etc. (***important***) 642.

Adv. by -heart, – rote; without book, ***memoriter***.

in memory of; ***in memoriam***; suggestive.

Phr. ***manet altâ mente repostum***; ***forsan et haec olim meminisse juvabit***.

506. Oblivion.—N. oblivion; forgetfulness etc. *adj.*; obliteration etc. 552, of –, insensibility etc. 823 to- the past.

short –, treacherous –, loose –, slippery –, failing- memory; decay –, failure –, lapse- of memory; memory like a sieve; waters of -Lethe, – oblivion, *amnesia*.

pardon, acquittal, amnesty, oblivion; absolution.

V. forget; be -forgetful etc. *adj.*; fall –, sink- into oblivion; have -a short memory etc. *n.* – no head.

forget one's own name, have on the tip of one's tongue, come in at one ear and go out at the other.

slip –, escape –, fade from –, die away from- the memory; lose, – sight of.

unlearn; efface etc. 552 –, discharge- from the memory; consign to -oblivion, – the tomb of the Capulets; think no more of etc. (***turn the attention from***) 458; cast behind one's back, wean one's thoughts from; let bygones be bygones etc. (***forgive***) 918.

Adj. forgotten etc. *v.*; unremembered, past recollection, bygone, out of mind; buried –, sunk- in oblivion; clean forgotten; gone out of one's -head, – recollection.

forgetful, oblivious, mindless, heedless, Lethean; insensible etc. 823- to the past.

Phr. ***non mi ricordo***; the memory -failing, – deserting one, – being at (***or*** in) fault.

507. Expectation.—N. expect-ation, -ance, -ancy; anticipation, reckoning, calculation; contingency; foresight etc. 510.

contemplation, prospection, look out; prospect, perspective, horizon, vista; destiny etc. 152.

suspense, waiting, abeyance; curiosity etc. 455; anxious –, ardent –, eager –, breathless –, sanguine- expectation; torment of Tantalus.

presumption, hope etc. 858; trust etc. (***belief***) 484; prognostication, auspices etc. (***prediction***) 511.

V. expect; look -for, – out for, – forward to; hope for, anticipate; have in -prospect, – contemplation; keep in view; contemplate, promise oneself; not -wonder etc. 870 -at, – if.

wait –, tarry –, lie in wait –, watch –, bargain- for; keep a -good, – sharp- look-out for; await; stand at 'attention,' abide, bide one's –, mark- time, watch.

foresee etc. 510; prepare for etc. 673; forestall etc. (***be early***) 132; count upon etc. (***believe in***) 484; think likely etc. (***probability***) 472; make one's mouth water.

lead one to expect etc. (***predict***) 511; have in store for etc. (***destiny***) 152.

prick up one's ears, hold one's breath.

Adj. expentant; expecting etc. *v.*; in -expectation etc. *n.*; on the watch etc. (***vigilant***) 459; open -eyed, -mouthed; agape, gaping, all agog; on -tenterhooks, – tiptoe, – the tiptoe of expectation; ***aux aguets***; ready; curious etc. 455; looking forward to; prepared for; on the rack.

expected etc. *v.*; long expected, foreseen; in prospect etc. *n.*; prospective; in -one's eye, – view, – the horizon; impending etc. (***destiny***) 152.

Adv. expectantly; in the event of; on the watch etc. *adj.*; with -breathless expectation etc. *n.*; – bated breath, – eyes, – ears strained; ***arrectis auribus***; on edge.

Phr. we shall see; ***nous verrons***.

508. Inexpectation.—N. in-, non-expectation; false expectation etc. (***disappointment***) 509; miscalculation etc. 481; unforeseen contingency, the unforeseen, the unexpected.

surprise, sudden burst, thunderclap, blow, shock; bolt out of the blue; eye-opener; wonder etc. 870.

V. not -expect etc. 507; be taken by surprise; start; miscalculate etc. 481; not bargain for; come –, fall- upon.

be -unexpected etc. *adj.*; come -unawares etc. *adv.*; turn up, pop, drop from the clouds; come –, burst –, flash –, bounce –, steal –, creep- upon one; come –, burst- like a thunder-clap; -bolt; take –, catch- -by surprise, – unawares, – napping.

pounce –, spring a mine- upon.

surprise, startle, take aback, electrify, stun, stagger, take away one's breath, throw off one's guard; astonish etc. (***strike with wonder***) 870.

Adj. non-expectant; surprised etc. *v.*; unwarned, -aware; off one's guard; inattentive etc. 458.

un-expected, -anticipated, -prepared for, -looked for, -foreseen, -hoped for; dropped from the clouds; beyond –, contrary to –, against- expectation; out of one's reckoning; unheard of etc. (*exceptional*) 83; startling; sudden etc. (*instantaneous*) 113.

Adv. abruptly, unexpectedly, plump, pop, *à l'improviste*, unawares; without -notice, – warning, – saying 'by your leave;' like a -thief in the night, – thunderbolt; in an unguarded moment; suddenly etc. (*instantaneously*) 113.

Int. heyday! etc. (*wonder*) 870.

Phr. little did one -think, – expect; nobody would ever -suppose, – think, – expect; who would have thought?'

509. Disappointment. [Failure of expectation.]—**N.** disappointment, disillusionment; blighted hope, balk; blow; slip 'twixt cup and lip; non-fulfilment of one's hopes; sad –, bitter- disappointment; trick of fortune; afterclap; false –, vain- expectation; miscalculation etc. 481; fool's paradise; much cry and little wool.

V. be disappointed; look -blank, – blue; look –, stand- -aghast etc. (*wonder*) 870; find to one's cost; laugh on the wrong side of one's mouth; find one a false prophet.

disappoint; crush –, dash –, balk –, disappoint –, blight –, falsify –, defeat –, not realize- one's -hope, – expectation; balk, jilt, bilk; play one -false, – a trick; dash the cup from the lips; tantalize; dumb-found, -founder; disillusion, -ize; dissatisfy, disgruntle.

Adj. disappointed etc. *v.*; disconcerted, aghast; out of one's reckoning; disgruntled.

Phr. the mountain brought forth a mouse; *nascitur ridiculus mus*; *parturiunt montes*; *diis aliter visum*, the bubble burst; one's countenance falling.

510. Foresight.—**N.** foresight, prospicience, prevision, longsightedness; anticipation; providence etc. (*preparation*) 673.

fore-thought, -cast; pre-deliberation, -surmise; foregone conclusion etc. (*prejudgment*) 481; prudence etc. (*caution*) 864.

foreknowledge; *prognosis*; pre-cognition, -science, -notion, -sentiment; second sight; sagacity etc. (*intelligence*) 498.

prospect etc. (*expectation*) 507; foretaste; prospectus etc. (*plan*) 626.

V. foresee; look -forwards to, – ahead, – beyond; scent from afar; feel in one's bones; look –, pry –, peep into the future.

see one's way; see how the -land lies, – wind blows, – cat jumps.

anticipate; expect etc. 507; be beforehand etc. (*early*) 132; predict etc. 511; fore-know, -judge, -cast; surmise; have an eye to the -future, – main chance; *respicere finem*; keep a sharp look-out etc. (*vigilance*) 459; forewarn etc. 668.

Adj. foreseeing etc. *v.*; prescient; anticipatory; far-seeing, -sighted; sagacious etc. (*intelligent*) 498; weather-wise; provident etc. (*prepared*) 673; prospective etc. 507.

Adv. against the time when.

511. Prediction.—**N.** prediction, announcement; program, programme etc. (*plan*) 626; premonition etc. (*warning*) 668; *prognosis*, prophecy, vaticination, Mantology, prognostication, premonstration, augur-y, -ation; a-, ha-riolation; fore-, a-boding; bode-, abode-ment; omin-ation, -ousness; auspices, forecast; sign, presage, prognostic; omen etc. 512; horoscope, nativity; sooth, -saying; fortune-telling; divination; crystal gazing, necromancy etc. 992; prophet etc. 512.

[Divination by the stars] astrology, horoscopy, astromancy, judicial astrology.*

[Place of prediction] *adytum*.

prefigur-ation, -ement; prototype, type.

V. predict, prognosticate, prophesy, vaticinate, divine, foretell, soothsay, augurate, tell fortunes; cast a -horoscope, – nativity; advise; forewarn etc. 668.

presage, augur, bode; a-, fore-bode, -cast; fore-, be-token; pre-figure, -show; portend; fore-show, -shadow, shadow forth, typify, ominate, signify, point to, precurse.

usher in, herald, premise, announce; lower.

hold out –, raise –, excite- -expectation, – hope; bid fair, promise, lead one to expect; be the -precursor etc. 64.

Adj. predicting etc. *v.*; predictive, prophetic, fatidical, vaticinal, oracular, Sibylline, haruspical, weatherwise.

ominous, presageful, portentous; augur-ous, -al, -ial; auspici-al, -ous; prescious, monitory, extispicious, premonitory, precusory, significant of, pregnant with, big with the fate of.

Phr. 'coming events cast their shadows before.'

*The following terms, expressive of different forms of divination, have been collected from various sources, and are here given as a curious illustration of bygone superstitions:

Divination *by oracles*, Theomancy; *by the Bible*, Bibliomancy; *by ghosts*, Psychomancy; *by spirits seen in a magic lens*, Cristallomantia; *by shadows or manes*, Sciomancy; *by appearances in the air*, Aeromancy, Chaomancy, *by the stars at birth*, Genethliacs; *by meteors*, Meteoromancy; *by winds*, Austromancy; *by sacrificial appearances*, Aruspicy (*or* Haruspicy), Hieromancy, Hieroscopy; *by the entrails of animals sacrificed*, Hieromancy; *by the entrails of a human sacrifice*, Anthropomancy; *by the entrails of fishes*, Ichthyomancy; *by sacrificial fire*, Pyromancy; *by red-hot iron*, Sideromancy; *by smoke from the alter*, Capnomancy; *by mice*, Myomancy; *by birds*, Orniscopy, Ornithomancy; *by a cock picking up grains*, Alectryomancy (*or* Alectoromancy); *by fishes*, Ophiomancy; *by herbs*, Botanomancy; *by water*, Hydromancy; *by fountains*, Pegomancy; *by a wand*, Rhabdomancy; *by dough of cakes*, Crithomancy; *by meal*, Aleuromancy, Alphitomancy; *by salt*, Halomancy; *by dice*, Cleromancy; *by arrows*, Belomancy; *by a balanced hatchet*, Axinomancy; *by a balanced sieve*, Coscinomancy; *by a suspended ring*, Dactyliomancy; *by dots made at random on paper*, Geomancy; *by precious stones*, Lithomancy; *by pebbles*, Pessomancy; *by pebbles drawn from a heap*, Psephomancy; *by mirrors*, Catoptromancy; *by writings in ashes*, Tephramancy; *by dreams*, Oneiromancy; *by the hand*, Palmistry, Chiromancy; *by nails reflecting the sun's rays*, Onychomancy; *by finger rings*, Dactylomancy; *by numbers*, Arithmancy; *by drawing lots*, Sortilege; *by passages in books*, Stichomancy; *by the letters forming the name of the person*, Onomancy, Nomancy; *by the features*. Anthroposcopy: *by the mode of laughing*. Geloscopy: *by ventriloquism*. Gastromancy: *by walking in a circle*. Gyromancy: *by dropping melted wax into water*. Ceromancy: *by currents*. Bletonism.

512. Omen.—N. omen, portent, presage, prognostic, augury, auspice; sigh etc. (*indication*) 550; herald, forerunner, harbinger etc. (*precursor*) 64.

bird of ill omen, signs of the times; gathering clouds; warning etc. 668.

prefigurement etc. 511.

513. Oracle.—N. oracle; prophet, -ess; seer, soothsayer, augur, fortune-teller, palmist, medium, clairvoyant, crystal gazer, witch, geomancer, *aruspex*; a-, ha-ruspice; Sibyl; Python, -ess; Pythia; Pythian –, Delphian- oracle; Monitor, Sphinx, Tiresias, Cassandra, Sibylline leaves; Zadkiel, Old Moore; sorcerer etc. 994; interpreter etc. 524.

514. Supposition.—N. supposition, assumption, postulation, condition, pre-supposition, hypothesis, postulate, *postulatum*, theory, *data*; pro-, position; *thesis*, theorem; proposal etc. (*plan*) 626.

bare –, vague –, loose- -supposition, – suggestion; conceit; conjecture; guess, – work; rough guess, shot; conjecturality; surmise, suspicion, inkling, , suggestion, suggestiveness, association of ideas, hint; presumption etc. (*belief*) 484; divination, speculation.

theorist, speculator, doctrinarian, hypothesist.

V. suppose, conjecture, surmise, suspect, guess, divine; theorize; pre-sume, -surmise, -suppose; assume, fancy, wis, take it; give a guess, speculate, believe, dare say, take it into one's head, take for granted.

put forth; pro-pound, -pose; moot; hypothesize; start, put a case, submit, move, make a motion; hazard –, throw out –, put forward- a - suggestion, – conjecture.

allude to, suggest, hint, put it into one's head.

suggest itself etc. (*thought*) 451; run in the head etc. (*memory*) 505; marvel –, wonder- -if, – whether.

Adj. supposing etc. *v.*; given, mooted, postulatory; assumed etc. *v.*; supposit-ive, -itious; gratuitous, speculative, conjectural, hypothetical, suppositional, theoretical, academic, supposable, presumptive, putative.

suggestive, allusive, stimulating.

Adv. if, – so be; an; on the -supposition etc. *n.*; *ex hypothesi*; in -case, – the event of; *quasi*, as if, provided; perhaps etc. (*by possibility*) 470; for aught one knows.

515. Imagination.—N. imagination; originality; invention; fancy; inspiration; *verve*; empathy.

warm –, heated –, excited –, sanguine –, ardent –, fiery –, boiling –, wild –, bold –, daring –, playful –, lively –, fertile- - imagination, – fancy.

'mind's eye;' 'such stuff as dreams are made of.'

ideal-ity, -ism; romanticism, utopianism, castle-building; dreaming; frenzy; ecs-, ex-tasy; calenture etc. (*delirium*) 503; reverie, brown study, trance; somnambulism.

conception, *vorstellung*, excogitation, 'a fine frenzy,' poetic frenzy, divine afflatus; cloud-, dream-land; flight –, fumes- of fancy; 'thick-coming fancies;' creation –, coinage- of the brain; imagery, word painting.

conceit, maggot, figment, myth, dream, vision, shadow, chimera; phan-tasm, -tasy; fantasy, fancy; whim, -sey; vagary, rhapsody, romance, *extravaganza*; air-drawn dagger, bugbear, nightmare; flying Dutchman, great sea-serpent, man in the moon, castle in the air, *château en Espagne*; Utopia, Atlantis, happy valley, millennium, fairy land; land of Prester John, kingdom of Micomicon; work of fiction etc. (*novel*) 594; poetry etc. 597; drama etc. 599; Arabian nights; *le pot au lait*; dream of Alnaschar etc. (*hope*) 858; day –, golden- dream

illusion etc. (*error*) 495; phantom etc. (*fallacy of vision*) 443; *Fata Morgana* etc. (*ignis fatuus*) 423; vapor etc. (*cloud*) 353; stretch of the imagination etc. (*exaggeration*) 549.

idealist, romanticist, visionary; mopus; romancer, dreamer; somnambulist; rhapsodist etc. (*fanatic*) 504.

V. imagine, fancy, conceive; ideal-, real-ize; dream, – of; 'give to airy nothing a local habitation and a name.'

create, originate, devise, invent, coin, fabricate; improvise, strike out something new.

set one's wits to work; strain –, crack- one's invention; rack –, ransack –, cudgel- one's brains; excogitate.

give -play, – the reins, – a loose- to the - imagination, – fancy; empathize; indulge in reverie.

conjure up a vision; fancy –, represent –, picture –, figure- to oneself; envisage.

float in the mind; suggest itself etc. (*thought*) 451.

Adj. imagined etc. *v.*; *ben trovato*; air-drawn, -built.

imagin-ing etc. *v.*, -ative; original, inventive, creative, fertile, productive; ingenious.

romantic, high-flown, flighty, extravagant, fanatic, enthusiastic, Utopian, Quixotic; preposterous, rhapsodical.

ideal, unreal; in the clouds, *in nubibus*; unsubstantial etc. 4; illusory etc. (*fallacious*) 495; fictitious, theoretical, hypothetical.

fabulous, legendary; myth-ic, -ological; chimerical; imagin-, vision-ary; notional; fan-cy, -ciful, -tastic, -tastical; whimsical; fairy, -like.

dreamy, entranced, vaporous.

516. Meaning. [Idea to be conveyed.] [Thing signified.]—**N.** meaning; signific-ation, -ance; sense, expression; im-, pur-port; drift, tenor, implication, connotation, essence, force, spirit bearing, coloring; scope.

matter; subject, -matter; argument, text, sum and substance; gist etc. 5.

general –, broad –, substantial – colloquial –, literal –, plain –, simple –, accepted –, natural –, unstrained –, true etc. (*exact*) 494 –, honest etc. 543 –, *primâ facie* etc. (*manifest*) 525- meaning.

literality; literal interpretation; after acceptation; allusion etc. (*latency*) 526; suggestion etc. (*information*) 527; synonym; figure of speech etc. 521; acceptation etc. (*interpretation*) 522.

V. mean, signify, express, connote, denote; im-, pur-port; convey, imply, breathe, indicate, bespeak, bear a sense; tell –, speak- of; touch on; point –, allude- to; drive at; involve etc. (*latency*) 526; delcare etc. (*affirm*) 535.

understand by etc. (*interpret*) 522.

Adj. meaning etc. *v.*; expressive, suggestive, meaningful, allusive; signific-ant, -ative, -atory; pithy; full of –, pregnant with- meaning.

declaratory etc. 535; intelligible etc. 518; literal, metaphrastic; synonymous; tantamount etc. (*equivalent*) 27; implied etc. (*latent*) 526; explicit etc. 525; literal etc. 562.

Adv. to that effect; that is to say etc. (*being interpreted*) 522.

literally; evidently, from the context.

517. Unmeaningness. [Absence of meaning.]—**N.** unmeaningness etc. *adj.*; scrabble, scribble, scrawl, daub, (*painting*), strumming (*music*).

empty sound, dead letter, *vox et praeterea nihil*; 'a tale told by an idiot, full of sound and fury, signifying nothing;' 'sounding brass and a tinkling cymbal.'

nonsense, jargon, gibberish, jabber, mere words, hocus-pocus, fustian, rant, bombast, balderdash, palaver, patter, flummery, *verbiage*, babble, *bavardage*, *baragouin*, platitude, *niaiserie*; inanity; rigmarole, rodomontade; truism; *nugae canorae*; twaddle, twattle, fudge, trash; stuff, – and nonsense; bosh, rubbish, rot, drivel, moonshine, wish-wash, fiddle-faddle, flapdoodle; absurdity etc. 497; vagueness etc. (*unintelligibility*) 519.

V. mean nothing; be -unmeaning etc. *adj.*; twaddle, quibble, rant, gabble, scrabble etc. *n.*

Adj. unmeaning; meaning-, sense-less; nonsensical; void of -sense etc. 516.

in-, un-expressive; vacant, fatuous; not significant; insignificant.

trashy, washy, inane, vague, trumpery, trivial, fiddle-faddle, twaddling, quibbling.

unmeant, not expressed; tacit etc. (*latent*) 526.

inexpressible, undefinable, incommunicable.

Int. rubbish! etc. 497.

518. Intelligibility.—**N.** intelligibility, clearness, clarity, explicitness etc. *adj.*; lucidity, perspicuity; legibility, plain speaking etc. (*manifestation*) 525; precision etc. 494; a word to the wise.

V. be -intelligible etc. *adj.*; speak -for itself, – volumes; tell its own tale, lie on the surface.

render -intelligible etc. *adj.*; popularize, simplify, clear up; elucidate etc. (*explain*) 522.

understand, comprehend; take, – in; catch, grasp, recognize, follow, collect, master, make out; see -with half an eye, – daylight, – one's way; enter into the ideas of; come to an understanding.

Adj. intelligible; clear, – as -day, – crystal, – noonday; lucid; per-, tran-spicuous; luminous, transparent; comprehensible.

easily understood, easy to understand, for the million, intelligible to the meanest capacity, popularized.

plain, distinct, explicit, clear-cut; positive; definite etc. (*precise*) 494.

graphic, vivid, telling; expressive etc. (*meaning*) 516; illustrative etc. (*explanatory*) 522.

un-ambiguous, -equivocal, -mistakable etc. (*manifest*) 525, -confused; legible, recognizable; obvious etc. 525.

Adv. in plain -terms, – words, – English.

Phr. he that runs may read etc. (*manifest*) 525.

519. Unintelligibility.—**N.** unintelligibility, incomprehensibility, imperspicuity; inconceivableness, vagueness etc. *adj.*; obscurity; ambiguity etc. 520; doubtful meaning; uncertainty etc. 475; perplexity etc. (*confusion*) 59; spinosity; *obscurum per obscurius*; mystification etc. (*concealment*) 528; latency etc. 526; transcendentalism.

paradox; enigma, riddle etc. (*secret*) 533; *dignus vindice nodus*; sealed book; steganography, freemasonry.

pons asinorum, asses' bridge; double –, high-Dutch, Greek, Hebrew; jargon etc. (*unmeaning*). 517.

obscurantist.

V. be -unintelligible etc. *adj.*; require -explanation etc. 522; have a doubtful meaning, pass comprehension.

render -unintelligible etc. *adj.*; conceal etc. 528; darken etc. 421; confuse etc. (*derange*) 61; perplex etc. (*bewilder*) 475.

not -understand etc. 518; lose, – the clue; miss; not know what to make of, be able to make nothing of, give it up; not be able to -account for, – make either head or tail of; be at sea etc. (*uncertain*) 475; wonder etc. 870; see through a glass darkly etc. (*ignorance*) 491.

not understand one another; play at cross purposes etc. (*misinterpret*) 523.

Adj. un-intelligible, -accountable, -decipherable, -discoverable, -knowable, -fathomable; incognizable, -explicable, -scrutable; inap-, incomprehensible; insol-vable, -uble; impenetrable.

illegible, indecipherable, as Greek to one, unexplained, paradoxical; enigmatic, -al; puzzling, baffling.

obscure, dark, muddy, clear as mud, seen through a mist, dim, nebulous, shrouded in mystery; undiscernible etc. (*invisible*) 447; misty etc. (*opaque*) 426; hidden etc. 528; latent etc. 526.

indefinite etc. (*indistinct*) 447; perplexed etc. (*confused*) 59; undetermined, vague, loose, ambiguous; mysterious; mystic, -al; transcendental; occult, recondite, esoteric, abstruse, crabbed.

incon-ceivable, -ceptible; searchless; above –, beyond –, past- comprehension; beyond one's depth; unconceived.

inexpressible, undefinable, incommunicable, unutterable, ineffable, unpronounceable.

520. Equivocalness. [Having a double sense.]—**N.** equivocalness etc. *adj.*; double -meaning etc. 516; ambiguity, *double entendre*, pun, paragram, *calembour*, quibble, *équivoque*, anagram; conundrum etc. (*riddle*) 533; word-play etc. (*wit*) 842; homonym, -y; amphibo-ly, -logy; ambiloquy.

Sphinx, Delphic oracle.

equivocation etc. (*duplicity*) 544; white lie, mental reservation etc. (*concealment*) 528.

V. be -equivocal etc. *adj.*; have two -meanings etc. 516; equivocate etc. (*palter*) 544.

Adj. equivocal, ambiguous, amphibolous, homonymous; double-tongued etc. (*lying*) 544.

521. Metaphor.—**N.** figure of speech; *facon de parler*, way of speaking, colloquialism.

phrase etc. 566; figure, trope, metaphor, tralatition, metonymy, enallage, *catachresis*, *synecdoche*, *autonomasia*; irony, satire, figurativeness etc. *adj.*; image, -ry; *metalepsis*, type, anagoge, simile, personification, *prosopopaeia*, allegory, apologue, parable, fable; allusion, adumbration; application; euphemism; euphuism.

V. employ -metaphor etc. *n.*; personify, allegorize, adumbrate, shadow forth, apply, allude –, refer- to.

Adj. metaphorical etc. *n.*; figurative, catachrestical, typical, tralatitious, parabolic, allegorical, allusive, anagogical; ironical; colloquial.

Adv. so to -speak, – say, – express oneself; as it were.

Phr. *mutato nomine de te fabula nattatur.*

522. Interpretation.—**N.** interpretation, definition; explan-, explic-ation; solution, answer; rationale; plain –, simple –, strict- interpretation; meaning etc. 516.

translation; rend-ering, -ition; reddition; literal –, free- translation; key, crib; secret; clew etc. (*indication*) 550; Rosetta stone.

exegesis; ex-pounding, -position; Hermeneutics; comment, -ary; inference etc. (*deduction*) 480; illustration, exemplification; gloss, annotation, *scholium*, note; e-, di-lucidation, enucleation; *éclaircissement*, *mot de l'énigme*.

symptomat-, semei-ology; metoposcopy, physiognomy; diagnosis, prognosis; paleography etc. (*philology*) 560.

accept-ion, -ation, -ance; light, reading, lection, construction, version.

equivalent, – meaning etc. 516; synonym; para-, meta-phrase; convertible terms, apposition; dictionary etc. 562; polyglot.

V. interpret, explain, define, construe, translate, render; do –, turn- into; transfuse the sense of.

find out etc. 480*a*- -the meaning etc. 516- of; read; spell –, figure –, make- out; decipher, decode, unravel, disentangle, puzzle out; find the key of, enucleate, resolve, solve; read between the lines.

account for; find –, tell- the cause etc. 153- of; throw –, shed- -light, – new light, – a fresh light- upon; clear up, elucidate.

illustrate, exemplify; unfold, expound, comment upon, annotate; popularize etc. (*render intelligible*) 518.

take –, understand –, receive –, accept- in a particular sense; understand by, put a construction on, be given to understand.

Adj. explanatory, expository; explica-tive, -tory; exegetical; hermeneutic, interpretive, illustrative, elucidative, annotative, scholiastic.

polyglot; literal; para-, meta-phrastic; cosignificative, synonymous; equivalent etc. 27.

Adv. in -explanation etc. *n.*; that is to say, *id est*, *videlicet*, to wit, namely, in other words.

literally, strictly speaking; in -plain, – plainer- -terms, – words, – English; more simply.

523. Misinterpretation.—**N.** misinterpretation, -apprehension, -understanding, -acceptation, -construction, -application; *catachresis*; cross -reading, – purposes; mistake etc. 495.

misrepresentation, perversion, exaggeration etc. 549; false -coloring, – construction; abuse of terms; parody, travesty; falsification etc. (*lying*) 544.

V. mis-interpret, -apprehend, -understand, -conceive, -judge, -doubt, -spell, -translate, -construe, -apply; mistake etc. 495.

misrepresent, pervert; garble etc. (*falsify*) 544; distort; detort; travesty, play upon words; stretch –, strain –, wrest- the -sense, – meaning; explain away; put a -bad, – false- construction on; give a false coloring, look through -rose colored –, – dark – spectacles.

be –, play- at cross purposes.

Adj. misinterpreted etc. *v.*; untranslat-ed, -able.

Adv. at cross purposes.

524. Interpreter.—**N.** interpreter, translator, ex-positor, -pounder, -ponent, -plainer; demonstrator.

scholiast, commentator, annotator; meta-, paraphrast.

spokesman, speaker, mouthpiece, prolocutor; diplomat etc. 758.

guide, courier, dragoman, *valet de place*, *cicerone*, showman; oneirocritic; Oedipus; oracle etc. 513.

525. Manifestation.—**N.** manifestation; unfolding; plainness etc. *adj.*; plain speaking; expression; showing etc. *v.*; exposition, demonstration, *séance*; exhibition, production; display, showing off etc. 882; premonstration. [Thing shown] exhibit, show.

indication etc. (*calling attention to*) 457; publicity etc. 531; disclosure etc. 529; openness etc. (*honesty*) 543, (*artlessness*) 703; *épachement*, prominence.

V. make –, render- -manifest etc. *adj.*; bring -forth, – forward, – to the front, – into view; give notice, express; represent, set forth, exhibit; show,

— up; expose; produce; hold up —, expose- to view; set —, place —, lay- before -one, — one's eyes; tell to one's face; trot out, put through one's paces, unfold, show off, show forth, unveil, bring to light, display, demonstrate, unroll; lay open; draw —, bring- out; bring out in strong relief; call —, bring- into notice; hold up the mirror; wear one's heart upon his sleeve; show one's -face, — colors; manifest oneself; speak out; make no -mystery, — secret- of; unfurl the flag; proclaim etc. (*publish*) 531.

indicate etc. (*direct attention to*) 457; disclose etc. 529; elicit etc. 480*a*; interpret etc. 522.

be -manifest etc. *adj.*; appear etc. (*be visible*) 446; transpire etc. (*be disclosed*) 529; speak for itself, stand to reason; stare one in the face; loom large, appear on the horizon, rear its head; give -token, — sign, — indication of; tell its own tale etc. (*intelligible*) 518; go without saying.

Adj. manifest, apparent; salient, striking, demonstrative, prominent, in the foreground, notable, pronounced.

flagrant; notorious etc. (*public*) 531; arrant; stark staring; unshaded, glaring.

defin-ed, -ite; distinct, conspicuous etc. (*visible*) 446; obvious, evident, incontestable, unmistakable, not to be mistaken, plain, clear, palpable, self-evident, autoptical; intelligible etc. 518; clear as -day, — daylight, — noonday; plain as -a pikestaff, — the sun at noonday, — the nose on one's face, — the way to the parish church.

ostensible; open, — as day; overt, patent, express, explicit; naked, bare, literal, downright, undisguised, exoteric.

unreserved; frank, plain spoken etc. (*artless*) 703; barefaced, brazen, bold, shameless, daring, flaunting, loud.

manifested etc. *v.*; disclosed etc. 529; expressible, capable of being shown, producible; in-, un-concealable.

Adv. manifestly, openly etc. *adj.*; before one's eyes, under one's nose, to one's face, face to face, above board, *cartes sur table*, on the stage, in plain sight, in open court, in the open, — streets; at the cross roads; in market overt; in the face of -day, — heaven; in -broad —, open- daylight; without reserve; at first blush, *primâ facie*, on the face of; in set terms.

Phr. *cela saute aux yeux*; he that runs may read; you can see it with half an eye; it needs no ghost to tell us; the meaning lies on the surface; *cela va sans dire*; *res ipsa loquitur*.

526. Latency.—N. latency, inexpression; hidden —, occult- meaning; occultness, occultism, mysticism, mystery, cabala, symbolism, anagoge; silence etc. (*taciturnity*) 585; concealment etc. 528; more than meets the -eye, — ear; Delphic oracle; *les dessous des cartes*, undercurrent.

allusion, insinuation, implication; innuendo etc. 527; adumbration; 'something rotten in the state of Denmark.'

snake in the grass etc. (*pitfall*) 667; secret etc. 533.

darkness, invisibility, imperceptibility.

latent influence, power behind the throne; friend at court, wire puller.

V. be -latent etc. *adj.*; lurk, smoulder, underlie, make no sign; escape -observation, — detection, — recognition; lie hid etc. 528.

laugh in one's sleeve; keep back etc. (*conceal*) 528.

involve, imply, implicate, connote, import, understand, allude to, infer, leave an inference; symbolize; whisper etc. (*conceal*) 528.

Adj. latent; lurking etc. *v.*; secret etc. 528; occult, symbolic, mystic; implied etc. *v.*; dormant.

un-apparent, -known, -seen etc. 441; in the background; invisible etc. 447; indiscoverable, dark; impenetrable etc. (*unintelligible*) 519; unspied, -suspected.

un-said, -written, -published, -breathed, -talked of, -told etc. 527, -sung, -exposed, -proclaimed, -disclosed etc. 529, -pronounced, -mentioned, -expressed; not expressed, tacit.

un-developed, -solved, -explained, -traced, -discovered etc. 480*a*, -tracked, -explored, -invented.

indirect, crooked, inferential; by -inference, — implication; implicit; constructive; allusive, covert, muffled; steganographic; under-stood, -hand, -ground; concealed etc. 528; delitescent.

Adv. by a side wind; *sub silentio*; in the background; behind -the scenes, — one's back, — the veil; below the surface; on the tip of one's tongue; secretly etc. 528; between the lines; by a mutual understanding.

Phr. 'thereby hangs a tale.' 'that is another story.'

527. Information.—N. information, enlightenment, acquaintance, knowledge etc. 490; publicity etc. 531.

communication, intimation; not-ice, -ification; e-an-nunciation; announcement; representation, round robin, presentment.

case, estimate, specification, report, advice, monition; news etc. 532; return etc. (*record*) 551; account etc. (*description*) 594; statement etc. (*affirmation*) 535.

mention; acquainting etc. *v.*; instruction etc. (*teaching*) 537; outpouring; intercommunication, communicativeness.

informant, authority, teller, announcer, annunciator, harbinger, herald, intelligencer, commentator, columnist, reporter, exponent, mouthpiece; informer, keek, eavesdropper, delator, detective, sleuth; *mouchard*, spy, stool pigeon, newsmonger; messenger etc. 534; *amicus curiae*.

valet de place, *cicerone*, pilot, guide; guide-, hand-book; *vade mecum*; manual; map, plan, chart, gazetteer; itinerary etc. (*journey*) 266.

hint, suggestion, wrinkle, innuendo, inkling, whisper, passing word, word in the ear, subaudition, cue, by-play; gesture etc. (*indication*) 550; gentle — broad- hint; *verbum sapienti*; word to the wise; insinuation etc. (*latency*) 526.

V. tell; inform, — of; acquaint, — with; impart, — to; make acquainted with, bring to the ears of, apprise, advise, enlighten, awaken.

let fall, mention, express, intimate, represent, communicate, make known; publish etc. 531; notify, signify, specify, convey the knowledge of.

let one —, have one to- know; serve notice, give one to understand; give notice; set —, lay —, put-before; point out, put into one's head; put one in possession of; instruct etc. (*teach*) 537; direct the attention to etc. 457.

an-nounce, -nunciate; report, – progress; bring –, send –, leave –, write- word; tele-graph, -phone; ring –, call- up; wire; retail, render an account; give an account etc. (*describe*) 594; state etc. (*affirm*) 535.

disclose etc. 529; show cause; explain etc. (*interpret*) 522.

hint; give an inkling of; give –, drop –, throw out- a hint; insinuate; allude –, make allusion- to; glance at; tip off, tip the wink etc. (*indicate*) 550; suggest, prompt, give the cue, breathe; whisper, – in the ear.

give a bit of one's mind; tell one plainly, – once for all; speak volumes.

un-deceive, -beguile; set right, correct, open the eyes of, disabuse.

be -informed of etc.; know etc. 490; learn etc. 539; get scent of, gather from; awaken –, open one's eyes- to; become -alive, – awake- to; keep posted; hear, overhear, understand

come to one's -ears, – knowledge; reach one's ears.

Adj. informed etc. *v.*; *communiqué*; reported etc. *v.*; published etc. 531; advisory.

expressive etc. 516; explicit etc. (*open*) 525, (*clear*) 518; plain-spoken etc. (*artless*) 703.

declara-, nuncupa-, exposi-tory; declarative, enunciative, communicat-ive, -ory; oral.

Adv. from information received; according to -rumor, – report; in the air; from what one can gather.

Phr. a little bird told me.

528. Concealment.—N. concealment; hiding etc. *v.*; occultation, mystification.

seal of secrecy; screen etc. 530; disguise etc. 530; masquerade; masked battery; hiding place etc. 530; cipher, code, cryp-, stegan-ography; invisible –, sympathetic- ink; palimpsest; freemasonry.

stealth, -iness; obreption; slyness etc. (*cunning*) 702.

latit-ancy, -ation; seclusion etc. 893; privacy, secrecy, secretness; *incognita*.

reticence; reserve; mental –, reservation, aside; *arrière pensée*, suppression, evasion, white lie, misprision; silence etc. (*taciturnity*) 585; suppression of truth etc. 544; underhand dealing; close-, secretive-ness etc. *adj.*; mystery.

latency etc. 526; snake in the grass; secret etc. 533.

V. conceal, hide, secrete, stow away, put out of sight; lock –, seal –, bottle- up.

cover, screen, cloak, veil, shroud; screen from -sight, – observation; draw the veil; draw –, close-the curtain; curtain, shade, eclipse, throw a veil over; be-cloud, -fog, -mask; mask, disguise; ensconce, muffle, smother; whisper.

keep -from, – back, – to oneself; keep -snug, – close, – secret, – dark; bury; sink, suppress; keep -from, – out of- -view, – sight; keep in –, throw into- the -shade, – background; cover up one's tracks; stifle, hush up, withhold, reserve; fence with a question; ignore etc. 460.

code, codify, use a cipher.

keep -a secret, – one's own counsel; hold one's tongue etc. (*silence*) 585; make no sign, not let it go further; not breathe a -word, – syllable- about; not let the right hand know what the left is doing; hide one's light under a bushel, bury one's talent in a napkin.

keep –, leave- in -the dark, – ignorance; blind, – the eyes; blindfold, hoodwink, mystify; puzzle etc. (*render uncertain*) 475; bamboozle etc. (*deceive*) 545.

be -concealed etc. *v.*; suffer an eclipse; retire from sight, couch; hide oneself; lie -hid, – in ambush, – low, – *perdu*, – snug, – close; seclude oneself etc. 893; lurk, sneak, skulk, slink, pussyfoot, prowl; steal -into, – out of, – by, – along; play at -bopeep, – hind and seek; hide in holes and corners.

Adj. concealed etc. *v.*; hidden; veiled, secret, recondite, mystic, cabalistic, occult, dark; cryptic, -al, private, privy, *in petto*, auricular, clandestine, close, inviolate.

behind a -screen etc. 530; under -cover, – an eclipse; in -ambush, – hiding, – disguise; in a -cloud, – fog, – mist, – haze, – dark corner; in the -shade, – dark; clouded, wrapt in clouds; invisible etc. 447; buried, underground, *perdu*; incommunicado; secluded etc. 893.

un-disclosed etc. 529; -told etc. 527; covert etc. (*latent*) 526; mysterious etc. (*unintelligible*) 519.

irrevealable, inviolable; confidential; esoteric; not ot be spoken of.

obreptitious, furtive, stealthy, feline; skulking etc. *v.*; surreptitious, underhand, hole and corner; sly etc. (*cunning*) 702; secretive, evasive, noncommittal, reserved, reticent, uncommunicative, buttoned up; close, – as wax; taciturn etc. 585.

Adv. secretly etc. *adj.*; in -secret, – private, – one's sleeve, – holes and corners; in the dark etc. *adj.*

janius clausis, with closed doors, *à huis clos*; hugger-mugger, *à la dérobée*; under the -cloak of, – rose, – table; *sub rosâ*, *en tapinois*, in the background, aside, on the sly, with bated breath, *sotto voce*, in a whisper, without beat of drum, *à la sourdine*.

in –, strict- confidence; confidentially etc. *adj.*; between -ourselves, – you and me; *entre nous*, *inter nos*, under the seal of secrecy; in -code, – cipher.

underhand, by stealth, like a thief in the night; stealthily etc. *adj.*; behind -the scenes, – the curtain, – one's back, – a screen etc. 530; *incognito*; *in camerâ*.

Phr. it -must, – will- go no further; 'tell it not in Gath,' nobody the wiser.

529. Disclosure.—N. disclosure; retection; unveiling etc. *v.*; deterration, revealment, revelation; divulgence, expos-ition, -ure; *exposé*; whole truth; tell-tale etc. (*news*) 532.

acknowledgment, avowal; confession, -al; shrift.

bursting of a bubble; *dénouement*.

V. dis-close, -cover, -mask; draw –, draw aside –, lift –, raise –, lift up –, remove –, tear- the -veil, – curtain; un-mask, -veil, -fold, -cover, -seal, -kennel; take off –, break- the seal; lay -open, – bare; expose; open, – up; bare, bring to light; evidence; make -clear, – evident, – manifest; evince.

divulge, reveal, break; let into the secret; reveal the secrets of the prison-house; tell etc. (*inform*) 527; breathe, utter, blab, peach; let -out, – fall, – drop, – the cat out of the bag; betray; tell tales, – out of school; come out with; give -vent, – utterance- to; open the lips, blurt out, vent, whisper about; speak out etc. (*make manifest*) 525; make public etc. 531; unriddle etc. (*find out*) 480*a*; split; blow the gaff; break the news.

acknowledge, allow, concede, grant, admit, own, confess, avow, throw off all disguise, turn inside out, make a clean breast; show one's -hand, – cards; unburden –, disburden- one's -mind, – conscience, – heart; open –, lay bare –, tell a piece of- one's mind; unbosom oneself, own to the soft impeachment; say –, speak- the truth; turn - King's, – Queen's, – States's- evidence.

raise –, drop –, lift –, remove –, throw off- the mask; expose; debunk; lay open; un-deceive, -beguile; disabuse, set right, correct, open the eyes of; *désillusionner*.

be -disclosed etc.; transpire, come to light; come in sight etc. (*be visible*) 446; become known, escape the lips; come –, ooze –, creep –, leak –, peep –, crop- out; show its -face, – colors; discover etc. itself; break through the clouds, flash on the mind.

Adj. disclosed etc. *v.*

Int. out with it!

Phr. the murder is out; a light breaks in upon one; the scales fall from one's eyes; the eyes are opened.

530. Ambush. [Means of concealment.]—**N.** hiding-place; secret -place, drawer; recess, hole, funk hole, holes and corners; closet, crypt, *adytum*, abditory, *oubliette*, safe, – deposit.

am-bush, -buscade; stalking horse; lurking-hole, -place; secret path, backstairs; retreat etc. (*refuge*) 666.

screen, cover, shade, blinder; veil, curtain, blind, *purdah*, cloak, cloud.

mask, vizor, visor, disguise, masquerade dress, domino; *camouflage*.

pitfall etc. (*source of danger*) 667; trap etc. (*snare*) 545.

v. ambush, ambuscade, lie in ambush etc. (*hide oneself*) 528; lie in wait for; set a trap for etc. (*deceive*) 545.

Adv. *aux aguets*.

531. Publication.—**N.** publication; public - announcement etc. 527; promulgation, propagation, proclamation, pronouncement, encylical, *pronunciamento*; circulation, indiction, edition, imprint, impression, printing; hue and cry.

publicity, notoriety, currency, flagrancy, cry, *bruit*; *vox populi*; report etc. (*news*) 532.

the Press, fourth estate, public press, newspaper, periodical, journal, gazette; house organ, trade publication, tabloid, daily, weekly, monthly, quarterly, annual, magazine, monograph, book; review; news sheet, special edition, supplement, feature, rotogravure, comic strips; leaflet, pamphlet; telegraphy; publisher etc. *v.*

circular, – letter; manifesto, advertisement, puff, placard, bill, *affiche*, broadside, poster; notice etc. 527; program.

V. publish; make -public, – known etc. (*information*) 527; speak –, talk- of; broach, utter; put forward; circulate, propagate, *promulgate*; spread –, abroad; rumor, diffuse, disseminate, evulgate; put –, give –, send- forth; emit, edit, get out; issue; cover, report; bring –, lay –, drag- before the public; give -out, – to the world; put –, bandy –, hawk –, buzz –, whisper –, bruit –, blaze- about; drag into the -open day, – limelight; voice.

proclaim, herald, blazon; blaze –, noise- abroad; sound a trumpet; trumpet –, thunder- forth; give tongue; announce with -beat of drum, – flourish of trumpets; proclaim -from the housetops, – at Charing Cross, at the cross roads; declare, declaim.

advertise, placard; post, – up; *afficher*, publish in the Gazette, send round the crier.

raise a -cry, – hue and cry, – report; set news afloat.

telegraph, cable, wireless, broadcast.

be -published etc; be –, become- public etc. *adj.*; come out; go –, fly –, buzz –, blow- about; get -about, – abroad, – afloat, – wind; find vent; see the light; go forth, take air, acquire currency, pass current; go -the rounds, – the round of the newspapers, – through the length and breadth of the land; *virum volitare per ora*; pass from mouth to mouth; spread; run –, spread- like wildfire.

Adj. published etc. *v.*; current etc. (*news*) 532; in circulation, public; notorious; flagrant, arrant; open etc. 525; trumpet-tongued; encyclical, promulgatory; exoteric.

Adv. publicly etc. *adj.*; in open court, with open doors; in the limelight.

Int. *Oyez!* O yes! notice!

Phr. notice is hereby given; this is –, these are- to give notice.

532. News.—**N.** news; information etc. 527; piece –, budget- of -news, – information; report, story, yarn, copy, filler, intelligence, tidings; stop press news.

word, advice, *aviso*, message; dis-, des-patch; telegram, cable, wireless telegram, radio-gram, marconi-gram, communication, errand, embassy; *bulletin*.

microphone; public address system, P.A.; walkie talkie, radio -telephone, -phone.

radio, wireless (Eng.), high fidelity, hi fi, radio set, transistor, receiver; speaker, loudspeaker, amplifier, tweeter, woofer; transmitter, broadcaster; AM –, FM –, short wave – transmitter; radio station, studio, control room, network, hookup, circuit; frequency, kilocycles, megacycles; band, channel, modulation, amplification; broadcast, program, newscast, network show, commerical announcement, serial, sound effects; signature, station – identification, – break, radio listener, audiophile.

television, TV, video, color television; television –, live – broadcast, telecast, TV show; televising, telecasting, transmission, television channel, video, audio, beam, reception, image, test pattern; rain, snow, ghost; television –, TV – station, mobile unit, TVmobile, transmitter, televisor, boost, camera; set, monitor, tube, screen.

rumor, hearsay, *on dit*, flying rumor, news stirring, cry, buzz, *bruit*, fame; talk, *oui-dire*, scandal, eavesdropping; town –, table- talk; tittle-tattle; *canard*, topic of the day, idea afloat.

fresh –, stirring –, old – stale- news; glad tidings; old –, stale- story.

narrator etc. (*describe*) 594; news-, scandal-monger; tale-bearer; tell-tale, gossip, tattler, busybody, chatterer; informer.

broad-, news-, sports-caster; commentator, announcer, master of ceremonies, M.C., programmer, sound man, radioman, ham, radioperator.

television technician, TV man, cameraman, soundman.

V. transpire etc. (*be disclosed*) 529; rumor etc. (*publish*) 531.

broadcast, radio, transmit, send, release, beam; sign – on, – off; go on –, go off – the air, monitor; listen –, tune – in.

tele-vise, -cast; color cast.

Adj. many-tongued; rumored; publicly –, currently- -rumored, – reported; rife, current, floating, afloat, going about, in circulation, in everyone's mouth, all over the town.

Adv. as the story -goes, – runs; as they say, it is said.

533. Secret.—N. secret; dead –, profound-secret; *arcanum*, mystery; latency etc. 526; Asian mystery; sealed book, secrets of the prison-house; *le dessous des cartes*.

enigma, riddle, puzzle, nut to crack, conundrum, charade, rebus, logogriph; mono-, ana-gram; acrostic, cross-word puzzle; Sphinx; *crux criticorum*.

maze, labyrinth, Hyrcynian wood.

problem etc. (*question*) 461; paradox etc. (*difficulty*) 704; unintelligibility etc. 519; *terra incognita* etc. (*ignorance*) 491.

Adj. secret etc. (*concealed*) 528.

534. Messenger.—N. messenger, envoy, emissary, legate; nuncio, internuncio; intermediary; ambassador etc. (*diplomatist*) 758.

marshal, flag-bearer, herald, crier, trumpeter, bellman, pursuivant, *parlementaire*, *apparitor*.

courier, runner, dawk, *estafette*; Hermes, Mercury, Iris, Ariel.

postman, letter carrier, telegraph boy, messenger boy, district messenger; despatch rider, commissionaire, erand-boy.

mail; post, -office; letter-bag; mail -boat, – train, – coach, – van, aerial mail; tele-graph, -phone; cable, wire; carrier-pigeon; wireless tele-graph, -phone; radiotele-graph, -phone.

journalist, newspaperman, reporter; gentleman –, representative- of the press; sob sister; penny-a-liner; special –, war –, own- correspondent; spy, scout; informer etc. 527.

535. Affirmation.—N. affirm-ance, -ation; statement, allegation, assertion, predication, declaration, word, averment.

asseveration, adjuration, swearing, oath, affidavit; deposition etc. (*record*) 551; avouchment, assurance; protest, -ation; profession; acknowledgment etc. (*assent*) 488; pledge.

vote, voice, suffrage, ballot.

remark, observation; position etc. (*proposition*) 514; saying, *dictum*, sentence, *ipse dixit*.

emphasis, positiveness, peremptoriness; dogmatism etc. (*certainty*) 474; dogmatist etc. 887.

V. assert; make -an assertion etc. *n.*; have one's say; say, affirm, predicate, declare, state, represent; protest, profess.

put -forth, – forward; advance, allege, propose, propound, enunciate, enounce, broach, set forth, hold out, maintain, contend, pronounce, pretend.

depose, depone, aver, avow, avouch, asseverate, swear; make –, take one's- oath; make –, swear –, put in- an affidavit; take one's Bible oath, kiss the book, vow, *vitam impendere vero*; swear till -one is black in the face, – all's blue; be sworn, call Heaven to witness; vouch, warrant, certify, assure, swear by bell, book and candle.

swear by etc. (*believe*) 484; insist –, take one's stand- upon; emphasize, lay stress on; assert -roundly, – positively; lay down, – the law; raise one's voice, dogmatize, have the last word; rap out; repeat; re-assert, -affirm.

announce etc. (*information*) 527; acknowledge etc. (*assent*) 488; attest etc. (*evidence*) 467; adjure etc. (*put to one's oath*) 768.

Adj. asserting etc. *v.*; declaratory, predicatory, pronunciative, affirmative, *soi-disant*; positive; certain etc. 474; express, explicit etc. (*patent*) 525; absolute, emphatic, flat, broad, round, pointed, marked, distinct, decided, confident, assertive, insistent, trenchant, dogmatic, definitive, formal, solemn, categorical, peremptory; unretracted; predicable, affirmable.

Adv. affirmatively etc. *adj.*; in the affirmative. with emphasis, *ex cathedrâ*, without fear of contradiction.

I must say, indeed, i' faith, let me tell you, why, give me leave to say, marry, you may be sure, I'd have you to know; upon my -word, – honor; by my troth, egad, I assure you; by -jingo, – Jove, – George, – etc.; troth, seriously, sadly; in –, in sober- -sadness, – truth, – earnest; of a truth, truly, pardi, perdy; in all conscience, upon oath; be assured etc. (*belief*) 484; yes etc. (*assent*) 488; I'll -warrant, – warrant you, – engage, – answer for it, – be bound, – venture to say, – take my oath; in fact, as a matter of fact, forsooth, joking apart; so help me God; not to mince the matter.

Phr. quoth he; *dixi*.

536. Negation.—N. ne-, abne-gation; denial; dis-avowal, -claimer; abjuration; contra-diction, -vention; recusation, protest; rebuttal; recusancy etc. (*dissent*) 489; flat –, emphatic- -contradiction, – denial; *démenti*.

qualification etc. 469; repudiation etc. 610; retraction etc. 607; confutation etc. 479; refusal etc. 764; prohibition etc. 761.

V. deny; contra-dict, -vene; controvert, give denial to, gainsay, negative, shake the head.

dis-own, -affirm, -claim, -avow; recant etc. 607; revoke etc. (*abrogate*) 756.

dispute, impugn, traverse, rebut, join issue upon; bring –, call- in question etc. (*doubt*) 485.

deny -flatly, – peremptorily, – emphatically, – absolutely, – wholly, – entirely; give the lie to, belie.

repudiate etc. 610; set aside, ignore etc. 460; rebut etc. (*confute*) 479; qualify etc. 469; refuse etc. 764.

Adj. denying etc. *v.*; denied etc. *v.*; contradictory; negat-ive, -ory; revocatory; recusant etc. (*dissenting*) 489; at issue upon.

Adv. no, nay, not, nowise; not a -bit, – whit, – jot; not -at all, – in the least, – so; no such thing; nothing of the -kind, – sort; quite the contrary, *tout au contraire*, far from it; *tant s'en faut*; on no account, in no respect; by -no, – no manner of- means; negatively.

phr. there never was a greater mistake; I know better; *non haec in foedera*.

537. Teaching.—N. teaching etc. *v.*; instruction; edification; education; pedagogy; tuition; tutor-, tutel-age; direction, guidance.

qualification, preparation; train-, school-ing etc. *v.*; discipline; exer-cise, -citation; drill, practice.

persuasion, proselytism, propagandism, *propaganda*; in-doctrination, -culcation, oculation.

explanation etc. (*interpretation*) 522; lesson, lecture, sermon, homily; apologue, parable; discourse, prelection, preachment, disquisition.

exercise, task; *curriculum*; course, – of study; grammar, three R's, initiation, A.B.C. etc. (*beginning*) 66.

elementary –, primary –, secondary –, grammar school –, high school –, college –, university –, technical –, liberal –, classical –, religious –, denominational –, moral –, secular- education; technical –, vocational- training; university extension lectures; propaedeutics, moral tuition; evening classes, correspondence course.

physical education, gymnastics, calisthenics, eurythmics; *sloyd*.

V. teach, instruct, edify, school, tutor; cram, prime, coach; enlighten etc. (*inform*) 527.

in-culcate, -doctrinate, -oculate, -fuse, -stil, -fix, -graft, -filtrate; im-bue, -pregnate, -plant; graft, sow the seeds of, disseminate, propagandize.

give an idea of; put -up to, – in the way of; set right.

sharpen the wits, enlarge the mind; give new ideas, open the eyes, bring forward, 'teach the young idea how to shoot;' improve etc. 658.

expound etc. (*interpret*) 522; lecture; prelect; read –, give- a -lesson, – lecture, – sermon, – discourse; hold forth, preach; sermon-, moral-ize; point a moral.

train, discipline; bring up, – to; educate, form, ground, prepare, qualify, drill, exercise, practice, habituate, familiarize with, nurture, dry-nurse, breed, rear, take in hand; break, – in; tame; preinstruct; initiate; inure etc. (*habituate*) 613.

put to nurse, send to school.

direct, guide; direct attention to etc. (*attention*) 457; impress upon the -mind, – memory; beat into, – the head; convince etc. (*belief*) 484.

Adj. teaching etc. *v.*; taught etc. *v.*; educational; scholastic, academic, doctrinal; disciplinal; instructive, didactic, hortative, pedagogic, tutorial.

Phr. the schoolmaster abroad.

538. Misteaching—N. *mis-teaching*, -information, -intelligence, -guidance, -direction, -persuasion, -instruction, -leading etc. *v.*; perversion, false teaching; sophistry etc. 477; college of Laputa; the blind leading the blind.

V. mis-inform, -teach, -direct, -guide, -instruct, -correct; pervert; put on a false –, throw off the- scent; deceive etc. 545; mislead etc. (*error*) 495; misrepresent; lie etc. 544; *ambiguas in vulgum spargere voces*, preach to the wise, teach one's grandmother to suck eggs.

render unintelligible etc. 519; bewilder etc. (*uncertainty*) 475; mystify etc. (*conceal*) 528; unteach.

Adj. misteaching etc. *v.*; unedifying.

Phr. *piscem natare doces*.

539. Learning.—N. learning; acquisition of -knowledge etc. 490, – *skill etc.* 698; acquirement, attainment; edification, scholarship, erudition; lore; information; self-instruction; study, reading, perusal; inquiry etc. 461.

ap-, prenticeship; pupil-age, -arity; tutelage, novitiate, matriculation.

docility etc. (*willingness*) 602; aptitude etc. 698.

V. learn; acquire –, gain –, receive –, take in –, drink in –, imbibe –, pick up –, gather –, get –, obtain –, collect –, glean- -knowledge, – information, – learning.

acquaint oneself with, master; make oneself -master of, – acquainted with; grind, cram; get –, coach- up; learn by -heart, – rote.

read, spell, peruse; con –, pore –, thumb- over; wade through; dip into; run the eye -over, – through; turn over the leaves.

study; be -studious etc. *adj.*; consume the midnight oil, mind one's book.

go to -school, – college, – the university; serve -an (*or* one's) apprenticeship, – one's time; learn one's trade; be -informed etc. 527; be -taught etc. 537.

Adj. studious; schol-astic, -arly; teachable; docile etc. (*willing*) 602; apt etc. 698; industrious etc. 682; learned erudite.

Adv. at one's books; *in statu pupillari* etc. (*learner*) 541.

540. Teacher.—N. teacher, trainer, instructor, institutor, master, tutor, don, director, Corypheus, dry nurse, coach, grinder, crammer; governor, bear-leader; governess, duenna; disciplinarian.

professor, lecturer, reader, prelector, prolocutor, preacher; Boanerges; pastor etc. (*clergy*) 996; schoolmaster, dominie, usher, pedagogue, abecedarian; schoolmistress, dame, monitor, proctor, pupil-teacher.

expositor etc. 524; preceptor, guide; mentor etc. (*adviser*) 695; pioneer, apostle, missionary, propagandist, moonshee; example etc. (*model for imitation*) 22.

professorship etc. (*school*) 542.

tutelage etc. (*teaching*) 537.

Adj. professorial, tutorial etc. 537.

541. Learner.—N. learner, scholar, student, *alumnus*, *élève*, pupil; ap-, prentice; articled clerk; school-boy, -girl, beginner, tyro, abecedarian, alphabetarian.

recruit, novice, neophyte, tenderfoot, inceptor, *débutant*, catechumen, probationer; undergraduate; freshman, frosh; sophomore, junior, senior; junior –, senior- soph; sophister, questionist, fellow-, commoner, pensioner, exhibitioner, sizar, scholar, fellow, advanced –, post graduate –, research- student.

class, form, grade, standard, remove; pupilage etc. (*learning*) 539.

disciple, follower, apostle, proselyte; fellow student, school-mate, -fellow, class mate, condisciple.

Adj. *in statu pupillari*, in leading strings, sophomoric.

542. School.—N. school, academy, university, *alma mater*, college, seminary, Lyceum; instit-ute, -ution, *conservatoire*; *palaestra*, *gymnasium*.

day –, boarding –, public –, preparatory –, elementary –, primary –, nursery –, dame's –, grammar –, Board –, County –, Council –, parochial –, denominational –, Sunday –, religious –, collegiate –, secondary –, continuation –, night –, correspondence –, secretarial –, military –, law –, medical –, business –, technical- school; technical –, training- college; Polytechnic; training ship; *Kindergarten*, nursery, *crèche*, reformatory.

pulpit, desk, reading desk, ambo, class-, lecture-room, theater, amphitheater, forum, stage, rostrum, platform, hustings, tribune.

school –, horn –, text-book; grammar, primer, abecedary, rudiments, manual, *vade mecum*, Lindley, Murray, Cocker.

professor-, lecture-, reader-ship; chair; schoolmaster etc. 540.

School Board, Council of Education; *propaganda*.

Adj. scholastic, academic, collegiate; educational.

Adv. *ex cathedrâ*.

543. Veracity.—N. veracity; truthfulness, frankness etc. *adj.*; truth, sooth, sincerity, candor, honesty, fidelity; plain dealing, *bona fides*; love of truth; probity etc. 939; ingenuousness etc. (*artlessness*) 703.

the truth the whole truth and nothing but the truth; honest –, sober- truth etc. (*fact*) 494; unvarnished tale; light of truth.

V. speak –, tell- the truth; speak by the card; paint in its –, show oneself in ones -true colors; make a clean breast etc. (*disclose*) 529; speak one's mind etc. (*be blunt*) 703; not -lie etc. 544, – deceive etc. 545.

Adj. truthful, true; ver-acious, -edical; scrupulous etc. (*honorable*) 939; sincere, candid, frank, open, straightforward, unreserved; open-, true-, simple- hearted; honest, trustworthy; undissembling etc. (dissemble etc. 544); guileless, pure; unperjured, ture blue, as good as one's word; unaffected, unfeigned, *bonâ fide*; outspoken, ingenuous etc. (*artless*) 703; undisguised etc. (*real*) 494.

Adv. truly etc. (*really*) 494; on oath; in plain words etc. 703; in –, with –, of a –, in good –, very- truth; as the -dial to the sun, – needle to the pole; honor bright; troth; in good -sooth, – earnest; unfeignedly, with no nonsense, in sooth, sooth to say, *bonâ fide*, *in foro conscientiae*; without equivocation; *cartes sur table*, from the bottom of one's heart; by my troth etc. (*affirmation*) 535.

544. Falsehood.—N. false-hood, -ness; fals-ity, -ification; misrepresentation; deception etc. 545; untruth etc. 546; guile; bad faith; lying etc. *v.*; misrepresentation; mendacity, perjury, false swearing; forgery, invention, fabrication; subreption; covin.

perversion –, suppression- of truth; *suppressio veri*; perversion, distortion, false coloring; exaggeration etc. 549; prevarication, equivocation, shuffling, fencing, evasion, fraud; *suggestio falsi* etc. (*lie*) 546; mystification etc. (*concealment*) 528; simulation etc. (*imitation*) 19; dis-simulation, -sembling; deceit.

sham; pretence, pretending, malingering.

lip-homage, – service; mouth honor; hollowness; mere -show, – outside, eye-wash, window dressing; duplicity, double dealing, insincerity, hypocrisy, cant, humbug, casuistry; jesuit-ism, -ry; pharisaism; Machiavelism, 'organized hypocrisy;' crocodile tears, mealy-mouthedness, quackery; charlatan-ism, -ry; gammon; bun-kum, -come; flam, ban, flim-flam, cajolery, flattery; Judas kiss; perfidy etc. (*bad faith*) 940; *il volto sciolto i pensieri stretti*.

unfairness etc. (*dishonesty*) 940; artfulness etc. (*cunning*) 702; misstatement etc. (*error*) 495.

V. be -false etc. *adj.*, – a liar etc. 548; speak -falsely etc. *adv.*; tell a -lie etc. 546; lie, fib; lie like a trooper; swear falsely, forswear, perjure oneself, bear false witness.

mis-state, -quote, -cite, -report, -represent; belie, falsify, pervert, distort; put a false construction upon etc. (*misinterpret*) 523.

prevaricate, equivocate, quibble; palter, – to the understanding; *répondre en Normand*; trim, shuffle, fence, mince the truth, beat about the bush, blow hot and cold, play fast and loose.

garble, gloss over, disguise, give a color to; give –, put- a -gloss, – false coloring- upon; color, varnish, cook, dress up, embroider; varnish right and puzzle wrong, exaggerate etc. 549.

invent, fabricate; trump –, get- up; forge, hatch, concoct; romance etc. (*imagine*) 515; cry 'wolf!'

dis-semble, -simulate; feign, assume, put on, pretend, make believe; play -false, – a double game; coquet; act –, play- a part; affect etc. 855; simulate, pass off for; counterfeit, fake, sham, make a show of; malinger; swing the lead; say the grapes are sour.

cant, play the hypocrite, sham Abraham, *faire pattes de velours*, put on the mask, clean the outside of the platter, lie like a conjuror; hang out –, hold out –, sail under- false colors; 'commend the poisoned chalice to the lips;' *ambiguas in vulgus spargere voces*; deceive etc. 545.

Adj. false, deceitful, mendacious, unveracious,

fraudulent, untruthful, dishonest; faith-, truth-, troth-less; un-fair, -candid; evasive; un-, dis-ingenuous; hollow, insincere, *Parthis mendacior*; forsworn.

canting; hypocrit-, jesuit-, pharisa-ical; tartuffish; Machiavelian; double-tongued, -faced, -handed, -minded, -hearted, -dealing; two-faced, bare-faced; Janus-faced; smooth-faced, -spoken, -tongued; plausible; mealy-mouthed; affected etc. 855.

collus-ive, -ory; artful etc. (*cunning*) 702; perfidious etc. 940, spurious etc. (*deceptive*) 545; untrue etc. 546; falsified etc. *v.*; covinous.

Adv. falsely etc. *adj.*; *à la Tartufe*, with a double tongue; out of whole cloth; slily etc. (*cunning*) 702.

545. Deception.—N. deception; falseness etc. 544; untruth etc. 546; impos-ition, -ture; fraud, deceit, guile; fraudulen-ce, -cy; covin; knavery etc. (*cunning*) 702; misrepresentation etc. (*falsehood*) 544.

delusion, gullery, bluff, spoof, *blague*; juggl-ing, -ery; sleight of hand, legerdemain; presti-giation, -digitation; magic etc. 992; conjur-ing, -ation; hocus pocus, jockeyship; trickery, coggery, hanky-panky, chicanery, pettifogging, sharp practice; *supercherie*, cozenage, circumvention, ingannation, collusion; treachery etc. 940; practical joke.

trick, cheat, wile, ruse, blind, feint, plant, bubble fetch, catch, chicane, juggle, reach, hocus, bite; thimble-rig, card-sharping, artful dodge, machination, swindle, hoax; tricks upon travellers; confidence trick; strategem etc. (*artifice*) 702; theft etc. 791.

snare, trap, pitfall, decoy, gin; sprin-ge, -gle; noose, hook; bait, decoy-duck, tub to the whale, baited trap, *guet-à-pens*; cobweb, net, meshes, toils, mouse-trap, bird-lime; ambush etc. 530; trap-door, sliding panel, false bottom; spring-net, -gun; mask, -ed battery; mine; booby trap.

Cornish hug; wolf in sheep's clothing etc. (*deceiver*) 548; disguise, -ment; false colors, masquerade, mummery, borrowed plumes; *pattes de velours*.

mockery etc. (*imitation*) 19; copy etc. 21; counterfeit, sham, brummagem, make-believe, forgery, fraud, fake; lie etc. 546; 'a mockery, a delusion, and a snare,' hollow mockery.

whited —, painted- sepulcher; tinsel, paste, false jewelry, scagliola, ormolu, German silver, Britannia metal, paint; jerry building; man of straw.

illusion etc. (*error*) 495; *ignis fatuus* etc. 423; *mirage* etc. 443.

V. deceive, take in; defraud, cheat, jockey, do, cozen, diddle, nab, gyp, chouse, double cross, play one false, bilk, cully, jilt, bite, pluck, swindle, victimize; abuse; mystify; blind one's eyes; blindfold, hoodwink, spoof, bluff; throw dust into the eyes, 'keep the word of promise to the ear and break it to the hope,' 'draw a herring across the trail.'

impose —, practice —, play —, put —, palm —, foist- upon; snatch a verdict.

circumvent, overreach; out-reach, -wit, maneuvre; steal a march upon, give the go-by to, leave in the lurch.

set —, lay- a -trap, — snare- for; bait the hook, forlay, spread the toils, lime; decoy, waylay, lure, beguile, delude, inveigle; tra-, tre-pan; kidnap; let-, hook-in; trick; en-, in-trap, -snare, entoil, benet; nick, springe; catch, — in a trap; sniggle, entangle, illaqueate, hocus, practice on one's credulity, dupe, gull, hoax, fool, befool, bamboozle; hum, -bug; gammon, stuff up, dope, sell; play a -trick, — practical joke- upon one; balk, trip up, throw a tub to a whale; fool to the top of one's bent, send on -a wild goose chase, — a fool's errand; make -game, — a fool, — an April fool, — an ass- of; trifle with, cajole, flatter; come over etc. (*influence*) 615; gild the pill, make things pleasant, divert, put a good face upon; dissemble etc. 544.

cog, — the dice, play with marked cards; live by one's wits, play at hide and seek; obtain money under false pretences etc. (*steal*) 791; conjure, juggle, practice chicanery; gerrymander.

play —, palm —, foist —, fob- off.

lie etc. 544; misinform etc. 538; mislead etc. (*error*) 495; betray etc. 940; be -deceived etc. 547.

Adj. deceived etc. *v.*; deceiving etc. *v.*; cunning etc. 702; prestigi-ous, -atory; decept-ive, -ious; deceitful, covinous; delus-ive, -ory; illus-ive, -ory; elusive, insidious, *ad captandum vulgus*.

untrue etc. 546; mock, sham, make-believe, counterfeit, faked, pseudo, spurious, so-called, pretended, feigned, trumped up, bogus, scamped, fraudulent, tricky, factitious, artificial, bastard; surreptitious, illegitimate, contraband, adulterated, sophisticated; unsound, rotten at the core; colorable; disguised; meretricious; tinsel, pinchbeck, plated; catch-penny; Brummagem; simulated etc. 544.

Adv. under -false colors, — the garb of, — cover of; over the left.

Phr. *fronti nulla fides.*

546. Untruth.—N. untruth, falsehood, lie, story, thing that is not, fib, bounce, crammer, taradiddle, whopper.

forgery, fabrication, invention; mis-statement, -representation; perversion, falsification, gloss, *suggestio falsi*; exaggeration etc. 549.

fiction; fable, nursery tale; romance etc. (*imagination*) 515; untrue —, false —, trumped up- -story, — statement; thing devised by the enemy; *canard*; shave, sell, hum, yarn, traveler's tale, Canterbury tale, cock and bull story, fairy tale, clap-trap.

myth, moonshine, bosh, all my eye, -and Betty Martin, mare's nest, farce.

irony; half truth, white lie, pious fraud; mental reservation etc. (*concealment*) 528.

pretence, pretext; false -plea etc. 617; subterfuge, evasion, shift, shuffle, make-believe; sham etc. (*deception*) 545.

profession, empty words; Judas kiss etc. (*hypocrisy*) 544; disguise etc. (*mask*) 530.

V. have a false meaning; not ring true.

pretend, sham, feign, counterfeit, make believe.

Adj. untrue, false, trumped up; void of —, without- foundation; far from the truth, false as dicer's oaths; unfounded, *ben trovato*, invented, fabulous, fabricated, forged; fict-, fact-, supposit-, surrept-itious; e-, il-lusory; ironical; satirical; evasive; *soi-disant* etc. (*misnamed*) 565.

Phr. *se non e vero e ben trovato.*

547. Dupe.—**N.** dupe, gull, gudgeon, *gobemouche*, cull, cully, victim, sucker, pigeon, April fool; laughing stock etc. 857; Cyclops, simple Simon, flat, mug, greenhorn; fool etc. 501; puppet, cat's paw.

V. be -deceived etc. 545, – the dupe of; fall into a trap; swallow –, nibble at- the bait; bite; catch a Tartar.

Adj. credulous etc. 486; mistaken etc. (*error*) 495.

548. Deceiver.—**N.** deceiver etc. (deceive etc. 545); dissembler, hypocrite; sophist, Pharisee, Jesuit, Mawworm, Pecksniff, Joseph Surface, Tartufe, Janus; serpent, snake in the grass, cockatrice, Judas, wolf in sheep's clothing; Molly Maguire; jilt; shuffler.

liar etc. (lie etc. 544; story-teller, perjurer, false-witness, *mentuer à triple étage*, Scapin.

imposter, pretender, capper, decoy, fraud, *soi-disant*, humbug; adventurer; Cagliostro, Fernam Mendez Pinto; ass in lion's skin etc. (*bungler*) 701; actor etc. (*stage player*) 599.

quack, *charlatan*, mountebank, saltimbanco, *saltimbanque*, empiric, quacksalver, medicaster.

conjuror, juggler, magician, necromancer, trickster, prestidigitator, medium, jockey; crimp; decoy-duck, stool pigeon; rogue, knave, cheat; swindler etc. (*thief*) 792; jobber.

549. Exaggeration.—**N.** exaggeration; expansion etc. 194; hyperbole, stretch, strain, coloring; high coloring, caricature, *caricatura*; extravagance etc. (*nonsense*) 497; Baron Munchausen; men in buckram, yarn, fringe, embroidery, traveler's tale; Pelion upon Ossa.

storm in a teacup; much ado about nothing etc. (*over-estimation*) 482; puffery etc. (*boasting*) 884; rant etc. (*turgescence*) 577.

figure of speech, *façon de parler*; stretch of- fancy, – the imagination; flight of fancy etc. (*imagination*) 515.

false coloring etc. (*falsehood*) 544; aggravation etc. 835.

V. exaggerate, magnify, pile up, aggravate; amplify etc. (*expand*) 194; overestimate etc. 482; hyperbolize; over-charge, -state, -draw, -lay, -shoot the mark, -praise; make -much, – the most- of; strain, – a point; stretch, – a point; go great lengths; spin a long yarn; draw –, shoot with- a long-bow; deal in the marvelous.

out -Herod Herod, run riot, talk at random.

heighten, overcolor; color -highly, – too highly; embroider, *broder*; flourish; color etc. (*misrepresent*) 544; puff etc. (*boast*) 884.

Adj. exaggerated etc. *v.*; overwrought; bombastic etc. (*magniloquent*) 577; hyperbolical, on stilts; fabulous, extravagant, preposterous, egregious, *outré*, high-flying.

Adv. hyperbolically etc. *adj.*

550. Indication.—**N.** indication; symbol-ism, -ization; semeio-logy, -tics; sign of the times.

lineament, feature, *trait*, characteristic, trick, diagnostic; divining-rod; cloven hoof; footfall; means of recognition; earmark.

sign, symbol; ind-ex, -ice, -icator; point, -er, marker; exponent, note, token, symptom.

type, figure, emblem, cipher, device; representation etc. 554; epigraph, motto, posy.

gest-ure, -iculation; pantomime; wink, glance, leer; nod, shrug, beck; touch, nudge; grip; dactylo-logy, -nomy; freemasonry, telegraphy, chirology, by-play, dumb-show; cue; hint etc. 527; clue, clew, key, scent, tract etc. 551.

signal, -post; rocket, blue light; watch-fire, -tower; telegraph, semaphore, flag-staff; cresset, fiery cross; calumet; heliograph, signal-, flash-lamp; radar, radar signal, pulse –, microwave –, radar; tracing, blips, pips.

mark, line, stroke, dash, score, stripe, streak, scratch, tick, dot, point, notch, nick, blaze; asterisk, red letter, Italics, heavy type, inverted commas, quotation marks, sublineation, underlining, jotting; print; impr-int, -ess, ession; note, annotation, mark of exclamation.

[For identification] badge, criterion; counter-check, -mark, -sign, -foil, duplicate, tally; label, tab, ticket, stub, billet, letter, counter, *tessera*, card, bill, check; witness, voucher; stamp; *cachet*; trade –, Hall- mark; broad arrow; signature; address –, visiting- card; *carte de visite*; credentials etc. (*evidence*) 467; passport, identity book; attestation; hand, – writing, sign-manual; cipher; monogram, – mark, seal, sigil, signet; autograph, -y, paraph, brand; superscription; in-, en-dorsement; title, heading, rubric, docket; *mot -de passe*, – *du guet*; *passe-parole*; shibboleth; watch-, catch-, pass-word; open *sesame*.

insignia, banner, -et, -ol; bandrol; flag, colors, streamer, standard, eagle, labarum, oriflamb, *oriflamme*; figure-head; ensign; pen-non, -nant, -dant; burgee, blue Peter, jack, ancient, gonfalon, union-jack; tricolor, stars and stripes; bunting.

hearldry, crest; coat of –, arms; armorial bearings, hatchment; e-, scutcheon; shield, supporters; livery, uniform; cockade, *epaulette*, brassard, chevron; garland, chaplet, love-knot, fillet, favor.

[Of locality] beacon, cairn, post, staff, flagstaff, hand, pointer, vane, cock, weathercock; guide-, hand-, finger-, directing-, sign-post; pillars of Hercules, pharos, signal fire; land-, sea-mark; lighthouse, balize; pole-, load-, lode-star; cynosure, guide; address, direction, name; sign, -board.

[Of the future] warning etc. 668; omen etc. 512; prefigurement etc. 511. [Of the past] trace record etc. 551. [Of danger] warning etc. 668; alarm etc. 669. [Of authority] scepter etc. 747. [Of triumph] trophy etc. 733. [Of quantity] gauge etc. 466. [Of distance] mile-stone, -post. [Of disgrace] brand, fool's cap, stigma, mark of Cain. [For detection] check, tell-tale; test etc. (*experiment*) 463.

notification etc. (*information*) 527; advertisement etc. (*publication*) 531.

word of command, call; bugle-, trumpet-call; reveille, taps; bell, alarum, cry; battle –, rallying-cry.

church, bell, angelus, sacring bell; muezzin.

exposition etc. (*explanation*) 522; proof etc. (*evidence*) 463; pattern etc. (*prototype*) 22.

V. indicate; be the -sign etc. *n.*- of; denote,

betoken; argue, testify etc. (*evidence*) 467; bear the -impress etc. *n.*- of; con-note, -notate.

represent, stand for; typify etc. (*prefigure*) 511; symbolize.

put -an indication, – a mark, – etc. *n.*; note, mark, tick, blaze, stamp, earmark; set one's seal upon; label, ticket, docket; dot, spot, score, dash, trace, chalk; print; im-print, -press, surprint; engrave, stereotype, electrotype.

signal, transmit, send, radiate, beam, deflect, echo, bounce back, return.

make a -sign etc. *n.*; signalize; give –, hang out- a signal; beck, -on; gesture; not; wink, glance, leer, nudge, shrug, tip the wink; gesticulate; raise –, hold up- the-finger, – hand; saw the air, suit the action to the word.

wave –, unfurl –, hoist –, hang out- a banner etc. *n.*; wave -the hand, – a kerchief; give the cue etc. (*inform*) 527; show one's colors; give –, sound- an alarm; beat the drum, sound the trumpets, raise a cry.

sign, seal, attest etc. (*evidence*) 467; underline etc. (*give importance to*) 642; call attention to etc. (*attention*) 457; give notice etc. (*inform*) 527.

Adj. indicat-ing etc. *v.*; -ive, -ory; de-, connotative; diacritical, representative, typical, symbolic, pantomimic, pathognomonic, symptomatic, ominous, characteristic, demonstrative, diagnostic, exponential, emblematic, armorial; individual etc. (*special*) 79.

known –, recognizable- by; indicated etc. *v.*; pointed, marked.

[Capable of being denoted] denotable; indelible.

Adv. in token of; symbolically etc. *adj.*; in dumb show.

Phr. *ecce signum*; *ex ungue leonem, ex pede Herculem*.

551. Record.—**N.** trace, vestige, relic, remains; scar, *cicatrix*; foot-step, -mark, -print; track, mark, wake, trail, spoor, scent, *piste*.

monument, hatchment, escutcheon, slab, tablet, trophy, achievement; obelisk, pillar, column, monolith, cromlech, dolmen; memorial; *memento* etc. (*memory*) 505; testimonial, medal, ribbon, order; commemoration etc. (*celebration*) 883.

record, note, minute; *dossier*; register, -try; census, roll etc. (*list*) 86; cartulary, diptych, Domesday book; entry, memorandum, indorsement, inscription, copy, duplicate, docket; notch etc. (*mark*) 550; muniment, deed etc. (*security*) 771; document; deposition, *procès-verbal*; affidavit; certificate etc. (*evidence*) 467.

note-, memorandum-, pocket-, commonplace-book; portfolio; scoring-board, -sheet; bulletin board; card index, file; pigeon-holes, *excerpta*, *adversaria*, jottings, dottings.

gazette, -er; newspaper, magazine etc. 531; alman-ac, -ack; calendar, ephemeris, noctuary, diary, log, journal, account-, cash-, day-book, ledger.

archive, scroll, state-paper, Congressional Record, return, blue-book; statistics etc. 86; *compte rendu*; Acts –, Transactions –, Proceedings- of; Hansard's Debates; chronicle, annals; legend; history, biography etc. 594.

registration; en-, in-rolment; tabulation; entry, booking; signature etc. (*identification*) 550; recorder etc. 553; journalism.

drawing, photograph etc. 554; phonograph –, gramophone- record; music roll.

V. record; put –, place- upon record; go on record; chronicle, calendar, hand down to posterity; keep up the memory of etc. (*remember*) 505; commemorate etc. (*celebrate*) 883; report etc. (*inform*) 527; commit to –, reduce to- writing; put –, set down- -in writing, – in black and white; put –, jot –, take –, write –, note –, set-down; note, minute, put on paper; take –, make- a -note, – minute, – memorandum; make a return.

mark etc. (*indicate*) 550; sign etc. (*attest*) 467.

enter, book; post, – up; insert, make an entry of; mark –, tick- off; register, list, docket, enroll, inscroll; file etc. (*store*) 636.

Adv. on record.

552. Obliteration. [Suppression of sign.]—**N.** obliteration; erasure, rasure; effacement; interference; cancel, -lation; cassation; circumduction; deletion, blot; *tabula rasa*.

V. efface, obliterate, erase, rase, expunge, cancel; blot –, take –, rub –, scratch –, strike –, wipe –, wash –, sponge- out; wipe –, rub- off; wipe away; deface, render illegible; draw the pen through, apply the sponge.

interfere, jam, black-, block-out; clutter, screen.

be -effaced etc.; leave no -trace etc. 449; 'leave not a rack behind.'

Adj. obliterated etc. *v.*; out of print; printless; leaving no trace; intestate; un-recorded, -registered, -written.

Int. *dele*; out with it!

553. Recorder.—**N.** recorder, notary, clerk; regis-trar, -trary, -ter; prothonotary; amanuensis, secretary, scribe, stenographer, remembrancer, book-keeper, *custos rotulorum*, Master of the Rolls.

annalist; histori-an, -ographer; chronicler, journalist, reporter, columnist; biographer etc. (*narrator*) 594; antiquary etc. (*antiquity*) 122; memorialist.

draughtsman etc. 559; engraver 558; photographer, cinematographer, camera man.

Recording instrument, recorder, camera, phonograph, gramophone, dictaphone, telegraphone, telautograph, printing telegraph, tape recorder, ticker, time recorder, cash register, turnstile, speedometer, voting machine, seismograph, radar, oscilloscope, teletypewriter, pari-mutuel, photostat.

554. Representation.—**N.** represent-ation, -ment; imitation etc. 19; illustration, delineation, depictment, portrayal; imagery, portraiture, iconography; design, -ing; art, fine arts; painting etc. 556; sculpture etc. 557; engraving etc. 558; photography, radiography, skiagraphy.

person-ation, -ification; impersonation; drama etc. 599.

picture, drawing, sketch, draught, draft; tracing; copy etc. 21; photo-, helio-graph; daguerreo-, talbo-, calo-, helio-type; cabinet, *carte-de-visite*, snapshot; X-ray photograph; radio-gram, -graph, skia-graph, -gram.

image, likeness, icon, portrait; striking –, speaking- likeness; very image; effigy, fac-simile.

figure, – head; puppet, doll, *figurine*, aglet, manikin, lay-figure, model, *marionnette*, *fantoccini*, bust; waxwork, statue, -tte, automaton, Robot.

hieroglyphic, anaglyph; dia-, mono-gram, graph.

map, plan, chart; ground plan, projection, elevation; ichno-, carto-graphy; atlas; outline, scheme; view etc. (*painting*) 556.

artist, draughtsman etc. 559.

V. represent, delineate; depict, -ure; portray; picture; take –, catch- a likeness etc. *n.*; hit off, photograph, daguerreotype; figure; shadow -forth, – out; adumbrate; body forth; describe etc. 594; trace, copy; mold.

dress up; illustrate, symbolize.

paint etc. 556; carve etc. 557; engrave etc. 558.

person-ate, -ify; impersonate; assume a character; pose as; act; play etc. (*drama*) 599; mimic etc. (*imitate*) 19; hold the mirror up to nature.

Adj. represent-ing etc. *v.*, -ative; illustrative; represented etc. *v.*; imitative, figurative.

like etc. 17; graphic etc. (*descriptive*) 594.

555. Misrepresentation.—N. misrepresentation, distortion, exaggeration; daubing etc. *v.*; bad likeness, daub, sign-painting; scratch, caricature; *anamorphosis*.

V. misrepresent, distort, overdraw, travesty, parody, burlesque, exaggerate, caricature, daub.

Adj. misrepresented etc. *v.*

556. Painting.—N. painting; depicting; drawing etc. *v.*; design; perspective, skiagraphy; *chiaroscuro* etc. (*light*) 420; composition; treatment, values, atmosphere, tone, technique.

historical –, portrait –, miniature –, landscape –, marine –, flower –, scene- painting; scenography.

school, style; the grand style, high art, *genre*, portraiture; ornamental art etc. 847.

mono-, poly-chrome; *grisaille*.

pallet, palette; easel; brush, pencil, stump; blacklead, charcoal, crayons, chalk, pastel; paint etc. (*coloring matter*) 428; water-, body-, oil-color; oils, oil-paint; varnish etc. 356*a*; *gouache*, tempera, distemper, fresco, water-glass; enamel; encaustic painting; *graffito*, *gesso*; mosiac; tapestry.

picture, painting, piece, *tableau*, canvas; oil etc.-painting; fresco, cartoon; easel –, cabinet- picture; drawing, draught, draft; pencil etc. –, watercolor-drawing; sketch; outline; study.

portrait etc. (*representation*) 554; whole –, full –, half- length; kitcat, head; miniature; shade, *silhouette*; profile.

landscape, sea-piece, -scape; view, scene, prospect; interior; bird's- eye view; pan-, di-orama; still life.

picture –, art- gallery; *studio*, *atelier*.

V. paint, design, limn, draw, sketch, pencil, scratch, shade, stipple, hatch, dash off, chalk out, square up; color, dead-color, wash, varnish; draw in -pencil etc. *n.*; paint in -oils etc. *n.*; stencil; depict etc. (*represent*) 554.

Adj. painted etc. *v.*; pictorial, graphic, picturesque, decorative; classical, romantic, pre-Raphaelite, modern, cubist, futurist, vorticist.

pencil, oil etc. *n.*

Adv. in -pencil etc. *n.*

Phr. *fecit, delineavit*.

557. Sculpture.—N. sculpture, insculpture; carving etc. *v.*; statuary, ceramics, plastic arts.

high –, low –, bas- relief; relievo; *basso-*, *alto-*, *mezzo-relievo*; *intaglio*, anaglyph; medal, -lion; *cameo*.

marble, bronze, *terra cotta*; ceramic ware, pottery, porcelain, china, earthenware, faïence, enamel, *cloisonné*.

statue etc. (*image*) 554; cast etc. (*copy*) 21; glyptotheca.

V. sculpture, carve, cut, chisel, model, mold; cast.

Adj. sculptured etc. *v.*; in relief, anaglyptic, ceroplastic, ceramic; parian; marble etc. *n.*

558. Engraving.—N. engraving, chalcography; line –, mezzotint –, stipple –, chalk- engraving; dry-point, bur; etching, aquatinta; plate –, copper-plate –, steel –, wood-, process-, photo-engraving; xylo-, ligno-, glypto-, cero-, litho-, chromolitho-, photolitho-, zinco-, glypho- -graphy, -graph.

impression, print, engraving, plate; steel-, copper-plate; etching; mezzo-, aqua-, litho-tint; cut, woodcut, block; stereo-, grapho-, auto-, helio-type; half-tone; *photogravure*, *rotogravure*.

graver, *burin*, etching-point, style; plate, stone, wood-block, negative; die, punch, stamp.

printing; plate –, copper-plate- –, intaglio –, anastatic –, lithographic –, color –, three color-printing; type-printing etc. 591.

illustr-, illumin-ation; *vignette*, initial letter, *cul de lampe*, tail-piece.

V. engrave, grave, stipple, scrape, etch; bite, – in; lithograph etc. *n.*; print.

Adj. insculptured; engraved etc. *v.*

Phr. *sculpsit, imprimit*.

559. Artist.—N. artist; painter, limner, drawer, sketcher, delineator; cartoon-, caricatur-ist, designer, engraver; draughtsman; copyist; enameller, -list.

historical –, landscape –, genre –, marine –, flower –, portrait –, miniature –, scene –, sign-painter; engraver; Apelles; sculptor, carver, chaser, modeller, lapidary, *figuriste*, statuary; Phidias, Praxiteles; Royal Academician.

photographer, retoucher.

560. Language.—N. language; phraseology etc. 569; speech etc. 582; tongue, lingo, vernacular, slang; mother –, vulgar –, native- tongue; household words; King's *or* Queen's English; idiom; dialect etc. 563.

volapuk, esperanto, ido, occidental, Ro.

confusion of tongues, Babel, *pasigraphie*; pantomime etc. (*signs*) 550; *onomatopaeia*.

phil-, gloss-, glott-ology; linguistics, chrestomathy; paleo-logy; -graphy; comparative grammar.

literature, letters, polite literature, *belles lettres*, muses, humanities, *literae humaniores*, republic of letters, dead languages, classics; genius of a language; scholarship etc. (*knowledge*) 490.

linguist etc. (*scholar*) 492.

V. speak, say, express by words etc. 566.

Adj. lingu-al, -istic; dialectic; vernacular, current, colloquial, slangy; bilingual, polyglot; literary.

561. Letter.—N. letter; character; hieroglyphic etc. (*writing*) 590; type etc. (*printing*) 591; capitals; majus-, minus-cule; alphabet, ABC, abecedary, christcross row, chrisscross row.

consonant, vowel, diphthong; mute, surd; sonant, liquid, labial, dental, palatal, gutteral.

syllable; mono-, dis-, poly-syllable; affix, prefix, suffix.

spelling, orthography; phon-ography, -etic spelling; ana-, meta-grammatism.

cipher, monogram, anagram; double – acrostic.

V. spell.

Adj. literal; alphabetical, abecedarian; syllabic; uncial etc. (*writing*) 590; phonetic, voiced, mute etc. *n*.

562. Word.—N. word, term, vocable; name etc. 564; phrase etc. 566; root, etymon; derivative; part of speech etc. (*grammar*) 567.

dictionary, vocabulary, word book, lexicon, index, glossary, thesaurus, *gradus, delectus*, concordance.

etymology, lexicology, derivation; phonology, orthoepy; gloss-, termin-, orism-ology; paleology etc. (*philology*) 560; comparative philology.

lexicograph-er, -y; glossographer etc. (*scholar*) 492; etymologist; logolept.

verbosity, verbiage, loquacity etc. 584.

Adj. verbal, literal; titular, nominal. [Similarly derived] conjugate, paraonymous; derivative.

Adv. verbally etc. *adj.*; *verbatim* etc. (*exactly*) 494.

563. Neology.—N. neolo-gy; -gism; newfangled expression; barbarism; caconym; archaism, black letter, monkish Latin; corruption; missaying, antiphrasis.

paronomasia, play upon words; wordplay etc. (*wit*) 842; *double-entente* etc. (*ambiguity*) 520; palindrome, paragram, clinch; abuse of -language, – terms.

dialect, brogue, *patois*, provincialism, broken English, *lingua franca*; Brit-, Gall-, Scott-, Hibernicism; American-ism; Gipsy lingo, Romany, pidgin English.

dog Latin, macaronics, gibberish, confusion of tongues, Babel; jargon.

colloquialism etc. (*figure of speech*) 521; byword; technicality, lingo, slang, cant, *argot*, St. Giles's Greek, thieves' Latin, peddler's French, flash tongue, Billingsgate, Wall Street slang.

pseudonym etc. (*misnomer*) 565; Mr. So-and-so; what d'ye call 'em, what's his name; thingum-my, -bob; *je ne sais quoi*.

neologist, coiner of words.

V. coin words.

Adj. neologic, -al; rare; archaic; obsolete etc. (*old*) 124; colloquial, dialectic, slang, cant.

564. Nomenclature.—N. nomenclature; naming etc. *v.*; nuncupation, nomination, baptism; orismology; *onomatopaeia*; antonomasia.

name; appella-tion, -tive; designation; title; head, -ing, caption; denomination; by-name, epithet.

style, proper name; prae-, ag-, cog-nomen; patronymic, surname; cognomination; compellation, description; empty -title, – name; handle to one's name; namesake, eponym.

synonym, antonym.

term, expression, noun; by-word; convertible terms etc. 522; technical term; cant etc. 563.

V. name, call, term, denominate, designate, style, entitle, intitule, clepe, dub, christen, baptize, nickname, characterize, specify, define, distinguish by the name of; label etc. (*mark*) 550.

be -called etc. *v.*; take –, bear –, go (*or* be known) by –, go (*or* pass) under –, rejoice in- the name of.

Adj. named etc. *v.*; hight, yclept, known as; what one may -well, – fairly, – properly, – fitly-call.

nuncupa-tory, -tive; cognominal, titular, nominal; orismological.

565. Misnomer.—N. misnomer; *lucus a non lucendo*; Mrs. Malaprop; what d'ye call 'em etc. (*neologism*) 563.

nickname, *sobriquet*, by-name, handle, moniker; assumed -name, – title; *alias*; *nom de - guerre*, – *plume*, – *theâtre*; pseudonym, pen name, stage name.

V. mis-name, -call, - term; nickname; assume -a name, – an alias.

Adj. misnamed etc. *v.*; pseudonymous; *soi-disant*; self-called, -styled, -christened; so-called.

nameless, anonymous; without a –, having no-name; innominate, unnamed.

Adv. in no sense.

566. Phrase.—N. phrase, expression, set phrase; sentence, paragraph; figure of speech etc. 521; idi-om, -otism; turn of expression.

paraphrase etc. (*synonym*) 522; periphrase etc. (*circumlocution*) 573; motto etc. (*proverb*) 496. phraseology etc. 569.

V. express, phrase; word, – it; give -words, – expression- to; voice; arrange in –, clothe in –, put into –, express by- words; couch in terms; find words to express; speak by the card.

Adj. expressed etc. *v.*; idiomatic.

Adv. in -round, – set, – good, set- terms; in set phrases.

567. Grammar.—N. grammar, accidence, syntax, *praxis*, analysis, paradigm, punctuation; parts of speech, inflexion, case, declension, conjugation; *jus et norma loquendi*; Lindley Murray etc. (*school-book*) 542; correct style; philology etc. (*language*) 560.

V. parse, analyze; decline, conjugate; punctuate.

Adj. grammatical; syntactic; inflexional.

568. Solecism.—N. solecism; bad –, false –, faulty- grammar; slip, error; slip of the -pen, – tongue; *lapsus calami-*, – *linguae*; *faux pas*; slipslop; bull.

V. use -bad, – faulty- grammar; solecize, commit a solecism; murder the -King's, – Queen's- English; break Priscian's head.

Adj. ungrammatical; in-correct, -accurate; faulty, improper, incongruous, abnormal.

569. Style.—N. style, diction, phraseology, wording; manner, strain; composition; mode of expression, choice of words, literary power, ready pen, pen of a ready writer; command of language etc. (*eloquence*) 582; authorship; *la morgue littéraire*.

V. express by words etc. 566; write.

570. Perspicuity.—N. perspicuity etc. (*intelligibility*) 518; plain speaking etc. (*manifestation*) 525; defin-iteness, -ition; exactness etc. 494; perspicuousness, logical acuteness.

Adj. lucid etc. (*intelligible*) 518; explicit etc. (*manifest*) 525; exact etc. 494.

571. Obscurity.—N. obscurity etc. (*unintelligibility*) 519; involution; hard words; ambiguity etc. 520; vagueness etc. 475, inexactness etc. 495; what d'ye call 'em etc. (*neologism*) 563; cloudiness, confusion.

Adj. obscure etc. *n.*; crabbed, involved, confused.

572. Conciseness.—N. conciseness etc. *adj.*; brevity, 'the soul of wit,' laconism; Tacitus; ellipsis; syncope; abridgment etc. (*shortening*) 201; compression etc. 195; epitome etc. 596; monostitch; portmanteau word, telescope word, protogram.

V. be -concise etc. *adj.*; condense etc. 195; abridge etc. 201; abstract etc. 596; come to the point.

Adj. concise, brief, short, terse, close; to the point, exact; neat, compact, condensed, pointed; laconic, curt, pithy, trenchant, summary; pregnant; compendious etc. (*compendium*) 596; succinct; elliptical, epigrammatic, crisp, sententious.

Adv. concisely etc. *adj.*; briefly, summarily; in -brief, – short, – a word, – few words, – a nutshell; for shortness sake; to -come to the point, – make a long story short, – cut the matter short, – be brief; it comes to this, the long and short of it is.

573. Diffuseness.—N. diffuseness etc. *adj.*; amplification etc. *v.*; dilating etc. *v.*; verbosity, *verbiage*, wordiness, cloud of words, *copia verborum*; flow of words etc. (*loquacity*) 584.

poly-, tauto-, batto-, perisso-logy; pleonasm, exuberance, redundance; thrice-told tale; prolixity; circumlocution, *ambages*; periphra-se, -sis; roundabout phrases; episode; expletive; penny-a-lining; padding, drivel, twaddle, rigmarole; richness etc. 577.

V. be -diffuse etc. *adj.*; run out on, descant, expatiate, enlarge, dilate, amplify, expand, inflate, pad; launch –, branch- out; rant.

maunder, prose; harp upon etc. (*repeat*) 104; dwell on, insist upon.

digress, ramble, *battre la campagne*, beat about the bush, perorate, spin a long yarn, protract; spin –, swell –, draw- out, drivel.

Adj. dif-, pro-fuse; wordy, verbose, largiloquent, copious, exuberant, effusive, pleonastic, lengthy; long, -some, -winded, -spun, -drawn out; diffusive, spun out, protracted, prolix, prosing, maundering; circumlocutory, periphrastic, ambagious, roundabout; digressive; dis-, ex-cursive; rambling, episodic; flatulent, frothy.

Adv. diffusely etc. *adj.*; at large, *in extenso*; about it and about it.

574. Vigor.—N. vigor, power, force; boldness, raciness etc. *adj.*; spirit, point, antithesis, piquancy; *verve*, glow, fire, warmth, ardor, enthusiasm; 'thoughts that breathe and words that burn;' strong language; punch; gravity, sententiousness; elevation, loftiness, sublimity.

eloquence; command of -words, – language.

Adj. vigorous, nervous, powerful, forcible, trenchant, mordant, biting, incisive, impressive; sensational.

spirited, lively, glowing, sparkling, racy, bold, slashing; pungent, *piquant*, full of point, pointed, pithy, antithetical; sententious.

lofty, elevated, sublime, grand, weighty, ponderous; eloquent; vehement, petulant, impassioned; poetic.

Adv. in -glowing, – good set, – no measured- terms.

575. Feebleness.—N. feebleness etc. *adj.*;

Adj. feeble, bald, tame, meager, insipid, nerve-les, jejune, vapid, trashy, cold, frigid, poor, dull, dry, languid; pros-ing, -y, -aic; unvaried, monotonous, weak, frail, washy, wishy-washy, sloppy; sketchy, slight; careless, slovenly, loose, lax; slip-shod, -slop; inexact; dis-jointed, -connected; puerile, childish; flatulent; rambling etc. (*diffuse*) 573.

576. Plainness.—**N.** plainness etc. *adj.*; simplicity, severity; plain -terms, – English; Saxon English; household words.

V. speak plainly; call a spade 'a spade;' plunge *in medias res*; come to the point.

Adj. plain, simple; un-ornamented, -adorned, -varnished; home-ly, -spun; neat; severe, chaste, pure, Saxon; commonplace, matter of fact, natural, prosaic, sober, unimaginative.

dry, unvaried, monotonous etc. 575.

Adv. in plain -terms, – words, – English, – common parlance; point blank.

577. Ornament.—**N.** ornament; floridness etc. *adj.*; turg-idity, -escence; altiloquence etc. *adj.*; orotundity; declamation, teratology; well-rounded periods; elegance etc. 578.

inversion, antithesis, alliteration, *paronomasia*; figurativeness etc. (*metaphor*) 521.

flourish; flowers of -speech, – rhetoric; euphuism, -emism.

big-, high-sounding words; macrology, *sesquipedalia verba*, sesquipedalianism; Alexandrine; inflation, pretension; rant, bombast, fustian, bunkum, balderdash, prose run mad; fine writing; Minerva press.

phrasemonger; euph-uist, -emist.

V. ornament, overlay with ornament, overcharge; smell of the lamp.

Adj. ornamented etc. *v.*; beautified etc. 847; ornate, florid, rich, flowery; euph-uistic, -emistic; sonorous; high-, big-sounding; inflated, swelling, tumid; turg-id, -escent; pedantic, pompous, stilted; high-flown, -flowing; sententious, rhetorical, declamatory; grandiose; grand-, magn-, altiloquent; sesquipedal, -ian; Johnsonian, mouthy; bombastic; fustian; frothy, flashy, flaming, flamboyant.

antithetical, alliterative; figurative etc. 521; artificial etc. (*inelegant*) 579.

Adv. *ore rotundo*; with rounded phrase.

578. Elegance.—**N.** elegance, purity, grace, ease, felicity, distinction, gracefulness, refinement, readiness etc. *adj.*; concinnity, euphony, numerosity, balance, rythym, symmetry, proportion; restraint; good taste, propriety.

well rounded –, well turned –, flowing-periods; the right word in the right place; antithesis etc. 577.

purist, stylist.

V. point an antithesis, round a period.

Adj. elegant, polished, classical, Attic, correct, Ciceronian, artistic; chaste, pure, Saxon, academical.

graceful, easy, readable, fluent, flowing, tripping; unaffected, natural, unlabored; mellifluous; euph-onious, -emistic; rhythmical, balanced, symmetrical.

felicitous, happy, neat; well –, neatly- -put, – expressed.

579. Inelegance.—**N.** inelegance; vulgarity, bad taste; stiffness etc. *adj.*; unlettered Muse; barbarism; slang etc. 563; solecism etc. 568; mannerism etc. (*affectation*) 855; euphuism; fustian etc. 577; cacophony; want of balance; words that -break the teeth, – dislocate the jaw.

V. be -inelegant etc. *adj.*

Adj. inelegant, graceless, ungraceful, unpolished; harsh, abrupt; dry, stiff, cramped, formal, *guindé*; forced, labored, awkward; artificial, mannered, ponderous; turgid etc. 577; affected, euphuistic; barbarous, uncouth, grotesque, rude, crude, halting; vulgar, offensive to ears polite.

580. Voice.—**N.** voice; vocality; organ, lungs, bellows; good –, fine –, powerful etc. (*loud*) 404 –, musical etc. 413- voice; intonation; tone etc. (*sound*) 402- of voice.

vocalization; cry etc. 411; strain, utterance, prolation; exclam-, ejacul-, vocifer-ation; enunci-, articul-ation; articulate sound; distinctness; clearness, – of articulation; stage whisper; delivery; attack.

accent, -uation; emphasis, stress; broad –, strong –, pure –, native –, foreign- accent; pronunciation.

[Word similarly pronounced] homonym.

orthoepy; euphony etc. (*melody*) 413.

gastri-, ventri-loquism; ventriloquist; polyphonism, -ist.

[Science of voice] phonology etc. (*sound*) 402.

V. sing, speak, utter, breathe, voice; give -utterance, – tongue; cry etc. (*shout*) 411; ejaculate, rap out; vocalize, prolate, articulate, enunciate, enounce, pronounce, accentuate, aspirate, deliver, mouth; emit, murmur, whisper, – in the ear, croon, yodel.

Adj. vocal, phonetic, oral; ejaculatory, articulate, distinct, stertorous; enunciative; accentuated, aspirated; euphonious etc. (*melodious*) 413.

581. Aphony—**N.** aphony, *aphonia*; dumbness etc. *adj.*; obmutescence; absence –, want- of voice; dysphony; silence etc. (*taciturnity*) 585; raucity; harsh etc. 410 –, unmusical etc. 414- voice; *falsetto*, 'childish treble;' mute, dummy, deaf mute.

V. keep silence etc. 585; speak -low, – softly; whisper etc. (*faintness*) 405.

silence; render -mute, – silent etc. 403; muzzle, muffle, suppress, smother, gag, strike dumb, dumbfound, -founder; drown the voice, put to silence, stop one's mouth, cut one short.

stick in the throat.

Adj. aphon-ous, -ic, dumb, mute; deaf-mute, –

and dumb; mum; tongue-tied; breath-, tongue-, voice-, speech-, word-less; mute as a -fish, – stockfish, – mackerel; silent etc. (*taciturn*) 585; muzzled; in-articulate, -audible.

croaking, raucous, hoarse, husky, dry, hollow, sepulchral, hoarse as a raven.

Adv. with -bated breath, – the finger on the lips; *sotto voce*; in a -low tone, – cracked voice, – broken voice; in an aside.

Phr. *vox faucibus haesit.*

582. Speech.—N. speech, faculty of speech; locution, talk, parlance, verbal intercourse, prolation, oral communication, word of mouth, *parole*, palaver, prattle; effusion.

oration, recitation, delivery, say, address, speech, lecture, harangue, sermon, *tirade*, screed, formal speech, salutatory, peroration; prelection; speechifying; soliloquy etc. 589; allocution etc. 586; interlocution etc. 588.

oratory; elo-cution, -quence; rhetoric, declamation; grandi-, multi-loquence; burst of eloquence; facundity; talkativeness; flow –, command- of -words, – language; *copia verborum*; power of speech, gift of the gab; *usus loquendi.*

speaker etc. *v.*; spokesman, pro-, inter-locutor; mouthpiece, Hermes; ora-tor, -trix, -tress; Demosthenes, Cicero; rhetorician; stump –, platform- orator, tub-thumper; elocutionist; speechmaker, patterer, *improvisatore*.

V. speak, – of; say, utter, pronounce, deliver, give utterance to; utter –, pour- forth; breathe, let fall, come out with; rap –, blurt- out; have on one's lips; have at the -end, – tip- of one's tongue.

break silence; open one's -lips, – mouth; lift –, raise- one's voice; give –, wag the- tongue; talk, outspeak; put in a word or two.

hold forth; make –, deliver- -a speech etc. *n.*; speechify, harangue, declaim, stump, flourish, spout, rant, recite, lecture, preach, sermonize, discourse, be on one's legs; have –, say- one's say; expatiate etc. (*speak at length*) 573; speak one's mind.

soliloquize etc. 589; tell etc. (*inform*) 527; speak to etc. 586; talk together etc. 588.

be -eloquent etc. *adj.*; have -a tongue in one's head, – the gift of the gab etc. *n.*

pass –, escape- one's lips; fall from the -lips, – mouth.

Adj. speaking etc., spoken etc. *v.*; oral, lingual, phonetic, not written, unwritten, outspoken; eloquent, -cutionary; orat-, rhetorical; declamatory; grandiloquent etc. 577; talkative etc. 584.

Adv. orally etc. *adj.*; by word of mouth, *vivâ voce*, from the lips of.

Phr. quoth –, said- he etc.

583. Stammering. [Imperfect Speech.]**—N.** inarticulateness; stammering etc. *v.*; hesitation etc. *v.*; impediment in one's speech; aphasia, titubancy, traulism; whisper etc. (*faint sound*) 405; lisp, drawl, tardiloquence; nasal -tone, – accent; twang; *falsetto* etc. (*want of voice*) 581; broken -voice, – accents, – sentences.

brogue etc. 563; slip of the tongue, *lapsus linguae.*

V. stammer, stutter, hesitate, falter, hammer; balbu-tiate, -cinate; haw, hum and haw, be unable to put two words together.

mumble, mutter; maund, -er; whisper etc. 405; mince, lisp; jabber, gabble, gibber; sp-, spl-utter; muffle, mump; drawl, mouth; croak; speak -thick, – through the nose; snuffle, clip one's words; murder the -language, – King's (*or* Queen's) English; mis-pronounce, -say.

Adj. stammering etc. *v.*; inarticulate, guttural, nasal; tremulous.

Adv. *sotto voce* etc. (*faintly*) 405.

584. Loquacity.—N. loquac-ity, -iousness; talkativeness etc. *adj.*; garrulity; multiloquence, much speaking, effusion, wordiness.

jaw; gab, -ble; jabber, chatter; prate, prattle, cackle, clack; twaddle, trattle, rattle; *caquet, -terie*; blabber, *bavardage*, bibble-babble, gibble-gabble; small talk etc. (*converse*) 588.

fluency, flippancy, volubility, flowing tongue; flow, – of words; *flux de -bouche, – mots, – paroles*; *copia verborum, cacoëthes loquendi*; verbosity etc. (*diffuseness*) 573; gift of the gab etc. (*eloquence*) 582.

talker; chatter-er, -box; babbler etc. *v.*; rattle; ranter; sermonizer, proser, driveller; wind bag; gossip etc. (*converse*) 588; magpie, jay, parrot, poll, Babel; *moulin à paroles.*

V. be -loquacious etc. *adj.*; talk glibly, pour forth, patter; prate, palaver, prose, chatter, prattle, clack, jabber, jaw; rattle, – on; twaddle, twattle; babble, gabble; out-talk; talk oneself -out of breath, – hoarse; maunder, gush, blatter; talk a donkey's hind leg off; expatiate etc. (*speak at length*) 573; gossip etc. (*converse*) 588; din in the ears etc. (*repeat*) 104; talk -at random, – nonsense etc. 497; be hoarse with talking.

Adj. loquacious, talkative, conversational, garrulous, linguacious, multiloquous; chattering etc. *v.*; chatty etc. (*sociable*) 892; declamatory etc. 582; open-mouthed.

fluent, voluble, glib, flippant; long-tongued, -winded etc. (*diffuse*) 573.

Adv. trippingly on the tongue; glibly etc. *adj.*

Phr. the tongue running -fast, – loose, – on wheels.

585. Taciturnity.—N. silence, muteness, obmutescence; taciturnity, pauciloquy, costiveness, curtness; reserve, reticence etc. (*concealment*) 528; *aposiopesis.*

man of few words.

V. be -silent etc. *adj.*; keep silence; hold one's -tongue, – peace, – jaw; not speak etc. 582; say nothing; seal –, close –, put a padlock on- the -lips, – mouth; put a bridle on one's tongue; keep one's tongue between one's teeth; make no sign, not let a word escape one; keep a secret etc. 528; not have a word to say; lay –, place- the finger on the lips; render mute etc. 581.

stick in one's throat.

Adj. silent, mute, mum; silent as -a post, – a stone, – the grave etc. (*still*) 403; dumb etc. 581.

taciturn, sparing of words; close, – mouthed, –

tongued; laconic, costive, inconversable, curt; reserved; reticent etc. (*concealing*) 528.

Int. tush! silence! mum! hush! *chut!* hist! tut! etc. 403.

586. Allocution.—**N.** allocution, alloquy, address; speech etc. 582; apostrophe, interpellation, appeal, invocation, salutation; word in the ear.

[Feigned dialogue] dialogism.

platform etc. 542; audience etc. (*interview*) 588.

V. speak to, address, accost, make up to, apostrophize, appeal to, invoke; hail, salute; call to, halloo.

take -aside, – by the button, button-hole; talk to in private.

lecture etc. (*make a speech*) 582.

Int. soho! halloo! hey! hist! hi!

587. Response etc.; *see* Answer 462.

588. Interlocution.—**N.** interlocution; collocution, colloquy, converse, conversation, confabulation, talk, discourse, verbal intercourse; communion, oral communication, commerce; dia-, duo-, tria-logue.

causerie, chat, chit-chat; small –, table –, teatable –, town –, village –, idle- talk; tattle, gossip, tittle-tattle; babble, -ment; *tripotage*, cackle, prittle-prattle, *on dit*; talk of the -town, – village.

conference, parley, interview, audience, *pourparler*; *tête-à-tête*; reception, *conversazione*; congress etc. (*council*) 696; pow-wow.

hall of audience, *durbar*, coliseum, assembly hall, auditorium.

palaver, debate, logomachy, war of words, controversy.

talker, gossip, tattler; Paul Pry; tabby; chatterer etc. (*loquacity*) 584; interlocutor etc. (*spokesman*) 582; conversation-ist, -alist; dialogist.

'the feast of reason and the flow of soul;' *mollia tempora fandi*.

V. talk together, converse, confabulate; hold –, carry on –, join in –, engage in- a conversation; put in a word; shine in conversation; bandy words; parley; palaver; chat, gossip, tattle; prate etc. (*loquacity*) 584.

discourse –, confer –, commune –, commerce- with; hold -converse, – conference, – intercourse; talk it over; be closeted with; talk with one -in private, – *tête-à-tête*.

Adj. conversing etc. *v.*; interlocutory; conversational, -able; discursive, -coursive; chatty etc. (*sociable*) 892; colloquial, *tête-à-tête*, confabulatory.

589. Soliloquy.—**N.** soliloquy, monologue, apostrophe.

solilo-quist, -quizer, monologist.

V. soliloquize; say –, talk- to oneself; say aside, think aloud, apostrophize.

Adj. soliloquizing etc. *v.*

Adv. aside.

590. Writing.—**N.** writing etc. *v.*; chiro-, stelo-, cero-graphy, graphology; stylography; pen-craft, -script, -manship; quill-driving; typewriting.

writing, manuscript, MS., *literae scriptae*; these presents.

stroke –, dash- of the pen; *coup de plume*; line; pen and ink.

letter etc. 561; uncial writing, cuneiform character, arrow-head, Ogham, Runes, futhorc; hieroglyphic, hieratic, demotic; script; contraction.

short-hand; steno-, brachy-, tachy-graphy; secret writing, writing in cipher; crypt-, stegan-ography; phono-, pasi-, poly-, logo-graphy.

copy; tran-, re-script; draft, rough –, fair- copy; handwriting; signature, sign-manual; auto-, mono-, holo-graph; hand, fist; mark.

calligraphy; good –, running –, flowing –, cursive –, legible –, copperplate –, round –, bold-hand.

cacography, *griffonage*, *barbouillage*; bad –, cramped –, crabbed –, illegible- hand; scribble etc. *v.*; *pattes de mouche*; ill-formed letters; pothooks and hangers.

stationery; pen, quill, goose-quill, reed; stylographic-, fountain-pen; pencil, style, stylus; paper, foolscap, parchment, vellum, papyrus, pad, tablet, block, note book, slate, marble, pillar, table, black board.

ink-bottle, -pot, -stand, -well, -horn; typewriter.

transcription etc. (*copy*) 21; inscription etc. (*record*) 551; superscription etc. (*indication*) 550.

composition, authorship; *cacoethes scribendi*.

writer, scribe, amanuensis, scrivener, secretary, clerk, penman, copyist, transcriber, quill-driver; writer for the press etc. (*author*) 593.

shorthand writer, stenographer; typewriter, typist.

V. write, pen; copy, engross; write out, – fair; transcribe; scribble, scrawl, scrabble, scratch; interline; stain paper; write down etc. (*record*) 551; sign etc. (*attest*) 467; take down, – in shorthand; typewrite, type.

compose, indite, draw up, redact, draft, formulate; dictate; inscribe, throw on paper, dash off; concoct.

take -up the pen, – pen in hand; shed –, spill –, dip one's pen in- ink.

Adj. writing etc. *v.*; written etc. *v.*; in -writing, – black and white; under one's hand.

uncial, Runic, cuneiform, hieroglyphical etc. *n.*

Adv. *currente calamo*; pen in hand.

591. Printing.—**N.** printing; block –, type-printing, lino-, mono-type; plate printing etc. (*engraving*) 558; the press etc. (*publication*) 531; composition.

print, letterpress, text, matter, standing type; context, note, page, column; over-running; head-, foot-line, title.

typography; stereo-, electro-, apro-type; type,

black letter, heavy type, font, fount; pi, pie; capitals etc. (*letters*) 561; diamond, pearl, nonpareil, minion, brevier, bourgeois, long primer, small pica, pica, english, great primer.

folio etc. (*book*) 593; copy, impression, pull, proof, galley –, author's –, page- proof, revise.

printer, compositor, reader; printer's devil.

V. print; compose; put –, go- to press; pass –, see- through the press; publish etc. 531; bring out; appear in –, rush into- print.

Adj. printed etc. *v.*; in type; typographical etc. *n.*

592. Correspondence.—N. correspondence, letter, epistle, note, *billet*, post-, letter-card, missive, circular, form letter; favor, *billet-doux*; des-, dis-patch; *bulletin*, communication etc. 532; these presents; rescript, -ion; post etc. (*messenger*) 534; letter writer, correspondent.

V. correspond, – with; write –, send a letter- to; keep up a correspondence; drop a line to; despatch; communicate with; circularize.

Adj. epistolary.

593. Book.—N. book, -let; writing, work, volume, tome, opuscule; tract, -ate; *livret*; *brochure, libretto*, handbook, treatise, text-book, codex, manual, pamphlet, monograph, enchiridion, circular, publication; book of poems; novel; chap-book.

part, issue, number, *livraison*; album, portfolio; periodical, serial, magazine, *ephemeris*, annual, journal.

paper, bill, sheet, broadsheet, screed; leaf, -let; fly-leaf, page; quire, ream.

chapter, section, head, article, paragraph, passage, clause, supplement, appendix; *feuilleton*.

folio, quarto, octavo; duo-, sexto-, octo-decimo.

en-, cyclopedia, dictionary, lexicon, thesaurus, concordance, anthology, bibliography; compilation, compendium, catalogue etc. 86; library, bibliotheca; the press etc. (*publication*) 531.

writer, author, *littérateur*, essayist, journalist, publicist; scribe, penman, war –, special –, correspondent; pen, scribbler, the scribbling race; ghost, hack, literary hack, Grub-street writer; writer for –, gentlemen of –, representative of- the press; reporter, penny-a-liner; editor, sub-editor; playwright etc. 599; poet etc. 597.

bookseller, publisher; biblio-pole, -polist, -grapher; librarian; book -collector, – worm.

book -shop, – club, circulating –, lending –, public- library; publishing house.

knowledge of books, bibliography; book-learning etc. (*knowledge*) 490.

594. Description.—N. description, account, statement, report; *exposé* etc. (*disclosure*) 529; specification, particulars, scenario, plot; state –, summary- of facts; brief etc. (*abstract*) 596; return etc. (*record*) 551; *catalogue raisonné* etc. (*list*) 86; guide-book etc. (*information*) 527.

delineation etc. (*representation*) 554; sketch, vignette; monograph; minute –, detailed –, particular –, circumstantial –, graphic- account; narration, recital, rehearsal, relation.

histori-, chron-ography; historic Muse, Clio; history; bi-, autobi-ography; necrology, obituary.

narrative, history; memoir, memorials; annals etc. (*chronicle*) 551; tradition, legend, saga, epic, epos, story, tale, historiette; personal narrative, journal, letters, life, adventures, fortunes, experiences, confessions; anecdote, ana, *trait*.

work of fiction, short story, novelette, novel, romance, penny dreadful, shilling, shocker, Minerva press; fairy –, nursery- tale; fable, allegory, parable, apologue.

relator etc. *v.*; *raconteur*; historian etc. (*recorder*) 553; biographer, fabulist, novelist, story teller, romancer, teller of tales, spinner of yarns, anecdotist.

V. describe; set forth etc. (*state*) 535; draw a picture, picture; portray etc. (*represent*) 554; characterize, particularize; narrate, relate, recite, recount, sum up, run over, recapitulate, rehearse, fight one's battles over again.

unfold etc. (*disclose*) 529- a tale; tell; give –, render- an account of; report, make a report, draw up a statement.

detail; enter into –, descend to- -particulars, – details.

Adj. descriptive, graphic, narrative, epic, suggestive, well-drawn; historic; auto-, biographical, realistic, expository, tradition-al, -ary; legendary; fabulous, mythical; anecdotic, storied; described etc. *v.*

595. Dissertation.—N. dissertation, treatise, essay; *thesis*, theme; tract, -ate, -ation, excursus; discourse, memoir, disquisition, lecture, sermon, homily, pandect.

commentary, review, *critique*, criticism, article; lead-er, -ing article, editorial; argument, running commentary.

investigation etc. (*inquiry*) 461; study etc. (*consideration*) 451; discussion etc. (*reasoning*) 476; exposition etc. (*explanation*) 522.

commentator, critic, essayist, pamphleteer; publicist, reviewer, leader writer, editor, annotator.

V. dissert –, descant –, write –, touch- upon a subject; dissertate; treat of –, take up –, ventilate –, discuss –, deal with –, go into –, canvass –, handle –, do justice to- a subject; comment, criticize, interpret etc. 522.

Adj. dis-cursive, -coursive; disquisitional, disquisitionary; expository, critical.

596. Compendium.—N. compend, -ium; abstract, *précis*, epitome, *multum in parvo*, analysis, pandect, digest, sum and substance, brief, abridgment, summary, *aperçu*, draft, minute, note; synopsis, textbook, *conspectus*, outlines, syllabus, contents, heads, prospectus.

album; scrap –, note –, memorandum –, commonplace- book; extracts, *excerpta*, cuttings; fugitive -pieces, – writings; *spicilegium*, flowers, anthology, miscellany, *collectanea, analecta*; compilation.

recapitulation, *résumé*, review.

abbrevia-tion, -ture; contraction; shortening etc. 201; compression etc. 195.

V. abridge, abstract, epitomize, summarize; make –, prepare –, draw –, compile- an abstract etc. *n.*

recapitulate, review, skim, run over, sum up.

abbreviate etc. (*shorten*) 201; condense etc. (*compress*) 195; compile etc. (*collect*) 72; edit, blue pencil.

Adj. compendious, synoptic, analectic, analytical; abridged etc. *v.*

Adv. in -short, – epitome, – substance, – few words.

Phr. it lies in a nutshell.

597. Poetry.—N. poetry, poetics, poesy, Muse, Calliope, tuneful Nine, Parnassus, Helicon, Pierides, Pierian spring, afflatus, inspiration.

versification, rhyming, making verses; prosody, scansion, orthometry.

poem; epic, – poem; epopee, *epopaea*, ode, epode, idyl, lyric, eclogue, pastoral, bucolic, georgic, dithyramb, anacreontic, sonnet, roundelay, *rondel, rondoletto, rondeau, rondo*, triolet; madrigal, canzonet, *cento*, monody, elegy, palinode; rhapsody.

dramatic –, lyric- poetry; opera; posy, anthology.

song, ballad, lay; love –, drinking –, war –, folk –, sea- song; lullaby; music etc. 415; nursery rhymes.

[Bad poetry] doggerel, Hudibrastic verse, prose run mad; macaronics; macaronic –, leonine- verse; runes.

canto, stanza, distich, verse, line, couplet, triplet, quatrain, sestet; *strophe, antistrophe*, refrain, chorus, burden.

verse, rhyme, assonance, crambo, meter, measure, foot, numbers, strain, rhythm; accentuation etc. (*voice*) 580; iambus, dactyl, spondee, trochee, anapaest etc.; hex-, pent-ameter; Alexandrine; blank verse, alliteration.

elegiacs etc. *adj.*; elegiac etc. *adj.* -verse, – meter, – poetry.

poet, – laureate; laureate; minor poet, bard, lyrist, scald, troubadour, *trouvère*; mistrel; minne-, meister-singer; *improvisatore*; versifier, sonneteer; ballad monger; rhym-er, -ist, -ester; poetaster.

V. poetize, sing, versify, make verses, rhyme, scan.

Adj. poetic, -al; lyric, -al; tuneful; epic; dithyrambic etc. *n.*; metrical; a-, catalectic; elegiac, iambic, trochaic, spondaic, anapest; Ionic, Sapphic, Alcaic, Pindaric.

598. Prose.—N. prose, – writer, pros-aism, -aist, -er.

V. prose, write prose.

write -prose, – in prose.

Adj. pros-y, -aic; unpoetical.

rhymeless, unrhymed, in prose, not in verse.

599. Drama.—N. drama, the -drama, – stage, – theater, – play; theatricals, dramaturgy, histrionic art, buskin, sock, *cothurnus*, Melpomene and Thalia, Thespis.

play, stage-play, piece, five-act play, tragedy, comedy, opera, comic opera, *vaudeville, comedietta, lever de rideau*, curtain raiser, interlude, afterpiece, exode, farce, *divertissement, extravaganza*, burletta, harlequinade, pantomime, mimodrama, burlesque, *opéra bouffe*, musical comedy, review, revue, intimate revue, variety, cabaret entertainment, *ballet, spectacle*, masque, *drame, comédie drame*; melo-drama, -drame; *comédie larmoyante*, emotional drama, sensation drama, tragi-, farcical-comedy; mono-drame, -logue; duologue; trilogy; charade, *proverbe*; mystery, miracle –, morality- play.

act, scene, *tableau*; in-, intro-duction; pro-, epi-logue, curtain; *libretto*, book, script.

performance, representation, show, *mise en scène*, stagery, *jeu de théâtre*, stage-craft; acting; gesture etc. 550; impersonation etc. 554; stage business, gag, patter, buffoonery.

theater; play-, opera-house; house; music hall; *cabaret*; amphitheater, circus, hippodrome; puppet-show, *fantoccini*; *marionnettes*, Punch and Judy.

cinema, -tograph-, picture –, theater, the pictures, the movies, the talkies.

auditory, *auditorium*, front of the house, stalls, boxes, balcony, dress –, upper- -circle, – boxes, amphitheater, pit, gallery; *foyer*; greenroom; dressing rooms, *coulisses*.

flat; drop, – scene; wing, screen, side-scene; transformation scene, curtain, act-drop, safety –, fire- curtain; *proscenium*, forestage.

stage, revolving stage, scene, the boards; star –, grave –, trap, mezzanine floor; flies; gridiron, floats, battens, footlights; lime –, spot –, flood –, bunch-lights; scenery, set, *décor*; orchestra.

theatrical -costume, – properties, props.

part, *rôle*, character, cast, *dramatis personae*; *répertoire*.

actor, player; stage –, strolling player; old –, stager, performer; mime, -r; *artiste*; com-, tragedian, straight man; *tragédienne*, Thespian, Roscius, star.

pantomimist, clown, harlequin, *buffo*, buffoon, *farceur, grimacier*, pantaloon, columbine; *Pierrot, Pierrette*; punch, -inello; *pulcinell-o, -a*; mute, *figurante*, general utility; super, -numerary, extra.

mummer, guiser, guisard, gysart, masque.

mountebank, Jack Pudding; tumbler, posture-master, acrobat, equilibrist, juggler, contortionist; *danseuse, ballerina*, ballet -dancer, – girl, *coryphée*; *bayadère, geisha*; chorus -singer, – girl.

company; first tragedian, *prima donna*, lead, leading lady, protagonist; *jeune premier*; juvenile lead, *débutant, -e*; light –, genteel –, low- -comedy, – comedian; *soubrette*, walking gentleman, *amoroso*, heavy, heavy father, *ingénue, jeune veuve, commère, compère*.

property man, *costumier*, machinist, stage hand, electrician, prompter, call-boy; director, manager; stage –, acting –, business- manager; *entrepreneur, impresario*, producer, press agent.

dramatic -author, – writer; play-writer, -wright; dramatist, mimographer; dramatic critic.

V. act, play, perform; stage, produce, put on the stage; personate etc. 554; mimic etc. (*imitate*) 19; enact; play –, act –, go through –, perform- a part; rehearse, spout, gag, rant; 'strut and fret one's hour upon a stage;' tread the -stage, – boards; come out; star.

Adj. dramatic; theatric, -al; scenic, histrionic, anctorial, comic, tragic, buskined, farcical, tragi-comic, melodramatic, operatic; stagey spectacular; stagestruck.

Adv. on the -stage, – boards; before -the floats, – an audience; in the limelight, behind the footlights; behind the scenes.

600. Will.—N. will, volition, conation, velleity; will and pleasure, free-will; freedom etc. 748; discretion; choice, inclination, intent, purpose, option etc. (*choice*) 609; voluntariness; spontane-ity, -ousness; originality.

pleasure, wish, desire, mind; frame of mind etc. (*inclination*) 602; intention etc. 620; predetermination etc. 611; self-control etc. determination etc. (*resolution*) 604; will-power.

V. will, list; see –, think- -fit; determine etc. (*resolve*) 604; settle etc. (*choose*) 609; volunteer.

have a will of one's own; do what one chooses etc. (*freedom*) 748; have it all one's own way; have one's -will, – own way.

use –, exercise- one's discretion; take -upon oneself, – one's own course, – the law into one's own hands; do -of one's own accord, – upon one's own -responsibility, – authority; take the bit between one's teeth; take responsibility; originate etc. (*cause*) 153.

Adj. voluntary, volitive, volitional, wilful; free etc. 748; optional; discretion-al, -ary; volitient; dictatorial.

minded etc. (*willing*) 602; prepense etc. (*predetermined*) 611; intended etc. 620; autocratic; unbidden etc. (bid etc. 741); spontaneous; original etc. (*causal*) 153.

Adv. voluntarily etc. *adj.*; at -will, – pleasure; *à -volonté*, – *discrétion*; *al piacere*; *ad -libitum*, – *arbitrium*; as -one thinks proper, – it seems good to.

of one's own -accord, – free will; *proprio* –, *suo* –, *ex mero- motu*; out of one's own head; by choice etc. 609; purposely etc. (*intentionally*) 620; deliberately etc. 611.

Phr. *stet pro ratione voluntas*; *sic volo sic jubeo.*

601. Necessity.—N. involuntariness; instinct, blind –, natural- impulse; inborn –, innate- proclivity; the force of circumstances.

necessi-ty, -tation, necessarianism; obligation; compulsion etc. 744; subjection etc. 749; stern –, hard –, dire –, imperious –, inexorable –, iron –, adverse- -necessity, – fate; what must be.

desti-ny, -nation; fatality, fate, *kismet*, doom, foredoom, election, predestination; pre-, fore- ordination; lot, fortune; fatalism, determinism; inevitableness etc. *adj.*; spell etc. 993.

star, -s; planet, -s; astral influence; sky, Fates, Norns, *Parcae*, Sisters three, Clotho, Lachesis, Atropos; book of fate; God's will, will of Heaven; wheel of Fortune, Ides of March, Hobson's choice.

last -shift, – resort; *dernier ressort*; *pis aller* etc. (*substitute*) 147; necessaries etc. (*requirement*) 630.

necess-arian, -itarian; fatalist, determinist; automaton.

V. lie under a necessity; be -fated, – doomed, – destined etc., – in for, – under the necessity of; have no -choice, – alternative; be- obliged –, forced –, driven –, one's -fate etc. *n.*- to; be - pushed to the wall, – driven into a corner, – unable to help, – drawn irresistibly.

destine, doom, foredoom, devote; pre-destine, - ordain; cast a spell etc. 992; necessitate; compel etc. 744.

Adj. necessary; needful etc. (*requisite*) 630.

fated; destined etc. *v.*; fateful; elect; spell-bound.

compulsory etc. (*compel*) 744; uncontrollable, inevitable, unavoidable, irrestible, irrevocable, inexorable, binding; avoid-, resist-less; written in the book of fate.

involuntary, instinctive, automatic, blind, mechanical; un-conscious, -witting, -thinking; unintentional etc. (*undesigned*) 621; impulsive etc. 612.

Adv. necessarily etc. *adv.*; of -necessity, – course; *ex necessitate rei*; needs must; perforce etc. 744; *nolens volens*; will he nil he, willy nilly, *bon gré mal gré*, willing or unwilling, *coûte que coûte*, forcefully.

faute de mieux; by stress of; if need be.

Phr. it cannot be helped; there is no- help for, – helping- it; it -will, – must, – must needs- be, – be so, – have its way; the die is cast; *jacta est alea*; *che sarà sarà*; 'it is written;' one's- days are numbered, – fate is sealed; *Fata obstant*; *diis aliter visum.*

602. Willingness.—N. willingness, voluntariness etc. *adj.*; willing mind, heart.

disposition, inclination, leaning, *animus*; frame of mind, humor, mood, vein; bent etc. (*turn of mind*) 820; *penchant* etc. (*desire*) 865; aptitude etc. 698.

doc-ility, -ibleness, tractability; persuasi-bleness, -bility; pliability etc. (*softness*) 324.

geniality, cordiality; goodwill; alacrity, readiness, earnestness, forwardness, enthusiasm; zeal, eagerness etc. (*desire*) 865.

assent etc. 488; compliance etc. 762; pleasure etc. (*will*) 600.

labor of love, self-appointed task; volunteer, - ing, gratuitous service; unpaid worker, amateur.

V. be -willing etc. *adj.*; incline, lean to, mind, propend; had as lief; lend –, give –, turn- a willing ear; have -a, – half a, – a great- mind to; hold –, cling- to; desire etc. 865.

see –, think- -good, – fit, – proper; acquiescence etc. (*assent*) 488; comply with etc. 762.

swallow –, nibble at- the bait; gorge the hook; swallow hook, line and sinker; have –, make- no scruple of; make no bones of; jump –, catch- at; meet half way; volunteer, offer oneself etc. 763.

Adj. willing, minded, fain, disposed, inclined, favorable, favorably- minded, -inclined, -disposed; nothing loth; in the -vein, – mood, – humor, – mind.

ready, forward, enthusiastic, earnest, eager; bent upon etc. (*desirous*) 865; predisposed, propense.

docile; persua-dable, -sible; suasible, easily persuaded, facile, easy-going; amenable; tractable etc. (*pliant*) 324; genial, gracious, cordial, hearty; content etc. (*assenting*) 488.

voluntary, gratuitous, spontaneous; unasked etc. (ask etc. 765); unforced etc. (*free*) 748.

Adv. willing etc. *adj.*; fain, freely, as lief, heart and soul; with -pleasure, – all one's heart, – open arms; with -good, – right good- will; *de bonne volonté, ex animo*; *con amore*, heart in hand, nothing loth, without reluctance, of one's own accord, graciously, with a good grace, without demur.

à la bonne heure; by all -means, – manner of means; to one's heart's content; yes etc. (*assent*) 488.

Int. sure, -ly! of course!

603. Unwillingness.—**N.** unwillingness etc. *adj.*; indispos-ition, -edness; disinclination, aversation, aversion; nolleity, nolition; renitence; reluctance; indifference etc. 866; backwardness etc. *adj.*; slowness etc. 275; want of -alacrity, – readiness; indocility etc. (*obstinacy*) 606.

scrupul-ousness, -osity; qualms of conscience, delicacy, demur, scruple, qualm, shrinking, recoil; hesitation etc. (*irresolution*) 605; fastidiousness etc. 868.

averseness etc. (*dislike*) 867; dissent etc. 489; refusal etc. 764.

slacker, scrimshanker, *embusqué*, unwilling worker, forced labor.

V. be -unwilling etc. *adj.*; nill; dislike etc. 867; grudge, begrudge; not be able to find it in one's heart to, not have the stomach to.

demur, stick at, scruple, stickle; hang fire, run rusty, slack, shirk, scamp, give up, fight shy of, not pull fair; recoil, shrink, swerve; hesitate etc. 605; avoid etc. 623.

oppose etc. 708; dissent etc. 489; refuse etc. 764.

Adj. unwilling; not in the vein, loth, shy of, disinclined, indisposed, averse, reluctant, not content; adverse etc. (*opposed*) 708; laggard, backward, remiss, slack, slow to; renitent; indifferent etc. 866; scrupulous; squeamish etc. (*fastidious*) 868; repugnant etc. (*dislike*) 867; rest-iff, -ive; demurring etc. *v.*; unconsenting etc. (*refusing*) 764; involuntary etc. 601; grudging, irreconcilable.

Adv. unwilling etc. *adj.*; grudgingly, with a heavy heart; with -a bad, – an ill- grace; against –, sore against- -one's wishes, – one's will, – the grain; *invitâ Minervâ*; *à contre coeur*; *malgré soi*; in spite of -one's teeth, – oneself; *nolens volens* etc. (*necessity*) 601; perforce etc. 744; under protest; no etc. 536; not for the world, far be it from me; not if I can help it; if I must I must.

604. Resolution.—**N.** determination, will; iron –, unconquerable- will; will of one's own, decision, resolution, backbone, grit; strength of -mind, – will; resolve etc. (*intent*) 620; *intransigeance*; firmness etc. (*stability*) 150; energy, manliness, vigor; game, pluck; resoluteness etc. (*courage*) 861; zeal etc. 682; *aplomb*; desperation; devot-ion, -edness.

mastery over self; self-control, -command, -mastery, -possession, -reliance, -government, -restraint, -conquest, -denial; moral -courage, – strength, – fiber; perseverance etc. 604*a*; tenacity; obstinacy etc. 606; bull-dog; British lion.

V. have -determination etc. *n.*; know one's own mind; be -resolved etc. *adj.*; make up one's mind, will resolve, determine; decide etc. (*judgment*) 480; form –, come to- a -determination, – resolution, – resolve; conclude, fix, seal, determine once for all, bring to a crisis, drive matters to an extremity; take a decisive step etc. (*choice*) 609; take upon oneself etc. (*undertake*) 676.

devote oneself –, give oneself up- to; throw away the scabbard, kick down the ladder, nail one's colors to the mast, set one's back against the wall, set one's teeth, put one's foot down, burn one's bridges, take one's stand; stand firm etc. (*stability*) 150; steel oneself; stand no nonsense, not listen to the voice of the charmer.

buckle to; put –, lay –, set- one's shoulder to the wheel; put one's heart into; run the gantlet, make a dash at, take the bull by the horns; beard the lion in his den; rush –, *plunge- in medias res*; go in for; insist upon, make a point of; set one's heart, – mind- upon.

stick at nothing; make short work of etc. (*activity*) 682; not stick at trifles; go -all lengths, – the whole hog; persist etc. (*persevere*) 604*a*; go down with colors flying, die game; go through fire and water, ride in the whirlwind and direct the storm.

Adj. resolved etc. *v.* determined; strong-willed, -minded; resolute etc. (*brave*) 861; self-possessed, plucky, tenacious; decided, definitive, peremptory; un-hesitating, -flinching, -shrinking; firm, cast iron, indomitable, game to the backbone; inexorable, relentless, not to be -shaken, – put down; *tenax propositi*; inflexible etc. (*hard*) 323; obstinate etc. 606; steady etc. (*persevering*) 604*a*; unbending, unyielding, irrevocable; firm as a rock; grim.

earnest, serious; set –, bent –, intent- upon.

steeled –, proof- against; *in utrumque paratus.*

Adv. resolutely etc. *adj.*; in –, in good- earnest; seriously, joking apart, earnestly, heart and soul; on one's metal; manfully, like a man, with a high hand; with a strong hand etc. (*exertion*) 686.

at any -rate, – risk, – hazard, – price, – cost, – sacrifice; at all -hazards, – risks, – events; cost what it may; *coûte que coûte*; *à tort et à travers*; once for all; neck or nothing; rain or shine; with colors nailed to the mast.

Phr. *spes sibi quisque.*

604a. Perseverance. —**N.** perseverance; continuance etc. (*inaction*) 143; permanence etc. (*absence of change*) 141; firmness etc. (*stability*) 150.

constancy, steadiness; singleness –, tenacity- of purpose; persistence, plodding, patience; sedulity etc. (*industry*) 682; pertina-cy, -city, -ciousness; iteration etc. 104.

bottom, game, pluck, stamina, backbone, grit; indefatiga-bility, -bleness; bulldog courage.

V. persevere, persist; hold -on, – out; die in the last ditch, be in at the death; stick –, cling –, adhere- to; stick to one's text, keep on; keep to –, maintain- one's -course, – ground; bear –, keep –, hold-up; plod; stick to work etc. (*work*) 686;

continue etc. 143; follow up; die -in harness, – at one's post.

Adj. persevering, constant; stead-y, -fast; undeviating, -wavering, -faltering, -swerving, -flinching, -sleeping, -flagging, -drooping; steady as time; uninter-, un-remitting; plodding; industrious etc. 682; strenuous etc. 686; pertinacious; persisting, -ent.

solid, sturdy, staunch, stanch, ture to oneself; unchangeable etc. 150; unconquerable etc. (*strong*) 159; indomitable, game to the last, indefatigable, untiring, unwearied, never tiring.

Adv. through -evil report and good report, – thick and thin, – fire and water; *per fas et nefas*; without fail, sink or swim, at any price, *vogue la galère*; in sickness and in health.

Phr. never say die; *vestigia nulla retrorsum*.

605. Irresolution.—N. irresolution, infirmity of purpose, indecision; in-, un-determination, loss of will power; unsettlement; uncertainty etc. 475; demur, suspense; hesi-tating etc. *v.*, -tation, -tancy; vacillation; ambivalence; changeableness etc. 149; fluctuation; alternation etc. (*oscillation*) 314; caprice etc. 608; lukewarmness.

fickleness, levity, *légèreté*; pliancy etc. (*softness*) 324; weakness; timidity etc. 860; cowardice etc. 862; half measures.

waverer, ass between two bundles of hay; shuttlecock, butterfly; timeserver, opportunist, turn coat.

V. be -irresolute etc. *adj.*; hang –, keep- in suspense; heave '*ad referendum*;' think twice about, pause; dawdle etc. (*inactivity*) 683; remain neuter; dilly dally. hesitate, boggle, hover, wobble, shilly-shally, hum and haw, demur, not know one's own mind; debate, balance; dally –, coquet- with; will and will not, *chasser-balancer*; go half-way, compromise, make a compormise; be thrown off one's balance, stagger like a drunken man; be afraid etc. 860; let 'I dare not' wait upon 'I would;' falter, waver.

vacillate etc. 149; change etc. 140; retract etc. 607; fluctuate; alternate etc. (*oscillate*) 314; keep off and on, play fast and loose; blow hot and cold etc. (*caprice*) 608.

shuffle, palter, blink; trim.

Adj. irresolute, infirm of purpose, double-minded, half-hearted; un-decided, -resolved, -determined; drifting; shilly-shally; fidgety, tremulous; wobbly; hesitating etc. *v.*; off one's balance; at a loss etc. (*uncertain*) 475.

vacillating etc. *v.*; unsteady etc. (*changeable*) 149; unsteadfast, fickle, unreliable, irresponsible, unstable, without ballast; capricious etc. 608; volatile, frothy; light, -some, -minded; giddy; fast and loose.

weak, feeble-minded, frail; timid etc. 860; cowardly etc. 862; facile; pliant etc. (*soft*) 324; unable to say 'no,' easy-going.

revocable, reversible.

Adv. irresolutely etc. *adj.*; irresolvedly; in faltering accents; off and on; from pillar to post; see-saw etc. 314.

Int. 'how happy could I be with either!'

606. Obstinacy.—N. obstinateness etc. *adj.*; obstinacy, tenacity; perseverance etc. 604*a*; immovability; old school; inflexibility etc. (*hardness*) 323; obdur-acy, -ation; dogged resolution; resolution etc. 604; ruling passion; blind side.

self-will, contumacy, perversity; pervica-cy, -city; indocility.

bigotry, intolerance, dogmatism; opinia-try, -tiveness; fixed idea etc.; intractibility, incorrigibility; (*prejudgment*) 481; fanaticism, zealotry, infatuation, monomania, opinionativeness.

mule; opin-ionist, -ionatist, -iator, -ator; stickler, dogmatist, die-hard, bitter-ender; bigot; zealot, enthusiast, fanatic.

V. be -obstinate etc. *adj.*; stickle, take no denial, fly in the face of facts; opinionate, be wedded to an opinion, hug a belief; have one's own way etc. (*will*) 600; persist etc. (*persevere*) 604*a*; have –, insist on having- the last word.

die -hard, – fighting, fight -against destiny, – to the last ditch; not yield an inch, stand out.

Adj. obstinate, tenacious, stubborn, obdurate, case-hardened; inflexible etc. (*hard*) 323; immovable, not to be moved; inert etc. 172; unchangeable etc. 150; inexorable etc. (*determined*) 604; mulish, obstinate as a mule, pig-headed.

dogged; sullen, sulky; un-moved, -influenced, -affected.

wilful, self-willed, perverse; res-ty, -tive, -tiff; pervicacious, wayward, refractory, unruly; head-y, -strong; *entete*; contumacious; cross-grained.

arbitrary, dogmatic, opinionated, positive, bigoted; prejudiced etc. 481; prepossessed, infatuated; stiff-backed, -necked, -hearted; hard-mouthed, hidebound; unyielding; im-pervious, -practicable, -persuasible; unpersuadable; in-, untractable; incorrigible, deaf to advice, impervious to reason; crotchety etc. 608.

Adv. obstinately etc. *adj.*

Phr. *non possumus*; no surrender.

607. Tergiversation.—N. change of -mind, – intention, – purpose; afterthought.

tergiversation, recantation; palinode, -ody; renunciation; abjur-ation, -ement; defection etc. (*relinquishment*) 624; going over etc. *v.*; apostasy; retract-ion, -ation; withdrawal, disavowal etc. (*negation*) 536; revo-cation, -kement; reversal; repentance etc. 950; *redintegratio amoris*.

coquetry, flirtation; vacillation etc. 605; backsliding, recidivation.

turn-coat, | -tippet; rat, apostate, renegade, mugwump; con-, per-vert; proselyte, deserter; backslider, recidivist; black leg.

time-server, -pleaser; timist, Vicar of Bray, trimmer, ambidexter; weathercock etc. (*changeable*) 149; Janus.

V. change one's -mind, – intention, – purpose, – note; abjure, renounce; withdraw from etc. (*relinquish*) 624; wheel –, turn –, veer- round; turn a *pirouette*; go over –, pass –, change –, skip- from one side to another; go to the right about; box the compass, shift one's ground, go upon another tack; back down, crawl, crawfish.

apostatize, change sides, go over, rat; recant, retract; revoke; rescind etc. (*abrogate*) 756; recall, forswear, abjure, unsay; come -over, – round- to an opinion.

draw in one's horns, eat one's words; eat –,

swallow- the leek; swerve, flinch, back out of, retrace one's steps, think better of it; come back –, return- to one's first love; turn over a new leaf etc. (*repent*) 950.

trim, shuffle, play fast and loose, blow hot and cold, coquet, flirt, hold with the hare but run with the hounds; straddle; *nager entre deux eaux*; wait to see how the -cat jumps, – wind blows.

Adj. changeful etc. 149; irresolute etc. 605; ductile, slippery as an eel, trimming, ambidextrous, timeserving; coquetting etc. *v.*

revocatory, reactionary.

Phr. 'a change came o'er the spirit of my dream.'

608. Caprice.—N. caprice, fancy, humor; whim, -sey, -wham; crotchet, *capriccio*, quirk, freak, maggot, fad, vagary, prank, fit, flim-flam, *escapade*, *boutade*, wild-goose chase; capriciousness etc. *adj.*; kink.

V. be -capricious etc. *adj.*; have a maggot in the brain; take it into one's head, strain at a gnat and swallow a camel; blow hot and cold; play -fast and loose, – fantastic tricks.

Adj. capricious; erratic, eccentric, fitful, hysterical; full of -whims etc. *n.*; maggoty; inconsistent, fanciful, fantastic, whimsical, crotchety, particular, humorsome, freakish, skittish, wanton, wayward; contrary; captious; arbitrary; unrestrained, undisciplined; not amenable to reason; uncomfortable etc. 83; penny wise and pound foolish; fickle etc. (*irresolute*) 605; frivolous, sleeveless, giddy, volatile.

Adv. by fits and starts, without rhyme or reason, at one's own sweet will.

Phr. *nil fuit unquam six impar sibi*; the deuce is in him.

609. Choice.—N. choice, option; discretion etc. (*volition*) 600; preoption; alternative; dilemma; *ambarras de choix*; adoption, cooptation; novation; decision etc. (*judgment*) 480.

election, poll, ballot, vote, voice, suffrage, plumper, cumulative vote; *plebiscitum*, *plébiscite*, *vox populi*; *referendum*, electioneering; voting etc. *v.*; franchise; ballot box; slate, ticket.

selection, excerption, gleaning, eclecticism; *excerpta*, gleanings, cuttings, scissors and paste; pick etc. (*best*) 650.

preference, prelation; predilection etc. (*desire*) 865.

V. offer for one's choice, set before; hold out –, present –, offer- the alternative; put to the vote.

use –, exercise –, one's- -discretion, – option; adopt, take up, embrace, espouse; choose, elect, coopt; take –, make- one's choice; make choice of, fix upon.

vote, poll, hold up one's hand; divide.

settle; decide etc. (*adjudge*) 480; list etc. (*will*) 600; make up one's mind etc. (*resolve*) 604.

select; pick, – and choose; pick –, single- out, excerpt; cull, glean, winnow; sift –, separate –, winnow- the chaff from the wheat; pick up, pitch upon; pick one's way; indulge one's fancy.

set apart, reserve, mark out for; mark etc. 550.

prefer; have -rather, – as lief; fancy etc. (*desire*) 865; be persuaded etc. 615.

take a -decided, – decisive- step; commit oneself to a course; pass –, cross- the Rubicon; cast in one's lot with; take for better or for worse.

Adj. optional; co-optative; discretional etc (*voluntary*) 600; on approval.

ecletic; choosing etc. *v.*; preferential; chosen etc. *v.*; choice etc. (*good*) 648.

Adv. optionally etc. *adj.*; at pleasure etc. (*will*) 600; either, – the one or the other; or; at the option of; whether or not; once for all; for one's money.

by -choice, – preference; in preference; rather, before.

609a. Absence of Choice.—N. no –, Hobson's- choice; first come, first served; necessity etc. 601; not a pin to choose etc. (*equality*) 27; any, the first that comes.

neutrality, indifference; indecision etc. (*irresolution*) 605.

V. be -neutral etc. *adj.*; have no choice; waive, not vote; abstain –, refrain- from voting; leave undecided; make a virtue of necessity.

Adj. neu-tral, -ter; indifferent; undecided etc. (*irresolute*) 605.

Adv. either etc. (*choice*) 609.

610. Rejection.—N. rejection, repudiation, exclusion; declination; refusal etc. 764.

V. reject; set –, lay- aside; give up; decline etc. (*refuse*) 764; exclude, except, eliminate; pluck, spin; cast.

repudiate, scout, set at naught; fling –, cast –, thrown –, toss- -to the winds, – to the dogs, – overboard, – away; send to the right about; disclaim etc. (*deny*) 536; discard etc. (*eject*) 297, (*have done with*) 678.

Adj. rejected etc. *v.*; reject-aneous, -itious; not -chosen etc. 609, – to be thought of; out of the question.

Adv. neither, – the one nor the other; no etc. 536.

Phr. *non haec in foedera*.

611. Predetermination.—N. premeditation, -deliberation, -determination, -destination; foreordination; foregone conclusion; *parti pris*; resolve, propendency; intention etc. 620; project etc. 626.

V. pre-determine, -destine, -meditate, -resolve, -concert; foreordain; resolve beforehand.

Adj. pre-pense, -meditated etc. *v.*, -designed; advised, studied, designed, calculated; aforethought; intended etc. 620; foregone.

well-laid, -devised, -weighed; maturely considered; cut and dried; cunning.

Adv. advisedly etc. *adj.*; with premeditation, deliberately, all things considered, with eyes open, in cold blood; intentionally etc. 620.

612. Impulse.—N. impulse, sudden thought; *impromptu*, improvisation; inspiration, hunch, flash, spurt.

improvisatore, *improvisatrice*, improviser, extemporizer; creature of impulse.

V. flash on the mind.

say what comes uppermost; improvise, extemporize; rise to the occasion; spurt.

Adj. extemporaneous, impulsive, indeliberate; improvis-ed, -ate, -atory; un-, unpre-meditated; *improvisé*; unprompted, -guided; natural, unguarded; spontaneous etc. (*voluntary*) 600; instinctive etc. 601.

Adv. extem-pore, -poraneously; offhand, *impromptu*, *à l'improviste*; improviso; on the spur of the -moment, – occasion.

613. Habit.—N. habit, -ude; assuetude, -faction; wont; run, way.

common –, general –, natural –, ordinary –, habitual- -course, – run, – state- of things; matter of course; beaten -path, – track, – ground.

prescription, custom, use, usage, immemorial usage, practice; tradition; prevalence, observance; conventionalism, -ity; mode, fashion, vogue; *etiquette* etc. (*gentility*) 852; order of the day, cry; conformity etc. 82.

habitué, addict.

one's old way, old school, consuetude, *veteris vestigia flammae*; *laudator temporis acti*.

rule, standing order, precedent, routine; red-tape, -tapism; pipe-clay; rut, groove.

cacoëthes; bad –, confirmed –, inveterate –, intrinsic etc. 5- habit; addiction, trick.

training etc. (*education*) 537; seasoning, hardening, inurement; radication; second nature, acclimatization; knack etc. (*skill*) 698.

V. be -wont etc. *adj.*

fall into a custom etc. (*conform to*) 82; tread –, follow- the beaten -track, – path; *stare super antiquas vias*; move in a rut, run on in a groove, go round like a horse in a mill, go on in the old jobtrot way.

habituate, inure, harden, season, caseharden; accustom, familiarize; naturalize, acclimatize; keep one's hand in; train etc. (*educate*) 537.

get into the -way, – knack- of; learn etc. 539; cling –, adhere- to; repeat etc. 104; acquire –, contract –, fall into- a -habit, – trick; addict oneself –, take- to; accustom oneself to.

be -habitual etc. *adj.*; prevail; come into use, become a habit, take root; gain –, grow- upon one.

Adj. habitual; ac-, customary; prescriptive; accustomed etc. *v.*; traditional; of -daily, – everyday- occurrence; wonted, usual, general, ordinary, common, frequent, every-day, household, jog-trot; well-trodden, -known; familiar, vernacular, trite, commonplace, banal, bromidic, conventional, regular, set, stock, officinal, established, stereotyped; pre-vailing, -valent; current, received, acknowledged, recognized, accredited; of course, admitted, understood.

conformable etc. 82; according to -use, – custom, – routine; in -vogue, – fashion; fashionable etc. (*genteel*) 852.

wont; used – given – addicted –, attuned –, habituated etc. *v.*- to; in the habit of; *habitué*; at home in etc. (*skilful*) 698; seasoned; permeated –, imbued- with; devoted –, wedded- to; never free from.

hackneyed, fixed, rooted, deep-rooted, ingrafted, permanent, inveterate, besetting; naturalized; ingrained etc. (*intrinsic*) 5.

Adv. habitually etc. *adj.*; always etc. (*uniformly*) 16.

as -usual, – is one's wont, – things go, – the world goes, – the sparks fly upwards; *more -suo*, – *solito*.

as a rule, for the most part; generally etc. *adj.*; most often, – frequently.

Phr. *cela s'entend*.

614. Desuetude.—N. desuetude, disusage; disuse etc. 678; want of -habit, – practice; inusitation; newness to; new brooms.

infraction of usage etc. (*unconformity*) 83; non-prevalence; 'a custom more honored in the breach than the observance.'

V. be -unaccustomed etc. *adj.*; leave off –, cast off –, break off –, wean oneself of –, violate –, break through –, infringe- -a habit, – a custom, – a usage; break one's fetters; disuse etc. 678; wear off.

Adj. un-accustomed, -used, -wonted, -seasoned, -inured, -habituated, -trained; new; green etc. (*unskilled*) 699; fresh, original, unhackneyed.

unusual etc. (*unconformable*) 83; unconventional, non-observant; disused etc. 678.

Adv. just for once.

615. Motive.—N. motive, springs of action.

reason, ground, call, principle; mainspring, *primum mobile*, key-stone; the why and the wherefore; *pro* and *con*, reason why; secret –, ulterior- motive, *arrière-pensée*; intention etc. 620.

inducement, consideration; attraction etc. 288; loadstone; magnet, -ism, -ic force; allect-ation, -ive; temptation, enticement, *agacerie*, allurement, witchery; bewitch-ment, -ery; charm; spell etc. 993; fascination, blandishment, cajolery; seduc-tion, -ement; honeyed words, voice of the tempter, son of the Sirens; forbidden fruit, golden apple.

persuasi-bility, -bleness; attractability; impress-, suscept-ibility; softness; persuas-, attract-iveness; tantalization.

influence, prompting, dictate, instance; impuls-e, -ion; incit-ement, -ation; press, instigation; provocation etc. (*excitation of feeling*) 824; inspiration; per-, suasion; encouragement, advocacy; exhortation, advice etc. 695; solicitation etc. (*request*) 765; lobbying.

incentive, stimulus, spur, fillip, whip, goad, rowel, provocative, whet, dram.

bribe, lure; decoy, – duck; bait, trail of a red herring; bribery and corruption; sop, – for Cerberus.

prompter, tempter; seduc-er, -tor; suggester, coaxer, wheedler; instigator, firebrand, incendiary; Siren, Circe; *agent provocateur*; lobbyist.

V. induce, move; draw, – on; bring in its train, give an -impulse etc. *n.*- to; inspire; put up to, prompt, call up; attract, beckon.

stimulate etc. (*excite*) 824; spirit up, inspirit; a-, rouse; ecphorize; animate, incite, provoke, instigate, set on, actuate; act –, work –, operate-upon; encourage; pat –, clap- on the -back, – shoulder.

influence, weigh with, bias, sway, incline, dispose, predispose, turn the scale, inoculate; lead, – by the nose; have –, exercise- influence- -with, – over, – upon; go –, come- round one; turn the head, magnetize.

persuade; prevail -with, – upon; overcome, carry; bring -round, – to one's senses; draw –, win –, gain –, come –, talk- over; procure, enlist, engage; invite, court.

tempt, seduce, overpersuade, entice, allure, captivate, fascinate, intrigue, bewitch, carry away, charm, conciliate, wheedle, coax, lure, suggest; inveigle; tantalize; cajole etc. (*deceive*) 545.

tamper with, bribe, suborn, grease the palm, bait with a silver hook, gild the pill, make things pleasant, put a sop into the pan, throw a sop to, bait the hook.

enforce, force; impel etc. (*push*) 276; propel etc. 284; whip, lash, goad, spur, prick, urge; egg –, hound –, hurry- on; drag etc. 285; exhort; advise etc. 695; call upon etc.; press etc. (*request*) 765; advocate.

set -an example, – the fashion; keep in countenance; back up.

be -persuaded etc.; yield to temptation, come round; concede etc. (*consent*) 762; obey a call; follow -advice, – the bent, – the dictates of; act on principle.

Adj. impulsive, motive; suas-, persuas-, hortat-ive, -ory; protreptical; inviting, tempting etc. *v.*; seductive, attractive, irresistible; fascinating etc. (*pleasing*) 829; provocative etc. (*exciting*) 824.

induced etc. *v.*; disposed; persuadable etc. (*docile*) 602; spellbound; instinct –, smitten- with; inspired etc. *v.*- by.

Adv. because, therefore etc. (*cause*) 155; from -this, – that- motive; for -this, – that- reason; for; by reason –, for the sake –, on the score –, on account of; out of, from, as, forasmuch as.

for all the world; on principle.

615a. Absence of Motive.—**N.** absence of motive; caprice etc. 608; chance etc. (*absence of design*) 621.

V. have no motive, scruple etc. (*be unwilling*) 603.

Adj. without rhyme or reason; aimless etc. (*chance*) 621.

Adv. capriciously; out of mere caprice.

616. Dissuasion.—**N.** dissuasion, dehortation, expostulation, remonstrance; deprecation etc. 766.

discouragement, damper, wet blanket; warning.

cohibition etc. (*restraint*) 751; curb etc. (*means of restraint*) 752; check etc. (*hindrance*) 706.

reluctance etc. (*unwillingness*) 603; contraindication.

V. dissuade, dehort, cry out against, remonstrate, expostulate, warn, contraindicate.

disincline, indispose, shake, stagger; dispirit; discourage, -hearten, -enchant; deter; hold –, keep-back etc. (*restrain*) 751; render -averse etc. 603; repel; turn aside etc. (*deviation*) 279; wean from; act as a drag etc. (*hinder*) 706; throw cold water on, damp, cool, chill, blunt, calm, quiet, quench; deprecate etc. 766.

Adj. dissuading etc. *v.*; dissuasive; dehortatory, expostulatory; monit-ive, -ory.

dissuaded etc. *v.*; uninduced etc. (induce etc. 615); unpersuadable etc. (*obstinate*) 606; averse etc. (*unwilling*) 603; repugnant etc. (*dislike*) 867.

617. Plea. [Ostensible motive, ground, or reason assigned.]—**N.** plea, pretext; allegation, advocation; ostensible -motive, – ground, – reason; excuse etc. (*vindication*) 937; color; gloss, guise.

loop-, starting-hole; how to creep out of, salvo, come off.

handle, peg to hang on room, *locus standi*; stalking horse, *cheval de bataille*, cue.

pretence etc. (*untruth*) 546; put off, subterfuge, dust thrown in the eyes; blind; moonshine; mere –, shallow- pretext; lame -excuse, – apology, tub to a whale; flase plea, sour grapes; makeshift, shift, white lie; special pleading etc. (*sophistry*) 477; soft sawder etc. (*flattery*) 933.

V. plead, allege; shelter oneself under the plea of; excuse etc. (*vindicate*) 937; gloss over; lend a color to; furnish a -handle etc. *n.*; make a -pretext, – handle- of; use as a plea etc. *n.*; take one's stand upon, make capital out of; pretend etc. (*lie*) 544.

Adj. ostensible etc. (*manifest*) 525; excusing; alleged, apologetic; pretended etc. 545.

Adv. ostensibly; under -color, – the plea, – the pretence- of.

618. Good.—**N.** good, benefit, advantage; improvement etc. 658; interest, service, behoof, behalf; weal; main chance, *summum bonum*, common weal; 'consummation devoutly to be wished;' gain, boot; profit, harvest.

boon etc. (*gift*) 784; good turn; blessing, benison; world of good; piece of good -luck, – fortune; nuts, prize, windfall, godsend, waif, treasure trove.

good fortune etc. (*prosperity*) 734; happiness etc. 827.

[Source of good] goodness etc. 648; utility etc. 644; remedy etc. 662; pleasure-giving etc. 829.

Adj. commendable etc. 931; useful etc. 644; good etc., beneficial etc. 648.

V. benefit, profit, advantage, serve, help, avail; do good to, gain, prosper, flourish.

Adv. well, aright, satisfactorily, favorably, not amiss; all for the best; to one's -advantage etc. *n.*; in one's -favor, – interest etc. *n.*

Phr. so far so good.

619. Evil.—**N.** evil, ill, harm, hurt, mischief, nuisance; machinations of the devil, Pandora's box, ills that flesh is heir to.

blow, buffet, stroke, scratch, bruise, wound, gash, mutilation; mortal -blow, – wound; *im-*

medicabile vulnus; damage, loss etc. (*deterioration*) 659.

disadvantage, prejudice, drawback.

disaster, accident, casualty; mishap etc. (*misfortune*) 735; bad job, devil to pay; calamity, bale, woe, catastrophe, tragedy; ruin etc. (*destruction*) 162; adversity etc. 735.

mental suffering etc. 828. [Evil spirit] demon etc. 980. [Cause of evil] bane etc. 663. [Production of evil] badness etc. 649; painfulness etc. 830; evil doer etc. 913.

outrage, wrong, injury, foul play; bad –, ill-turn; disservice; spoliation etc. 791; grievance, crying evil.

V. be in trouble etc. (*adversity*) 735; harm, injure, hurt, do disservice to.

Adj. disastrous, bad etc. 649; awry, out of joint; disadvantageous, injurious, harmful.

Adv. amiss, wrong, ill, to one's cost.

620. Intention.—N. intent, -ion, -ionality; purpose; *quo animo*; project etc. 626; undertaking etc. 676; predetermination etc. 611; design, ambition.

contemplation, mind, *animus*, view, purview, proposal; study; look out.

final cause; *raison d'être*; *cui bono*; object, aim, end; 'the be all and the end all;' drift etc. (*meaning*) 516; tendency etc. 176; destination, mark, point, butt, goal, target, bull's-eye, quintain; prey, quarry, game.

decision, determination, resolve; set –, settled-purpose; *ultimatum*; resolution etc. 604; wish etc. 865; *arrière-pensée*; motive etc. 615.

[Study of final causes] teleology.

V. intend, purpose, design, mean; have to; propose to oneself; harbor a design; have in -view, – contemplation, – one's eye, – *petto*; have an eye to.

bid –, labor- for; be –, aspire –, endeavour-after; be –, aim –, drive –, point –, level- at; take aim; set before oneself; study to.

take upon oneself etc. (*undertake*) 676; take into one's head; meditate, contemplate; think –, dream –, talk- of; premeditate etc. 611; compass, calculate; dest-ine, -inate, propose.

project etc. (*plan*) 626; have a mind to etc. (*be willing*) 602; desire etc. 865; pursue etc. 622.

Adj. intended etc. *v.*; intentional, advised, express, determinate; prepense etc. 611; bound for; intending etc. *v.*; minded, disposed, inclined; bent upon etc. (*earnest*) 604; at stake, on the -anvil, – *tapis*; in -view; – prospect, – the breast of; *in petto*; teleological.

Adv. intentionally etc. *adj.*; advisedly, wittingly, knowingly, designedly, purposely, on purpose, by design, studiously, pointedly; with -intent etc. *n.*; deliberately etc. (*with premeditation*) 611; with one's eyes open, in cold blood.

for; with -a view, – an eye- to; in order -to, – that; to the end –, with the intent- that; for the purpose –, with the view –, in contemplation –, on account- of.

in pursuance of, pursuant to; *quo animo*; to all intents and purposes.

621. Chance.† [Absence of purpose in the succession of events.]—**N.** chance etc. 156; lot, fate etc. (*necessity*) 601; luck; good luck etc. (*good*) 618; bad luck etc. 735; wheel of fortune; mascot; swastika.

speculation, venture, stake, flutter, flier, gamble, game of chance; mere –, random- shot; blind bargain, leap in the dark; pig in a poke etc. (*uncertainty*) 475; fluke, pot-luck.

drawing lots; sorti-legy, -tion; *sortes*, – *Virgilianae*; *rouge et noir*, hazard, *roulette*, pitch and toss, chuck-farthing, cup-tossing, heads or tails, cross and pile, wager; bet, -ting; risk, stake, plunge; gambling; the turf.

stock exchange, bourse, board of trade, curb exchange.

gaming-, gambling-, betting-house; hell; betting ring, totalizator; dice, – box; dicer; gam-bler, -ester, plunger, stock operator, manipulator, punter; man of the turf; adventurer, speculator; bookmaker, layer, backer.

V. chance etc. (*hap*) 156; stand a chance etc. (*be possible*) 470.

toss up; cast –, draw- lots; leave –, trust- -to chance, – to the chapter of accidents; tempt fortune; chance it, take one's chance; run –, incur –, encounter- the -risk, – chance; stand the hazard of the die.

speculate, try one's luck, set on a cast, raffle, put into a lottery, buy a pig in a poke, shuffle the cards.

risk, venture, hazard, stake; lay, – a wager; make a bet, wager, bet, gamble, game, play for; play at chuck-farthing.

Adj. fortuitous etc. 156; unintentional, -ded; accidental; not meant; un-designed, -purposed; unpremeditated etc. 612; never thought of.

indiscriminate, promiscuous; undirected, random; aim-, drift-, design-, purpose-, cause-less; without purpose.

possible etc. 470.

Adv. casually etc. 156; unintentionally etc. *adj.*; unwittingly.

en passant, by the way, incidentally; as it may happen; at -random, – a venture, – haphazard; as luck would have it, by -chance, – good fortune; un-, -luckily.

† See note on 156.

622. Pursuit. [Purpose in action.]—**N.** pursuit; pursuing etc. *v.*; prosecution; pursuance; enterprise etc. (*undertaking*) 676; business etc. 625; adventure etc. (*essay*) 675; quest etc. (*search*) 461; scramble, hue and cry, game; hobby.

chase, hunt, *battue*, race, steeplechase, hunting, coursing; ven-ation, -ery; fox-chase; sport, -ing; shooting, angling, fishing, hawking.

pursuer; hunt-er, -sman; sportsman, Nimrod, the field; hound etc. 366.

V. pursue, prosecute, follow; run –, make –, be –, hunt – prowl- after; shadow; carry on etc. (*do*) 680; engage in etc. (*undertake*) 676; set about etc. (*begin*) 66; endeavor etc. 675; court etc. (*request*) 765; seek etc. (*search*) 461; aim at etc. (*intention*) 620; follow the trail etc. (*trace*) 461; fish for etc. (*experiment*) 463; press on etc. (*haste*) 684; run a race etc. (*velocity*) 274.

chase, give chase, course, dog, hunt, hound, stalk; tread –, follow- on the heels of etc. (*sequence*) 281.

rush upon; rush headlong etc. (*violence*) 173;

ride –, run- full tilt at; make a leap –, jump –, snatch- at; run down; start game.

tread a path; take –, hold- a course; shape –, direct –, bend- one's -steps, – course; play a game; fight –, elbow- one's way; follow up; take - to, – up; go in for; ride one's hobby.

Adj. pursuing etc. *v.*; in quest of etc. (*inquiry*) 461; in -pursuit, – full cry, – hot pursuit; on the scent.

Adv. in pursuance of etc. (*intention*) 620; after.

Int. tally-ho! yoicks! so-ho!

623. Avoidance. [Absence of pursuit.]—**N.** abst-ention, -inence; forbearance; refraining etc. *v.*; inaction etc. 681; neutrality.

avoidance, evasion, elusion; seclusion etc. 893.

avolation, flight; escape etc. 671; retreat etc. 287; recoil etc. 277; departure etc. 293; rejection etc. 610.

shirker etc. *v.*; slacker; truant; fugitive, refugee; runa-way, -gate; renegade; deserter.

V. abstain, refrain, spare, not attempt; not do etc. 681; maintain the even tenor of one's way.

eschew, keep from, let alone, have nothing to do with; keep –, stand –, hold- -aloof, – off; take no part in, have no hand in.

avoid, shun; steer –, keep- clear of; fight shy of; keep -one's, – at a respectful- distance; keep –, get- out of the way; evade, elude, turn away from; set one's face against etc. (*oppose*) 708; deny oneself.

shrink; hang –, hold –, draw- back; recoil etc. 277; retire etc. (*recede*) 287; flinch, blink, blench, shy, shirk, dodge, parry, make way for, give place to.

beat a retreat; turn -tail, – one's back; take to one's heels; run, -away, – for one's life; cut and run; be off, – like a shot; fly, flee; fly –, flee –, run away- from; take –, take to- flight; desert, elope; make –, scamper –, sneak –, shuffle –, sheer- off; break –, burst –, tear oneself –, slip –, slink –, steal- -away, – away from; slip cable, part company, turn on one's heel; sneak out of, play truant, give one the go by, give leg bail, take French leave, slope, decamp, flit, bolt, abscond, levant, skedaddle, absquatulate, cut one's stick, walk one's chalks, show a light pair of heels, make oneself scarce; escape etc. 671; go away etc. (*depart*) 293; abandon etc. 624; reject etc. 610.

lead one a -dance, – a merry chase, – pretty dance; throw off the scent, play at hide and seek.

Adj. unsought, unattempted; avoiding etc. *v.*; neutral; shy of etc. (*unwilling*) 603; elusive, evasive, distant; fugitive, runaway; shy, wild.

Adj. lest, in order to avoid.

Int. forebear! keep –, hands- off! *sauve qui peut!* devil take the hindmost.

624. Relinquishment.—N. relinquish-, abandon-ment; desertion, defection, secession, withdrawal; cave of Adullam; *nolle prosequi.*

discontinuance etc. (*cessation*) 142; renunciation etc. (*recantation*) 607; abrogation etc. 756; resignation etc. (*retirement*) 757; desuetude etc. 614; cession etc. (*of property*) 782.

V. relinquish, give up, abandon, desert, forsake, leave in the lurch; depart –, secede –, withdraw- from; back – out of, – down from, leave, go back on one's word, quit, take leave of, bid a long farewell; vacate etc. (*resign*) 757.

renounce etc. (*abjure*) 607; forego, have done with, drop; write off; disuse etc. 678; discard etc. 782; wash one's hands of; drop all idea of; *nolle-pros.*; lose interest in.

break –, leave- off; desist; stop etc. (*cease*) 142; hold –, stay- one's hand; quit one's hold; give over, shut up shop.

throw up the -game, – cards; give up the -point, – argument; pass to the order of the day, move the previous question, table the motion.

Adj. unpursued; relinquished etc. *v.*; relinquishing etc. *v.*

Int. avast etc.! (*stop*) 142.

625. Business.—N. business, occupation, employment; pursuit etc. 622; what one is doing-, – about; affair, concern, matter, case, undertaking.

matter in hand, irons in the fire; thing to do, *agendum*, task, work, job, chore, errand, transaction, commission, mission, charge, care; duty etc. 926.

part, *rôle*, cue; province, function, look-out, department, capacity, sphere, orb, field, line; walk, – of life; beat, round, routine; race, career.

office, place, post, incumbency, living situation, appointment, billet, berth, employ; service etc. (*servitude*) 749; engagement; undertaking etc. 676.

vocation, calling, profession, *métier*, cloth, faculty; industry, art; industrial arts; craft, mystery, handicraft; trade etc. (*commerce*) 794.

exercise; work etc. (*action*) 680; avocation; press of business etc. (*activity*) 682.

V. pass –, employ –, spend- one's time in; employ oneself -in, – upon; occupy –, concern- oneself with; make it one's -business etc. *n.*; undertake etc. 676; enter a profession; betake oneself to, turn one's hand to; have to do with etc. (*do*) 680.

drive a trade; carry on –, do –, transact- -business, – a trade etc. *n.*; keep a shop; ply one's task, – trade; labor in one's vocation; pursue the even tenor of one's way; attend to -business, – one's work.

officiate, serve, act; act –, play- one's part; do duty; serve –, discharge –, perform- the -office, – duties, – functions- of; hold –, fill- -an office, – a place, – a situation; hold a portfolio.

be -about, – doing, – engaged in, – employed in, – occupied with, – at work on; have one's hands in, have in hand; have on one's -hands, – shoulders; bear the burden; have one's hands full etc. (*activity*) 682.

be -in the hands of, – on the stocks, – on the anvil; pass through one's hands.

Adj. business-like; work-a-day; professional; official, functional; busy etc. (*actively employed*) 682; on –, in- -hand, – one's hands; afoot; on - foot, – the anvil; going on; acting.

Adv. in the course of business, all in a day's work; professionally etc. *adj.*

626. Plan.—N. plan, scheme, design, project; propos-al, -ition; suggestion; resolution, motion;

precaution etc. (*provision*) 673; deep-laid etc. (*premeditated*) 611- plan etc.; racket.

system etc. (*order*) 58; organization etc. (*arrangement*) 60; germ etc. (*cause*) 153; Five Year Plan.

sketch, skeleton, outline, draught, draft, *ébauche*, *brouillon*; rough-cast, – draft, – draught, – copy; proof, revise.

forecast, *programme*, prospectus, scenario; *carte du pays*; card; bill, protocol; order of the day, list of agenda, *memorandum*; bill of fare etc. (*food*) 298; base of operations; platform, plank.

rôle; policy etc. (*line of conduct*) 692.

contrivance, invention, expedient, receipt, nostrum, artifice, device, gadget; stratagem etc. (*cunning*) 702; trick etc. (*deception*) 545; alternative, loophole, shift etc. (*substitute*) 147; last shift etc. (*necessity*) 601.

measure, step; stroke, – of policy; master stroke; trump-, court-card; *chaval de bataille*, great gun; *coup*, – *d'état*; clever –, bold –, good- -move, – hit, – stroke; bright -thought, – idea, great idea.

intrigue, cabal, plot, frame-up, conspiracy, complot, machination; under-, counter-plot.

schem-ist, -atist; stragetist, machinator, schemer; projector, author, builder, artist, promoter, designer etc. *v.*; conspirator; *intrigant* etc. (*cunning*) 702.

V. plan, scheme, design, frame, contrive, project, forecast, sketch; çonceive, devise, invent etc. (*imagine*) 515; set one's wits to work etc. 515; spring a project; fall –, hit- upon; strike –, chalk –, cut –, lay –, map-out; lay down a plan; shape –, mark- out a course; predetermine etc. 611; concert, preconcert, preestablish; prepare etc. 673; hatch, – a plot; concoct; take -steps, – measures.

cast, recast, systematize, organize; arrange etc. 60; digest, mature.

plot; counter-plot, -mine; dig a mine; lay a train; intrigue etc. (*cunning*) 702.

Adj. planned etc. *v.*; strategic, -al; planning etc. *v.*; in course of preparation etc. 673; under consideration; on the *-tapis*, – carpet, – table.

627. Method. [Path.]—**N.** method, way, manner, wise, gait, form, mole, fashion, tone, guise; *modus operandi*; procedure etc. (*line of conduct*) 692.

path, road, route, course; line of -way, – road; trajectory, orbit, track, beat, tack.

steps; stair, -case; flight of stairs, ladder, stile.

bridge, viaduct, gauntry, pontoon, stepping stone, plank, gangway, catwalk, drawbridge; pass, ford, ferry, tunnel, subway, elevated; pipe etc. 260.

door; gateway etc. (*opening*) 260; channel, passage, avenue, means of access, approach, perron, adit, entrance; artery, lane, alley, aisle, lobby, corridor, cloister; back- door, -stairs; secret passage; covert-way.

road-, path-, stair-way; thoroughfare; highway, pike, turnpike, trail, parkway, *boulevard*; turnpike –, royal –, coach- road; broad –, King's –, Queen's- highway; beaten -track, – path; horse –, bridle- road, – track, – path; pathway; walk, *trottoir*, foot-path, pavement, flags, side-walk; by –, cross- -road, – path, – way; cut; short -cut etc. (*mid-course*) 628; *carrefour*; private –, occupation- road; highways and byways; rail-, tram-road, -way; funicular, ropeway, causeway; defile, cutting; canal etc. (*conduit*) 350; street etc. (*abode*) 189.

Adv. how; in what -way, – manner; by what mode; so, in this way, after this fashion, on these lines.

one way or another, anyhow; somehow or other etc. (*instrumentality*) 631; by way of; *viâ*; *in transitu* etc. 270; on the high road to.

Phr. *hae tibi erunt artes.*

628. Mid-course.—**N.** middle-, mid-course; moderation, mean etc. 29; middle etc. 68; *juste milieu*, *mezzo termine*, golden mean, *aurea mediocritas*.

straight etc. (*direct*) 278 -course, – path; short –, cross- cut; short- circuit; great circle sailing.

neutrality; half –, half and half- measures; compromise.

V. keep in –, steer –, preserve- -a middle, – an even- course; go straight etc. (*direct*) 278.

go half way, compromise, make a compromise.

Adj. neutral, average, even, impartial, moderate, straight etc. (*direct*) 278.

629. Circuit.—**N.** circuit, round-about way, digression, divagation, *détour*, circum-ambience, -ambulation, bendibus, *ambages*, loop; winding etc. (*circuition*) 311; zigzag etc. (*deviation*) 279.

V. perform –, make- a circuit; go -round about, – out of one's way; make a *détour*; meander etc. (*deviate*) 27; circumambulate.

lead a pretty dance; beat about, – the bush; make two bites of a cherry.

adj. circuitous, indirect, round-about; zig-zag etc. (*deviating*) 279; circum-ambient, -ambulatory.

Adv. by -a side wind, – an indirect course; in a roundabout way; from pillar to post.

630. Requirement.—**N.** requirement, need, wants, necessities; necessaries, – of life; stress, exigency, pinch, *sine quâ non*, matter of necessity; case of -need, – life or death.

needfulness, essentiality, necessity, indispensability, urgency, prerequisite.

requisition etc. (*request*) 765, (*exaction*) 741; run upon; demand –, call- for.

desideratum etc. (*desire*) 865; want etc. (*deficiency*) 640.

charge, claim, command, injunction, requisition, mandate, order, *ultimatum*.

V. require, need, want, have occasion for, entail; not be able to -do without, – dispense with; prerequire.

render necessary, necessitate, create a necessity for, call for, put in requisition; make a requisition etc. (*ask for*) 765, (*demand*) 741,

stand in need of; lack etc. 640; desiderate; desire etc. 865; be -necessary etc. *adj.*

Adj. required etc. *v.*; requisite, needful,

necessary, imperative, essential, indispensable, prerequisite; called for; in -demand, – request.

urgent, exigent, pressing, instant, crying, absorbing.

in want of; destitute of etc. 640.

Adv. *ex necessitate rei* etc. (*necessarily*) 601; of –, out of stern- necessity; at a pinch.

Phr. there is no time to lose; it cannot be - spared, – dispensed with.

631. Instrumentality.—N. instrumentality; aid etc. 707; subservien-ce, -cy; mediation, intervention, -mediacy, medium, inter-medium, -mediary, vehicle, hand; agency etc. 170.

minister, handmaid, servant, slave, maid, valet; midwife, *accoucheur*, obstetrician; go-between; cat's paw; stepping-stone.

key; master –, pass –, latch- key; 'open sesame;' passport, *passe partout*, safe-conduct; influence.

instrument etc. 633; expedient etc. (*plan*) 626; means etc. 632.

V. subserve, minister, tend, mediate, intervene; come –, go- between, interpose; pull the strings; be -instrumental etc. *adj.*; pander to.

Adj. instrumental; useful etc. 644; ministerial, subservient, mediatorial; inter-mediate, -vening; conducive.

Adv. through, by, *per*; where-, there-, here-by; by the -agency etc. 170- of; by dint of; by –, in- virtue of; through the -medium etc. *n.*- of; along with; on the shoulders of; by means of etc. 632; by –, with- -the aid etc. (*assistance*) 707- of.

per fas et nefas, by fair means or foul; somehow, – or other; by hook or by crook.

632. Means.—N. means, resources, revenue, wherewithal, ways and means, income; capital etc. (*money*) 800; stock in trade etc. 636; provision etc. 637; a shot in the locker; appliances etc. (*machinery*) 633; means and appliances; conveniences; cards to play; expendients etc. (*measures*) 626; two strings to one's bow; sheet anchor etc. (*safety*) 666; aid etc. 707; medium etc. 631.

V. find –, have –, possess- means etc. *n.*; provide the wherewithal.

Adj. instrumental etc. 631; mechanical etc. 633.

Adv. by means of, with; by -what, – all, – any, – some- means; where-, here-, there-with; wherewithal.

how etc. (*in what manner*) 627; through etc. (*by the instrumentality of*) 631; with –, by- the aid etc. (*assistance*) 707- of; by the -agency etc. 170- of.

633. Instrument.—N. machinery, mechanism, engineering.

instrument, organ, tool, implement, utensil, contrivance, machine, motor, engine, lathe, gin, mill, pump.

gear; tack-le, -ling, trice, rigging, gear, apparatus, appliances; plant, *matériel*; harness, trappings, fittings, accouterments; equip-ment, -age; appointments, furniture, upholstery; chattels; paraphernalia etc. (*belongings*) 780; *impedimenta.*

mechanical powers; lever, -age; mechanical advantage; crow, -bar; handspike, gavelock, jemmy, arm, limb, wing; oar, paddle; pulley, sheave; parbuckle; wheel and axle; wheel-, clock-work; wheels within wheels; pinion, gear wheel, spur –, bevel-gearing, chains, belting, crank, winch, capstan, windlass, crane, derrick, hoist, lift etc. 307; cam; pedal; wheel etc. (*rotation*) 312; inclined plane; wedge; screw; jack; spring, mainspring.

handle, hilt, haft, shaft, heft, shank, blade, trigger, tiller, helm, treadle, key; turnscrew, screwdriver, spanner, wrench.

hammer etc. (*impulse*) 276; edge tool etc. (*cut*) 253; borer etc. 262; vice, teeth etc. (*hold*) 781; nail, rope etc. (*join*) 45; peg etc. (*hang*) 214; support etc. 215; spoon etc. (*vehicle*) 272; arms etc. 727; oar etc. (*navigation*) 267.

Adj. instrumental etc. 631; mechanical, machinal, automatic, self-acting; brachial.

634. Substitute.—N. substitute etc. 147; deputy etc. 759; proxy, alternative, understudy.

635. Materials.—N. material, raw material, stuff, stock, staple; building materials, bricks and mortar; metal; stone; clay, brick; crockery etc. 384; compo, -sition; reinforced –, ferro-, concrete; cement; wood, ore, timber; gravel, cobbles, macadam, asphalt, tarmac.

materials; supplies, munition, fuel, grist, household stuff; *pabulum* etc. (*food*) 298; ammunition etc. (*arms*) 727; contingents; relay, reinforcement; baggage etc. (*personal property*) 780; means etc. 632.

Adj. raw etc. (*unprepared*) 674; wooden etc. *n.*

636. Store.—N. stock, fund, mine, vein, lode, quarry; spring; fount, -ain; well, -spring; milch-cow.

stock in trade, supply; heap etc. (*collection*) 72; treasure; reserve, *corps de réserve*, reserve fund, nest-egg, savings, *bonne bouche*.

crop, harvest, mow, vintage; yield, product, gleanings.

store, accumulation, hoard, rick, stack; lumber; relay etc. (*provision*) 637.

store-house, -room, -closet; depository, *dépôt*, *cache*, safe deposit, vault, pantechnicon, repository, -servatory, -pertory; *repertorium*; promptuary, warehouse, *entrepôt*, magazine, dump, buttery, larder, pantry, panary, lanary, still-room, spence; crib, garner, granary, silo, barn; bunker; thesaurus; bank etc. (*treasury*) 802; armoury; arsenal; dock; gallery, museum, library, conservatory, hot-house; manag-ery, -erie, aquarium, zoological gardens.

reservoir, cistern, tank, sump, pond, mill-pond; gasometer.

budget, quiver, bandolier, portfolio; coffer etc. (*receptacle*) 191.

conservation; storing etc. *v.*; storage.
dictionary etc. 562; list etc. 86.

V. store; put –, lay –, set- by; stow away; set –, lay- apart; store –, hoard –, treasure –, lay –, heap –, put –, garner –, save- up; *cache*; accumulate, amass, hoard, fund, garner, save, bank.
conserve, reserve; keep –, hold- back; husband, – one's resources.
deposit; stow, stack, load, dump; harvest; heap, collect etc. 72; lay -in, – down, – by, store etc. *adj.*; keep, file [papers] lay in etc. (*provide*) 637; preserve etc. 670; put by for a rainy day.

Adj. stored etc. *v.*; in -store, – reserve, – ordinary; spare, supernumerary.

637. Provision.—N. provision, supply; grist, – to the mill; subvention etc. (*aid*) 707; resources etc. (*means*) 632.
provising etc. *v.*; purveyance; reinforcement; commissary, commissariat.
rations; iron –, emergency- rations; provender etc. (*food*) 298; *viaticum*; ensilage.
caterer, purveyor, commissary, quartermaster, steward, housekeeper, manciple, feeder, batman, victualler, storekeeper, grocer, provision merchant, green-, grocer, *comprador*, *restaurateur*; sutler etc. (*merchant*) 797; innkeeper, publican, confectioner, baker, butcher, wine merchant, vintner.

V. provide; make -provision, – due provision for; lay in, – a stock, – a store.
sup-ply, -peditate; furnish; find, – one in; arm.
cater, victual, provision, purvey, forage; beat up for; stock, – with; make good, replenish; fill, – up; recruit, feed, ration.
have in -store, – reserve; keep, – by one, – on foot; have to fall back upon; store etc. 636; provide against a rainy day etc. (*economy*) 817.

638. Waste.—N. consumption, expenditure, exhaustion; dispersion etc. 73; ebb; leakage etc. (*exudation*) 295; loss etc. 776; wear and tear; waste; prodigality etc. 818; misuse etc. 679; wasting etc. *v.*; rubbish etc. (*useless*) 645.
mountain in labor.

v. spend, expend, use, consume, swallow up, exhaust, deplete; impoverish; spill, drain, empty; disperse etc. 73.
cast –, throw –, fling –, fritter- away; burn the candle at both ends, waste; squander etc. 818.
'waste its sweetness on the desert air;' cast -one's bread upon the waters, – pearls before swine; employ a steam engine to crack a nut, waste powder and shot, break a butterfly on a wheel; labor in vain etc. (*useless*) 645; cut a whetstone with a razor, pour water into a sieve; tilt at windmills.
leak etc. (*run out*) 295; run to waste; ebb; melt away, run dry, dry up.

Adj. wasted etc. *v.*; at a low ebb.
wasteful etc. (*prodigal*) 818; penny wise and pound foolish.

Phr. *magno conatu magnas nugas; le jeu n'en vaut pas la chandelle.*

639. Sufficiency.—N. sufficiency, adequacy, enough, withal, *quantum sufficit*, satisfaction, competence; no less.
mediocrity etc. (*average*) 29.
fill; fullness etc (*completeness*) 52; plen-itude, -ty; abundance; copiousness etc. *adj.*; amplitude, galore, lots, profusion; full measure; 'good measure pressed down, shaken together and running over.'
luxuriance etc. (*fertility*) 168; affluence etc. (*wealth*) 803; fat of the land; 'a land flowing with milk and honey;' cornucopia; horn of -plenty, – Amalthaea; mine etc. (*stock*) 636.
outpouring; flood etc. (*great quantity*) 31; tide etc. (*river*) 348; repletion etc. (*reduncance*) 641; satiety etc. 869; rich man etc. 803.

V. be -sufficient etc. *adj.*; suffice, do, just do, satisfy, pass muster; have -enough etc. *n.*; eat –, drink –, have- one's fill; roll –, swim- in; wallow in etc. (*superabundance*) 641.
abound, exuberate, teem, flow, stream, rain, shower down; pour, – in; swarm; bristle with.
render -sufficient etc. *adj.*; replenish etc. (*fill*) 52.

Adj. sufficient, enough, adequate, up to the mark, commensurate, competent, satisfactory, valid, tangible.
measured; moderate etc. (*temperate*) 953.
full etc. (*complete*) 52; ample; plen-ty, -tiful, -teous; plenty as blackberries; copious, abundant, abounding etc. *v.*; replete, enough and to spare, flush; choke-full; well-stocked, -provided; liberal; unstint-ed, -ing; stintless; without stint; un-sparing, -measured; lavish etc. 641; wholesale.
rich, luxuriant etc. (*fertile*) 168; affluent etc. (*wealthy*) 803; wantless; big with etc. (*pregnant*) 161.
un-exhausted, -wasted; exhaustless, inexhaustible.

Adv. sufficiently, amply etc. *adj.*; full; in -abundance etc. *n.*; with no sparing hand; to one's heart's content, *ad libitum*, without stint.

Phr. cut and come again.

640. Insufficiency.—N. insufficiency; inadequa-cy, -teness; incompetence etc. (*impotence*) 158; deficiency etc. (*incompleteness*) 53; imperfection etc. 651; shortcoming etc. 304; paucity; stint; scantiness etc. (*smallness*) 32; none to spare; bare subsistence.
scarcity, dearth; want, need, lack, poverty, exigency; inanition, starvation, famine, drought.
dole, pittance, mite; short -allowance, – commons; half-rations; banyan –, fast- day, Lent.
emptiness, poorness etc. *adj.*; depletion, vacancy, flaccidity; ebb-tide; low water; 'a beggarly account of empty boxes;' indigence etc. (*poverty*) 804; insolvency etc. (*non-payment*) 808; poor man etc. 804; bankrupt etc. 808.

V. be -insufficient etc. *adj.*; not -suffice etc. 639; come short of etc. 304; run dry.
want, lack, need, require; *caret*; be in want etc. (*poor*) 804; live from hand to mouth.
render- insufficient etc. *adj.*; drain of resources; impoverish etc. (*waste*) 638; stint etc. (*begrudge*) 819; put on short -commons, – allowance.
do -insufficiently etc. *adv.*; scotch the snake.

Adj. insufficient, inadequate; too -little etc. 32; not -enough etc. 639; unequal to; incompetent etc. (*impotent*) 158; 'weighed in the balance and found wanting;' perfunctory etc. (*neglect*) 460; deficient etc. (*incomplete*) 53; wanting etc. *v.*; imperfect etc. 651; ill-furnished, -provided, -stored, -off.

slack, at a low ebb; empty, vacant, bare; short –, out –, destitute –, devoid –, bereft etc. 789 –, denuded- of; dry, drained.

un -provided, -supplied, -furnished; unreplenished, -fed; un-stored, -treasured; empty-handed.

meager, poor, thin, scrimp, sparing, spare, stinted, stunted; skimpy; starv-ed, -eling; half-starved, emaciated, famine-stricken, famished, underfed, undernourished; jejune.

scant etc. (*small*) 32; scarce; not to be had, – for love or money, – at any price; scurvy; stingy etc. 819; at the end of one's tether; without - resources etc. 632; in want etc. (*poor*) 804; in debt etc. 806.

Adv. insufficiently etc. *adj.*; in default –, for want- of; failing.

641. Redundance.—N. redundance; too - much, – many; superabundance, -fluity, -fluence, -saturation; nimiety, transcendency, exuberance, profuseness; profusion etc. (*plenty*) 639; repletion, enough in all conscience, *satis superque*, lion's share; more than -enough etc. 639; plethora, engorgement, congestion, load, surfeit, sickener; turgescence etc. (*expansion*) 194; over-dose, - measure, -supply, -flow; inundation etc. (*water*) 348; *avalanche*.

accumulation etc. (*store*) 636; heap etc. 72; drug, – in the market; glut; crowd; burden.

excess; sur-, over-plus, epact; margin; remainder etc. 40; duplicate; surplusage; expletive; work of –, supererogation; *bonus*, *bonanza*.

luxury; intemperance etc. 954; extravagance etc. (*prodigality*) 818; exorbitance, lavishment.

pleonasm etc. (*diffuseness*) 573; too many irons in the fire; embarassment of riches; money to burn.

V. super-, over-abound; know no bounds, swarm; meet one at every turn; creep –, bristle-with; overflow; run –, flow –, well –, brim-over; run riot; over-run, -stock, -lay, -charge, -dose, -feed, -burden, -load, -do, -whelm, -shoot the mark etc. (*go beyond*) 303; surcharge, supersaturate, gorge, glut, load, drench, whelm, inundate, deluge, flood; drug, – the market.

choke, cloy, accloy, suffocate; pile up, lay it on, – with a trowel, lay on thick; impregnate with; lavish etc. (*squander*) 818.

send –, carry- coals to Newcastle, – owls to Athens; teach one's grandmother to suck eggs; *pisces natare docere*; kill the slain, 'gild refined gold,' 'paint the lily;' butter one's bread on both sides, put butter upon bacon; employ a steam-engine to crack a nut etc. (*waste*) 638.

exaggerate etc. 549; wallow in; roll in etc. (*plenty*) 639; remain on one's hands, hang heavy on hand, go a begging.

Adj. redundant; too -much, – many; exuberant, inordinate, superabundant, excessive, overmuch, replete, profuse, lavish; prodigal etc. 818; exorbitant; overweening; extravagant; overcharged etc. *v.*; supersaturated, drenched, overflowing; running -over, – to waste, – down.

crammed –, filled- to overflowing; gorged, stuffed, ready to burst; dropsical, turgid, plethoric, full-blooded; obese etc. 194; voluminous.

superfluous, unnecessary, needless, supervacaneous, uncalled for, to spare, in excess; over and above etc. (*remainder*) 40; *de trop*; adscititious etc. (*additional*) 37; supernumerary etc. (*reserve*) 636; on one's hands, spare, duplicate, supererogatory, expletive; *un peu fort*.

Adj. over, too, over and above; over –, too-much; too far; without –, beyond – out of- measure; with ... to spare; over head and ears; up to one's eyes, – ears; *extra*; beyond the mark etc. (*transcursion*) 303; over one's head.

Phr. It never rains but it pours.

642. Importance.—N. importance, consequence, moment, prominence, consideration, mark, materialness.

import, significance, concern; emphasis, interest.

greatness etc. 31; superiority etc. 33; notability etc. (*repute*) 873; weight etc. (*influence*) 175; value etc. (*goodness*) 648; usefulness etc. 644.

gravity, seriousness, solemnity; no -joke, – laughing matter; pressure, urgency, stress; matter of life and death.

memorabilia, *notabilia*, great doings; red-letter day.

great -thing, – point; main chance, 'the be all and end all,' cardinal point, outstanding feature; substance, gist etc. (*essence*) 5; sum and substance, *gravamen*, head and front; important –, principal –, prominent –, essential- part; half the battle; *sine quâ non*; breath of one's nostrils etc. (*life*) 359; cream, salt, core, kernel, heart, nucleus; key, -note, -stone; corner stone; trumpcard etc. (*device*) 626; salient points.

top-sawyer, first fiddle, *prima donna*, chief, bigwig; triton among the minnows.

V. be -important etc. *adj.*, – somebody, – something; import, signify, matter, be an object; carry weight etc. (*influence*) 175; make a figure etc. (*repute*) 873; be in the ascendant, come to the front, lead the way, take the lead, play first fiddle, throw all else into the shade; lie at the root of; deserve –, merit –, be worthy- -of notice, – regard, – consideration.

attach –, ascribe –, give- importance etc. *n.*- to; value, care for; set store -upon, – by; mark etc. 550; mark with a white stone, underline; write –, put –, print- in -italics, – capitals, – large letters, – large type, – letters of gold; accentuate, emphasize, lay stress on.

make -a fuss, – a stir, – a piece of work, – much ado- about; make -of, – much of.

Adj. important; of -importance etc. *n.*; momentous, material; to the point; not to be -overlooked, – despised, – sneezed at; egregious; weighty etc. (*influential*) 175; of note etc. (*repute*) 873; notable, prominent, salient, signal; memorable, remarkable; worthy of -remark, – notice; never to be forgotten; stirring, eventful.

grave, serious, earnest, noble, grand, solemn, impressive, commanding, imposing.

urgent, pressing, critical, instant.

paramount, essential, vital, all-absorbing, radical, cardinal, chief, main, prime, primary, principal, leading, capital, foremost, overruling; of vital etc. importance.

in the front rank, first-rate, A1; superior etc. 33; considerable etc. (*great*) 31; marked etc. *v.*; rare etc. 137.

significant, telling, trenchant, emphatic, pregnant; *tanti*.

Adv. materially etc. *adj.*; in the main; above all, *par excellence*, to crown all.

643. Unimportance.—N. unimportance, insignificance, nothingness, immateriality.

triviality, trivia, fribble, levity, frivolity; paltriness etc. *adj.*; poverty; smallness etc. 32; vanity etc. (*uselessness*) 645; matter of -indifference etc. 866; no object; side issue.

nothing, – to signify, – worth speaking of, – particular, – to boast of, – to speak of; small –, no great –, trifling etc. *adj.*-matter; mere -joke, – nothing; hardly –, scarcely- anything; nonentity, cipher, figurehead; no great shakes, *peu de chose*; child's play; small beer.

toy, plaything, popgun, paper pellet, gimcrack, geegaw, bauble, trinket, *bagatelle*, kickshaw, knicknack, whim-wham, trifle, 'trifles light as air.'

trumpery, trash, rubbish, stuff, *fatras*, frippery; 'leather or prunello;' chaff, drug, froth, bubble, smoke, cobweb; weed; refuse etc. (*inutility*) 645; scum etc. (*dirt*) 653.

joke, jest, snap of the fingers; fudge etc. (*unmeaning*) 517; fiddlestick, – end; pack of nonsense, mere farce.

straw, pin, fig, continental, button, rush; bulrush, feather, halfpenny, farthing, brass farthing, doit, peppercorn, jot, rap, pinch of snuff, old song.

minutiae, details, minor details, small fry; dust in the balance, feather in the scale, drop in the ocean, flea-bite, molehill; fingle-fangle.

nine days' wonder, *ridiculus mus*; flash in the pan etc. (*impotence*) 158; much ado about nothing etc. (*overestimation*) 482; storm in a teacup.

V. be -unimportant etc. *adj.*; not -matter etc. 642; go for –, matter –, signify- -little, – nothing, – little or nothing; not matter a -straw etc. *n.*

make light of etc. (*underestimate*) 483; catch at straws etc. (*overestimate*) 482.

Adj. unimportant; of -little, – small, – no- -account, – importance etc. 642; immaterial; un-, non-essential; not vital; irrelevant, incidental, indifferent.

subordinate etc. (*inferior*) 34; *médiocre* etc. (*average*) 29; passable, fair, respectable, tolerable, commonplace; uneventful, mere, common; ordinary etc. (*habitual*) 613; inconsiderable, so-so, insignificant, inappreciable, nugatory.

trifling, trivial; slight, slender, light, flimsy, frothy, idle; puerile etc. (*foolish*) 499; airy, shallow; weak etc. 160; powerless etc. 158; frivolous, petty, niggling; pid-, ped-dling; fribble, inane, ridiculous, farcical; fini-cal, -kin; fiddle-faddle, namby-pamby, wishy-washy, milk and water.

poor, paltry, pitiful; contemptible etc. (*contempt*) 930; sorry, mean, meager, shabby, miserable, wretched, vile, scrubby, scrannel, weedy, niggardly, scurvy, putid, beggarly, worthless, twopenny-half penny, cheap, trashy, catchpenny, gimcrack, trumpery, one-horse; toy.

not worth -the pains, – while, – mentioning, – speaking of, – a thought, – a curse, – a straw, – rap etc. *n.*; beneath –, unworthy of- -notice, – regard, – consideration, – contempt; *de lanâ caprinâ*; vain etc. (*useless*) 645.

Adv. slightly etc. *adj.*; rather, somewhat, pretty well, fairly well, tolerably.

for aught one cares.

Int. no matter! pish! tush! tut! pshaw! pugh! pooh, -pooh! fudge! bosh! humbug! fiddle-stick, – end! fiddlededee! never mind! *n'importe!* what -signifies, – matter, – boots it, – of that, –'s the odds! a fig for! stuff ! nonsense! stuff and nonsense!

Phr. *magno conatu magnas nugas*; *le jeu n'en vaut pas la chandelle*; it -matters not, – does not signify; it is of no -consequence, – importance.

644. Utility.—N. utility; usefulness etc. *adj.*; efficacy, efficiency, adequacy; service, use, stead, avail; help etc. (*aid*) 707; applicability etc. *adj.*; subservience etc. (*instrumentality*) 631; function etc. (*business*) 625; value; worth etc. (*goodness*) 648; money's worth; productiveness etc. 168; *cui bono* etc. (*intention*) 620; utilization etc. (*use*) 677; step in the right direction.

common weal, public good; utilitarianism etc. (*philanthropy*) 910.

V. be -useful etc. *adj.*; avail, serve; subserve etc. (*be instrumental to*) 631; conduce etc. (*tend*) 176; answer –, serve- -one's turn, – a purpose.

act a part etc. (*action*) 680; perform –, discharge- -a function etc. 625; do –, render- -a service, – good service, – yeoman's service; bestead, stand one in good stead; be the making of; help etc. 707.

bear fruit etc. (*produce*) 161; bring grist to the mill; profit, remunerate; benefit etc. (*do good*) 648.

find one's -account, – advantage- in; reap the benefit of etc. (*be better for*) 658.

render useful etc. (*use*) 677.

Adj. useful; of -use etc. *n.*; serviceable, usable, proficuous, good for; subservient etc. (*instrumental*) 631; conducive etc. (*tending*) 176; subsidiary etc. (*helping*) 707.

advantageous etc. (*beneficial*) 648; profitable, gainful, remunerative, worth one's salt; in-, valuable; prolific etc. (*productive*) 168.

adequate; ef-ficient, -ficacious; effect-ive, -ual; practicable, expedient etc. 646.

applicable, available, ready, handy, at hand, tangible; commodious, adaptable; of all work.

Adv. usefully etc. *adj.*; *pro bono publico*.

645. Inutility.—N. inutility; uselessness etc. *adj.*; inefficacy, futility; inep-, inap-titude; un-subservience; inadequacy etc. (*insufficiency*) 640; inefficiency etc. (*incompetence*) 158; unskilfulness etc. 699; disservice; unfruitfulness etc. (*unproductiveness*) 169; labor -in vain, – lost, – of Sisyphus; lost -trouble, – labor; work of Penelope; sleeveless errand, wild goose chase, mere farce.

tautology etc. (*repetition*) 104; supererogation etc. (*redundance*) 641.

vanitas vanitatum, vanity, inanity, worthlessness, nugacity; triviality etc. (*unimportance*) 643.

caput mortuum, waste paper, dead letter; blunt tool.

litter, rubbish, lumber, odds and ends, cast-off clothes; button-top; shoddy; rags, orts, trash, refuse, sweepings, scourings, off-scourings, dross, slag, waste, rubble, dottle, drast, *débris*; stubble, leavings; broken meat; dregs etc. (*dirt*) 653; weeds, tares; rubbish heap, dust hole; *rudera*, deads.

fruges consumere natus etc. (*drone*) 683.

V. be -useless etc. *adj.*; go a begging etc. (*redundant*) 641; fail etc. 732.

seek –, strive- after impossibilities; use vain efforts, labor in vain, roll the stone of Sisyphus, beat the air, lash the waves; *battre l'eau avec un bâton, donner un coup d'épée dans l'eau*, fish in the air, milk the ram, drop a bucket into an empty well, sow the sand; bay the moon; preach –, speak- to the winds; whistle jigs to a milestone; kick against the pricks, *se battre contre des moulins*; lock the stable door when the steed is stolen etc. (*too late*) 135; hold a farthing candle to the sun; cast pearls before swine etc. (*waste*) 638; carry coals to Newcastle etc. (*redundance*) 641; wash a blackamoor white etc. (*impossible*) 471.

render -useless etc. *adj.*; dis-mantle, -mast, -mount, -qualify, -able; unrig; cripple, lame etc. (*injure*) 659; spike guns, clip the wings; put out of gear.

Adj. useless, inutile, inefficacious, futile, unavailing, bootless; inoperative etc. 158; inadequate etc. (*insufficient*) 640; in-, un- subservient; inept, inefficient etc. (*impotent*) 158; of no -avail etc. (*use*) 644; ineffectual etc. (*failure*) 732; incompetent etc. (*unskilful*) 699; 'stale, flat and unprofitable;' superfluous etc. (*redundant*) 641; dispensable; thrown away etc. (*wasted*) 638; abortive etc. (*immature*) 674.

worth-, value-less; unsaleable; not worth a straw etc. (*trifling*) 643; dear at any price.

vain, empty, inane; gain-, profit-, fruit-less; unserviceable, -profitable; ill-spent; unproductive etc. 169; *hors de combat*; barren, sterile, impotent, unproductive, effete, past work etc (*impaired*) 659; obsolete etc. (*old*) 124; fit for the -dust-hole, – wastepaper basket; good for nothing; of no earthly use; not worth -having, – powder and shot; leading to no end, uncalled for; un-necessary, -needed, superfluous.

Adv. uselessly etc. *adj.*; to -little, – no, – little or no- purpose.

Int. *cui bono?* what's the good!

646. Expedience. [Specific subservience.]—**N.** expedien-ce, -cy; desirableness, -bility etc. *adj.*; fitness etc. (*agreement*) 23; utility etc. 644; propriety; advantage; opportunism, pragmatism.

high time etc. (*occasion*) 134.

V. be -expedient etc. *adj.*; suit etc. (*agree*) 23; befit; suit –, befit- the -time, – season, – occasion.

conform etc. 82.

Adj. expedient; desir-, advis-, accept-able; convenient; worth while, meet; fit, -ting; due, proper, eligible, seemly, becoming; befitting etc. *v.*; opportune etc. (*in season*) 134; *in loco*; suitable etc. (*accordant*) 23; applicable etc. (*useful*) 644; practical, effective, pragmatical; suitable, handy.

Adv. in the right place; conveniently etc. *adj.*; in the nick of time.

Phr. *operae pretium est.*

647. Inexpedience.—N. enexpedien-ce, -cy; undesira-bleness, -bility etc. *adj.*; discommodity, impropriety; unfitness etc. (*disagreement*) 24; inutility etc. 645; inconvenience, inadvisability; disadvantage.

V. be -inexpedient etc. *adj.*; come amiss etc. (*disagree*) 24; embarrass etc. (*hinder*) 706; put to inconvenience; pay too dear for one's whistle.

Adj. inexpedient, undesirable; un-, in-advisable; objectionable; troublesome, in-apt, -eligible, -admissable, -convenient; in-, dis-commodious; disadvantageous; inappropriate, unsuitable, unfit etc. (*inconsonant*) 24.

ill-contrived, -advised; unsatsifactory; unprofitable etc., unsubservient etc. (*useless*) 645; inopportune etc. (*unseasonable*) 135; out of –, in the wrong- place; improper, unseemly.

clumsy, awkward; cum-brous, -bersome; lumbering, unwieldy, hulky; unmanageable etc. (*impracticable*) 704; impedient (*in the way*) 706.

unnecessary etc. (*redundant*) 641.

Phr. it will never do.

648. Goodness. [Capability of producing good. Good qualities.]—**N.** goodness etc. *adj.*; excellence, merit; virtue etc. 944; value, worth, price.

super-excellence, -eminence; superiority etc. 33; perfection etc. 650; *coup de maître*; master-piece, *chef d'oeuvre*, prime, flower, cream, *élite*, pick, A1, none such, *nonpareil*, *crême de la crême*, flower of the flock, cock of the roost, salt of the earth; champion.

tid-bit; gem, – of the first water; *bijou*, precious stone, jewel, pearl, diamond, ruby, brilliant, treasure; good thing; *rara avis*, one in a thousand.

beneficence etc. 906; good man etc. 948.

V. be -beneficial etc. *adj.*; produce –, do- -good etc. 618; profit etc. (*be of use*) 644; benefit; confer a -benefit etc. 618.

be the making of, do a world of good, make a man of.

produce a good effect; do a good turn, confer an obligation; improve etc. 658.

do no harm, break no bones.

be -good etc. *adj.*; excel, transcend etc. (*be superior*) 33; bear away the bell.

stand the -proof, – test; pass -muster, – an examination.

challenge comparison, vie, emulate, rival.

Adj. harm-, hurt-less; unobnoxious; in-nocuous, -nocent, -offensive.

beneficial, valuable, of value; serviceable etc. (*useful*) 644; advantageous, profitable, edifying; salutary etc. (*healthful*) 656.

favorable; propitious etc. (*hopegiving*) 858; fair.

good, – as gold; excellent; better; superior etc. 33; above par; nice, fine; genuine etc. (*true*) 494.

best, choice, select, picked, elect, eximious, *recherché*, rare, priceless; unpara-goned, -lleled etc. (*supreme*) 33; superlatively etc. 33- good; super-fine, -excellent; bonzer; of the first water; first-rate, -class; high-wrought; exquisite, very best, crack, prime, tip-top, gilt-edged, capital, cardinal; standard etc. (*perfect*) 650; inimitable.

admirable, estimable; praiseworthy etc. (*approve*) 931; pleasing etc. 829; *couleur de rose*, precious, of great price; costly etc. (*dear*) 814; worth -its weight in gold, – a Jew's eye, – a king's ransom; matchless, peerless, invaluable, inestimable, precious as the apple of the eye.

tolerable etc. (*not very good*) 651; up to the mark, un-exceptionable, -objectionable; satisfactory, tidy.

in -good, – fair- condition; fresh; unspoiled; sound etc. (*perfect*) 650.

Adv. beneficially etc. *adj.*; well etc. 618.

649. Badness. [Capability of producing evil. Bad qualities.]—**N.** hurtfulness etc. *adj.*; virulence.

evil doer etc. 913; bane etc. 663; plague-spot etc. (*insalubrity*) 657; evil star, ill wind; snake in the grass, skeleton in the closet; *amari aliquid*, thorn in the side; Jonah, jinx, hoodoo.

malignity; malevolence etc. 907; tender mercies [ironically].

ill-treatment, annoyance, molestation, abuse, oppression, persecution, outrage; misusage etc. 679; injury etc. (*damage*) 659.

badness etc. *adj.*; peccancy, abomination; painfulness etc. 830; pestilence etc. (*disease*) 655; guilt etc. 947; depravity etc. 945.

V. be -hurtful etc. *adj.*; cause –, produce –, inflict –, work –, do- evil etc. 619; damnify, endamage, hurt, harm, scathe; injure etc. (*damage*) 659; pain etc. 830.

wrong, aggrieve, oppress, persecute; trample –, tread –, bear hard –, put-upon; overburden; weigh -down, – heavy on; victimize; run down; molest etc. 830.

maltreat, abuse; ill-use, -treat; thwart, buffet, bruise, scratch, maul; smite etc. (*scourge*) 972; do - violence, – harm, – a mischief; stab, pierce, outrage.

do –, make- mischief; bring –, get- into trouble.

destroy etc. 162.

Adj. hurt-, harm-, scath-, bane-, bale-ful; injurious, deleterious, detrimental, noxious, pernicious, mischievous, full of mischief, mischief-making, malefie, malignant, nocuous, noisome; prejudicial; dis-serviceable, advantageous; wide-wasting.

unlucky, sinister; obnoxious, untoward, disastrous.

oppressive, burdensome, onerous; malign etc. (*malevolent*) 907.

corrupting etc. (corrupt etc. 659) virulent, venomous, envenomed, corrosive; poisonous etc. (*morbific*) 657; deadly etc. (*killing*) 361; destructive etc. (*destroying*) 162; inauspicious etc. 859.

bad, ill, arrant, as bad bad can be, dreadful; horrid, -rible; dire; rank, peccant, foul, fulsome; rotten, – at the core.

vile, base, villainous; mean etc. (*paltry*) 643; injured etc., deteriorated etc. 659; unsatisfactory, exception, -able, indifferent; below par etc. (*imperfect*) 651; ill-contrived, -conditioned; wretched, sad, grievous, deplorable, lamentable; piti-ful, -able, woeful etc. (*painful*) 830.

evil, wrong; depraved etc. 945; shocking; reprehensible etc. (*disapprove*) 932.

hateful, – as a toad; abominable, detestable, execrable, cursed, accursed, confounded; damn-ed, -able; infernal; diabolic etc. (*malevolent*) 907.

inadvisable etc. (*inexpedient*) 647; unprofitable etc. (*useless*) 645; incompetent etc. (*unskilful*) 699; irremediable etc. (*hopeless*) 859.

Adv. badly etc. *adj.*; wrong, ill; to one's cost; where the shoe pinches.

Phr. bad is the best; the worst come to the worst.

650. Perfection.—N. perfection; perfectness etc. *adj.*; indefectibility; inpecc-ancy, -ability.

pink, *beau idéal*, phoenix, paragon; pink –, acme- of perfection; *ne plus ultra*; summit etc. 210.

cygne noir; philosopher's stone; chrysolite, Koh-i-noor, black tulip.

model, standard, pattern, mirror, admirable Chrichton; trump; very prince of.

master-piece, -stroke, super-excellence etc. (*goodness*) 648; transcendence etc. (*superiority*) 33.

V. be -perfect etc. *adj.*: transcend etc. (*be supreme*) 33.

bring to perfection, perfect, ripen, mature; consummate, complete etc. 729; put in trim etc. (*prepare*) 673: put the finishing touch to.

Adj. perfect, faultless, ideal; indefective, -ficient, -fectible; immaculate, spotless, impeccable; free from -imperfection etc. 651; un-blemished, -injured etc. 659; sound, – as a roach; in perfect condition; scathless, intact, harmless; seaworthy etc. (*safe*) 644; right as a trivet; *in seipso totus teres atque rotundus*; consummate etc. (*complete*) 52; finished etc. 729; complete in itself.

best etc. (*good*) 648; model, standard; inimitable, unparagoned, unparalleled etc. (*supreme*) 33; superhuman, divine; beyond all praise etc. (*approbation*) 931; *sans peur et sans reproche*.

Adj. to perfection, to the limit; perfectly etc. *adj.*: *ad unguem*; clean, – as a whistle.

651. Imperfection.—N. imperfection; imperfectness etc. *adj.*; deficiency; inadequacy etc. (*insufficiency*) 640; peccancy etc. (*badness*) 649; immaturity etc. 674.

fault, defect, weak point; screw loose; rift within the lute; fly in the ointment; flaw etc. (*break*) 70; gap etc. 198; twist etc. 243; taint, attainder; bar sinister, hole in one's coat; blemish etc. 848; weakness etc. 160; half-blood, touch of the tar brush; shortcoming etc. 304; drawback; seamy side.

mediocrity; no great -shakes, – catch; not much to boast of.

V. be -imperfect etc. *adj.*; have a -defect etc. *n.*; lie under a disadvantage; spring a leak.

not –, barely- pass muster; fall short etc. 304.

Adj. imperfect; not -perfect etc. 650; de-ficient, -fective; faulty, unsound, mutilated, tainted; out of -order, – tune; cracked, leaky; sprung; warped etc. (*distort*) 243; lame; injured etc. (*deteriorated*) 659; peccant etc. (*bad*) 649; frail etc. (*weak*) 160; inadequate etc. (*insufficient*) 640; crude etc. (*unprepared*) 674; incomplete etc. 53; found wanting; below par; shorthanded; below –, under- its full - strength, – complement.

indifferent, middling, ordinary, mediocre; average etc. 29; so-so; *così-così*, milk and water; tolerable, fair, passable; pretty -well, – good; rather –, moderately- good; good –, well-enough; decent; not -bad, – amiss; inobjectionable, admissable, bearable, only better than nothing.

secondary, inferior; second-rate, -best, one-horse.

Adv. almost etc.; to a limited extent, rather etc. 32; pretty, moderately; only; considering, all things considered, enough.

Phr. *surgit amari aliquid.*

652. Cleanness.—N. cleanness etc. *adj.*; purity; cleaning etc. *v.*; purification, defecation etc. *v.*; purgation, lustration; de-, abs-tersion; epuration, mundation, ablution, lavation, colature; disinfection etc. *v.*; drain-, sewerage.

lavatory, bath, -room; swimming pool, natatorium; public baths; hot –, cold –, Turkish –, Swedish –, Russian – vapor- bath; *hammam*, laundry, washhouse; washerwoman, laundress, laundryman; scavenger, cleaner, sweeper, goodie; crossing sweeper, white wings, dustman, sweep.

brush; broom, besom, carpet-sweeper, vacuum-cleaner, mop, squilgee, rake, shovel, sieve, riddle, screen, filter; scraper, strigil.

napkin, *serviette*, cloth, table-, carving-cloth, table-linen, napery, maukin, handkerchief, towel, sudary; doyley, doily, duster, sponge, mop, swab.

cover, drugget, mat, doormat.

soap, wash, lotion, detergent, cathartic, purgative; purifier etc. *v.*; dentifrice, tooth-powder, -paste; mouth wash; disinfectant.

V. be –, render- clean etc. *adj.*

clean, -se; mundify, rinse, wring, flush, full, wipe, mop, sponge, scour, swab, scrub, holystone, brush up.

wash, shampoo, lave, launder, buck; abs-, deterge; clear, purify; de-purate, -spumate, -fecate; purge, expurgate; Bowdlerize; elutriate, lixiviate, edulcorate, clarify, refine, rack; fil-ter, -trate; drain, strain.

disinfect, sterilize, pasteurize, fumigate, ventilate, deodorize; whitewash.

sift, winnow, screen, riddle, pick, weed, comb, rake, brush, sweep.

rout –, clear –, sweep etc.- out; make a clean sweep of.

Adj. clean, -ly; pure; immaculate; spot-, stain-, taint-less; without a stain, un-stained, -spotted, -soiled, -sullied, -tainted, -infected, -adulterated; aseptic; sweet, – as a nut.

neat, spruce, tidy, trim, gimp, clean as a new penny, like a cat in pattens; cleaned etc. *v.*; kempt.

Adv. neatly etc. *adj.*; clean as a whistle.

653. Uncleanness.—N. uncleanness etc. *adj.*; impurity; immundi-ty, -city; impurity etc. [of mind] 961.

defilement, contamination etc. *v.*; defedation; soil-ure, -iness; abomination; leaven; taint, -ure; fetor etc. 401.

decay; putre-scence, -faction; corruption; mold, must, mildew, dry-rot, *mucor*, rubigo, caries.

slovenry; slovenliness etc. *adj.*; squalor.

dowdy, drab, slut, malkin, slattern, sloven, slammerkin, scrub, draggletail, mudlark, dustman, sweep; beast.

dirt, filth, soil, slop; dust, cobweb, flue; smoke, soot, smudge, smut, grime, raff.

sordes, dregs, grounds, lees; sedi-, settle-ment; heel-tap; dross, -iness; mother, precipitate, *scoria*, ashes, cinders, recrement, slag; scum, froth.

hog-wash, swill, ditch-, dish-, bilge-water; rinsings, cheese-parings; sweepings etc. (*useless refuse*) 645; off-, out-scourings; off-scum; *caput mortuum*, *residuum*, sprue, feculence, clinker, draff; scurf, -iness; *exuviae*, morphew; fur, -fur; dandruff; tartar.

riffraff; vermin, louse, cootie, flea, bug.

mud, mire, quagmire, *alluvium*, silt, sludge, slime, slush, slosh.

spawn, offal, garbage, carrion; *excreta* etc. 299; slough, peccant humor, pus, matter, suppuration, *lienteria*; *feces*, excrement, ordure, dung; sew-, sewer-age; muck, coprolite; guano, manure, compost.

dunghill, *coluvies*, mixen, midden, bog, laystall, sink, w.c., water-, earth-closet, latrine, privy, jakes, John's, cess, -pool; sump, sough, *cloaca*, drain, sewer, common sewer; Cloacina; dust-hole.

sty, pig-sty, lair, den, Augean stable, sink of corruption; slum, rookery.

V. be –, become- unclean etc. *adj.*; rot, putrefy, fester, rankle, reek; stink etc. 401; mold, -er; go -bad etc. *adj.*

render -unclean etc. *adj.*; dirt, -y; soil, smoke, tarnish, slaver, spot, smear, daub, blot, blur, smudge, smutch, smirch; d-, dr-abble, -aggle; spatter, slubber; be-smear etc.; -mire, -slime, -grime, -foul; splash, stain, distain, maculate, sully, pollute, defile, debase, contaminate, taint, leaven; corrupt etc. (*injure*) 659; cover with -dust etc. *n.*; drabble in the mud.

wallow in the mire; slob-, slab-ber.

Adj. unclean, dirty, filthy, grimy; soiled etc. *v.*; not to be handled with kid gloves; dusty, snuffy, smutty, sooty, smoky; thick, turbid, dreggy; slimy.

uncleanly, slovenly, untidy, sluttish, dowdy, slatternly, draggletailed; un-combed, -kempt, -scoured, -swept, -wiped, -washed, -strained, -purified; squalid.

nasty, coarse, foul, impure, offensive, abominable, beastly, reeky, reechy; fetid etc. 401.

moldy, lentiginous, musty, mildewed, rusty, moth-eaten, mucid, rancid, bad, gone bad, touched, fusty, reasty, rotten, corrupt, tainted, high, fly-blown, maggoty; putr-id, -escent, -efied; purulent, carious, peccant, fec-al, -ulent; stercoraceous, excrementitious; scurfy, impetiginous; gory, bloody; rotting etc. *v.*; rotten as -a pear, – cheese.

crapulous etc. (*intemperate*) 954; gross etc. (*impure in mind*) 961.

654. Health.—N. health, sanity; soundness etc. *adj.*; vigor; good –, perfect –, excellent –, rude –, robust- health; bloom, *mens sana in corpore sano*; Hygeia; incorrupti-on, -bility; good state –, clean bill- of health, eupepsia.

V. be in health etc. *adj.*; bloom, flourish.

keep -body and soul together, – on one's legs; enjoy -good, – a good state of - health; have a clean bill of health.

return to health; recover etc. 660; get better etc. (*improve*) 658; take a -new, – fresh- lease of life; convalesce, be convalescent, recruit; restore to health; cure etc. (*restore*) 660.

Adj. health-y, -ful; in -health etc. *n.*; well, sound, strong, fit, hearty, hale, fresh, blooming, green, whole; florid, flush, hardy, stanch, staunch, brave, robust, vigorous, weather-proof; convalescent.

un-scathed, -injured, -maimed, -marred, -tainted; sound of wind and limb, safe and sound; without a scratch.

on one's legs; sound as a -roach, – bell; fresh as -a daisy, – a rose, – April; picture of health; bursting with health; fit as a fiddle; hearty as a buck; in -fine, – high- feather; in -good case, – full bloom; in fine fettle; pretty bobbish, tolerably well, as well as can be expected.

sanitary etc. (*health-giving*) 656; sanatory etc. (*remedial*) 662.

655. Disease.*—**N.** disease, illness, sickness etc. *adj.*; ailing etc. *v.*; 'the ills that flesh is heir to;' morb-idity, -osity; infirmity, ailment, indisposition; complaint, disorder, malady; distemper, -ature.

visitation, attack, seizure, stroke, fit, epilepsy, apoplexy, shock, shell-shock.

delicacy, loss of health, valetudinarianism, invalidism, cachexy; *cachexia*, atrophy, *marasmus*; indigestion, *dyspepsia*; decay etc. (*deterioration*) 659; malnutrition, decline, consumption, palsy, paralysis, prostration; occupational diseases.

taint, pollution, infection, contagion, septicity, septicaemia, blood poisoning, pyaemia, epi-, endemic; murrain, plague, pestilence, virus, pox.

sore, ulcer, abscess, fester, boil; pimple etc. (*swelling*) 250; carbuncle, gathering, whitlow, imposthume, peccant humor, issue; rot, canker, cancer, *carcinoma*, *caries*, mortification, corruption, gangrene, *sphacelus*, leprosy, eruption, rash, breaking out, venereal disease.

fever, calenture; inflammation.

fatal etc. (*hopeless*) 859- -disease etc.; dangerous illness, galloping consumption, churchyard cough; general breaking up, break up of the system.

[Disease of the mind] neurasthenia; idiocy etc. 499; insanity etc. 503.

martyr to disease; cripple; 'the halt, the lame and the blind;' valetudinar-y, -ian; invalid, patient, case; sick-room, -chamber, hospital etc. 662.

[Science of disease] path-, eti-, nos-ology, therapeutics, diagnosis, prognosis.

V. be -ill etc. *adj.*; ail, suffer, labor under, be affected with, complain of; droop, flag, languish, halt; sicken, peak, pine, waste away, fail, lose strength; gasp.

keep one's bed; feign sickness etc. (*falsehood*) 544; malinger.

lay -by, – up; take –, catch- -a disease etc. *n.*, – an infection; be stricken by; break out.

Adj. diseased; ailing etc. *v.*; ill, – of; taken ill, seized with; indisposed, unwell, sick, squeamish, poorly, seedy; affected –, afflicted- with illness; laid up, confined, bed-ridden, invalided, in hospital, on the sick list; out of -health, – sorts; valetudinary.

un-sound, -healthy; sickly, morbose, healthless, infirm, chlorotic, unbraced, drooping, flagging, lame, halt, crippled, halting.

morbid, tainted, vitiated, peccant, contaminated, poisoned, septic, tabid, mangy, leprous, cankered; rotten, – to, – at- the core; withered, palsied, paralytic, tuberculous; dyspeptic.

touched in the wind, broken-winded, spavined, gasping; *hors de combat* etc. (*useless*) 645.

weak-ly, -ened etc. (*weak*) 160; decrepit; decayed etc. (*deteriorated*) 659; incurable etc. (*hopeless*) 859; in declining health; cranky; in a bad way, in danger, prostrate; moribund etc. (*death*) 360.

morbific, epidemic etc. 657.

*Extended lists of different diseases are beyond the scope of this work.

656. Salubrity.—**N.** salubrity, salubriousness; healthiness etc. *adj.*

fine -air, – climate; eudiometer.

[Preservation of health] *hygiène*; valetudinarian, -ism, preventorium, sanitarian; *sanitarium*, *sanitorium*, immunity.

V. be -salubrious etc. *adj.*; agree with, be good for; assimilate etc. 23.

Adj. salu-brious, -tary, -tiferous, wholesome; health-y, -ful; sanitary, prophylactic, benign, bracing, tonic, invigorating, good for, nutritious, hyg-eian, -ienic.

in-noxious, -nocuous, -nocent; harmless, uninjurious, uninfectious; immune.

sanative etc. (*remedial*) 662; restorative etc. (*reinstate*) 660; useful etc. 644.

657. Insalubrity.—**N.** insalubrity, unhealthiness etc. *adj.*; non-naturals; plague spot; malaria etc. (*poison*) 663; death in the pot, contagion.

Adj. insalubrious; un-healthy, -wholesome; noxious, noisome, foul; morbi-fic, -ferous; mephitic, septic, azotic, deleterious; pesti-lent, -ferous, -lential; virulent, venomous, envenomed, poisonous, toxic, narcotic.

contagious, infectious, catching, taking, communicable, epidemic, zymotic, sporadic, endemic, pandemic, epizoötic.

innutritious, indigestible, ungenial; uncongenial etc. (*disagreeing*) 24.

deadly etc. (*killing*) 361.

658. Improvement.—**N.** improvement; a-, melioration; betterment; mend, amendment, emendation; mending etc. *v.*; advancement; advance etc. (*progress*) 282; ascent etc. 305; promotion, preferment; elevation etc. 307; increase etc. 35.

cultiv-, civiliz-ation; menticulture, culture, march of intellect; eugenics, euthenics, meliorism, telesis.

reform, -ation; revision, radical reform; second thoughts, correction, *limae labor*, refinement, elaboration; purification etc. 652; repair etc. (*restoration*) 660; recovery etc. 660.

revise; revised –, new- edition.

reformer, radical, progressive.

V. improve; be –, become –, get- better; mend, amend.

advance etc. (*progress*) 282; ascend etc. 305; increase etc. 35; fructify, ripen, mature; pick up, come about, rally, take a favorable turn; turn -over a new leaf, – the corner; raise one's head, sow one's wild oats; recover etc. 660.

be -better etc. *adj.*, – improved by; turn to -right, – good, – best- account; profit by, reap the benefit of; make -good use of, – capital out of; place to good account; take advantage of.

render better, improve, emend, make over, better; a-, meliorate; correct.

improve –, refine- upon; rectify; enrich, mellow, elaborate, fatten.

promote, cultivate, advance, forward, enhance; bring -forward, – on; foster etc. 707; invigorate etc. (*strengthen*) 159.

touch –, rub –, brush –, furbish –, bolster –, vamp –, brighten –, warm- up; polish, cook, make the most of, set off to advantage; prune; repair etc. (*restore*) 660; put in order etc. (*arrange*) 60.

review, revise, edit, redact; make -corrections, – improvements etc. *n.*; doctor etc. (*remedy*) 662; purify etc. 652.

relieve, refresh, revive, infuse new blood into, recruit, re-invigorate, renew, revivify, freshen, build -afresh, – anew; uplift, inspire.

re-form, -model, -organize; new model, civilize.

view in a new light, think better of, appeal from Philip drunk to Philip sober.

palliate, mitigate; lessen etc. 36- an evil.

Adj. improving etc. *v.*; progressive, improved etc. *v.*; better, – off, – for; all the better for; better advised.

reform-, emend-atory; reparatory etc. (*restorative*) 660; remedial etc. 662.

corrigible, improvable, curable, accultural.

Adv. on -consideration, – reconsideration, – second thoughts, – better advice; *ad melius inquirendum*; on the -mend, – up grade.

659. Deterioration.—N. deterioration, debasement; want, ebb; recession etc. 287; retrogradation etc. 283; decrease etc. 36.

degenera-cy, -tion, -teness; degradation; deprav-ation, -ement; depravity etc. 945; demoralization, retrogression.

impairment, inquination, injury, damage, loss, detriment, delaceration, outrage, havoc, inroad, ravage, scath; perversion, prostitution, vitiation, discoloration, oxidation, pollution, defedation, poisoning, venenation, leaven, contamination, canker, corruption, adulteration, alloy.

decl-ine, -ension, -ination; decadence, -cy; falling off etc. *v.*; caducity, decreptitude, senility.

decay, dilapidation, ravages of time, wear and tear; cor-, e-rosion; mouldi-, rotten-ness; moth and rust, dry-rot, blight, marasmus, atrophy, collapse; disorganization; *délabrement* etc. (*destruction*) 162.

wreck, mere wreck, honeycomb, *magni nominis umbra.*

V. be –, become- -worse, – deteriorated etc. *adj.*; have seen better days, deteriorate, degenerate, fall off; wane etc. (*decrease*) 36; ebb; retrograde etc. 283; decline, droop; go down etc. (*sink*) 306; go -downhill, – on from bad to worse, – farther and fare worse; jump out of the frying pan into the fire.

run to -seed, – waste; swale, sweal; lapse, be the worse for; break, – down; spring a leak, crack, start; shrivel etc. (*contract*) 195; fade, go off, wither, molder, rot, rankle, decay, go bad; go to – fall into- decay; 'fall into the sear and yellow leaf,' rust, crumble, shake; totter, – to its fall; perish etc. 162; die etc. 360.

[Render less good] deteriorate; weaken etc. 160; put back; taint, infect, contaminate, poison, empoison, envenom, canker, corrupt, exulcerate, pollute, vitiate, inquinate; de-, em-base; denaturalize, leaven; de-flower, -bauch, -file, -prave, -grade; stain etc. (*dirt*) 653; discolor; alloy, adulterate, sophisticate, tamper with, prejudice.

pervert, prostitute, demoralize, brutalize; render vicious etc. 945; compromise.

embitter, ex-, acerbate, aggravate.

injure, impair, labefy, damage, harm, hurt, shend, scathe, spoil, mar, despoil, dilapidate, waste; overrun; ravage; pillage etc. 791.

wound, stab, pierce, maim, lame, surbate, cripple, hough, hamstring, hit between the wind and water, scotch, mangle, mutilate, disfigure, blemish, deface, warp.

blight, rot; cor-, e-rode, eat away; wear -away, – out; gnaw, – at the root of; sap, mine, undermine, shake, sap the foundations of, break up; dis-organize, -mantle, -mast; destroy etc. 162.

damnify etc. (*aggrieve*) 649; do one's worst; knock down; deal a blow to; play -havoc, – sad havoc, – the mischief, – the deuce, – the very devil- -with, – among; decimate.

Adj. unimproved etc. (improve etc. 658); deteriorated etc. *v.*; altered, – for the worse; injured etc. *v.*; sprung; withering, spoiling, etc. *v.*; on the -wane, – decline; tabid; degenerate; worse; the –, all the- worse for; out of -repair, – tune; imperfect etc. 651; the worse for wear; battered; weather-ed, -beaten; stale, *passé*, shaken, dilapidated, frayed, faded, wilted, shabby, second-hand, second-rate, threadbare; worn, – to- -a thread, – a shadow, – the stump, rags; reduced, – to a skeleton, skeletonized; far gone.

decayed etc. *v.*; moth-, worn-eaten; mildewed, rusty, moldy, spotted, seedy, time-worn, moss-grown; discolored; effete, wasted, crumbling, moldering, rotten, cankered, blighted, tainted; depraved etc. (*vicious*) 945; decrep-id, -it; broken down; done, – for, – up; worn out, used up; fit for the -dust-hole, – wastepaper basket; past work etc. (*useless*) 645.

at a low ebb, in a bad way, on one's last legs, washed -up; – out; undermined, deciduous; nodding to its fall etc. (*destruction*) 162; tottering etc. (*dangerous*) 665; past cure etc. (*hopeless*) 859; fatigued etc. 688; backward, retrograde etc. (*retrogressive*) 283; deleterious etc. 649; behind the times.

Adv. on the down grade; beyond hope.

Phr. out of the frying pan into the fire; *aegrescit medendo.*

660. Restoration.—N. restor-ation, -al; re-instatement, -placement, -habilitation, establishment, -construction; reporduction etc. 163; re-novation, -newal; reviv-al, -escence; refreshment etc. 689; re-suscitation, -animation, -vivification, -viction; Phoenix; reorganization.

renaissance, renascence, rebirth, second youth, rejuvenation, rejuvenescence, new birth; regenera-tion, -cy, -teness; palingenesis, reconversion, resurgence, resurrection.

redress, retrieval, reclamation, recovery; con-valescence; resumption, *résumption*.

recurrence etc. (*repetition*) 104; *réchauffé, rifacimento*.

cure, recure, sanation; healing etc. *v.*; redin-tegration; rectification, instauration.

repair, reparation, mending; recruiting etc. *v.*; cicatrization; disinfection; tinkering.

reaction; redemption etc. (*deliverance*) 672; restitution etc. 790; relief etc. 834.

mender, repairer, renewer; tinker, cobbler; doc-tor etc. 662; *vis medicatrix* etc. (*remedy*) 662.

curableness.

V. return to the original state; recover, rally, revive; come -to, – round, – to oneself; pull through, weather the storm, be oneself again; get -well, – round, – the better of, – over, – about; rise from -one's ashes, – the grave; resurge, resurrect; survive etc. (*outlive*) 110; resume, reap-pear; come to, – life again; live –, rise- again; relive.

heal, skin over, cicatrize; right itself.

restore, put back, place *in statu quo*; re-instate, -place, -seat, -habilitate, -establish, -estate, -install.

re-construct, -build, -organize, -constitute; reconvert; re-new, -novate; recondition; regenerate; rejuvenate.

re-deem, -claim, -cover, -trieve; rescue etc. (*deliver*) 672.

redress, recure; cure, heal, remedy, doctor, physic, medicate; break of; bring round, set on one's legs.

re-suscitate, -vive, -animate, -vivify, -call to life; reproduce etc. 163; warm up; reinvigorate, refresh etc. 689.

redintegrate, make whole; recoup etc. 790; make -good, – all square; rectify; put –, set- -right, – to rights, – straight; set up, correct; put in order etc. (*arrange*) 60; refit, recruit; fill up, – the ranks; reinforce.

repair, mend; put in -repair, – thorough repair, – complete repair; retouch, botch, vamp, tinker, doctor, cobble; do –, patch –, plaster –, vamp-up; darn, fine-draw, heel-piece; stop a gap, stanch, staunch, caulk, calk, careen, splice, bind up wounds.

Adj. restored etc. *v.*; *redivivus*, convalescent; in a fair way; none the worse; rejuvenated, renascent.

restoring etc. *v.*; restorative, recuperative; sana-, repara-tive, -tory; curative, remedial.

restor-, recover-, san-, remedi-, retriev-, cur-able.

Adv. *in statu qho*; as you were.

Phr. *revenons a nos moutons*.

661. Relapse.—**N.** relapse, lapse; falling back etc. *v.*; retrogradation etc. (*retrogression*) 283; deterioration etc. 659.

[Return to, or recurrence of a bad state] backsliding, recidivation, recrudescence.

V. relapse, lapse; fall –, slide –, sink- back; have a relapse; return; retrograde etc. 283; recidivate; fall off etc. 659- again.

662. Remedy.—**N.** remedy, help, redress; an-tidote, anti-toxin, -biotic; anti-, counter-poison, prophylactic, antiseptic, germicide, bactericide, corrective, restorative, stimulant, pick-me-up, tonic; sedative etc. 174; palliative; febrifuge; alter-ant, -ative; specific; emetic, carminative; narcotic etc. *adj.*; Nepenthe, Mithridate.

cure; radical –, perfect –, certain- cure; sovereign remedy.

physic, medicine, patent medicine, Galenicals, simples, drug, wonder –, miracle – drugs; potion, draught, dose, pill, bolus, lozenge, tablet, tabloid, capsule; electuary; linct-us, -ure; medicament.

nostrum, receipt, recipe, prescription; catholicon, panacea, elixir, *elixir vitae*, philosopher's stone; balm, balsam, cordial, theriac, ptisan.

salve, ointment, cerate, oil, lenitive, lotion, cosmetic; plaster; epithem, embrocation, liniment, cataplasm, sinapism, arquebusade, traumatic, vulnerary, pepastic, poultice, collyrium, depilatory.

compress, pledget; bandage etc. (*support*) 215.

treatment, medical treatment, regimen; diet-ary, -etics; *vis medicatrix*, – *naturae*; *médicine ex-pectante*; seton, blood-letting, bleeding, venesec-tion, phlebotomy, cupping, leeches; operation, surgical operation; tonsillectomy, appendectomy; injection, electrolysis, massage.

pharma-cy, -cology, -ceutics; acology; materia medica, pharmacopoeia, therapeutics, therapy, posology, pathology etc. 655; home-, hetero-, all-, hydr-opathy; cold water –, open air- cure; dietetics; sur-, chirur-gery, osteopathy; healing art, leechcraft, practice of medicine; ortho-paedy, -praxy; dentistry, midwifery, obstetrics, gynecology.

faith -cure, – healing, Christian science; psycho-therapy, -analysis, psychiatry.

hospital, infirmary, clinic; pest-, lazar-house; lazaretto, lazaret; lock hospital; *maison de santé*; *ambulance*; dispensary; *sanatorium*, *sanitarium*, spa, baths, pump-room, well; *hospice*; Red Cross; nursing home; asylum.

doctor, physician, surgeon; medical –, general-practitioner, consultant, specialist; medical at-tendant; medical student, medico; chemist, apothecary, pharmacopolist, druggist; leech; Aesculapius, Hippocrates, Galen; *accoucheur*, gynecologist, midwife, oculist, aurist, dentist; operator; osteopath, bonesetter; nurse, monthly nurse, sister; dresser; *masseur*, *masseuse*.

V. apply a -remedy etc. *n.*; doctor, dose, physic, nurse, minister to, attend, dress the wounds, plaster, bandage, poultice; heal, cure, work a cure, kill or cure, remedy, stay (disease), snatch from the jaws of death; prevent etc. 706; relieve etc. 834; palliate etc. 658; restore etc. 660; drench with physic; consult, operate, extract, deliver; bleed, cup, let blood, transfuse; electrolyse; psycho-analyse.

Adj. remedial; restorative etc. 660; corrective, palliative, healing; sana-tory, -tive; prophylactic; salutiferous etc. (*salutary*) 656; medic-al, -inal; therapeutic, surgical, chirurgical, orthopedic, epulotic, paregoric, tonic, corroborant, analeptic, balsamic, anodyne, hypnotic, neurotic, narcotic, sedative, lenitive, demulcent, emollient; depuratory; deter-sive, -gent; abstersive, disinfectant, febrifugal, alternative; traumatic, vulnerary.

dietetic, alimentary; nutrit-ious, -ive; peptic; alexi-pharmic, -teric; remedi-, cur-able.

663. Bane.—N. bane, curse, thorn in the -side, -flesh, bugbear, *bête noire*; evil etc. 619; hurtfulness etc. (*badness*) 649; painfulness etc. (*cause of pain*) 830; scourge etc. (*punishment*) 975; *damnosa hereditas*; white elephant.

sting, fang, thorn, tang, bramble, briar, nettle.

poison, leaven, virus, venom; intoxicant; arsenic, Prussic acid, antimony, tartar emetic, strychnine, nicotine, cyanide of potassium, corrosive sublimate; curare; hyoscine etc.; poison-, mustard-, tear-gas; carbon di-, mon-oxide; ptomaine poisoning, botulism; miasm, mephitis, malaria, azote, sewer gas; pest, stench etc. 401.

rust, worm, moth, moth and rust, fungus, mildew; dry-rot; canker, -worm; cancer; torpedo; viper etc. (*evil-doer*) 913; demon etc. 980.

hemlock, hellebore, nightshade, *belladonna*, henbane, aconite; Upas tree.

drugs, dope, opium, morphia, morphine, cocaine, heroin, hashish, bhang.

[*Science of poisons*] Toxicology.

Adj. baneful etc. (*bad*) 649; poisonous etc. (*unwholesome*) 657.

664. Safety.—N. safety, security, impregnability; invulnera-bility, -bleness etc. *adj.*; danger -past, – over; storm blown over; coast clear; escape etc. 671; means of escape, safety-valve; safeguard, palladium, sheet anchor, rock, tower of strength.

guardian-, ward-, warden-ship; tutelage, custody, safe keeping; preservation etc. 670; protection, auspices.

safe-conduct, escort, convoy; guard, sheild etc. (*defense*) 717; guardian angel, tutelary -god, – deity, – saint; *genius loci*.

protector, guardian; ward-en, -er; preserver, custodian, *duenna chaperon*, third person.

watch-, ban-dog; Cerberus; watch-, patrol-, police-man, constable, peeler, bobby, copper, cop, bull, flat-foot, detective, armed guard; sentinel, sentry, scout etc. (*warning*) 668; garrison; guardship.

[Means of safety] refuge etc., anchor etc. 666; precaution etc. (*preparation*) 673; quarantine, *cordon sanitaire*. [Sense of security] confidence etc. 858.

V. be -safe etc. *adj.*; keep one's head above water, tide over, save one's bacon; ride out –, weather- the storm; light upon one's feet; bear a charmed life; escape etc. 671; possess nine lives.

make –, render- -safe etc. *adj.*; protect, watch over; take care of etc. (*care*) 459; preserve etc. 670; cover, screen, shelter, shroud, flank, ward; guard etc. (*defend*) 717; secure etc. (*restrain*) 751; intrench, fence round etc. (*circumscribe*) 229; house, nestle, ensconce; take charge of.

escort, convoy; garrison; watch, mount guard, patrol, scout, spy.

make assurance double sure etc. (*caution*) 864; take up a loose thread; take precautions etc. (*prepare for*) 673; take in a reef; double reef topsails.

seek safety; take –, find- shelter etc. 666; run into port.

Adj. safe, secure, sure; in -safety, – security; have an anchor to windward; on the safe side; under the -shield of, – shade of, – wing of, – shadow of one's wing; under -cover, – lock and key; out of -danger, – the meshes, – harm's way; in -harbor, – port; on sure ground, at anchor, high and dry, above water, on *terra firma*; unthreatened, -molested; protected etc. *v.*; cavendo tutus; panoplied etc. (*defended*) 717.

snug, sea-, air-worthy; weather-, water-, fire-, bomb-proof.

defensible, tenable, proof against, invulnerable; un-assailable, -attackable; im-pregnable, -perdible; founded on a rock; inexpugnable.

safe and sound etc. (*preserved*) 670; harmless; scathless etc. (*perfect*) 650; unhazarded; not -dangerous etc. 665.

protecting etc. *v.*; guardian, tutelary; perservative etc. 670; trustworthy etc. 939.

Adv. *ex abundanti cautelâ*; with impunity.

Phr. all's well; all clear; *salva res est*; *suave mari magno*; safety first.

665. Danger.—N. danger, peril, insecurity, jeopardy, risk, hazard, venture, precariousness, slipperiness; instability etc. 149; defenselessness etc. *adj.*

exposure etc. (*liability*) 177; vulnerability; vulnerable point, heel of Achilles; forlorn hope etc. (*hopelessness*) 859.

[Dangerous course] leap in the dark etc. (*rashness*) 863; road to ruin, *facilis descensus Averni*, hair-breadth escape.

cause for alarm; source of danger etc. 667. [Approach of danger] rock –, breakers- ahead; storm brewing; clouds -in the horizon, – gathering; warning etc. 668; alarm etc. 669. [Sense of danger] apprehension etc. 860.

V. be -in danger etc. *adj.*; be exposed to –, run into –, incur –, encounter- -danger etc. *n.*; run a risk; lay oneself open to etc. (*liability*) 177; lean on –, trust to- a broken reed; feel the ground sliding from under one, have to run for it; have the -chances, – odds- against one.

hang by a thread, totter; tremble on the -verge, – brink; sleep – stand -on a volcano; sit on a barrel of gunpowder, live in a glass house.

bring –, place –, put- in -danger etc. *n.*; endanger, expose to danger, imperil; jeopard, -ize, compromise; sail too near the wind etc. (*rash*) 863; put one's head in the lion's mouth.

adventure, risk, hazard, venture, stake, set at hazard; run the gauntlet etc. (*dare*) 861; engage in a forlorn hope.

threaten etc. 909- danger; run one hard; lay a trap for etc. (*deceive*) 545.

Adj. in -danger etc. *n.*; endangered etc. *v.*; fraught with danger; danger-, hazard-, peril-, parl-, pericul-ous; unsafe, unprotected etc. (safe, protect etc. 664); insecure, untrustworthy, unreliable; built upon sand, on a sandy basis.

defence-, fence-, guard-, harbor-less; unshielded; vulnerable, expugnable, unsheltered, exposed; open to etc. (*liable*) 177.

aux abois, at bay; on -the wrong side of the wall, – a lee shore, – the rocks.

at stake, in question; precarious, aleatory, critical, ticklish; slip-pery, -py; hanging by a thread etc. *v.*; with a halter round one's neck; between -the hammer and the anvil, – Scylla and Charybdis, – two fires; on the -edge, – brink, – verge of a- -precipice, – volcano; in the lion's den, on slippery ground, under fire; not out of the wood.

un-warned, -admonished, -advised; unprepared etc. 674; off one's guard etc. (*inexpectant*) 508.

tottering; un-stable, -steady; shaky, top-heavy, tumble-down, ramshackle, crumbling, waterlogged; help-, guide-less; in a bad way; reduced to –, at- the last extremity; trembling in the balance; nodding to its fall etc. (*destruction*) 162.

threatening etc. 909; ominous, ill-omened; alarming etc. (*fear*) 860; explosive; poisonous etc. 657.

adventurous etc. (*rash*) 863, (*bold*) 861.

Int. stop! look out! beware! take care!

Phr. *incidit in Scyllam qui vult vitare Charybdim; nam tua res agitur paries dum proximus ardet.*

666. Refuge. [Means of safety.]—**N.** refuge, sanctuary, retreat, fastness; stronghold, keep, last resort; ward; prison etc. 752; asylum, ark, home, almshouse, refuge for the destitute; hiding-place etc. (*ambush*) 530; *sanctum sanctorum* etc. (*privacy*) 893.

roadstead, anchorage; breakwater, mole, port, haven; harbor, – of refuge; sea-port; pier, jetty, embankment, quay.

covert, shelter, abri, screen, lee-wall, wing, shield, umbrella; splash-, dash-board, mudguard.

wall etc. (*inclosure*) 232; fort etc. (*defence*) 717.

anchor, kedge; grap-nel, -pling iron; sheet-, mushroom-anchor, main-stay; support etc. 215; check etc. 706; ballast.

jury-mast; vent-peg; safety -valve, – lamp; lightning conductor.

means of escape etc. (*escape*) 671; life-boat, swimming belt, cork jacket; life preserver, breeches buoy; parachute, plank, stepping-stone.

safeguard etc. (*protection*) 664.

V. seek –, take –, find- refuge etc. *n.*; seek –, find- safety etc. 664; throw oneself into the arms of; claim sanctuary; take to the -hills, – woods; make port, reach shelter, bar –, bolt –, lock -the door, – gete; let the portcullis down; raise the drawbridge.

667. Pitfall. [Source of danger.]—**N.** rocks, reefs, coral reef, sunken rocks, snags; sands, quicksands, Goodwin sands, sandy foundation; slippery ground; breakers, shoals, shallows, bank, shelf, flat, lee shore, iron-bound coast; rock –, breakers- ahead; derelict.

precipice; abyss, chasm, pit, crevasse; maelstrom, whirlpool, eddy, vortex, rapids, current, bore, tidal wave; storm, squall, hurricane, whirlwind; volcano; ambush etc. 530; pitfall, trap-door; trap etc. (*snare*) 545.

sword of Damocles; wolf at the door, snake in the grass, viper in one's bosom, death in the pot; latency etc. 526.

ugly customer, dangerous person, *le chat qui dort*; firebrand, hornet's nest.

Phr. *latet anguis in herbâ; proximus ardet Ucalegon.*

668. Warning.—**N.** warning, caution, *caveat*; notice etc. (*information*) 527; premoni-tion, -shment; prediction etc. 511; contraindication; symptom; lesson, dehortation; admonition, monition; alarm etc. 669.

handwriting on the wall, *tekel upharsin*, yellow flag; fog-signal, -horn; siren; monitor, warning voice, Cassandra, signs of the times, Mother Carey's chickens, stormy petrel, bird of ill omen, gathering clouds, clouds in the horizon, cloud no bigger than a man's hand, death-watch.

watch-tower, beacon, signal-post; light-house etc. (*indication of locality*) 550.

sent-inel, -ry; watch, -man; watch and ward; watch-, ban-, house-dog; patrol, vedette, picket, bivouac, scout, spy, spial; advanced –, rear-guard, lookout, flagman.,

cautiousness etc. 864.

V. warn, caution; fore-, pre-warn; ad-, premonish; give -notice, – warning; menace etc. (*threaten*) 909; put on one's guard; sound the alarm etc. 669; croak.

beware, ware; take -warning, – heed at one's peril; watch out for; keep watch and ward etc. (*care*) 459.

Adj. warning etc. *v.*; premonitory, monitory, cautionary; admonitory, -tive; ominous, threatening, lowering, minatory, symptomatic.

warned etc. *v.*; on one's guard etc. (*careful*) 459; (*cautious*) 864.

Adv. *in terrorem* etc. (*threat*) 909.

Int. beware! ware! take care! mind –, take care-what you are about; mind! look out!

Phr. *ne reveillez pas le chat qui dort*; *foenum habet in cornu.*

669. Alarm. [Indication of danger.]—**N.** alarm; alarum, larum, alarm bell, tocsin, *alerte*, beat of drum, sound of trumpet, note of alarm, hue and cry, signal of distress, S.O.S.; blue-lights; war-cry, -whoop; warning etc. 668; fog-signal, -horn; siren; yellow flag; danger signal; red -light, – flag; fire -bell, – alarm; burglar alarm, police whistle, watchman's rattle.

false alarm, cry of wolf; bug-bear, -aboo.

V. give –, raise –, sound –, beat- the *or* an -alarm etc. *n.*; alarm; warn etc. 668; ring the tocsin; *battre la générale*; cry wolf.

Adj. alarming etc. *v.*

Int. *sauve qui peut! qui vive?* who goes there?

670. Preservation.—**N.** preservation; safe keeping; conservation etc. (*storage*) 636; maintenance, upkeep, support, sustentation, conservatism; *vis conservatrix*; salvation etc. (*deliverance*) 672; drying etc. *v.*

[Means of preservation] prophylaxis; preserv-er, -ative; canned goods; cold pack; hygi-astics, -antics; cover, durgget; *cordon sanitaire.*

[Superstitious remedies] charm etc. 993.

V. preserve, maintain, keep, sustain, support; keep -up, – alive; not willingly let die; shore –, bank- up; nurse; save, rescue; be –, make- safe etc. 664; take care of etc. (*care*) 459; guard etc. (*defend*) 717.

stare super antiquas vias; hold one's own; hold –, stand- -one's ground etc. (*resist*) 719.

embalm, dry, cure, smoke, salt, pickle, season, kyanize, bottle, pot, tin, can; husband etc. (*store*) 636.

Adj. preserving etc. *v.*; conservative; prophylatic; preserva-tory, -tive; hygienic.

preserved etc. *v.*; un-impaired, -broken, -injured, -hurt, -singed, -marred; safe, – and sound; intact, with a whole skin, without a scratch.

Phr. *nolumus leges Angliae mutari.*

671. Escape.—N. escape, scape; avolation, elopment, flight, get-away; evasion etc. (*avoidance*) 623; retreat; narrow –, hairbreadth- escape; close –, near- shave; come off, impunity.

[Means of escape] loophole etc. (*opening*) 260; path etc. 627; secret -door, – passage; refuge etc. 666; vent, – peg; safety-valve; drawbridge, fire-escape.

reprieve etc. (*deliverance*) 672; liberation etc. 750.

refugee etc. (*fugitive*) 623.

V. escape, scape; make –, effect –, make good- one's escape, make a get-away; get -off, – clear off, – well out of; *échapper belle*, save one's bacon; weather the storm etc. (*safe*) 664; escape scot-free.

elude etc., make off etc. (*avoid*) 623; march off etc. (*go away*) 293; give one the slip; slip through the -hands, – fingers; slip the collar, wriggle out of; break -loose, – from prison; break –, slip –, get- away; find -vent, – a hole to creep out of.

Adj. escap-ing, -ed etc. *v.*; stolen away, fled.

Phr. the bird has flown.

672. Deliverance.—N. deliverance, extrication, rescue; repriev-e, -al; respite; ransom; liberation etc. 750; truce, armistice; redemption, salvation; riddance; gaol delivery; exemption, day of grace; redeemableness.

V. deliver, extricate, rescue, save, redeem, ransom, free, liberate, release, set free, redeem, emancipate; bring -off, – through; *tirer d'affaire*, get the wheel out of the rut; snatch from the jaws of death, come to the rescue; rid; retrieve etc. (*restore*) 660; be –, get- rid of.

Adj. saved etc. *v.*; extric-, redeem-, rescu-able.

Phr. to the rescue!

673. Preparation.—N. preparation; providing etc. *v.*; provi-sion, -dence; anticipation etc. (*foresight*) 510; precaution, -concertation, disposition; forecast etc. (*plan*) 626; rehearsal, not of preparation.

[Putting in order] arrangement etc. 60; clearance; adjustment etc. 23; tuning; equipment, outfit, accoutrement, armament, array.

ripening etc. *v.*; maturation, evolution; elaboration, concoction, digestion; gestation, hatching, incubation, sitting.

groundwork, datum, first stone, cradle, stepping-stone; foundation, scaffold etc. (*support*) 215; scaffolding, *échafaudage*.

[Preparation -of men] training etc. (*education*) 537; inurement etc. (*habit*) 613; novitiate; [– of food] cook-ing, -ery; brewing, culinary art; [– of the soil] till-, plough-, sow-ing; semination, cultivation.

[State of being prepared] prepared-, readi-, ripe-, mellow-ness; maturity; *un impromptu fait à loisir.*

[Preparer] preparer, teacher, coach, trainer, pioneer; *avant-courrier*, *-coureur*; sappers and miners, paver, navvy; packer, stevedore; warmingpan; precursor etc. 64.

V. prepare; get –, make- ready; make preparations, settle preliminaries, get up, sound the note of preparation; address oneself to.

set –, put- in order etc. (*arrange*) 60; forecast etc. (*plan*) 626; prepare –, plough –, dress- the ground; till –, cultivate- the soil; predispose, sow the seed, lay a train, dig a mine; lay –, fix- the -foundations, – basis, -groundwork; dig the foundations, erect the scaffolding; lay the first stone etc. (*begin*) 66.

rough-hew; cut out work; block –, hammer-out; lick into shape etc. (*form*) 240.

elaborate, mature, ripen, mellow, season, bring to maturity; nurture etc.

(*aid*) 707; hatch, cook, brew; temper; anneal, smelt; dry, cure etc. 670.

equip, arm, man; fit-out, -up; furnish, rig, dress, garnish, betrim, accouter, array, fettle, fledge; dress –, furbish –, brush –, vamp- up; refurbish; sharpen one's tools, trim one's foils, set, prime, attune; whet the -knife, – sword; wind –, screw- up; adjust etc. (*fit*) 27; put in- trim, – train, – gear, – working order, – tune, – a groove for, – harness; pack, stow away, store.

train etc. (*teach*) 537; inure etc. (*habituate*) 613; breed; prepare etc.- for; rehearse; make provision for; take -steps, – measures, – precautions; provide, – against; beat up for recruits; open the door to etc. (*facilitate*) 705.

set one's house in order, make all snug; clear -decks, – for action; close one's ranks; shuffle the cards.

prepare oneself; serve an apprenticeship etc. (*learn*) 539; lay oneself out for, get into harness, gird up one's loins, buckle on one's armor, *reculer pour mieux sauter*, prime and load, shoulder arms, get the steam up, put the horses to.

guard –, make sure- against; forearm, make sure, prepare for the evil day, have a rod in pickle, provide against a rainy day, feather one's nest; lay in provisions etc. 637; make investments; keep on foot.

be -prepared, – ready etc. *adj.*; hold oneself in readiness, watch and pray, keep one's powder dry; lie in wait for etc. (*expect*) 507; anticipate etc. (*foresee*) 510; *principiis obstare*; *veniente occurrere morbo.*

Adj. preparing etc. *v.*; in -preparation, – course

of preparation, – agitation, – embryo, – hand, – train; afoot, afloat; on -foot, – the stocks, – the anvil; under consideration etc. (*plan*) 626; brewing, hatching, forthcoming, brooding; in -store for, – reserve.

precautionary, provident; prepara-tive, -tory; provisional, inchoate, under revision; preliminary etc. (*precedent*) 62.

prepared etc. *v.*; in readiness; ready, – to one's hand, – made, cut and dried; ready for use, reach me down; made to one's hand, handy, on the table, made to order; in gear; in working -order, – gear; snug; in practice.

ripe, mature, mellow; practiced etc. (*skillet*) 698; labored, elaborate, highly-wrought, smelling of the lamp, worked up.

in -full feather, – best bib and tucker; in –, at- harness; in – the saddle, – arms, – battle array, – war paint; up in arms; armed -at all points, – to the teeth, – *cap-à-pie*; sword in hand; booted and spurred.

in utrumque –, semper- paratus; on the alert etc. (*vigilant*) 459; at one's post.

Adv. in -preparation, – anticipation of; afoot, astir, abroad; abroach.

674. Non-preparation.—N. non-, absence of –, want of- preparation; unpreparedness; inculture, inconcoction, improvidence.

immaturity, crudity; rawness etc. *adj.*; abortion; disqualification.

[Absence of art] nature, state of nature; virgin soil, unweeded garden; rough diamond, neglect etc. 460.

rough copy etc. (*plan*) 626; germ etc. 153; raw material etc. 635.

improvisation etc. (*impulse*) 612.

V. be -unprepared etc. *adj.*; want –, lack- preparation; lie fallow; *s'embarquer sans biscuits*; live from hand to mouth.

[Render unprepared] dismantle etc. (*render useless*) 645; undress etc. 226.

extemporize, improvise.

surprise, pay a surprise visit, take by surprise, drop in upon, take unawares; take pot-luck.

Adv. un-prepared etc. prepare etc. 673] without -preparation etc. 673; incomplete etc. 53; rudimental, embryonic, abortive; immature, unripe, raw, green, crude; coarse; rough, -cast, -hewn; in the rough; un-hewn, -formed, -fashioned, -wrought, -labored, -blown, -cooked, -boiled, -concocted, -cut, -polished.

callow, un-hatched, -fledged, -nurtured, -licked, -taught, -educated, -cultivated, -trained, -tutored, -drilled, -exercised; precocious, premature; un-, indigested; un-mellowed, -seasoned, -leavened.

fallow; un-sown, -tilled; natural, in a state of nature; undressed; in dishabille, *en déshabille, en négligé*.

un-, dis-qualified; unfitted; ill-digested; unbegun, -ready, -arranged, -organized, -furnished, -provided, -equipped, -trimmed; out of -gear, – order; dismantled etc. *v.*

shiftless, improvident, unthrifty, thoughtless, unguarded; happy-go-lucky; caught napping etc. (*inexpectant*) 508; unpremeditated etc. 612.

Adv. extempore etc. 612.

675. Essay.—N. essay, trial, endeavor, aim, attempt; venture, adventure, speculation, *coup d'essai, début*; probation etc. (*experiment*) 463.

V. try, essay; experiment etc. 463; endeavor, strive; tempt, tackle, take on, attempt, make an attempt; venture, adventure, speculate, take one's chance, tempt fortune; try one's -fortune, – luck, – hand; use one's endeavor; feel –, grope –, pick- one's way.

try hard, push, make a bold push, use one's best endeavor; do one's best etc. (*exertion*) 686.

Adj. essaying etc. *v.*; experimental etc. 463; tentative, empirical, probationary.

Adv. experimentally etc. *adj.*; on trial, at a venture; by rule of thumb.

if one may be so bold.

676. Undertaking.—N. undertaking, compact etc. 769; engagement etc. (*promise*) 768; enter-, em-prise; venture etc. 675; pilgrimage; matter in hand etc. (*business*) 625; move; first move etc. (*beginning*) 66.

V. undertake; engage –, embark- in; launch –, plunge- into; volunteer; apprentice oneself to; engage etc. (*promise*) 768; contract etc. 769; take upon -oneself, – one's shoulders; devote oneself to etc. (*determination*) 604.

take -up, – in hand; tackle; set –, go- about; set –, fall- -to, – to work; launch forth; set up shop; put in -hand, – execution; set forward; break the neck of a business, be in for; put one's hand to; betake oneself to, turn one's hand to, go to do; begin etc. 66; broach, institute, etc. (*originate*) 153; put –, lay- one's -hand to the plough, – shoulder to the wheel.

have in hand etc. (*business*) 625; have many irons in the fire etc. (*activity*) 682.

Adj. undertaking etc. *v.*; on the anvil etc. 625; adventurous, venturesome.

Int. here goes!

677. Use.—N. use; employ, -ment; exer-cise, -citation; appli-cation, -ance; adhibition, disposal; consumption; agency etc. (*physical*) 170; usufruct; usefulness etc. 644; recourse, resort, avail, pragmatism.

[Conversion to use] utilization, service, wear.

[Way of using] usage.

V. use, make use of, employ, put to use; apply, put in -action, – operation, – practice; set -in motion, – to work.

ply, work, wield, handle, manipulate; play, – off; exert, exercise, practice, avail oneself of, profit by; resort –, have recourse –, recur –, take –, betake oneself- to; take -up with, – advantage of; lay one's hands on, try.

render useful etc. 644; mold; turn to -account, – use; convert to use, utilize, administer; work up; call –, bring- into play; put into requisition; call –, draw- forth; press –, enlist- into the service; bring to bear upon, devote, dedicate, consecrate, apply, adhibit, dispose of; make a -handle, – cat's paw- of.

fall beak upon, make a shift with; make the -most, – best- of.

use –, swallow- up; consume, absorb, expend; tax, task, wear, put to task.

Adj. in use; used etc. *v.*; well-worn, -trodden.
useful etc. 644; subservient etc. (*instrumental*) 631; utilitarian; pragmatical.

678. Disuse.—N. forbearance, abstinence; disuse; relinquishment etc. 782; desuetude etc. (*want of habit*) 614.

V. not use; do without, dispense with, let alone, not touch, forbear, abstain, spare, waive, neglect; keep back, reserve.

lay -up, – by, – on the shelf, – up in a napkin; shelve; set –, put –, lay- aside; disuse, leave off, have done with; supersede; discard etc. (*eject*) 297; dismiss, give warning.

throw aside etc. (*relinquish*) 782; make away with etc. (*destroy*) 162; cast –, heave –, throw- overboard; cast to the -dogs, – winds; dismantle etc. (*render useless*) 645.

lie –, remain- unemployed etc. *adj.*

Adj. not used etc. *v.*; un-employed, -applied, -disposed of, -spent, -exercised, -touched, -trodden, -essayed, -gathered, -culled; uncalled for, not required.

disused etc. *v.*; done with; run down, used up, cast off.

679. Misuse.—N. mis-use, -usage, -employment, -application, -appropriation.

abuse, profanation, prostitution, desecration; waste etc. 638.

V. mis-use, -employ, -apply, -appropriate.

desecrate, abuse, profane, prostitute; waste etc. 638; over-task, -tax, -work; squander etc. 818.

cut a whetstone with a razor, employ a steam-engine to crack a nut; catch at a straw.

Adj. misused etc. *v.*

680. Action.—N. action, performance; doing etc. *v.*; perpetration; exercise, -citation; movement, operation, evolution, work; labor etc. (*exertion*) 686; *praxis*, execution; procedure etc. (*conduct*) 692; handicraft; business etc. 625; agency etc. (*power at work*) 170.

deed, act, overt act, stitch, touch, gest; transaction, job, doings, dealings, proceeding, measure, step, maneuver, bout, passage, move, stroke, blow; *coup*, – *de main*, – *d'état*; *tour de force* etc. (*display*) 882; feat, exploit, stunt; achievement etc. (*completion*) 729; handiwork, workmanship, craftsmanship; manufacture; stroke of policy etc. (*plan*) 626.

actor etc. (*doer*) 690.

V. do, perform, execute; achieve etc. (*complete*) 729; transact, enact; commit, perpetrate, inflict; exercise, prosecute, carry on, work, practice, play.

employ oneself, ply one's task; officiate, have in hand etc. (*business*) 625; labor etc. 686; be at work; pursue a course; shape one's course etc. (*conduct*) 692.

act, operate; take -action, – steps; strike a blow, lift a finger, stretch forth one's hand; take in hand etc. (*undertake*) 676; put oneself in motion; put in practice; carry into execution etc. (*complete*) 729; act upon.

be -an actor etc. 690; take –, act –, play –, perform- a part in; participate in; have a -hand in, – finger in the pie; have to do with; be a -party to, – participator in; bear –, lend- a hand; pull an oar, run in a race; mix oneself up with etc. (*meddle*) 682.

be in action; come into operation etc. (*power at work*) 170.

Adj. doing etc. *v.*; acting; in action; in harness; on duty; at work; in operation etc. 170; up to one's ears in work, in the midst of things.

Adv. in the -act, – midst of, – thick of; red-handed, *in flagrante delicto*; while one's hand is in.

681. Inaction.—N. inaction, passiveness, abstinence from action; non-interference; Fabian –, conservative- policy; neglect etc. 460; stagnation, vegetation; loafing.

inactivity etc. 683; rest etc. (*repose*) 687; quiescence etc. 265; want of –, in- occupation; unemployment; idle hours, time hanging on one's hands, *dolce far niente*; sinecure.

V. not -do, – act, – attempt; be -inactive etc. 683; abstain from doing, do nothing, hold, spare; not -stir, – move, – lift- a -finger, – foot, – peg; fold one's -arms, – hands; leave –, let- alone; let -be, – pass, – things take their course, – it have its way, – well alone; *quieta non movere*; *stare super antiquas vias*; rest and be thankful, live and let live; lie –, rest- upon one's oars; *laisser -aller*, – *faire*; stand aloof; refrain etc. (*avoid*) 623; keep oneself from doing; remit –, relax- one's efforts; desist etc. (*relinquish*) 624; stop etc. (*cease*) 142; pause etc. (*be quiet*) 265.

wait, lie in wait, bide one's time, take time, tide it over.

cool –, kick- one's heels; loaf, while away the -time, – tedious hours; pass –, fill –, beguile- the time; talk against time; waste time etc. (*inactive*) 683.

lie -by, – on the shelf, – in ordinary, – idle, – to, – fallow; keep quiet, slug; have nothing to do, whistle for want of thought; twiddle one's thumbs.

undo, do away with; take -down, – to pieces; destroy etc. 162.

Adj. not doing etc. *v.*; not done etc. *v.*; undone; passive; un-occupied, -employed; out of -employ, – work, – a job; fallow; *désoeuvré*.

Adv. *re infectâ*, at a stand, *les bras croisés*, with folded arms; with the hands -in the pockets, – behind one's back; *pour passer le temps*.

Int. so let it be! stop! etc. 142; hands off!

Phr. nothing doing; *cunctando restituit rem*.

682. Activity.—N. activity; briskness, liveliness etc. *adj.*; animation, life, vivacity, spirit, verve, dash, energy, go.

nimbleness, agility; smartness, quickness etc. *adj.*; velocity etc. 274; alacrity, promptitude; des-, dis-patch; expedition; haste etc. 684; punctuality etc. (*early*) 132.

eagerness, zeal, ardor, *perfervidum ingenium*, *empressement*, earnestness, intentness; *abandon*; vigor etc. (*physical energy*) 171; devotion etc. (*resolution*) 604; exertion etc. 686.

industry, assiduity; assiduousness etc. *adj.*; sedulity; laboriousness; drudgery etc. (*labor*) 686; painstaking, diligence; perseverance etc. 604*a*; indefatigation; habits of business.

vigilance etc. 459; wakefulness; sleep-, restlessness; *pervigilium, insomnia*; racketing.

movement, bustle, hustle, stir, fuss, ado, bother, pottering; fidget, -iness; flurry etc. (*haste*) 684.

officiousness; dabbling, meddling; inter-ference, -position, -meddling, butting in, intrusiveness; tampering with, intrigue.

press of business, no sinecure, plenty to do, many irons in the fire, great doings, busy hum of men, battle of life, thick of -things, – the action; the madding corwd.

housewife, busy bee; new brooms; sharp fellow, blade; hustler, devotee, enthusiast, fan, zealot, fanatic; meddler, intermeddler, intriguer, busybody, kibitzer, pickthank.

V. be -active etc. *adj.*; busy oneself in; stir, -about, – one's stumps; bestir –, rouse- oneself; speed, hasten, peg away, lay about one, bustle, fuss; raise –, kick up- a dust; push; make a -push, – fuss, – stir; go ahead, push forward; flight –, elbow- one's way; make progress etc. 282; toil etc. (*labor*) 686; drudge, plod, persist etc. (*persevere*) 604*a*; keep -up the ball, – the pot boiling.

look sharp; have all one's eyes about one etc. (*vigilance*) 459; rise, arouse oneself, get up early, hustle, push; be about, keep moving, steal a march, kill two birds with one stone; seize the opportunity etc. 134; lose no time, not lose a moment, make the most of one's time, not suffer the grass to grow under one's feet, improve the shining hour, make short work of; dash off; make haste etc. 684; do one's best, take pains etc. (*exert oneself*) 686; do –, work- wonders.

have -many irons in the fire, – one's hands full, – much on one's hands; have other -things to do, – fish to fry; be busy; not have a moment -to spare, – that one can call one's own.

have one's fling, run the round of; go all lengths, stick at nothing, run riot.

outdo; over-do, -act, -lay, -shoot the mark; make a toil of a pleasure.

have a hand in etc. (*act in*) 680; take an active part, put in one's oar, have a finger in the pie, mix oneself up with, trouble one's head about, intrigue; agitate.

tamper with, meddle, moil; inter-meddle, -fere, -pose; obtrude; poke –, thrust- one's nose in, butt in.

Adj. active; brisk, – as a lark, – as a bee; lively, animated, vivacious; alive, – and kicking; frisky, spirited, stirring.

nimble, – as a squirrel; agile; light-, nimble-footed; featly, tripping.

quick, prompt, yare, instant, ready, alert, spry, sharp, smart, slick, go-ahead; fast etc. (*swift*) 274; quick as a lamplighter, expeditious; awake, broad awake; wide awake etc. (*intelligent*) 498.

forward, eager, ardent, strenuous, zealous, enterprising, pushing, in earnest; resolute etc. 604.

industrious, assiduous, diligent, sedulous, notable, painstaking; intent etc. (*attention*) 457; indefatigable etc. (*persevering*) 604*a*; unwearied; unsleeping, sleepless, never tired; plodding, hardworking etc. 686; business-like, workaday.

bustling; restless, – as a hyena; fussy, fidgety, pottering; busy, – as a hen with one chicken.

working, laboring, at work, on duty, in harness; up in arms; on one's legs, at call; up and -doing, – stirring.

busy, occupied; hard at -work, – it; up to one's ears in, full of business, busy as a bee.

meddling etc. *v.*; meddlesome, pushing, officious, overofficious, *intrigant*.

astir, stirring; a-going, -foot; on foot; in full swing; eventful; on the alert etc. (*vigilant*) 459.

Adv. actively etc. *adj.*; with -life and spirit, – might and main etc. 686, – haste etc. 684, – wings; full tilt, *in mediis rebus*.

Int. be –, look- -alive, – sharp! move –, push- on! keep moving! go ahead! stir your stumps! *age quod agis!*

Phr. *carpe diem* etc. (*opportunity*) 134; *nulla dies sine lineâ*; *nec mora nec requies*; no sooner said than done etc. (*early*) 132; catch a weasel asleep.

683. Inactivity.—N. inactivity; inaction etc. 681; inertness etc. 172; obstinacy etc. 606.

lull etc. (*cessation*) 142; quiescence etc. 265; rust, -iness.

idle-, remiss-ness etc. *adj.*; sloth, indolence, indiligence; otiosity, dawdling etc. *v.*

dullness etc. *adj.*; languor; segni-ty, -tude; lentor; sluggishness etc. (*slowness*) 275; procrastination etc. (*delay*) 133; torp-or, -idity, -escence; stupor etc. (*insensibility*) 823; somnolence; drowsiness etc. *adj.*; nodding etc. *v.*; oscitation, -ancy; pandiculation, hypnotism, lethargy; heaviness, heavy eye-lids, sand in the eyes.

sleep, slumber; sound –, heavy –, balmy-sleep; Morpheus, dreamland; coma, trance, catalepsy, hypnosis, *ecstasis*, dream, hibernation, nap, doze, snooze, *siesta*, wink of sleep, forty winks, snore; Hypnology.

dull work; pottering; relaxation etc. (*loosening*) 47; Castle of Indolence.

[Cause of inactivity] lullaby, *berceuse*; anesthetic, sedative etc. 174; torpedo.

idler, drone, droil, dawdle, mopus; do-little, *fainéant*, dummy, sleeping partner; afternoon farmer; truant etc. (*runaway*) 623; lounger, *lazzarone*, floater, loafer, tramp, beggar, cadger; lubber, -bard; slow-coach etc. (*slow*) 275; opium –, lotus- eater; slug; lag-, slug-gard, lie-abed; slumberer, dormouse, marmot; waiter on Providence, *fruges consumere natus*.

V. be -inactive etc. *adj.*; do nothing etc. 681; move slowly etc. 275; let the grass grow under one's feet; take one's time, dawdle, poke, drawl, droil, lag, hang back, slouch; loll, -op; lounge, loaf, loiter; go to sleep over; sleep at one's post; *ne battre que d'une aile*.

take -it easy, – things as they come; lead an easy life, vegetate, swim with the stream, eat the bread of idleness; loll in the lap of -luxury, – indolence; waste –, consume –, kill –, lose time; burn daylight, waste the precious hours.

idle –, trifle –, fritter –, fool- away time; spend –, take- time in; ped-, pid-dle; potter, putter, dabble, faddle, fribble, fiddle-faddle; dally, dilly-dally.

sleep, slumber, be asleep; hibernate; oversleep; sleep like a -top, – log, – dormouse; sleep -soundly, – heavily; doze, drowze, snooze, nap; take a -nap etc. *n.*; dream; snore; settle –, go –, go off- to sleep; drop off; fall –, drop- asleep; close –, seal up- -the -eyes, – eyelids; weigh down the eyelids; get sleepy, nod, yawn; go to bed, turn in.

languish, expend itself, flag, hang fire; relax.

render -idle etc. *adj.*; sluggardize; mitigate etc. 174.

Adj. inactive; motionless etc. 265; unoccupied etc. (*doing nothing*) 681.

indolent, lazy, slothful, idle, otiose, lusk, remiss, slack, inert, torpid, sluggish, languid, supine, heavy, dull, leaden, lumpish: exanimate, soulless; listless; dron-y, -ish; lazy as Ludlam's dog.

dilatory, laggard; lagging etc. *v.*; slow etc. 275; rusty, flagging; lackadaisical, maudlin, fiddle-faddle; pottering etc. *v.*; shilly-shally etc. (*irresolute*) 605.

sleeping etc. *v.*; alseep; fast –, dead –, sound-alseep; in a sound sleep; sound as a top, dormant, comatose; in the -arms, – lap- of Morpheus.

sleep-y, -ful; dozy, drowsy, somnolent, torpescent; lethargic, -al; heavy, – with sleep; napping; somni-fic, -ferous; sopor-ous, -ific, -iferous; hypnotic; balmy, dreamy; un-, una-wakened.

sedative etc. 174.

Adv. inactively etc. *adj.*; at leisure etc. 685.

Phr. the eyes begin to draw straws.

684. Haste.—N. haste, urgency; des-, dis-patch; acceleration, spurt, spirt, forced march, rush, dash; velocity etc. 274; precipit-ancy, -ation, -ousness etc. *adj.*; impetuosity; *brusquerie*; hurry, scurry, scuttle, drive, scramble, push, hustle, bustle, fuss, fidget, flurry, flutter, splutter.

V. haste, hasten; make -haste, – a dash etc. *n.*; hurry –, dash –, whip –, push –, press- -on, – forward; hurry, skurry, scuttle along, bundle on, dart to and fro, bustle, flutter, scramble; plunge, – headlong; run, race, speed; dash off; rush etc. (*violence*) 173.

bestir oneself etc. (*be active*) 682; lose -no time, – not a moment, – not an instant; make short work of; make the best of one's -time, – way.

be -precipitate etc. *adj.*; jump at; be in -haste, – a hurry etc. *n.*; have -no time, – not a moment- -to lose, – to spare; work -under pressure, – against time.

quicken etc. 274; accelerate, expedite, put on, precipitate, urge, whip, spur, flog, goad.

Adj. hasty, hurried, *brusque*; scrambling, cursory, precipitate, headlong, furious, boisterous, impetuous, hot-headed; feverish, fussy; pushing.

in -haste, – a hurry etc. *n.*; in -hot, – all- haste; breathless, pressed for time, hard pressed, urgent.

Adv. with -haste, – all haste, – breathless speed; in haste etc. *adj.*; apace etc. (*swiftly*) 274; amain; all at once etc. (*instantaneously*) 113; at short notice etc., immediately etc. (*early*) 132; posthaste; by -express, – telegraph, – wire, – wireless, – air mail.

hastily, precipitately etc. *adj.*; helter-skelter, hurry-skurry, holusbolus; slap-dash, -bang; full-tilt, -drive; heels over head, head and shoulders, headlong, *à corps perdu*.

by -fits and starts, – spurts; hop, skip and jump.

Phr. *sauve qui peut*, devil take the hindmost, no time to be lost; no sooner said than done etc. (*early*) 132; a word and a blow.

Int. hurry up! look alive! get a move on! buck up! double march! rush! urgent!

685. Leisure.—N. leisure; spare -time, – hours, – moments; vacant hour; time, – to spare, – on one's hands; holiday etc. (*rest*) 687; *otium cum dignitate*, ease.

V. have -leisure etc. *n.*; take one's -time, – leisure, – ease; repose etc. 687; move slowly etc. 275; while away the time etc. (*inaction*) 681; be -master of one's time, – an idle man; *desipere in loco*.

Adj. leisurely; slow etc. 275; deliberate, quiet, calm, undisturbed; at -leisure, – one's ease, – a loose end.

Phr. time hanging heavy on one's hands.

686. Exertion.—N. exertion, effort, strain, tug, pull, stress, force, pressure, throw, stretch, struggle, spell, spurt, spirt; stroke –, stitch- of work.

'a stong pull, a long pull and a pull all together;' dead lift; heft; gymnastics, sports; exer-cise, -citation; wear and tear; ado; toil and trouble; uphill –, hard –, warm- work; harvest time.

labor, work, toil, travail, manual labor, sweat of one's brow, swink, operoseness, drudgery, slavery, fagging, hammering; *limae labor*.

trouble, pains, duty; resolution etc. 604; energy etc. (*physical*) 171.

V. exert oneself; exert –, tax- one's energies; use exertion.

labor, work, toil, moil, sweat, fag, drudge, slave, drag a lengthened chain, wade through, strive, strain; make –, stretch- a long arm; pull, tug, ply; ply –, tug at- the oar; do the work; take the laboring oar.

bestir oneself (*be active*) 682; take trouble, trouble oneself.

work hard; rough it; put forth -one's strength, – a strong arm; fall to work, bend the bow; buckle to, set one's shoulder to the wheel etc. (*resolution*) 604; work like a -Briton, – horse, – carthorse, – galley-slave, – coalheaver; labor –, work-day and night; redouble one's efforts; do double duty; work double -hours, – tides; sit up, burn the -midnight oil, – candle at both ends; stick to etc. (*persevere*) 604*a*; work –, fight- one's way; lay about one, hammer at.

take pains; do one's -best, – level best, – utmost; do -the best one can, – all one can, – all in one's power, – as much as in one lies, – what lies in one's power; use one's -best, – utmost- endeavor; try one's -best, – utmost; play one's best card; put one's -best, – right- leg foremost; have one's whole soul in one's work, put all one's strength into, strain every nerve; spare no -efforts, – pains; go all lengths; go through fire and water etc. (*resolution*) 604; move heaven and earth, leave no stone unturned.

Adj. laboring etc. *v.*

laborious, operose, elaborate; strained; toil-, trouble-, burden-, weari-some; uphill; herculean, gymnastic, athletic, palestric.

hardworking, painstaking, strenuous, energetic. hard at work, on the stretch.

Adv. laboriously etc. *adj.*; lustily; with -might and main, – all one's might, – a strong hand, – sledge-hammer, – much ado; to the best of one's abilities, *totis viribus*, *vi et armis*, *manibus pedibusque*, tooth and nail, *unguibus et rostro*,

hammer and tongs, heart and soul; through thick and thin etc. (*perseverance*) 604*a*.
by the sweat of one's brow, *suo Marte*.

687. Repose.—N. repose, rest, silken repose; sleep etc. 683.
relaxation, breathing time; halt, pause etc. (*cessation*) 142; respite.
day of rest, *dies non*, Sabbath, Lord's day, holiday, red-letter day, vacation, recess.
V. repose; rest, – and be thankful; take -rest, – one's ease.
relax, unbend, slacken; take breath etc. (*refresh*) 689; rest upon one's oars; pause etc. (*cease*) 142; stay one's hand.
lie down; recline, – on a bed of down, – on an easy chair; go to -rest, – bed, – sleep etc. 683.
take a holiday, shut up shop; lie fallow etc. (*inaction*) 681.
Adj. reposing etc. *v.*; unstrained.
Adv. at rest.

688. Fatigue.—N. fatigue; weariness etc. 841; yawning, drowsiness etc. 683; lassitude, tiredness, fatigation, exhaustion; sweat.
anhelation, shortness of breath, panting; faintness; collapse, prostration, swoon, fainting, *deliquium*, syncope, lipothymy.
V. be -fatigued etc. *adj.*; yawn etc. (*get sleepy*) 683; droop, sink, flag; lose -breath, – wind; gasp, pant, puff, blow, drop, swoon, faint, succumb.
fatigue, tire, weary, bore, irk, fag, jade, harass, exhaust, knock up, wear out, prostrate.
tax, task, strain; over-task, -work, -burden, -tax, -strain.
Adj. fatigued etc. *v.*; weary etc. 841; drowsy etc. 683; drooping etc. *v.*; haggard; toil-, way-worn; footsore, surbated, weatherbeaten; faint; done –, used –, knock- up; exhausted, prostrate, spent; over-tired, -spent, -fatigued; forspent; unre-freshed, -stored.
worn, – out; battered, shattered, pulled down, seedy, altered.
breath-, wind-less; short of –, out of -breath, – wind; blown, puffing and blowing; short-breathed; anhelous; broken-, short-winded.
ready to drop, more dead than alive, dog -tired, – weary, walked off one's legs, tired to death, on one's last legs, played out, *hors de combat*.
fatiguing etc. *v.*; tire-, irk-, weari-some; weary; trying.

689. Refreshment.—N. bracing etc. *v.*; recovery of -strength etc. 159; restoration, revival etc. 660; repair, refection, refocillation, refreshment, regalement, bait; relief etc. 834.
V. brace etc. (*strengthen*) 159; reinvigorate; air, freshen up, refresh, recruit; repair etc. (*restore*) 660; fan, revocillate.
breathe, respire; draw –, take –, gather –, take a long –, regain –, recover- breath; get better, raise one's head; recover –, regain –, renew- one's strength etc. 159; perk up.
come to oneself etc. (*revive*) 660; feel like a giant refreshed.
Adj. refreshing etc. *v.*; recuperative etc. 660.
refreshed etc. *v.*; un-tired, -wearied.

690. Agent.—N. doer, actor, agent, performer, perpetrator, operator; execu-tor, -trix; practitioner, worker, stager.
bee, ant, working bee, laboring oar, shaft horse, servant –, maid- of all work, general servant, factotum.
workman, artisan; crafts-, handicrafts-man; mechanic, operative; working –, laboring- man; hewers of wood and drawers of water, laborer, navvy; hand, man, day laborer, journeyman, hack; mere -tool etc. 633; porter, docker, stevedore, beast of burden, drudge, fag.
maker, artificer, artist, wright, manufacturer, architect, contractor, builder, mason, bricklayer, smith, forger, Vulcan; black-, tin-smith; carpenter; ganger, platelayer.
machinist, mechanician, engineer, electrician, plumber, gasfitter etc.
semp-, sem-, seam-stress; needle-, char-, work-woman; tailor, cordwainer.
minister etc. (*instrument*) 631; servant etc. 746; representative etc. (*commissioner*) 758; (*deputy*) 759.
co-worker, fellow-worker, party to, participator in, co-operator, colleague, associate, collaborator, *particeps criminis, dramatis personae*; *personnel*.
Phrs. *'quorum pars magna fui.'*

691. Workshop.—N. work-shop, -house; laboratory; manufactory, mill, factory, armory, arsenal, mint, forge, loom; cabinet, *studio*, *bureau*, *atelier*; hive, – of industry; nursery; hot-house, -bed; kitchen, kitchenette; dock, -yard; slip, yard, wharf; found-ry, -ery; furnace; vineyard, orchard, farm, kitchen garden.
melting pot, crucible, alembic, caldron, mortar, *matrix*.

692. Conduct.—N. dealing, transaction etc. (*action*) 680; business etc. 625.
tactics, game, policy, polity; general-, statesman-, seaman-ship; strate-gy, -gics; plan etc. 626.
husbandry; house-keeping, -wifery; stewardship; *ménage*; regimen, *régime*; econom-y, -ics; political economy; management; government etc. (*direction*) 693.
execution, manipulation, treatment, campaign, career, life, course, walk, race.
conduct; behavior; de-, com-portment; carriage, *maintien*, demeanor, guise, bearing, manner, mien, air, observance.
course –, line- of -conduct, – action, – proceeding; *rôle*; process, ways, practice, procedure, *modus operandi*; method etc., path etc. 627.
V. transact, execute; des-, dis-patch; proceed with, discharge; carry -on, – through, – out, – into effect; work out; go –, get- through; enact; put into practice; officiate etc. 625.

behave —, comport —, demean —, carry —, bear —, conduct —, acquit- oneself.

run a race, lead a life, play a game; take —, adopt- a course; steer —, shape- one's course; play one's- part, — cards; shift for oneself; paddle one's own canoe.

conduct; manage etc. (*direct*) 693.

deal —, have to do- with; treat, handle a case; take -steps, — measures.

Adj. conducting etc. *v.*; strategical, business-like, practical, economic, executive.

693. Direction.—N. direction; manage-ment, -ry; government, gubernation, conduct, legislation, regulation, guidance; steer-, pilot-age; reins, — of government; helm, rudder, controls, joy stick, needle, compass, binnacle; guiding —, load —, lode —, pole- star; cynosure.

super-vision, -intendence; *surveillance*, oversight; eye of the master; control, charge, auspices; board of control etc. (*council*) 696; command etc. (*authority*) 737.

premier-, senator-ship; director etc. 694; chair, seat, portfolio.

statesmanship; state-, king-craft.

minis-try, -tration; administration; steward-, proctor-ship; agency.

V. direct, manage, govern, conduct; order, prescribe, cut out work for; head, lead; lead —, show- the way; take the lead, lead on; regulate, guide, steer, pilot; take —, be at- the helm; have —, handle —, hold —, take- the reins, handle the ribbons; drive, tool; tackle.

super-intend, -vise; overlook, control, keep in order, look after, see to, oversee, legislate for; administer, ministrate; patronize; have the -care, — charge- of; have —, take- the direction; pull the -strings, — wires; rule etc. (*command*) 737; have —, hold- -office, — the portfolio; preside, — at the board; take —, occupy —, be in- the chair; pull the stroke oar.

Adj. directing etc. *v.*; executive, supervisory, hegemonic.

Adv. at the -helm, — head of, in charge of; under the auspices of.

694. Director.—N. director, manager, governor, rector, comptroller; super-intendent, -visor; intendant; over-seer, -looker; foreman, boss, straw boss; supercargo, husband, inspector, visitor, ranger, surveyor, aedile, moderator, monitor, task-master; master etc. 745; leader, ringleader, demagogue, corypheus, conductor, fugleman, precentor, bellwether, agitator.

guiding star etc. (*guidance*) 693; adviser etc. 695; guide etc. (*information*) 527; pilot; helmsman; steers-man, -mate; man at the wheel; wire-puller.

driver, whip, Jehu, charioteer; coach-, car-, cab-man, jarvey; postilion, *vetturino*, muleteer, team-ster; whipper in; engineer, engine driver, motor-man, *chauffeur*.

head, — man; principal, president, speaker; chair, -man; captain etc. (*master*) 745; superior; dean; mayor etc. (*civil authority*) 745; vice-president, prime minister, premier, vizier, grand vizier; dictator.

officer, functionary, minister, official, red-tapist, bureaucrat; man —, Jack- in office; office-bearer; person in authority etc. 745.

statesman, strategist, legislator, lawgiver, politician, administrator, statist, statemonger; Minos, Draco; arbiter etc. (*judge*) 967; king maker, power behind the throne.

board etc. (*council*) 696.

secretary, — of state; Reis Effendi; vicar etc. (*deputy*) 759; steward, factor; agent etc. 758; bailiff, middleman; ganger, clerk of works; land-reeve; factotum, major-domo, seneschal, house-keeper, shepherd, *croupier*; proctor, procurator, curator, librarian.

Adv. *ex officio*.

695. Advice.—N. advice, counsel, adhortation; word to the wise; suggestion, submonition, recommendation, advocacy, consultation.

exhortation etc. (*persuasion*) 615; expostulation etc. (*dissuasion*) 616; admonition etc. (*warning*) 668; guidance etc. (*direction*) 693.

instruction, charge, injunction.

adviser, prompter; counsel, -lor; monitor, mentor, Nestor, *magnus Apollo*, senator; teacher etc. 540.

guide, manual, chart etc. (*information*) 527.

physician, leech, archiater; arbiter etc. (*judge*) 967.

refer-ence, -ment; consultation, conference, parley, *pourparler* etc. 696.

V. advise, counsel; give -advice, — counsel, — a piece of advice; suggest, prompt, submonish, recommend, prescribe, advocate; exhort etc. (*persuade*) 615.

enjoin, enforce, charge, instruct, call; call upon etc. (*request*) 765; dictate.

expostulate etc. (*dissuade*) 616; admonish etc. (*warn*) 668.

advise with; lay heads —, consult- together; compare notes; hold a council, deliberate, be closeted with.

confer, consult, refer to, call in; take —, follow-advice; follow implicitly; be advised by, have at one's elbow, take one's cue from.

Adj. recommendatory; hortative etc. (*persuasive*) 615; dehortatory etc. (*dissuasive*) 616; admonitory etc. (*warning*) 668; consultative.

Int. go to!

696. Council.—N. council, committee, sub-committee, *comitia*, court, chamber, cabinet, board, bench, staff; consultation.

senate, *senatus*, parliament, house, — of Lords, — Peers, — Commons, legislature, legislative assembly, federal council, chamber of deputies, directory, *reichsrath*, *rigsdag*, *cortes*, storthing, witenagemote, *junta*, divan, *musnud*, *sanhedrim*, Amphictyonic council; *duma*, *zemstvo*, *soviet*, *cheka*, *ogpu*; *Dail Eireann*; caput, consistory, chapter, syndicate; court of appeal etc. (*tribunal*) 966; board of -control, — works; vestry; county —, borough —, district —, parish —, town- council, local board.

cabinet –, privy- council, royal commission; cockpit, convocation, synod, congress, congregation, convention, diet, states-general, aulic council.

League of Nations, assembly, *caucus*, conclave, *clique*, conventicle; meeting, sitting, *séance*, conference, session, hearing, palaver, *pourparler*, *durbar*, pow-wow, house; *quorum*.

senator; member, – of parliament; councilor, M.P., representative of the people.

Adj. senatorial, curule, parliamentary.

697. Precept.—N. precept, direction, instruction, charge; prescript, -ion; *recipe*, receipt; golden rule; maxim etc. 496.

commandment, rule, ruling, canon, law, code, *corpus juris*, *lex scripta*, common –, unwritten –, canon- law; the Ten Commandments; act, statute, convention, rubric, stage direction, regulation; form, -ula, -ulary; technicality; nice point.

order etc. (*command*) 741.

698. Skill.—N. skill, skilfulness, address; dexter-ity, -ousness; adroitness, expertness etc. *adj.*; proficiency, competence, craft, callidity, facility, knack, trick, sleight; master-y, -ship; excellence, panurgy; ambidext-erity, -rousness; sleight of hand etc. (*deception*) 545.

sea-, air-, marks-, horse-manship; tight-, rope-dancing.

accomplish-, acquire-, attain-ment; art, science; techn-icality, -ology, -ique; practical –, technical- knowledge; technocracy; finish, technic.

knowledge of the world, world wisdom, *savoir-faire*; tact; mother wit etc. (*sagacity*) 498; discretion etc. (*caution*) 864; *finesse*; craftiness etc. (*cunning*) 702; management etc. (*conduct*) 692; *ars celare artem*; self-help.

cleverness, talent, ability, ingenuity, capacity, parts, talents, faculty, endowment, *forte*, turn, gift, genius, flair, feeling; intelligence etc. 498; sharpness, readiness etc. (*activity*) 682; invention etc. 515; apt-ness, -itude; turn –, capacity –, genius- for; felicity, capability, *curiosa felicitas*, qualification, habilitation.

proficient etc. 700.

masterpiece, *coup de maître*, *chef- d'oeuvre*, *tour de force*; good stroke etc. (*plan*) 626.

V. be -skilful etc. *adj.*; excel in, be master of; have -a turn for etc. *n.*

know -what's what, – a hawk from a handsaw, – what one is about, – on which side one's bread is buttered, – what's o'clock, – a thing or two; have cut one's -eye, – wisdom- teeth.

see -one's way, – where the wind lies, – which way the wind blows; have -all one's wits about one, – one's hand in; *savoir vivre*; *scire quid valeant humeri quid ferre recusent*

look after the main chance; cut one's coat according to one's cloth; live by one's wits; exercise one's discretion, feather the oar, sail near the wind; stoop to conquer etc. (*cunning*) 702; play one's -cards well, – best card; hit the right nail on the head, put the saddle on the right horse.

take advantage of, make the most of; profit by etc. (*use*) 677; make a hit etc. (*succeed*) 731; make a virtue of necessity; make hay while the sun shines etc. (*occasion*) 134.

Adj. skilful, dexterous, adroit, expert, apt, slick, handy, quick, deft, ready, resourceful, gain; smart etc. (*active*) 682; proficient, good at, up to, at home in, master of, a good hand at, *au fait*, thoroughbred, masterly, crack, accomplished; conversant etc. (*knowing*) 490.

experienced, practiced, skilled; up –, well up- in; in -practice, – proper cue; competent, efficient, qualified, capable, fitted, fit for, up to the mark, trained, initiated, prepared, primed, finished.

clever, able, ingenious, felicitous, gifted, talented, endowed, cute, inventive etc. 515; shrewd, sharp etc. (*intelligent*) 498; cunning etc. 702; alive to, up to snuff, not to be caught with chaff; discreet.

neat-handed, fine-fingered, ambidextrous, sure-footed; cut out –, fitted- for.

technical, artistic, scientific, daedalian, shipshape; workman-, business-, statesman-like.

Adv. skilfully etc. *adj.*; well etc. 618; artistically; with -skill, – consummate skill; *secundum artem, suo Marte*; to the best of one's abilities etc. (*exertion*) 686; like a machine.

699. Unskillfulness.—N. unskillfulness etc. *adj.*; want of -skill etc. 698; incompeten-ce, -cy; in-ability, -felicity, -dexterity, -experience; clumsiness; disqualification, unproficiency; quackery.

folly, stupidity etc. 499; indiscretion etc. (*rashness*) 863; thoughtlessness etc. (*inattention*) 458, (*neglect*) 460.

mis-management, -conduct; impolicy; maladministration; mis-rule, -government, -application, -direction, -feasance.

absence of rule, rule of thumb; bungling etc. *v.*; failure etc. 732; screw loose; too many cooks.

blunder etc. (*mistake*) 495; *étourderie*, *gaucherie*, act of folly, *balourdise*; botch, -ery; bad job, sad work.

sprat sent out to catch a whale, much ado about nothing, wildgoose chase.

bungler etc. 701; fool etc. 501.

layman, amateur.

V. be -unskillful etc. *adj.*; not see an inch beyond one's nose; blunder, bungle, boggle, fumble, muff, botch, bitch, flounder, loppet, stumble, trip; hobble etc. 275; put one's foot in it; make a -mess, – hash, – sad work- of; overshoot the mark.

play -tricks with, – Puck; mismanage, -conduct, -direct, -apply, -send.

stultify –, make a fool of –, commit- oneself; act foolishly; play the fool; put oneself out of court; lose one's -head, – cunning.

begin at the wrong end; do things by halves etc. (*not complete*) 730; make two bites of a cherry; play at cross purposes; strain at a gnat and swallow a camel etc. (*caprice*) 608; put the cart before the horse; lock the stable door when the horse is stolen etc. (*too late*) 135.

not know -what one is about, – one's own interest, – on which side one's bread is buttered; stand in one's own light, quarrel with one's bread and butter, throw a stone in one's own garden, kill the goose which lays the golden eggs, pay dear for one's whistle, cut one's own throat, burn one's fingers; knock –, run- one's head against a stone wall; fall into a trap, catch a Tartar, bring the house about one's ears; have too many -eggs in one basket (*imprudent*) 863, – irons in the fire.

mistake etc. 495; take the shadow for the substance etc. (*credulity*) 486; be in the wrong box, aim at a pigeon and kill a crow; take –, get- the wrong sow by the ear, – the dirty end of the stick; put -the saddle on the wrong horse, – a square peg into a round hole, – new wine into old bottles.

cut a whetstone with a razor; hold a farthing candle to the sun etc. (*useless*) 645; fight with –, grasp at- a shadow; catch at straws, lean on a broken reed, reckon without one's host, pursue a wildgoose chase; go on a fool's –, sleeveless- errand; go further and fare worse; loose –, miss- one's way; fail etc. 732.

Adj. un-skillful etc. 698; unskilled, inexpert; bungling etc. *v.*; awkward, clumsy, unhandy, lubberly, *gauche*, *maladroit*; left-, heavy-handed; slovenly, slatternly; gawky.

adrift, at fault.

in-, un-apt; inhabile; un-tractable, -teachable; giddy etc. (*inattentive*) 458; inconsiderate etc. (*neglectful*) 460; stupid etc. 499; inactive etc. 683; incompetent; un-, dis-, ill-qualified; unfit; quackish; raw, green, inexperienced, rusty, out of practice.

un-accustomed, -used, -trained etc. 537; -initiated, -conversant etc. (*ignorant*) 491; shiftless; unbusinesslike, unpractical; unstatesmanlike.

un-, ill-, mis-advised; ill-devised, -imagined, -judged, -contrived, -conducted; un-, mis-guided; misconducted, foolish, wild; infelicitous; penny wise and pound foolish etc. (*inconsistent*) 608.

Phr. one's fingers being all thumbs; the right hand forgets its cunning.

il se noyerait dans une goutte d'eau.

incidit in Scyllam qui vult vitare Charybdim; *out of the frying pan into the fire*

700. Proficient.—N. proficient, expert, adept, dab; *connoisseur* etc. (*scholar*) 492; master, -hand; top-sawyer, *prima donna*, first fiddle, *chef de cuisine*; protagonist; past master; profess-or, -ional, specialist.

picked man; medalist, prizeman.

veteran; old -stager, – campaigner, – soldier, – file, – hand; man of -business, – the world.

nice –, good –, clean- hand; practised –, experienced- -eye, – hand; marksman; good –, dead –, crack- shot; rope-dancer, funambulist, acrobat, contortionist; cunning man; conjuror etc. (*deceiver*) 548; wizard etc. 994.

genius; master-mind, – head, – spirit.

cunning –, sharp -blade, – fellow; jobber; cracksman etc. (*thief*) 792; politician, tactician, diplomat, -ist, strategist.

pantologist, admirable Crichton, Jack of all trades; prodigy of learning; walking encyclopedia; mine of information.

701. Bungler.—N. bungler; blunderer, -head; marplot, fumbler, lubber, lout, oaf, duffer, stick, clown; bad –, poor- -hand, – shot; butter-fingers.

no conjuror, flat, muff, slow coach, looby, lubber, swab; clod, yokel, hick, awkward squad, novice, greenhorn, jaywalker, *blanc-bec*.

land lubber; fresh water –, fair weather- sailor; horse-marine; fish out of water, ass in lion's skin, jackdaw in peacock's feathers; quack etc. (*deceiver*) 548; Lord of Misrule.

sloven, slattern, trapes.

Phr. *il n'a pas inventé la poudre*; he will never set the Thames on fire.

702. Cunning.—N. cunning, craft; cunningness, craftiness etc. *adj.*; subtlety, artificiality; maneuvring etc. *v.*; temporization; circumvention.

chicane, -ry; sharp practice, knavery, jugglery; concealment etc. 528; nigger in the woodpile; guile, duplicity etc. (*falsehood*) 544; foul play.

diplomacy, politics; Machiavellism; jobbery, back-stairs influence, gerrymandering.

art, -ifice; device, machination; plot etc. (*plan*) 626; maneuver, stratagem, dodge, artful dodge, wile; trick, -ery etc. (*deception*) 545; *ruse*, *– de guerre*; *finesse*, side-blow, thin end of the wedge, shift, go by, subterfuge, evasion; white lie etc. (*untruth*) 546; juggle, *tour de force*; tricks -of the trade, – upon travelers; imposture, deception; *espièglerie*, net, trap etc. 545.

Ulysses, Machiavel, sly boots, fox, reynard; Scotch-, Yorkshire-man; Jew, Yankee; intriguer, *intrigant*, schemer, trickster.

V. be -cunning etc. *adj.*; have cut one's eyeteeth; contrive etc. (*plan*) 626; live by one's wits; maneuver; intrigue, gerrymander, *finesse*, double, temporize, stoop to conquer, *reculer pour mieux sauter*, circumvent, steal a march upon; overreach etc. 545; throw off one's guard; surprise etc. 508; outdo, get the better of, snatch from under one's nose; snatch a verdict; waylay, undermine, introduce the thin end of the wedge; play -a deep game, – tricks with; have an axe to grind; *ambiguas in vulgum spargere voces*; flatter, make things pleasant.

Adj. cunning, crafty, artful; skilful etc. 698; subtle, feline, vulpine; cunning as a -fox, – serpent; deep, – laid; profound; designing, contriving; intriguing etc. *v.*; strategic, diplomatic, politic, Machiavellian, time-serving; artificial; trick-y, -sy; wily, sly, slim, insidious, stealthy, foxy; underhand etc. (*hidden*) 528; subdolous; deceitful etc. 545; double-tongued, -faced; shifty; crooked; arch, pawky, shrewd, acute; sharp, – as a needle; canny, astute, leery, knowing, up to snuff, too clever by half, not to be caught with chaff.

Adv. cunningly etc. *adj.*; slily, on the sly, by a side wind.

Phr. diamond cut diamond.

703. Artlessness.—N. artlessness etc. *adj.*; nature, simplicity; innocence etc. 946; *bonhomie*, *naiveté*, *abandon*, candor, sincerity; singleness of -purpose, – heart; honesty etc. 939; plain speaking; *épanchement*.

rough diamond, matter of fact man; *le palais de vérité*; *enfant terrible*.

V. be -artless etc. *adj.*; look one in the face; wear one's heart upon his sleeves for daws to peck at; think aloud; speak -out, – one's mind; be free with one, call a spade a spade.

Adj. artless, natural, pure, native, simple, plain, inartificial, untutored, unsophisticated, *ingenu*, unaffected, *naïve*; sincere, frank; open, – as day; candid, ingenuous, guileless, unsuspicious, childlike; honest etc. 939; innocent etc. 946; Arcadian; undesigning, straightforward; unreserved, unvarnished, above-board; simple-, single-minded; frank-, open-, single-, simple-hearted; open and above-board.

free-, plain-, out-spoken; blunt, downright, direct, matter of fact, unpoetical; unflattering.

Adv. in plain -words, – English; without mincing the matter; not to mince the matter etc. (*affirmation*) 535.

Phr. *Davus sum non Oedipus*; *liberavi animam meam.*

704. Difficulty.—N. difficulty; hardness etc. *adj.*; impracticability etc. (*impossibility*) 471; tough –, hard –, uphill- work; hard –, Herculean –, Augean- task; task of Sisyphus, Sisyphean labor, tough job, teaser, rasper, dead lift.

dilemma, embarrassment; perplexity etc. (*uncertainty*) 475; involvement; intricacy; entanglement etc. 59; cross fire; awkwardness, delicacy, ticklish card to play, deadlock, knot, Gordian knot, *dignus vindice nodus*, net, meshes, maze; coil etc. (*convolution*) 248; crooked path.

nice –, delicate –, subtle –, knotty-point; vexed question, *vexata quaestio*, poser; puzzle etc. (*riddle*) 533; paradox; hard –, nut to crack; bone to pick, *crux*, *pons asinorum*, where the shoe pinches.

nonplus, quandary, strait, pass, pinch, pretty pass, stress, brunt; critical situation, crisis; trial, rub, emergency, exigency, scramble.

scrape, hobble, slough, quagmire, hot water, hornet's nest; sea –, peck- of troubles; pretty kettle of fish; pickle, stew, *imbroglio*, mess, muddle, botch, fuss, bustle, ado; false position; set fast, stand; dead -lock, – set; fix, horns of a dilemma, *cul de sac*; hitch; stumbling block etc. (*hindrance*) 706.

V. be -difficult etc. *adj.*; run one hard, go against the grain, try one's patience, put one out; put to one's -shifts, – wit's end; go hard with –, try- one; pose, perplex etc. (*uncertain*) 475; bother, nonplus, gravel, bring to a dead lock; be -impossible etc. 471; be in the way of etc. (*hinder*) 706.

meet with –, labor under –, get into –, plunge into –, struggle with –, contend with –, grapple with- difficulties; labor under a disadvantage; be -in difficulty etc. *adj.*

fish in troubled waters, buffet the waves, swim against the stream, scud under bare poles.

have -much ado with, – a hard time of it; come to the -push, – pinch; bear the brunt.

grope in the dark, lose one's way, weave a tangled web, walk among eggs.

get into a -scrape etc. *n.*; bring a hornet's nest about one's ears; be put to one's shifts; flounder, boggle, struggle; not know which way to turn etc. (*uncertain*) 475; get -tangled up, – wound up; *perdre son latin*; stick - at, – in the mud, – fast; come to a -stand, – dead lock; hold the wolf by the ears.

render -difficult etc. *adj.*; encumber, embarrass, ravel, entangle; put a spoke in the wheel etc. (*hinder*) 706; lead a pretty dance.

Adj. difficult, not easy, hard, tough; trouble-, toil-, irk-some; operose, laborious, onerous, arduous, Herculean, formidable; sooner –, more easily- said than done; difficult –, hard- to deal with; ill-conditioned, crabbed; not -to be handled with kid gloves, – made with rosewater.

awkward, unwieldy, unmanageable; intractable, stubborn etc. (*obstinate*) 606; perverse, refractory, plaguy, trying, thorny, rugged; knot-ted, -ty; invious; path-, track-less; labyrinthine etc. (*convoluted*) 248; intricate, complicated etc. (*tangled*) 59; impracticable etc. (*impossible*) 471; not -feasible etc. 470; desperate etc. (*hopeless*) 859.

embarrassing, perplexing etc. (*uncertain*) 475; delicate, ticklish, critical; beset with –, full of –, surrounded by –, entangled by –, encompassed with- difficulties.

under a difficulty; in -difficulty, – hot water, – the suds, – a cleft stick, – a fix, – the wrong box, – a scrape etc. *n.*; – deep water, – a fine pickle; *in extremis*; between -two stools, – Scylla and Charybdis; surronded by -shoals, – breakers, – quicksands; at cross purposes; not out of the wood.

reduced to straits; hard –, sorely- pressed; run hard; pinched, put to it, straitened; hard -up, – put to it, – set; put to one's shifts; puzzled, at a loss etc. (*uncertain*) 475; at -the end of one's tether, – one's wit's end, – a nonplus, – a standstill; graveled, nonplussed, stranded, aground; stuck –, set- fast; up a tree, at bay, *aux abois*, driven -into a corner, – from post to pillar, – to extremity, – to one's wit's end, – to the wall; *au bout de son latin*; out of one's -depth, – reckoning; put –, thrown -out.

accomplished with difficulty; hard-fought, -earned.

Adv. with -difficulty, – much ado; hardly etc. *adj.*; uphill; against the -stream, – grain; *à rebours*; *invitâ Minervâ*; in the teeth of; at –, upon- a pinch; at long odds.

Phr. ay there's the rub; *hic labor hoc opus*; things are come to a pretty pass.

705. Facility.—N. facility, ease; easiness etc. *adj.*; capability; feasibility etc. (*practicability*) 470; flexibility, pliancy etc. 324; smoothness etc. 255; convenience.

plain –, smooth –, straight- sailing; mere child's play, holiday task.

smooth water, fair wind; smooth – royal- road; clear -coast, – stage; *tabula rasa*; *full play* etc. (*freedom*) 748.

disen-cumbrance, -tanglement; deoppilation; permission etc. 760.

V. be -easy etc. *adj.*; go on –, run- smoothly; have -full play etc. *n.*; go –, run- on all fours; obey the helm, work well.

flow –, swim –, drift –, go- with the- -stream, – tide; see one's way; have -it all one's own way, – the game in one's own hands; walk over the course, win -at a canter, – hands down; make -light of, – nothing of; be at home in etc. (*skilful*) 698.

render -easy etc. *adj.*; facilitate, smooth, ease; popularize; lighten, – the labor; free, clear; dis-encumber, -embarrass, -entangle, -engage; deobstruct, unclog, extricate, unravel; untie –, cut- the knot; disburden, unload, exonerate, emancipate, free from, deoppilate; humor etc. (*aid*) 707; lubricate etc. 332; relieve etc. 834.

leave -a hole to creep out of, – a loophole, – the matter open; give -the reins to, – full play, – full swing; make way for; open the -door to, – way; prepare –, smooth –, clear- the -ground, – way, – path, – road; pave the way, bridge over; permit etc. 760.

Adj. easy, facile; feasible etc. (*practicable*) 470; easily -managed, – accomplished; within reach, accessible, easy of access, for the million, open to.

manageable, wieldy; towardly, tractable; submissive; yielding, ductile; pliant etc. (*soft*) 324; glib, slippery; smooth etc. 255; on -friction wheels, – velvet; convenient.

un-, dis-burdened, -encumbered, -embarrassed; exonerated; un-loaded, -obstructed, -trammeled, -impeded, -restrained etc. (*free*) 748; at ease, light.

at –, quite at- home; in -one's element, – smooth water.

Adv. easily etc. *adj.*; readily, smoothly, swimmingly, *ad lib.*, on easy terms, single-handed.

Phr. touch and go.

Int. all clear!

706. Hindrance.—N. prevention, preclusion, obstruction, stoppage; prohibition; inter-ruption, -ception, -clusion; hindrance, impedition; retardment, -ation; constriction; embarrassment, oppilation; coarctation, stricture, restriction; anchor etc. 666; restraint etc. 751 & 752; inhibition etc. 761; blockade etc. (*closure*) 261; picketing.

inter-ference, -position; obtrusion; discouragement, -countenance, -approval, -approbation; opposition etc. 708.

impediment, let, obstacle, obstruction, knot, knag; check, hitch, *contretemps, impasse*, screw loose, grit in the oil.

bar, stile, barrier; turn-stile, -pike; gate, portcullis; bulwark, parapet, barricade etc. (*defence*) 717; wall, dead wall, breakwater, groyne; bulkhead, block, buffer; stopper etc. 263; boom, dam, weir, burrock.

drawback, objection; stumbling-block, -stone; lion in the path; snag; snags and sawyers.

en-, in-cumbrance; clog, skid, shoe, spoke; brake, drag, – chain, – weight; stay, stop; preventive, prophylactic; contraception; load, burden, fardel, *onus*, millstone round one's neck, *impedimenta*; dead weight; lumber, pack; nightmare, Ephialtes, incubus, old man of the sea; remora.

difficulty etc. 704; insuperable etc. 471- obstacle; estoppel; ill wind; head wind etc. (*opposition*) 708; trammel, tether etc. (*means of restraint*) 752; hold back, counterpoise; damper, wet blanket, hinderer, marplot, kill-joy, dog in the manger, interloper; trail of a red herring; opponent etc. 710.

V. hinder, impede, impedite, embarrass.

keep –, stave –, ward- off; picket; obviate; a-, ante-vert; turn aside, draw off, prevent, forefend, nip in the bud; retard, slacken, check, let; counter-act, -check; preclude, debar, foreclose, estop; inhibit etc. 761; shackle etc. (*restrain*) 751; restrict, restrain, cohibit.

obstruct, filibuster, stop, stay, bar, bolt, lock; block, – up; belay, barricade; block –, stop- the way; dam up etc. (*close*) 261; put on the -brake etc. *n.*; scotch –, lock –, put a spoke in- the wheel; put a stop to etc. 142; traverse, contravene; inter-rupt, -cept; oppose etc. 708; hedge -in, – round; cut off; interclude.

inter-pose, -fere, -meddle etc. 682.

cramp, hamper; clog, – the wheels; cumber; en-, in-cumber; handicap; choke; saddle –, load-with; overload, lay; lumber, trammel, tie one's hands, put to inconvenience; in-, discommode; discompose; hustle, drive into a corner; choke off.

run –, fall- foul of; cross the path of, break in upon.

thwart, frustrate, disconcert, balk, foil, baffle, snub, override, circumvent; defeat etc. 731; spike guns etc. (*render useless*) 645; spoil, mar, clip the wings of; cripple etc. (*injure*) 659; put an extinguisher on; damp; dishearten etc. (*dissuade*) 616; discountenance, throw cold water on, spoil sport; lay –, throw- a wet blanket on; cut the ground from under one, take the wind out of one's sails, undermine; be –, stand- in the way of; act as a drag; hang like a millstone round one's neck.

Adj. hindering etc. *v.*; obstr-uctive, -uent; impedi-tive, -ent; intercipient; prophylactic etc. (*remedial*) 662.

in the way of, unfavorable; onerous, burdensome; cumb-rous, -ersome; obtrusive.

hindered etc. *v.*; wind-bound, water-logged, heavy laden; hard pressed.

unassisted etc. (*see* assist etc. 707); single-handed, alone; deserted etc. 624.

707. Aid.—N. aid, -ance; assistance, help, opitulation, succor; support, lift, advance, furtherance, promotion, coadjuvancy etc. (*co-operation*) 709.

patronage, championship, countenance, favor, interest, advocacy, auspices.

sustentation, subvention, subsidy, bounty, alimentation, nutrition, nourishment, maintenance; manna in the wilderness; food etc. 298; means etc. 632.

ministr-y, -ation, subministration; accomodation.

relief, rescue; help at a dead lift; supernatural aid; *deus ex machinâ*.

supplies, reinforcements, succors, contingents, recruits; support etc. (*physical*) 215; adjunct, ally etc. (*helper*) 711.

V. aid, assist, help, succor, lend one's aid; come to the aid etc. *n*- of; contribute, subscribe to; bring –, give –, furnish –, afford –, supply- -aid etc. *n.*; render assistance; give –, stretch –, lend –, bear –, hold out- a -hand, – helping hand; give one a -lift, – cast, – turn; take -by the hand, – in tow; help a lame dog over a stile, lend wings to.

relieve, rescue; set -up, – agoing, – on one's legs; bear –, pull- through; give new life to, be the making of; reinforce, recruit; set –, put –, push-forward; give -a lift, – a shove, – an impulse- to; promote, further, forward, advance; speed, expedite, quicken, hasten.

support, sustain, uphold, prop, hold up, bolster.

cradle, nourish; nurture, nurse, dry nurse, suckle, put out to nurse; manure, cultivate, force; foster; cherish, foment; feed –, fan- the flame.

serve; do service to, tender to, pander to; ad-, sub-, minister to; tend, attend, wait on; take care of etc. 459; entertain; smooth the bed of death.

oblige, accomodate, consult the wishes of; humor, cheer, encourage.

second, stand by; back, – up; pay the piper, abet; work –, make interest –, stick up –, take up the cudgels- for; take up –, espouse –, adopt- the cause of; advocate, beat up for recruits, press into the service; squire, give moral support to, keep in countenance, countenance, patronize; lend - oneself, – one's countenance- to; smile –, shine- upon; favor, befriend, take up, take in hand, enlist under the banners of; side with etc. (*co-operate*) 709.

be of use to; subserve etc. (*instrument*) 631; benefit etc. 648; render a service etc. (*utility*) 644; conduce etc. (*tend*) 176.

Adj. aiding etc. *v.*; auxiliary, adjuvant, helpful; coadjuvant etc. 709; subservient, ministrant, ancillary, accessory, subsidiary.

at one's beck; friendly, amicable, favorable, propitious, well-disposed; neighborly; obliging etc. (*benevolent*) 906.

Adv. with –, by- -the aid etc. *n.*- of; on –, in- behalf of; in -aid, – the service, – the name, – favor, – furtherance- of; on account of; for the sake of, on the part of; *non obstante*.

Int. help! save us! to the rescue! S.O.S.!

708. Opposition.—N. opposition, antagonism, oppug-nancy, -nation; impugnation; contravention; counteraction etc. 179; counterplot.

cross-fire, under-current, head-wind.

clashing, collision, conflict, lack of harmony, contest.

competition, two of a trade, rivalry, emulation, race; war to the knife.

absence of -aid etc. 707; resistance etc. 719; restraint etc. 751; hindrance etc. 706.

V. oppose, conteract, run counter to; withstand etc. (*resist*) 719; control etc. (*restrain*) 751; hinder etc. 706; antagonize, oppugn, fly in the face of, go dead against, kick against, fall foul of; set –, pit- against; face, confront, cope with; make a -stand, – dead set- against; set -oneself, one's face- against; protest –, vote –, raise one's voice- against; disfavor, turn one's back upon; set at naught, slap in the face, slam the door in one's face.

be –, play- at cross purposes; counter-work, - mine; thwart, overthwart.

stem, breast, encounter; stem –, breast- the - tide, – current, – flood; buffet the waves; beat up –, make head- against; grapple with; kick against the pricks etc. (*resist*) 719; contend etc. 720 –, do battle etc. (*warfare*) 722- -with, – against.

contra-dict, -vene; belie; go –, run –, beat –, militate- against; come in conflict with.

emulate etc. (*compete*) 720; rival, spoil one's trade.

Adj. oppos-ing, -ed etc. *v.*; adverse, antagonistic; ambivalent; contrary etc. 14; at variance etc. 24; at issue, at war with; in opposition; 'agin the Government.'

un-favorable, -friendly; hostile, inimical, cross, unpropitious.

in hostile array, front to front, with crossed bayonets, at daggers drawn; up in arms; resistant etc. 791.

competitive, emulous.

Adv. against, *versus*, counter to, in conflict with, at cross purposes.

against the -grain, – current, – stream, – wind, – tide; with a headwind; with the wind - ahead, – in one's teeth.

in spite, in despite, in defiance; in the -way, – teeth, – face- of; across; a-, over-thwart; where the shoe pinches.

though etc. 30; even; *quand même*; *per contra*.

Phr. *nitor in adversum*.

709. Co-operation.—N. co-operation; coadjuvancy, -tancy; coagency, coefficiency; concert, concurrence, complicity, participation; union etc. 43; amalgamation, combination etc. 48; collusion.

association, alliance, colleagueship, jointstock, copartnership, trust, cartel, pool, ring, combine, interlocking directorate; confederation etc. (*party*) 712; federation, coalition, fusion; a long pull, a strong pull and a pull all together; log-rolling, freemasonry.

unanimity etc. (*assent*) 488; *esprit de corps*, party spirit; clan-, partisan-ship; reciprocity, concord etc. 714.

V. co-operate, co-adjute, concur; conduce etc. 178; combine, cartelize, unite one's efforts; keep –, draw –, pull –, club –, hang –, hold –, league –, band –, be banded- together; stand –, put- shoulder to shoulder; act in concert, join forces, fraternize, cling to one another, conspire, concert, lay one's heads together; confederate, be in league with; collude, understand one another, play into the hands of, hunt in couples.

side –, take side –, go along –, go hand in hand –, join hands –, make common cause –, strike in –, unite –, join –, mix oneself up –, take part –, play along –, cast in one's lot- with; join –, enter into- partnership with; rally round, follow the lead of; come to, pass over to, come into the views of; be –, row –, sail- in the same boat; sail on the same tack.

be a party to, lend oneself to; participate; have a -hand in, – finger in the pie; take –, bear- part in; second etc. (*aid*) 707; take the part of, play the game of; espouse a -cause, – quarrel.

Adj. co-operating etc. *v.*; in -co-operation etc. *n.*- league etc. (*party*) 712; coadju-vant, -tant; hand and glove with.

favorable etc. 707- to; un-opposed etc. 708.

Adj. as one man etc. (*unanimously*) 488; shoulder to shoulder; in co-operation with.

710. Opponent.—N. opponent, antagonist, adversary; adverse party, opposition; enemy etc. 891; assailant.

oppositionist, obstructive; obscurantist; brawler, wrangler, brangler, disputant, extremist, irreconcilable, diehard, bitter-ender.

malcontent; Jacobin, Fenian etc. 742; demagogue, reactionist.

passive resister, conscientious objector.

rival, competitor, contestant.

711. Auxiliary.—N. auxiliary; recruit; assistant; adju-vant, -tant; adjunct; help, er, -mate, -ing hand; midwife; colleague, partner, mate, *confrère*, co-operator; coadju-tor, -trix; collaborator.

ally; friend etc. 890; confidant, *fidus Achates*, pal, chum, buddy, *alter ego*.

confederate; ac-, complice; accessory, – after the fact; *particeps criminis*.

aide-de-camp, secretary, clerk, associate, marshal; right-hand; candle-, bottle-holder; hand-maid; servant etc. 746; puppet, cat's-paw; stooge, dependent, creature, jackal; tool, *âme damnée*; satellite, adherent, parasite.

votary, disciple; secta-rian, -ry; seconder, backer, upholder, supporter, abettor, advocate, partisan, champion, patron, friend at court, mediator.

friend in need, Jack at a pinch, *deus ex machinâ*, guardian angel, fairy godmother; special providence, tutelary genius.

712. Party.—N. party, faction, side, denomination, class, communion, set, crowd, crew, band, horde, posse, phalanx; regiment etc. 726; family, clan etc. 166.

Tories, Conservatives, Unionists, Whigs, Liberals, Radicals, Labour party, Socialists, Communists etc.; Republicans, Democrats, Farmer-Labor; *Fascisti*, Revolutionaries etc. 742.

community, body, fellowship, sodality, solidarity; con-, fraternity; sorority; brother-, sisterhood.

Freemasons, Knights Templars, Odd Fellows, Ku Klux Klan etx.

knot, gang, *clique*, ring, circle; *coterie*, club, *casino*.

corporation, corporate body, guild; establishment, company, copartnership, firm, house, joint concern, joint-stock company, trust, investment trust, combine etc. 709.

society, association; instit-ute, -ution; union; trade-union; league, syndicate, alliance, *Verein*, *Bund*, *Zollverein*, combination; league –, alliance- offensive and defensive; coalition; federation; confedera -tion, -cy; junto, cabal, *camarilla*, *camorra*, *brigue*; freemasonry; party spirit etc. (*co-operation*) 709.

staff; cast, *dramatis personae*.

V. unite, join; club together etc. (*co-operate*) 709; cement –, form- a party etc. *n.*; associate etc. (*assemble*) 72.

Adj. in -league, – partnership, – alliance etc. *n.*

bonded –, banded –, linked etc. (*joined*) 43- together; embattled; confederated, federative, joint, corporate, leagued, fraternal, masonic, cliquish.

Adv. hand in hand, side by side, shoulder to shoulder, *en masse*, in the same boat.

713. Discord.—N. disagreement etc. 24; discord, -accord, -sidence, -sonance; jar, clash, shock; jarring, jostling etc. *v.*; screw loose.

variance, difference, dissension, misunderstanding, cross purposes, odds, *brouillerie*; division, split, rupture, disruption, division in the camp, house divided against itself, rift within the lute; disunion, breach; schism etc. (*dissent*) 489; feud, faction.

quarrel, dispute, rippet, spat, tiff, *tracasserie*, squabble, altercation, words, high words; wrangling etc. *v.*; jangle, brabble cross questions and crooked answers, snip-snap; family jars.

polemics; litigation; strife etc. (*contention*) 720; warfare etc. 722; outbreak, open rupture; breaking off of negotiations, recall of ambassadors; declaration of war.

broil, brawl, row, racket, hubbub, rixation; embroilment, embranglement, *imbroglio*, *fracas*, breach of the peace, piece of work, scrimmage, rumpus; breeze, squall; riot, disturbance etc. (*disorder*) 59; commotion etc. (*agitation*) 315; bear garden, Donnybrook Fair.

subject of dispute, ground of quarrel, battle ground, disputed point; bone -of contention, – to pick; apple of discord, *casus belli*; question at issue etc. (*subject of inquiry*) 461; vexed question, *vexata quaestio*, brand of discord.

troublous times; cat-and-dog life; contentiousness etc. *adj.*; enmity etc. 889; hate etc. 898; Kilkenny cats; disputant etc. 710; strange bedfellows.

V. be -discordant etc. *adj.*; disagree, come amiss etc. 24; clash, jar, jostle, pull different ways, conflict, have no measures with, misunderstand one another; live like cat and dog; differ; dissent etc. 489; have a -bone to pick, – crow to pluck- with.

fall out, quarrel, dispute; litigate; controvert etc. (*deny*) 536; squabble, wrangle, jangle, brangle, bicker, nag; spar etc. (*contend*) 720; have -words etc. *n.* with; fall foul of.

split; break –, break squares –, part company- with; declare war, try conclusions; join –, put in- issue; pick a quarrel, fasten a quarrel on; sow –, stir up- -dissension etc. *n.*; embroil, estrange, entangle, disunite, widen the breach; set -at odds, – together by the ears; set –, pit- against; rub up the wrong way.

get into hot water, fish in troubled waters, brawl; kick up a -row, – dust; turn the house out of window.

Adj. discordant; disagreeing etc. *v.*; out of tune, dissonant, inharmonious, harsh, grating, jangling, ajar, on bad terms; dissentient etc. 489; inconsistent, contradictory, incongruous, discrepant; un- reconciled, -pacified.

quarrelsome, unpacific; gladiatorial, controversial, polemic, disputatious; factious; liti-gious, -gant; pettifogging.

at odds, at loggerheads, at daggers drawn, at variance, at issue, at cross purposes, at sixes and sevens, at feud, at high words; up in arms, together by the ears, in hot water, embroiled.

torn, disunited.

Phr. *quot homines tot sententiae*; no love lost between them, *non nostrum tantas componere lites*.

714. Concord.—N. concord, accord, harmony, symphony, homology; aggreement etc. 23; sympathy etc. (*love*) 897; response; union, unison, unity; bonds of harmony; peace etc. 721; unanimity etc. (*assent*) 488; league etc. 712; happy family.

rapprochement; *réunion*; amity etc. (*friendship*) 888; reciprocity; alliance, *entente cordiale*, good understanding, conciliation, arbitration, peacemaker etc. 724.

V. agree etc. 23; accord, harmonize with; fraternize; be -concordant etc. *adj.*; go hand in hand; blend –, tone in- with; run parallel etc. (*concur*) 178; understand one another; pull together etc. (*co-operate*) 709; put up one's horses together, sing in chorus.

side –, sympathize –, go –, chime in –, fall in- with; come round; be pacified etc. 723; assent etc. 488; enter into the -ideas, – feelings- of; reciprocate.

hurler avec les loups; go –, swim- with the stream.

pour oil on troubled waters, keep in good humor, render accordant, put in tune; come to an understanding, meet half-way; keep the –, remain at- peace.

Adj. concordant, congenial; agreeing etc. *v.*; in-accord etc. *n.*; harmonious, united, cemented; banded together etc. 712; allied; friendly etc. 888; fraternal; conciliatory; at one with; of one mind etc. (*assent*) 488.

at peace, in still water; tranquil etc. (*pacific*) 721.

Adv. with one voice etc. (*assent*) 488; in concert with, hand in hand; on one's side, unanimously.

715. Defiance.—N. defiance; daring etc. *v.*; dare, challenge, *cartel*; threat etc. 909; war-cry, -whoop.

V. defy, dare, beard; brave etc. (*courage*) 861; bid defiance to; set at -defiance, – naught; hurl defiance at; dance the war dance; snap the fingers at, laugh to scorn; disobey etc. 742.

show -fight, – one's teeth, – a bold front; bluster, look big, stand akimbo; double –, shake- the fist; threaten etc 909.

challenge, call out; throw –, fling- down the -gauntlet, – gage, – glove.

Adj. defiant; defying etc. *v.*; with arms akimbo; rebellious, insolent; reckless, greatly daring.

Adv. in -defiance, – the teeth- of; under one's very nose.

Int. do your worst! come if you dare! come on! marry come up! hoity toity!

Phr. *noli me tangere*; *nemo me impune lacessit*.

716. Attack.—N. attack; assault, – and battery; onset, onslaught, charge.

aggression, drive, offence; incursion, inroad; invasion; irruption; outbreak; *estrapade*, *ruade*; *coup de main*, sally, *sortie*, *camisade*, raid, foray; run -at, – against; dead set at.

storm, -ing; boarding, *escalade*; siege, investment, obsession, bombardment, cannonade; air raid.

fire, volley; platoon –, file –, rapid-fire; *fusillade*; sharp-shooting, sniping; broadside; raking –, cross –, machine gun- fire; – volley of grapeshot, *feu d'enfer*; salvo.

cut, thrust, lunge, pass, *passado*, *carte* and *tierce*, home thrust, *coup de pied*; kick, punch, etc. (*impulse*) 276.

battue, *razzia*, *Jacquerie*, *dragonnade*; devastation etc. 162.

assailant, aggressor, invader.

base of operations, point of attack.

V. attack, assault, assail; set –, fall- upon; charge, impugn, break a lance with, enter the lists.

assume –, take- the offensive; be –, become- the aggressor; strike the first blow, fire the first shot, throw the first stone at; lift a hand –, draw the sword- against; take up the cudgels; advance –, march- against; march upon, invade, harry; come on, show fight.

strike at, poke at, thrust at; aim –, deal- a blow at; give –, fetch- one a -blow, – kick; have a -cut, – shot, – fling, – shy- at; be down –, pounce- upon; fall foul of, pitch into, launch out against; bait, slap on the face; make a -thrust, – pass, – set, – dead set- at; dunt; bear down upon.

close with, come to close quarters, bring to bay.

ride full tilt against; let fly at, dash at, run a tilt at, rush at, tilt at, run at, fly at, hawk at, have at, let out at; make a -dash, – rush at; attack tooth and nail; strike home; drive –, press- one hard; be hard upon, run down, strike at the root of.

lay about one, run amuck.

fire -upon, – at, – a shot at; shoot at, pop at, level at, let off a gun at; open fire, pepper, bombard, shell, pour a broadside into; fire -a volley, – red-hot shot; spring a mine.

throw -a stone, – stones- at; stone, lapidate, pelt; hurl -at, – against, – at the head of.

beset, besiege, beleaguer; lay siege to, invest, open the trenches, plant a battery, sap, mine; storm, board, scale the walls.

cut and thrust, bayonet, butt; kick, strike etc. (*impulse*) 276; whip etc. (*punish*) 972.

Adj. attacking etc. *v.*; aggressive, offensive, obsidional.

up in arms; on the warpath; over the top.

Adv. on the offensive.

Int. 'up and at them!'

717. Defense.—N. defense, protection, guard, ward; shielding etc. *v.*; propugnation; preservation etc. 670; guardianship.

self-defense, -preservation; resistance etc. 719.

safeguard etc. (*safety*) 664; screen etc. (*shelter*) 666, (*concealment*) 530; barrage; fortification; muni-tion, -ment; bulwark, fosse, moat, ditch, intrenchment, trench, dugout, gas mask; dike, dyke; parapet, parados, sunk fence, embankment, mound, mole, bank; earth- field-work, gabions; fence, wall, dead wall, contravallation; paling etc. (*inclosure*) 232; palisade, haha, stockade, *stoccado, laager, sangar*; barri-er, -cade; boom; portcullis, *chevaux de frise*; aba-, abat-, abba-tis; *vallum*, circumvallation, battlement, rampart, scarp; e-, counter-scarp; glacis, casemate.

mine, countermine.

buttress, abutment; shore etc. (*support*) 215.

breastwork, *banquette*, curtain, mantlet, bastion, demilune, redan, ravelin; advanced –, horn –, out- work, lunette; barb-acan, -ican; redoubt; fortelage, -alice; lines; coast defense.

loop-hole, machicolation; sally-port, postern gate.

hold, stronghold, fastness; asylum etc. (*refuge*) 666; keep, donjon, fortress, citadel; capitol, castle; tower, – of strength; fort, barracoon, pah, sconce, martello tower, peel-house, block-house, rath; wooden walls; turret, barbette.

buffer, corner-stone, fender, apron, mask, gauntlet, thimble, carapace, armor, shield, buckler; target, targe, aegis, breastplate, cuirass, plastron, habergeon, mail, coat of mail, brigandine, hauberk, lorication, helmet, helm, basinet, sallet, salade, heaume, morion, murrion, armet, cabaset, vizor, casquetel, siege-cap, head-piece, casque, steel helmet, tin hat; *pickelhaube*, csako; shako etc. (*dress*) 225; bearskin; panoply; truncheon etc. (*weapon*) 727.

garrison, picket, piquet; defender, protector; guardian etc. (*safety*) 664; trabant, body guard, champion; knight-errant, Paladin; propugner.

V. defend, forfend, fend; shield, screen, shroud; fence round etc. (*circumscribe*) 229; fence, intrench; guard etc. (*keep safe*) 664; guard against; take care of etc. (*vigilance*) 459; bear harmless; keep –, ward –, beat- off; hinder etc. 706.

parry, repel, propugn, put to flight; give a warm reception to [*ironical*]; hold –, keep- at -bay, – arm's length.

stand –, act- on the defensive; show fight; maintain –, stand- one's ground; stand by; hold one's own; bear –, stand- the brunt; fall back upon, hold, stand in the gap.

Adj. defending etc. *v.*; defensive; mural; armed, – at all points, – *cap-à-pie*, – to the teeth; panoplied; accoutred, harnessed; iron-plated, -clad; loop-holed, castellated, machicolated; casemated; defended etc. *v.*; proof against, bomb-, bullet-proof; protective.

Adv. defensively; on the -defense, – defensive; in defense; at bay, *pro aris et focis*.

Int. no surrender! *il ne passeront pas!*

Phr. defense not defiance.

718. Retaliation.—N. retaliation, reprisal, retort; counter-stroke, -blast, -plot, -project; retribution, *lex talionis*; reciprocation etc. (*reciprocity*) 12.

requital, desert, tit for tat, give and take, blow for blow, *quid pro quo*, a Roland for an Oliver, measure for measure, an eye for an eye, diamond cut diamond, the biter bit, a game at which two can play; boomerang.

recrimination etc. (*accusation*) 938; revenge etc. 919; compensation etc. 30; reaction etc. (*recoil*) 277.

V. retaliate, retort, turn upon; pay -off, – back; pay in -one's own, – the same- coin; cap; reciprocate etc. 148; turn the tables upon, return the compliment; give -a *quid pro quo* etc. *n.*, – as much as one takes; give and take, exchange -blows, – fisticuffs; be -quits, – even- with; pay off old scores.

serve one right, be hoist on one's own petard, throw a stone in one's own garden, cathch a Tartar.

Adj. retaliating etc. *v.*; retalia-tory, -tive; retributive, recriminatory, reciprocal.

Adv.. in retaliation; *en revanche*.

Phr. *mutato nomine de te fabula narratur; par pari refero; tu quoque*; you're another; *suo sibi gladio hunc jugulo*.

719. Resistance.—N. resistance, stand, front, oppugnation; opposition etc. 708; renitence, reluctation, recalcitration, recalcitrance; repugnance; kicking etc. *v.*

repulse, rebuff.

insurrection etc. (*disobedience*) 742; strike; turn –, lock –, barring- out; *levée en masse*, *Jacquerie*; riot etc. (*disorder*) 59.

V. resist; not -submit etc. 725; repugn, reluctate, withstand; stand up –, strive –, bear up –, be proof –, make head- against; stand, – firm, – one's ground, – the brunt of, – out; hold -one's ground, – one's own, – out.

breast the -wave, – current; stem the -tide, – torrent; face, confront, grapple with; show a bold front etc. (*courage*) 861; present a front; make a –, take one's- stand.

kick, – against; recalcitrate, kick against the pricks; oppose etc. 708; fly in the face of; lift the hand against etc. (*attack*) 716; rise up in arms etc. (*war*) 722; strike, turn out; draw up a round robin etc. (*remonstrate*) 932; revolt etc. (*disobey*) 742; make a riot.

prendre le mors aux dents; take the bit between the teeth; sell one's life dearly, die hard, keep at bay; repel, repulse.

Adj. resisting etc. *v.*; resist-ive, -ant; refractory etc. (*disobedient*) 742; recalcitrant, re-nitent, -pulsive, -pellant; up in arms.

proof against; unconquerable etc. (*strong*) 159; stubborn, unconquered; indomitable etc. (*persevering*) 604*a*; unyielding etc. (*obstinate*) 606.

Int. hands off! keep off!

720. Contention.—N. contention, strife; contest, -ation; struggle; belligerency; opposition etc. 708.

controversy, polemics; debate etc. (*discussion*) 476; war of words, logomachy, litigation; paper war, ink slinging; high words etc. (*quarrel*) 713; sparring etc. *v.*

competition, rivalry; corrival-ry, -ship; agonism, *concours*, match, race, horse-racing, heat, steeple chase, point-to-point race, handicap; boat race, regatta; field-day; sham fight, Derby day; turf, sporting, bull-fight, tauromachy, *gymkhana*, rodeo, Olympiad.

wrestling, *ju-jitsu*, pugilism, boxing, fisticuffs, spar, mill, set-to, scrap, round, bout, event; prize-fighting; quarter-staff, single stick; gladiatorship, gymnastics; athletic-s, – sports; games of skill etc. 840.

shindy; *fracas* etc. (*discord*) 713; clash of arms; tussle, scuffle, broil, fray; affray, -ment; velitation; col-, luctation; brabble, *brique*, scramble, *mêlée*, scrimmage, stramash, bush-fighting.

free –, stand up –, hand to hand –, running- fight.

conflict, skirmish; ren-, en-counter; *rencontre*, collision, affair, brush, fight; battle, – royal; combat, action, engagement, joust, tournament; tilt, -ing; tourney, list; pitched battle, guerilla warfare.

death-struggle, struggle for life or death, Armageddon; hard knocks, sharp contest, tug of war.

naval -engagement, – battle; *naumachia*, sea-fight.

duel, -lo; single combat, monomachy, satisfaction, *passage d'armes*, passage of arms, affair of honor; triangular duel; hostile meeting, digladiation; appeal to arms etc. (*warfare*) 722.

deeds –, feats- of arms; pugnacity; combativeness etc. *adj.*; bone of contention etc. 713.

V. contend; contest, strive, struggle, scramble, wrestle; spar, square; exchange -blows, – fisticuffs; scrap, mix with, fib, justle, tussle, tilt, box, stave, fence; skirmish; fight etc. (*war*) 722; wrangle etc. (*quarrel*) 713.

contend etc. –, grapple –, engage –, close –, buckle –, bandy –, try conclusions –, have a brush etc. *n.* –, tilt- with; encounter, fall foul of, pitch into, clapperclaw, run a tilt at; oppose etc. 708; reluct.

join issue, come to blows, be at loggerheads, set-to, come to the scratch, exchange shots, measure swords, meet hand to hand; take up the -cudgels, – glove, – gauntlet; enter the lists; couch one's lance; give satisfaction; appeal to arms etc. (*warfare*) 722.

lay about one; break the peace.

compete –, cope –, vie –, race- with; outvie, emulate, rival; run a race; contend etc. –, stipulate –, stickle- for; insist upon, make a point of.

Adj. contending etc. *v.*; together by the ears, at loggerheads, at war, at issue.

competitive, rival; belligerent; contentious, combative, bellicose, unpeaceful; warlike etc. 722; quarrelsome etc. 901; pugnacious; pugilistic, gladiatorial; palestric, -al.

Phr. *a verbis ad verbera*; a word and a blow.

721. Peace.—N. peace; amity etc. (*friendship*) 888; harmony etc. (*concord*) 714; tranquility etc. (*quiescence*) 265; truce etc. (*pacification*) 723; pacificism; pipe –, calumet- of peace.

piping time of peace, quiet life; neutrality.

V. be at peace; keep the peace etc. (*concord*) 714; make peace etc. 723.

Adj. pacific; peace-able, -ful; calm, tranquil, untroubled, halcyon; bloodless; neutral.

Phr. the storm blown over; the lion lies down with the lamb.

722. Warfare.—N. warfare; fighting etc. *v.*; hostilities; war, arms, the sword; Mars, Bellona, grim visaged war, *horrida bella*, Armageddon.

appeal to -arms, – the sword; ordeal –, wager- of battle; *ultima ratio regum*, arbitrament of the sword.

battle array, campaign, crusade, expedition; mobilization; state of siege; battle-field etc. (*arena*) 728; warpath.

art of war, tactics, strategy, castrametation; general-, soldier-ship; aerial –, submarine –, naval –, chemical-, atomic-, guerilla- warfare; military evolutions, ballistics, gunnery; chivalry; poison gas; gun-powder, shot, – and shell.

battle, tug of war etc. (*contention*) 720; service, campaigning, active service, tented field; fiery cross, trumpet, clarion, bugle, pibroch, slogan; war-cry, -whoop; battle cry, beat of drum, rappel, tom-tom; word of command; pass-, watch-word.

war to the -death, – knife; *guerre à -mort*, – *outrance*; open –, internecine –, civil- war.

V. arm; raise –, mobilize- troops; raise up in arms; take up the cudgels etc. 720; take up –, fly to –, appeal to- -arms, – the sword; draw –, unsheathe- the sword; dig up the hatchet; go to –, declare –, wage –, let slip the dogs of- war; cry havoc; kindle –, light- the torch of war; raise one's banner, send round the fiery cross; hoist the black flag; throw –, fling- away the scabbard; enrol, enlist, join up; take the field; take the law into one's own hands; do –, give –, join –, engage in –, go to- battle; flesh one's sword; set to, fall to, engage, measure swords with, draw the trigger, cross swords; come to -blows, – close quarters; fight; combat; contend etc. 720; battle –, break a lance- with.

serve; see –, be on- -service, – active service; campaign; wield the sword, shoulder a musket, smell powder, be under the fire; spill –, imbrue the hands in- blood; be on the warpath.

carry on -war, – hostilities; keep the field; fight the good fight; go over the top; cut one's way through; fight -it out, – like devils, – one's way, – hand to hand; sell one's life dearly.

Adj. conten-ding, -tious etc. 720; armed, – to the teeth, – cap-à-pie; sword in hand; in –, under –, up in- arms; at war with; bristling with arms; in -battle array, – open arms, – the field; embattled.

unpacific, unpeaceful; belligerent, combative, armigerous, bellicose, martial, warlike; mili-tary, -tant; soldier-like, -ly; chivalrous; strategical, internecine.

Adv. *flagrante bello*, in the -thick of the fray, – cannon's mouth; at the -swords's point, – point of the bayonet.

Int. *vae victis!* to arms! to your tents O Israel!

Phr. the battle rages.

723. Pacification.—N. pacification, conciliation; reconcil-iation, -ement; shaking of hands, accomodation, arrangement, adjustment; terms, compromise; amnesty, deed of release.

peace-offering; olive-branch; overtures; pipe –, calumet –, preliminaries- of peace.

truce, armistice; suspension of -arms, – hostilities; breathing-time; convention; *modus vivendi*; flag of truce, white flag, *parlementaire*, *cartel*.

hollow truce, *pax in bello*; drawn battle.

V. pacify, tranquilize, compose; allay etc. (*moderate*) 174; reconcile, propitiate, placate, conciliate, meet half-way, hold out the olive-branch, heal the breach, make peace, restore harmony, bring to terms.

settle –, arrange –, accommodate- -matters, – differences; set straight; make up a quarrel, *tantas componere lites*; come to -an understanding, – terms; bridge over, hush up; make -it, – matters- up; shake hands.

raise a siege; put up –, sheathe- the sword; bury the hatchet, lay down one's arms, turn swords into ploughshares; smoke the calumet of peace, close the temple of Janus; keep the peace etc. (*concord*) 714; be -pacified etc.; come round.

Adj. conciliatory, pacificatory; composing etc *v.*; pacified etc. *v.*

Phr. *requiescat in pace*.

724. Mediation.—**N.** media-tion, -torship, -tization; inter-vention, -position, -ference, -meddling, -cession; parley, negotiation, arbitration; flag of truce etc. 723; good offices, peace -offering; diploma-tics, -cy; compromise etc. 774.

mediator, intercessor, peacemaker, make-peace, negotiator, go-between; diplomatist etc. (*consignee*) 758; moderator, propitiator, umpire, arbitrator.

V. media-te, -tize; inter-cede, -pose, -fere, -vene; step in, negotiate; meet half-way; arbitrate; *magnas componere lites*.

Adj. mediatory, propitiatory, diplomatic.

725. Submission.—**N.** submission, yielding, acquiescence, compliance; non-resistance; obedience etc. 743; submissiveness, deference.

surrender, cession, capitulation, resignation.

obeisance, homage, kneeling, genuflexion, courtesy, curtsy, *salaam*, *kowtow*, prostration.

V. succumb, submit, yield, bend, resign, defer to, accede.

lay down –, deliver up- one's arms; hand over one's sword; lower –, haul down –, strike- one's flag, – colors; deliver the keys of the city.

surrender, – at discretion; cede, capitulate, come to terms, retreat, beat a retreat; draw in one's horns etc. (*humility*) 879; give -way, – ground, – in, – up; cave in; suffer judgment by default; bend, – to one's yoke, – before the storm; reel back; bend –, knuckle- -down, – to, – under; knock under.

humble oneself; eat -dirt, – the leek, – humble pie; bite –, lick- the dust; be –, fall- at one's feet; craven; crouch before, throw oneself at the feet of; swallow the -leek, – pill; kiss the rod; turn the other cheek; *avaler des couleuvres*, gulp down.

obey etc. 743; kneel to, bow to, pay homage to, cringe to, truckle to; bend the -neck, – knee; kneel, fall on one's knees, bow submission, courtesy, curtsy, *kowtow*; make obeisance.

pocket the affront; make -the best of, – a virtue of necessity; grin and abide, shrug the shoulders, resign oneself; submit with a good grace etc. (*bear with*) 826.

Adj. surrendering etc. *v.*; submissive, resigned, crouching; down-trodden; down on one's marrow bones; on one's bended knee; weak-kneed, un-, non-resisting; pliant etc. (*soft*) 324; undefended.

untenable, indefensible; humble etc. 879.

Phr. have it your own way; it can't be helped; amen etc. (*assent*) 488.

726. Combatant.—**N.** combatant; disputant, controversialist, polemic, litigant, belligerent; competitor, rival, corrival; fighter, assailant, aggressor; champion, Paladin; moss-trooper, swashbuckler, fire-eater, duellist, bully, bludgeon-man, rough, fighter, fighting-man, prize-fighter, pugilist, pug, boxer, bruiser, the fancy, gladiator, athlete, wrestler; fighting-, game-cock; swordsman, *sabreur*.

warrior, soldier, Amazon, man-at-arms, armigerent; campaigner, veteran; red-coat, military man, *rajpoot*, brave.

armed force, troops, soldiery, military, forces, sabaoth, the army, standing army, regulars, the line, troops of the line, militia, territorials, yeomanry, volunteers, trainband, fencible; auxiliary –, reserve- forces; reserves, *posse comitatus*, national guard, *gendarme*, beefeater; guards, -man; yeoman of the guard, life guards, household troops.

janissary; myrmidon; Mama-, Mame-luke; spahee, *spahi*, Cossack, Croat, Pandour; irregular, free lance, *franc-tireur*, *bashi-bazouk*, *guerilla*, *condottiere*; mercenary.

levy, draught, commando; *Land-wehr*, *-sturm*; conscript, recruit, rookie, cadet, raw levies.

private, – soldier; Tommy Atkins, rank and file, peon, trooper, doughboy, sepoy, *askari*, *legionnaire*, legionary, food for powder, cannon fodder; officer etc. (*commander*) 745; subaltern, ensign, shave-tail, standard bearer, non-com; spear-

pike-man; halberdier, lancer; musketeer, carabineer, rifleman, sharpshooter, yager, skirmisher; grenadier, fusileer; archer, bowman.

horse and foot; horse –, foot- soldier; cavalry, horse, artillery, horse –, field –, heavy –, mountain- artillery, infantry, light horse, *voltigeur*, *Uhlan*, mounted rifles, dragoon, hussar, trooper; light –, heavy- dragoon; heavy; *cuirassier*; gunner, cannoneer, bombardier, artillery-man, matross; sapper, – and miner; engineer; light infantry, rifles, *chasseur*, *zouave*; military train, supply and transport, coolie.

army, – corps, *corps d'armée*, host, division, column, wing, detachment, *escadrille*, garrison, flying column, brigade, regiment, *corps*, battalion, squadron, company, platoon, battery, subdivision, section, squad; piquet, picket, guard, rank, file; legion, phalanx, cohort; cloud of skirmishers; impi.

war-horse, charger, *destrier*.

armored -train, – car; tank.

marine, man of war's man etc. (*sailor*) 269; navy, first line of defense, wooden walls; naval forces, fleet, flotilla, armada, squadron.

man-of-war, warship; H.M.S., U.S.S.; capital ship; line-of-battle ship, battle ship; super-, dreadnought, battle –, armored –, protected – light-cruiser; scout, flotilla leader; destroyer, torpedo boat; submarine, submersible, U-boat; submarine chaser, eagle boat, mystery ship, Q-boat; mine-layer, -sweeper; ship of the line, iron-clad, turret-ship, ram, Monitor, floating battery; first-rate, frigate, sloop of war, corvette, gunboat, bomb-vessel, fire-boat; flag ship, guard ship, cruiser; airplane carrier; privateer; tender; depot –, parent-ship; store –, troop- ship; transport, catamaran.

aircraft etc. 273; air force, scout, fighter, bomber, troop carrier, aerial patrol, seaplane, flying boat, torpedo plane; airship, Zeppelin; rigid –, semi-rigid –, non-rigid- airship; dirigible –, free –, captive –, kite –, observation- balloon.

anti-aircraft guns, searchlights, sound locators; catapult.

727. Arms.—**N.** arm, -s; weapon, deadly weapon; arma-ment, -ture; panoply, stand of arms; armor etc. (*defense*) 717; armory etc. (*store*) 636.

ammunition; powder, – and shot; explosive; propellant; gun-powder, -cotton; dynam-, melin-, cord-, lydd-ite; trinitrotoluene, T.N.T., ammonal; cartridge; ball cartridge, *cartouche*, fire-ball; dud, black Marie; 'villainous saltpeter;' poison –, mustard –, lachrymatory –, tear- gas.

sword, saber, broadsword, cutlass, falchion, scimitar, cimeter, brand, whinyard, bilbo, glaive, glave, rapier, skean, Toledo, Ferrara, tuck, claymore, creese, kris, *kukri*, dagger, dirk, hanger, poniard, stiletto, stylet, dudgeon, bayonet; sword-bayonet, -stick; side arms, foil, blade, steel; axe, bill; pole-, battle-axe; gisarm, halberd, partisan, tomahawk, bowie-knife; at-, att-, yat-aghan; yatachan; good –, trusty –, naked- sword; cold –, naked-steel.

club, mace, truncheon, staff, bludgeon, cudgel, life-preserver, shillelagh, sprig; hand-, quarter-staff; bat, cane, stick, knuckle-duster, sand bag.

gun, piece; fire-arms; artillery, ordnance; siege –, battering-train; park, battery; cannon, gun of position, heavy –, siege –, field –, mountain –, anti-aircraft –, breech loading –, quick firing-gun; field piece, mortar, trench mortar; mine –, flame- -thrower, napalm; howitzer, carronade, culverin, basilisk; falconet jingal, swivel, *pederero, bouche à feu*; smooth bore, rifled cannon; Armstrong –, Lancaster –, Paixhan –, Whitworth –, Parrott –, Krupp –, Gatling –, Maxim –, Vickers –, Hotchkiss –, Lewis –, machine- gun; tommy gun, Thompson's submachine gun; *mitrailleu-r, -se*; pompom; blow pipe.

small arms; musket, -ry, firelock, flintlock, fowling-piece, shot gun, rifle, *fusil*, caliver, carbine, blunderbuss, musketoon, Brown Bess, matchlock, harquebuss, *arquebuse*, haguebut; petronel; smallbore; breech-, muzzle-loader; Minie –, Enfield –, Westly Richards –, Snider –, Springfield –, Martini-Henry –, Lee-Metford –, Lee-Enfield –, Mauser –, Männlicher –, magazine –, repeating- rifle; needle-gun, *chassepot*; pis-tol, -et; revolver, automatic pistol, automatic; wind-, air-gun; flame –, gas- projector.

bow, cross-bow, arbalest, balister, catapult, sling; battering-ram etc. (*impulse*) 276; gunnery; ballistics etc. (*propulsion*) 284.

missile, bolt, projectile, shot, pellet, ball; grape; grape –, canister –, bar –, cannon –, langrel –, langrage –, round –, chain- shot; explosive; incendiary –, expanding –, soft-nosed –, dum-dum- bullet; slug, stone, brickbat; hand –, rifle-grenade; high explosive –, incendiary –, stink-, A-, H-, atomic –, hydrogen – bomb; petard, torpedo, carcass, rocket; congreve, – rocket; shrapnel, *mitraille*; thunderbolt; mine, land mine, infernal machine.

pike, lance, spear, spontoon, javelin, assagai, throwing stick, dart, djerrid, arrow, reed, shaft, bolt, boomerang, harpoon, gaff.

728. Arena.—N. arena, field, platform; scene of action, theater; walk, course; hustings; stage, boards etc. (*playhouse*) 599; amphitheater; Coli-, Colos-seum; Flavian amphitheater, hippodrome, circus, race-course, track, *stadium*, *corso*, turf, cockpit, bear-garden, play-ground, playing fields, *gymnasium, palaestra*, ring, lists; tilt-yard, -ing ground; *Campus Martius, Champ de Mars*; aerodrome, airport, air base, flying field.

theater –, seat- of war; battle-field, -ground; field of -battle, – slaughter; no man's land; Aceldama, camp; the enemy's camp; trysting- place etc. (*place of meeting*) 74.

729. Completion.—N. completion; accomplish-, achieve-, fulfil-ment; performance, execution; des-, dis-patch; consummation, culmination, climax; finish, conclusion, effectuation; close etc. (*end*) 67; terminus etc. (*arrival*) 292; winding up; *finale, dénouement*, catastrophe, issue, upshot, result; final –, last –, crowning –, finishing- -touch, – stroke; last finish, *coup de grâce*; crowning of the edifice; coping-, keystone; missing link etc. 53; super-structure, *ne plus ultra*, work done, *fait accompli*.

elaboration; finality; completeness etc. 52.

V. effect, -uate; accomplish, achieve, compass, consummate, hammer out; bring to -maturity, – perfection; perfect, complete; elaborate.

do, execute, make; go –, get- through; work out, enact; bring -about, – to bear, – to pass, – through, – to a head.

des-, dis-patch; knock –, finish –, polish- off; make short work of; dispose of, set at rest; perform, discharge, fulfil, realize; put in -practice, – force; carry -out, – into effect, – into execution; make good; be as good as one's word.

do thoroughly, not do by halves, go the whole hog; drive home; be in at the death etc. (*persevere*) 604*a*; carry through, play out, exhaust, deliver the goods, fill the bill.

finish, bring to a close etc. (*end*) 67; wind up, stamp, clinch, seal, set the seal on, put the seal to; give the -final touch etc. *n.* to; put the -last, – finishing- hand to; crown, – all; cap.

ripen, culminate; come to a -head, – crisis; come to its end; die -a natural death, – of old age; run -its course, – one's race; touch –, reach –, attain- the goal; reach etc. (*arrive*) 292; get in the harvest.

Adj. completing, final; conclu-ding, -sive; crowning etc. *v.*; exhaustive, complete, mature, perfect, consummate.

done, completed etc. *v.*; done for, sped, wrought out; highly wrought etc. (*preparation*) 673; thorough etc. 52; ripe etc. (*ready*) 673.

Adv. completely etc. (*thoroughly*) 52; to crown all, out of hand.

Phr. the race is run; *actum est*; *finis coronat opus*; *consummatum est*; *c'en est fait*; it is all over; the game is played out, the bubble has burst.

730. Non-Completion.—N. non-completion, -fulfilment; shortcoming etc. 304; incompleteness etc. 53; drawn -battle, – game; work of Penelope, task of Sisyphus.

non-performance, inexecution; neglect etc. 460.

V. not -complete etc. 729; leave -unfinished etc. *adj.*, – undone; neglect etc. 460; let -alone, – slip; lose sight of.

fall short of etc. 304; do things by halves; scotch the snake, not kill it; hang fire; be slow to; collapse etc. 304.

Adj. not completed etc. *v.*; incomplete etc. 53; uncompleted, unfinished; unaccomplished; un-performed, unexecuted; sketchy, addle.

in progress, in hand; going on, proceeding; on one's hands; on the fire; on the stocks; in preparation; lacking the finishing touch.

Adv. *re infectâ*.

731. Success.—N. success, -fulness; speed; advance etc. (*progress*) 282.

trump card; hit, stroke; lucky —, fortunate —, good- -hit, — stroke; bold —, master- stroke; *coup de maître*, checkmate; half the battle, prize; profit etc. (*acquisition*) 775; best seller.

continued success; good fortune etc. (*prosperity*) 734; time well spent.

advantage over; edge; upper-, whiphand; ascendancy, mastery; expugnation, conquest, victory, subdual; subjugation etc. (*subjection*) 749.

triumph etc. (*exultation*) 884; proficiency etc. (*skill*) 698; conqueror, victor, winner, champion; master of the -situation, — position.

V. succeed; be -successful etc. *adj.*; gain one's -end, — ends; crown with success.

gain —, attain —, carry —, secure —, win- -a point, — an object; put over; make a go of; manage to, contrive to; accomplish etc. (*effect, complete*) 729; do —, work- wonders.

come off -well, — successfully, — with flying colors; make short work of; take —, carry- by storm; bear away the bell; win -one's spurs, — the battle; win —, carry —, gain- the -day, — prize, — palm; climb on the bandwagon; have -the best of it, — it all one's own way, — the game in one's own hands, — the ball at one's feet, — one on the hip; walk over the course; carry all before one, remain in possession of the field; score a success, win hands down.

speed; make progress etc. (*advance*) 282; win —, make —, work —, find- one's way; strive to some purpose; prosper etc. 734; drive a roaring trade; make profit etc. (*acquire*) 775; reap —, gather- the -fruits, — benefit of, — harvest; make one's fortune, get in the harvest, turn to good account; turn to account etc. (*use*) 677.

triumph, be triumphant; gain —, obtain- -a victory, — an advantage; chain victory to one's car.

surmount —, overcome —, get over- -a difficulty, — an obstacle etc. 706; *se tirer d'affaire*; make head against; stem the -torrent, — tide, — current; weather -the storm, — a point; turn a corner, keep one's head above water, tide over; master; get —, have —, gain- the -better of, — best of, — upper hand, — ascendancy, — whip hand, — start of; distance; surpass etc. (*superiority*) 33.

defeat, conquer, vanquish, discomfit; over-come, throw, -power, -master, -match, -set, -ride, -reach; out-wit, -do, -flank, -maneuver, -general, vote; take the wind out of one's adversary's sails; beat, — hollow; rout, lick, drub, floor, worst; put -down, — to flight, — to the rout, — *hors de combat*; — out of court.

silence, quell, nonsuit, checkmate, upset, confound, nonplus, trump; baffle etc. (*hinder*) 706; circumvent, elude; trip up — the heels of; drive -into a corner, — to the wall; run hard, put one's nose out of joint.*

settle, do for; break the -neck of, — back of; capsize, sink, shipwreck, drown, swamp; subdue; subjugate etc. (*subject*) 749; reduce; make the enemy bite the dust; victimize, roll in the dust, trample under foot, put an extinguisher upon.

answer, — the purpose; avail, prevail, take effect, do, turn out well, work well, take, tell, bear fruit; hit -it, — the mark, — the right nail on the head; nick it; turn up trumps, make a hit; find one's account in.

Adj. succeeding etc. *v.*; successful; prosperous etc. 734; triumphant; flushed —, crowned- with success; victorious; set up; in the ascendant; unbeaten etc. (*see* beat etc. *v.*); well-spent; felicitous, effective, in full swing.

Adv. successfully etc. *adj.*; with flying colors, in triumph, swimmingly; *à merveille*, beyond all hope; to some —, good- purpose; to one's heart's content.

Phr. *veni vidi vici*, the day being one's own, one's star in the ascendant; *omne tulit punctum*.

732. Failure.—N. failure; non-success, -fulfilment; dead failure, successlessness; abortion, miscarriage; *brutum fulmen* etc. 158; labor in vain etc. (*inutility*) 645; no go; inefficacy; inefficaciousness etc. *adj.*; vain —, ineffectual —, abortive- -attempt, — efforts; flash in the pan, 'lame and impotent conclusion;' frustration; slip 'twixt cup and lip etc. (*disappointment*) 509.

blunder etc. (*mistake*) 495; fault, omission, miss, oversight, slip, trip, stumble, claudication, footfall; false —, wrong- step; *faux pas*, titubation, *bévue, faute*, lurch; botchery etc. (*want of skill*) 699; scrape, jam, mess, muddle, foozle, *fiasco*, breakdown.

mishap etc. (*misfortune*) 735; split, collapse, smash, blow, explosion.

repulse, rebuff, defeat, rout, overthrow, discomfiture; beating, drubbing; *quietus*, nonsuit, subjugation; check-, fool's-mate.

fall, downfall, ruin, perdition; wreck etc. (*destruction*) 162; death-blow; bankruptcy etc. (*non-payment*) 808.

losing game, *affaire flambée*.

victim, prey; bankrupt.

V. fail; be -unsuccessful etc. *adj.*; not -succeed etc. 731; make -vain efforts etc. *n.*; do —, labor —, toil- in vain; lose one's labor, take nothing by one's motion; bring to naught, make nothing of; wash a blackamoor white etc. (*impossible*) 471; roll the stone of Sisyphus etc. (*useless*) 645; do by halves etc. (*not complete*) 730; lose ground etc. (*recede*) 283; flunk; fall -short of etc. 304.

miss, — one's aim, — the mark, — one's footing, — stays; slip, trip, stumble; make a -slip etc. *n.*, — blunder etc. 495, — mess of, — botch of; bitch it, miscarry, abort, go up like a rocket and come down like the stick, reckon without one's host; get the wrong sow by the ear etc. (*blunder, mismanage*) 699.

limp, halt, hobble, titubate; fall, tumble; lose one's balance; fall -to the ground, — between two stools; flounder, falter, stick in the mud, run aground, split upon a rock; run —, knock —, dash- one's head against a stone wall; break one's back; break down, sink, drown, founder, have the ground cut from under one; get into -trouble, — a mess, — a scrape; come to grief etc. (*adversity*) 735; go to -the wall, — the dogs, — pot; lick —, bite- the dust; be -defeated etc. 731; have the worst of it, lose the day, come off second best, lose; fall a prey to; succumb etc. (*submit*) 725; not have a leg to stand on.

come to nothing, end in smoke; fall -to the ground, — through, — dead, — still-born, — flat; slip through one's fingers; hang —, miss- fire; flash in the pan, collapse; topple down etc. (*descent*) 305; go to wrack and ruin etc. (*destruction*) 162.

go amiss, go wrong, go cross, go hard with, go on a wrong tack; go on —, come off —, turn out

–, work- ill; take -a wrong, – an ugly- turn; gang agley.

be all -over with, – up with; explode; dash one's hopes etc. (*disappoint*) 509; defeat the purpose; upset the apple cart; sow the wind and reap the whirlwind, jump out of the frying pan into the fire.

Adj. unsuccessful, successless; failing, tripping etc. *v.*; at fault; unfortunate etc. 735.

abortive, addle, still-born; fruitless, sterile, bootless; ineffect-ual, -ive; inefficient etc. (*impotent*) 158; inefficacious; lame, hobbling, *décousu*; insufficient etc. 640; unavailing etc. (*useless*) 645; of no effect.

aground, grounded, swamped, stranded, cast away, wrecked, foundered, capsized, shipwrecked, non-suited; foiled; defeated etc. 731; struck –, borne –, broken- down; down-trodden; overborne, -whelmed; all up with; beaten to a frazzle.

lost, undone, ruined, broken; bankrupt etc. (*not paying*) 808; played out; done -up, – for; dead beat, ruined root and branch, *flambé*, knocked on the head; destroyed etc. 162.

frustrated, thwarted, crossed, unhinged, disconcerted, dashed; thrown -off one's balance, – on one's back, – on one's beam ends; unhorsed, in a sorry plight; hard hit.

stultified, befooled, dished, hoist on one's own petard, victimized, sacrificed.

wide of the mark etc. (*error*) 495; out of one's reckoning etc. (*inexpectation*) 508; left in the lurch; thrown away etc. (*wasted*) 638; unattained; uncompleted etc. 730.

Adv. unsuccessfully etc. *adj.*; to little or no purpose, in vain, *re infectâ*.

Phr. the bubble has burst, the game is up, all is lost; the devil to pay; *parturiunt montes* etc. (*disappointment*) 509.

733. Trophy.—N. trophy; medal, prize, palm; ribbon, blue ribbon, *cordon bleu*; citation; cup, laurel, -s; bays, crown, chaplet, wreath, civic crown; Victoria Cross, V.C., *Croix de Guerre*, Iron Cross; Distinguished Service Cross, Medal of Honor, Congressional Medal; insignia etc. 550; feather in one's cap etc. (*honor*) 873; decoration etc. 877; garland, triumphal arch.

triumph etc. (*celebration*) 883; flying colors etc. (*show*) 882.

monumentum aere perennius.

734. Prosperity.—N. prosperity, welfare, well-being; affluence etc. (*wealth*) 803; success etc. 731; thrift, roaring trade; chicken in every pot, the full dinner paid; good –, smiles of- fortune; blessings, godsend.

luck; good –, run of- luck; sunshine; fair -weather, – wind; palmy –, bright –, halcyon- days; piping times, tide, flood, high tide.

Saturnia regna, Saturnian age; golden -time, – age; bed of roses; fat of the land, milk and honey, loaves and fishes, fleshpots of Egypt.

made man, lucky dog, *enfant gâté*, spoiled child of fortune.

upstart, *parvenu, nouveau riche*, profiteer, skipjack, mushroom.

V. prosper, thrive, flourish; be -prosperous etc. *adj.*; drive a roaring trade; go on -well, – smoothly, – swimmingly; sail before the wind, swim with the tide; run -smooth, – smoothly, – on all fours.

rise –, get on- in the world; work –, make- one's way; look up; lift –, raise- one's head, make one's -fortune, – pile, feather one's nest.

flower, blow, blossom, bloom, fructify, bear fruit, fatten, batten.

keep oneself afloat; keep –, hold- one's head above water; light –, fall- on one's -legs, – feet; drop into a good thing; bear a charmed life; bask in the sunshine; have a -good, – fine- time of it; have a run, – of luck; have the -good fortune etc. *n.* to; take a favorable turn; live -on the fat of the land, – in clover.

Adj. prosperous; thriving etc. *v.*; in a fair way, buoyant; well -off, – to do, – to do in the world; set up, at one's ease; rich etc. 803; in good case; in -full, – high- feather; fortunate, lucky, in luck; born -with a silver spoon in one's mouth, – under a lucky star; on the sunny side of the hedge.

auspicious, propitious, providential.

palmy, halcyon; agreeable etc. 829; *couleur de rose*.

Adv. prosperously etc. *adj.*; swimmingly; as good luck would have it; beyond all -expectation, – hope, – one's wildest dreams.

Phr. one's star in the ascendant, all for the best, one's course runs smooth.

735. Adversity.—N. adversity, evil etc. 619; failure etc. 732; bad –, ill –, evil –, adverse –, hard- -fortune, – hap, – luck, – lot; frowns of fortune; evil -dispensation, – star, – genius; ups and downs of life, broken fortunes; hard -case, – lines, – life; sea –, peck- of troubles; hell upon earth; slough of despond; jinx.

trouble, humiliation, hardship, curse, blight, blast, load, pressure.

pressure of the times, iron age, evil day, time out of joint; hard –, bad –, sad- times; rainy day, cloud, dark cloud, gathering clouds, ill wind; visitation, infliction; affliction etc. (*painfulness*) 830; bitter -pill, – cup; care, trial; the sport of fortune.

mis-hap, -chance, -adventure, -fortune; disaster, calamity, catastrophe; accident, casualty, cross, reverse, check, *contretemps*, rub, pinch, setback.

losing game; falling etc. *v.*; fall, down-fall, come-down; ruin-ation, -ousness; undoing; extremity; ruin etc. (*destruction*) 162.

V. be -ill off etc. *adj.*; go hard with; fall on evil, – days; go on ill; not -prosper etc. 734.

go -downhill, – to rack and ruin etc. (*destruction*) 162, – to the dogs; fall, – from one's high estate; decay, sink, decline, go down in the world; have seen better days; bring down one's grey hairs with sorrow to the grave; come to grief; be all -over, – up- with; bring a -wasp's, – hornet's- nest about one's ears.

Adj. unfortunate, unblest, unhappy, unlucky; im-, un-prosperous; luck-, hap-less; out of luck; in trouble, in a bad way, in an evil plight; under a cloud; clouded; ill –, badly- off; in adverse circumstances; poor etc. 804; behindhand, down in the world, decayed, undone; on the road to ruin, on its last legs, on the wane; in one's utmost need.

planet-struck, devoted; born -under an evil star, – with a wooden ladle in one's mouth; ill-fated, -starred, -omened; inconspicuous, ominous, doomed, unpropitious.

adverse, untoward; disastrous, calamitous, ruinous, dire, deplorable.

Adv. if the worst come to the worst, as ill luck would have it, from bad to worse, out of the frying pan into the fire.

Phr. one's star is on the wane; one's luck -turns, – fails; the game is up, one's doom is sealed, the ground crumbles under one's feet, *sic transit gloria mundi, tant va la cruche à l'eau qu'à la fin elle se casse.*

736. Mediocrity.—**N.** moderate –, average-circumstances; respectability; middle classes, *bourgeoisie*; mediocrity; golden mean etc. (*mid-course*) 628, (*moderation*) 174.

V. jog on; go –, get on- -fairly, – quietly, – peaceably, – tolerably, – respectably; steer a middle course etc. 628.

Adj. middling, so-so, fair, medium, moderate, mediocre, second-, third- etc. -rate.

737. Authority.—**N.** authority; influence, patronage, power, preponderance, credit, *prestige*, prerogative, jurisdiction; right etc. (*title*) 924.

divine right, dynastic rights, authoritativeness; absolut-eness, -ism; despotism, tyranny; *jus nocendi.*

command, empire, sway, rule; domin-ion, -ation; sovereignty, supremacy, suzerainty; lord-, head-ship; chiefdom; seignior-y, -ity, hegemony, patriarchate, patriarchy; master-y, -ship, -dom; government etc. (*direction*) 693; dictation, control.

hold, grasp; grip, -e; reach; iron sway etc. (*severity*) 739; fangs, clutches, talons; rod of empire etc. (*scepter*) 747.

reign, regnancy, *régime*, dynasty; director-, dictator-ship; protector-ate, -ship; caliphate, pashalic, electorate; presiden-cy, -tship; administration; pro-, consulship; prefecture; seneschalship; magistra-ture, -cy; raj.

empire; monarchy; king-hood, -ship; royalty, regality, autocracy, monocracy, arist-archy, -ocracy; oligarchy, democracy, demogogy; republic, -anism, federalism; socialism, collectivism; communism, bolshevism, syndicalism; mob law, mobocracy, ochlocracy, ergatocracy; *vox populi, imperium in imperio*; bureaucracy; beadle-, bumble-dom; stratocracy; martial law, military -power, – government; feodality, feudal system, feudalism.

Thearchy, diarchy; du-, tri-, heter-archy; du-, triumvirate; auto-cracy, -nomy; limited monarchy; constitutional -government, – monarchy; home rule, autonomy; self-government, -determination; representative government; Soviet government.

gyn-archy, -ocracy, -aeocracy; petticoat government, matriarchate, matriarchy.

[Vicarious authority] commission etc. 755; deputy etc. 759; permission etc. 760.

country, state, realm, commonwealth, canton, constituency, toparchy, municipality, polity, body politic, *posse comitatus.*

person in authority etc. (*master*) 745; judicature etc. 965; cabinet etc. (*council*) 696; usurper; seat of -government, – authority; head-quarters.

[Acquisition of authority] accession; installation etc. 755; usurpation.

V. authorize etc. (*permit*) 760; warrant etc. (*right*) 924; dictate etc. (*order*) 741; have –, hold –, possess –, exercise –, exert –, wield- -authority etc. *n.*

be -at the head of etc. *adj.*; hold –, be in –, fill an- office; hold –, occupy- a post; be -master etc. 745.

rule, sway, command, control, administer; govern etc. (*direct*) 693; lead, preside over, reign; possess –, be seated on –, occupy- the throne; sway –, wield- the scepter; wear the crown.

have –, get- the -upper, – whip- hand; gain a hold upon, preponderate, dominate, boss, rule the roost; over-ride, -rule, -awe; lord it over, hold in hand, keep under, make a puppet of, lead by the nose, hold in the hollow of one's hand, turn round one's little finger, bend to one's will, hold one's own, wear the breeches; have -the ball at one's feet, – it all one's own way, – the game in one's own hand, – on the hip, – under one's thumb; be master of the situation; take the lead, play first fiddle, set the fashion; give the law to; carry with a high hand; lay down the law; 'ride in the whirlwind and direct the storm;' rule with a rod of iron etc. (*severity*) 739.

ascend –, mount- the throne, take the reins, – into one's hand; assume -authority etc. *n.*, – the reins of government; take –, assume the- command.

be -governed by, – in the power of; be under -the rule of, – the domination of.

Adj. ruling etc. *v.*; regnant, at the head, dominant, paramount, supreme, predominant, preponderant, in the ascendant, influential; gubernatorial; imperious; authoritative, executive, administrative, clothed with authority, official, *ex officio*, ministerial, bureaucratic, departmental, imperative, peremptory, overruling, absolute; hegemonic, -al; arbitrary; compulsory etc. 744; stringent.

regal, sovereign; royal, -ist; monarchical, kingly; imperial, -istic; princely; feudal; aristo-, auto-cratic; oligarchic etc. *n.*; democratic, republican, dynastic.

at one's command; in one's -power, – grasp; under control; authorized etc. (*due*) 924.

Adv. in the name of, by the authority of, *de par le Roi*, in virtue of; under the auspices of, in the hands of.

at one's pleasure; by a -dash, – stroke- of the pen; *ex mero motu*; *ex cathedrâ.*

Phr. the grey mare the better horse; 'every inch a king.'

738. Laxity. [Absence of authority.]—**N.** laxity; lax-, loose-, slack-ness; toleration etc. (*lenity*) 740; freedom etc. 748.

anarchy, interregnum; relaxation; loosening etc. *v.*; remission; dead letter, *brutum fulmen*, misrule; license, licentiousness; insubordination etc. (*disobedience*) 742; lynch law etc. (*illegality*) 964; nihilism.

[Deprivation of power.] dethronement, deposition, usurpation, abdication.

V. be -lax etc. *adj.*; *laisser -faire*, – *aller*; hold a loose rein; give -the reins to, – rope enough, – a loose to; tolerate; relax; misrule.

go beyond the length of one's tether; have one's -swing, – fling; act without -instructions, – authority; act on one's own responsibility, usurp authority.

dethrone, depose; abdicate.

Adj. lax, loose; slack; remiss etc. (*careless*) 460; weak.

relaxed; licensed; reinless, unbridled; anarchical; unauthorized etc. (*unwarranted*) 925.

739. Severity.—N. severity; strictness, formalism, harshness etc. *adj.*; rigor, stringency, austerity; inclemency etc. (*pitilessness*) 914*a*; arrogance etc. 885.

arbitrary power; absolut-, despot-ism; dictatorship, autocracy, tyranny, domineering, oppression; assumption, usurpation; inquisition, reign of terror, martial law; iron -heel, – rule, – hand, – sway; tight grasp; brute -force, – strength; coercion etc. 744; strong –, tight- hand.

hard -lines, – measure; tender mercies [ironical.]; sharp practice; bureaucracy, red tape; pipe-clay, officialism.

tyrant, disciplinarian, martinet, stickler, formalist, bashaw, despot, hard master, Draco, oppressor, inquisitor, extortioner, harpy, vulture, bird of prey.

V. be -severe etc. *adj.*

assume, usurp, arrogate, take liberties; domineer, bully etc. 885; tyrannize, inflict, wreak, stretch a point, put on the screw; be hard upon; bear –, lay- a heavy hand on; be –, come- down upon; ill-treat; deal-hardly with, – hard measure to; rule with a rod of iron, chastise with scorpions; dye with blood; oppress, override; trample –, tread- -down, – upon, – under foot; crush under an iron heel, ride roughshod over; rivet the yoke; hold –, keep- a tight hand; force down the throat; coerce etc. 744; give no quarter etc. (*pitiless*) 914*a*.

Adj. severe; strict, hard, harsh, dour, rigid, stiff, stern, rigorous, uncompromising, exacting, exigent, *exigeant*, inexorable, inflexible, obdurate, austere, relentless, Spartan, Draconian, stringent, strait-laced, puritanical, prudish, searching, unsparing, ironhanded, hard-headed, peremptory, absolute, positive, arbitrary, imperative; coercive etc. 744; tyrannical, despotic, masterful, extortionate, grinding, withering, oppressive, inquisitorial; inclement etc. (*ruthless*) 914*a*; cruel etc. (*malevolent*) 907; haughty, arrogant etc. 885.

Adv. severely etc. *adj.*; with a -high, – strong, – tight, – heavy-hand.

at the point of the -sword, – bayonet.

Phr. *Delirant reges plectuntur Achivi.*

740. Leniency.—N. leni-ency, -ence, -ty; moderation etc. 174; toler-ance, -ation; mildness, gentleness; favor; indulgen-ce, -cy; clemency, mercy, forbearance, quarter; compassion etc. 914.

V. be -lenient etc. *adj.*; tolerate, bear with; *parcere subjectis*, give quarter.

indulge, allow one to have his own way, spoil.

Adj. lenient; mild, – as milk; gentle, soft; tolerant, indulgent, easy-going; clement etc. (*compassionate*) 914; forbearing; complaisant, long-suffering.

741. Command.—N. command, order, ordinance, act, *fiat*, bidding, *dictum*, hest, behest, call, beck, nod.

des-, dis-patch; message, direction, injunction, charge, instructions; appointment, fixture.

demand, exaction, imposition, requisition, claim, reclamation, revendication; *ultimatum* etc. (*terms*) 770; request etc. 765; requirement.

dictation; dict-, mand-ate; *caveat*, decree, decree -nisi, – absolute, *senatus consultum*; precept; pre-, re-script; writ, ordination, bull, edict, decretal, dispensation, prescription, brevet, placet, ukase, *firman*, hatti-sheriff, warrant, passport, *mittimus*, *mandamus*, summons, subpoena, *nisi prius*, interpellation, citation; word, – of command; *mot d'ordre*; bugle –, trumpet- call; beat of drum, tattoo; order of the day; enactment etc. (*law*) 963; *plébiscite* etc. (*choice*) 609.

V. command, order, decree, enact, ordain, dictate, direct, give orders.

prescribe, set, appoint, mark out; set –, prescribe –, impose- a task; set to work, put in requisition etc. 926.

bid, enjoin, charge, call upon, instruct; require, – at the hands of; exact, impose, tax, task; demand; insist on etc. (*compel*) 744.

claim, lay claim to, revendicate, reclaim.

cite, summon; call –, send- for; subpoena; beckon.

issue a command; make –, issue –, promulgate- -a requisition, – a decree, – an order etc. *n.*; give the -word of command, – word, – signal; call to order; give –, lay down- the law; assume the command etc. (*authority*) 737; remand.

be -ordered etc.; receive an order etc. *n.*

Adj. commanding etc. *v.*; authoritative etc. 737; decret-ory, -ive, -al; imperative, jussive, decisive, final.

Adv. in a commanding tone; by a -stroke, – dash- of the pen; by order, at beat of drum, on the first summons; at the word of command.

Phr. the decree is gone forth; *sic volo sic jubeo*; *le Roi le veut.*

742. Disobedience.—N. disobedience, insubordination, contumacy; infraction, -fringement; violation, non-compliance; non-observance etc. 773.

revolt, rebellion, mutiny, outbreak, rising, uprising, putsch, insurrection, *émeute*; riot, tumult etc. (*disorder*) 59; strike etc. (*resistance*) 719; barring out; defiance etc. 715.

mutinousness etc. *adj.*; mutineering; sedition, treason; high –, petty –, misprison of- treason; *premunire*; *lèse- majesté*; violation of law etc. 964; defection, secession, revolution, *sabotage*, bolshevism, *Sinn Fein.*

insurgent, mutineer, rebel, revolter, rioter, traitor, *carbonaro*, *sansculottes*, red republican, communist, Fenian, chartist, *frondeur*; seceder, runagate, brawler, anarchist, demagogue; suffragette; Spartacus, Masaniello, Wat Tyler, Jack Cade; bolshevist, bolshevik, maximalist, ringleader.

V. disobey, violate, infringe; shirk; set at defiance etc. (*defy*) 715; set authority at naught, run riot, fly in the face of, bolt, take the law into one's own hands; kick over the traces.

turn –, run- restive; champ the bit; strike etc. (*resist*) 719; rise, – in arms; secede; mutiny, rebel.

Adj. disobedient; uncompl-ying, -iant; unsubmissive; unruly, ungovernable; insubordinate, impatient of control; rest-iff, -ive; refractory, contumacious; recusant etc. (refuse) 764; recalcitrant; resisting etc. 719; lawless, mutinous, seditious, insurgent, riotous, revolutionary.

disobeyed, unobeyed; unbidden.

743. Obedience.—**N.** obedience; observance etc. 772; compliance; submission etc. 725; subjection etc. 749; non-resistance; passiveness, passivity, resignation.

allegiance, loyalty, fealty, homage, deference, devotion, fidelity, constancy.

submiss-ness, -iveness; ductility etc. (*softness*) 324; obsequiousness etc. (*servility*) 886.

V. be -obedient etc. *adj.*; obey, bear obedience to; submit etc. 725; comply, answer the helm, come at one's call; do -one's bidding, – what one is told, – suit and service; attend to orders, serve -devotedly, –, loyally, – faithfully.

follow, – the lead of, – to the world's end; serve etc. 746; play second fiddle.

Adj. obedient; compl-ying, -iant; law-abiding, loyal, faithful, leal, devoted; at one's -call, – command, – orders, – beck and call; under -beck and call, – control.

restrainable; resigned, passive; submissive etc. 725; henpecked, pliant etc. (*soft*) 324.

unresist-ed, -ing.

Adv. obediently etc. *adj.*; in compliance with, in obedience to.

Phr. to hear is to obey; as –, if- you please; at your service.

744. Compulsion.—**N.** compulsion, coercion, coaction, constraint, eminent domain, duress, enforcement, press, conscription.

force; brute –, main –, physical- force; the sword, *ultima ratio*; club –, mob –, lynch- law; *argumentum baculinum, le droit du plus fort*, martial law.

restraint etc. 751; necessity etc. 601; *force majeure*; Hobson's choice; the spur of necessity.

V. compel, force, make, drive, coerce, constrain, enforce, necessitate, oblige.

force upon, press; cram –, thrust –, force- down the throat; say it must be done, make a point of, insist upon, take no denial; put down, dragoon.

extort, wring from; put –, turn- on the screw; drag into; bind, – over; pin –, tie- down; require, tax, put in force; commandeer; restrain etc. 751.

Adj. compelling etc. *v.*; coercive, coactive; inexorable etc. 739; compuls-ory, -atory; obligatory, stringent, peremptory, binding.

forcible, not to be trifled with; irresistible etc. 601; compelled etc. *v.*; fain to.

Adv. by -force etc. *n.*, – force of arms; on compulsion, perforce; *vi et armis*, under the lash; at the point of the -sword, – bayonet; forcibly; by a strong arm.

under protest, in spite of one's teeth; against one's will etc. 603; *nolens volens* etc. (*of necessity*) 601; by stress of -circumstances, – weather; under press of; *de rigueur*.

745. Master.—**N.** master, *padrone*; lord, – paramount; command-er, -ant; captain; chief, -tain; *sahib*, sirdar, sachem, sheik, head, senior, governor, *duce*, ruler, dictator; leader etc. (*director*) 694.

lord of the ascendant; cock of the -walk, – roost; grey mare; mistress.

potentate; liege, – lord; suzerain, sovereign, monarch, autocrat, despot, tyrant, oligarch, overlord.

crowned head, emperor, king, anointed king, majesty, *imperator*, protector, president, stadtholder, judge.

caesar, kaiser, czar, sultan, grand Turk, caliph, imaum, shah, padishah, sophi, mogul, great mogul, khan, cham; lama, tycoon, mikado, inca, cazique; domn; vaivode; wai-, way-wode; landamman; seyyid, cacique.

prince, duke etc. (*nobility*) 875; arch-duke, doge, elector; seignior; mar-, land-grave; rajah, emir, nizam, nawab, negus.

empress, queen, sultana, czarina, princess, infanta, duchess, margravine, begum, maharani.

regent, viceroy, exarch, palatine, khedive, hospodar, beglerbeg, three-tailed bashaw, pasha, pashaw, bashaw, bey, beg, dey, scherif, tetrarch, satrap, mandarin, subhadar, nabob, maharajah; burgrave; laird etc. (*proprietor*) 779; High Commissioner.

the -authorities, – powers that be, – government; staff, *état major*, aga, official, man in office, person in authority.

[Naval authorities] admiral, -ty, – of the fleet; rear-, vice-, port-admiral; senior-, naval officer, S.N.O., commodore, captain, commander, lieutenant-commander, lieutenant, sub-lieutenant, midshipman, warrant –, petty- officer, leading seaman; skipper, mate, master.

[Military authorities] marshal, field-marshal, *maréchal*; general, -issimo; commander-in-chief, *seraskier, hetman*; lieutenant-, major-general; commandant; colonel, lieutenant-colonel, major, captain, centurion, skipper, lieutenant, second-lieutenant, officer, staff-officer, *aide de camp*, brigadier, brigade-major, adjutant, *jemidar*, ensign, cornet, cadet, subaltern, warrant officer, quartermaster, noncommissioned officer, N.C.O.; sergeant, -major; top-sergeant, color sergeant; corporal, -major; lance-, acting-corporal; drum major; shavetail.

[Air authorities] air -marshal, – commodore; group captain, squadron leader, wing commander, flight lieutenant, flying –, pilot- officer.

[Civil authorities] judge etc. 967; mayor, -alty; prefect, chancellor, archon, provost, magistrate, syndic; alcalde, alcaid; burgomaster, *corregidor*, seneschal, alderman, warden, constable, portreeve; lord mayor, sheriff; officer etc. (*executive*) 965.

746. Servant.—**N.** subject, liegeman; servant, retainer, follower, henchman, servitor, domestic, menial, help, lady help, *employé, attaché*; official.

retinue, suite, *cortège*, staff, court.

attendant, squire, usher, page, buttons, donzel, footboy; dog robber; train-, cup-bearer; waiter, busboy, tapster, butler, livery servant, lackey, footman, flunkey, valet, *valet de chambre*; boots; scout, gyp; equerry, groom; jockey, hostler, ostler, tiger, orderly, messenger, cad, gillie, caddie; *wallah*; journeyman, herdsman, swineherd.

bailiff, castellan, seneschal, chamberlain, *major-domo*, groom of the chambers.

secretary; under –, assistant- secretary; clerk; clerical staff, stenographer, subsidiary; agent etc. 758; subaltern; under-ling, -strapper; man.

maid, -servant, waitress; handmaid; *confidente*, lady's maid, abigail, *soubrette*; nurse, *bonne*, *ayah*; nurse-, nursery-, house-, parlor-, waiting-, chamber-, kitchen-, scullery-, between –, laundry –, dairy-maid; *femme* –, *fille- de chambre*; *camarista*; *chef de cuisine*, *cordon bleu*, cook, scullion, Cinderella; maid –, servant- of all work, tweeny, general servant, girl, slavey; laundress, bed-maker, goodie, char-woman etc. (*worker*) 690.

serf, vassal, slave, negro, helot; bondsman, -woman; bondslave; *âme damnée, odalisque*, ryot, *adscriptus glebae*; vill-ain, -ein; bead-, bede-sman; sizar; pension-er, -ary; client; dependant, -ent; hanger on, stooge, satellite; parasite etc. (*servility*) 886; led captain; *protégé*, ward, hireling, mercenary, puppet, creature.

badge of slavery; bonds etc. 752.

V. serve; minister to, wait –, attend –, dance attendance –, pin oneself- upon; squire, tend, hang on the sleeve of, char, do for; fag; valet.

Adj. in the train of; in one's -pay, – employ; at one's call etc. (*obedient*) 743; in bonds.

747. Scepter. [Insignia of authority.]—**N.** scepter, regalia, rod of empire, sword of state, mace, *fasces*, wand; staff, – of office; *bâton*, truncheon; flag etc. (*insignia*) 550; ensign –, emblem –, badge –, insignia- of authority, rank marks, brassard, badge, sash; cocked –, brass- hat.

epaulette, aiguilette, crown, star, eagle, bar, double bar, pip, stripe, chevron, curl, ring, anchor, shoulder-strap, tab.

throne, chair, musnud, divan, dais, woolsack.

toga, pall, mantle, robes of state, ermine, purple.

crown, coronet, diadem, tiara, triple crown, miter, crozier, cardinal's hat etc.; cap of maintenance; decoration; title etc. 877; portfolio.

key, signet, seals, talisman; helm; reins etc. (*means of restraint*) 752.

748. Freedom.—**N.** freedom, liberty, independence; license etc. (*permission*) 760; facility etc. 705.

scope, range, latitude, play; free –, full- -play, – scope; free stage and no favor; swing, full swing, elbow-room, margin, rope, wide berth; Liberty Hall.

franchise, denization; free –, freed-, liveryman; denizen.

autonomy, self-government, homerule, self-determination, liberalism, free trade; non-interference etc. 706.

immunity, exemption; emancipation etc. (*liberation*) 750; en-, af-franchisement; rights, privileges.

free land, freehold; allodium; frankalmoigne, mortmain.

independent, free-lance, -thinker, -trader.

V. be -free etc. *adj.*; have -scope etc. *n.*, – the run of, – one's own way, – a will of one's own, – one's fling; do what one -likes, – wishes, – pleases, – chooses; go at large, feel at home, paddle one's own canoe; stand on one's -legs, – rights; shift for oneself.

take a liberty; make -free with, – oneself quite at home; use a freedom; take -leave, – French leave.

set free etc. (*liberate*) 750; give the reins to etc. (*permit*) 760; allow –, give- scope etc. *n.* to; give a horse his head.

make free of; give the -freedom of, – franchise; en-, af-franchise.

laisser -faire, – *aller*; live and let live; leave to oneself; leave –, let- alone; mind one's own business.

Adj. free, – as air; out of harness, independent, at large, loose, scot free; left -alone, – to oneself.

in full swing; uncaught, unconstrained, unbuttoned, unconfined, unrestrained, unchecked, unprevented, unhindered, unobstructed, unbound, uncontrolled, untrammeled.

unsubject, ungoverned, unenslaved, unenthralled, unchained, unshackled, unfettered, unreined, unbridled, uncurbed, unmuzzled, unimpeded.

unrestricted, unlimited, unconditional; absolute; discretionary etc. (*optional*) 600.

unassailed, unforced, uncompelled.

unbiassed, unprejudiced, uninfluenced, spontaneous.

free and easy; at –, at one's- ease; *dégagé*, quite at home; wanton, rampant, irrepressible, unvanquished.

exempt; freed etc. 750; freeborn; autonomous, freehold, allodial; *gratis* etc. 815.

unclaimed, going a begging.

Adv. freely etc. *adj.*; *ad libitum* etc. (*at will*) 600.

749. Subjection.—**N.** subjection; depend-ence, -ance, -ency; subordination; thrall, thraldom, enthralment, subjugation, bondage, serfdom; feudal- -ism, -ity; vassalage, villenage; slavery, enslavement, involuntary servitude.

service; servi-tude, -torship; tendence, employ, tutelage, clientship; liability etc. 177; constraint etc. 751; oppression etc. (*severity*) 739; yoke etc. (*means of restraint*) submission etc. 725; obedience etc. 743.

V. be -subject etc. *adj.*; be –, lie- at the mercy of; depend –, lean –, hang- upon; fall -a prey to, – under; play second fiddle.

be a -mere machine, – puppet, – football; not dare to say one's soul is his own; drag a chain.

serve etc. 746; obey etc. 743; submit etc. 725.

break in, tame; subject, subjugate; master etc. 731; tread -down, – under foot; weigh down; drag at one's chariot wheels; reduce to -subjection, –

slavery; en-, in-, be-thral; enslave, lead captive; take into custody etc. (*restrain*) 751; rule etc. 737; drive into a corner, hold at the sword's point; keep under; hold in -bondage, – leading strings, – swaddling clothes.

Adj. subject, dependent, subordinate; feud-al, -atory; in subjection to, under control; in -leading strings, – harness; subjected, enslaved etc. *v.*; con-strained etc. 751; subservient, servile, fawning, slavish, obsequious, cringing; down-trodden; over-borne, -whelmed; under the lash, on the hip, led by the nose, henpecked; the -puppet, – sport, – plaything- of; under one's -orders, – command, – thumb; like dirt under one's feet; a slave to; at the mercy of; in the -power, – hands, – clutches- of; at the feet of; at one's beck and call etc. (*obedient*) 743; liable etc. 177; parasitical; stipendiary.

Adv. under.

750. Liberation.—N. liberation, disengagement, release, disenthrallment, enlargement, emancipation; af-, en-franchisement; manumission; discharge, dismissal.

deliverance etc. 672; redemption, extrication, acquittance, absolution; acquittal etc. 970; escape etc. 671.

V. liberate, free; set -free, – clear, – at liberty; render free, emancipate, release; en-, af-franchise; manumit; enlarge; dis-band, -charge, -miss, -enthral; let -go, – loose, – out, – slip; cast –, turn- adrift; deliver etc. 672; absolve etc. (*acquit*) 970; reprieve.

unfetter etc. 751; untie etc. 44; loose etc. (*disjoin*) 44; loosen, relax; un-bolt, -bar, -close, -cork, -clog, -hand, -bind, -latch, -chain, -harness; dis-engage, -entangle; clear, extricate, unloose.

gain –, obtain –, acquire- one's -liberty etc. 748; get -rid, – clear- of; deliver oneself from; shake off the yoke, slip the collar; break -loose, – prison; tear asunder one's bonds, cast off trammels; escape etc. 671.

Adj. at -liberty, – large, free, liberated etc. *v.*; out of harness etc. 748; adrift.

Int. unhand me! let me go!

751. Restraint.—N. restraint; hindrance etc. 706; coercion etc. (*compulsion*) 744; cohibition, constraint, repression; discipline, control, self-restraint etc. 604.

confinement; durance, duress; im-, prisonment; incarceration, coarctation, entombment, mancipation, durance vile, thrall, -dom, limbo, captivity; blockade; quarantine; detention.

arrest, -ation; custody, keep, care, charge, ward, restringency.

curb etc. (*means of restraint*) 752; *lettres de cachet*.

limitation, restriction, protection, monopoly; prohibition etc. 761; economic pressure.

prisoner etc. 754.

V. restrain, check; put –, lay- under restraint; en-, in-, be-thral; restrict; debar etc. (*hinder*) 706; constrain; coerce etc. (*compel*) 744; curb, control; hold –, keep- -back, – from, – in, – in check, – within bounds; hold in -leash, – leading strings; withhold.

keep under; repress, suppress; smother; pull in, rein in; hold, – fast; keep a tight hand on; prohibit etc. 761; in-, co-hibit.

enchain; fasten etc. (*join*) 43; fetter, shackle; en-, trammel; bridle, muzzle, gag, pinion, manacle, handcuff, tie one's hands, hobble, bind hand and foot; swathe, swaddle; pin –, peg- down; tether, picket; tie, – up, – down; secure; forge fetters.

confine; shut –, clap –, lock –, box –, mew –, bottle –, cork –, seal –, button- up; shut –, hem –, bolt –, wall –, rail- in; impound, pen, coop; enclose etc. (*circumscribe*) 229; cage; in-, en-cage; close the door upon, cloister; imprison, immure; incarcerate, entomb; clap –, lay- under hatches; put in -irons, – a strait waistcoat; throw –, cast- into prison; put into bilboes.

arrest; take -up, – charge of, – into custody; take –, make- -prisoner, – captive; captivate; lead -captive, – into captivity; send –, commit- to prison; commit; give in -charge, – custody; subjugate etc. 749.

Adj. re-, con-strained; imprisoned etc. *v.*; pent up; jammed in, wedged in; under -restraint, – lock and key, – hatches; serving –, doing- time; in swaddling clothes; on *parole*; in custody etc. (*prisoner*) 754; cohibitive; coactive etc. (*compulsory*) 744.

stiff, restringent, straitlaced, hide-bound.

ice-, wind-, weather-bound; 'cabined, cribbed, confined;' in Lob's pound, laid by the heels.

Adv. in captivity, under arrest, behind the bars, in -prison, – jail, – durance vile.

752. Prison. [Means of restraint.]—**N.** prison, -house; jail, gaol, cage, coop, den, death house, condemned –, cell; stronghold, fortress, keep, donjon, dungeon, *Bastille*, *oubliette*, bridewell, house of correction, hulks, tool-booth, panopticon, penitentiary, guard-room, clink, can, stir, tronk, jug, lock-up, hold; round , watch , station –, sponging-house; station; house of detention, black hole, pen, fold, pound; enclosure etc. 232; penal settlement; chain gang; debtors' prison; reformatory; federal penitentiary, state prison; criminal lunatic asylum; bilboes, stocks, limbo, quod.

Dartmoor, Newgate, Fleet, Marshalsea; King's (*or* Queen's) Bench; Sing Sing, Dannemora.

bond; strap, bandage, splint, tourniquet; irons, pinion, gyve, fetter, shackle, trammel, manacle, handcuff, bracelets, darbies, strait waistcoat, strait-jacket.

yoke, collar, halter, harness; muzzle, gag, bit, brake, curb, snaffle, bridle; rein, -s; ribbons, lines, bearing-rein; martingale, leading string; tether, picket, band, guy, chain; cord etc. (*fastening*) 45.

bolt, bar, lock, padlock, rail, wall; paling, palisade; fence; barrier, barricade.

brake, drag etc. (*hindrance*) 706.

753. Keeper.—N. keeper, custodian, *custos*, ranger, warder, jailer, gaoler, turnkey, castellan, guard; watch, -dog, -man; Charley; sen-try, -tinel; watch and ward; *concierge*, coast-guard, *guarda costa*, gamekeeper.

escort, body guard, convoy.

protector, governor, duenna; guardian; governess etc. (*teacher*) 540; nurse, *bonne*, *ayah*, *amah*.

754. Prisoner.—**N.** prisoner, captive, *détenu*, close prisoner.
jail-bird, ticket-of-leave man.
V. stand committed; be -imprisoned etc. 751.
Adj. imprisoned etc. 751; in -prison, – quod, – durance vile, – limbo, – custody, – charge, – chains; under -lock and key, – hatches; on *parole*; detained at his Majesty's pleasure.

755. Commission. [Vicarious authority.]—**N.** commission, delegation; con-, as-signment; procuration; deputation, legation, mission, embassy; agency, agentship; power of attorney, proxy; clerkship.
errand, charge, *brevet*, diploma, *exequatur*, permit etc. (*permission*) 760.
appointment, nomination, return; charter; ordination; installation, inauguration, investiture; accession, coronation, enthronement.
vicegerency; regency, regentship.
viceroy etc. 745; consignee etc. 758; deputy etc. 759.
V. commission, delegate, depute; consign, assign; charge; in-, en-trust; turn over to; commit, – to the hands of; authorize etc. (*permit*) 760.
put in commission, accredit, engage, hire, bespeak, appoint, name, nominate, return, ordain; install, induct, inaugurate, invest, crown; en-roll, -list.
employ, empower; give power of attorney to; set –, place- over; send out.
be commissioned, be accredited; represent, stand for; stand in the -stead, – place, – shoes- of.
Adj. commissioned etc. *v.*
Adv. *per procuratione.*

756. Abrogation.—**N.** abrogation, annulment, nullification; cancelling etc. *v.*; cancel; revo-cation, -kement; repeal, rescission, defeasance.
dismissal, *congé*, demission; depos-al, -ition; sack, dethronement; disestablish-, disendow-ment; deconsecration.
aboli-tion, -shment; dissolution.
counter-order, -mand; repudiation, retractation; recantation etc. (*tergiversation*) 607.
V. abrogate, annul, cancel; destroy etc. 162; abolish; revoke, repeal, rescind, reverse, retract, recall; over-rule, -ride; set aside; disannul, dissolve, quash, nullify, declare null and void; dis-establish, -endow; deconsecrate.
disclaim etc. (*deny*) 536; ignore, repudiate; recant etc. 607; divest oneself, break off.
counter-mand, -order; do away with; sweep –, brush- away; throw -overboard, – to the dogs; scatter to the winds, cast behind.
dismiss, discard; cast –, turn- -off, – out, – adrift, – out of doors, – aside, – away; send -off, – away, – about one's business; discharge, get rid of, fire out, fire etc. (*eject*) 297; jilt.
cashier; break; oust; set down, unseat, -saddle; un-, de-, disen-throne; depose, uncrown; unfrock, strike off the roll; dis-bar, -bench.
be -abrogated etc.; receive its quietus.
Adj. abrogated etc. *v.*; *functus officio.*
Int. get along with you! begone! go about your business! away with!

757. Resignation.—**N.** resignation, retirement, abdication, renunciation, abjuration, disclaimer, abandonment, relinquishment.
V. resign; give –, throw- up; lay down, throw up the cards, wash one's hands of, abjure, renounce, forego, disclaim, abandon, relinquish, retract, demit; deny etc. 536.
abrogate etc. 756; desert etc. (*relinquish*) 624; get rid of etc. 782.
abdicate; vacate, – one's seat; accept the stewardship of the Chiltern Hundreds; retire; tender –, send in –, hand in- one's resignation.
Adj. abdicant, renunciatory etc. *v.*
Phr. 'Othello's occupation's gone.'

758. Consignee.—**N.** consignee, trustee, nominee, committee.
delegate; commiss-ary, -ioner; emissary, envoy, commissionaire; messenger etc. 534.
diplomatist, diplomat, *corps diplomatique*, embassy; am-, em-bassador; representative, resident, consul, legate, nuncio, internuncio, *chargé d' affaires, attaché*.
vicegerent etc. (*deputy*) 759; plenipotentiary.
functionary, placeman, curator; treasurer etc. 801; agent, factor, bailiff, steward, clerk, secretary, attorney, solicitor, proctor, broker, underwriter, commission agent, auctioneer, one's man of business; factotum etc. (*director*) 694; caretaker.
negotiator, go between; middleman; under agent, *employé*; servant etc. 746.
salesman; commercial, – traveler; bagman, *commis-voyageur*, touter.
newspaper –, own –, war –, special- correspondent; reporter.

759. Deputy.—**N.** deputy, substitute, vice, proxy, *locum tenens*, delegate, representative, next friend, surrogate, secondary.
regent, vicegerent, vizier, minister, vicar; premier etc. (*director*) 694; chancellor, prefect, provost, warden, lieutenant, archon, consul, proconsul; viceroy etc. (*governor*) 745; commissioner etc. 758; plenipotentiary, *alter ego.*
team, eight, eleven; champion.
V. be -deputy etc. *n.*; stand –, appear –, hold a brief –, answer- for; represent; stand –, walk- in the shoes of; stand in the stead of.
substitute, ablegate, accredit; commission, empower, delegate etc. 755.
Adj. acting; vice, -regal; accredited to.
Adv. in behalf of, by proxy.

760. Permission.—**N.** permission, leave; allow-, suffer-ance; toler-ance, -ation; liberty, law, license, concession, grace; indulgence etc. (*lenity*) 740; favor, dispensation, exemption, release; connivance; vouchsafement.
authorization, warranty, accordance, admission.
permit, warrant, *brevet*, precept, sanction, authority, *firman*; pass, -port; furlough, license, *carte blanche*, ticket of leave; grant, charter, patent.
V. permit; give -permission etc. *n.*, – power;

let, allow, admit; suffer, bear with, tolerate, recognize; concede etc. 762; accord, vouchsafe, favor, humor, gratify, indulge, stretch a point; wink at, connive at; shut one's eyes to.

grant, empower, charter, enfranchise, privilege, confer a privilege, license, authorize, warrant; sanction; entrust etc. (*commission*) 755.

give -*carte blanche*, – the reins to, – scope to etc. (*freedom*) 748; leave -alone, – it to one, – the door open; open the -door to, – floodgates; give a loose to.

let off; absolve etc. (*acquit*) 970; release, exonerate, dispense with.

ask –, beg –, request- -leave, – permission.

Adj. permitting etc. *v.*; permissive, indulgent; permitted etc. *v.*; patent, chartered, permissible, allowable, lawful, legitimate, legal; legalized etc. (*law*) 963; licit; unforbid, -den; unconditional.

Adv. permissibly; by –, with –, on- -leave etc. *n.*; *speciali gratiâ*; under favor of; *pace*; *ad libitum* etc. (*freely*) 748, (*at will*) 600; by all means etc. (*willingly*) 602; yes etc. (*assent*) 488.

761. Prohibition.—N. pro-, in-hibition; *veto*, disallowance; interdict, -ion; injunction; embargo, ban, *verboten*, taboo, proscription; *index expurgatorius*; restriction etc. (*restraint*) 751; hindrance etc. 706; forbidden fruit.

V. pro-, in-hibit; forbid, put one's *veto* upon, disallow; bar; debar etc. (*hinder*) 706, forefend.

keep -in, – within bounds; restrain etc. 751; cohibit, withhold, limit, circumscribe, clip the wings of, restrict, narrow; interdict, taboo; put –, place- under -an interdiction, – the ban; proscribe, censor; exclude, shut out; shut –, bolt –, show- the door; warn off; dash the cup from one's lips; forbid the banns.

Adj. prohibit-ive, -ory; interdictive; proscriptive; restrictive, exclusive; forbidding etc. *v.*

prohibited etc. *v.*; not -permitted etc. 760; unlicensed, contraband, under the ban of; illegal etc. 964; unauthorized, not to be thought of.

Adv. on no account etc. (*no*) 536.

Int. forbid it heaven! etc. (*deprecation*) 766. hands –, keep- off! hold! stop! avast!

Phr. that will never do.

762. Consent.—N. consent; assent etc. 488; acquiescence; approval etc. 931; compliance, agreement, concession; yield-ance, -ingness; accession, acknowledgment, acceptance, agnition.

settlement, ratification, confirmation, adjustment.

permit etc. (*permission*) 760; promise etc. 768.

V. consent; assent etc. 488; yield assent, admit, allow, concede, grant, yield; come -over, – round; give in to, acknowledge, agnize, give consent, comply with, acquiesce, agree to, fall in with, accede, accept, embrace an offer, close with, take at one's word, have no objection.

satisfy, meet one's wishes, settle, come to terms etc. 488; not -refuse etc. 764; turn a willing ear etc. (*willingness*) 602; jump at; deign, vouchsafe; promise etc. 768.

Adj. consenting etc. *v.*; agreeable, compliant; agreed etc. (*assent*) 488; unconditional.

Adv. yes etc. (*assent*) 488; by all means etc. (*willingly*) 602; if –, as- you please; be it so, so be it, well and good, of course.

763. Offer.—N. offer, proffer, presentation, tender, bid, overture; propos-al, -ition; motion, invitation; candidature; offering etc. (*gift*) 784.

V. offer, proffer, present, tender; bid; propose, move; make -a motion, – advances; start; invite, hold out, place- at one's disposal, – in one's way, put forward.

hawk about; offer for sale etc. 796; press etc. (*request*) 765; lay at one's feet.

offer –, present- oneself; volunteer, come forward, be a candidate; stand –, bid- for; seek; be at one's service; go a begging; bribe etc. (*give*) 784.

Adj. offer-ing, -ed etc. *v.*; in the market, for sale, to let, disengaged, on hire.

764. Refusal.—N. refusal, rejection; non-, incompliance; denial; declining etc. *v.*; declension; peremptory –, flat –, point blank- refusal; repulse, rebuff; discountenance.

recusancy, renunciation, abnegation, negation, protest, disclaimer; dissent etc. 489; revocation etc. 756.

V. refuse, reject, deny, decline; nill, negative; refuse –, withhold- one's assent; shake the head; close the -hand, – purse; grudge, begrudge, be slow to, hang fire.

be deaf to; turn -a deaf ear to, – one's back upon; set one's face against, discountenance, not hear of, have nothing to do with, wash one's hands of, stand aloof, forswear, set aside, cast behind one; not yield an inch etc. (*obstinacy*) 606.

resist, cross; not -grant etc. 762; repel, repulse; shut –, slam- the door in one's face; rebuff; send -back, – to the right about, – away with a flea in the ear; deny oneself, not be at home to; discard etc. (*repudiate*) 610; rescind etc. (*revoke*) 756; disclaim, protest; dissent etc. 489.

Adj. refusing etc. *v.*; rest-ive, -iff; recusant; uncomplying, noncompliant, unconsenting, uncomplaisant, protestant; not willing to hear of, deaf to.

refused etc. *v.*; ungranted, out of the question, not to be thought of, impossible.

Adv. no etc. 536; on no account, not for the world; no thank you.

Phr. *non possumus*; [ironically] your humble servant; *bien obligé*.

765. Request.—N. requ-est, -isition; claim etc. (*demand*) 741; petition, suit, prayer; begging letter, round-robin.

motion, overture, application, canvass, address, appeal, apostrophe; imprecation; rogation; proposal, proposition.

orison etc. (*worship*) 990; incantation etc. (*spell*) 993.

mendicancy; asking, panhandling, begging etc. *v.*; postulation, solicitation, invitation, entreaty, importunity, supplication, instance, impetration, imploration, obsecration, obtestation, invocation, interpellation.

V. request, ask; beg, crave, sue, pray, petition, solicit, invite, pop the question, make bold to ask; beg -leave, – a boon; apply to, call to, put to; call -upon, – for; make –, address –, prefer –, put up- a -request, – prayer, – petition; make -application, – a requisition; ask –, trouble- one for; claim etc. (*demand*) 741; offer up prayers etc. (*worship*) 990; whistle for.

beg hard, entreat, beseech, plead, supplicate, implore, apostrophize; conjure, adjure; obtest; cry to, kneel to, appeal to; invoke, evoke; impetrate, imprecate, ply, press, urge, beset, importune, dun, tax, clamor for; cry -aloud, – for help; fall on one's knees; throw oneself at the feet of; come down on one's marrow-bones.

beg from door to door, send the hat round, go a begging; mendicate, mump, cadge, panhandle, beg one's bread.

dance attendance on, besiege, knock at the door.

bespeak, canvass, tout, make interest, court; seek, bid for etc. (*offer*) 763; publish the banns.

Adj. requesting etc. *v.*; precatory; suppli-ant, -cant, -catory; invoc-, imprec-, rog-atory; postulant, mendicant.

importunate, clamorous, urgent; solicitous; cap in hand; on one's -knees, – bended knees, – marrow-bones.

Adv. prithee, do, please, pray; be so good as, be good enough; have the goodness, vouchsafe, will you, I pray thee, if you please.

Int. for -God's, – heaven's, – goodness', – mercy's- sake.

766. Deprecation. [Negative request.]—**N.** deprecation, expostulation; remonstrance; intercession, mediation.

V. deprecate, protest, expostulate, enter a protest, intercede for.

Adj. deprecatory, expostulatory, intercessory, mediatorial.

deprecated, protested.

un-, unbe-sought; unasked etc. (*see* ask etc. 765).

Int. cry you mercy! God forbid! forbid it Heaven! Heaven -forefend, – forbid! far be it from! hands off! etc. (*prohibition*) 761.

767. Petitioner.—**N.** petitioner, solicitor, applicant; suppli-ant, -cant; suitor, candidate, claimant, postulant, aspirant, competitor, bidder; place –, pot- hunter; prizer.

beggar, mendicant, mumper, sturdy beggar, cadger, panhandler.

canvasser, barker, touter etc. 768.

sycophant, parasite etc. 886.

768. Promise.—**N.** promise, undertaking, word, troth, plight, pledge, *parole*, word of honor, vow; oath etc. (*affirmation*) 535; profession, assurance, warranty, guarantee, insurance, obligation; contract etc. 769.

engagement, pre-engagement; affiance; betroth, -al, -ment; marriage -compact, – vow.

V. promise; give a -promise etc. *n.*; undertake, engage; make –, form- an engagement; enter -into, – on- an engagement; bind –, tie –, pledge –, commit –, take upon- oneself; vow; swear etc. (*affirm*) 535; give –, pass –, pledge –, plight- one's -word, – honor, – credit, – troth; betroth, plight faith; take the vows.

assure, warrant, guarantee, vouch for, avouch, covenant etc. 769; attest etc. (*bear witness*) 467.

hold out an expectation; contract an obligation; become -bound to, – sponsor for; answer –, be answerable- for; secure; give security etc. 771; underwrite.

adjure, administer an oath, put to one's oath, swear a witness.

Adj. promising etc. *v.*; promissory; votive; under hand and seal; upon -oath, – affirmation.

promised etc. *v.*; affianced, pledged, bound; committed, compromised; in for it.

Adv. as one's head shall answer for; upon my honor.

Phr. in for a penny, in for a pound.

768a. Release from engagement.—**N.** release etc. (*liberation*) 750.

Adj. absolute; unconditional etc. (*free*) 748.

769. Compact.—**N.** compact, contract, agreement, bargain, deal, transaction; affidation; pact, -ion; bond, covenant, indenture.

stipulation, settlement, convention; compromise, *cartel*.

protocol, treaty, *concordat*, *Zollverein*, *Sonderbund*, charter, *Magna Charta*, Pragmatic Sanction.

negotiation etc. (*bargaining*) 794; diplomacy etc. (*mediation*) 724; negotiator etc. (*agent*) 758.

ratification, completion, signature, seal, sigil, signet.

V. contract, covenant, agree for, engage etc. (*promise*) 768.

treat, negotiate, stipulate, make terms; bargain etc. (*barter*) 794.

make –, strike- a bargain; come to -terms, – an understanding; compromise etc. 774; set at rest; close, – with; conclude, complete, settle; confirm, ratify, clench, subscribe, underwrite; en-, in-dorse; put the seal to; sign, seal etc. (*attest*) 467; indent.

take one at one's word, bargain by inch of candle.

Adj. contractual, agreed etc. *v.*; conventional; under hand and seal; signed, sealed and delivered.

Phr. *caveat emptor*.

770. Conditions.—**N.** conditions, terms; articles, – of agreement.

clauses, provisions; proviso etc. (*qualification*) 469; covenant, stipulation, obligation, *ultimatum*, *sine quâ non*; *casus foederis*.

V. make –, come to- -terms etc. (*contract*) 769; make it a condition, stipulate, insist upon, make a point of; bind, tie up.

Adj. conditional, provisional, guarded, fenced, hedged in.

Adv. conditionally etc. (*with qualification*) 469; provisionally, *pro re natâ*; on condition; with a reservation.

771. Security.—N. security; guaran-ty, -tee; gage, waranty, bond, tie, pledge, plight, mortgage, debenture, hypothecation, bill of sale, lien, pignus, pawn, pignoration; real security; bottomry; collateral, vadium.

stake, deposit, earnest, handsel, caution.

promissory note; bill, – of exchange; I.O.U.; personal security, covenant, specialty; *parole* etc. (*promise*) 768.

acceptance, indorsement, signature, execution, stamp, seal.

spon-sor, -sion, -sorship; surety, bail; mainpernor, hostage.

recognizance; deed –, covenant- of indemnity.

authentication, verfication, warrant, certificate, voucher, docket, doquet; record etc. 551; probate, attested copy.

receipt; ac-, quittance; discharge, release.

muniment, title-deed, instrument; deed, – poll; assurance, insurance, indenture; charter etc. (*compact*) 769; charter-poll; paper, parchment, settlement, will, testament, last will and testament, codicil.

V. give -security, – bail, – substantial bail; go bail; pawn, impawn, hock, spout, mortgage, hypothecate, impignorate.

guarantee, warrant, assure; accept, indorse, underwrite, insure.

execute, stamp; sign, seal etc. (*evidence*) 467.

let, set; grant –, take –, hold- a lease; hold in pledge; lend on security etc. 787.

Adj. secure, -ed; pledged etc. *v.*; in pawn, on deposit.

772. Observance.—N. observance, performance, compliance; obedience, etc. 743; fulfilment, satisfaction, discharge; acquit-tance, -tal.

adhesion, acknowledgment; fidelity etc. (*probity*) 939; exact etc. 494- observance.

V. observe, comply with, respect, acknowledge, abide by; cling to, adhere to, be faithful to, act up to; meet, fulfil; carry -out, – into execution; execute, perform, keep, satisfy, discharge; do one's office.

perform –, fulfill –, discharge –, acquit oneself of- an obligation; make good; make good –, keep- one's -word, – promise; redeem one's pledge; keep faith with, stand to one's engagement.

Adj. observant, faithful, true, loyal; honorable etc. 939; true as the -dial to the sun, – needle to the pole; punct-ual, -ilious; meticulous; literal etc. (*exact*) 494; as good as one's word.

Adv. faithfully etc. *adj.*

773. Non-observance.—N. non-observance etc. 772; evasion, inobservance, failure, omission, neglect, laches, laxity, informality.

infringement, infraction; violation, transgression. retractation, repudiation, nullification; protest; forfeiture.

lawlessness; disobedience etc. 742; bad faith etc. 940.

V. fail, neglect, omit, elude, evade, give the go by to, cut, set aside, ignore; shut –, close- one's eyes to, avoid.

infringe, transgress, pirate, violate, break, trample under foot, do violence to, drive a coach and six through.

discard, protest, repudiate, fling to the winds, set at naught, nullify, declare null and void; cancel etc. (*wipe off*) 552.

retract, go back from, be off, forfeit, go from one's word, palter; stretch –, strain- a point.

Adj. violating etc. *v.*; lawless, transgressive; elusive, evasive; lax, casual; non-observant.

unfulfilled etc. (*see* fulfil etc. 772).

774. Compromise.—N. com-promise, -mutation, -position; middle term, *mezzo termine*; compensation etc. 30; adjustment, mutual concession.

V. com-promise, -mute, -pound; take the mean; split the difference, meet one half way, give and take; come to terms etc. (*contract*) 769; submit to –, abide by- arbitration; patch up, bridge over, fix up, arrange; adjust, – differences; agree; make -the best of, – a virtue of necessity; take the will for the deed.

775. Acquisition.—N. acquisition; gaining etc. *v.*; obtainment; procur-ation, -ement; purchase, descent, inheritance; gift etc. 784.

recovery, retrieval, revendication, replevin; redemption, salvage, trover; find, *trouvaille*, foundling.

gain, thrift; money-making, -grubbing; lucre, filthy lucre, loaves and fishes, the main chance, pelf; emolument etc. 973; wealth etc. 803.

profit, earnings, winnings, innings, clean-up, pickings, perquisite, net profit; income etc. (*receipt*) 810; pro-ceeds, -duce, -duct; out-come, -put; return, fruit, crop, harvest, tilth; second crop, aftermath; benefit etc. (*good*) 618.

sweepstakes, trick, prize, pool.

[Fraudulent acquisition] subreption; theft, stealing etc. 791.

V. acquire, get, gain, win, earn, obtain, procure, gather, annex; collect etc. 72; pick, – up; glean, take etc. 789.

find; come –, pitch –, light- upon; scrape -up, – together; get in, reap and carry, net, bag, sack, bring home, secure, come across, derive, draw, get in the harvest.

profit; make –, draw- profit; turn to -profit, – account; make -capital out of, – money by; obtain a return, reap the fruits of; reap –, gain- an advantage; turn -a penny, – an honest penny; make the pot boil, bring grist to the mill; make –, coin –, raise- money; raise -funds, – the wind; fill one's pocket etc. (*wealth*) 803.

treasure up etc. (*store*) 636; realize, clear; produce etc. 161; take etc. 789.

get back, recover, regain, retrieve, revendicate, replevy, redeem, come by one's own.

come -by, – in for; receive etc. 785; inherit; step into, – a fortune, – the shoes of; succeed to.

get -hold of, – between one's finger and thumb, – into one's hand, – at; take –, come into –, enter into- possession.

be -profitable etc. *adj.*; pay, answer.

accrue etc. (*be received*) 785.

Adj. acquir-ing, -ed etc. *v.*; acquisitive; productive, profitable, advantageous, gainful, remunerative, paying, lucrative.

776. Loss.—**N.** loss; de-, perdition; forfeiture, lapse.

privation, bereavement; deprivation etc. (*dispossession*) 789; riddance.

V. lose; incur –, experience –, meet with- a loss; miss; mislay, let slip, allow to slip through the fingers, squander; be without etc. (*exempt*) 777*a*; forfeit.

get rid of etc. 782; waste etc. 638.

be lost, lapse.

Adj. losing etc. *v.*; not having etc. 777*a*.

shorn of, deprived of; denuded, bereaved, bereft, *minus*, cut off; dispossessed etc. 789; rid of, quit of; out of pocket.

lost etc. *v.*; long lost; irretrievable etc. (*hopeless*) 859; irredentist; off one's hands.

Int. farewell to! adieu to! good riddance!

777. Possession.—**N.** possession, seisin; ownership etc. 780; occupancy; hold, -ing; tenure, tenancy, feodality, dependency; villenage; socage, chivalry, knight service.

exclusive possession, impropriation, monopoly, corner; retention etc. 781; pre-possession, -occupancy; nine points of the law.

future possession, heritage, inheritance, heirship, reversion, fee, seigniority, feud, fief.

bird in hand, *uti possidetis*, *chose* in possession.

V. possess, have, hold, occupy, enjoy; be -possessed of etc. *adj.*; have -in hand etc. *adj.*; own etc. 780; command.

inherit; come -to, – in for.

engross, monopolize, forestall, regrate, impropriate, have all to oneself, corner; have a firm hold of etc. (*retain*) 781; get into one's hand etc. (*acquire*) 775.

belong to, appertain to, pertain to; be -in one's possession etc. *adj.*; vest in.

Adj. possessing etc. *v.*; worth; possessed of, seized of, master of, in possession of; endowed –, blest –, instinct –, fraught –, laden –, charged –, instilled –, with.

possessed etc. *v.*; on hand, by one; in hand, in store, in stock; in one's -hands, – grasp, – possession; at one's -command, – disposal; one's own etc. (*property*) 780.

unsold, unshared.

777a. Exemption.—**N.** exemption; exception, immunity, privilege, release etc. 927*a*; absence etc. 187.

V. not -have etc. 777; be -without etc. *adj.*

Adj. exempt from, devoid of, without, unpossessed of, unblest with, immune from.

not -having etc. 777; unpossessed; untenanted etc. (*vacant*) 187; without an owner.

unobtained, unacquired.

778. Participation. [Joint possession.]—**N.** participation; co-, joint-tenancy; possession –, tenancy- in common; joint –, common- stock; co-, partnership; communion; community of -possessions, – goods; communalism, communism, socialism, collectivism; co-operation etc. 709; profit sharing.

snacks, co-portion, picnic, hotchpotch; co-heirship, -parceny, -parcenary; gavelkind.

participator, sharer; co-, partner; shareholder; co-, joint-tenant; tenants in common; co-heir, -parcener.

communist, socialist.

V. par-ticipate, -take; share, – in; come in for a share; go -shares, – snacks, – halves; share and share alike.

have –, possess –, be seized- -in common, – as joint tenants etc. *n.*

join in; have a hand in etc. (*co-operate*) 709.

Adj. partaking etc. *v.*; communistic, socialistic, co-operative, profit sharing.

Adv. share and share alike.

779. Possessor.—**N.** possessor, holder; occupant, -ier; tenant; person –, man- -in possession etc. 777; renter, lodger, lessee, under-lessee; zemindar, ryot; tenant -on sufferance, – at will, – from year to year, – for years, – for life.

owner; propriet-or, -ress, -ary; impropriator, master, mistress, lord.

land-holder, -owner, -lord, -lady; lord -of the manor, – paramount; heritor, laird, vavasor, landed gentry, mesne lord.

cestui-que-trust, beneficiary, mortgagor.

grantee, feoffee, relessee, devisee; legat-ee, -ary.

trustee; holder etc.- of the legal estate; mortgagee.

right –, rightful- owner.

[Future possessor] heir, – apparent; – presumptive; heiress; inherit-or, -ress, -rix; reversioner, remainder-man.

780. Property.—**N.** property, possession, *suum cuique*, *meum et tuum*.

owner-, proprietor, lord-ship; seignority; empire etc. (*dominion*) 737.

interest, stake, estate, right, title, claim, demand, holding; tenure etc. (*possession*) 777; vested –, contingent –, beneficial –, equitable- interest; use, trust, benefit; legal –, equitable- estate; seisin.

absolute interest, paramount estate, freehold; fee, – simple, – tail; estate -in fee, – in tail, – tail; estate in tail -male, – female, – general.

limitation, term, lease, settlement, strict settlement, particular estate; estate -for life, – for years, – *pur autre vie*; remainder, reversion, expectancy, possibility.

dower, dowry, *dot*, jointure, marriage portion, appanage, inheritance, heritage, patrimony, alimony; legacy etc. (*gift*) 784.

assets, belongings, means, resources, circumstances; wealth etc. 803; money etc. 800; what one -is worth, – will cut up for; estate and effects.

landed –, real- -estate, – property; realty; land, -s; subdivision; plot, site; tenements; hereditaments; corporeal –, incorporeal- hereditaments; acres; ground etc. (*earth*) 342; acquest; messuage.

territory, state, kingdom, principality, realm, empire, protectorate, margravate, dependancy, colony, sphere of influence, mandate.

manor, honor, domain, demesne; farm, ranch, plantation, *hacienda*; allodium etc. (*free*) 748; fieff, feoff, feud, zemindary, dependency.

free-, copy-, lease-holds; chattels real; fixtures, plant, heirloom easement; folkland; right of -common, – user.

personal -property, – estate, – effects; personalty, chattels, goods, effects, movables; stock, – in trade; things, traps, rattle-traps, paraphernalia; equipage etc. 633.

parcels, appurtenances.

impedimenta; lug-, bag-gage; bag and baggage; pelf; cargo, lading.

rent-roll; income etc. (*receipts*) 810.

patent, copyright; *chose* in action; credit etc. 805; debt etc. 806.

V. possess etc. 777; be the -possessor etc. 779- of own; have for one's own, – very own; come in for, inherit; enfeoff.

savor of the realty.

be one's own -property etc. *n.*; belong to; ap-, pertain to.

Adj. one's own; landed, predial, manorial, allodial, seignorial; free-, copy-, lease-hold; feu-, feo-dal; hereditary, entailed, personal.

Adv. to one's -credit, – account; to the good.

to one and -his heirs for ever, – the heirs of his body, – his heirs and assigns, – his executors, administrators and assigns.

781. Retention.—N. retention; retaining etc. *v.*; keep, detention, custody; tenacity, firm hold, grasp, gripe, grip, iron grip.

fangs, teeth, claws, talons, nail, hook, tentacle, *tenaculum*; bond etc. (*vinculum*) 45.

clutches, tongs, forceps, pincers, nippers, pliers, tweezers, vise.

paw, hand, finger, wrist, fist, neaf, neif.

bird in hand; captive etc. 754.

V. retain, keep; hold, – fast, – tight, – one's own, – one's ground; clinch, clench, clutch, grasp, gripe, hug, have a firm hold of.

secure, withold, detain; hold –, keepback; keep close; husband etc. (*store*) 636; reserve; have –, keep- in stock etc. (*possess*) 777; enfail, tie up, settle.

Adj. retaining etc. *v.*; retentive, tenacious.

unforfeited, undeprived, undisposed, uncommunicated.

incommunicable, inalienable; in mortmain; in strict settlement.

Phr. *uti possidetis*.

782. Relinquishment.—N. relinquishment, abandonment etc. (*of a course*) 624; renunciation, expropriation, dereliction; cession, surrender, dispensation; resignation etc. 757; riddance.

derelict etc. *adj.*; jetsam; waif, foundling, orphan.

v. relinquish, give up, surrender, yield, cede; let -go, – slip; spare, drop, resign, forego, renounce, abjure, abandon, expropriate, give away, dispose of, part with; lay -aside, – apart, – down, – on the shelf etc. (*disuse*) 678; set –, put- aside; make away with, cast behind; discard, cast off, dismiss; maroon.

give -notice to quit, – warning; supersede; be –, get- -rid of, – quit of; eject etc. 297.

rid –, disburden –, divest –, dispossess- oneself of; wash one's hands of; divorce, desert; disinherit, cut off.

cast –, throw –, pitch –, fling- -away, – aside, – overboard, – to the dogs; cast –, throw –, sweep- to the winds; put –, turn –, sweep- away; jettison.

quit one's hold.

Adj. relinquished etc. *v.*; cast off, derelict; unowned, unappropriated, unculled; left etc. (*residuary*) 40; divorced; disinherited.

Int. away with!

783. Transfer.—N. transfer, conveyance, assignment, alienation, abalienation; demise, limitation; conveyancing; transmission etc. (*transference*) 270; enfeoffment, bargain and sale, lease and release; exchange etc. (*interchange*) 148; barter etc. 794; substitution etc. 147.

succession, reversion; shifting -use, – trust; devolution.

V. transfer, convey; alien, -ate; assign; grant etc. (*confer*) 784; consign; make –, hand- over; pass, hand, transmit, negotiate; hand down; exchange etc. (*interchange*) 148.

change -hands, – from one to another; devolve, succeed; come into possession etc. (*acquire*) 775; take over.

abalienate; disinherit; dispossess etc. 789; substitute etc. 147.

Adj. alienable, negotiable, transferable, reversional.

Phr. estate coming into possession.

784. Giving.—N. giving etc. *v.*; bestowal, donation; present-ation, -ment; accordance; con-, cession; delivery, consignment, dispensation, communication, endowment; invest-ment, -iture; award.

almsgiving, charity, liberality, generosity; philanthropy etc. 910.

[Thing given] gift, donation, present, *cadeau*; fairing; free gift, boon, favor, benefaction, grant, offering, oblation, sacrifice, immolation.

grace, act of grace, *bonus*, *bonanza*.

allowance, contribution, subscription, subsidy, tribute, subvention.

bequest, legacy, devise, will, dotation, appanage; dowry; voluntary -settlement, – conveyance etc. 783; amortization.

alms, largess, bounty, dole, sportule, donative, help, oblation, offertory, Peter's pence, *honorarium*, gratuity, Maundy money, Christmas box, Easter offering, vail, tip, *douceur*, drink money, *pourboire, trinkgeld, backsheesh*; fee etc. (*recompense*) 973; consideration.

bribe, bait, ground-bait; peace-offering, handsel.

giver, grantor etc. *v.*; donor, feoffer, settlor; almoner; testator; investor, subscriber, contributor; fairy godmother; Santa Claus, benefactor etc. 816.

V. deliver, hand, pass, put into the hands of; hand –, make –, deliver –, pass –, turn- over.

present, give away, dispense, dispose of; give –, deal –, dole –, mete –, fork –, shell –, squeeze- out.

pay etc. 807; render, impart, communicate.

concede, cede, yield, part with, shed cast; spend etc. 809.

give, bestow, confer, grant, accord, award, assign.

entrust, consign, vest in.

make a present; allow, contribute, subscribe, donate, furnish its quota.

invest, endow, settle upon; bequesth, leave, devise.

furnish, supply, help; ad-, minister to; afford, spare; accommodate –, indulge –, favor- with; shower down upon; lavish, pour on, thrust upon; tip, bribe; tickle –, grease- the palm; offer etc. 763; sacrifice, immolate.

Adj. giving etc. *v.*; given etc. *v.*; allow-ed, -able; concessional; communicable; charitable, eleemosynary, sportulary, tributary; *gratis* etc. 815.

785. Receiving.—**N.** receiving etc. *v.*; acquisition etc. 775; reception etc. (*introduction*) 296; suscipiency acceptance, admission.

re-, ac-cipient; assignee, devisee; lega-tee, -tary; grantee, feoffee, donee, relessee, lessee.

sportulary, stipendiary; beneficiary; pension-er, -ary; almsman.

income etc. (*receipt*) 810.

v. receive; take etc. 789; acquire etc. 775; admit.

take in, catch, touch; pocket; put into one's - pocket, – purse; accept; take off one's hands.

be received; come -in, – to hand; pass –, fall- into one's hand; go into one's pocket; fall to one's - lot, – share; come –, fall- to one; accrue; have - given etc. 784 to one.

Adj. receiving etc. *v.*; re-, suscipient.

received etc. *v.*; given etc. 784; second-hand.

not given, unbestowed etc. (*see* give, bestow etc. 784).

786. Apportionment.—**N.** apportion-, allot-, consign-, assign-, appoint-ment; appropriation; dispensation, -tribution; allocation, division, deal; repartition; administration.

dividend, portion, contingent, share, allotment, lot, cut, split, measure, dose; dole, meed, pittance; *quantum*, ration; ratio, proportion, quota, *modicum*, mess, allowance.

V. apportion, divide; cut, split, divvy; distribute, administer, dispense; billet, allot, detail, cast, share, mete; portion –, parcel –, dole- out; deal, carve.

partition, assign, appropriate, appoint.

come in for one's share etc. (*participate*) 778.

Adj. apportioning etc. *v.*; respective.

Adv. respectively, each to each.

787. Lending.—**N.** lending etc. *v.*; loan, advance, accommodation, feneration; mortgage etc. (*security*) 771; investment.

mont de piété, pawnshop, hock shop, spout, my uncle's.

lender, pawnbroker, money lender, usurer, Jew, Shylock.

V. lend, advance, loan, accommodate with; lend on security; pawn etc. (*security*) 771.

intrust, invest; place –, put- out to interest; sink, risk.

let, demise, lease, set, under-, sub-let.

Adj. lending etc. *v.*; lent etc. *v.*; unborrowed etc. (*see* borrowed etc. 788).

Adv. in advance; on -loan, – security.

788. Borrowing.—**N.** borrowing, pledging, pawning.

borrowed plumes; plagiarism etc. (*thieving*) 791.

replevin.

V. borrow, desume; pawn.

hire, rent, farm; take a -lease, – demise; take –, hire- by the -hour, – mile, – year etc.

raise –, take up- money; float bonds; raise the wind; fly a kite, borrow of Peter to pay Paul; run into debt etc. (*debt*) 806.

make use of, plagiarize, pirate.

replevy.

789. Taking.—**N.** taking etc. *v.*; reception etc. (*taking in*) 296; deglutition etc. (*taking food*) 298; appropriation, prehension, prensation; capture, caption; ap-, de-prehension; abreption, seizure; abduction, -lation; subtraction etc. (*subduction*) 38; abstraction, ademption.

dispossession; depriv-ation, -ement; bereavement; divestment; disherison; distraint, distress; sequestration, confiscation, attachment, execution; eviction etc. 297.

rapacity, extortion, vampirism, predacity, blood-sucking; theft etc. 791.

resumption; repris-e, -al; recovery etc. 775.

clutch, swoop, wrench; grip etc. (*retention*) 781; haul, take, catch; scramble.

taker, captor, capturer; vampire; extortioner.

V. take, catch, hook, nab, bag, sack, pocket, put into one's pocket, scrounge; receive; accept.

reap, crop, cull, pluck; gather etc. (*get*) 775; draw.

ap-, im-propriate; assume, possess oneself of; take possession of; commandeer; lay –, clap- one's hands on; help oneself to; make free with, dip one's hands into, lay under contribution; intercept; scramble for; deprive of.

take –, carry –, bear- -away, – off; abstract; hurry off –, run away- with; abduct; steal etc. 791; ravish; seize; pounce –, spring- upon; swoop -to, – down upon; take by -storm, – assault; snatch, reave.

snap up, nip up, whip up, catch up; kidnap, crimp, capture, lay violent hands on.

get –, lay –, take –, catch –, lay fast –, take firm- hold of; lay by the heels, take prisoner; fasten upon, grip, grapple, embrace, gripe, clasp, grab, clutch, collar, throttle, take by the throat, claw, clinch, clench, make sure of.

catch at, jump at, make a grab at, snap at, snatch at; reach, make a long arm, stretch forth one's hand.

take -from, – away from; deduct etc. 38; retrench etc. (*curtail*) 201; dispossess, ease one of, snatch from one's grasp; tear –, tear away –, wrench –, wrest –, wring- from; extort; deprive of, bereave; disinherit, cut off with a shilling.

oust etc. (*eject*) 297; divest; levy, distrain, confiscate; sequest-er, -rate, accroach; usurp; despoil, strip, fleece, shear, displume, impoverish, eat out of house and home; drain, – to the dregs; gut, dry, exhaust, swallow up; absorb etc. (*suck in*) 296; draw off; suck, – like a leech, – the blood of.

retake, resume; recover etc. 775.

Adj. taking etc. *v.*; privative, prehensile; predaceous, -al, -atory, -atorial; rap-acious, -torial; ravenous; parasitic; all-devouring, -engulfing.

bereft etc. 776.

Adv. at one fell swoop.

Phr. give an inch and take an ell.

790. Restitution.—N. restitution, return; ren-, red-dition; reinstatement, restoration; reinvestment, recuperation; repatriation; rehabilitation etc. (*reconstruction*) 660; reparation, atonement, indemnity, compensation, recompense.

release, replevin, redemption; recovery etc. (*getting back*) 775; remitter, reversion.

V. return, restore; recondition; give –, carry –, bring- back; render, – up; give up; let go, unclutch; dis-, re-gorge; regurgitate; recoup, reimburse, repay, indemnify, reinvest, remit, rehabilitate; repair etc. (*make good*) 660.

redeem, recover etc. (*get back*) 775; take back again; revest, revert.

Adj. restoring etc. *v.*; recuperative etc. 660; in full restitution, to compensate for.

Phr. *suum cuique*.

791. Stealing.—N. stealing etc. *v.*; theft, thievery, robbery, latrociny, direption; abstraction, appropriation; plagiar-y, -ism; rape, kidnapping, depredation; raid, hold up.

spoliation, plunder, pillage; sack, -age; rapine, *brigandage*, highway robbery, foray, *razzia*; blackmail; piracy, privateering, buccaneering; filibustering, -ism; burglary; house-breaking; cattle-stealing, -rustling, -lifting.

peculation, embezzlement; fraud etc. 545; larceny, petty larceny, pilfering, shop-lifting.

thievishness, rapacity, kleptomania, Alsatia; den of -Cacus, – thieves.

license to plunder, letters of marque.

V. steal, thieve, rob, purloin, pilfer, filch, lift, prig, bag, nim, crib, cabbage, palm; abstract; appropriate, plagiarize.

convey away, carry off, abduct, kidnap, shanghai, impress, crimp; make –, walk –, run- off with; run away with; spirit away; seize etc. (*lay violent hands on*) 789.

plunder, pillage, rifle, sack, loot, ransack, spoil, spoliate, despoil, strip, sweep, gut, forage, levy black-mail, pirate, pickeer, maraud, lift cattle, rustle, poach, smuggle, run.

stick –, hold- up.

swindle, peculate, embezzle; sponge, mulct, rook, bilk, pluck, pigeon, skin, fleece, diddle; defraud etc. 545; obtain under false pretences; live by one's wits

rob –, borrow of- Peter to Paul; set a thief to catch a thief.

disregard the distinction between *meum* and *tuum*.

Adj. thieving etc. *v.*; thievish, light-fingered; furacious, -tive; piratical; pred-aceous, -al, -atory, -atorial; raptorial etc. (*rapacious*) 789.

stolen etc. *v.*

Phr. *sic vos non vobis.*

792. Thief.—N. thief, robber, *homo trium literarum*, pilferer, rifler, filcher, plagiarist.

spoiler, depredator, pillager, marauder; harpy, shark, land-shark, falcon, moss-trooper, bushranger, Bedouin, brigand, freebooter, bandit, thug, dacoit, pirate, corsair, viking, Paul Jones; buccan-eer, -ier; piqu-, pick-eerer; rover, ranger, privateer, filibuster; rapparee, wrecker, picaroon; smuggler, poacher, plunderer; racketeer.

highwayman, Dick Turpin, Claude Duval, Macheath, knight of the road, footpad, sturdy beggar; abductor, kidnapper.

cut-, pick-purse; pick-pocket, light-fingered gentry; sharper; card-, skittle-sharper; crook; thimble-rigger; rook, Greek, blackleg, leg, welsher, defaulter; Autolycus, Cacus, Barabbas, Jeremy Diddler, Robert Macaire, artful dodger, trickster; swell mob, *chevalier d'industrie*; shop-lifter.

swindler, peculator; forger, coiner, counterfeiter, shoful; fence, receiver of stolen goods, duffer; smasher.

burglar, housebreaker; cracks-, mags-man; Bill Sikes, Jack Sheppard, Jonathan Wild, Raffles, cat burglar.

793. Booty.—N. booty, spoil, plunder, price, loot, graft, swag, pickings, boodle; *spolia opima*, prey; blackmail; stolen goods.

Adj. looting etc. *n.*; manubial, spoliative.

794. Barter.—N. barter, exchange, scorse, truck system; interchange etc. 148.

a Roland for an Oliver; *quid pro quo*; commutation, -position.

trade, commerce, mercature, buying and selling, bargain and sale; traffic, business, nundination, custom, shopping; commercial enterprise, speculation, jobbing, stock-jobbing, *agiotage*, brokery, arbitrage.

dealing, transaction, negotiation, bargain.

free trade.

V. barter, exchange, truck, scorse, swop; interchange etc. 148; commutate etc. (*substitute*) 147; compound for.

trade, traffic, buy and sell, give and take, nundinate; carry on –, ply –, drive- a trade; be in -

business, – the city; keep a shop, deal in, employ one's capital in.
trade –, deal –, have dealings- with; transact –, do- business with; open –, keep- an account with.
bargain; drive –, make- a bargain; negotiate, bid for; dicker, haggle, higgle; chaffer, huckster, cheapen, beat down; stickle, – for; out-, under-bid; ask, charge; strike a bargain etc. (*contract*) 769.
speculate, give a sprat to catch a herring; buy in the cheapest and sell in the dearest market; rig the market.
Adj. commercial, mercantile, trading; interchangeable, marketable, staple, in the market, for sale.
wholesale, retail.
Adv. across the counter; on 'change.

795. Purchase.—**N.** purchase, emption; buying, purchasing, shopping; pre-emption, refusal.
coemption, bribery; slave trade.
buyer, purchaser, *emptor*, vendee; patron, employer, client, customer, *clientèle*.
V. buy, purchase, invest in, procure; rent etc. (*hire*) 788; repurchase, buy in.
keep in one's pay, bribe, suborn; pay etc. 807; spend etc. 809.
make –, complete- a purchase; buy over the counter; pay cash for.
shop, market, go a shopping.
Adj. purchased etc. *v.*
Phr. *caveat emptor.*

796. Sale.—**N.** sale, vent, disposal; auction, roup, Dutch auction; custom etc. (*traffic*) 794.
vendi-bility, -bleness.
seller, salesman; peddler, smous; vender, vendor, consignor; merchant etc. 797; auctioneer.
V. sell, vend, dispose of, effect a sale; sell -over the counter, – by auction etc. *n.*; dispense, retail; deal in etc. 794; sell -off, – out; turn into money; realize; bring -to, – under- the hammer; put up to auction; auction, offer –, put up- for sale; hawk, peddle, bring to market; offer etc. 763; undersell; dump, unload.
let; mortgage etc. (*security*) 771.
Adj. under the hammer, in the market, for sale.
saleable, marketable, vendible, in demand, having a ready sale; unsaleable etc., unpurchased, unbought; on one's hands.

797. Merchant.—**N.** merchant, trader, dealer, monger, chandler, salesman; changer; regrater; shop-keeper, -man; trades-man, -people, -folk.
retailer; chapman, hawker, huckster, higgler; peddler, smous, pedlar, *colporteur*, cadger, Autolycus; sutler, *vivandière*; coster-man, -monger; market woman; cheap jack; caterer etc. 637; tallyman.
money-broker, -changer, -lender; stock-broker, -jobber; cambist, usurer, moneyer, banker.
jobber; broker etc. (*agent*) 758; buyer etc. 795; seller etc. 796.
concern; firm etc. (*partnership*) 712.

798. Merchandise.—**N.** merchandise, ware, commodity, effects, goods, article, stock, produce, staple commodity; stock in trade etc. (*store*) 636; cargo etc. (*contents*) 190.

799. Mart.—**N.** mart; market, -place, *forum*; fair, bazaar, staple; stock –, exchange; 'change, *bourse*, Wall Street, Rialto, hall, guildhall; toll-booth, custom-house; Tattersalls.
shop, stall, booth; wharf; office, chambers, counting-house, *bureau*; coun-, comp-ter.
ware-house, -room; *dépôt*, interposit, *entrepôt*, *emporium*, establishment; store etc. 636.
open market, market-overt.

800. Money.—**N.** money -matters, – market; finance; accounts etc. 811; funds, treasure; capital, stock; assets etc. (*property*) 780; wealth etc. 803; supplies, ways and means, wherewithal, sinews of war, almighty dollar, needful, cash.
sum, amount; balance, -sheet; sum total; proceeds etc. (*receipts*) 810.
currency, circulating medium, specie; coin, – of the realm; piece, hard cash, dollar, sterling coin; pounds, shillings and pence; L s. d., guineas; pocket, breeches pocket, purse; money in hand; the best, ready, – money; filthy lucre, shekels, roll, jack, rhino, blunt, dust, bawbees, brass, dibs, dough, mopus, tin, salt, chink, oof, spondulics, pile, wads.
precious metals, gold, silver, copper, nickel; bullion, bar, ingot, nugget.
petty cash; pocket-, pin-money; small –, change; small coin, loose cash; doit, stiver, rap, mite, farthing, *sou*, penny, shilling, bob, tanner, tester, groat, guinea, ducat; *rouleau*; *wampum*; good –, round –, lump- sum; power –, mint –, tons- of money; plum, lac of rupees, millions, money-bags, miser's hoard, stocking, mine of wealth etc. 803.
[Science of coins] numismatics, chrysology.
paper-money; money –, postal –, Post Office-order; note, – of hand; bank –, treasury- note; Bradbury; promissory note; I.O.U., bond; bill, – of exchange; draft, check, order, warrant, *coupon*, debenture, exchequer bill, *assignat*, greenback, gold –, silver- certificate.
copper, nickel, dime, quarter, two bits, half a dollar, dollar, buck, simoleon, fiver, tenner, a twenty, a sawbuck, a century, a grand; eagle, double eagle.
gold standard, bimetallism, fiat money; rate of –, exchange; in-, de-flation.
remittance etc. (*payment*) 807; credit etc. 805; liability etc. 806; solvency etc. 803.
draw-er, -ee; oblig-or, -ee; moneyer, coiner, counterfeiter, forger.
false –, bad- money; base –, counterfeit- coin, flash note, slip, kite; Bank of Elegance.
argumentum ad crumenam.
V. amount to, come to, mount up to; touch the pocket; draw, – upon; endorse etc. (*security*) 771; issue, utter, circulate; discount etc. 813.
forge, counterfeit, coin, circulate –, pass- bad money.
Adj. monetary, pecuniary, crumenal, fiscal, financial, sumptuary, numismatical; sterling; solvent etc. 803.

801. Treasurer.—N. treasurer; bursar, -y; purser, purse-bearer; cash-keeper, banker; depositary; questor, receiver, steward, trustee, chartered –, accountant; Accountant-General, almoner, liquidator, paymaster, cashier, teller; cambist; money-changer etc. (*merchant*) 797.

financier, Chancellor of the Exchequer, minister of finance; Secretary of the Treasury, Director of the Budget, Controller of Currency.

802. Treasury.—N. treasury, bank, exchequer, almonry, fisc, hanaper, bursary; safe; strong-box, -hold, -room; coffer; chest etc. (*receptacle*) 191; depository etc. 636; till, -er; cash-box, -register, purse, pocketbook, wallet; money-bag, -belt, -box, *porte-monnaie*.

purse-strings; pocket, breeches pocket.

sinking fund; stocks; government –, public –, parliamentary- -stocks, – funds, – securities, bonds; gild-edged securities; Consols, Liberty bonds, government bonds, *crédit mobilier*.

803. Wealth.—N. wealth, riches, fortune, handsome fortune, opulence, affluence; good –, easy- circumstances; independence; competence etc. (*sufficiency*) 639; solvency, soundness, solidity.

provision, livelihood, maintenance; alimony, dowry; means, resources, substance; property etc. 780; command of money.

income etc. 810; capital, money; round sum etc. (*treasure*) 800; mint of money, mine of wealth, *El Dorado*, Pactolus, Golconda, Potosi, *bonanza*; philosopher's stone.

long –, full –, well lined –, heavy- purse; purse of Fortunatus.

pelf, Mammon, lucre, filthy lucre; loaves and fishes; fleshpots of Egypt.

rich –, moneyed –, warm- man; man of substance; capitalist, millionaire, Nabob, Croesus, Midas, Plutus, Dives, Timon of Athens; Timo-, Pluto-cracy; Danaë.

V. be -rich etc. *adj.*; roll –, wallow- in -wealth, – riches; have money to burn.

afford, well afford; command -money, – a sum; make both ends meet, hold one's head above water.

become -rich etc. *adj.*; fill one's -pocket etc. (*treasury*) 802; feather one's nest, clean up –, make- a fortune; make money etc. (*acquire*) 775.

enrich, imburse.

worship -Mammon, – the golden calf.

Adj. wealthy, rich, affluent, opulent, moneyed, monied, worth -a great deal, – much; well -to do, – off; warm; well –, provided for.

made of money; rich as Croesus; rolling in -riches, – wealth.

flush, – of -cash, – money, – tin; in -funds, – cash, – full feather; solvent, solid, sound, pecunious, out of debt, all straight; able to pay 20s in the L.

Phr. one's ship coming in.

804. Poverty.—N. poverty, indigence, penury, pauperism, destitution, want; need, -iness; lack, necessity, privation, distress, difficulties, wolf at the door.

bad –, poor –, needy –, embarrassed –, reduced –, straitened- circumstances; slender –, narrow- means; straits; hand to mouth existence, *res angusta domi*, low water, impecuniosity.

beggary; mendi-cancy, -city; broken –, loss of- fortune; insolvency etc. (*non-payment*) 808.

empty -purse, – pocket; light purse; beggarly account of empty boxes.

poor man, pauper, mendicant, mumper, beggar, starveling; *pauvre diable*.

V. be -poor etc. *adj.*; want, lack, starve, live from hand to mouth, have seen better days, go down in the world, be on one's uppers, come upon the parish; go to -the dogs, – wrack and ruin; not have a -penny etc. (*money*) 800, – shot in one's locker; beg one's bread; *tirer le diable par la queue*; run into debt etc. (*debt*) 806.

render -poor etc. *adj.*; impoverish; reduce, – to poverty; pauperize, fleece, ruin, bring to the parish.

Adj. poor, indigent; poverty-striken; badly –, poorly –, ill- off; poor as -a rat, – a church mouse, – Job's turkey, – Job; fortune-, dower-, money-, penni-less; unportioned, unmoneyed; impecunious; broke, flat; out –, short- of -money, – cash; without –, not worth- a rap etc. (*money*) 800; *qui n'a pas le sou*, out of pocket, hard up; out at -elbows, – heels; seedy, bare-footed; beggar-ly, -ed; destitute; fleeced, strapped, stripped; bereft, bereaved; reduced.

in -want etc. *n.*; needy, necessitous, distressed, pinched, straitened; put to one's -shifts, – last shifts; unable to -keep the wolf from the door, – make both ends meet; embarrassed, under hatches; involved etc. (*in debt*) 806; insolvent etc. (*not paying*) 808.

Adv. *in formâ pauperis*.

Phr. *zonam perdidit*.

805. Credit.—N. credit, trust, tick, score, tally, account.

letter of credit, circular note; duplicate; mortgage, lien, debenture, paper credit, floating capital; draft; securities.

creditor, lender, lessor, mortgagee; dun; usurer.

V. keep –, run up- an account with; entrust, credit, accredit.

place to one's -credit, – account; give –, take- credit; fly a kite.

Adj. credit-ing, -ed; accredited.

Adv. on -credit etc. *n.*; to the -account, – credit- of.

806. Debt.—N. debt, obligation, liability, indebtment, debit, score.

arrears, deferred payment, deficit, default; insolvency etc. (*non-payment*) 808; bad debt.

interest; usance, usury; premium; floating -debt, – capital.

debtor, debitor; mortgagor; defaulter etc. 808; borrower.

V. be -in debt etc. *adj.*; owe; incur –, contract- a debt etc. *n.*; run up -a bill, – a score, – an account; go on tick, put on the cuff; borrow etc. 788; run –, get- into debt; outrun the constable.

answer –, go bail- for; back one's note.

Adj. indebted; liable, chargeable, answerable for.

in -debt, — embarrassed circumstances, — difficulties; incumbered, involved; involved —, plunged —, deep —, over head and ears- in debt; deeply involved; fast tied up; insolvent etc. (*not paying*) 808; *minus*, out of pocket.

unpaid; unrequieted, unrewarded; owing, due, in arrear, outstanding.

807. Payment.—N. pay-, defray-ment; discharge; ac-, quittance; settlement, clearance, liquidation, satisfaction, reckoning, arrangement.

acknowledgment, release; receipt, — in full, — in full of all demands; voucher.

repayment, reimbursement, retribution; pay etc. (*reward*) 973; money paid etc. (*expenditure*) 809.

ready money etc. (*cash*) 800; stake, remittance, instalment.

payer, liquidator etc. 801.

V. pay, defray, make payment; pay -down, — on the nail, — ready money, — at sight, — in advance; cash, honor a bill, acknowledge; redeem; pay in kind.

pay one's -way, — shot, — footing; pay -the piper, — sauce for all, — costs; do the needful; come across; shell —, fork- out; come down with, — the dust; tickle —, grease- the palm; expend etc. 809; put —, lay- down.

discharge, settle, quit, acquit oneself of; account —, reckon —, settle —, be even —, be quits- with; strike a balance; settle —, balance —, square- accounts with; quit scores; foot the bill; wipe —, clear- off old scores; satisfy; pay in full; satisfy —, pay in full of- all demands; clear, liquidate; pay - up, — old debts.

disgorge, make repayment; repay, refund, reimburse, retribute; make compensation etc. 30.

Adj. paying etc., paid etc. *v.*; owing nothing, out of debt, all straight, clear of -debt, — encumbrance; unowed, never indebted.

Adv. to the tune of; on the nail; money —, cash- down; cash on delivery.

808. Non-payment.—N. non-payment; default, defalcation; protest, repudiation; application of the sponge; whitewashing.

insolvency, bankruptcy, failure; overdraft, overdrawn account; insufficiency etc. 640; run upon a bank.

waste paper bonds; dishonored —, protested- bills; bogus cheque.

bankrupt, insolvent debtor, lame duck, man of straw, welsher, stag, defaulter, absconder, levanter.

V. non -pay etc. 807; fail, break, stop payment; become -insolvent, — bankrupt; be gazetted.

protest, dishonor, repudiate, nullify.

pay under protest; button up one's pockets, draw the purse strings; apply the sponge; pay over the left shoulder, get whitewashed; swindle etc. 791; run up bills, fly kites.

Adj. not paying; in debt etc. 806; behindhand, in arrear; beggared etc. (*poor*) 804; unable to make both ends meet; *minus*; worse than nothing.

insolvent, bankrupt, in the gazette, gazetted, ruined.

unpaid etc. (*outstanding*) 806; *gratis* etc. 815; unremunerated.

809. Expenditure.—N. expenditure, money going out; out-goings, -lay; expenses, disbursement; prime cost etc. (*price*) 812; circulation; run upon a bank.

[Money paid] payment etc. 807; pay etc. (*remuneration*) 973; bribe etc. 973; fee, footing, garnish; subsidy; tribute, Peter's pence; contingent, quota; donation etc. 784.

pay in advance, earnest, handsel, deposit, instalment.

investment; purchase etc. 795.

V. expend, spend; run —, get- through; pay, disburse; open —, loose —, untie- the purse strings; lay —, shell —, fork- out; bleed; make up a sum, invest, sink money.

fee etc. (*reward*) 973; pay one's way etc. (*pay*) 807; subscribe etc. (*give*) 784; subsidize, bribe.

Adj. expend-ing, -ed etc. *v.*; sumptuary, liberal etc. 816; openhanded, lavish etc. 818; extensive etc. 814.

810. Receipt—N. receipt, accountable —, conditional —, binding —, return- receipt; value received, money coming in; income, incomings, innings, revenue, return, proceeds; gross receipts, net profit; earnings etc. (*gain*) 775.

rent, — roll; rent-al, -age; rack-rent.

premium, *bonus*; sweepstakes, tontine, prize, drawing.

pension, annuity; jointure etc. (*property*) 780; alimony, pittance; emolument etc. (*remuneration*) 973.

V. receive etc. 785; take money; draw —, derive- from; get, be in receipt of, acquire etc. 775; take etc. 789.

bring in, yield, afford, pay, return; accrue etc. (*be received from*) 785.

Adj. receiv-ing, -ed etc. *v.*; profitable etc. (*gainful*) 775.

811. Accounts.—N. accounts, accompts; commercial —, monetary- arithmetic; statistics etc. (*numeration*) 85; money matters, finance, budget, bill, score, reckoning, account.

books, account book, ledger; day —, cash —, pass- book; journal; debtor and creditor —, cash —, petty cash —, running- account; account-current; balance, — sheet; *compte rendu*, account settled.

book-keeping, audit; double —, single- entry; reckoning etc. 85.

chartered —, certified public —, accountant; auditor, actuary, bookkeeper; financier etc. 801; accounting party.

V. keep accounts, enter, post, book, credit, debit, carry over; take stock; balance —, make up —, square —, settle —, wind up —, cast up —, add up —, tot up- accounts; make accounts square.

bring to book, audit, tax, surcharge and falsify.

falsify —, garble —, cook —, doctor- an account.

Adj. monetary etc. 800; account-able, -ing; statistical.

812. Price.—N. price, amount, cost, expense, prime cost, charge, figure, demand, damage, fare, hire; wages etc. (*remuneration*) 973.

dues, duty, toll, tax, impost, cess, sess, tallage, levy, capitation-, poll-, income-, sur-, sales-, super-tax; gabel, *gabelle*; gavel, *octroi*, custom, tariff, excise, assessment, taxation, benevolence, tithe, tenths, exactment, ransom, salvage; broker-, wharf-, lighter-, ton-, freight-age.

worth, rate, value, valuation, appraisement, money's worth, par value; penny etc. -worth; price current, market price, quotation; what it will -fetch etc. *v*.

bill etc. (*account*) 811; shot.

V. bear –, set –, fix- a price; appraise, assess, price, charge, demand, ask, require, exact, run up; distrain; run up a bill etc. (*debt*) 806; have one's price; liquidate.

amount to, come to, mount up to; stand one in. fetch, sell for, cost, bring in, yield, afford.

Adj. priced etc. *v*.; to the tune of, *ad valorem*; mercenary, venal.

Phr. no penny, no paternoster; *point d'argent, point de Suisse*, no longer pipe, no longer dance, no song, no supper.

one may have it for.

813. Discount.—N. discount, abatement, concession, reduction, depreciation, allowance, qualification, set off, drawback, poundage, *agio*, percentage; rebate, -ment; backwardation, contango; salvage; tare and tret.

V. discount, bate; a-, re-bate; deduct, reduce, mark down, take off, allow, give, make allowance; tax, depreciate.

Adj. discounting etc. *v*.

Adv. at a discount, below par.

814. Dearness.—N. dearness etc. *adj*.; high –, famine –, fancy- price; overcharge; extravagance; exorbitance, extortion; heavy pull upon the purse; Pyrrhic victory.

V. be -dear etc. *adj*.; cost -much, – a pretty penny; rise in price, look up.

overcharge, bleed, fleece, skin, extort.

pay -too much, – through the nose, –, too dear for one's whistle.

Adj. dear; high, -priced; of great price, expensive, costly, precious, worth a Jew's eye, dear bought; unreasonable, extravagant, exorbitant, extortionate.

at a premium; not to be had, – for love or money; beyond –, above- price; priceless, of priceless value.

Adv. dear, -ly; at great –, heavy- cost; *à grands frais*.

Phr. prices looking up; *le jeu ne vaut pas la chandelle*.

815. Cheapness.—N. cheapness, low price; depreciation; bargain; good penny etc.- worth, *bon marché*.

[Absence of charge] gratuity; free -quarters, – seats, – admission, – warren; pass, Annie Oakley; run of one's teeth; nominal price, peppercorn rent; labor of love.

drug in the market.

V. be -cheap etc. *adj*.; cost little; come down –, fall- in price.

buy for -a mere nothing, – an old song; have one's money's worth; cheapen, beat down.

Adj. cheap; low, – priced; moderate, reasonable; in-, un-expensive; well –, worth the money; *magnifique et pas cher*; good –, cheap- at the price; dirt –, dog- cheap; cheap, -as dirt, – and nasty; catchpenny.

reduced, marked down, half-price, depreciated, unsaleable.

gratuitous, *gratis*, free, for love, – nothing; cost-, expense-less; without charge, not charged, untaxed; scot –, shot –, rent- free; free of -cost, – expense; honorary, unbought, unpaid, complimentary.

Adv. for a mere song; at -cost price, – prime cost, – a reduction, – a bargain; on the cheap.

816. Liberality.—N. liberality, generosity, munificence; bount-y, -eousness, -ifulness; hospitality; charity etc. (*beneficence*) 906.

benefactor, free giver, Lady Bountiful.

V. be -liberal etc. *adj*.; spend –, bleed- freely; shower down upon; open one's purse strings etc. (*disburse*) 809; spare no expense, give -with both hands, – *carte blanche*.

Adj. liberal, free, generous; charitable etc. (*beneficent*) 906; hospitable; bount-iful, -eous; handsome; unsparing, ungrudging; open-, free-, full-handed; open-, large-, free-hearted; munificent, princely, unstinting.

overpaid.

Adv. liberally, ungrudgingly, with open hand.

817. Economy.—N. economy, frugality; thrift, -iness; prudence, care, husbandry, good housewifery, savingness, retrenchment.

savings; prevention of waste, save-all; cheese parings and candle ends; parsimony etc. 819.

V. be -economical etc. *adj*.; economize, save; retrench; cut- down expenses, – one's coat according to one's cloth, make both ends meet, keep within compass, meet one's expenses, pay one's way; keep one's head above water; husband etc. (*lay by*) 636; save –, invest- money; put out to interest; provide –, save- -for, – against- a rainy day; feather one's nest; look after the main chance.

Adj. economical, frugal, careful, thrifty, saving, chary, spare, sparing; parsimonious etc. 819.

underpaid.

Adv. sparingly etc. *adj*.; *ne quid nimis*.

818. Prodigality.—N. prodi-gality, -gence; unthriftiness, waste, -fulness; profus-ion, -eness; extravagance; squandering etc. *v*.; lavishness; malversation.

prodigal; spend-, waste-thrift; losel, play-boy, spender, squanderer, locust.

V. be -prodigal etc. *adj*.; squander, lavish, sow broadcast; pour forth like water; pay through the nose etc. (*dear*) 814; spill, waste, dissipate, exhaust, drain, eat out of house and home, overdraw, outrun the constable; run -out, – through; misspend; throw -good money after bad, – the helve after the hatchet; burn the candle at both ends; make ducks and drakes of one's money;

squander one's substance, spend money like water; fool —, potter —, muddle —, fritter —, throw-away one's money; pour water into a sieve, kill the goose that lays the golden eggs; ***manger son blé en herbe.***

Adj. prodigal, profuse, thriftless, unthrifty, improvident, wasteful, losel, extravagant, lavish, dissipated, over liberal; full-handed etc. (*liberal*) 816.

penny wise and pound foolish

Adv. with an unsparing hand; money burning one's pocket; recklessly profuse.

Int. hang the expense!

819. Parsimony.—N. parsimony, parcity; parsimoniousness, stinginess etc. *adj.*; stint; illiberality, avarice, tenacity, avidity, rapacity, extortion, venality, cupidity; selfishness etc. 943; *auri sacra fames.*

miser, niggard, churl, screw, tightwad, skinflint, crib, codger, muckworm, money-grubber, pinch-fist, scrimp, lickpenny, hunks, curmudgeon, *Harpagon*, Silas Marner, harpy, extortioner, Jew, usurer.

V. be -parsimonious etc. *adj.*; grudge, begrudge, stint, skimp, pinch, gripe, screw, dole out, hold back, withhold, starve, famish, live upon nothing, skin a flint.

drive a -bargain, — hard bargain; cheapen, beat down; stop one hole in a sieve; have an itching palm, grasp, grab.

Adj. parsimonious, penurious, stingy, miserly, mean, shabby, peddling, scrubby, pennywise, near, niggardly, frugal to excess; close; fast-, close-, strait-handed; close-, hard-, tight-fisted; tight, sparing; chary; grudging, griping etc. *v.*; illiberal, ungenerous, churlish, hidebound, sordid, mercenary, venal, covetous, usurious, avaricious, greedy, extortionate, rapacious.

Adv. with a sparing hand.

820. Affections.—N. affections, character, qualities, disposition, nature, spirit, tone; temper, -ament; *diathesis*, idiosyncrasy; cast —, habit —, frame- of -mind, — soul; predilection, turn; natural —, turn of mind; bent, bias, predisposition, proneness, proclivity; propen-sity, -sedness, -sion, -dency; vein, humor, mood, grain, mettle; sympathy etc. (*love*) 897.

soul, heart, breast, bosom, inner man; heart's -core, — strings, — blood; heart of hearts, *penetralia mentis*; secret and inmost recesses of the —, cockles of one's- heart; inmost -heart, — soul; back-bone.

passion, pervading spirit; ruling —, master-passion; *furore*; fulness of the heart, heyday of the blood, flesh and blood, flow of soul, force of character.

V. have —, possess- -affections etc. *n.*; be of a -character etc. *n.*; be -affected etc. *adj.*; breathe.

Adj. affected, characterized, formed, molded, cast; at-, tempered; framed; pre-, disposed; prone, inclined; having a -bias etc. *n.*; tinctured —, imbued —, penetrated —, eaten up- with.

inborn, inbred, ingrained, in the grain, congenital, inherent, bred in the bone; deep-rooted, ineffaceable, inveterate; pathoscopic.

Adv. in one's -heart etc. *n.*; at heart; heart and soul etc. 821; in the -vein, — mood.

821. Feeling.—N. feeling; suffering etc. *v.*; endurance, tolerance, sufferance, supportance, experience, response; sympathy etc. (*love*) 897; impression, inspiration, affection, sensation, emotion, pathos, deep sense.

fire, warmth, glow, unction, *gusto*, vehemence; ferv-or, -ency; heartiness, cordiality; earnestness, eagerness; *empressment*, ardor, zeal, passion, enthusiasm, *verve*, *furore*, fanaticism; excitation of feeling etc. 824; fulness of the heart etc. (*disposition*) 820; passion etc. (*state of excitability*) 825; ecstasy etc. (*pleasure*) 827.

blush, suffusion, flush; hectic; tingling, thrill, kick, turn, shock; agitation etc. (*irregular motion*) 315; quiver, heaving, flutter, flurry, fluster, twitter, tremor; throb, -bing; pulsation, palpitation, painting; trepid-, perturb-ation; ruffle, hurry of spirits, pother, stew, ferment.

V. feel; receive an -impression etc. *n.*; be -impressed with etc. *adj.*; entertain —, harbor —, cherish- -feeling etc. *n.*

respond; catch the -flame, — infection; enter the spirit of.

bear, suffer, support, sustain, endure, brook, thole, aby; abide etc. (*be composed*) 826; experience etc. (*meet with*) 151; taste, prove; labor —, smart- under; bear the brunt of, brave, stand.

swell, glow, warm, flush, blush, change color, mantle; turn -color, — pale, — red, — black in the face; blench, crimson, whiten, pale, tingle, thrill, heave, pant, throb, palpitate, go pit-a-pat, tremble, quiver, flutter, twitter; stagger, reel; shake etc. 315; be -agitated, — excited etc. 824; look -blue, — black; wince, draw a deep breath.

impress etc. (*excite the feelings*) 824.

Adj. feeling etc. *v.*; sentient; sensuous; sensorial, -y; emo-tive, -tional; of —, with- feeling etc. *n.*

warm, quick, lively, smart, strong, sharp, acute, cutting, piercing, incisive; keen, — as a razor; trenchant, pungent, racy, *piquant*, poignant, caustic.

impressive, deep, profound, indelible; deep-, home-, heart-felt; swelling, soul-stirring, deep-mouthed, heart-expanding, electric, thrilling, rapturous, ecstatic.

earnest, wistful, eager, breathless; fer-vent, -vid; gushing, passionate, warmhearted, hearty, cordial, sincere, zealous, enthusiastic, glowing, ardent, burning, red-hot, fiery, flaming; boiling, — over.

pervading, penetrating, absorbing; rabid, raving feverish, fanatical, hysterical; impetuous etc. (*excitable*) 825; overmastering.

impressed —, moved —, touched —, affected —, penetrated —, seized —, imbued etc. 820- with; devoured by; wrought up etc. (*excited*) 824; struck all of a heap; rapt; in a -quiver etc. *n.*; enraptured etc. 829.

Adv. heart and soul, from the bottom of one's heart, *ab imo pectore*, *de profundis*, at heart, *con amore*, heartily, devoutly, over head and ears.

Phr. the heart -big, — full, — swelling, — beating, — pulsating, — throbbing, — thumping, — beating high, — melting, — overflowing, — bursting, — breaking.

822. Sensibility.—N. sensi-bility, -bleness, -tiveness; moral sensibility; impress-, affect-ibility; suscepti-bleness, -bility, -vity; mobility; viva-city, -ciousness; tender-, soft-ness; sentimental-ity, -ism.

excitability etc. 825; fastidiousness etc. 868; physical sensibility etc. 375.

sore -point, – place; where the shoe pinches.

V. be -sensible etc. *adj.*; have a -tender, – warm, – sensitive- heart.

take to –, treasure up in the- heart; shrink. 'die of a rose in aromatic pain;' touch to the quick.

Adj. sensi-ble, -tive; impressi-ble, -onable; suscepti-ve, -ble; alive to, impassion-able, -ed; gushing; warm-, tender-, soft-hearted; tender –, as a chicken; soft, sentimental, romantic; enthusiastic, highflying, spirited, mettlesome, vivacious, lively, expressive, mobile, tremblingly alive; excitable etc. 825; over-sensitive, without skin, thin-skinned; fastidious etc. 868.

Adv. sensibly etc. *adj.*; to the -quick, – inmost core.

823. Insensibility.—N. insensi-bility, -bleness; moral insensibility; inertness, *inertia, vis inertiae*; impassi-bility, -bleness; inappetency, apathy, phlegm, dulness, hebetude, supineness, lukewarmness, insusceptibility, unimpressibility.

cold -fit, – blood, – heart; cold-, cool-ness; frigidity, *sang-froid*; stoicism, imperturbation etc. (*inexcitability*) 826; *nonchalance*, unconcern, dry eyes; *insouciance* etc. (*indifference*) 866; recklessness etc. 863; callousness; heart of stone, stock and stone, marble, deadness.

torp-or, -idity; obstupefaction, lethargy, coma, trance; sleep etc. 683; suspended animation; stupor, -efaction; paralysis, palsy; numbness etc. (*physical insensibility*) 376.

neutrality; quietism, vegetation.

V. be -insensible etc. *adj.*; have a rhinoceros hide; show -insensibility etc. *n.*; not -mind, – care, – be affected by; have no desire for etc. 866; have –, feel –, take- no interest in; *nil admirari*; not care a -straw etc. (*unimportance*) 643 for; disregard etc. (*neglect*) 460; set at naught etc. (*make light of*) 483; turn a deaf ear to etc. (*inattention*) 458; vegetate.

render -insensible, – callous; blunt, obtund, numb, benumb, paralyze, chloroform, deaden, hebetate, stun, stupefy; brut-ify, -alize.

inure; harden, – the heart; steel, case-harden, sear.

Adj. insensible, unconscious; impassi-ve, -ble; blind to, deaf to, dead to; un-, in-susceptible; unimpress-ionable, -ible; passion-, spirit-, heart-, soulless; unfeeling, unmoral.

apathetic; leuco-, phlegmatic; dull, frigid; cold, -blooded, -hearted; unemotional; cold as charity; flat, obtuse, inert, supine, sluggish, torpid; sleepy etc. (*inactive*) 683; languid, half-hearted, tame; numb, -ed; comatose; anesthetic etc. 376; stupefied, chloroformed, palsy-stricken.

indifferent, lukewarm; Laodicean; careless, mindless, regardless; inattentive etc. 458; neglectful etc. 460; disregarding.

unconcerned, *nonchalant, pococurante, insouciant, sans souci*; unambitious etc. 866.

un-affected, -ruffled, -impressed, -inspired, -excited, -moved, -stirred, -touched, -shocked, -struck; unblushing etc. (*shameless*) 885; unanimated; vegetative.

callous, thick-skinned, pachydermatous, impervious; hard, -ened; inured, case-hardened; steeled –, proof- against; imperturbable etc. (*inexcitable*) 826; unfelt.

Adv. insensibly etc. *adj.*; *aequo animo*; without being -moved, – touched, – impressed; in cold blood; with -dry eyes, – withers unwrung.

Phr. never mind; it is of no consequence etc. (*unimportant*) 643; it cannot be helped; nothing coming amiss; it is all -the same, – one- to.

824. Excitation.—N. excitation of feeling; mental –, excitement; suscitation, galvanism, stimulation, piquancy, provocation inspiration, calling forth, infection; interest, animation, agitation, perturbation; subjugation, fascination, intoxication; en-, ravishment; entrancement, high pressure.

unction, impressiveness etc. *adj.*; emotional appeal; melodrama; psychological moment, crisis; sensationalism.

trail of temper, *casus belli*; irritation etc. (*anger*) 900; passion etc. (*state of excitability*) 825; thrill etc. (*feeling*) 821; repression of feeling etc. 826.

V. excite, affect, touch, move, impress, strike, interest, intrigue, animate, inspire, impassion, smite, infect; stir –, fire –, warm- the blood; set astir; a-, wake; a-, waken; call forth; e-, pro-voke; raise up, summon up, call up, wake up, blow up, get up, light up; raise; get up steam, rouse, arouse, stir, fire, kindle, enkindle, apply the torch, set on fire, inflame, illuminate.

stimulate; ex-, suscitate; inspirit; spirit up, stir up, work up; infuse life into, five new life to; bring –, introduce- new blood; quicken; sharpen, whet; work upon etc. (*incite*) 615; hurry on, give a fillip, put on one's mettle.

fan the -fire, – flame; blow the coals, stir the embers; fan, – into a flame; foster, heat, warm, foment, raise to a fever heat; keep -up, – the pot boiling; revive, rekindle; rake up, rip up.

stir –, play on –, come home to- the feelings; touch -a string, – a chord, – the soul, – the heart; go to one's heart, penetrate, pierce, go through one, touch to the quick, open the wound; possess –, pervade –, penetrate –, imbrue –, absorb –, affect –, disturb- the soul.

absorb, rivet the attention; sink into the -mind, – heart; prey on the mind; intoxicate; over-whelm, -power; *bouleverser*, upset, turn one's head.

fascinate; enrapture etc. (*give pleasure*) 829.

agitate, perturb, ruffle, fluster, flutter, shake, disturb, faze, startle, shock, stagger; give one a shock, – turn; strike -dumb, – all of a heap; stun, astound, electrify, galvanize, petrify.

irritate, sting; cut, – to the -heart, – quick; try one's temper; fool to the top of one's bent, pique; infuriate, madden, make one's blood boil; lash into fury etc. (*wrath*) 900.

be -excited etc. *adj.*; flash up, flare up; catch the infection; thrill etc. (*feel*) 821; mantle; work oneself up; seethe, boil, simmer, foam, fume, flame, rage, rave; run mad etc. (*passion*) 825.

Adj. excited etc. *v.*; wrought up, on the *qui vive*, astir, sparkling; in a -quiver etc. 821, – fever, – ferment, – blaze, – state of excitement; in hysterics; black in the face, over-wrought; hot, red-hot, flushed, feverish; all -of a twitter, – of a flutter, – of a dither, – in a pucker; with -quivering lips, – tears in one's eyes.

flaming; boiling, – over; ebullient, seething; foaming, – at the mouth; fuming, raging, carried away by passion, wild, raving, frantic, mad, distracted, distraught, beside oneself, out of one's wits, amuck, ready to burst, *bouleversé*, demoniacal.

lost, *eperdu*, tempest-tossed; haggard; ready to sink.

stung to the quick, up, on one's high ropes.

exciting etc. *v.*; impressive, warm, glowing, fervid, swelling, imposing, spirit-stirring, thrilling; high-wrought; soul-stirring, -subduing; heart-swelling, -thrilling; agonizing etc. (*painful*) 830; telling, sensational, melodramatic, hysterical; overpowering, -whelming; more than flesh and blood can bear.

piquant etc. (*pungent*) 392; spicy, appetizing, provocative, *provaquant*, tantalizing.

Adv. till one is black in the face.

Phr. the heart -beating high, – going pit-a-pat, – leaping into one's mouth; the blood -being up, – boiling in one's veins; the eye -glistening, – 'in a fine frenzy rolling;' the head turned.

825. Excitability. [Excess of sensitiveness.]—**N.** excitability, impetuosity, vehemence; boisterousness etc. *adj.*; turbulence; impatience, intolerance, non-endurance; irritability etc. (*irascibility*) 901; itching etc. (*desire*) 865; wincing; disquiet, -ude; restlessness; fidge-ts, -tiness; agitation etc. (*irregular motion*) 315.

trepidation, perturbation, ruffle, hurry, -skurry, fuss, flurry; fluster, flutter; pother, stew, ferment; whirl; thrill etc. (*feeling*) 821; state –, fever- of excitement; transport.

passion, excitement, flush, heat; fever, -heat; fire, flame, fume, blood boiling; tumult; effervescence, ebullition; boiling, – over; whiff, gust, storm, tempest; scene, breaking out, burst, fit, paroxysm, explosion; out-break, -burst; agony.

violence etc. 173; fierceness etc. *adj.*; rage, fury, *furor*, *furore*, desperation, madness, distraction, raving, delirium, brain storm; frenzy, hysterics; intoxication; tearing –, raging- passion, towering rage; anger etc. 900.

fascination, infatuation, fanaticism; Quixot-ism, -ry; *tête montée*.

V. be -impatient etc. *adj.*; not be able to -bear etc. 826; bear ill, wince, chafe, champ the bit; be in a -stew etc. *n.*; be out of all patience, fidget, fuss, not have a wink of sleep; toss, – on one's pillow.

lose one's temper etc. 900; break –, burst –, fly- out; go –, fly- -off, – off the handle, – off at a tangent; explode; flare up, flame up, fire up, burst into a flame, take fire, fire, burn; boil, – over; foam, fume, rage, rave, rant, tear; go –, run- -wild, – mad; go into hysterics; run -riot, – amuck; *battre la campagne, faire le diable à quatre*, play the deuce; raise -Cain, – the devil.

Adj. excitable, easily excited, in an excitable state; high strung; irritable etc. (*irascible*) 901; impatient, intolerant.

feverish, febrile, hysterical; delirious, mad, moody, maggoty-headed.

unquiet, mercurial, electric, galvanic, hasty, hurried, restless, fidgety, fussy; chafing etc. *v.*

startlish, mettlesome, high mettled, skittish.

vehement, demonstrative, violent, wild, furious, fierce, fiery, hot-headed, mad-cap.

over-zealous, enthusiastic, impassioned, fanatical; rabid etc. (*eager*) 865.

rampant, clamorous, uproarious, turbulent, tempestuous, tumultuary, boisterous.

impulsive, impetuous, passionate; uncontroll-ed, -able; ungovernable, irrepressible, stanchless, inextinguishable, burning, simmering, volcanic, ready to burst forth.

excit-ed, -ing etc. 824.

Int. pish! pshaw!

Phr. *noli me tangere*.

826. Inexcitability. [Absence of excitability, or of excitement.]—**N.** inexcit-, imperturb-, inirritability; even temper, tranquil mind, dispassion; tolerance, toleration, patience.

passiveness etc. (*physical inertness*) 172; hebetude, -ation; impassibility etc. (*insensibility*) 823; stupefaction.

coolness, calmness etc. *adj.*; composure, placidity, indisturbance, imperturbation, *sang-froid*, tranquility, serenity; quiet, -ude; peace of mind, mental calmness.

staidness etc. *adj.*; gravity, sobriety, Quakerism; philosophy, equanimity, stoicism, command of temper; self-possession, -control, -command, -restraint; presence of mind.

submission etc. 725; resignation; suffer-, support-, endur-, long-suffer-, forbear-ance; longanimity; fortitude; patience -of Job, – 'on a monument,' – 'sovereign o'er transmuted ill;' moderation; repression –, subjugation- of feeling; restraint etc. 751.

tranquilization etc. (*moderation*) 174.

V. be -composed etc. *adj.*

laisser -faire, – *aller*; take things -easily, – as they come; take it easy, run on, live and let live; take -easily, – cooly, – in good part; *aequam serva e mentem*.

bear, – well, – the brunt; go through, support, endure, brave, disregard.

tolerate, suffer, stand, bide; abide, aby; bear –, put up –, abide- with; acquiesce; submit etc. (*yield*) 725; submit with a good grace; resign –, reconcile- oneself to; brook, digest, eat, swallow, pocket, stomach; make -light of, – the best of, – a virtue of necessity; put a good face on, keep one's countenance; carry -on, – through; check etc. 751- oneself.

compose, appease etc. (*moderate*) 174; propitiate; repress etc. (*restrain*) 751; render insensible etc. 823; overcome –, allay –, repress- one's -excitability etc. 825; master one's feelings.

make -oneself, – one's mind- easy; set one's mind at -ease, – rest.

calm –, cool- down; thaw, grow cool.

be -borne, – endured; go down.

Adj. in-, un-excitable; imperturbable; unsusceptible etc. (*insensible*) 823; un-, dispassionate; cold-blooded, inirritable; enduring etc. *v.*; stoical, Platonic, philosophic, staid, stayed; sober, – minded; grave; sober –, grave- as a judge; sedate, demure, cool-, level-headed; steady.

easy-going, peaceful, placid, calm; quiet, – as a mouse; tranquil, serene; cool, – as -a cucumber, – custard; undemonstrative.

temperate etc. (*moderate*) 174; composed, collected; un-excited, -stirred, -ruffled, -disturbed, -perturbed, -impassioned; unoffended; unresisting.

meek, tolerant; patient, – as- Job; submissive etc. 725; tame; content, resigned, chastened, subdued, lamblike; gentle, – as a lamb; *suaviter in modo*; mild, – as mother's milk; soft as peppermint; armed with patience, bearing with, clement, forbearant, long-suffering.

Adv. 'like patience on a monument smiling at grief;' *aequo animo*, in cold blood etc. 823; more in sorrow than in anger.

Int. patience! and shuffle the cards.

827. Pleasure.—N. pleasure, gratification, enjoyment, fruition; ob-, de-lectation; relish, zest; *gusto* etc. (*physical pleasure*) 377; satisfaction etc. (*content*) 831; complacency.

well-being; good etc. 618; snugness, comfort, ease; cushion etc. 215; *sans souci*, mind at ease.

joy, gladness, delight, glee, cheer, sunshine; cheerfulness etc. 836.

treat, refreshment; frolic, fun, lark, gambol, merry-making; amusement etc. 840; luxury etc. 377; hedonism.

mens sana in corpore sano.

happiness, felicity, bliss; beati-tude, -fication; enchantment, transport, rapture, ravishment, ecstasy; *summum bonum*; paradise, elysium etc. (*heaven*) 981; third —, seventh- heaven; unalloyed - happiness etc.

honeymoon; palmy —, halcyon- days; golden - age, — time; *Saturnia regna*, Eden, Arcadia, happy valley, Agapemone; Cockaigne.

V. be pleased etc. 829; feel —, experience- pleasure etc. *n.*; joy; enjoy —, hug- oneself; be in - clover etc. 377, — elysium etc. 981; tread on enchanted ground; fall —, go- into raptures.

feel at home, breathe freely, bask in the sunshine.

be -pleased etc. 829- with; receive —, derive- pleasure etc. *n.*- from; take -pleasure etc. *n.*- in; delight in, rejoice in, indulge in, luxuriate in; gloat over etc. (*physical pleasure*) 377; enjoy, relish, like; love etc. 897; take -to, — a fancy to; have a liking for; enter into the spirit of.

take in good part.

treat oneself to, solace oneself with.

Adj. pleased etc. 829; not sorry; glad, -some; pleased as Punch.

happy, blest, blessed, blissful, beatified; happy as -a king, — the day is long; thrice happy, *ter quaterque beatus*; enjoying etc. *v.*; joyful etc. (*in spirits*) 836; hedonic.

in -a blissful state, — paradise etc. 981; — raptures, — ecstasies, — a transport of delight.

comfortable etc. (*physical pleasure*) 377; at ease; content etc. 831; *sans souci*, in clover.

overjoyed, entranced, enchanted; enraptured; en-, ravished; transported; fascinated, captivated.

with -a joyful face, — sparkling eyes.

pleasing etc. 829; ecstatic, beat-ic, -ific; painless, unalloyed, without alloy, cloudless.

Adv. happily etc. *adj.*; with pleasure etc. (*willingly*) 60; with -glee etc. *n.*

phr. one's heart leaping with joy.

828. Pain.—N. mental suffering, pain, dolor; suffer-ing, -ance; ache, smart etc. (*physical pain*) 378; passion.

displeasure, dissatisfaction, discomfort, discomposure, disquiet; *malaise*; inquietude, uneasiness, vexation of spirit; taking; discontent etc. 832.

dejection etc. 837; weariness etc. 841.

annoyance, irritation, worry, infliction, visitation; plague, bore; bother, -ation; stew, vexation, mortification, chagrin, *esclandre*; *mauvais quart d'heure.*

care, anxiety, solicitude, trouble, trial, ordeal, fiery ordeal, shock, blow, cark, dole, fret, burden, load.

concern, grief, sorrow, distress, affliction, woe, bitterness, gloom, heartache; heavy —, aching —, bleeding —, broken- heart; heavy affliction, gnawing grief; unhappiness, infelicity, misery, tribulation, wretchedness, desolation; despair etc. 859; extremity, prostration, depth of misery.

nightmare, *ephialtes*, incubus.

anguish, agony; throe, tor-ture, -ment; crucifixion, martyrdom; pang, twinge, stab; the rack, the stake; purgatory etc. (*hell*) 982.

hell upon earth; iron age, reign of terror; slough of despond etc. (*adversity*) 735; peck —, sea- of troubles; ills that flesh is heir to etc. (*evil*) 619; miseries of human life; unkindest cut of all.

sufferer, victim, prey, martyr, object of compassion, wretch, shorn lamb.

V. feel —, suffer —, experience —, undergo —, bear —, endure- pain etc. *n.*; smart, ache etc. (*physical pain*) 378; suffer, bleed, ail; be the victim of; bear — take up- the cross.

labor under afflictions; quaff the bitter cup, have a bad time of it; fall on evil days etc. (*adversity*) 735; go hard with, come to grief, fall a sacrifice to, drain the cup of misery to the dregs, sup full of horrors.

sit on thorns, be on pins and needles, wince, fret, chafe, worry oneself, be in a taking, fret and fume, take -on, — to heart.

grieve; mourn etc. (*lament*) 839; yearn, repine, pine, droop, languish, sink; give way; despair etc. 859; break one's heart; weigh upon the heart etc. (*inflict pain*) 830.

Adj. in —, in a state of —, full of- pain etc. *n.*; suffering etc. *v.*; pained, afflicted, worried, displeased etc. 830; aching, griped, sore etc. (*physical pain*) 378; on the rack; in limbo; between hawk and buzzard.

un-comfortable, -easy; ill at ease; in a -taking, — way; disturbed; discontented etc. 832; out of humor etc. 901*a*; weary etc. 841.

heavy laden, stricken, crushed, a prey to, victimized, ill-used.

unfortunate etc. (*hapless*) 735; to be pitied, doomed, devoted, accursed, undone, lost, stranded.

unhappy, infelicitous, poor, wretched, miserable, woe-begone; cheerless etc. (*dejected*) 837; careworn.

concerned, sorry; sorrow-ing, -ful; cut up, chagrined, horrified, horror-stricken; in —, plunged in —, a prey to- grief etc. *n.*; in tears etc. (*lamenting*) 839; steeped to the lips in misery; heart-stricken, -broken, -scalded; broken-hearted; in despair etc. 859.

Phr. 'the iron entered into our soul;' *haeret lateri lethalis arundo*;' one's heart bleeding.

829. Pleasurableness. [Capability of giving pleasure; cause or source of pleasure.]—**N.** pleasurable-, pleasant-, agreeable-ness etc. *adj.*; pleasure giving, jocundity, delectability; amusement etc. 840.

attraction etc. (*motive*) 615; attractiveness, -

ability; invitingness etc. *adj.*; charm, fascination, captivation, enchantment, witchery, seduction, winsomeness, winning ways, amenity, amiability, sweetness.

loveliness etc. (*beauty*) 845; sunny –, bright- side; sweets etc. (*sugar*) 396; goodness etc. 648; manna in the wilderness, land flowing with milk and honey.

treat; regale etc. (*physical pleasure*) 377; dainty; tit-, tid-bit; nuts, *sauce piquante*.

V. cause –, produce –, create –, give –, afford –, procure –, offer –, present –, yield- pleasure etc. 827.

please, charm, delight; gladden etc. (*make cheerful*) 836; take, captivate, fascinate; enchant, entrance, enrapture, transport, bewitch; en-, ravish.

bless, beatify; satisfy; gratify –, desire etc. 865; slake, satiate, quench; indulge, humor, flatter, tickle; tickle the palate etc. (*savory*) 394; regale, refresh; enliven; treat; amuse etc. 840; take –, tickle –, hit- one's fancy; meet one's wishes; win –, gladden –, rejoice –, warm the cockles of- the heart; do one's heart good.

attract, allure etc. (*move*) 615; stimulate etc. (*excite*) 824; interest, intrigue.

make things pleasant, popularize, gild the pill, sweeten.

Adj. causing pleasure etc. *v.*; pleasure-giving; pleas-ing, -ant, -urable; agreeable, cushy; grat-eful, -ifying; leef, lief, acceptable; welcome, – as the roses in May; welcomed; favorite; to one's -taste, – mind, – liking, – heart's content; satisfactory etc. (*good*) 648.

refreshing; comfortable; cordial; genial; glad, -some; sweet, delectable, nice, dainty; delic-ate, -ious; dulcet; luscious etc. 396; palatable etc. 394; luxurious, voluptuous; sensual etc. 377.

attractive etc. 615; inviting, prepossessing, engaging; win-ning, -some; taking, fascinating, captivating, killing; seduc-ing, -tive; alluring, enticing; appetizing etc. (*exciting*) 824; cheering etc. 836; bewitching; interesting, absorbing, enchanting, entrancing, enravishing.

charming; delightful, felicitous, exquisite; lovely etc. (*beautiful*) 845; ravishing, rapturous; heartfelt, thrilling, ecstatic; beat-ic, -ific; seraphic; empyrean; elysian etc. (*heavenly*) 981.

palmy, halcyon, Saturnian.

Phr. *decies repetita placebit.*

830. Painfulness. [Capability of giving pain; cause or source of pain.]—**N.** painfulness etc. *adj.*; trouble, care etc. (*pain*) 828; trial; af-, in-fliction; cross, blow, stroke, burden, load, curse; bitter -pill, – draught, – cup; waters of bitterness.

annoyance, grievance, nuisance, vexation, mortification, sickener; bore, bother, pother, hot water, sea of troubles, hornet's nest, plague, pest.

cancer, ulcer, sting, thorn; canker etc. (*bane*) 663; scorpion etc. (*evil-doer*) 913; dagger etc. (*arms*) 727; scourge etc. (*instrument of punishment*) 975; carking –, canker worm of- care.

mishap, misfortune etc. (*adversity*) 735; *désagrément, esclandre*, rub.

source of -irritation, – annoyance; wound, sore subject, skeleton in the closet; thorn in -the flesh, – one's side; where the shoe pinches, gall and wormwood.

sorry sight, heavy news, provocation; affront etc. 929; head and front of one's offending.

infestation, molestation; malignity etc. (*malevolence*) 907.

V. cause –, occasion –, give –, bring –, induce –, produce –, create –, inflict- pain etc. 828; pain, hurt, wound.

pinch, prick, gripe etc. (*physical pain*) 378; pierce, lancinate, cut.

hurt –, wound –, grate upon –, jar upon- the feelings; wring –, pierce –, lacerate –, break –, rend- the heart; make the heart bleed; tear –, rend- the heart-strings; draw tears from the eyes.

sadden; make -unhappy etc. 828; plunge into sorrow, grieve, fash, afflict, distress; cut -up, – to the heart.

displease, annoy, incommode, discommode, discompose, trouble, disquiet, disturb, thwart, cross, perplex, molest, tease, rag, tire, irk, vex, mortify, wherret, worry, plague, bother, pester, bore, pother, harass, harry, badger, heckle, bait, beset, infest, persecute, importune, be troublesome.

wring, harrow, torment, torture; put to the -rack, – question; break on the wheel, rack, scarify; cruci-ate, -fy; convulse, agonize; barb the dart; plant a -dagger in the breast, – thron in one's side.

irritate, provoke, sting, nettle, try the patience, pique, fret, rile, tweak the nose, chafe, gall; sting –, wound –, cut- to the quick; aggrieve, affront, enchafe, enrage, ruffle, sour the temper; give offence etc. (*resentment*) 900.

maltreat, bite, snap at, assail, bully; smite etc. (*punish*) 972.

sicken, disgust, revolt, nauseate, disenchant, repel, offend, shock, stink in the nostrils; go against –, turn- the stomach; make one sick, set the teeth on edge, go against the grain, grate on the ear; stick in one's -throat, – gizzard; rankle, gnaw, corrode, horrify, appal, freeze the blood; chill the spine; make the -flesh creep, – hair stand on end; make the blood -curdle, – run cold; make one shudder.

haunt, – the memory; weigh –, prey- on the -heart, – mind, – spirits; bring one's grey hairs with sorrow to the grave; add a nail to one's coffin.

Adj. causing pain, hurting etc. *v.*; hurtful etc. (*bad*) 649; painful; dolor-ific, -ous; unpleasant; un-, dis-pleasing; disagreeable, unpalatable, bitter, distasteful; uninviting; unwelcome; undesir-able, -ed; obnoxious; unacceptable, unpopular, thankless.

unsatisfactory, untoward, unlucky, uncomfortable.

distressing; afflict-ing, -ive; joy-, cheer-, comfortless; dismal, disheartening; depress-ing, -ive; dreary, melancholy, grievous, piteous; woeful, rueful, mournful, deplorable, pitiable, lamentable; sad, affecting, touching, pathetic.

irritating, provoking, stinging, annoying, aggravating, mortifying, galling; unaccommodating, invidious, vexatious; trouble-, tire-, irk-, weari-some; plagu-ing, -y; awkward.

importunate; teas-, pester-, bother-, harass-, worry-, torment-, cark-ing.

in-toler-, -suffer-, -support-able; un-bear-, -endur-able; past bearing; not to be -borne, – endured; more than flesh and blood can bear; enough to -drive one mad, – provoke a saint, – make a parson swear, – try the patience of Job.

shocking, terrific, grim, appalling, crushing; dreadful, fearful, frightful; thrilling, tremendous, dire; heart-breaking, -rending, -wounding, -corroding, -sickening; harrowing, rending.

odious, hateful, execrable, repulsive, repellent, abhorrent; horri-d, -ble, -fic, -fying; offensive; nause-ous, -ating; disgust-, sicken-, revolt-ing; nasty; loath-some, -ful; fulsome; vile etc. (*bad*) 649; hideous etc. 846.

sharp, acute, sore, severe, grave, hard, harsh, cruel, biting, acrimonious, caustic; cutting, corroding, consuming, racking, excruciating, searching, searing, grinding, grating, agonizing; envenomed.

ruinous, disastrous, calamitous, tragical; desolating, withering; burdensome, onerous, oppressive; cumb-rous, -ersome.

Adv. painfully etc. *adj.*; with -pain etc. 828; deuced.

Int. *hinc illae lachrymae!* woe is me!

Phr. *surgit amari aliquid*; the place being too hot to hold one; the iron entering the soul.

831. Content.—N. content, -ment, -edness; complacency, satisfaction, entire satisfaction, ease, heart's ease, peace of mind; serenity etc. 826; cheerfulness etc. 836; ray of comfort; comfort etc. (*well-being*) 827.

re-, conciliation; resignation etc. (*patience*) 826. waiter on Providence.

V. be -content etc. *adj.*; rest -satisfied, – and be thankful; take the good the gods provide, let well alone, feel oneself at home, hug oneself, lay the flattering unction to one's soul.

take -up with, – in good part; assent etc. 488; be reconciled to, make one's peace with; get over it; take -heart, – comfort; put up with etc. (*bear*) 826.

render -content etc. *adj.*; set at ease, comfort; set one's -heart, – mind- at -ease, – rest; speak peace; conciliate, reconcile, win over, propitiate, disarm, beguile; content, satisfy; gratify etc. 829.

be -tolerated etc. 826; go down, – with; do.

Adj. content, -ed; satisfied etc. *v.*; at -ease, – one's ease, – home; with the mind at ease, *sans souci, sine curâ*, easy-going, not particular; conciliatory; unrepining, of good comfort; resigned etc. (*patient*) 826; cheerful etc. 836.

un-afflicted, -vexed, -molested, -plagued; serene etc. 826; at rest; snug, comfortable; in one's element.

satisfactory, satisfying, ample, sufficient, adequate, tolerable.

Adv. to one's heart's content; *à la bonne heure*; all for the best.

Int. amen etc. (*assent*) 488; very well, so much the better, well and good; it –, that- will do; it cannot be helped.

Phr. nothing comes amiss.

832. Discontent.—N. discontent, -ment; dissatisfaction; dissent etc. 489; labor unrest.

disappointment, mortification; cold comfort; regret etc. 833; repining, taking on etc. *v.*; inquietude, vexation of spirit, soreness; heart-burning, -grief; querulousness etc. (*lamentation*) 839; hypercriticism.

malcontent, grumbler, growler, croaker, *laudator temporis acti*; censurer, complainer, faultfinder, murmurer, Adullamite, Diehard, Bitterender.

the Opposition, cave of Adullam, indignation meeting, 'winter of our discontent.'

V. be -discontented etc. *adj.*; quarrel with one's bread and butter; repine; regret etc. 833; wish one at the bottom of the Red Sea; take -on, – to heart; shrug the shoulders; make a wry –, pull a long- face; knit one's brows; look -blue, – black, – black as thunder, – blank, – glum.

take -in bad part, – ill; fret, chafe, make a piece of work; grumble, croak, grouse; lament etc. 839.

cause -discontent etc. *n.*; dissatisfy, disappoint, mortify, put out, disconcert; cut up; dishearten.

Adj. discontented; dissatisfied etc. *v.*; unsatisfied, ungratified; dissident; dissentient etc. 489; malcontent, exigent, exacting, hypercritical.

repining etc. *v.*; regretful etc. 833; down in the mouth etc. (*dejected*) 837.

in -high dudgeon, – a fume, – the sulks, – the dumps, – bad humor; glum, sulky; sour, – as a crab; soured, sore; out of -humor, – temper.

disappointing etc. *v.*; unsatisfactory.

Int. so much the worse!

Phr. that –, it- will never do.

833. Regret.—N. regret, repining; home sickness, nostalgia; *mal –, maladie- du pays*; lamentation etc. 839; contrition, compunction, penitence etc. 950.

bitterness, heart-burning.

laudator temporis acti etc. (*discontent*) 832.

V. regret, deplore; bewail etc. (*lament*) 839; repine, cast a longing lingering look behind; rue, – the day; repent etc. 950; *infandum renovare dolorem*.

prey –, weigh –, have a weight- on the mind; leave an aching void.

Adj. regretting etc. *v.*; regretful; home-sick.

regretted etc. *v.*; much to be regretted, regrettable; lamentable etc. (*bad*) 649.

Int. what a pity! hang it!

Phr. 'tis -pity, – too true.

834. Relief.—N. relief; deliverance; refreshment etc. 689; easement, softening, alleviation, mitigation, palliation etc. 174; soothing, lullaby; cradle song, *berceuse*.

solace, consolation, comfort, encouragement.

lenitive, restorative etc. (*remedy*) 662; poultice etc. *v.*; cushion etc. 215; crumb of comfort, balm in Gilead; aspirin.

V. relieve, ease, alleviate, mitigate, palliate, soothe, addulce; salve; soften, – down; foment, stupe, poultice; assuage, allay.

cheer, comfort, console; encourage, bear up, pat on the back, give comfort, set at ease; enliven, gladden –, cheer- the heart.

remedy; cure etc. (*restore*) 660; refresh; pour -balm into, – oil on.

smoothe the ruffled brow of care, temper the wind to the shorn lamb, lay the flattering unction to one's soul.

disburden etc. (*free*) 705; take off a load of care.

be relieved; breathe more freely, draw a long breath; take comfort; dry –, wipe- the -tears, – eyes.

Adj. relieving etc. *v.*; consolatory, soothing; assua-ging, -sive; bal-my, -samic; lenitive, palliative; anodyne etc. (*remedial*) 662; curative etc. 660.

835. Aggravation.—N. aggravation, heightening; exacerbation; exasperation; overestimation etc. 482; exaggeration etc. 549.

V. aggravate, render worse, heighten, embitter, sour; ex-, acerbate; exasperate, envenom; tease, provoke, enrage.

add fuel to the -fire, – flame; fan the flame etc. (*excite*) 824; go from bad to worse etc. (*deteriorate*) 659.

Adj. aggravated etc. *v.*; worse, unrelieved; aggravable; aggravating etc. *v.*

Adv. out of the frying pan into the fire, from bad to worse, worse and worse.

Int. so much the worse!

836. Cheerfulness.—N. cheerfulness etc. *adj.*; geniality, gaiety, *l'allegro*, cheer, good humor, spirits; high –, animal –, flow of- spirits; glee, high glee, light heart; sunshine of the -mind, – breast; *gaieté de coeur, bon naturel.*

liveliness etc. *adj.*; life, alacrity, vivacity, animation, *allégresse*; jocundity, joviality, jollity; levity; jocularity etc. (*wit*) 842.

mirth, merriment, hilarity, exhilaration; laughter etc. 838; merry-making etc. (*amusement*) 840; heyday, rejoicing etc. 838; marriage bells.

nepenthe, Euphrosyne.

optimism etc. (*hopefulness*) 858; self-complacency.

V. be -cheerful etc. *adj.*; have the mind at ease, smile, put a good face upon, keep up one's spirits; view -the bright side of the picture, – things *en couleur de rose*; *ridentem dicere verum*, cheer up, brighten up, light up, bear up; chirp, take heart, cast away care, drive dull care away, perk up.

rejoice etc. 838; carol, chirrup, lilt; frisk, rollick, give a loose to mirth.

cheer, enliven, elate, exhilarate, gladden, in-spirit, animate, raise the spirits, inspire; put in good humor; cheer –, rejoice- the heart; delight etc. (*give pleasure*) 829.

Adj. cheerful; happy etc. 827; cheer-y, -ly; of good cheer, smiling; blithe; in –, in good- spirits; in high -spirits, – feather; happy as -the day is long, – a king; gay, – as a lark; *allegro*; light, -some, -hearted; buoyant, *débonnaire*, bright, free and easy, airy; janty, jaunty, canty; spright-ly, -ful; spry; spirit-ed, -ful; lively; animated, breezy, vivacious; brisk, – as a bee; sparkling; sportive; full of -play, – spirit; all alive.

sunny, palmy; hopeful etc. 858.

merry, – as a -cricket, – grig, – marriage bell; joyful, joyous, jocund, jovial; jolly, – as a thrush, – as a sandboy; blithesome; glee-ful, -some; hilarious, rattling.

winsome, bonny, hearty, buxom.

play-ful, -some; *folâtre*, playful as a kitten, tricksy, frisky, frolicsome; gamesome; jocose, jocular, waggish; mirth-, laughter-loving; mirthful, rollicking.

elate, -d; exulting, jubilant, flushed; rejoicing etc. 838; cock-a-hoop.

cheering, inspiriting, exhilarating; cardiac, -al; pleasing etc. 829; flourishing, halcyon.

Adv. cheerfully etc. *adj.*

Int. never say die! come! cheer up! hurrah! etc. 838; 'hence loathed melancholy!' begone dull care! away with melancholy!

837. Dejection.—N. dejection; dejectedness etc. *adj.*; depression, prosternation; lowness –, depression- of spirits; weight –, oppression –, damp- on the spirits; low –, bad –, drooping –, depressed- spirits; heart sinking; heaviness –, failure- of heart.

heaviness etc. *adj.*; infestivity, gloom; weariness etc. 841; *taedium vitae*, disgust of life; *mal du pays* etc. (*regret*) 833.

melancholy; sadness etc. *adj.*; *il penseroso*, *melancholia*, dismals, mumps, mopes, lachrymals, dumps, blues, blue devils, doldrums, vapors, megrims, spleen, horrors, hypochondriasis, pessimism; despondency, slough of Despond; disconsolateness etc. *adj.*; hope deferred, blank despondency.

prostration, – of soul; broken heart; despair etc. 859; cave of -despair, – Trophonius.

demureness etc. *adj.*; gravity, solemnity; long –, grave- face.

hypochondriac, seek-sorrow, self-tormentor, *heautontimorumenos, malade imaginaire, médecin tant pis*; croaker, pessimist; mope, mopus.

[Cause of dejection] affliction etc. 830; sorry sight; *memento mori*; damper, wet blanket, Job's comforter; death's head, skeleton at the feast.

V. be -dejected etc. *adj.*; grieve; mourn etc. (*lament*) 839; take on, give way, lose heart, despond, droop, sink.

lower, look downcast, frown, pout; hang down the head; pull –, make- a long face; laugh on the wrong side of the mouth; grin a ghastly smile; look -blue, – like a drowned man; lay –, take- to heart.

mope, brood over; fret; sulk; pine, – away; yearn; repine etc. (*regret*) 833; despair etc. 859.

refrain from laughter, keep one's countenance; be –, look- grave etc. *adj.*; repress a smile, keep a straight face.

depress; dis-courage, -hearten; dis-pirit; damp, dull, deject, lower, sink, dash, knock down, un-man, prostrate, break one's heart; frown upon; cast a -gloom, – shade- on; sadden; damp –, dash –, wither- one's hopes; weigh –, lie heavy –, prey- on the -mind, – spirits; damp –, depress- the spirits.

Adj. cheer-, joy-, spirit-less; uncheer-ful, -y; unlively; unhappy etc. 828; melancholy, dismal, somber, dark, gloomy, adust, *triste*, clouded, murky, lowering, frowning, lugubrious, Acherontic, funereal, mournful, lamentable, dreadful.

dreary, flat; dull, – as -a beetle, – ditchwater; depressing etc. *v.*

'melancholy as a gib cat;' oppressed with –; a prey to- melancholy; down-cast, -hearted; down -in the mouth, – on one's luck; heavy-hearted; in the -dumps, – suds, – sulks, – doldrums; in doleful dumps, in bad humor; sullen; mumpish, dumpish; mopish, moping; moody, glum; sulky etc. (*discontented*) 832; out of -sorts, – humor, – heart, – spirits; ill at ease, low-spirited, in low spirits, a cup too low; weary etc. 841; dis-couraged, -heartened; desponding; chop-, jaw-, crest-fallen.

sad, pensive, *penseroso*, tristful; dole-some, -ful; woebegone, lachrymose, in tears, melancholic, hypped, hypochondriacal, bilious, jaundiced, atrabilious, saturnine, splenetic; lackadaisical.

serious, sedate, staid, stayed; grave, – as -a judge, – an undertaker, – a mustard pot; sober, solemn, demure; grim; grim-faced, -visaged; rueful, wan, long-faced.

disconsolate; un-, in-consolable; forlorn, comfortless, desolate, *désolé*, sick at heart; soul-, heart-sick; *au désepoir*; in despair etc. 859; lost.

overcome; broken-, borne-, bowed-down; heart-stricken etc. (*mental suffering*) 828; cut up, dashed, sunk; unnerved, unmanned; down-fallen, -trodden; broken-hearted; care-worn.

Adv. with -a long face, – tears in one's eyes; sadly etc. *adj*.

Phr. the countenance falling; the heart -failing, – sinking within- one.

838. Rejoicing. [Expression of pleasure.]—**N.** rejoicing, exultation, triumph, jubilation, heyday, flush, revelling; merry-making etc. (*amusement*) 840; jubilee etc. (*celebration*) 883; *paean*, *Te Deum* etc. (*thanksgiving*) 990; congratulation etc. 896; applause etc. 971.

smile, simper, smirk, grin; broad –, sardonic-grin.

laughter, giggle, titter, crow, cheer, chuckle, snicker, snigger, shout; Homeric laughter, horse –, hearty- laugh; guffaw; burst –, fit –, shout –, roar –, peal- of laughter; cachinnation.

risibility; derision etc. 856.

Momus; Democritus the Abderite; rollicker; Laughter holding both his sides.

V. rejoice; thank –, bless- one's stars; congratulate –, hug- oneself; rub –, clap- one's hands; smack the lips, fling up one's cap; dance, skip, caleer; sing, carol, chirrup, chirp; hurrah; cry for –, leap with- joy; exult etc. (*boast*) 884; triumph; hold jubilee etc. (*celebrate*) 883; make merry etc. (*sport*) 840; sing a paean of joy.

smile, simper, smirk; grin, – like a Cheshire cat; mock, laugh in one's sleeve; laugh, – outright; giggle, titter, snigger, crow, smicker, chuckle, snicker, cackle; burst -out, – into a fit of laughter; shout, split, roar.

shake –, split –, hold both- one's sides, roar –, die- with laughter.

raise laughter etc. (*amuse*) 840.

Adj. rejoicing etc. *v.*; jubilant, exultant, triumphant; flushed, elated; laughing etc. *v.*; risible; ready to -burst, – split, – die with laughter; convulsed with laughter.

laughable etc. (*ludicrous*) 853.

Int. hip, hip, -hurrah! huzza! aha! hail! tolderolloll! tra-la la! Heaven be praised! *io triumphe! tant mieux!* so much the better.

Phr. the heart leaping with joy.

839. Lamentation. [Expression of pain.]—**N.** lament, -ation; wail, complaint, plaint, murmur, mutter, grumble, groan, moan, whine, whimper, sob, sigh, suspiration, heaving, deep sigh.

cry etc. (*vociferation*) 411; scream, howl; outcry, wail of woe, frown, scowl.

tear; weeping etc. *v.*; flood of tears, fit of crying, lachrymation, melting mood, weeping and gnashing of teeth.

plaintiveness etc. *adj.*; languishment; condolence etc. 915.

mourning, weeds, willow, cypress, crêpe, crape, deep mourning; sackcloth and ashes; knell etc. 363; dump, deathsong, dirge, coronach, keen, *nenia*, requiem, elegy, *epicedium*; threne; mon-, thren-ody; jeremiad; ululation.

mourner, professional mourner, keener; grumbler etc. (*discontent*) 832; Niobe; Heraclitus.

V. lament, mourn, deplore, grieve, weep over; be-wail, -moan; keen; condole with etc. 915; fret etc. (*suffer*) 828; wear –, go into –, put on-mourning; wear -the willow, – sackcloth and-ashes; *infandum renovare dolorem* etc. (*regret*) 833; give sorrow words.

sigh; give –, heave –, fetch- a sigh; 'waft a sigh from Indus to the pole;' sigh 'like furnace;' wail.

cry, weep, sob, greet, blubber, pipe, snivel, bibber, whimper, pule; pipe one's eye; drop –, shed- -tears, – a tear; melt –, burst- into tears; *fondre en larmes*; cry -oneself blind, – one's eyes out.

scream etc. (*cry out*) 411; mew etc. (*animal sounds*) 412; groan, moan, whine, yammer; roar; roar –, bellow- like a bull; cry out lustily, rend the air, yell.

frown, scowl, make a wry face, grimace, gnash one's teeth, wring one's hands, tear one's hair, beat one's breast, roll on the ground, burst with grief.

complain, murmur, mutter, grumble, growl, clamor, make a fuss about, croak, grunt, maunder; deprecate etc. (*disapprove*) 932.

cry out before one is hurt, complain without cause.

Adj. lamenting etc. *v.*; in mourning, in sackcloth and ashes; crying, sorrowing, -ful etc. (*unhappy*) 828; mourn-, tear-ful; lachrymose; plaint-ive, -ful, quer-ulous, -imonious; in the melting mood.

in tears, with tears in one's eyes; with -moistened, – watery- eyes; bathed –, dissolved-in tears; 'like Niobe all tears.'

elagiac, epicedial, threnetic.

Adv. *de profundis*; *les larmes aux yeux*.

Int. heigh-ho! alas! alack! O dear! ah –, woe is-me! lackadaisy! well –, lack –, alack- a day! well-a-way! alas the day! *O tempora! O mores!* what a pity! *miserabile dictu!* O lud lud! too true!

Phr. tears -standing in, – starting from- the eyes; eyes -suffused, – swimming, – brimming –, over- flowing- with tears.

840. Amusement.—**N.** amuse-, entertain-ment; diver-sion, -tissement; reaction, relaxation, solace; pastime, *passetemps*, sport; labor of love; pleasure etc. 827.

fun, frolic, merriment, whoopee, jollity; jovial-ity, -ness; heyday; laughter etc. 838; jocos-ity, -eness; droll-, buffoon-, tomfool-ery; mummery, masquing, pleasantry; wit etc. 842; quip, quirk.

play; game, – at romps; gambol, romp, prank, antic, rig, lark, spree, skylarking, vagary, trick, monkey trick, *gambade*, *fredaine*, *escapade*, *échappée*, bout, *espièglerie*; practical joke etc. (*ridicule*) 856.

dance; round –, square –, solo –, step –, tap –, clog –, skirt –, sand –, folk –, morris-dance, *pas seul*, step, turn, *chassé*, cut, shuffle, double shuffle; hop, reel, rigadoon, saraband, hornpipe, bolero, fandango, pavan, tarantella, minuet, waltz, polka; galop, -ade; Schottische, *pas de quatre*, Boston, one-, two-step, rumba, tango, maxixe, fox-, turkey-trot, shimmy, ragtime, cakewalk, jazz, blues, Charleston; jig, breakdown, fling, strathspey; *allemande*; gavot, -te; mazurka, morisco; quadrille, lancers, country dance, *cotillon*, polonaise, Sir Roger de Coverley, Swedish dance; *ballet* etc. (*drama*) 599; ball; *bal*, – *masqué*, – *costumé*; masquerade, fancy dress ball; *thé dansant*; Terpsichore, choreography, Russian ballet, classical dancing; eurythmics; nautch dance, *danse du ventre*, cancan.

festivity, merry-making; party etc. (*social gathering*) 892; *fête*, festival, gala, *ridotto*; revel-s, -ry, -ling; carnival, brawl, saturnalia, high jinks; feast, banquet etc. (*food*) 298; regale, *symposium*, wassail; carous-e, -al; jollification, junket, wake, pic-nic, *fête champêtre*, garden party, gymkhana, regatta, track meet, field day, jamboree, treat.

round of pleasures, dissipation, a short life and a merry one, racketing, holiday making, high jinks.

rejoicing etc. 838; jubilee etc. (*celebration*) 883.

bonfire, fireworks, *feu-de-joie*, rocket, catherine wheel, roman candle etc.

holiday; gala –, red letter –, play- day; high days and holidays; high –, Bank- holiday; May –, Derby- day; Saint –, Easter –, Whit- Monday; King's birthday, Empire Day; *mi-carême*; *Bairam*; wayzgoose, bean feast, beano.

place of amusement, theater etc. 599; concert-, ball-, assembly-room; music-hall, cinema, movies, talkies, vaudeville; hippodrome, circus, rodeo; *casino*, *kursaal*; winter garden; park, pleasance, arbor; garden etc. 371; pleasure-, play-, cricket-, football-, polo-, croquet-, archery-, hunting-ground; golf links, race course, stadium, gridiron, bowl, speedway, racing track, ring; gymnasium, swimming pool; shooting gallery; tennis-, racket-court; bowling-green, -alley; croquet-lawn, rink, skating rink; roller-coaster, roundabout, carousel, merry-go-round; swing; *montagne russe*; switch-back, scenic railway etc.

game, – of -chance, – skill; athletic sports, gymnastics; fencing; archery, rifle-shooting; tournament, pugilism etc. (*contention*) 720; sporting etc. 622; horse-racing, the turf; aquatics etc. 267; skating, roller skating; ski-running, -joring, -jumping, bobsleighing, luging, tobogganing, winter sports; sliding; cricket, tennis, lawn –, table –, deck-tennis, rackets, fives, squash, ping pong, trap bat and ball, battledore and shuttlecock, badminton, *la grâce*; pall mall, tip-cat, croquet, golf, curling, hockey, basketball, soccer, football, Rugby, Association, *pallone*, polo; tent-pegging, tilting at the ring, quintain, greasy pole; quoits, *discus*; throwing the hammer, putting the -weight, – shot, tossing the caber; knurr and spell; leap-frog; hop, skip and jump; French and English, tug of war; blind man's buff, hunt the slipper, hide-and-seek, kiss in the ring; snapdragon; cross questions and crooked answers; jig-saw puzzle; rounders, base-ball, *la crosse* etc.; angling; swimming, diving, water-polo.

billiards, pool, pyramids, snooker, bagatelle; bowls, skittles, ninepins, kail, American bowls.

cards; bridge, auction, contract, whist, rubber; round game, coon-can, loo, cribbage, *bésique*, pinocle, euchre, drole, *écarté*, skat, picquet, all-fours, quadrille, ombre, reverse, Pope Joan, commit; bo-, boa-ston; *vingt-et-un*; *quinze*, thirty-one, put-and-take, speculation, connections, brag, cassino, lottery, commerce, snip-snap-snorem, lift smoke, blind hookey, Polish bank, poker, banker; faro; Earl of Coventry, Napoleon, nap, patience, pairs; old maid, fright, beggar-my-neighbor; *baccarat*, *chemin de fer*, *monté*, *roulette*.

chess, draughts, backgammon, dominoes, checkers, mah jong, merelles, nine men's morris, go-bang, solitaire; game of –, fox and-goose; lotto; etc.

morra; gambling etc. (*chance*) 621.

toy, plaything, bauble; doll etc. (*puppet*) 554; teetotum; knick-knack etc. (*trifle*) 643; magic lantern etc. (*show*) 448; peep-, puppet-, raree-, gallanty-show; marionettes, Punch and Judy; toy-shop; 'quips and cranks and wanton wiles, nods and becks and wreathed smiles.'

sportsman, gamester, gambler etc. 621; reveler, master of the -ceremonies, – revels; *arbiter elegantiarum*.

V. amuse, entertain, divert, eliven; tickle, – the fancy; titillate, raise a smile, put in good humor; cause –, create –, occasion –, raise –, excite –, produce –, convulse with- laughter; set the table in a roar, be the death of one.

recreate, solace, cheer, rejoice; please etc. 829; interest; treat, regale.

amuse oneself; game; play, – a game, – pranks, – tricks; sport, disport, toy, wanton, revel, junket, feast, carouse, banquet, make merry; drown care; drive dull care away; frolic, gambol, frisk, romp; caper; dance etc. (*leap*) 309; keep up the ball; run a rig, sow one's wild oats, have one's fling, paint the town red, take one's pleasure; see life; *desipere in loco*, play the fool.

make –, keep- holiday; go a Maying.

while away –, beguile- the time; kill time, dally.

Adj. amusing, entertaining, diverting etc. *v.*; recreative, lusory; pleasant etc. (*pleasing*) 829; laughable etc. (*ludicrous*) 853; witty etc. 842; festive, -al; jovial, jolly, jocund, roguish, rompish; sporting; playful – as a kitten; sportive, ludibrious.

amused etc. *v.*; 'pleased with a feather, tickled with a straw.'

Adv. 'on the light fantastic toe,' at play, in sport.

Int. *vive la bagatelle! vogue la galère!*

Phr. *Deus nobis haec otia fecit*; *dum vivimus vivamus*.

841. Weariness.—N. weariness, defatigation, boredom, *ennui*; lassitude etc. (*fatigue*) 688; drowsiness etc. 683.

disgust, nausea, loathing, sickness; satiety etc. 869; *taedium vitae* etc. (*dejection*) 837.

wearisome-, tedious-ness etc. *adj.*; dull work, tedium, monotony, twice told tale.

bore, button-hole, proser, wet blanket; heavy hours, 'the enemy' [time].

V. weary; tire etc. (*fatigue*) 688; bore; bore –, weary –, tire- -to death, – out of one's life, – out of all patience; set –, send- to sleep.

pall, sicken, nauseate, disgust.

harp on the same string; drag its -slow, – weary-length along.

never hear the last of; be -tired etc. *adj.* -of, – with; yawn; died with *ennui*.

Adj. wearying etc. *v.*; wearing; weari-, tire-, irksome; uninteresting, stupid, bald, devoid of interest, dry, monotonous, dull, arid, tedious, humdrum, mortal, flat; pros-y, -ing; slow; soporific, somniferous, dormitive.

disgusting etc. *v.*; unenjoyed.

weary; tired etc. *v.*; drowsy etc. (*sleepy*) 683; uninterested, flagging, used up, worn out, *blasé*, life-weary, weary of life; sick of.

Adv. wearily etc. *adj.*; *usque ad nauseam*.

Phr. time hanging heavily on one's hands; *toujours perdrix*; *crambe repetita*.

842. Wit.—N. wit, -tiness; attic -wit, – salt; atticism; salt, *esprit*, point, fancy, whim, humor, drollery, pleasantry.

farce, buffoonery, fooling, tomfoolery; harlequinade etc. 599; broad -farce, – humor; fun, *espièglerie*; *vis comica*.

jocularity; jocos-ity, -eness; facetiousness; waggery, -ishness; whimsicality; comicality etc. 853.

smartness, ready wit, banter, *badinage, persiflage*, retort, repartee, *quid pro quo*; ridicule etc. 856.

facetiae, quips and cranks; jest, joke, capital joke; standing -jest, – joke; conceit, quip, quirk, crank, quiddity, *concetto, plaisanterie*, brilliant idea; merry –, bright –, happy- thought; sally; flash, – of wit, – of merriment; scintillation; *mot*, – pour rire; witticism, smart saying, *bon mot, jeu d'esprit*, epigram; jest book; dry joke, *quodlibet*, cream of the jest.

word-play, *jeu de mots*; play -of, – uponwords; pun, -ning; *double entente* etc. (*ambiguity*) 520; quibble, verbal quibble; conundrum etc. (*riddle*) 533; anagram, acrostic, double acrostic, *nugae canorae*, trifling, idle conceit, *turlupinade*.

old joke, Joe Miller, chestnut, hoary-headed jest.

V. joke, jest, cut jokes; crack a joke; perpetrate a -joke, – pun; make -fun of, – merry with; set the table in a roar etc. (*amuse*) 840; scintillate.

retort, flash back; banter etc. (*ridicule*) *856*; *ridentem dicere verum*; joke at one's expense.

Adj. witty, attic, salty; quick-, nimble-witted; keen, clever, smart, brilliant, pungent, jocular, jocose, funny, waggish, facetious, whimsical, humorous, gilbertian; playful etc. 840; merry and wise; pleasant, sprightly, *spirituel*, sparkling, epigrammatic, full of point, *ben trovato*; comic etc. 853.

Adv. in joke, in jest, in sport, in play.

843. Dullness.—N. dullness, heaviness, flatness; infestivity etc. 837; stupidity etc. 499; want of originality, dearth of ideas.

prose, matter of fact; heavy book, *conte à dormir debout*; platitude.

V. be -dull etc. *adj.*; prose, platitudinize, take *au sérieux*, be caught napping.

render -dull etc. *adj.*; damp, depress, throw cold water on, lay a wet blanket on; fall flat upon the ear; hang fire.

Adj. dull, – as ditch water; dry, insipid, jejune; unentertaining, uninteresting, unlively, unimaginative; heavisome, heavy-gaited; insulse; dry as dust; pros-y, -ing, -aic; matter of fact, commonplace, banal, pointless; 'weary, flat, stale and unprofitable.'

stupid, slow, flat, sluggish, ponderous, humdrum, monotonous; melancholic etc. 837; stolid etc. 499; plodding.

Phr. *Davus sum non Oedipus*.

844. Humorist.—N. humorist, wag, wit, reparteeist, epigrammatist, gag man, punster; *bel esprit*, life of the party; wit-snapper, -cracker, worm; joker, jester, jokesmith, Joe Miller, *drôle de corps, gaillard*, spark, *persiffleur*, banterer.

buffoon, *farceur*, merry-andrew, mime, tumbler, acrobat, mountebank, charlatan, posturemaster, harlequin, punch, *pulcinella*, scaramouch, clown; wearer of the -cap and bells, – motley; motley, fool; pantaloon, gipsy; jack -pudding, – in the green, – a dandy; zany; mad-cap, pickle-herring, witling, caricaturist, *grimacier*.

845. Beauty.—N. beauty, the beautiful, *le beau ideal*, loveliness.

[Science of the perception of beauty] Callaesthetics.

form, elegance, grace, beauty unadorned; symmetry etc. 242; comeliness, fairness etc. *adj.*; pulchritude, polish, gloss; good -effect, – looks; *belle tournure*; bloom, brilliancy, radiance, splendor, gorgeousness, magnificence; sublimi-ty, -fication.

concinnity, delicacy, refinement; charm, *je ne sais quoi*, style, *chic*, swank.

Venus, – of Milo; Aphrodite, Hebe, the Graces, Peri, Houri, Cupid, Apollo, Hyperion, Adonis, Antinous, Narcissus; Helen of Troy.

peacock, butterfly; flower, flow'ret gay, rose, lily, asphodel; garden; flower of, pink of; *bijou*; jewel etc. (*ornament*) 847; work of art.

pleasurableness etc. 829.

beautifying; landscape gardening; decoration etc. 847; calisthenics.

V. be -beautiful etc. *adj.*; shine, beam, bloom; become one etc. (*accord*) 23; set off, grace, flatter one.

render -beautiful etc. *adj.*; beautify; polish, burnish; gild etc. (*decorate*) 847; set out.

'snatch a grace beyond the reach of art.'

Adj. beaut-iful, -eous; handsome; pretty; lovely, graceful, elegant; delicate, dainty, refined, exquisite; fair, personable, comely, seemly; bonny; good-looking; well-favored, -made, -formed, -proportioned; proper, shapely; symmetrical etc. (*regular*) 242; harmonious etc. (*color*) 428; sightly.

fit to be seen, passable, not amiss.

goodly, dapper, tight, jimp; gimp; janty, jaunty; natty, quaint, trim, tidy, neat, spruce, smart, tricksy.

bright, -eyed; rosy-, cherry-cheeked; rosy, ruddy; blooming, in full bloom.

brilliant, shining; beam-y, -ing; sparkling, swanky, splendid, resplendent, dazzling, glowing; glossy, sleek.

showy, specious; rich, gorgeous, superb, magnificent, grand, fine, sublime, imposing; majestic 873.

artistic, -al; aesthetic; pict-uresque, -orial; *fait à piendre*, paintable; well-composed, -grouped, -varied; curious.

enchanting etc. (*pleasure-giving*) 829; attractive etc. (*inviting*) 615; becoming etc. (*accordant*) 23; ornamental etc. 847.

undeformed, undefaced, unspotted; spotless etc. (*perfect*) 650.

846. Ugliness.—N. ugliness etc. *adj.*; deformity, inelegance; disfigurement etc. (*blemsih*) 848; want of symmetry, inconcinnity; distortion etc. 243; squalor etc. (*uncleanness*) 653.

forbidding countenance, vinegar aspect, hanging look, wry face, *'spretae injuria formae.'*

eyesore, object, figure, sight, fright, specter, scarecrow, hag, harridan, satyr, witch, toad, baboon, monster, Caliban, Aesop, *'monstrum horrendum informe ingens cui lumen ademptum.'*

V. be -ugly etc. *adj.*; look ill, grin horribly a ghastly smile, make faces.

render -ugly etc. *adj.*; deface; dis-, de-figure; deform, spoil, distort etc. 243; blemish etc. (*injure*) 659; soil etc. (*render unclean*) 653.

Adj. ugly, — as -sin, — a toad, — a scarecrow, — a dead monkey; plain, bald etc. 226; homely etc. (*unadorned*) 849; ordinary, unornamental, inartistic; unsightly, unseemly, uncomely, unshapely, unlovely; sightless, seemless; not fit to be seen; unbeaut-eous, -iful; beautiless; shapeless etc. (*amorphous*) 241; course; garish, over-decorated etc. 882.

mis-shapen, -proportioned; monstrous; gaunt etc. (*thin*) 203; dumpy etc. (*short*) 201; curtailed of its fair proportions; ill-made, -shaped, -proportioned; crooked etc. (*distorted*) 243; hard-featured, -visaged; ill-, hard-, evil-favored; ill-looking; unprepossessing.

graceless, inelegant; ungraceful, ungainly, uncouth; stiff; rugged, rough, gross, rude, awkward, clumsy, slouching, rickety; gawky; lump-ing, -ish; lumbering; hulk-y, -ing; unwieldy.

squalid, haggard; grim, -faced, -visaged; grisly, ghastly; ghost-, death-like; cadaverous, gruesome.

frightful, hideous, odious, uncanny, forbidding, repellant, repulsive; horri-d, -ble; shocking etc. (*painful*) 830.

foul etc. (*dirty*) 653; dingy etc. (*colorless*) 429; gaudy etc. (*color*) 428; disfigured etc. *v.*; discolored (*blemished*) etc. 848.

847. Ornament.—N. ornament, -ation, -al art; ornat-ture, -eness; adorn-ment, 'decoration, embellishment; architecture.'

garnish, polish, varnish, French polish, gilding, japanning, lacquer, ormolu, enamel.

cosmetics, rouge, powder, lipstick, lip salve, mascara; manicure, nail polish; permanent —, Marcel —, finger-wave.

pattern, diaper, powdering, panelling, graining, pargeting, inlay, detail; texture etc. 329; richness; tracery, molding, beading, reeding, fillet, listel, strapwork, *coquillage*, flourish, *fleur-de-lis*, arabesque, fret, *anthemion*; egg and -tongue, — dart; *astragal*, zigzag, *acanthus, cartouche*; pilaster etc. (*projection*) 250; cyma, ogee.

em-, broidery, needlework; knitting, crochet, tatting, brocade, *brocatelle*, beads, bugles; galloon, lace, gimp, *guipure*, fringe, trapping, border, edging, insertion, *motif*, trimming; *passementerie*; drapery, hanging, tapestry, arras; millinery, ermine.

wreath, festoon, garland, lei, chaplet, flower, nosegay, *bouquet*, posy, 'daisies pied and violets blue.'

tassle, knot; shoulder-knot, *épaulette*, epaulet, aigulet, *aiguilette*, frog; star, rosette, bow; feather, plume, *panache*, *aigrette*.

jewel, -ry, -lery; bijoutry; *bijou*, *-terie*; diadem, tiara; pendant, trinket, locket, necklace, armilla, bracelet, bangle, armlet, anklet, ear-, nose- ring, carcanet, chain, *châtelaine*, albert, brooch, torque.

gem, precious stone; diamond, brilliant, beryl, aquamarine, alexandrite, cat's eye, emerald, calcedony, chrysoprase, cornelian, jasper, bloodstone, agate, heliotrope; girasol, -e; onyx, plasma; sard, -onyx; garnet, lapis-lazuli, opal, peridot, chrysolite, sapphire, ruby; spinel, -le; balais; oriental —, topaz; turquois, -e; zircon, jacinth, hyacinth, carbuncle, amethyst; moonstone; pearl, coral.

finery, frippery, gewgaw, gimcrack, knick-knack, tinsel, spangle, sequin, *clinquant*, pinch-beck, paste; excess of ornament etc. (*vulgarity*) 851; gaud, pride, ostentation; frills and furbelows.

illustration, illumination, *vignette*; *fleuron*; head-, tail-piece; *cul-de-lampe*; flowers of rhetoric etc. 577; work of art, article of vertu, *bric-à-brac*, curio, *bibelot*.

V. ornament, embellish, enrich, decorate, adorn, beautify, adonize.

smarten, furbish, polish, gild, varnish, whitewash, enamel, japan, lacquer, paint, grain.

garnish, trim, dizen, bedizen, prink, prank; trick —, fig- out; deck, bedeck, dight, bedight, array; dress, — up, preen, spruce up, titivate; spangle, bespangle, powder; embroider, work; chase, tool, emboss, fret; emblazon, blazon, illuminate; illustrate.

become etc. (*accord with*) 23.

Adj. ornamented, beautified etc. *v.*; ornate, rich, gilt, begilt, tesselated, enamelled, inlaid; festooned; topiary.

smart, gay, tricksy, flowery, glittering; new-gilt, -spangled; fine, — as -a Mayday queen, — fivepence, — a carrot fresh scraped; pranked out, bedight, well-groomed.

in full dress etc. (*fashion*) 852; *en grande -tenue*, — *toilette*; in best bib and tucker, in Sunday best, *endimanché*; dressed to advantage.

showy, flashy; gaudy etc. (*vulgar*) 851; garish; gorgeous.

ornamental, decorative; becoming etc. (*accordant*) 23.

848. Blemish.—N. blemish, disfigurement, deformity; defect etc. (*imperfection*) 651; flaw; injury etc. (*deterioration*) 659; spots on the sun; eyesore.

stain, blot, slur; spot, -tiness; speck, -le; blur, freckle, mole, *macula*, patch, blotch, birthmark, blain, maculation, tarnish, smudge, smear; dirt etc. 653; bruise, black eye, scar, wem; pustule; excrescence, pimple etc. (*protuberance*) 250.

V. disfigure etc. (*injure*) 659; speckle; render ugly etc. 846.

Adj. pitted, freckled, discolored, bloodshot, bruised, disfigured; stained etc. *n.*; imperfect etc. 651; injured etc. (*deteriorated*) 659.

849. Simplicity.—N. simplicity; plain-, homeli-ness; undress, nudity, nakedness, beauty unadorned, chastity, chasteness.

V. be -simple etc. *adj.*

render -simple etc. *adj.*; simplify, chasten, strip of ornament.

Adj. simple, plain; home-ly, -spun; ordinary, household.

natural, unaffected; free from -affectation, – ornament; *simplex munditiis*; *sans façon, en déshabillé*, nude, naked.

chaste, inornate, severe.

un-adorned, -ornamented, -decked, -garnished, -arranged, -trimmed, -varnished.

bald, flat, dull, blank.

850. Taste. [Good taste.]—**N.** taste; good –, refined –, cultivated- taste; delicacy, refinement, fine feeling, gust, *gusto*, tact, *finesse*; nicety etc. (*discrimination*) 465; polish, elegance, grace.

virtu; dilettanteism, virtuosity; fine art; cul-ture, -ivation.

[Science of taste] esthetics.

man of -taste etc.; *connoisseur*, judge, critic, *conoscente, virtuoso, amateur, dilettante*, Aristarchus, Corinthian, *arbiter elegantarum*, stagirite, euphemist.

'caviar to the general.'

V. appreciate, judge, criticize, discriminate etc. 465.

Adj. in good taste; tasteful, tasty; unaffected, pure, chaste, classical, attic; cultivated, refined; dainty; esthetic, artistic; elegant etc. 578; euphemistic.

to one's -taste, – mind; after one's fancy; *comme il faut*; *tiré à quatre épingles*.

Adv. elegantly etc. *adj.*

Phr. *nihil tetigit quod non ornavit*.

851. Vulgarity. [Bad taste.]—**N.** vulgar-ity, -ism; barbar-, Vandal-, Gothic-ism; *mauvais goût*, bad taste; Babbittry; *gaucherie*, awkwardness, want of tact; ill-breeding etc. (*discourtesy*) 895; ungentlemanly behavior.

coarseness etc. *adj.*; indecorum, misbehavior.

low-, homeli-ness; low life, *mauvais ton*, rusticity; boorishness etc. *adj.*; brutality; rowdy-, ruffian-, blackguard-ism; ribaldry; slang etc. (*neology*) 563.

bad joke, *mauvaise plaisanterie*.

[Excell of ornament] gaudi-, tawdri-ness; false ornament; finery, frippery, trickery, tinsel, gewgaw, *clinquant*.

rough diamond, tomboy, hoyden, cub, unlicked cub; clown etc. (*commonalty*) 876; Hun, Goth, Vandal, Boeotian; vulgarian; snob, cad, bounder, gent; *parvenu* etc. 876; frump, dowdy; slattern etc. 653.

V. be -vulgar etc. *adj.*; misbehave; talk –, smell of the- shop.

Adj. in bad taste, vulgar, unrefined, gutter.

coarse, indecorus, ribald, gross; unseemly, unbeseeming, unpresentable; *contra bonos mores*; ungraceful etc. (*ugly*) 846.

dowdy, slovenly etc. (*dirty*) 653; ungenteel, shabby genteel; low etc. (*plebeian*) 876; uncourtly; uncivil etc. (*discourteous*) 895; ill-bred, -mannered; underbred; ungentleman-ly, -like; unladylike, unfeminine; wild, – as an unbacked colt.

unkempt, uncombed, untamed, unlicked, unpolished, uncouth, plebeian; incondite; heavy, rude, awkward; home-ly, -spun, -bred; provincial, hick, countrified, rustic, uncultivated, freshwater; boorish, clownish; savage, brutish, blackguard, rowdy, snobbish; barbar-ous, -ic; Gothic, unclassical, doggerel, heathenish, tramontane, outlandish; Bohemian.

obsolete etc. (*antiquated*) 124; unfashionable, old-fashioned, out of date; new-fangled etc. (*unfamiliar*) 83; fantastic, odd etc. (*ridiculous*) 853.

particular; affected etc. 855; meretricious; extravagant, monstrous, horrid; shocking etc. (*painful*) 830.

gaudy, tawdry, bedizened, tricked out, gingerbread; obtrusive, flaunting, loud, flashy, garish, showy.

852. Fashion.—N. fashion, style, *ton*, *bon ton*, society; good –, polite- society; drawing room, civilized life, civilization, town, *beau monde*, high life, court; world; fashionable –, gay- world; Vanity Fair; show etc. (*ostentation*) 822.

manners, breeding etc. (*politeness*) 894; air, demeanor etc. (*appearance*) 448; *savoir faire*; gentlemanliness, gentility, decorum, propriety, *bienséance*; conventions –, dictates- of society; Mrs. Grundy; convention, -ality; punctilio; form, -ality; etiquette, point of etiquette; custom etc. 613; mode, vogue, style, go; rage etc. (*desire*) 865; prevailing taste, *dernier cri*, dress etc. 225.

man –, woman- of -fashion, – the world; height –, pink –, star –, glass –, leader- of fashion; *arbiter elegantiarum* etc. (*taste*) 850; upper ten thousand etc. (*nobility*) 875; *élite* etc. (*distinction*) 873.

V. be -fashionable etc. *adj.*, – the rage etc. *n.*; have a run, pass current.

follow –, conform to –, fall in with- the fashion etc. *n.*; go with the stream etc. (*conform*) 82; *savoir -vivre*, – *faire*; keep up appearances, behave oneself.

set the –, bring into- fashion; give a tone to –, cut a figure in- society, rub shoulders with nobility, keep one's carriage.

Adj. fashionable; in -fashion etc. *n.*; *à la mode, comme il faut*; admitted –, admissible- in -society etc. *n.*; presentable, decorous, punctilious, conventional etc. (*customary*) 613; genteel; well-bred, -mannered, -behaved, -spoken; gentleman-like, -ly; ladylike; civil, polite etc. (*courteous*) 894.

polished, refined, thoroughbred, courtly; *distingué*, aristocratic, unembarrassed, poised, *dégagé*; ja-, jau-nty; dashing, fast, showy, high toned, toney.

modish, stylish, in the latest style, *recherché*; new-fangled etc. (*unfamiliar*) 83.

in -court, – full, – evening- dress; *en grande tenue* etc. (*ornament*) 847.

Adv. fashionably etc. *adj.*; for fashion's sake.

853. Ridiculousness.—N. ridiculousness etc. *adj.*; comical-, odd-ity etc. *adj.*; extravagance, drollery.

farce, comedy; burlesque etc. (*ridicule*) 856; buffoonery etc. (*fun*) 840; frippery; doggerel verses; Irish bull, Hibernianism, Hibernicism; Spoonerism; absurdity etc. 497; bombast etc. (*unmeaning*) 517; anticlimax, bathos; monstrosity etc. (*unconformity*) 83; laughing stock etc. 857.

V. be -ridiculous etc. *adj.*; pass from the sublime to the ridiculous; make one laugh; play the fool, make a fool of oneself, commit an absurdity.

play a joke on, make a -fool of, – sucker of, – monkey of.

Adj. ridiculous, ludicrous; comic, -al; droll, funny, laughable, *pour rire*, grotesque, farcical, odd; whimsical, – as a dancing bear; fanciful, fantastic, queer, rum, quizzical, waggish, quaint, *bizarre*; eccentric etc. (*unconformable*) 83; strange, outlandish, out of the way, *baroque*, *rocaille*, rococo; awkward etc. (*ugly*) 846.

absurd, extravagant, *outré*, monstrous, preposterous, bombastic, inflated, stilted, burlesque, mock heroic.

drollish; serio-, tragic-comic; gimcrack, contemptible etc. (*unimportant*) 643; doggerel; ironical etc. (*derisive*) 856; risible.

Phr. *'risum teneatis amici?' rideret Heraclitus.*

854. Fop.—N. fop, fine gentleman; swell; dand-y, -iprat; exquisite, coxcomb, toff, beau, macaroni, blade, blood, buck, man about town, fast man; fribble, jemmy, spark, popinjay, puppy, prig, *petit maître*; jacka-napes, -dandy; man milliner; Jemmy Jessamy, carpet-knight, masher, Dundreary, Johnnie, dude.

belle, fine lady, *coquette*, flirt.

855. Affectation.—N. affectation; affectedness etc. *adj.*; acting a part etc. *v.*; pretence etc. (*falsehood*) 544; (*ostentation*) 882; boasting etc. 884.

charlatanism, quakery, shallow profundity, humbug, pretension, airs, pedantry, purism, precisianism, euphuism, prunes and prisms; teratology etc. (*altiloquence*) 577.

mannerism, *simagrée*, grimace.

conceit, foppery, dandyism, man millinery, coxcombry, puppyism.

stiffness, formality, buckram; prudery, demureness, coquetry, mock modesty, *minauderie*, sentimentalism; *mauvaise honte*, false shame.

affector, performer, actor; pedant, pedagogue, *doctrinaire*, purist, euphuist, mannerist; shoneen; *grimacier*; lump of affectation, *précieuse ridicule*, *bas bleu*, blue stocking, poetaster; prig, hypocrite; charlatan etc. (*deceiver*) 548; *petit maître* etc. (*fop*) 854; flatterer etc. 935; *coquette*, prude, puritan; precisian, formalist.

V. affect, act a part, put on; give oneself airs etc. (*arrogance*) 885; boast etc. 884; coquet; simper, mince, attitudinize, strike a pose, pose; flirt a fan; over-act, -play, -do.

Adj. affected, full of affectation, pretentious, pedantic, stilted, stagey, theatrical, big-sounding, *ad captandum*, canting, insincere.

not natural, unnatural; self-conscious; *maniéré*; artificial; over-wrought, -done, -acted; euphuistic etc. 577.

stiff, starch, formal, prim, smug, demure, *tiré à quatre épingles*, quakerish, puritanical, prudish, pragmatical, priggish, conceited, coxcomical, foppish, dandified; fini-cal, -kin, -cky, mincing, simpering, namby-pamby, sentimental, languishing.

856. Ridicule.—N. ridicule, derision; sardonic -smile, – grin; irrision; snigger; scoffing etc. (*disrespect*) 929; mockery, quiz, banter, irony, *persiflage*, raillery, chaff, *badinage*; quizzing etc. *v.*

squib, satire, skit, quip, quib, grin.

parody, burlesque, travesty; farce etc. (*drama*) 599; caricature, take-off.

buffoonery etc. (*fun*) 840; practical joke, horse-play.

V. ridicule, deride; laugh at, grin at, smile at; snigger; laugh in one's sleeve; banter, rally, chaff, joke, twit, quiz, poke fun at, jolly, roast, rag; fleer; play –, play tricks- upon; fool, – to the top of one's bent; show up.

satirize, parody, caricature, burlesque, travesty.

turn into ridicule; make merry with; make -fun, – game, – a fool, – an April fool- of; rally; scoff etc. (*disrespect*) 929.

raise a laugh etc. (*amuse*) 840; play the fool, make a fool of oneself.

be ridiculous etc. 853.

Adj. deris-ory, -ive; mock; sarcastic, ironical, quizzical, burlesque, Hudibrastic; scurrilous etc. (*disrespectful*) 929.

Adv. in -ridicule etc. *n.*

857. Laughing-stock. [Object and cause of ridicule.]**—N.** laughing-, jesting-, gazing-stock; butt, game, fair game; April fool etc. (*dupe*) 547.

original, oddity; queer –, odd- fish; quiz, square toes; old –, fogey *or* fogy.

monkey; buffoon etc. (*jester*) 844; pantomimist etc. (*actor*) 599.

jest etc. (*wit*) 842.

858. Hope.—N. hope, -s; desire etc. 865; fervent hope, sanguine expectation, trust, confidence, reliance; faith etc. (*belief*) 484; affiance, assurance; secur-eness, -ity; reassurance.

good -omen, – auspices; promise; well-grounded hopes; good –, bright- prospect; clear sky.

as-, pre-sumption; anticipation etc. (*expectation*) 507.

hopefulness, buoyancy, optimism, enthusiasm, heart of grace, aspiration; optimist, utop-ian, -ist; Pollyanna.

castles in the air, *châteaux en Espagne*, hope chest, *le pot au lait*, Utopia, millennium; day –, golden- dream; dream of Alnaschar; airy hopes, fool's paradise; *mirage* etc. (*fallacies of vision*) 443; fond hope.

beam –, ray –, gleam –, glimmer –, dawn –, flash –, star- of hope; cheer; bit of blue sky, silver lining of the cloud, bottom of Pandora's box, balm in Gilead.

anchor, sheet-anchor, main-stay; staff etc. (*support*) 215; heaven etc. 981.

V. hope, trust, confide, rely on, put one's trust in, lean upon; pin one's -hope, – faith- upon etc. (*believe*) 484.

feel –, entertain –, harbor –, indulge –, cherish –, feed –, foster –, nourish –, encourage –, cling to –, live in- hope etc. *n.*; see land; feel –, rest- -assured, – confident etc. *adj.*

presume; promise oneself; expect etc. (*look forward to*) 507.

hope for etc. (*desire*) 865; anticipate.

be -hopeful etc. *adj.*; look on the bright side of, view on the sunny side, make the best of it, hope for the best; put -a good, – a bold, – the best- face upon; keep one's spirits up; take heart, – of grace; be of good -heart, – cheer; flatter oneself, lay the flattering unction to one's soul.

catch at a straw, hope against hope, count one's chickens before they are hatched.

give –, inspire –, raise –, hold out- hope etc. *n.*; raise expectations; encourage, hearten, cheer, assure, reassure, buoy up, embolden; promise, bid fair, augur well, be in a fair way, look up, flatter, tell a flattering tale.

Adj. hoping etc. *v.*; in -hopes etc. *n.*; hopeful, confident; secure etc. (*certain*) 484; sanguine, in good heart, buoyed up, buoyant, elated, flushed, exultant, enthusiastic; utopian.

unsus-pecting, -picious; fearless, free –, exempt from- -fear, – suspicion, – distrust, – despair; undespairing, self-reliant.

probable, on the high road to; within sight of -shore, – land; promising, propitious; of –, full of- promise; of good omen; auspicious, *de bon augure*; reassuring; encouraging, cheering, inspiriting, looking up, bright, roseate, *couleur de rose*, rose-colored.

Adv. hopefully etc. *adj.*

Phr. *nil desperandum*; never say die, *dum spiro spero, latet scintillula forsan*, all is for the best, *spero meliora*; the wish being father to the thought; 'hope told a flattering tale;' *rusticus expectat dum defluat amnis*.

859. Hopelessness. [Absence, want, or loss of hope.]—**N.** hopelessness etc. *adj.*; despair, desperation; despondency etc. (*dejection*) 837; pessimism.

hope deferred, dashed hopes; vain expectation etc. (*disappointment*) 509.

airy hopes etc. 858; forlorn hope; bad -job, – business; *enfant perdu*; gloomy –, black spots in the- horizon; slough of Despond, cave of Despair.

Job's comforter; bird of -bad, – ill-omen.

V. despair; lose –, give up –, abandon –, relinquish- -all hope, – the hope of; give -up, – over; yield to despair; falter; despond etc. (*be dejected*) 837; *jeter le manche après la cognée*.

inspire –, drive to- despair etc. *n.*; disconcert; dash –, crush –, shatter –, destroy- one's hopes; hope against hope.

Adj. hopeless, desperate, despairing, in despair, *au désespoir*, forlorn; inconsolable etc. (*dejected*) 837; broken-hearted.

out of the question, not to be thought of; impracticable etc. 471; past -hope, – cure, – mending, – recall; at one's last gasp etc. (*death*) 360; given -up, – over.

incurable, cureless, immedicable, remediless, beyond remedy; incorrigible; irre-parable, -mediable, -coverable, -versible, -trievable, -claimable, -deemable, -vocable; ruined, undone; immitigable.

unpromising, unpropitious; inauspicious, ill-omened, threatening, clouded over, lowering, ominous.

Phr. '*lasciate ogni speranza voi ch' entrate*;' its days are numbered; the worst come to the worst.

860. Fear.—**N.** fear, timidity, diffidence, want of confidence; apprehensive-, fearful-ness etc. *adj.*; solicitude, anxiety, care, apprehension, misgiving; mistrust etc. (*doubt*) 485; suspicion, qualm; hesitation etc. (*irresolution*) 605.

nervous-, restless-ness etc. *adj.*; in-, dis-quietude; flutter, trepidation, fear and trembling, perturbation, tremor, quivering, shaking, trembling, throbbing heart, palpitation, ague fit, cold sweat; abject fear etc. (*cowardice*) 862; mortal funk, heart-sinking, despondency; despair etc. 859.

fright; affright, -ment; alarm, pavor, dread, awe, terror, horror, dismay, consternation, panic, scare, stampede [of horses].

intimidation, terrorism, reign of terror.

[Object of fear] bug-bear, -aboo; scarecrow; hobgoblin etc. (*demon*) 980; daymare, nightmare, Gorgon, Medusa, mormo, ogre, Hurlothrumbo, raw head and bloody bones, fee faw fum, *bête noire, enfant terrible*.

alarmist etc. (*coward*) 862.

V. fear, stand in awe of; be -afraid etc. *adj.*; have -qualms etc. *n.*; apprehend, sit upon thorns, eye askance; distrust etc. (*disbelieve*) 485.

hesitate etc. (*be irresolute*) 605; falter, funk, cower, crouch; skulk etc. (*cowardice*) 862; let 'I dare not' wait upon 'I would;' take -fright, alarm; start, wince, flinch, shy, shrink; fly etc. (*avoid*) 623.

tremble, shake; shiver, – in one's shoes; shudder, flutter; shake –, tremble- -like an aspen leaf, – all over; quake, quaver, quiver, quail; get the wind up.

grow –, turn- pale; blench, stand aghast; not dare to say one's soul is one's own.

inspire –, excite- -fear, – awe; raise apprehensions; give –, raise –, sound- an alarm; alarm, startle, scare, cry 'wolf,' disquiet, dismay; fright, -en; affright, terrify; astound; frighten from one's propriety; frighten out of one's -wits, – senses, – seven senses; awe; strike -all of a heap, – an awe into, – terror; harrow up the soul, appal, unman, petrify, horrify.

make one's -flesh creep, – hair stand on end, – blood run cold, – teeth chatter; chill one's spine; take away –, stop- one's breath; make one -tremble etc.

haunt, obsess, beset; prey –, weigh- on the mind.

put in -fear, – bodily fear; terrorize, intimidate, cow, daunt, over-awe, abash, deter, discourage; browbeat, bully; threaten etc. 909.

Adj. fearing etc. *v.*; frightened etc. *v.*; in -fear, – a fright etc. *n.*; haunted with the -fear etc. *n.*- of.

afraid, fearful; tim-id, -orous; nervous, diffident, coy, faint-hearted, tremulous, shaky, afraid of one's shadow, apprehensive, restless, fidgety; more frightened than hurt.

aghast; awe-, horror-, terror-, panic- -struck, -stricken; frightened to death, white as a sheet; pale, – as -death, – ashes, – a ghost; breathless, in hysterics.

inspiring fear etc. *v.*; alarming; formidable, redoubtable; perilous etc. (*danger*) 665; portentous; fear-ful, -some; dread, -ful; fell; dire, -ful; shocking; terri-ble, -fic; tremendous; horri-d, -ble, -fic; ghastly; awful, awe-inspiring, eerie, weird; revolting etc. (*painful*) 830.

Adv. *in terrorem.*

Int. 'angels and ministers of grace defend us!'

Phr. *ante tubam trepidat*; *horresco referens*, one's heart failing one, *obstupui steteruntque comae et vox faucibus haesit.*

861. Courage. [Absence of fear.]—**N.** courage, bravery, valor; resolute-, bold-ness etc. *adj.*; spirit, daring, gallantry, intrepidity; contempt –, defiance- of danger; derring-do; audacity; rashness etc. 863; dash; defiance etc. 715; confidence, self-reliance.

man-liness, -hood; nerve, pluck, mettle, game; heart, – of grace; spunk, gameness, grit, face, virtue, hardihood, fortitude; firmness etc. (*stability*) 150; heart of oak; bottom, backbone etc. (*perseverance*) 604*a*.

resolution etc. (*determination*) 604; tenacity, bull-dog courage.

prowess, heroism, chivalry.

exploit, feat, achievement; heroic -deed, – act; bold stroke.

man, – of mettle; hero, demigod, paladin, heroine, Amazon, Hector, Joan of Arc; lion, tiger, panther, bulldog; game-, fighting-cock; bully, fire-eater etc. 863; dare-devil.

V. be -courageous etc. *adj.*; dare, venture, make bold; face –, front –, affront –, confront –, brave –, defy –, despise –, mock- danger; look in the face; look -full, – boldly, – danger- in the face; face; meet, – in front; brave, beard; defy etc. 715.

take –, muster –, summon up –, pluck up- courage; nerve oneself, take heart; take –, pluck up- heart of grace; hold up one's head, screw one's courage to the sticking place; come -to, – up to- the scratch; stand, – to one's guns, – fire, – against; bear up – against; hold out etc. (*persevere*) 604*a*.

put a bold face upon; show –, present- a bold front, face the music; envisage; show fight.

bell the cat, take the bull by the horns, beard the lion in his den, march up to the cannon's mouth, go through fire and water, run the gauntlet, go over the top.

give –, infuse –, inspire- courage; reassure, encourage, embolden, inspirit, cheer, hearten, nerve, put upon one's mettle, rally, raise a rallying cry; pat on the back, make a man of, keep in countenance.

Adj. courageous, brave; val-iant, -orous; gallant, intrepid; spirit-ed, -ful; high-spirited, -mettled; mettlesome, game, plucky; man-ly, -ful; resolute; stout, -hearted; iron-, lion-hearted; heart of oak; Penthesilean.

bold, – spirited; daring, audacious; fear-, daunt-, dread-, awe-less; un-daunted, -appalled, -dismayed, -awed, -blenched, -abashed, -*alarmed*, -flinching, -shrinking, -blenching; apprehensive; confident, self-reliant; bold as -a lion, – brass.

enterprising, adventurous; ventur-ous, -esome; dashing, chivalrous; soldierly etc. (*warlike*) 722; heroic.

fierce, savage; pugnacious etc. (*bellicose*) 720.

strong-minded, hardy, doughty; firm etc. (*stable*) 150; determined etc. (*resolved*) 604; dogged, indomitable etc. (*persevering*) 604*a*.

up to, – the scratch; upon one's mettle; reassured etc. *v.*; unfeared, undreaded.

Phr. one's blood being up.

862. Cowardice. [Excess of fear.]—**N.** cowardice, pusillanimity; cowardliness etc. *adj.*; timidity, effeminacy.

poltroonery, baseness; dastard-ness, -y; abject fear, funk; Dutch courage; fear etc. 860; white feather, faint heart.

coward, poltroon, dastard, sneak, recreant; shy –, dunghill- cock; coistril, milksop, white-liver, nidget, cur, craven, one that cannot say 'Boo' to a goose; Bob Acres, Jerry Sneak.

alarm-, terror-, pessim-ist; runagate etc. (*fugitive*) 623; shirker.

V. quail etc. (*fear*) 860; be -cowardly etc. *adj.*, – a coward etc. *n.*; funk; cower, skulk, sneak; flinch, shy, fight shy, slink, turn tail; run away etc. (*avoid*) 623; show the white feather, have cold feet, show a yellow streak.

Adj. coward, -ly; fearful, shy; tim-id, -orous; skittish; poor-spirited, spirit-less, soft, effeminate.

weak-minded; infirm of purpose etc. 605; weak-, faint-, chicken-, lily-, pigeon-hearted; yellow; white-, lily-, milk-livered; milksop, smock-faced; unable to say 'Boo' to a goose.

dastard, -ly; base, craven, sneaking, dunghill, recreant; unwar-, unsoldier-like.

'in face a lion but in heart a deer.'

unmanned; frightened etc. 860.

Int. *sauve qui peut!* devil take the hindmost!

Adv. in fear and trembling, in fear of one's life, in a blue funk.

Phr. *ante tubam trepidat*, one's courage oozing out.

863. Rashness.—**N.** rashness etc. *adj.*; temerity, want of caution, imprudence, indiscretion; over-confidence, presumption, audacity.

precipit-ancy, -ation; impetuosity; levity; foolhardi-hood, -ness; heed-, thought-lessness etc. (*inattention*) 458; carelessness etc. (*neglect*) 460; desperation; Quixotism, knight-errantry; fire-eating.

gam-ing, -bling; blind bargain, leap in the dark, fool's paradise; too many eggs in one basket.

desperado, rashling, mad-cap, dare-devil, Hotspur, fire-eater, bully, *bravo*, Hector, scapegrace, *enfant perdu*; Don Quixote, knight-errant, Icarus; adventurer; gam-bler, -ester; dynamitard.

V. be -rash etc. *adj.*; stick at nothing, play a desperate game; run into danger etc. 665; play with -fire, – edge tools.

carry too much sail, sail too near the wind, ride at single anchor, go out of one's depth.

take a leap in the dark, buy a pig in a poke.

donner tête baissée; knock one's head against a wall etc. (*be unskilful*) 699; rush on destruction; kick against the pricks, tempt Providence, go on a forlorn hope.

count one's chickens before they are hatched; reckon without one's host; catch at straws; trust to –, lean on- a broken reed.

Adj. rash, incautious, indiscreet, injudicious; imprudent, improvident, temerarious; uncalculating; heedless; careless etc. (*neglectful*) 460; without ballast, heels over head; giddy etc. (*inattentive*) 458; wanton, reckless, wild, madcap; desperate, devil-may-care.

hot-blooded, -headed, -brained; head-long, -strong; break-neck; fool-hardy; harebrained; precipitate, impulsive.

over-confident, -weening; ventur-esome, -ous; adventurous, Quixotic; fire-eating, cavalier; free-and-easy.

off one's guard etc. (*inexpectant*) 508.

Adv. post haste, *à corps perdu*, hand over head, *tête baissée*, head- foremost; happen what may.

Phr. neck or nothing, the devil being in one.

864. Caution.—N. caution; cautiousness etc. *adj.*; discretion, prudence, cautel, heed, circumspection, calculation, deliberation; safety first.

foresight etc. 510; vigilance etc. 459; warning etc. 668.

coolness etc. *adj.*; self-possession, -command; presence of mind, *sang froid*; well-regulated mind; worldly wisdom, Fabian policy.

V. be -cautious etc. *adj.*; take -care, – heed, – good care; have a care; mind, – what one is about; be on one's guard etc. (*keep watch*) 459; make assurance double sure; ca' canny.

bespeak etc. (*be early*) 132.

think twice, look before one leaps, keep one's weather eye open, count the cost, look to the main chance, cut one's coat according to one's cloth; feel one's -ground, – way; see how the land lies etc. (*foresight*) 510; wait to see how the cat jumps; bridle one's tongue; *reculer pour mieux sauter* etc. (*prepare*) 673; let well alone, let sleeping dogs lie, *ne pas réveiller le chat qui dort*.

keep out of -harm's way, – troubled waters; keep at a respectful distance, stand aloof; keep –, be- on the safe side.

husband one's resources etc. 636.

caution etc. (*warn*) 668.

Adj. cautious, wary, guarded; on one's guard etc. (*watchful*) 459; *cavendo tutus*; *in medio tutissimus*.

care-, heed-ful; cautelous, stealthy, chary, shy of, circumspect, prudent, canny, safe, non-committal, discreet, politic; sure-footed etc. (*skilful*) 698.

unenterprising, unadventurous, cool, steady, self-possessed; over-cautious.

suspicious, leery, vigilant.

Adv. cautiously, gingerly etc. *adj.*

Int. have a care! look out! *cave canem!*

Phr. *timeo Danaos*; *festina lente*.

865. Desire.—N. desire, wish, fancy, fantasy; want, need, exigency.

mind, inclination, leaning, bent, *animus*, partiality, *penchant*, predilection; propensity etc. 820; willingness etc. 602; liking, love, fondness, relish.

longing, hankering; solicitude, anxiety; yearning, coveting; aspiration, ambition, vaulting ambition; eagerness, zeal, ardor, *empressement*, breathless impatience, over-anxiety; solicitude, impetuosity etc. 825.

appet-ite, -ition, -ence, -ency; sharp appetite, keenness, hunger, stomach, twist; thirst, -iness; drouth, mouth-watering; itch, -ing; prurience, *cacoëthes*, cupidity, lust, concupiscence.

edge of -appetite, – hunger; torment of Tantalus; sweet –, lickerish- tooth; itching palm; longing –, wistful –, sheep's-eye.

avidity; greed, -iness; covetous-, ravenous-ness etc. *adj.*; grasping, craving, canine appetite, rapacity; voracity etc. (*gluttony*) 957.

passion, rage, *furore*, mania, *manie*; inextinguishable desire; dips-, klept-, mon-omania.

[Person desiring] desirer, lover, *amateur*, votary, devotee, aspirant, solicitant, candidate; cormorant etc. 957; sycophant.

[Object of desire] *desideratum*; want etc. (*requirement*) 630; 'consumation devoutly to be wished;' attraction, magnet, allurement, fancy, temptation, seduction, lure, fascination, *prestige*, height of one's ambition, idol; whim, -sey; maggot; hobby, -horse.

Fortunatus's cap, wishing cap, love potion.

V. desire; wish, – for; be -desirous etc. *adj.*; have a -longing etc. *n.*; hope etc. 858.

care for, affect, like, list; take to, cling to, take a fancy to; fancy; prefer etc. (*choose*) 609.

have -an eye, – a mind- to; find it in one's heart etc. (*be willing*) 602; have a fancy for, set one's eyes upon; cast a sheep's eye –, look sweet- upon; take into one's head, have a heart, be bent upon; set one's -cap at, – heart upon, – mind upon; covet.

want, miss, need, lack, desiderate, feel the want of; would fain -have, – do; would be glad of.

be -hungry etc. *adj.*; have a good appetite, play a good knife and fork; hunger –, thirst –, crave –, lust –, itch –, hanker –, run mad- after; raven –, die- for; burn to.

desiderate; sigh –, cry –, gape –, gasp –, pine –, pant –, languish –, yearn –, long –, be on thorns –, hope- for; aspire after; catch at, grasp at, jump at.

woo, court, solicit; fish –, spell –, whistle –, put up- for; ogle.

cause –, create –, raise –, excite –, provoke- desire; whet the appetite; appetize, titillate, allure, attract, take one's fancy, tempt; hold out -temptation, – allurement; tantalize, make one's mouth water, *faire venir l'eau à la bouche*.

gratify desire etc. (*give pleasure*) 829.

Adj. desirous; desiring etc. *v.*; orectic, appetitive; inclined etc. (*willing*) 602; partial to; fain, wishful, optative; anxious, wistful, curious; at a loss for, sedulous, solicitous.

craving, hungry, sharp-set, peckish, ravening, with an empty stomach, esurient, lickerish, thirsty, athirst, parched with thirst, pinched with hunger, famished, dry, drouthy; hungry as a -hunter, – hawk, – horse, – church mouse.

greedy, – as a hog; over-eager, voracious; ravenous, – as a wolf; open-mouthed, covetous, rapacious, grasping, extortionate, exacting, sordid,

alieni appetens; insati-able, -ate; unquenchable, quenchless; omnivorous.
unsatisfied, unsated, unslaked.
eager, avid, keen; burning, fervent, ardent; agog; all agog; breathless; impatient etc. (*impetuous*) 825; bent –, intent –, set- -on, – upon; mad after, *enragé*, rabid, dying for, devoured by desire.
aspiring, ambitious, vaulting, sky-aspiring.
desirable; popular; desired etc. *v.*; in demand; pleasing etc. (*giving pleasure*) 829; appeti-zing, -ble; tantalizing.
Adv. wistfully etc. *adj.*; fain.
Int. would -that, – it were! O for! *esto perpetua!* if only!
Phr. the wish being the father to the thought; *sua cuique voluptas*; *hoc erat in votis*, the mouth watering, the fingers itching; *aut Caesar aut nullus*.

866. Indifference.—N. indifference, neutrality; coldness etc. *adj.*; unconcern, *insouciance, nonchalance*; want of -interest, – earnestness; anorexy, inappetency; apathy etc. (*insensibility*) 823; supineness etc. (*inactivity*) 683; disdain etc. 930; recklessness etc. 863; inattention etc. 458.
V. be -indifferent etc. *adj.*; stand neuter; take no interest in etc. (*insensibility*) 823; have no -desire etc. 865, – taste, – relish- for; not care for; care nothing -for, – about; not care a -straw etc. (*unimportance*) 643 -about, – for; not mind.
set at naught etc. (*make light of*) 483; spurn etc. (*disdain*) 930.
Adj. indifferent, cold, frigid, lukewarm; cool, – as a cucumber; unconcerned, *insouciant*, phlegmatic, *pococurante*, easy-going, devil-may-care, careless, listless, lackadaisical, feckless; half-hearted; un-ambitious, -aspiring, -desirous, -solicitous, -attracted.
un-attractive, -alluring, -desired, -desirable, -cared for, -wished, -valued, all one to.
insipid etc. 391; vain.
Adv. for aught one cares.
Int. never mind.

867. Dislike.—N. dis-like, -taste, -relish, -inclination, -placency.
reluctance; backwardness etc. (*unwillingness*) 603.
repugnance, disgust, queasiness, turn, nausea, loathing; avers-eness, -ation, -ion; abomination, antipathy, abhorrence, horror; mortal –, rooted- -antipathy, – horror; hatred, detestation; hate etc. 898; animosity etc. 900; hydrophobia.
sickener; gall and wormwood etc. (*unsavory*) 395; shuddering, cold sweat.
V. dis-, mis-like, -relish; mind, object to; have rather not, not care for; have –, conceive –, entertain –, take- -a dislike, – an aversion- to; have no -taste, – stomach- for.
shun, avoid etc. 623; eschew; withdraw –, shrink –, recoil- from; not be able to -bear, – abide, – endure; shrug the shoulders at, shudder at, turn up the nose at, look askance at; make a -mouth, – wry face, – grimace; make faces.
loathe, nauseate, abominate, detest, abhor; hate etc. 898; take amiss etc. 900; have enough of etc. (*be satiated*) 869.
cause –, excite- dislike; disincline, repel, sicken; make –, render- sick; turn one's stomach, nauseate, wamble, disgust, shock, stink in the nostrils; go against the -grain, – stomach; stick in the throat; make one's blood run cold etc. (*give pain*) 830; pall.
Adj. disliking etc. *v.*; averse to, loth, adverse; shy of, sick of, out of conceit with; disinclined; heart-, dog-sick; queasy.
disliked etc. *v.*; uncared for, unpopular; out of favor; repulsive, repugnant, repellent; abhorrent, insufferable, fulsome, nauseous; loath-some, -ful; offensive; disgusting etc. *v.*; disagreeable etc. (*painful*) 830; unsavory etc. 395.
Adv. *usque ad nauseam*.
Int. faugh! foh! ugh!

868. Fastidiousness.—N. fastidiousness etc. *adj.*; nicety, meticulosity, hypercriticism, difficulty in being pleased, *friandise*, epicurism, *omnia suspendens naso*.
discrimination, discernment, good taste, perspicacity.
epicure, gourmet.
[Excess of delicacy] prudery, prudishness, primness.
V. be -fastidious etc. *adj.*; split hairs, discriminate, have a sweet tooth.
mince the matter; turn up one's nose at etc. (*disdain*) 930; look a gift horse in the mouth, see spots on the sun.
Adj. fastidious, meticulous, exacting, nice, delicate, *délicat*, finical, finicky, difficult, dainty, lickerish, squeamish, thin-skinned; s-, queasy; hard –, difficult- to please; querulous, particular, over-particular, straitlaced, prudish, prim, scrupulous; censorious etc. 932; hypercritical, discriminating, discerning, perspicacious.
Phr. *noli me tangere*.

869. Satiety.—N. satiety, satisfaction, saturation, repletion, glut, surfeit; weariness etc. 841.
spoiled child; *enfant gâté*; too much of a good thing, *toujours perdrix*; *crambe repetita*.
V. sate, satiate, satisfy, saturate; cloy, quench, slake, pall, glut, gorge, surfeit; bore etc. (*weary*) 841; tire etc. (*fatigue*) 688; spoil.
have -enough of, – quite enough of, – one's fill, – too much of; be -satiated etc. *adj.*
Adj. satiated etc. *v.*; overgorged; *blasé*, used up, sick of, heart-sick.
Int. enough! hold! *eheu jam satis!*

870. Wonder.—N. wonder, marvel; astonish-, amaze-, wonder-, bewilder-ment; amazedness etc. *adj.*; admiration, awe; stup-or, -efaction; stound, fascination; sensation; surprise etc. (*inexpectation*) 508; cynosure.
note of admiration; thaumaturgy etc. (*sorcery*) 992.
V. wonder, marvel, admire; be -surprised etc. *adj.*; start; stare; open –, rub –, turn up- one's eyes; gloar; gape, open one's mouth, hold one's breath; look –, stand- -aghast, – agog; look blank

etc. (*disappointment*) 509; *tomber des nues*; not believe one's -eyes, – ears, – senses.

not be able to account for etc. (*unintelligible*) 519; not know whether one stands on one's head or one's heels.

surprise, astonish, amaze, astound; dumbfound, -er; startle, dazzle; strike, – with -wonder, – awe; electrify; stun, stupefy, petrify, confound, bewilder, flabbergast; stagger, throw on one's beam ends, fascinate, turn the head, take away one's breath, strike dumb; make one's -hair stand on end, – tongue cleave to the roof of one's mouth; make one stare.

take by surprise etc. (*be unexpected*) 508.

be -wonderful etc. *adj.*; beggar –, baffle-description; stagger belief.

Adj. surprised etc. *v.*; aghast, all agog, breathless, agape; open-mouthed; awe-, thunder-, moon-, planet-struck; spell-bound; lost in -amazement, – wonder, – astonishment; struck all of a heap, unable to believe one's senses, like a duck in thunder.

wonderful, wondrous; surprising etc. *v.*; unexpected etc. 508; unheard of; mysterious etc. (*inexplicable*) 519; miraculous; *foudroyant*.

in-describable, -expressible, -effable; unutterable, -speakable.

monstrous, prodigious, stupendous, marvelous; in-conceivable, -credible; in-, un-imaginable; strange etc. (*uncommon*) 83; passing strange.

striking etc. *v.*; over-whelming; wonder-working.

Adv. wonderfully etc. *adj.*; fearfully; for a –, in the name of- wonder; strange to say; *mirabile -dictu*, – visu; to one's great surprise.

with -wonder etc. *n.*, – gaping mouth, – open eyes, – upturned eyes; eyes starting out of one's head.

Int. lo, – and behold! O! hey-day! halloo! what! indeed! really! surely! humph! hem! good -lack, – heavens, – gracious! – lord! by jove! gad so! well a day! dear me! only think! lack-a-daisy! my -stars, – goodness! gracious goodness! goodness gracious! mercy on us! heavens and earth! God bless me! bless -us, – my heart! odzookens! *O gemini!* adzooks! hoity-toity! strong! Heaven save –, bless-the mark! can such things be! zounds! 'sdeath! what -on earth, – in the world! who would have thought it! etc. (*inexpectation*) 508; fancy! did you ever? you don't say so! what do you say to that! how now! where am I? well I'm blowed! etc.

Phr. *vox faucibus haesit*; one's hair standing on end.

871. Expectance. [Absence of wonder.]—**N.** expectan-ce, -cy etc. (*expectation*) 507; calmness, composure, tranquillity, serenity, coolness, imperturbability etc. 826.

nine days' wonder.

V. expect etc. 507; not -be surprised, – wonder etc. 870; *nil admirari*, make nothing of.

Adj. expecting etc. *v.*; unamazed, astonished at nothing, *blasé* etc. (*weary*) 841; unimaginative, calm, serene, imperturbable etc. 826; expected etc. *v.*; foreseen.

common, ordinary etc. (*habitual*) 613.

Int. no wonder; of course; why not?

872. Prodigy.—**N.** prodigy, phenomenon; wonder, -ment; genius, marvel, miracle; freak, monster etc. (*unconformity*) 83; curiosity, lion, infant prodigy, sight, spectacle; *jeu –, coup- de théâtre*; gazing-stock; sign; portent etc. 512.

bursting of a -shell, – bomb; volcanic eruption, peal of thunder; thunder-clap, -bolt.

what no words can paint; wonders of the world; *annus mirabilis*; *dignus vindice nodus*.

873. Repute.—**N.** distinction, mark, name, figure; repute, reputation, character; good –, high-repute; note, notability, notoriety, *éclat*, 'the bubble reputation,' vogue, celebrity; fame, famousness; renown; populairty, *aura popularis*; esteem, approval, approbation etc. 931; credit, *succès d'estime*, *prestige*, talk of the town; name to conjure with.

glory, honor; luster etc. (*light*) 420; illustriouness etc. *adj*.

account, regard, respect; reputableness etc. *adj.*; respectability etc. (*probity*) 939; good -name, – report; fair name.

dignity; stateliness etc. *adj.*; solemnity, grandeur, splendor, nobility, majesty, sublimity.

rank, standing, brevet rank, precedence, *pas*, station, place, *status*; position, – in society; order, degree, *locus standi*, caste, condition.

greatness etc. *adj.*; eminence; height etc. 206; importance etc. 642; pre-, super-eminence; high mightiness, primacy; top of the -ladder, – tree.

elevation; ascent etc. 305; super-, ex-altation; dignification, aggrandizement.

dedication, consecration, enthronement, canonization, apotheosis, deification, celebration, enshrinement, glorification.

hero, man of mark, great card, celebrity, worthy, lion, *rara avis*, notability, somebody; man of rank etc. (*nobleman*) 875; pillar of the -state, – society, – church.

chief etc. (*master*) 745; first fiddle etc. (*proficient*) 700; scholar etc. 492; cynosure, mirror; flower, pink, pearl; paragon etc. (*perfection*) 650; choice and master spirits of the age; *élite*, star, sun, constellation, galaxy.

ornament, honor, feather in one's cap, halo, aureole, nimbus; halo –, blaze- of glory; blushing honors; laurels etc. (*trophy*) 733.

memory, posthumous fame, niche in the temple of fame; immor-tality, -tal name; *magni nominis umbra*.

V. be conscious of glory; be proud of etc. (*pride*) 878; exult etc. (*boast*) 884; be vain of etc. (*vanity*) 880.

be -distinguished etc. *adj.*; shine etc. (*light*) 420; shine forth, figure; make –, cut- a -figure, – dash, – splash.

rival, surpass; out-shine, -rival, -vie, -jump; emulate, vie with, eclipse; throw –, cast- into the shade; overshadow.

live, flourish, glitter, scintillate, flaunt; gain –, acquire- honor etc. *n.*; play first fiddle etc. (*be of importance*) 642; bear the -palm, – bell; lead the way; take -precedence, – the wall of; gain –, win- -laurels, – spurs, – golden opinions etc. (*approbation*) 931; graduate, take one's degree, pass one's examination, win a -scholarship, – fellowship.

make -a, – some- -noise, – noise in the world; leave one's mark, exalt one's horn, star, have a run, be run after; enjoy popularity, come -into vogue, – to the front; raise one's head.

enthrone, signalize, immortalize, deify, exalt to the skies; hand one's name down to posterity.

consecrate; dedicate to, devote to; enshrine, inscribe, blazon, lionize, blow the trumpet, crown with laurel.

confer –, reflect- honor etc. *n.* on; shed a luster on; redound to one's honor, ennoble.

give –, do –, pay –, render- honor to; honor, accredit, pay regard to, dignify, glorify; sing praises to etc. (*approve*) 931; look up to; exalt, aggrandize, elevate, nobilitate.

Adj. distinguished, *distingué*, noted; of -note etc. *n.*; honored etc. *v.*; popular; fashionable etc. 852.

in good odor; in –, in high- favor; reput-, respect-, credit-able.

remarkable etc. (*important*) 642; notable, notorious; celebrated, renowned, in every one's mouth, talked of; fam-ous, -ed; far-famed; conspicuous, to the front; foremost; in the -front rank, – ascendant.

imperishable, deathless, immortal, never fading, *aere perennius*; time-honored.

illustrious, glorious, splendid, brilliant, radiant; bright etc. 420; full-blown; honorific.

eminent, prominent; high etc. 206; in the zenith; at the -head of, – top of the tree; peerless, of the first water; superior etc. 33; super-, pre-eminent.

great, dignified, proud, noble, honorable, worshipful, lordly, grand, stately, august, princely, imposing, solemn, transcendent, majestic, sacred, sublime, heaven-born, heroic, *sans peur et sans reproche*; sacrosanct.

Int. hail! all hail! *ave! viva! vive!* long life to! glory –, honor- be to!

Phr. one's name -being in every mouth, – living for ever; *sic itur ad astra, fama volat, aut Caesar aut nullus*; not to know him argues oneself unknown; none but himself could be his parallel, *palmam qui meruit ferat.*

874. Disrepute.—N. disrepute, discredit; ill-, bad- -repute, -name, -odor, -favor; disapprobation etc. 932; in-gloriousness, derogation; a-, debasement; abjectness etc. *adj.*; degradation, dedecoration; 'a long farewell to all one's greatness;' odium, obloquy, opprobrium, ignominy.

dishonor, disgrace; shame, humiliation; scandal, baseness, vileness; perfidy, turpitude etc. (*improbity*) 940; infamy.

tarnish, taint, defilement, pollution.

stain, blot, spot, blur, stigma, brand, reproach, imputation, slur.

crying –, burning- shame; *scandalum magnatum*, badge of infamy, blot in one's escutcheon; bend –, bar- sinister; champain, point champain; by- word of reproach; Ichabod.

argumentum ad verecundiam; sense of shame etc. 879.

V. be -inglorious etc. *adj.*; incur -disgrace etc. *n.*; have –, earn- a bad name; put –, wear- a halter round one's neck; disgrace –, expose- oneself.

play second fiddle; lose caste; pale one's ineffectual fire; recede into the shade; fall from one's high estate; keep in the background etc. (*modesty*) 881; be conscious of disgrace etc. (*humility*) 879; look -blue, – foolish, – like a fool; cut a -poor, – sorry- figure; laugh on the wrong side of the mouth; make a sorry face, go away with a flea in one's ear, slink away.

cause -shame etc. *n.*; shame, disgrace, put to shame, dishonor; throw –, cast –, fling –, reflect- dishonor etc. *n.* upon; be a -reproach etc. *n.* to; derogate from.

tarnish, stain, blot, sully, taint; discredit, degrade, debase, defile; beggar; expel etc. (*punish*) 972.

impute shame to, brand, post, stigmatize, vilify, defame, slur, cast a slur upon, hold up to shame, send to Coventry; tread –, trample- under foot; show up, drag through the mire, heap dirt upon; reprehend etc. 932.

bring low, put down, snub; take down a peg, – lower, – or two.

obscure, eclipse, outshine, take the shine out of; throw –, cast- into the shade; overshadow; leave –, put- in the background; push into a corner, put one's nose out of joint; put out, – of countenance.

upset, throw off one's center; discompose, disconcert; put to the blush etc. (*humble*) 879.

Adj. disgraced etc. *v.*; blown upon; shorn of -its beams, – one' glory; overcome, down-trodden; loaded with -shame etc. *n.*; in -bad repute etc. *n.*; out of -repute, – favor, – fashion, – countenance; at a discount; under -a cloud, – an eclipse; unable to show one's face; in the -shade, – background; out at elbows, down in the world, down and out.

inglorious; nameless, renownless, obscure, unknown to fame; un-noticed, -noted, -honored, -glorified.

shameful; dis-graceful, -creditable, -reputable; despicable; questionable; unbecoming, unworthy; derogatory; degrading, humiliating, *infra dignitatem*, dedecorous; scandalous, infamous, too bad, unmentionable; ribald, opprobrious; arrant, shocking, outrageous, notorious, shady.

ignominious, scrubby, dirty, abject, vile, beggarly, pitiful, low, mean, shabby; base etc. (*dishonorable*) 940.

Adv. to one's shame be it spoken.

Int. fie! shame! for shame! *proh pudor! O tempora! O mores!* ough! *sic transit gloria mundi!*

875. Nobility.—N. nobility, rank, condition, distinction, optimacy, blood, *pur sang*, birth, high descent, order; quality, gentility; blue blood of Castile; *ancien régime*.

high life, *haut monde*; upper -classes, – ten thousand; *élite*, aristocracy, great folks; fashionable world etc. (*fashion*) 852; salariat.

peer, -age; house of -lords, – peers; lords, – temporal and spiritual; *noblesse*; baronage, knightage; noble, -man; lord, -ling; grandee, *magnifico, hidalgo*; don, -ship; aristocrat, swell, three-tailed bashaw; gentleman, squire, squireen, patrician, laureate.

gentry, gentlefolk; squirarchy, better sort, *magnates, primates, optimates*.

king etc. (*master*) 745; prince, crown prince, *Dauphin*; duke; marquis, -ate; earl, viscount, baron, thane, banneret; baronet, -cy; knight, -hood; count, armiger, laird; sig-, seig-nior; esquire, boyar, margrave, vavasor, sheik, emir, ameer, scherif, *pasha*, effendi, sahib.

queen etc. 745; princess, begum, duchess, marchioness; countess etc.; lady, dame.

personage –, man- of -distinction, – mark, – rank; nota-bles, -bilities; celebrity, big-wig, magnate, great man, star; *magni nominis umbra*; 'every inch a king;' grand Panjandrum

V. be -noble etc. *adj.*

Adj. noble, exalted; of -rank etc. *n.*; princely, titled, patrician, aristocratic; high-, well-born; of gentle blood; genteel, *comme il faut*, gentlemanlike, courtly etc. (*fashionable*) 852; highly respectable.

Adv. in high quarters.

876. Commonalty.—N. commonalty, democracy; obscruity; low -condition, – life, – society, – company; *bourgeoisie*; mass of -the people, – society; Brown, Jones, and Robinson; Tom, Dick, and Harry; lower –, humbler- -classes, – orders; vulgar –, common- herd; rank and file, *hoc genus omne*; the -many, – general, – crowd, – people, – populace, – multitude, – million, – masses, – mobility, – peasantry; king Mob; proletariat, *fruges consumere nati*, great unwashed; man in the street

mob; rabble, – rout; chaff, rout, horde, *canaille*; scum –, *residuum* –, dregs- of -the people, – society; swinish multitude, *faex populi*; *profanum* –, *ignobile- vulgus*; vermin, riff-raff, tag-rag and bobtail; small fry.

commoner, one of the people, democrat, plebeian, republican, proletary, *prolétaire*, *roturier*, Mr. Snooks, *bourgeois*, *épicier*, Philistine, cockney; *grisette*, *demi-monde*.

peasant, countryman, boor, carle, churl; vill-ain, -ein; serf, kern, tyke, tike, chuff, ryot, fellah; longshoreman; swain, clown, hind; clod, -hopper; hobnail, yokel, hick, rube, cider squeezer, bog-trotter, bumpkin; ploughman, -boy; rustic, chawbacon, tiller of the soil; hewers of wood and drawers of water, groundling; gaffer, loon, put, cub, Tony Lumpkin, looby, lout, under-ling; *gamin*, guttersnipe, street arab, mudlark; rough, rowdy, ruffian, roughneck; pot-wallopper, slubberdegullion; vulgar –, low- fellow; cad, curmudgeon.

upstart, *parvenu*, *nouveau-riche*, skipjack; nobody, – one knows; *hesterni quirites*, *pessoribus orti*; *bo. ~eois gentilhomme*, *novus homo*, snob, gent, mushroom, no one knows who, adventurer; man of straw.

beggar, panhandler, gaberlunzie, muckworm, mudlark, *sans-culotte*, raff, tatterdemalion, caitiff, ragamuffin, Pariah, outcast of society, tramp, weary Willie, bum, vagabond, *chiffonaier*, rag-picker, Cinderella, cinderwench, scrub, jade; boots, gossoon.

Goth, Vandal, Hottentot, savage, barbarian, Yahoo; unlicked cub, rough diamond.

barbar-ousness, -ism; Boeotia.

V. be -ignoble etc. *adj.*, – nobody etc. *n.*

Adj. ignoble, common, mean, low, base, vile, sorry, scrubby, beggarly, below par; no great shakes etc. (*unimportant*) 643; home-ly, -spun; vulgar, low-minded; snobbish, *parvenu*.

plebeian, proletarian; of -low, – mean- -parentage, – origin, extraction; low-, base-, earth-born, low bred; mushroom, dunghill, risen from the ranks; unknown to fame, obscure, untitled.

rustic, uncivilized; lout-, boor-, clown-, churl-, brut-, raff-ish; rude, unlicked, unpolished.

barbar-ous, -ian, -ic, -esque; cockney, born within sound of Bow bells.

underling, menial, servile, subaltern.

Adv. below the salt.

877. Title.—N. title, honor; knighthood etc. (*nobility*) 875.

royal –, serene- highness, excellency, grace; lordship, worship, Rt. Hon., rever-ence, -end; esquire, sir; madam, *madame*; master, mistress, Mr., Mrs., *signor*, *señor*, *Mein Herr*, *mynheer*; your –, his- honor; handle to one's name.

decoration, laurel, palm, wreath, garland, bays, medal, ribbon, riband, blue ribbon, *cordon*, cross, crown, coronet, star, garter; feather, – in one's cap; chevron, epaulet, *épaulette*, colors, cockade; livery; order, arms, armorial bearings, shield, scutcheon, crest, reward etc. 973.

878. Pride.—N. dignity, self-respect, *mens sibi conscia recti*.

pride; haughtiness etc. *adj.*; high notions, *hauteur*; vainglory, crest; arrogance etc. (*assumption*) 885; pomposity etc. 882.

proud man, highflier; fine -gentleman, – lady; *grande dame*.

V. be -proud etc. *adj.*; put a good face on; look one in the face; stalk abroad, perk oneself up; presume, swagger, strut; rear –, lift up –, hold up- one's head; hold one's head high, look big, take the wall, 'bear like the Turk no rival near the throne,' carry with a high hand; ride the –, mount on one's- high horse; set one's back up, bridle, toss the head; give oneself airs etc. (*assume*) 885; boast etc. 884.

pride oneself on; glory in, take pride in; pique –, plume –, hug oneself; stand upon, be proud of; put a good face on; not -hide one's light under a bushel, – put one's talent in a napkin; not think small beer of oneself etc. (*vanity*) 880.

Adj. dignified; stately; proud, -crested; lordly, baronial; lofty-minded; high-souled, -minded, -mettled, -handed, -plumed, -flown, -toned.

haughty, paughty, insolent, lofty, high, mighty, swollen, puffed up, flushed, blown; vain-glorious; purse-proud, fine; proud as -a peacock, Lucifer; bloated with pride.

supercilious, disdainful, bumptious, magisterial, imperious; high-handed, – and mighty; overweening, consequential; arrogant etc. 885; unblushing etc. 880.

stiff, -necked; starch; perked –, stuck- up; in buckram, straitlaced; prim etc. (*affected*) 855.

on one's -high horses, – tight ropes, – high ropes; on stilts; *en grand seigneur*.

Adv. with head erect, with one's nose in the air.

Phr. *odi profanum vulgus et arceo*.

879. Humility.—N. hum-ility, -bleness; meek-, low-ness; lowli-ness, -hood; abasement, self-abasement, -effacement; submission etc. 725; resignation.

condescension; affability etc. (*courtesy*) 894.

modesty etc. 881; verecundity, blush, suffusion, confusion; sense of -shame, – disgrace; humiliation, mortification; let –, set- down.

V. be -humble etc. *adj.*; deign, vouchsafe, condescend; humble –, demean- oneself; stoop, – to conquer; carry coals; submit etc. 725; submit with a good grace etc. (*brook*) 826; yield the palm.

lower one's -tone, – note; sing small, draw in one's horns, sober down; hide one's -face, – diminished head; not dare to show one's face, take shame to oneself, not have a word to say for oneself; feel –, be conscious of- -shame, – disgrace; drink the cup of humiliation to the dregs; eat -humble pie, – one's words, – dirt; be humiliated, receive a snub.

blush -for, – up to the eyes; redden, change color; color up; hang one's head, look foolish, feel small.

render humble; humble, humiliate; let –, set –, take –, tread –, frown- down; snub, abash, abase, make one sing small, strike dumb; teach one -his distance, – his place; take down a peg, – lower; throw –, cast- into the shade etc. 874; stare –, put- out of countenance; put to the blush; confuse, ashame, mortify, disgrace, crush; send away with a flea in one's ear.

get a set down.

Adj. humble, lowly, meek; modest etc. 881; humble-, sober-minded; unoffended; submissive etc. 725; servile etc. 886.

condescending; affable etc. (*courteous*) 894.

humbled etc. *v.*; bowed down, resigned; abashed, ashamed, dashed; out of countenance; down in the mouth; down on one's -knees, – marrow-bones; humbled in the dust, brow-beaten; chap-, crest-fallen; dumbfoundered, flabbergasted, struck all of a heap.

shorn of one's glory etc. (*disrepute*) 874.

Adv. with -downcast eyes, – bated breath, – bended knee; on all fours, on one's feet.

under correction, with due deference.

Phr. I am your -obedient, – very humble- servant; my service to you.

880. Vanity.—N. vanity; conceit, -edness; self-conceit, -complacency, -confidence, -sufficiency, -esteem, -love, -approbation, -praise, -glorification, -laudation, -gratulation, -applause, -admiration; *amour-propre*; selfishness etc. 943.

airs, pretensions, mannerism; egotism; prigg-ism, -ishness; coxcombery, gaudery, vainglory, elation; pride etc. 878; ostentation etc. 882; assurance etc. 885.

vox et praeterea nihil; *cheval de bataille*.

ego-ist, -tist; peacock, coxcomb etc. 854; Sir Oracle etc. 887.

V. be -vain etc. *adj.*, – vain of; pique oneself etc. (*pride*) 878; lay the flattering unction to one's soul.

have -too high, – an overweening- opinion of -oneself, – one's talents; blind oneself as to one's own merit; not think -small beer, – *vin ordinaire*- of oneself; put oneself forward; fish for compliments; give oneself airs etc. (*assume*) 885; boast etc. 884.

render -vain etc. *adj.*; inspire with -vanity etc. *n.*; inflate, puff up, turn up, turn one's head.

Adj. vain, – as a peacock; conceited, assured, overweening, pert, forward, perky; vain-glorious, high-flown; ostentatious etc. 882; puffed up, inflated, flushed.

self-satisfied, -confident, -sufficient, -flattering, -admiring, -applauding, -glorious, -opinionated; *entêté* etc. (*wrong-headed*) 481; wise in one's own conceit, pragmatical, overwise, pretentious, priggish; egotistic, -al; *soi-disant* etc. (*boastful*) 884; arrogant etc. 885.

un-abashed, -blushing; un-constrained, -ceremonious; free and easy.

Adv. vainly etc. *adj.*

Phr. how we apples swim!

881. Modesty.—N. modesty; humility etc. 879; diffidence, timidity; retiring disposition, unobtrusiveness, bashfulness etc. *adj.*; *mauvaise honte*; blush, -ing; verecundity; self-knowledge.

reserve, constraint; demureness etc. *adj.*; blushing honors.

V. be -modest etc. *adj.*; retire, reserve oneself; give way to; draw in one's horns etc. 879; hide one's face.

keep -private, – in the background, – one's distance; pursue the noiseless tenor of one's way, 'do good by stealth and blush to find it fame,' hide one's light under a bushel, cast a sheep's eye.

Adj. modest, diffident; humble etc. 879; timid, timorous, bashful; shy, nervous, skittish, coy, sheepish, shamefaced, blushing, over-modest.

unpreten-ding, -tious; un-obtrusive, -assuming, -ostentatious, -boastful, -aspiring; poor in spirit.

out of countenance etc. (*humbled*) 879.

reserved, constrained, demure.

Adv. humbly etc. *adj.*; quietly, privately; without -ceremony, – beat of the drum; *sans façon*.

882. Ostentation.—N. ostentation, display, show, flourish, parade, *étalage*, pomp, array, state, solemnity; dash, splash, glitter, strut, swank, side, swagger, pomposity; preten-se, -sions; showing off; fuss.

magnificence, splendor; *coup d'oeil*; grand doings.

coup de théâter; stage -effect, – trick; clap-trap; *mise en scène*; *tour de force*; *chic*.

demonstration, flying colors; tomfoolery; flourish of trumpets etc. (*celebration*) 883; pageant, -ry; spectacle, exhibition, procession; turn –, set- out; grand function; *fête*, gala, field-day, review, march past, promenade, insubstantial pageant.

dress; court –, full –, evening –, ball –, fancy- dress; tailoring, millinery, man-millinery, frippery; foppery, equipage.

ceremon-y, -ial; ritual; form, -ality; etiquette; punct-o, -ilio, -ilious-ness; starched-, stateli-ness.

mummery, solemn mockery, mouth honor.

attitudinarian; fop etc. 854.

V. be -ostentatious etc. *adj.*; come –, put oneself- forward; attract attention, star it.

make –, cut- a -figure, – dash, – splash; strut, blow one's own trumpet; figure, – away; make a show, – display; glitter.

show -off, – one's paces; parade, march past;

display, exhibit, put forward, hold up; trot –, hang- out; sport, brandish, blazon forth; dangle, – before the eyes.

cry up etc. (*praise*) 931; *prôner*, flaunt, emblazon, prink, set off, mount, have framed and glazed.

put a good, – smiling- face upon; clean the outside of the platter etc. (*disguise*) 544.

Adj. ostentatious, showy, dashing, pretentious, ja-, jau-nty; grand, pompous, palatial; high sounding; turgid etc. (*big-sounding*) 577; garish, gorgeous; gaudy, – as a -peacock, – butterfly, – tulip; flaunting, flashing, flaming, glittering; gay etc. (*ornate*) 847; colorful.

splendid, magnificent, sumptuous.

theatrical, dramatic, spectacular, scenic, ceremonial, ritual, -istic.

solemn, stately, majestic, formal, stiff, ceremonious, punctilious, starch-ed, -y.

en grande tenue, in best bib and tucker, in Sunday best, *endimanché*.

Adv. with -flourish of trumpet, – beat of drum, – flying colors, – a brass band.

ad captandum vulgus.

883. Celebration.—**N.** celebration, solemnization, jubilee, diamond jubilee, commemoration, ovation, paean, triumph, jubilation.

triumphal arch, bonfire, salute; salvo, – of artillery; *feu de joie*, flourish of trumpets, *fanfare*, colors flying, illuminations, fireworks.

inauguration, installation, presentation; *début*, coming out, birthday anniversary, bi-, ter-, centenary; silver –, golden –, diamond- wedding, -day; coronation; Lord Mayor's show; harvest home, red letter day, festival; trophy etc. 733; *Te Deum* etc. (*thanksgiving*) 990; fête etc. 882; holiday etc. 840.

V. celebrate, keep, signalize, do honor to, commemorate, solemnize, hallow, mark with a red letter, hold high festival, maffick.

pledge, drink to, toast, hob and nob.

inaugurate, install, instate, induct, chair.

rejoice etc. 838; kill the fatted calf, hold jubilee, roast an ox, fire a salute.

Adj. celebrating etc. *v.*; commemorative, celebrated, immortal.

Adv. in -honor, – commemoration, – celebration of.

Int. hail! all hail! *io -paean*, – *triumphe!* 'see the conquering hero comes!'

884. Boasting.—**N.** boasting etc. *v.*; boast, vaunt, crake; preten-ce, -sions; puff, -ery; flourish, *fanfaronnade*; gasconade; bluff, swank, brag, -gardism; bravado, bunkum, Buncombe; highfalutin; jact-itation, -ancy; bounce, rant, bluster; venditation, vaporing, rodomontade, bombast, fine talking, tall talk, magniloquence, teratology, heroics; jingoism, Chauvinism; exaggeration etc. 549; gas, hot air.

vanity etc. 880; *vox et praeterea nihil*; much cry and little wool, *brutum fulmen*.

exultation; glorification; flourish of trumpets; triumph etc. 883.

boaster; bragg-art, -adocio; hot air merchant; Gascon, *fanfaron*, pretender, fourflusher, *soi-disant*; windbag, blowhard, bluffer; chauvinist; blusterer etc. 887; charlatan, jack-pudding, trumpeter; puppy etc. (*fop*) 854.

V. boast, make a boast of, brag, vaunt, puff, show off, flourish, crake, crack, trumpet, strut, swagger, vapor, bluff; draw the long bow.

exult, crow over, neigh, chuckle, triumph; glory, gloat, jubilate; throw up one's cap; talk big, *se faire valoir*, *faire claquer son fouet*, take merit to oneself, make a merit of, sing *Io triumphe*, holloa before one is out of the wood.

Adj. boasting etc. *v.*; magniloquent, flaming, Thrasonic, stilted, gasconading, braggart, boastful, pretentious, *soi-disant*; vain-glorious etc. (*conceited*) 880.

elate, -d; jubilant, triumphant, exultant; in high feather; flushed, – with victory; cock-a-hoop; on stilts.

vaunted etc. *v.*

Adv. vauntingly etc. *adj.*; with a brass band.

Phr. 'let the galled jade wince.'

885. Insolence. [Undue assumption of superiority.]—**N.** insolence; haughtiness etc. *adj.*; arrogance, airs; overbearance, brashness, bumptiousness, contumely, disdain; domineering etc. *v.*; tyranny etc. 739.

impertinence; cheek, nerve, sauce; sauciness etc. *adj.*; flippancy, dicacity, petulance, procacity, bluster; swagger, -ing etc. *v.*; bounce; terrorism; jingoism, chauvinism.

as-, pre-sumption; beggar on horseback; usurpation.

impudence, assurance, audacity, self-assertion, hardihood, front, face, brass; shamelessness etc. *adj.*; effrontery, hardened front, face of brass.

assumption of infallibility.

malapert, saucebox etc. (*blusterer*) 887.

V. be -insolent etc. *adj.*; bluster, vapor, swagger, swell, give oneself airs; snap one's fingers, kick up a dust; swear etc. (*affirm*) 535; rap out oaths; roister.

arrogate; as-, pre-sume; make -bold, – free; take a liberty, give an inch and take an ell.

domineer, bully, dictate, hector; lord it over, bulldoze; *traiter de haut*, *regarder de haut en bas*; exact; snub, huff, beard, fly in the face of; put to the blush; bear –, beat- down; browbeat, intimidate; trample –, tread- -down, – under foot; dragoon, ride roughshod over, terrorize.

out-face, -look, -stare, -brazen, -brave; stare out of countenance; brazen out; lay down the law; teach one's grandmother to suck eggs; assume a lofty bearing; talk –, look- big; put on big looks, act the *grand seigneur*; mount –, ride- the high horse; toss the head, carry with a high hand.

tempt Providence, want snuffing.

Adj. insolent, haughty, arrogant, imperious, magisterial, dictatorial, arbitrary; high-handed, high and mighty; contumelious, supercilious, overbearing, intolerant, domineering; overweening, high-flown.

flippant, pert, cavalier, saucy, forward, impertinent, fresh, malapert.

precocious, assuming, would-be, bumptious.

bluff; brazen-, browed-faced, shameless, aweless, unblushing, unabashed; bold-, bare-faced; dead –, lost- to shame.

impudent, audacious, presumptuous, free and easy, devil-may-care, rollicking; janty, jaunty; roistering, blustering, hectoring, swaggering, vaporing; thrasonic, fire-eating, 'full of sound and fury.'

Adv. insolently, with a high hand; *ex cathedrâ*.

Phr. one's bark being worse than his bite.

886. Servility.—N. servility; slavery etc. (*subjection*) 749; obsequiousness etc. *adj.*; subserviency; abasement; pros-tration, -ternation; genuflexion etc. (*worship*) 990; fawning etc. *v.*; tuft-hunting, time-serving, flunkeyism; sycophancy etc. (*flattery*) 933; humility etc. 879.

sycophant, parasite, yes-man; toad, -y, -eater; tuft-hunter; snob, flunkey, lap-dog, spaniel, lick-spittle, smell-feast, *Graeculus esuriens*, hanger on, stooge, *cavaliere servente*, led captain, carpet knight; time-server, fortune-hunter, Vicar of Bray, Sir Pertinax Mac Sycophant, pick-thank; flatterer etc. 935; doer of dirty work; *âme damnée*, tool; reptile; slave etc. (*servant*) 746; courtier; sponge, jackal; truckler.

V. cringe, bow, stoop, kneel, bend the knee; fall on one's knees, prostrate oneself; worship etc. 990.

sneak, crawl, crouch, cower, truckle to, grovel, fawn, toady, lick the feet of, kiss the hem of one's garment.

pay court to; feed –, fatten –, batten- on; dance attendance on, pin oneself upon, hang on the sleeve of, *avaler des couleuvres*, keep time to, fetch and carry, do the dirty work of.

go with the stream, follow the crowd, worship the rising sun, hold with the hare and run with the hounds.

Adj. servile, obsequious; supple, – as a glove; soapy, oily, pliant, cringing, fawning, slavish, groveling, sniveling, mealy-mouthed; beggarly, sycophantic, parasitical; abject, prostrate, down on one's marrow-bones; base, mean, sneaking; crouching etc. *v.*

Adv. hat –, cap- in hand.

887. Blusterer.—N. bluster-, swagger-, vapor-, roister-, brawl-er; brazen-face; *fanfaron*; braggart etc. (*boaster*) 884; bully, terrorist, rough, rough-neck; hooligan, hoodlum, larrikin, ruffian; Mohock, -hawk; drawcansir, swashbuckler, Captain Boabdil, Sir Lucius O'Trigger, Thraso, Pistol, Parolles, Bombastes Furioso, Hector, Chrononhotonthologos; jingo; desperado, dare-devil, fire-eater; fury etc. (*violent person*) 173; rowdy.

puppy etc. (*fop*) 854; prig; Sir Oracle, dogmatist, *doctrinaire*, stump orator, jack-in-office; saucebox, malapert, jackanapes, minx; bantam-cock.

888. Friendship.—N. friendship, amity; friendliness etc. *adj.*; brotherhood, fraternity, sodality, confraternity, sorosis, sisterhood; harmony etc. (*concord*) 714; peace etc. 721.

firm –, staunch –, intimate –, familiar –, bosom –, cordial –, tried –, devoted –, lasting –, fast –, sincere –, warm –, ardent- friendship.

cordiality, fraternization, *entente cordiale*, good understanding, *rapprochement*, sympathy, fellow-feeling, response, welcomeness; *camaraderie*.

affection etc. (*love*) 897; favoritism; goodwill etc. (*benovolence*) 906; partiality.

acquaintance, familiarity, intimacy, intercourse, fellowship, knowledge of; introduction.

V. be -friendly etc. *adj.*, – friends etc. 890; – acquainted with etc. *adj.*; know; have the ear of; keep- company with etc. (*sociality*) 892; hold communication –, have dealings –, sympathize- with; have a leaning to; bear good will etc. (*benevolence*) 906; love etc. 897; make much of; befriend etc. (*aid*) 707; introduce to.

set one's horses together; hold out –, extend the right hand of -friendship, – fellowship; become -friendly etc. *adj.*; make -friends etc. 890 with; break the ice, be introduced to; make –, pick –, scrape- acquaintance with; get into favor, gain the friendship of.

shake hands with, fraternize, embrace; receive with open arms, throw oneself into the arms of; meet half way, take in good part.

Adj. friendly, amic-able, -al; well affected, unhostile, neighborly, brotherly, fraternal, sisterly, sympathetic, harmonious, hearty, cordial, warm-hearted, devoted.

friends –, well –, at home –, hand in hand- with; on -good, – friendly, – amicable, – cordial, – familiar, – intimate- -terms, – footing; on -speaking, – visiting- terms; in one's good -graces, – books.

acquainted, familiar, intimate, thick, hand and glove, hail fellow well met, free and easy; welcome.

Adv. amicably etc. *adj.*; with open arms; *sans cérémonie*; arm in arm.

889. Enmity.—N. enmity, hostility; unfriendliness etc. *adj.*; discord etc. 713.

alienation, estrangement; dislike etc. 867; hate etc. 898; antagonism.

heartburning; animosity etc. 900; malevolence etc. 907.

V. be -inimical etc. *adj.*; keep –, hold- at arm's length; be at loggerheads; bear malice etc. 907; fall out; take umbrage etc. 900; harden the heart, alienate, estrange.

Adj. inimical, unfriendly, hostile; at -enmity, – variance, – swords points, – daggers drawn, – open war with; up in arms against; in bad odor with.

on bad –, not on speaking- terms; cool; cold, -hearted; estranged, alienated, disaffected, irreconcilable.

890. Friend.—N. friend, – of one's bosom, intimate acquaintance, neighbor, well-wisher; *alter ego*; best –, bosom –, fast- friend; *amicus usque ad aras*; *fidus Achates*; *persona grata*.

favorer, *fautor*, patron, backer, Maecenas; tutelary saint, good genius, advocate, partisan, sympathizer; ally; friend in need etc. (*auxiliary*) 711.

associate, compeer, comrade, mate, companion, *confrère*, *camarade*, *confidante*, colleague; old –, crony; side-kick; chum, buddy, bunkie, roommate, pal; play-fellow, -mate; classmate, schoolfellow; bed-fellow, -mate; maid of honor.

compatriot; fellow –, countryman, – townsman.

shop-, ship-, mess-mate; fellow –, boon –, pot-companion; co-partner.

Arcades ambo, Pylades and Orestes, Castor and Pollux, Nisus and Euryalus, Damon and Pythias, *par nobile fratrum*.

host, Amphitryon, Boniface; guest, visitor, frequenter, *habitué*; *protégé*.

891. Enemy.—N. enemy; antagonist, foeman; open –, bitter- enemy; opponent etc. 710; back friend.

public enemy, enemy to society, traitor, anarchist etc. 743.

Phr. every hand being against one.

892. Sociality.—N. soci-ality, -ability, -ableness etc. *adj.*; social intercourse; consociation; intercourse, -community; consort-, companion-, fellow-, comrade-ship; clubbism; *esprit de corps*.

conviviality; good -fellowship, – company, *camaraderie*; joviality, jollity, *savoir -vivre*, festivity, festive board, merry-making; loving cup; hospitality, heartiness; cheer.

welcome, -ness; greeting; hearty –, warm –, welcome- reception; urbanity etc. (*courtesy*) 894; intimacy, familiarity.

good –, jolly- fellow, good mixer, Rotarian; *bon enfant*.

social –, family- circle; circle of acquaintance, *coterie*, society, company.

social -gathering, – *réunion*; assembly etc. (*assemblage*) 72; party, entertainment, reception, *levée*, at home, *conversazione*, *soirée*, *matinée*, evening –, morning –, afternoon –, garden –, dinner –, tea –, cocktail- party; symposium, sing-song; kettle-, drum; *partie carrée*, dish of tea, *ridotto*, rout, housewarming; ball, prom, hop, dance, *thé dansant*; festival etc. (*amusement*) 840; wedding breakfast; 'the feast of reason and the flow of soul.'

visit, -ing; round of visits; call, morning call; interview etc. (*interlocution*) 588; assignation; tryst, -ing place; appointment.

club etc. (*association*) 712.

V. be -sociable etc. *adj.*; know; be -acquainted etc. *adj.*; associate –, sort –, keep company –, walk hand in hand -with; eat off the same trencher, club together, consort, bear one company, join; make acquaintance with etc. (*friendship*) 888; make advances, fraternize, embrace; intercommunicate.

be –, feel –, make oneself- at home with; make free with; crack a bottle with; take pot luck with, receive hospitality, live at free quarters.

visit, pay a visit; interchange -visits, – cards; call -at, – upon; leave a card; drop in, look in; look one up, beat up one's quarters.

entertain; give a -party etc. *n.*; be at home, see one's friends, hang out, keep open house, do the honors; receive, – with open arms; welcome; give a warm reception etc. *n.* to; kill the fatted calf.

Adj. sociable, companionable, clubbable, clubby, conversable, cosy, cosey, chatty, conversational; homiletical.

convivial; fest-ive, -al; jovial, jolly, hospitable.

welcome, – as the roses in May; *fêté*, entertained.

free and easy, hail fellow well met, familiar, on visiting terms, acquainted.

social, neighborly; international, cosmopolitan, gregarious.

Adv. *en famille*, in the family circle; *sans -façon*, – *cérémonie*, arm in arm.

893. Seclusion. Exclusion.—N. seclusion, privacy; retirement; concealment; reclusion, recess; snugness etc. *adj.*; delitescence; rustication, *rus in urbe*; solitude; solitariness etc. (*singleness*) 87; isolation; loneliness etc. *adj.*; estrangement from the world, anchoritism, voluntary exile; aloofness.

cell, hermitage; convent etc. 1000; *sanctum sanctorum*; study, library, den; hide-out.

depopulation, desertion, desolation; wilderness etc. (*unproductive*) 169; howling wilderness; rotten borough, Old Sarum.

exclusion, excommunication, banishment, exile, ostracism, proscription; cut, – direct; dead cut.

inhospit-ality, -ableness etc. *adj.*; un-, dis-sociability; domesticity, Darby and Joan.

recluse, hermit, eremite, cenobite; anchor-et, -ite; Simon Stylites; Troglodyte, Timon of Athens, Santon, *solitaire*, ruralist, disciple of Zimmermann, closet cynic, Diogenes; outcast, Pariah, castaway, outsider, pilgarlic; wastrel, foundling, orphan.

V. be –, live- secluded etc. *adj.*; keep –, stand –, hold oneself- -aloof, – in the background; keep snug; shut oneself up; deny –, seclude- oneself; creep into a corner, rusticate, *aller planter ses choux*; retire, – from the world; hermetize, take the veil; abandon etc. 624.

cut, – dead; refuse to -associate with, – acknowledge; look cool –, turn one's back –, shut the door- upon; repel, blackball, excommunicate, exclude, exile, expatriate; banish, outlaw, maroon, ostracize, proscribe, cut off from, send to Coventry, keep at arm's length, draw a cordon round; boycott, blockade, lay an embargo on, isolate.

depopulate; dis-, un-people.

Adj. secluded, sequestered, retired, delitescent, private, bye; out of the -world, -way; in a backwater; 'the world forgetting by the world forgot.'

snug, domestic, stay-at-home.

unsociable; un-, dis-social; inhospitable, cynical, inconversable, unclubbable, *sauvage*, eremetic.

solitary; lone-ly, -some; isolated, single.

excluded, estranged; unfrequented; uninhabitable, -ed; tenantless; un-tenanted, -occupied; abandoned; deserted, – in one's utmost need; unfriended; kith-, friend-, home-less; lorn, forlorn, desolate.

un-visited, -introduced, -invited, -welcome; under a cloud, left to shift for oneself, derelict, outcast, outside the gates.

banished etc. *v.*; under an embargo.

Phr. *noli me tangere*.

894. Courtesy.—N. courtesy; respect etc. 928; good -manners, – behavior, – breeding; manners; politeness etc. *adj.*; *bienséance*, urbanity, comity, gentility; gentle –, breeding; polish, presence, cultivation, culture; civili-ty, -zation; amenity, suavity; good -temper, – humor; amiability, easy temper, complacency, soft tongue, mansuetude; condescension etc. (*humility*) 879; affability, complaisance, *prévenance*; amiability, gallantry, chivalry; pink of -politeness, – courtesy.

compliment; fair –, soft –, sweet- words; honeyed phrases, flattering remarks, ceremonial; salutation, reception, presentation, introduction, *accueil*, greeting, recognition; welcome, *abord*, respects, *devoir*, regards, remembrances; kind -regards, – remembrances; love, best love, duty; deference.

obeisance etc. (*reverence*) 928; bow, courtesy, curtsy, scrape, *salaam*, *kow-tow*, bowing and scraping; kneeling; genuflexion etc. (*worship*) 990; obsequiousness etc. 886; capping, shaking hands etc. *v.*; grip of the hand, embrace, hug, squeeze, *accolade*, loving cup, *vin d'honneur*, pledge; love token etc. (*endearment*) 902; kiss, buss, salute.

mark of recognition, not; 'nods and becks and wreathed smiles;' valediction etc. 293; condolence etc. 915.

V. be -courteous etc. *adj.*; show -courtesy etc. *n.* mind one's P's and Q's, behave oneself, be all things to all men, conciliate, speak one fair, take in good part; make –, do- the amiable; look as if butter would not melt in one's mouth; mend one's manners.

receive, do the honors, usher, greet, hail, bid welcome; welcome, – with open arms; shake hands; hold out –, press –, squeeze- the hand; bid God speed; speed the parting guest; cheer, serenade.

salute; embrace etc. (*endearment*) 902; kiss, – hands; drink to, pledge, hob and nob; move to, nod to; smile upon.

uncover, cap; touch –, take off- the hat; doff the cap; pull the forelock; present arms; make way for; bow; make one's bow; scrape, curtsy, courtesy; bob a -curtsy, – courtesy; kneel; bow –, bend- the knee; salaam, *kowtow*.

visit, wait upon, present oneself, pay one's respects, pay a visit etc. (*sociability*) 892; dance attendance on etc. (*servility*) 886; pay attentions to; do homage to etc. (*respect*) 928.

prostrate oneself etc. (*worship*) 990.

give –, send- one's duty etc. *n.* to.

render -polite etc. *adj.*; polish, civilize, humanize.

Adj. courteous, polite, civil, mannerly, urbane; well-behaved, -mannered, -bred, -brought up, gently bred, of gentle -breeding, – manners, good-mannered, polished, civilized, cultivated; refined etc. (*taste*) 850; gentlemanlike etc. (*fashion*) 852; gallant, chivalrous, on one's good behavior.

fine –, fair –, soft- spoken; honey-mouthed, -tongued; oily, unctuous, bland, suave; obliging, conciliatory, complaisant, complacent; obsequious etc. 886.

ingratiating, winning; gentle, mild; good-humored, cordial, gracious, amiable, tactful, addressful, affable, genial, friendly, familiar; neighborly.

Adv. courteously etc. *adj.*; with a good grace; with -open, – outstretched- arms; *à bras ouverts*; *suaviter in modo*, in good humor.

Int. hail! welcome! well met! *ave!* all hail! good -day, – morning etc., – morrow! God speed! *pax vobiscum!* may your shadow never be less! *chin-chin!*

895. Discourtesy.—N. discourtesy; ill-breeding; ill –, bad –, ungainly- manners; insuavity; grouchiness; un-courteousness etc. *adj.*, tactlessness; rusticity, inurbanity; illiberality, incivility, displacency.

disrespect etc. 929; procacity, impudence; barbar-ism, -ity; misbehavior, brutality, blackguard-ism, conduct unbecoming a gentleman, *grossièreté*, *brusquerie*; vulgarity etc. 851.

churlishness etc. *adj.*; spinosity, perversity; moroseness etc. (*sullenness*) 901*a*.

bad-, ill-temper; sternness etc. *adj.*; austerity; moodishness, captiousness etc. 901; cynicism; tartness etc. *adj.*; acrimony, acerbity, virulence, asperity.

scowl, black looks, frown; short answer, rebuff; hard words, contumely; unparliamentary language, personality.

bear, bruin, brute, grouch, blackguard, beast; unlicked cub; frump, cross-patch; saucebox etc. 887.

V. be -rude etc. *adj.*; insult etc. 929; treat with discourtesy; take a name in vain; make -bold, – free- with; take a liberty; stare out of countenance, ogle, point at, put to the blush.

cut; turn -one's back upon, – on one's heel; give the cold shoulder; keep at -a distance, – arm's length; look -cool, – coldly, – black- upon; show the door to, send away with a flea in the ear.

lose one's temper etc. (*resentment*) 900; sulk etc. 901*a*; frown, scowl, glower, pout; snap, snarl, growl.

render -rude etc. *adj.*; brut-alize, -ify.

Adj. dis-, un-courteous; uncourtly; ill-bred, -mannered, -behaved, -conditioned; unbred; unmanner-ly, -ed; im-, un-polite; un-polished, -civilized, -genteel; ungentleman-like, -ly; unladylike; blackguard; vulgar etc. 851; dedecorous; foul-mouthed, -spoken; abusive.

un-civil, -gracious, -ceremonious; cool; pert, forward, obtrusive, impudent, rude, saucy, precocious; insolent etc. 885.

repulsive; un-complaisant, -accommodating, -neighborly, -gallant; inaffable; un-gentle, -gainly; rough, rugged, bluff, blunt, gruff; churl-, boor-, bear-ish; brutal, *brusque*; stern, harsh, austere; cavalier.

tart, sour, crabbed, sharp, short, trenchant, sarcastic, crusty, biting, caustic, virulent, bitter, acrimonious, venomous, contumelious; snarling etc., *v.*; surly, – as a bear; perverse; grim, sullen etc. 901*a*; peevish etc. (*irascible*) 901.

Adv. discourteously etc. *adj.*; with -discourtesy etc. *n.*, – a bad grace.

896. Congratulations.—N. con-, gratulation; felicitation; salute etc. 894; condolence etc. 915; compliments of the season; good –, best- wishes.

V. con-, gratulate; felicitate, compliment; give –, wish one- joy; tender –, offer- one's congratulations; wish -many happy returns of the day, – a merry Christmas and a happy new year.

congratulate oneself etc. (*rejoice*) 838.

Adj. con-, gratulatory.

897. Love.—N. love; fondness etc. *adj.*; liking; inclination etc. (*desire*) 865; regard, dilection, admiration, fancy.

affection, sympathy, fellow-felling; tenderness etc. *adj.*; heart, brotherly love; benevolence etc. 906; attachment.

yearning, tender passion, *affaire de coeur*, *amour*, gallantry, passion, flame, devotion, fervor, enthusiasm, transport of love, rapture, enchantment, infatuation, adoration, idolatry.

narcissism, Oedipus complex, Electra complex.

Cupid, Venus, Eros; myrtle; true lover's knot; love -token, – suit, – affair, – tale, – story; the old story, plighted love; courtship etc. 902; *amourette*.

maternal love.

attractiveness, charm; popularity; favorite etc. 899.

lover, suitor, follower, admirer, adorer, wooer, amoret, beau, sweetheart, inamorato, swain, young man, flame, love, truelove; leman, Lothario, gallant, paramor, *amoroso*, *cavaliere servente*, captive, *cicisbeo*; *caro sposo*, Don Juan, sheik, ladies' man, squire of dames, Knave of Hearts.

inamorata, lady-love, idol, darling, duck, Dulcinea, angel, goddess, *cara sposa*; mistress.

betrothed, affianced, *fiancée*.

flirt, *coquette*; amorette; pair of turtle doves; abode of love, *agapemone*.

V. love, like, affect, fancy, care for, take an interest in, be partial to, sympathize with; be -in love etc. *adj.*- with; have –, entertain –, harbor –, cherish- a -love etc. *n.* for; regard, revere; take to, bear love to, be wedded to; set one's affections on; make much of, feast one's eyes on; hold dear, prize, treasure; hug, cling to, cherish, pet, caress etc. 902.

burn; adore, idolize, love to distraction, *aimer eperdument*; dote -on, – upon.

take a fancy to, fall for, be stuck on, look sweet upon; become -enamored etc. *adj.*; fall in love with, lose one's heart; desire etc. 865.

excite love; win –, gain –, secure –, engage- the -love, – affections, – heart; take the fancy of; have a place in –, wind round- the heart; attract, attach, endear, charm, fascinate, captivate, bewitch, seduce, enamor, enrapture, turn the head.

get into favor; ingratiate –, insinuate –, worm- oneself; propitiate, curry favor with, pay one's court to, make a date with, *faire l'aimable*, set one's cap at, flirt, coquet.

Adv. loving etc. *v.*; fond of; taken –, struck- with; smitten, bitten; attached to, wedded to; enamored; charmed etc. *v.*; in love; lovesick; over head and ears in love.

affectionate, tender, sweet upon, sympathetic, loving, fond, amorous, amatory; erotic, uxurious, ardent, passionate, rapturous, devoted, motherly.

loved etc. *v.*; beloved; well –, dearly- beloved; dear, precious, darling, pet, little; favorite, popular.

congenial; to –, after- one's -mind, – taste, – fancy, – own heart.

in one's good -graces etc. (*friendly*) 888; dear as the apple of one's eye, nearest to one's heart.

lovable, adorable; lovely, sweet; attractive, seductive, winning; charming, engaging, interesting, enchanting, captivating, fascinating, intriguing, bewitching; amiable, like an angel, angelic, seraphic.

898. Hate.—N. hate, hatred, vials of hate; Hymn of Hate.

dis-affection, -favor; alienation, estrangement, coolness; enmity etc. 889; animosity etc. 900.

umbrage, pique, grudge; dudgeon, spleen; bitterness, – of feeling; ill –, bad- blood; acrimony; malice etc. 907; implacability etc. (*revenge*) 919.

repugnance etc. (*dislike*) 867; odium, unpopularity; loathing, detestation, antipathy; object of -hatred, – execration; abomination, aversion, *bête noire*; enemy etc. 891; bitter pill; source of annoyance etc. 830.

V. hate, detest, abominate, abhor, loathe; recoil –, shudder- at; shrink from, view with horror, hold in abomination, revolt against, execrate; scowl etc. 895; disrelish etc. (*dislike*) 867.

owe a grudge; bear -spleen, – a grudge, – malice etc. (*malevolence*) 907; conceive an aversion to.

excite –, provoke- hatred etc. *n.*; be -hateful etc. *adj.*; stink in the nostrils; estrange, alienate, repel, set against, sow dissension, set by the ears, envenom, incense, irritate, rile, ruffle, vex; horrify etc. 830.

Adj. hating etc. *v.*; abhorrent; averse from etc. (*disliking*) 867; set against.

bitter etc. (*acrimonious*) 895; implacable etc. (*revengeful*) 919.

un-loved, -beloved, -lamented, -deplored, -mourned, -cared for, -endured, -valued; disliked etc. 867.

crossed in love, forsaken, rejected, love-lorn, jilted.

obnoxious, hateful, odious, abominable, repulsive, offensive, shocking; disgusting etc. (*disagreeable*) 830.

invidious, spiteful; malicious etc. 907.

insulting, irritating, provoking.

[Mutual hate] at -daggers drawn, – swords points; not on speaking terms etc. (*enmity*) 889.

Phr. no love lost between.

899. Favorite.—N. favorite, pet, cosset, minion, idol, jewel, spoiled child, *enfant gâté*; led captain; crony; fondling; apple of one's eye, man after one's own heart; *persona grata*.

love, dear, darling, duck, honey, jewel; mopsey, moppet; sweetheart etc. (*love*) 897.

general –, universal- favorite; idol of the people; matinée idol, movie –, radio- star.

900. Resentment.—N. resentment, displeasure, animosity, anger, wrath, indignation; vexation, exasperation, bitter resentment, wrathful indignation.

pique, umbrage, huff, miff, soreness, dudgeon, acerbity, virulence, bitterness, acrimony, asperity, spleen, gall; heart-burning, -swelling; rankling.

ill –, bad- -humor, – temper; irascibility etc. 901; ill blood etc. (*hate*) 898; revenge etc. 919.

excitement, irritation; warmth, bile, choler, ire, fume, pucker, dander, ferment, ebullition; towering -passion, – rage, *acharnement*, angry mood, taking, pet, tiff, passion, fit, tantrums.

burst, explosion, paroxysm, storm, rage, fury, desperation; violence etc. 173; fire and fury; vials of wrath; gnashing of teeth, hot blood, high words.

scowl etc. 895; sulks etc. 901*a*.

[Cause of umbrage] affront, provocation, offence; indignity etc. (*insult*) 929; grudge, crow to pluck, sore subject; red rag to a bull; *casus belli*.

Furies, Erinys, Eumenides, Alecto, Megaera, Tisiphone.

buffet, slap in the face, box on the ear, rap on the knuckles.

V. resent; take -amiss, – ill, – to heart, – offence, – umbrage, – huff, – exception; take in -ill part, – bad part, – dudgeon; *ne pas entendre raillerie*; breathe revenge, cut up rough.

fly –, fall –, get- into a -rage, – passion; bridle –, bristle –, froth –, fire –, flare- up; open –, pour out- the vials of one's wrath.

pout, knit the brow, frown, scowl, lower, snarl, growl, gnarl, gnash, snap; redden, color; look -black, – black as thunder, – daggers; bite one's thumb; show –, grind- one's teeth; champ the bit.

chafe, mantle, fume, kindle, fly out, take fire; boil, – over; boil with -indignation, – rage; rage, storm, foam; vent one's -rage, – spleen; lose one's temper, stand on one's hind legs, stamp the foot, kick up a row, fly off the handle, cut up rough; stamp –, quiver –, swell –, foam- with rage; burst with anger; raise Cain, breathe fire and fury.

have a fling at; bear malice etc. (*revenge*) 919.

cause –, raise- anger; affront, offend; give -offence, – umbrage; anger; hurt the feelings; insult, discompose, fret, ruffle, nettle, heckle, huff, pique; excite etc. 824; irritate, stir the blood, stir up bile; sting, – to the quick; rile, provoke, chafe, wound, incense, inflame, enrage, aggravate, add fuel to the flame, fan into a flame, widen the breach, envenom, embitter, exasperate, infuriate, kindle wrath; stick in one's gizzard; rankle etc. 919.

put out of humor; put one's -monkey, – back-up; set –, get- one's back up; raise one's -gorge, – dander, – choler; work up into a passion; make -one's blood boil, – the ears tingle; throw into a ferment, madden, drive one mad; lash into -fury, – madness; fool to the top of one's bent; set by the ears.

bring a hornet's nest about one's ears.

Adj. angry, wrath, irate; ire-, wrath-ful; cross etc. (*irascible*) 901; sulky etc. 901*a*; bitter, virulent; acrimonious etc. (*discourteous*) etc. 895; violent etc. 173.

warm, burning; boiling, – over; fuming, raging; foaming, – at the mouth; convulsed with rage.

offended etc. *v.*; waxy, *acharné*; wrought, worked up; indignant, hurt, sore, peeved; set against.

fierce, wild, rageful, furious, mad with rage, fiery, infuriate, rabid, savage; relentless etc. 919.

flushed with -anger, – rage; in a -huff, – stew, – fume, – pucker, – passion, – rage, – fury; on one's high ropes, up in arms; in high dudgeon.

Adv. angrily etc. *adj.*; in the height of passion; in the heat of -passion, – the moment.

Phr. one's -blood, – back, – monkey- being up; *fervens difficili bile jecur*; the gorge rising, eyes flashing fire; the blood -rising, – boiling; *haeret lateri lethalis arundo*.

901. Irascibility.—N. irascibility, temper; crossness etc. *adj.*; susceptibility, procacity, petulance, irritability, tartness, acerbity, protervity; pugnacity etc. (*contentiousness*) 720.

excitability etc. 825; bad –, fiery –, crooked –, irritable etc. *adj.*- temper; *genus irritabile*, hot blood.

ill humor etc. (*sullenness*) 901*a*; asperity etc., churlishness etc. (*discourtesy*) 895.

huff etc. (resentment) 900; a word and a blow.

Sir Fretful Plagiary; brabbler, Tartar; shrew, vixen, virago, termagant, dragon, scold, Xanthippe; porcupine; spit-fire; fire-eater etc. (*blusterer*) 887; fury etc. (*violent person*) 173.

V. be -irascible etc. *adj.*; have a -temper etc. *n.*, – devil in one; fire up etc. (*be angry*) 900.

Adj. irascible; bad-, ill-tempered; irritable, susceptible; excitable etc. 825; thin-skinned etc. (*sensitive*) 822; fretful, fidgety; on the fret.

hasty, over-hasty, quick, warm, hot, testy, touchy, techy, tetchy; like -touchwood, – tinder; huffy; pet-tish, -ulant; waspish, snapp-y, -ish, peppery, fiery, passionate, choleric, shrewish, 'sudden and quick in quarrel.'

querulous, captious, mood-y, -ish; quarrelsome, contentious, disputatious; pugnacious etc. (*bellicose*) 720; cantankerous, exceptious; restive etc. (*perverse*) 901*a*; churlish etc. (*discourteous*) 895.

cross, – as -crabs, – two sticks, – a cat, – a dog, – the tongs; like a bear with a sore head; fractious, peevish, *acariâtre*.

in a bad temper; sulky etc. 901*a*; angry etc. 900.

resent-ful, -ive; vindictive etc. 919.

Int. pish!

901a. Sullenness.—N. sullenness etc. *adj.*; morosity, spleen; churlishness etc. (*discourtesy*) 895; irascibility etc. 901.

moodiness etc. *adj.*; perversity; obstinacy etc. 606; torvity, spinosity; crabbedness etc. *adj.*

ill –, bad- -temper, – humor; sulks, dudgeon, mumps, doleful dumps, doldrums, fit of the sulks, *bouderie*, black looks, scowl; huff etc. (*resentment*) 900.

V. be -sullen etc. *adj.*; sulk; frown, scowl, lower, glower, grouse, grouch, crab, gloam, pout, have a hang-dog look, glout.

Adj. sullen, sulky; ill-tempered, -humored, -affected, -disposed; in -an ill, – a bad, – a shocking- -temper, – humor; out of -temper, – humor; knaggy, torvous, crusty, crabbed; sore as a boil; surly etc. (*discourteous*) 895.

moody; spleen-ish, -ly; splenetic, cankered.

cross, -grained; perverse, wayward, humorsome; restive; cantankerous, refractory, intractable, exceptious, sinistrous, deaf to reason, unaccommodating, rusty, crust, froward.

dogged etc. (*stubborn*) 606.

grumpy, glum, grim, grum, morose, frumpish; in the -sulks etc. *n.*; out of sorts; scowl-, glower-, growl-ing.

peevish etc. (*irascible*) 901.

902. Endearment. [Expression of affection or love.]—**N.** endearment, caress; blandish-, blandiment; *épanchement*, fondling, billing and cooing, dalliance.

embrace, salute, kiss, buss, smack, osculation,

deosculation; amorous glances; ogle, side glance, sheep's eyes.

courtship, wooing, suit, addresses, the soft impeachment; love-making; an affair; serenading; caterwauling.

flirting etc. *v.*; flirtation, gallantry; coquetry, spooning.

ture lover's knot, plighted love, engagement, bethrothal; love -tale, – token, – letter; *billet-doux*, valentine.

honeymoon; Strephon and Chloe, 'Arry and 'Arriet.

V. caress, fondle, pet, dandle, nurse; pat, – on the -head, – cheek; chuck under the chin, smile upon, coax, wheedle, cosset, coddle, cocker; make -of, – much of, pamper; cherish, foster, kill with kindness.

clasp, hug, cuddle; fold –, strain- in one's arms; nestle, nuzzle, neck, embrace, kiss, buss, smack, blow a kiss; salute etc. (*courtesy*) 894.

bill and coo, spoon, toy, dally, flirt, coquet; galli-, gala-vant; philander; make love; pay one's -court, – addresses, – attentions- to; serenade; court, woo; set one's cap at; be –, look- sweet upon; ogle, cast sheep's eyes upon; *faire les yeux doux*.

fall in love with, win the affections etc. (*love*) 897; die for.

propose; make –, have- an offer; pop the question; plight one's -troth, – faith; become -engaged, – betrothed.

Adj. caressing etc. *v.*; 'sighing like furnace;' love-sick, spoony.

carressed etc. *v.*

903. Marriage.—N. marriage, matrimony, wedlock, union, intermarriage, *vinculum matrimonii*, nuptial tie, knot.

married state, coverture, bed, cohabitation.

match; betrothment etc. (*promise*) 768; wedding, nuptials, Hymen, bridal; e-, spousals; leading to the altar etc. *v.*; nuptial benediction, *epithalamium*.

torch –, temple- of Hymen; hymeneal altar; honeymoon.

bride, bridegroom; brides-maid; -man.

best –, grooms-man, page, usher.

married -man, – woman, – couple; neogamist, Benedick, partner, spouse, mate, yokemate; husband, man, consort, baron; old –, good- man; wife of one's bosom; help-meet, -mate, rib, better half, grey mare, old woman, good wife; feme, – coverte; squaw, lady; matron, -age, -hood; man and wife; wedded pair, Darby and Joan.

affinity, soul-mate.

mono-, bi-, di-, deutero-, tri-, poly-gamy; mormonism; poly-andry; Turk, Bluebeard.

unlawful –, left-handed –, companionate –, morganatic –, ill-assorted- marriage; *mésalliance*; *mariage de convenance*; an affair.

match-maker, marriage broker, matrimonial agent.

V. marry, wive, take to oneself a wife; be -married, – spliced; go –, pair- off; wed, espouse, lead to the hymeneal altar, take 'for better, for worse,' give one's hand to, bestow one's hand upon; remarry; intermarry.

marry, join, handfast; couple etc. (*unite*) 43; tie the nuptial knot; give -away, – in marriage; affy, affiance; betroth etc. (*promise*) 768; publish –, bid- the banns; be asked in church.

Adj. married etc. *v.*; one, – bone and one flesh.

marriageable, nubile.

engaged, betrothed, affianced.

matrimonial, marital, conjugal, connubial, wedded; nuptial, hymeneal, spousal, bridal.

Phr. the gray mare the better horse.

904. Celibacy.—N. celibacy, singleness, single blessedness; bachelor-hood, -ship; miso-gamy, -gyny.

virginity, *pueelage*; maiden-hood, -head.

unmarried man, bachelor, agamist, old bachelor; miso-gamist, -gynist; celibate.

unmarried woman, spinster; maid, -en; virgin, *feme sole*, old maid; bachelor girl; nun etc.

V. live single; keep bachelor hall.

Adj. un-married, -wedded; wife-, spouse-less; single, virgin, celibate.

905. Divorce.—N. divorce, -ment; separation; judicial separation, separate maintenance; *separatio a -mensâ et thoro*, – *vinculo matrimonii*.

widowhood, viduage, viduity, weeds.

widow, -er; relict; dowager; *divorcée*; cuckold.

V. live -separately, – apart; separate, divorce, disespouse, put away; wear the horns.

906. Benevolence.—N. benevolence, Christian charity; God's -love, – grace; good-will; philanthropy etc. 910; unselfishness etc. 942.

good -nature, – feeling, – wishes; kind-, kindliness etc. *adj.*; lovingkindness, benignity, brotherly love, charity, humanity, fellow-feeling, sympathy; goodness –, warmth- of heart; *bon-homie*; kindheartedness; amiability, milk of human kindness, tenderness; love etc. 897; friendship etc. 888.

toleration, consideration, generosity; mercy etc. (*pity*) 914.

charitableness etc. *adj.*; bounty, alms-giving; good works, beneficence, the luxury of doing good.

acts of kindness, a good turn; good –, kind- -offices, – treatment.

good Samaritan, sympathizer, well-wisher, philanthropist, *bon enfant*; altruist.

V. be -benevolent etc. *adj.*; have one's heart in the right place, bear good will; wish -well, – God speed; view –, regard- with an eye of favor; take in good part; take –, feel- an interest in; be –, feel-interested- in; sympathize with, feel for; fraternize etc. (*be friendly*) 888.

enter into the feelings of others, do as you would be done by, meet halfway.

treat well; give comfort, smooth the bed of death; do -good, – a good turn; benefit etc. (*goodness*) 648; render a service, be of use; aid etc. 707.

Adj. benevolent; kind, -ly; wellmeaning; amiable; obliging, accommodating, indulgent, considerate, gracious, complacent, good-humored.

warm-, soft-, kind-, tender-, large-, broad-hearted; merciful etc. 914; philanthropic etc. 910; charitable, beneficent, humane, benign, benignant; bount-eous, -iful etc. 816.

good-, well-natured; spleenless; sympath-izing, -etic; complaisant etc. (*courteous*) 894; kindly, well-meant, -intentioned.

fatherly, motherly, brotherly, sisterly; pat-, mat-, frat-ernal; friendly etc. 888.

Adv. with -a good intention, – the best intentions.

Int. God speed! much good may it do!

907. Malevolence.—N. malevolence; bad intent, -ion; un-, dis-kindness; ill -nature, – will, – blood; bad blood; enmity etc. 889; hate etc. 898; malignity; malice, – aforethought, – prepense; maliciousness etc. *adj.*; spite, despite; resentment etc. 900.

uncharitableness etc. *adj.*; incompassionateness etc. 914*a*; gall, venom, rancor, rankling, virulence, mordacity, acerbity; churlishness etc. (*discourtesy*) 895.

hardness of heart, heart of stone, obduracy; cruelty; cruelness etc. *adj.*; brutality, savagery; ferity, -ocity; barbarity, inhumanity, immanity, truculence, ruffianism; evil eye, cloven -foot, – hoof; Inquisition; torture.

ill –, bad- turn; affront etc. (*disrespect*) 929; outrage, atrocity; ill usage; intolerance, bigotry, persecution; tender mercies [ironical]; 'unkindest cut of all.'

V. be -malevolent etc. *adj.*; bear –, harbor- -spleen, – a grudge, – malice; betray –, show- the cloven foot.

hurt etc. (*physical pain*) 378; annoy etc. 830; injure, harm, wrong; do -harm, – an ill office- to; outrage; disoblige, malign, plant a thorn in the breast.

molest, worry, harass, haunt, harry, bait, tease, throw stones at; play the devil with; hunt down, dragoon, hound; persecute, oppress, grind; maltreat; ill-treat, -use.

wreak one's malice on, do one's worst, break a butterfly on the wheel; dip –, imbrue- one's hands in blood; have no mercy etc. 914*a*.

Adj. male-, unbene-volent; unbenign; ill-disposed, -intentioned, -natured, -conditioned, -contrived; evil-minded, -disposed.

malicious; malign, -ant; rancorous; de-, spiteful; mordacious, caustic, bitter, envenomed, acrimonious, virulent; un-amiable, -charitable; maleficent, venomous, grinding, galling.

harsh, disobliging; un-kind, -friendly, -gracious; treacherous; inofficious; invidious; uncandid; churlish etc. (*uncourteous*) 895; surly, sullen etc. 901*a*.

cold, -blooded, -hearted; hard-, flint-, marble-, stony-hearted; hard of heart, unnatural; ruthless etc. (*unmerciful*) 914*a*; relentless etc. (*revengeful*) 919.

cruel; brut-al, -ish; savage, – as a -bear, – tiger; ferine, feral, ferocious; inhuman; barbarous, fell, untamed, tameless, truculent, incendiary; bloodthirsty etc. (*murderous*) 361; atrocious.

fiend-ish, -like; demoniacal; diabolic, -al; devilish, infernal, hellish, Satanic.

Adv. malevolently etc. *adj.*; with -bad intent etc. *n.*

908. Malediction.—N. malediction, malison, curse, imprecation, denunciation, execration, anathema, ban, proscription, excommunication, commination, thunders of the Vatican, fulmination, *maranatha*, aspersion, vilification, vituperation, scurrility.

abuse; foul –, bad –, strong –, unparliamentary- language, Limehouse; Billingsgate, sauce, evil speaking; cursing etc. *v.*; profane swearing, oath.

threat etc. 909; more bark than bite; invective etc. (*disapprobation*) 932.

V. curse, accurse, imprecate, damn, swear at; slang; curse with bell, book and candle; invoke –, call down- curses on the head of; devote to destruction.

execrate, beshrew, scold; anathematize etc. (*censure*) 932; hold up to execration, denounce, proscribe, excommunicate, fulminate, thunder against; threaten etc. 909; curse up hill and down dale.

curse and swear; swear, – like a trooper; fall a cursing, rap out an oath, damn, cuss.

Adj. curs-ing, -ed etc. *v.*; maledictory.

Int. woe to! beshrew! *ruat coelum!* ill –, woebetide! confusion seize! damn! confound! blast! curse! devil take! hang! out with! a plague –, outupon! aroynt! *honi soit!*

Phr. *delenda est Carthago.*

909. Threat.—N. threat, menace; defiance etc. 715; abuse, minacity, intimidation; fulmination; commination etc. (*curse*) 908; gathering clouds etc. (*warning*) 668.

V. threat, -en; menace; snarl, growl, gnarl, mutter, bark, bully.

defy etc. 715; intimidate etc. 860; keep –, hold up –, hold out- *in terrorem*; shake –, double –, clinch- the fist at; thunder, talk big, fulminate, use big words, bluster, look daggers.

Adj. threatening, menacing; mina-tory, -cious; comminatory, abusive; *in terrorem*; ominous etc. (*predicting*) 511; defiant etc. 715; under the ban.

Int. *vae victis!* at your peril! do your worst!

910. Philanthropy.—N. philanthropy; altruism, humanit-y, -arianism; universal benevolence; ***deliciae humani generis;*** cosmopolitanism, utilitarianism, the greatest happiness of the greatest number, social science, sociology.

common weal, public welfare, socialism, communism.

patriotism, civism, nationality, love of country, *amor patriae*, public spirit.

chivalry, knight errantry; generosity etc. 942.

philanthropist, altruist etc. 906; utilitarian, Benthamite, socialist, communist, cosmopolite, citizen of the world, *amicus humani generis*; knight errant; patriot.

Adj. philanthropic, altruistic, humanitarian, utilitarian, cosmopolitan; public-spirited, patriotic; humane, large-hearted etc. (*benevolent*) 906; chival-ric, -rous, generous etc. 942.

Adv. *pro -bono publico, – aris et focis.*

Phr. *'humani nihil a me alienum puto.'*

911. Misanthropy.—N. misanthropy, incivism; egotism etc. (*selfishness*) 943; moroseness etc. 901*a*; cynicism; defeatism.

misanthrope, misanthropist, egotist, cynic, man-hater, Timon, Diogenes.
woman-hater, misogynist.
Adj. misanthropic, antisocial, unpatriotic; egotistical etc. (*selfish*) 943; morose etc. 901*a*.

912. Benefactor.—N. benefactor, savior, good genius, tutelary saint, patron, guardian angel, fairy godmother, good Samaritan; *pater patriae*; salt of the earth etc. (*good man*) 948; auxiliary etc. 711.

913. Evil-doer.[*Maleficent being.*]**—N.** evil-doer, – worker; wrong doer etc. 949; mischief maker, marplot; oppressor, tyrant; firebrand, incendiary, pyromaniac, anarchist, destroyer, Hun, *Boche*, Vandal, iconoclast; communist; terrorist, *apache*, gunman, gangster, racketeer.
savage, brute, ruffian, barbarian, semi-barbarian, caitiff, desperado; Mo-hock, -hawk; bludgeon man, bully, rough, hooligan, larrikin, dangerous classes, ugly customer; thief etc. 792.
cockatrice, scorpion, hornet; viper, adder; snake, – in the grass; serpent, cobra, asp, rattlesnake, anaconda; canker-, wire-worm; locust, Colorado beetle; torpedo; bane etc. 663.
cannibal; Anthropophag-us, -ist; bloodsucker, vampire, ogre, ghoul, gorilla; vulture; gyr-, gerfalcon.
wild beast, tiger, hyaena, butcher, hangman; cut-throat etc. (*killer*) 361; blood-, sleuth-, hell-hound.
hag, hellhag, beldam, Jezebel.
monster; fiend etc. (*demon*) 980; homicidal maniac, devil incarnate, demon in human shape; Frankenstein's monster.
harpy, siren, vampire; Furies, Eumenides etc. 900.
Attila, scourge of the human race.
Phr. *foenum habet in cornu*.

914. Pity.—N. pity, compassion, commiseration; bowels, – of compassion; condolence etc. 915; sympathy, fellow-feeling, tenderness, yearning, forbearance, humanity, mercy, clemency, exorability; leniency etc. (*lenity*) 740; charity, ruth, long-suffering.
melting mood; *argumentum ad misericordiam*; quarter, grace, *locus poenitentiae*.
sympathizer, champion, partisan.
V. pity; have –, show –, take- pity etc. *n.*; commiserate, compassionate; condole etc. 915; sympathize; feel –, be sorry –, yearn- for; weep, melt, thaw, enter into the feelings of.
forbear, relent, relax, give quarter, wipe the tears, *parcere subjectis*, give a *coup de grâce*, put out of one's misery; be cruel to be kind.
raise –, excite- pity etc. *n.*; touch, soften; melt, – the heart; appeal to one's better feelings; propitiate, disarm.
ask for -mercy etc. *n.*; supplicate etc. (*request*) 765; cry for quarter, beg one's life, kneel; deprecate.
Adj. pitying etc. *v.*; pitiful, compassionate, sympathetic, touched.
merciful, clement, ruthful; humane; humanitarian etc. (*philanthropic*) 910; tender, – hearted, – as a chicken; soft, – hearted; unhardened; lenient etc. 740; exorable, forbearing; melting etc. *v.*; weak.
Int. for pity's sake! mercy! have –, cry you-mercy! God help you! poor -thing, – dear, – fellow! woe betide! *quis talia fando temperet a lachrymis!*
Phr. one's heart bleeding for; *haud ignara mali miseris succurrere disco*.

914a. Pitilessness.—N. pitilessness etc. *adj.*; inclemency; inexorability, hardness of heart; inflexibility; severity etc. 739; malevolence etc. 907.
V. have no –, shut the gates of- mercy etc. 914; give no quarter.
Adj. piti-, merci-, ruth-, bowel-less; unpitying, unmerciful, inclement; in-, un-compassionate; inexorable, inflexible; harsh etc. 739; cruel etc. 907; unrelenting etc. 919.

915. Condolence.—N. condolence; lamentation etc. 839; sympathy, consolation.
V. condole with, console, sympathize etc. 914; share one's misery; feel for; express –, testify- pity; afford –, supply- consolation; lament etc. 839-with; send one's condolences.

916. Gratitude.—N. gratitude, thankfulness, gratefulness, feeling of obligation.
acknowledgement, recognition, thanksgiving, giving thanks.
thanks, praise, benediction; paean; *Te Deum* etc. (*worship*) 990; grace, – before, – after-meat; thank-offering.
requital.
V. be -grateful etc. *adj.*; thank; give –, render –, return –, offer –, tender- thanks etc. *n.*; acknowledge, requite.
feel –, be –, lie- under an obligation; *savoir gré*; not look a gift horse in the mouth; never forget, overflow with gratitude; thank –, bless- one's stars; fall on one's knees.
Adj. grateful, thankful, obliged, beholden, indebted to, under obligation.
Int. thanks! many thanks! gramercy! much obliged! thank you! thank Heaven! Heaven be praised!

917. Ingratitude.—N. ingratitude, thanklessness, oblivion of benefits; unthankfulness.
'benefits forgot;' thankless -task, – office.
V. be -ungrateful etc. *adj.*; forget benefits; look a gift horse in the mouth.
Adj. un-grateful, -mindful, -thankful; thankless, ingrate, wanting in gratitude, insensible of benefits.
forgotten; un-acknowledged, -thanked, -requited, -rewarded; ill-requited.
Int. thank you for nothing! *'et tu Brute!'*

918. Forgiveness.—N. forgiveness, pardon, condonation, grace, remission, absolution, amnesty, oblivion; indulgence; reprieve.

conciliation; reconciliation etc. (*pacification*) 723; propitiation.

excuse, exoneration, quittance, release, indemnity; bill –, act –, covenant –, deed- of indemnity; exculpation etc. (*acquittal*) 970.

longanimity, placability, forbearance; *amantium irae*; *locus poenitentiae*.

V. forgive, – and forget; pardon, condone, think no more of, let bygones be bygones, shake hands; forget an injury, bury the hatchet; clean the slate.

excuse, pass over, overlook; wink at etc. (*neglect*) 460; bear with; allow –, make allowances- for; let one down easily, not be too hard upon, pocket the affront; blot out one's transgression.

let off, remit, absolve, give absolution, reprieve; acquit etc. 970.

beg –, ask –, implore- pardon etc. *n.*; conciliate, propitiate, placate; make up a quarrel etc. (*pacify*) 723; let the wound heal.

Adj. forgiving, placable, conciliatory.

forgiven etc. *v.*; un-resented, -avenged, revenged.

Adv. cry you mercy.

Phr. *veniam petimusque damusque vicissim*; more in sorrow than in anger.

919. Revenge.—N. revenge, -ment; vengeance; avenge-ment, -ance; sweet revenge, *vendetta*, death-feud, eye for an eye, blood for blood, a Roland for an Oliver; retaliation etc. 718; day of reckoning.

rancor, vindictiveness, implacability; malevolence etc. 907; ruthlessness etc. 914*a*.

avenger, vindicator, Nemesis, Eumenides.

V. re-, a-venge; take –, have one's- revenge; breathe -revenge, – vengeance; wreak one's -vengeance, – anger; give no quarter.

have -accounts to settle, – a crow to pluck, – a rod in pickle; pay off old scores.

keep the wound green; harbor -revenge, – vindictive feeling; bear malice; rankle, – in the breast; have at one's mercy.

Adj. revenge-, venge-ful; vindictive, rancorous; pitiless etc. 914*a*; ruthless, rigorous, avenging, retaliative.

unforgiving, unrelenting; inexorable, stony-hearted, implacable; relent-, remorse-less.

aeternum servans sub pectore vulnus; rankling, immitigable.

Phr. *manet -cicatrix,– altâ mente repostum.* revenge is sweet.

920. Jealousy.—N. jealous-y, -ness; jaundiced eye, heartburning; green-eyed monster; yellows; Juno.

V. be -jealous etc. *adj.*; view with -jealousy, – a jealous eye.

Adj. jealous, – as a Barbary pigeon; jaundiced, yellow-eyed, horn-mad.

921. Envy.—N. envy; enviousness etc. *adj.*; rivalry; *jalousie de métier*.

V. envy, covet, lust after, crave, burst with envy, regard with envious eyes.

Adj. envious, invidious, covetous; *alieni appetens*.

922. Right.—N. right; what -ought to, – should- be; fitness etc. *adj.*; *summum jus*.

justice, equity; equitableness etc. *adj.*; propriety; fair play, impartiality, measure for measure, give and take, *lex talionis*, square deal.

Astraea, Nemesis, Themis.

scales of justice, even-handed justice, retributive justice, *suum cuique*; clear stage –, fair field- and no favor; Queensberry rules.

morals etc. (*duty*) 926; law etc. 963; honor etc. (*probity*) 939; virtue etc. 944.

V. be -right etc. *adj.*; stand to reason.

see -justice done, – one righted, – fair play; do justice to; recompense etc. (*reward*) 973; hold the scales even, give and take; serve one right, put the saddle on the right horse; give -every one, – the devil- his due; *audire alteram partem*.

deserve etc. (*be entitled to*) 924.

Adj. right, good; just, reasonable; fit etc. 924; equ-al, -able, -itable; evenhanded, fair, – and square.

legitimate, justifiable, rightful; as it -should, – ought to- be; lawful etc. (*permitted*) 760, (*legal*) 963.

deserved etc. 924.

Adv. rightly etc. *adj.*; in -justice, – equity, – reason.

without -distinction of, – regard to, – respect to- persons; upon even terms.

Int. all right!

923. Wrong.—N. wrong; what -ought not to, – should not- be; *malum in se*; unreasonableness, grievance; shame.

injustice; unfairness etc. *adj.*; iniquity, foul play, partiality, leaning; favor, -itism; nepotism, party spirit, partisanship; undueness etc. 925; unlawfulness etc. 964.

robbing Peter to pay Paul etc. *v.*; the wolf and the lamb; vice etc. 945.

a custom more honored in the breach than the observance.

V. be -wrong etc. *adj.*; cry to heaven for vengeance.

do -wrong etc. *n.*; be -inequitable etc. *adj.*; favor, lean towards; encroach; impose upon; reap where one has not sown; give an inch and take an ell; rob Peter to pay Paul.

Adj. wrong, -ful; bad, too bad; unjust, -fair; in-, un-equitable; unequal, partial, one-sided.

objectionable; un-reasonable, -allowable, -warrantable, -justifiable; not cricket, not playing the game; improper, unfit; unjustified etc. 925; illegal etc. 964; iniquitous, criminal; immoral etc. 945; injurious etc. 649.

in the wrong, – box.

Adv. wrongly etc. *adj.*

Phr. it will not do; this is too bad.

924. Dueness.—N. due, -ness; right, privilege, prerogative, prescription, title, claim, pretension, demand, birthright.

immunity, license, liberty, franchise; vested -interest, – right; licitness.

sanction, authority, warranty, charter; warrant etc. (*permission*) 760; constitution etc. (*law*) 963; tenure; bond etc. (*security*) 771.

deserts, merits, dues.

claimant, appellant; plaintiff etc. 938.

V. be -due etc. *adj.* to, – the due etc. *n.* of; have -right, – title, – claim- to; be entitled to; have a claim upon; belong to etc. (*property*) 780.

deserve, merit, be worthy of, richly deserve.

demand, claim; call upon –, come upon –, appeal to- for; re-vendicate, -claim; exact; insist -on, – upon; challenge; take one's stand, make a point of, require, lay claim to, assert, assume, arrogate, make good; substantiate; vindicate a -claim, – right; make out a case.

give –, confer- a right; sanction, entitle; authorize etc. 760; sanctify, legalize, ordain, prescribe, allot.

give every one his due etc. 922; pay one's dues; have one's -due, – rights; stand upon one's rights.

use a right, assert, enforce, put in force, lay under contribution.

Adj. having a right to etc. *v.*; entitled to; claiming; deserving, meriting, worthy of.

privileged, allowed, sanctioned, warranted, authorized; ordained, prescribed, constitutional, chartered, enfranchised.

prescriptive, presumptive; absolute, indefeasible; un-, in-alienable.

imprescriptible, inviolable, unimpeachable, unchallenged; sacrosanct.

due to, merited, deserved, condign, richly deserved, *emeritus*.

allowable etc. (*permitted*) 760; lawful, licit, legitimate, legal; legalized etc. (*law*) 963.

square, unexceptionable, right; equitable etc. 922; due, *en règle*; fit, -ting; correct, proper, meet, befitting, becoming, seemly; decorous; creditable, up to the mark, right as a trivet; just –, quite- the thing; *selon les règles*.

Adv. duly, *ex officio*, *de jure*; by -right, – divine right; as is -fitting, – proper, – fitting and proper; *jure divino*, *Dei gratiâ*, in the name of.

Phr. *civis Romanus sum*.

925. Undueness. [Absence of right.]—**N.** undueness etc. *adj.*; *malum prohibitum*; impropriety; illegality etc. 964.

falseness etc. *adj.*; emptiness –, invalidity- of title; illegitimacy.

loss of right, disfranchisement, forfeiture.

usurpation, assumption, tort, violation, breach, encroachment, presumption, seizure, stretch, exaction, imposition, lion's share.

usurper, pretender, Carlist; imposter.

V. be -undue etc. *adj.*; not be -due etc. 924.

infringe, encroach, trench on, exact; arrogate, – to oneself; give an inch and take an ell; stretch –, strain- a point; usurp, violate, do violence to; sail under false colors.

dis-franchise, -entitle, -qualify; invalidate.

relax etc. (*be lax*) 738; misbehave etc. (*vice*) 945; misbecome.

Adj. undue; unlawful etc. (*illegal*) 964; unconstitutional, *ultra vires*; illicit; un-authorized, -warranted, -allowed, -sanctioned, -justified; un-, dis-entitled, -qualified; un-privileged, -chartered.

illegitimate, bastard, spurious, false; usurped, tortious.

un-deserved, -merited, -earned; unfulfilled.

forfeited, disfranchised.

improper; un-meet, -fit, -befitting, -seemly; un-, mis-becoming; seemless; *contra bonos mores*; not the thing, out of the question, not to be thought of; preposterous, pretentious, would- be.

926. Duty.—N. duty, what ought to be done, moral obligation, accountableness, liability, *onus*, responsibility; bounden –, imperative- duty; call, – of duty.

allegiance, fealty, tie; engagement etc. (*promise*) 768; part; function, calling etc. (*business*) 625.

morality, morals, decalogue; case of conscience; conscientiousness etc. (*probity*) 939; conscience, inward monitor, still small voice within, sense of duty, tender conscience.

dueness etc. 924; propriety, fitness, seemliness, amenableness, decorum; the -thing, – proper thing; the -right, – proper- thing to do.

[Science of morals] eth-ics, -ology; deon-, aretology; moral –, ethical-philosophy; casuistry, polity.

observance, fulfilment, discharge, performance, acquittal, satisfaction, redemption; good behavior.

V. be -the duty of, – incumbent etc. *adj.* on, – responsible etc. *adj.*; behoove, become, befit, beseem; belong –, pertain- to; fall to one's lot; devolve on; lie -upon, – on one's head, – at one's door; rest -with, – on the shoulders of.

take upon oneself etc. (*promise*) 768.

be –, become- -bound to, – sponsor for; be responsible for; incur a -responsibility etc. *n.*; be –, stand –, lie- under an obligation; have to answer for, owe it to oneself.

impose a -duty etc. *n.*; enjoin, require, exact; bind, – over; saddle with, prescribe, assign, call upon, look to, oblige.

enter upon –, perform –, observe –, fulfil –, discharge –, adhere to –, acquit oneself of –, satisfy- -a duty, – an obligation; act one's part, redeem one's pledge, do justice to, be at one's post; do duty; do one's duty etc. (*be virtuous*) 944.

be on one's good behavior, mind one's P's and Q's.

Adj. obligatory, binding; imperative, peremptory; stringent etc. (*severe*) 739; behooving etc. *v.*; incumbent –, chargeable- on; under obligation; obliged –, bound –, tied- by; saddled with.

due –, beholden –, bound –, indebted- to; tied down; compromised etc. (*promised*) 768; in duty bound.

amenable, liable, accountable, responsible, answerable.

right, meet etc. (*due*) 924; moral, ethical, casuistical, conscientious, ethological.

Adv. with a safe conscience, as in duty bound, on one's own responsibility, at one's own risk, *suo periculo*; *in foro conscientiae*; *quamdiu se bene gesserit*; at one's post, on duty.

Phr. *dura lex sed lex*.

927. Dereliction of Duty.—N. dere; liction of duty; fault etc. (*guilt*) 947- sin etc. (*vice*) 945; non-observance, -performance, -co-operation; neglect, carelessness, laziness, incompetence, eye-service, relaxation, infraction, violation, transgression, failure, evasion, indolence; dead letter.

slacker, loafer, striker, non-co-operator.

V. violate; break, – through; infringe; set -aside, – at naught; trample -on, – under foot; slight, neglect, evade, renounce, forswear, repudiate; wash one's hands of; escape, transgress, fail.

call to account etc. (*disapprobation*) 932.

927a. Exemption.—N. exemption, freedom, irresponsibility, immunity, liberty, license, release, exoneration, excuse, dispensation, absolution, franchise, renunciation, discharge; exculpation etc. 970; *aegrotat*.

V. be -exempt etc. *adj.*

exempt, release, acquit, discharge, quit-claim, remise, remit; free, set at liberty, let off, pass over, spare, excuse, dispense with, give dispensation, license; stretch a point; absolve etc. (*forgive*) 918; exonerate etc. (*exculpate*) 970; save the necessity.

Adj. exempt, free, immune, at liberty, scot free; released etc. *v.*; unbound, unencumbered; irresponsible, unaccountable, not answerable; excusable.

928. Respect.—N. respect, regard, consideration; courtesy etc. 894; attention, deference, reverence, honor, esteem, estimation, veneration, admiration; approbation etc. 931.

homage, fealty, obeisance, genuflexion, kneeling, prostration; obsequiousness etc. 886; salaam, *kowtow*, bow, presenting arms, salute.

respects, regards, duty, *devoirs*, *égards*.

devotion etc. (*piety*) 987.

V. respect, regard; revere, -nce; hold in reverence, honor, venerate, hallow; esteem etc. (*approve of*) 931; think much of; entertain –, bear- respect for; have a high opinion of; look up to, defer to; pay -attention, – respect etc. *n.*- to; do –, render- honor to; do the honors, hail; show courtesy etc. 894; salute, present arms; do –, pay- homage to; pay tribute to; kneel to, bow to, bend the knee to; fall down before, prostrate oneself, kiss the hem of one's garment; worship etc. 990.

keep one's distance, make room, observe due decorum, stand upon ceremony.

command –, inspire- respect; awe, impose, overawe, dazzle.

Adj. respecting etc. *v.*; respectful, deferential, decorous, reverential, obsequious, ceremonious, bare-headed, cap in hand, on one's knees; prostrate etc. (*servile*) 886.

respected etc. *v.*; in high -esteem, – estimation; time-honored, venerable, *emeritus*.

Adv. in deference to; with -all, – due, – the highest- respect; with submission.

saving your -grace, – presence; *salva sit reverentia*; *pace tanti nominis*.

Int. hail! all hail! *esto perpetua!* may your shadow never be less!

929. Disrespect.—N. dis-respect, -esteem, -estimation, -favor, -repute; low estimation; disparagement etc. (*dispraise*) 932; (*detraction*) 934.

irreverence; slight, neglect; *spretae injuria formae*; superciliousness etc. (*contempt*) 930.

vilipendency, contumely, affront, dishonor, insult, indignity, outrage, discourtesy etc. 895; practical joking; scurrility, scoffing, sibilation; ir-, derision; mockery; irony etc. (*ridicule*) 856; sarcasm.

hiss, hoot, gibe, flout, jeer, scoff, gleek, taunt, sneer, quip, fling, wipe, slap in the face.

V. hold in disrespect etc. (*despise*) 930; misprize, disregard, slight, undervalue, depreciate, trifle with, set at naught, pass by, push aside, overlook, turn one's back upon, laugh in one's sleeve; be -disrespectful etc. *adj.*, – discourteous etc. 895; treat with -disrespect etc. *n.*; set down, browbeat.

dishonor, desecrate; insult, affront, outrage.

speak slightingly of; disparage etc. (*dispraise*) 932; vilipend, call names; throw –, fling- dirt; drag through the mud, point at, indulge in personalities; make -mouths, – faces; bite the thumb; take –, pluck- by the beard; toss in a blanket, tar and feather.

have –, hold- in derision; deride, scoff, sneer, laugh at, snigger, ridicule, gibe, mock, jeer, taunt, twit, niggle, gleek, gird, flout, fleer; roast, turn into ridicule; guy, burlesque etc. 856; laugh to scorn etc. (*contempt*) 930; smoke; fool; make -game, – a fool, – an April fool- of; play a practical joke; rag; lead one a dance, run the rig upon, have a fling at, scout, hiss, hoot, mob.

Adj. disrespectful; aweless, irreverent; disparaging etc. 934; insulting etc. *v.*; supercilious etc. (*scornful*) 930; rude, derisive, contemptuous, sarcastic; scurri-le, -lous; contumelious.

un-respected, -worshipped, -envied, -saluted; un-dis-regarded.

Adv. disrespectfully etc. *adj.*

930. Contempt.—N. contempt, disdain, scorn, sovereign contempt; despi-sal, -ciency; vilipendency, contumely; slight, sneer, spurn, by-word.

contemptuousness etc. *adj.*; scornful eye; smile of contempt; derision etc. (*disrespect*) 929.

[State of being despised] despisedness.

V. despise, contemn, scorn, disdain, feel contempt for, view with a scornful eye, disregard, slight, not mind; pass by etc. (*neglect*) 460.

look down upon; hold -cheap, – in contempt, – in disrespect; think -nothing, – small beer- of; make light of; underestimate etc. 483; esteem -slightly, – of small or no account; take no account of, care nothing for; set no store by; not care a -straw etc. (*unimportance*) 643; set at naught, laugh in one's sleeve, snap one's fingers at, shrug one's shoulders, turn up one's nose at, pooh-pooh, damn with faint praise; sneeze –, whistle –, sneer- at; curl up one's lip, toss the head, *traiter de haut*; laugh at etc. (*be disrespectful*) 929.

point the finger of –, hold up to –, laugh to- scorn; scout, hoot, flout, hiss, scoff at.

turn -one's back, – a cold shoulder- upon; tread –, trample- -upon, – under foot; spurn, kick; fling to the winds etc. (*repudiate*) 610; send away with a flea in the ear.

Adj. contemptuous; disdain-, scorn-ful; withering, contumelious, supercilious, cynical, haughty, bumptious, cavalier; derisive.

contemptible, despicable; pitiable; pitiful etc. (*unimportant*) 643; despised etc. *v.*; downtrodden; unenvied.

Adv. contemptuously etc. *adj*.

Int. a fig for etc. (*unimportant*) 643; bah! never mind! away with! hang it! fiddle-de-dee!

931. Approbation.—N. approbation; approval, -ement; sanction, advocacy; nod of approbation; esteem, estimation, good opinion, golden opinions, admiration; love etc. 897; appreciation, regard, account, popularity, *kudos*, credit; repute etc. 873.

commendation, praise; laud, -ation; good word; meed –, tribute- of praise; encomium; eulog-y, -ium; *éloge*, panegyric; homage, hero worship; benediction, blessing, benison.

applause, plaudit, clap; clapping, – of hands; accl-aim, -amation; cheer; paean, hosannah; shout –, peal –, chorus –, thunders- of -applause etc. Kentish fire; Prytaneum; blurb.

V. approve; think -good, – much of, – well of, – highly of; esteem, value, prize; set great store -by, – on.

do justice to, appreciate; honor, hold in esteem, look up to, admire; like etc. 897; be in favor of, wish God speed; hail, – with satisfaction.

stand –, stick- up for; uphold, hold up, countenance, sanction; clap –, pat- on the back; keep in countenance, endorse, give credit, recommend; mark with a white -mark, – stone.

commend, praise; be-, laud; compliment, pay a tribute, bepraise; clap, – the hands; applaud, cheer, acclaim, acclamate, encore; panegyrize, eulogize, cry up, *prôner*, puff; extol, – to the skies; magnify, glorify, exalt, boost, swell, make much of; flatter etc. 933; bless, give a blessing to; have –, say- a good word for; speak -well, – highly, – in high terms- of; sing –, sound –, chaunt –, resound- the praises of; sing praises to; cheer –, applaud- to the -echo, – very echo.

redound to the -honor, – praise, – credit- of; do credit to, deserve -praise etc. *n.*; recommend itself; pass muster.

be -praised etc.; receive honorable mention; be in -favor, – high favor- with; ring with the praises of, win golden opinions, gain credit, find favor with, stand well in the opinion of; *laudari a laudato viro*.

Adj. approving etc. *v.*; in favor of; lost in admiration.

commendatory, complimentary, benedictory, laudatory, panegyrical, eulogistic, encomiastic, acclamatory, lavish of praise, uncritical.

approved, praised etc. *v.*; un-censured, -impeached; popular, in good odor; in high esteem etc. (*respected*) 928; in –, in high- favor.

deserving –, worthy of- praise etc. *n.*; praiseworthy, commendable, of estimation; good etc. 648; meritorious, estimable, creditable, plausible, unimpeachable; beyond all praise.

Adv. commendably, with credit, to admiration; well etc. 681; with three times three.

Int. hear, hear! well done! *brav-o! -a! -i! bravissimo! euge! macte virtute!* so far so good, that's right, quite right; *optime!* one cheer more; may your shadow never be less! *esto perpetua!* long life to! *viva! enviva!* God speed! *valete et plaudite! encore! bis!*

Phr. *probatum est.*

932. Disapprobation.—N. disappro-bation, -val; improbation; , dis-esteem, -valuation, -placency; odium; dislike etc. 867; dissent etc. 489.

dis-praise, -commendation; blame, censure, obloquy; detraction etc. 934; disparagement, depreciation; denunciation; condemnation etc. 971; ostracism; boycott; black-list, -ball; *index -expurgatorius, – librorum prohibitorum*.

animadversion, reflection, stricture, objection, exception, criticism; sardonic -grin, – laugh; sarcasm, insinuation, innuendo; bad –, poor –, left-handed- compliment.

satire; sneer etc. (*contempt*) 930; taunt etc. (*disrespect*) 929; cavil, carping, censoriousness; hypercriticism etc. (*fastidiousness*) 868.

reprehension, remonstrance, expostulation, reproof, reprobation, admonition, increpation, reproach; rebuke, reprimand, castigation, jobation, lecture, curtain lecture, blow up, wigging, dressing, – down; rating, scolding, trimming; correction, set down, rap on the knuckles, *coup de bec*, rebuff; slap, – on the face; home thrust; hit; frown, scowl, black look.

diatribe; jeremiad; *tirade*, philippic.

clamor, outcry, hue and cry; hiss, -ing; sibilation, cat-call; execration etc. 908.

chiding, upbraiding etc. *v.*; exprobration, abuse, vituperation, invective, objurgation, contumely, personal remarks; hard –, cutting –, bitter- words.

evil-speaking; bad language etc. 908; personality.

V. disapprove; dislike etc. 867; lament etc. 839; object to, take exception to; be scandalized at, think ill of; view with -disfavor, – dark eyes, – jaundiced eyes; *nil admirari*, disvalue, improbate.

frown upon, look grave; bend –, knit- the brows; shake the head at, shrug the shoulders; turn up the nose etc. (*contempt*) 930; look -askance, – black upon; look with an evil eye; make a wry -face, – mouth- at; set one's face against.

dis-praise, -commend, -parage; deprecate, speak ill of, not speak well of, slate, condemn etc. (*find guilty*) 971.

blame; lay –, cast- blame upon; censure, *fronder*, reproach, pass censure on, reprobate, impugn.

remonstrate, expostulate, recriminate.

reprehend, chide, admonish; bring –, call- -to account, – over the coals, – to order; take to task, reprove, lecture, bring to book; read a -lesson, – lecture- to; rebuke, correct.

reprimand, chastise, castigate, lash, blow up, trounce, trim, *laver la tête*, overhaul; give it one, – finely; gibbet.

accuse etc. 938; impeach, denounce; hold up to -reprobation, – execration; expose, brand, gibbet, stigmatize; show –, pull –, take- up; cry 'shame' upon; be outspoken; raise a hue and cry against.

execrate etc. 908; exprobrate, speak daggers, vituperate; abuse, –, like a pickpocket; scold, rate, objurage, upbraid, fall foul of; jaw; rail, – at, – in good set terms; bark at; anathematize, call names; call by -hard, – ugly- names; a-, re-vile; vili-fy, -pend; bespatter; backbite; clapperclaw; rave –, thunder –, fulminate- against; load with reproaches; lash with the tongue.

exclaim –, protest –, inveigh –, declaim –, cry out –, raise one's voice- against.

decry; cry –, run –, frown- down; clamor, hiss,

hoot, mob, ostracize; draw up –, sing- a round robin; black-ball, -list.

animadvert –, reflect- upon; glance at; cast - reflection, – reproach, – a slur- upon; insinuate, damn with faint praise; 'hint a fault and hesitate dislike;' not to be able to say much for.

scoff at, point at; twit, taunt etc. (*disrespect*) 929; sneer at etc. (*despise*) 230; satirize, lampoon; defame etc. (*detract*) 934; depreciate, find fault with, criticize, cut up; pull –, pick- to pieces; take exception; cavil; peck –, nibble –, carp- at; be - censorious etc. *adj.*; pick -holes, – a hole, – a hole in one's coat; make a fuss about.

take –, set- down; snub, snap one up, give a rap on the knuckles; throw a stone -at, – in one's garden; have a -fling, – snap- at; have words with, pluck a crow with; give one a -wipe, – lick with the rough side of the tongue.

incur blame, excite disapprobation, scandalize, shock, revolt; get a bad name, forfeit one's good opinion, be under a cloud, come under the ferule, bring a hornet's nest about one's ears.

take blame, stand corrected; have to answer for.

Adj. disapproving etc. *v.*; scandalized.

disparaging, condemnatory, damnatory, denunciatory, reproachful, abusive, objurgatory, clamorous, vituperative; defamatory etc. 934.

satirical, sarcastic, sardonic, cynical, dry, sharp, cutting, biting, severe, virulent, withering, trenchant, hard upon; censorious, critical, captious, carping, hypercritical; fastidious etc. 868; sparing of –, grudging- praise.

disapproved, chid etc. *v.*; in bad odor, blown upon, unapproved; unblest; at a discount, exploded; weighed in the balance and found wanting.

blameworthy, reprehensible etc. (*guilt*) 947; to –, worthy of- blame, answerable, uncommendable, exceptionable, not to be thought of, bad etc. 649; vicious etc. 945.

un-lamented, -bewailed, -pitied.

Adv. with a wry face; reproachfully etc. *adj.*

Int. it is too bad! it -won't, – will never- do! marry come up! Oh! come! 'sdeath!

forbid it Heaven! God –, Heaven- forbid! out –, fie- upon it! away with! tut! *O tempora! O mores!* shame! fie, – for shame! out on you!

tell it not in Gath!

933. Flattery.—N. flattery, adulation, gloze; bland-ishment, -iloquence; cajolery; fawning, wheedling etc. *v.*; captation, coquetry, sycophancy, obsequiousness, flunkeyism, toad-eating, tuft-hunting; snobbishness.

incense, honeyed words, flummery; bun-kum, -combe; blarney, *placebo*, butter; soft -soap, – sawder; rose water.

voice of the charmer, mouth honor; lip-homage; euphemism; unctuousness etc. *adj.*

V. flatter, praise to the skies, puff; wheedle, cajole, glaver, coax; fawn, –, upon; humor, gloze, soothe, pet, coquet, slaver, butter; be-spatter, -slubber, -plaster, -slaver; lay it on thick, overpraise; earwig, cog, collogue; truckle –, pander *or* pandar –, pay court- to; court; creep into the good graces of; curry favor with, hang on the sleeve of; fool to the top of one's bent; lick the dust.

lay the flattering unction to one's soul, gild the pill, make things pleasant.

overestimate etc. 482; exaggerate etc. 549.

Adj. flattering etc. *v.*; adulatory; mealy-, honey-mouthed; honeyed; smooth, – tongued; soapy, oily, unctuous, blandiloquent, specious; fine-, fair-spoken; plausible, servile, sycophantic, fulsome; courtier-ly, -like.

Adv. *ad captandum.*

934. Detraction.—N. detraction, disparagement, depreciation, vilification, obloquy, scurrility, scandal, defamation, aspersion, traducement, slander, calumny, obtrectation, evil-speaking, backbiting, *scandalum magnatum.*

personality, libel, squib, lampoon, skit, pasquinade; *chronique scandaleuse.*

sarcasm, cynicism; criticism (*disapprobation*) 932; invective etc. 932; envenomed tongue; *spretae injuria formae.*

detractor etc. 936.

V. detract, derogate, decry, depreciate, disparage; run –, cry- down; minimize, make light of; belittle, sneer at etc. (*contemn*) 930; criticize, pull to pieces, pick a hole in one's coat, asperse, cast aspersions, blow upon, bespatter, blacken; vilify, -pend; avile; give a dog a bad name, brand, malign, backbite, libel, lampoon, traduce, slander, defame, calumniate, bear false witness against; speak ill of behind one's back.

'damn with faint praise, assent with civil leer; and without sneering, others teach to sneer.'

fling dirt etc. (*disrespect*) 929; anathematize etc. 932; dip the pen in gall, view in a bad light.

Adj. detracting etc. *v.*; defamatory, detractory, derogatory; disparaging, libellous; scurril-e, -ous; abusive; foul-spoken, -tongued, -mouthed; slanderous; calumni-ous, -atory; sar-castic, -donic; satirical, cynical.

935. Flatterer.—N. flatterer, adulator; eulogist, -phemist; optimist, encomiast, *laudator*, whitewasher, booster.

toad-y, -eater; sycophant, courtier, pickthank, Sir Pertinax MacSycophant; *flâneur, prôneur*; puffer, touter, *claqueur*; claw-back, ear-wig, doer of dirty work; parasite, hanger on etc. (*servility*) 886.

936. Detractor.—N. detractor, reprover; cens-or, -urer; cynic, critic, caviller, carper, word-catcher.

defamer, backbiter, slanderer, knocker, Sir Benjamin Backbite, lampooner, satirist, traducer, libeller, calumniator, dearest foe, dawplucker, Thersites; Zoilus; good-natured –, candid- friend [satirically]; reviler, vituperator, castigator; shrew etc. 901.

disapprover, *laudator temporis acti.*

937. Vindication.—N. vindication, justification, warrant; exoneration, exculpation; acquittal etc. 970; whitewashing.

extenuation; pallia-tion, -tive; softening, mitigation.

reply, defense; recrimination etc. 938.

apology, gloss, varnish; plea etc. 617; salvo; excuse, extenuating circumstances; allowance, – to be made; *locus poenitentiae*.

apologist, vindicator, justifier; defendant etc. 938.

justifiable charge, true bill.

V. justify, warrant; be an -excuse etc. *n.*- for; lend a color, furnish a handle; vindicate; ex-, disculpate; acquit etc. 970; clear, set right, exonerate, whitewash.

extenuate, palliate, excuse, soften, apologize, varnish, slur, gloze; put a -gloss, – good face- upon; mince; gloss over, bolster up, help a lame dog over a stile.

advocate, defend, plead one's cause; stand –, stick –, speak- up for; contend –, speak- for; bear out, keep in countenance, support; plead etc. 617; say in defense; plead ignorance; confess and avoid, propugn, put in a good word for.

take the will for the deed, make allowance for, do justice to; give -one, – the Devil- his due.

make good; prove -the truth of, – one's case; be justified by the event.

Adj. vindicat-ed, -ing etc. *v.*; vindicat-ive, -ory; palliative; exculpatory; apologetic.

excusable, defensible, pardonable; veni-al, -able; specious, plausible, justifiable.

Phr. *'honi soit qui mal y pense.'*

938. Accusation.—**N.** accusation, charge, imputation, slur, inculpation, exprobration, delation; crimination; in-, ac-, re-crimination; *tu quoque* argument; invective etc. 932.

de-nunciation, -nouncement; libel, challenge, citation, arraignment; im-, ap-peachment; indictment, bill of indictment, true bill; lawsuit etc. 969; condemnation etc. 971.

gravamen of a charge, head and front of one's offending, *argumentum ad hominem*; scandal etc. (*detraction*) 934; *scandalum magnatum*.

accuser, prosecutor, plaintiff, complainant, petitioner; relator, informer; appellant.

accused, defendant, prisoner, panel co-, respondent; litigant.

V. accuse, charge, tax, impute, twit, taunt with, reproach.

brand with reproach; stigmatize, slur; cast a -stone at, – slur on; incriminate; inculpate, implicate; call to account etc. (*censure*) 932; take to- blame, – task; put in the black book.

inform against, indict, denounce, arraign; im-, ap-peach; have up, show up, pull up, challenge, cite, lodge a complaint; prosecute, bring an action against etc. 969.

charge –, saddle- with; lay to one's -door, – charge; lay the blame on, bring home to; cast –, throw- in one's teeth; cast the first stone at.

have –, keep- a rod in pickle for; have a crow to pluck with.

trump up a charge.

Adj. accusing etc. *v.*; accusat-ory, -ive; imputative, denunciatory; re-, criminatory.

accused etc. *v.*; suspected; under -suspicion, – a cloud, – *surveillance*; in -custody, – detention; in the -lock up, – watch house, – house of detention.

accusable, imputable; in-defensible, -excusable; un-pardonable, -justifiable; vicious etc. 945.

Int. look at home; *tu quoque* etc. (*retaliation*) 718.

939. Probity.—**N.** probity, integrity, rectitude; uprightness etc. *adj.*; honesty, faith; honor; good faith, *bona fides*; purity, clean hands.

fairness etc. *adj.*; fair play, justice, equity, impartiality, principle; grace.

constancy; faithfulness etc. *adj.*; fidelity, loyalty; incorrupt-ion, -ibility.

trustworthiness etc. *adj.*; truth, candor, singleness of heart; veracity etc. 543; tender conscience etc. (*sense of duty*) 926.

punctil-iousness, -io; delicacy, nicety; scrupulosity, -ousness etc. *adj.*; scruple; point, – of honor; punctuality.

dignity etc. (*repute*) 873; respectability, -bleness etc. *adj.*; gentleman; man of -honor, – his word; *fidus Achates*, *preux chevalier*; *galantuomo*; truepenny, trump, brick; true Briton, white man, sportsman.

court of honor, a fair field and no favor; *argumentum ad verecundiam*.

V. be -honorable etc. *adj.*; deal -honorably, – squarely, – impartially, – fairly; speak the truth etc. (*veracity*) 543; tell the truth and shame the devil, *vitam impendere vero*; show a proper spirit, make a point of; do one's duty etc. 944; play the game.

redeem one's pledge etc. 926; keep –, be as good as- one's -promise, – word; keep faith with, not fail.

give and take, *audire alteram partem*, give the devil his due, put the saddle on the right horse.

redound to one's honor.

Adj. upright; honest, – as daylight; veracious etc. 543; virtuous etc. 944; honorable; fair, right, just, equitable, impartial, even-handed, square; fair –, open- and aboveboard.

constant, – as the northern star; faithful, loyal, staunch; true, – blue, – to one's colors, – to the core, – as the needle to the pole; true-hearted, trust-y, -worthy; as good as one's word, to be depended on, incorruptible.

manly, straightforward etc. (*ingenuous*) 703; frank, candid, open-hearted.

conscientious, tender-conscienced, right-minded; high-principled, -minded; scrupulous, religious, strict; nice, punctilious, correct, punctual; respect-, reput-able; gentlemanlike.

inviol-able, -ate; un-violated, -broken, -betrayed; un-bought, -bribed.

innocent etc. 946; pure; stainless; un-stained, -tarnished, -sullied, -tainted, -perjured; uncorrupt, -ed; unde-filed, -praved, -bauched; *integer vitae scelerisque purus*; *justus et tenax propositi*.

chivalrous, jealous of honor, *sans peur et sans reproche*; high-spirited.

supra-mundane, unworldly, overscrupulous.

Adv. honorably etc. *adj.*; *bona fide*; on the square, in good faith, honor bright, *foro conscientiae*, with clean hands; by fair means.

940. Improbity.—**N.** improbity; dishon-esty, -our; deviation from rectitude; disgrace etc. (*disrepute*) 874; fraud etc. (*deception*) 545; lying etc. 544; bad –, Punic- faith; *mala –, Punica, fides*; infidelity; faithlessness etc. *adj.*; Judas kiss, betrayal; scrap of paper.

breach of -promise, – trust, – faith; prodition, disloyalty, divided allegiance, treason, high treason; apostacy etc. (*tergiversation*) 607; non-observance etc. 773.

shabbiness etc. *adj.*; villainy; baseness etc. *adj.*; abjection, debasement, turpitude, moral turpitude, laxity, trimming, shuffling.

perfidy; perfidiousness etc. *adj.*; treachery, double-dealing; unfairness etc. *adj.*; knavery, roguery, rascality, foul-play; jobb-ing, -ery; Tammany, graft; venality, nepotism; corruption, job, shuffle, fishy transaction, barratry; sharp practice, heads I win, tails you lose; mouth-honor etc. (*flattery*) 933.

V. be -dishonest etc. *adj.*; play false; break one's -word, – faith, – promise; jilt, betray, forswear; shuffle etc. (*lie*) 544; live by one's wits, sail near the wind; play with marked cards.

disgrace –, dishonor –, demean –, degrade- oneself; derogate, stoop, grovel, sneak, lose caste; sell oneself, go over to the enemy; seal one's infamy.

Adj. dishon-est, -orable; un-conscientious, -scrupulous; fraudulent etc. 545; knavish; disgraceful etc. (*disreputable*) 874; wicked etc. 945.

false-hearted, disingenuous; unfair, one-sided; double, -tongued, -faced; time-serving, crooked, tortuous, insidious, Machiavellian, dark, slippery; questionable; fishy; perfidious, treacherous, perjured.

infamous, arrant, foul, base, vile, low, ignominious, blackguard;

contemptible, abject, mean, shabby, little, paltry, dirty, scurvy, scabby, sneaking, groveling, scrubby, rascally, pettifogging; beneath one; not cricket.

low-minded, -thoughted; base-minded.

undignified, indign; unbe-coming, -seeming, fitting; de-rogatory, -grading; *infra dignitatem*; ungentleman-ly, -like; un-knightly, -chivalric, -manly, -handsome; recreant, inglorious.

corrupt, venal; debased, mongrel.

faithless, of bad faith, false, unfaithful, disloyal; untrustworthy; trust-, troth-less; lost to shame, dead to honor.

Adv. dishonestly etc. *adj.*; *malâ fide*, like a thief in the night, by crooked paths; by foul means.

Int. *O tempora! O mores!*

941. Knave.—N. knave, rogue, villain; Scapin, rascal; Lazarillo de Tormes; bad man etc. 949; blackguard etc. 949.

traitor, betrayer, arch-traitor, conspirator, stool pigeon, Judas, Catiline; reptile, serpent, snake in the grass, wolf in sheep's clothing, sneak, Jerry Sneak, tell-tale, squealer, mischief-maker, trimmer; renegade etc. (*tergiversation*) 607; truant, recreant; sycophant etc. (*servility*) 886.

942. Disinterestedness.—N. disinterestedness etc. *adj.*; generosity; liberal-ity, -ism; altruism; benevolence etc. 906; elevation, loftiness of purpose, exaltation, magnanimity; chival-ry, -rous spirit; heroism, sublimity.

self-denial, -abnegation, -effacement, -sacrifice, -immolation, -control etc. (*resolution*) 604; stoicism, devotion, martyrdom, *suttee*.

labor of love.

V. be -disinterested etc. *adj.*; make a sacrifice, lay one's head on the block; put oneself in the place of others, do as one would be done by, do unto others as we would men should do unto us.

Adj. disinterested; unselfish; self-denying, -sacrificing, -devoted; generous.

handsome, liberal, noble; noble-, high-minded; princely, great, high, elevated, lofty, exalted, spirited, stoical, magnanimous; great-, large-hearted, chivalrous, heroic, sublime.

un-bought, -bribed; uncorrupted etc. (*upright*) 939.

943. Selfishness.—N. selfishness etc. *adj.*; self-love, -indulgence, -worship, -interest; ego-tism, -ism; egocentrism, narcissism; *amour propre* etc. (*vanity*) 880; nepotism.

worldliness etc. *adj.*; world wisdom.

illiberality; meanness etc. *adj.*

time-server; tuft-, fortune-hunter; self-seeker; jobber, worldling; egotist, egoist, monopolist, nepotist, profiteer; temporizer, trimmer; dog in the manger, charity that begins at home.

V. be -selfish etc. *adj.*; please –, indulge –, coddle- oneself; consult one's own -wishes, – pleasure; look after one's own interest; feather one's nest; take care of number one, have an eye to the main chance, know on which side one's bread is buttered; give an inch and take an ell; wangle.

Adj. selfish; self-seeking, -indulgent, -interested; wrapt up –, centered- in self; egotistic, -al; egoistical; egocentric.

illiberal, mean, ungenerous, narrowminded; mercenary, venal; covetous etc. 819.

unspiritual; earthly, -minded; mundane; worldly, -minded, -wise; time-serving.

interested; *alieni appetens sui profusus*.

Adv. ungenerously etc. *adj.*; to gain some private ends; from selfish –, interested- motives.

Phr. *après nous le déluge*.

944. Virtue.—N. virtue; virtuousness etc. *adj.*; morality; moral rectitude; integrity etc. (*probity*) 939; nobleness etc. 873.

morals; ethics etc. (*duty*) 926; cardinal virtues.

merit, worth, desert, excellence, credit; self-control etc. (*resolution*) 604; self-denial etc. (*temperance*) 953.

well-doing; good -actions, – behavior; discharge –, fulfilment –, performance- of duty; well spent life; innocence etc. 946.

V. be -virtuous etc. *adj.*; practice -virtue etc. *n.*; do –, fulfil –, perform –, discharge- one's duty; redeem one's pledge etc. 926; act well, – one's part; fight the good fight; acquit oneself well; command –, master- one's passions; keep -straight, – in the right path.

set -an, – a good- example; be on one's -good, – best- behavior.

Adj. virtuous, good; innocent etc. 946; meritorious, deserving, worthy, desertful, correct; dut-iful, -eous; moral; right, -eous, -minded; well-intentioned, creditable, laudable, commendable, praiseworthy; above –, beyond- all praise; excellent, admirable; sterling, pure, noble.

exemplary; match-, peer-less; saint-ly, -like; heaven-born, angelic, seraphic, godlike.

Adv. virtuously etc. *adj.*; *e merito*.

945. Vice.—N. vice; evil-doing, – courses; wrong doing; wickedness, viciousness etc. *adj.*; iniquity, peccability, demerit; sin, Adam; old – offending- Adam.

immorality, impropriety, indecorum, scandal, laxity, looseness of morals; want of -principle, – ballast; obliquity, backsliding, infamy, demoralization, pravity, depravity, pollution; hardness of heart; brutality etc. (*malevolence*) 907; corruption etc. (*debasement*) 659; knavery etc. (*improbity*) 940; profligacy; lust etc. 961; flagrancy, atrocity; cannibalism.

infirmity; weakness etc. *adj.*; weakness of the flesh, frailty, imperfection; error; weak side; foible; fail-ing, -ure; crying –, besetting- sin; defect, deficiency, shortcoming; cloven foot.

lowest dregs of vice, sink of iniquity, Alsatian den; *gusto picaresco*.

fault, crime; criminality etc. (*guilt*) 947.

sinner etc. 949.

V. be -vicious etc. *adj.*; sin, commit sin, do amiss, err, transgress; misdemean –, forget –, misconduct- oneself; mis-do, -behave; fall, lapse, slip, trip, offend, trespass; deviate from the -line of duty, – path of virtue etc. 944; take a wrong course, go astray; hug a -sin, – fault; sow one's wild oats.

render -vicious etc. *adj.*; demoralize, brutalize; corrupt etc. (*degrade*) 659.

Adj.* vicious; sinful; sinning etc. *v.*; wicked, iniquitous, bad, immoral, unrighteous, wrong, criminal; naughty, incorrect; undut-eous, -iful.

unprincipled, lawless, disorderly, *contra bonos mores*, indecorous, unseemly, improper; dissolute, profligate, scampish; unworthy; worth-, desert-less; disgraceful, recreant; reprehensible, blameworthy, uncommendable; dis-creditable, -reputable.

base, sinister, scurvy, foul, gross, vile, black, grave, facinorous, felonious, nefarious, shameful, scandalous, infamous, villainous, of a deep dye, heinous; flag-rant, -itious; atrocious, incarnate, accursed.

Mephistophelian, satanic, diabolic, hellish, infernal, stygian, fiend-ish, -like, hell-born, demoniacal, devilish.

mis-created, -begotten; demoralized, corrupt, depraved.

evil-minded, -disposed; ill-conditioned; malevolent etc. 907; heart-, grace-, shame-, virtueless; abandoned, lost to virtue; unconscionable; sunk –, lost –, deep –, steeped- in iniquity.

incorrigible, irreclaimable, obdurate, reprobate, past praying for; culpable, reprehensible etc. (*guilty*) 947.

unjustifiable; in-defensible, -excusable; inexpiable, unpardonable, irremissible.

weak, frail, lax, infirm, imperfect, indiscreet; demoralizing, degrading.

Adv. wrong; sinfully etc. *adj.*; without excuse.

Int. *O tempora! O mores!*

*Most of these adjectives are applicable both to the act and to the agent.

946. Innocence.—N. innocence; guiltlessness etc. *adj.*; incorruption, impeccability.

clean hands, clear conscience, *mens sibi conscia recti*.

innocent, new born babe, lamb, dove.

V. be -innocent etc. *adj.*; *nil conscire sibi nullâ pallescere culpâ*.

acquit etc. 970; exculpate etc. (*vindicate*) 937.

Adj. innocent, not guilty, unguilty; guilt-, fault-, sin-, stain-, blood-, spot-less; clear, immaculate; *rectus in curiâ*; un-spotted, -blemished, -erring; undefiled etc. 939; unhardened, Saturnian; Arcadian etc. (*artless*) 703.

in-, un-culpable; unblam-ed, -able; blameless, inerrable, above suspicion; irrepr-oachable, -ovable, -ehensible; un-exceptionable, -objectionable, -impeachable; salvable; venial etc. 937.

harmless; in-offensive, -noxious, -nocuous; dove-, lamb-like; pure, harmless as doves; innocent as -a lamb, – the babe unborn; more sinned against than sinning.

virtuous etc. 944; un-reproved, -impeached, -reproached.

Adv. innocently etc. *adj.*; with clean hands; with a -clear, – safe- conscience.

947. Guilt.—N. guilt, -iness; culpability; crimin-ality, -ousness; deviation from rectitude etc. (*improbity*) 940; sinfulness etc. (*vice*) 945; peccability.

mis-conduct, -behavior, -doing, -deed; malpractice, fault, sin, error, transgression; dereliction, delinquency; indiscretion, lapse, slip, trip, *faux pas*, *peccadillo*; flaw, blot, omission; fail-ing, -ure.

offence, trespass; mis-demeanor, -feasance, -prision, tort; mal-efaction, -feasance, -versation; crime, felony.

enormity, atrocity, outrage; deadly –, mortal –, unpardonable- sin; died without a name.

corpus delicti.

Adj. guilty, to blame, culpable, peccable, in fault, censurable, reprehensible, blameworthy, uncommendable, illaudable; weighed in the balance and found wanting; exceptionable, objectionable.

Adv. *in flagrante delicto*; red-handed, in the very act.

948. Good Man.—N. good man, worthy.

good woman, goddess, *madonna*, virgin.

model, paragon etc. (*perfection*) 650; good example; hero, demigod, seraph, angel; innocent etc. 946; saint etc. (*piety*) 987; benefactor etc. 912; philanthropist etc. 910; Aristides.

brick, trump, rough diamond, ugly duckling.

salt of the earth; one in ten thousand; one of the best.

Phr. *si sic omnes!*

949. Bad Man.—N. bad man, wrongdoer, worker of iniquity; evil-doer etc. 913; sinner; the -wicked etc. 945; bad example.

rascal, scoundrel, villain, miscreant, caitiff; wretch, reptile, viper, serpent, cockatrice, basilisk, urchin; tiger, monster; devil etc. (*demon*) 980; devil incarnate; demon in human shape, Nana Sahib; hell-hound, -cat; rake-hell.

bad woman, jade, Jezebel, adultress, etc. 962.

scamp, scapegrace, rip, runagate, ne'er-do-well, reprobate, *roué*, rake; limb; one who has sold himself to the devil, fallen angel, *âme damnée*, *vaurien*, *mauvais sujet*, loose fish, sad, dog; lost –, black-sheep; castaway, recreant, defaulter; prodigal etc. 818; libertine etc. 962.

rough, rowdy, ugly customer, ruffian, hoodlum, bully; Jonathan Wild; hangman; incendiary; thief etc. 792; murderer etc. 361.

culprit, delinquent, criminal, melefactor, misdemeanant; felon; convict, jail-bird, ticket-of-leave man; outlaw.

blackguard, *polisson*, loafer, sneak; raps-, rascallion; cullion, mean wretch, varlet, kern, *âme-de-boue*, *drôle*; cur, dog, hound, whelp, mongrel; lown, loon, runnion, outcast, vagabond; rogue etc. (*knave*) 941; scum of the earth, riff-raff; *Arcades ambo*.

Int. sirrah!

950. Penitence.—N. penitence, contrition, compunction, repentance, remorse; regret etc. 833.

self-reproach, -reproof, -accusation, -condemnation, -humiliation; stings –, pangs –, qualms –, prickings –, twinge –, twitch –, touch –, voice- of conscience; compunctious visitings of nature.

acknowledgment, confession etc. (*disclosure*) 529; apology etc. 952; recantation etc. 607; penance etc. 952; resipiscence.

awakened conscience, deathbed repentance, *locus poenitentiae*, stool of repentance, cutty stool.

penitent, Magdalen, prodigal son, returned prodigal, a sadder and wiser man.

V. repent, be sorry for; be -penitent etc. *adj.*; rue; regret etc. 833; think better of; recant etc. 607; knock under etc. (*submit*) 725; plead guilty; sing -*miserere*, – *de profundis*; cry *peccavi*; own oneself in the wrong; acknowledge, confess etc. (*disclose*) 529; humble oneself; beg pardon etc. (*apologize*) 952; turn over a new leaf, put on the new man, turn from sin; reclaim; repent in sackcloth and ashes etc. (*do penance*) 952; learn by experience.

Adj. penitent; repenting etc. *v.*; repentant, contrite; conscience-smitten, -stricken; self-accusing, -convicted.

penitenti-al, -ary; chastened, reclaimed; not hardened; un-hardened.

Adv. *meâ culpâ*.

Phr. *peccavi*; *erubuit*; *salva res est*; *vous l'avez voulu, Georges Dandin*.

951. Impenitence.—N. impenitence, irrepentance, recusance.

hardness of heart, seared conscience, induration, obduracy.

V. be -impenitent etc. *adj.*; steel –, harden- the heart; die -game, – and make no sign.

Adj. impenitent uncontrite, obdurate; hard, -ened; seared, recusant; unrepentant; relent-, remorse-, grace-, shrift-less.

lost, incorrigible, irreclaimable.

unre-claimed, -formed; unrepented, unatoned.

952. Atonement.—N. atonement, reparation; compromise, composition; compensation etc. 30; quittance, quits; indemni-ty, -fication; expiation, redemption, reclamation, conciliation, propitiation.

amends, apology, *amende honorable*, satisfaction; peace –, sin –, burnt- offering; scapegoat, sacrifice.

penance, fasting, maceration, sackcloth and ashes, white sheet, shrift, flagellation, lustration; purga-tion, -tory.

V. atone, – for; expiate; propitiate; make -amends, – good; reclaim, redeem, repair, ransom, absolve, purge, shrive, do penance, stand in a white sheet, repent in sackcloth and ashes.

set one's house in order, wipe off old scores, make matters up; pay the -forfeit, – penalty.

apologize, beg pardon, express regret, *faire amende honorable*, give satisfaction; come –, fall-down on one's -knees, – marrow bones.

Adj. propitiatory, expiatory; sacrific, -ial, -atory; piacul-ar, -ous.

953. Temperance.—N. temperance, moderation, sobriety, soberness.

forbearance, abnegation; self-denial, -restraint, -control etc. (*resolution*) 604.

frugality; vegetarianism, teetotalism, total abstinence, prohibition; abst-inence, -emiousness, asceticism etc. 955; system of -Pythagoras, – Cornaro; Pythagorism, Stoicism.

vegetarian; Pythagorean, gymnosophist; teetotaler etc. 958; abstainer.

V. be -temperate etc. *adj.*; abstain, forbear, refrain, deny oneself, spare; know when one has had enough; take the pledge; look not upon the wine when it is red.

Adj. temperate, moderate, sober, frugal, sparing; abst-emious, -inent; within compass; measured etc. (*sufficient*) 639.

Pythagorean; vegetarian; teetotal, pussy-foot.

954. Intemperance.—N. intemperance; sensuality, animalism, carnality; pleasure; effeminacy, silkiness; luxur-y, -iousness; lap of -pleasure, – luxury.

indulgence; high-, free- living, in-abstinence, self-indulgence; voluptuousness etc. *adj.*; epicur-ism, -eanism; sybaritism.

dissipation; licentiousness etc. *adj.*; debauchery; crapulence.

revel-s, -ry; debauch, carousal, jollification, drinking bout, wassail, Saturnalia, orgies; excess, too much; intoxication etc. 959.

Circean cup; drug habit etc. 663.

V. be -intemperate etc. *adj.*; indulge, exceed; live -well, – high, – on the fat of the land; give a loose to -indulgence etc. *n.*; dine not wisely but too well; wallow in -voluptuousness etc. *n.*; plunge into dissipation.

revel, rake, live hard, run riot, sow one's wild oats; slake one's -appetite, – thirst; swill; pamper.

Adj. intemperate, inabstinent, intoxicated etc. 958; sensual, self-indulgent; voluptuous, luxurious, licentious, wild, dissolute, rakish, fast, debauched.

brutish, crapulous, swinish, piggish, hoggish, bestial.

Paphian, Epicurean, Sybaritical; bred –, nursed- in the lap of luxury; indulged, pampered, full-fed.

954a. Sensualist.—N. Sybarite, voluptuary, Sardanapalus, man of pleasure, carpet knight; epicure, -an; *gourm-et, -and;* gormandizer, gutling, glutton, pig, hog; votary –, swine- of Epicurus; sensualist; Heliogabalus; free –, hard- liver; libertine etc. 962; hedonist.

955. Asceticism.—N. asceticism, puritanism, sabbatarianism; cynicism, austerity; total abstinence.

mortification, maceration, sackcloth and ashes, flagellation; penance etc. 952; fasting etc. 956; martyrdom.

ascetic; anchor-et, -ite; martyr; *Heautontimorumenos*; hermit etc. (*recluse*) 893; puritan, sabbatarian, cynic.

Adj. ascetic, austere, puritanical; cynical; over-religious.

956. Fasting.—N. fasting; exrophagy; famishment, starvation; banting.

fast, *jour maigre*; fast –, banyan-day; Lent, quadragesima; Rama-dan, -zan; spare –, meager-diet; lenten -diet, – entertainment; *soupe maigre*, short -rations, – commons; Barmecide feast; hunger strike.

V. fast, starve, clem, famish, perish with hunger; dine with Duke Humphrey; make two bites of a cherry.

Adj. lenten, quadragesimal; unfed; starved etc. *v.*; half-starved; fasting etc. *v.*; hungry etc. 865.

957. Gluttony.—N. gluttony; greed; greediness etc. *adj.*; voracity.

epicurism; good –, high- living; edacity, gulosity, crapulence; gutt-, guzz-ling; over-indulgence.

good cheer, blow out; feast etc. (*food*) 298; gastronomy.

epicure, *bon vivant*, *gourmand*; glutton, cormorant, hog, belly-god, Apicius, gastronome, gormandizer.

V. gormandize, gorge; over-gorge, -eat- oneself; engorge, eat one's fill, cram, stuff, stodge, glut, satiate; gutt-le, guzz-le; bolt, devour, gobble up; gulp etc. (*swallow food*) 298; raven, eat out of house and home.

have the stomach of an ostrich; play a good knife and fork etc. (*appetite*) 865.

Adj. gluttonous, greedy; gormandizing etc. *v.*; edacious, omnivorous, crapulent, swinish, voracious, devouring.

pampered; over-fed, -gorged.

958. Sobriety.—N. sobriety; teetotalism, temperance etc. 953.

water-drinker; teetotal-er, -ist; abstainer, Good Templar, Rechabite, band of hope; prohibitionist, pussyfoot.

V. take the pledge.

Adj. sober, – as a judge; dry, on the water wagon.

959. Drunkenness.—N. drunkenness etc. *adj.*; intemperance; drinking etc. *v.*; inebri-ety, -ation; ebri-ety, -osity; befuddlement; insobriety; intoxication; temulency, bibacity, wine-bibbing; com-, potation; deep potations, bacchanals, *bacchanalia*, libations.

oino-, dipso-mania; *delirium tremens*, d.t., alcohol, -ism.

drink; alcoholic drinks, alcohol, booze; gin, blue ruin, grog, brandy, port wine; punch, -bowl; cup, rosy wine, flowing bowl; drop, – too much; dram; beer, wine, spirits etc. (*beverage*) 298; cocktail, nip, peg; stirrup cup.

drunkard, sot, toper, tippler, bibber, wine-bibber; hard –, gin –, dram- drinker; soak, soaker, sponge, tun; love-, toss-pot; thirsty soul, reveller, carouser; Bacchanal, -ian; Bacch-al, -ante; devotee to Bacchus, dipsomaniac.

V. get –, be- drunk etc. *adj.*; see double; take a -drop, – glass- too much; drink, tipple, tope, booze, bouse, guzzle, swill, soak, sot, lush, bib, swig, carouse; sacrifice at the shrine of Bacchus; take to drinking; drink -hard, – deep, – like a fish; have one's swill, drain the cup, splice the main brace, take a hair of the dog that bit you.

liquor, – up; wet one's whistle, take a whet; lift one's elbow; crack a –, pass the- bottle; toss of etc. (*drink up*) 298; go to the -ale, – public house.

make one-drunk etc. *adj.*; inebriate, fuddle, fuzzle, get into one's head.

Adj. drunk, tipsy; intoxicated; inebri-ous, -ate, -ated; in one's cups; in a state of -intoxication etc. *n.*; temulent, -ive; fuddled, mellow, cut, boosy, fou, fresh, merry, elevated, squiffy; plastered, befuddled, sozzled; flush, -ed; flustered, disguised, groggy, beery; topheavy; potvaliant, glorious; potulent; over-come, -taken; whittled, screwed, tight, primed, oiled, corned, raddled, sewed up, lushy, nappy, muddled, muzzy, bosky, obfuscated, maudlin; crapulous, dead –, blind- drunk.

inter pocula; in –, the worse for- liquor, having had a drop too much, half seas over, three sheets in the wind; under the table, blind to the world, one over the eight.

drunk as -a piper, – a fiddler, – a lord, – Chloe, – an owl, – David's sow, – a wheelbarrow.

drunken, bibacious, bibulous, sottish; given –, addicted- to -drink, – the bottle; toping etc. *v.*; wet.

Phr. *nunc est bibendum*.

960. Purity.—N. purity; decency, decorum, delicacy; continence, chastity, honesty, virtue, modesty, shame; pudicity, *pucelage*, virginity.

vestal, virgin, Joseph, Hippolytus; Lucretia, Diana; prude.

Adj. pure, undefiled, modest, delicate, decent, decorous; *virginibus puerisque*; chaste, continent, virtuous, honest, Platonic.

961. Impurity.—N. impurity; uncleanness etc. (*filth*) 653; immodesty; grossness etc. *adj.*; indelicacy, indecency; impudicity; obscenity, ribaldry, smut, bawdry, *double entendre*, *équivoque*; Aretinism; pornography.

concupiscence, lust, carnality, flesh, salacity; pruriency, lechery, lasciviency, lubricity, lewdness.

incontinence, intrigue, *faux pas*; *amour*, *-ette*; gallantry; dabauchery, libertinism, *libertinage*, fornication; *liaison*; wenching, venery, dissipation.

seduction; defloration, defilement, abuse, violation, rape; incest.

social evil, harlotry, stupration, whoredom, concubinage, cuckoldom, adultery, advoutry, *crim. con.*; free love.

seraglio, harem, zenana; brothel, bagnio, stew, bawdy-house, *lupanar*, house of ill fame, *bordel*, kip.

V. be -impure etc. *adj.*; intrigue; debauch, defile, assault, attack, seduce; prostitute; abuse, violate, deflower; commit -adultery etc. *n.*

Adj. impure; unclean etc. (*dirty*) 653; not to be mentioned to ears polite; immodest, shameless; indecorous, -delicate, -decent; loose, suggestive, *risqué*, coarse, gross, broad, free, equivocal, smutty, fulsome, ribald, obscene, bawdy, pornographic.

concupiscent, prurient, lickerish, rampant, lustful; carnal, -minded; lewd, lascivious, lecherous, libidinous, erotic, ruttish, salacious; Paphian; voluptuous; incestuous.

unchaste, -light, wanton, licentious, adulterous, debauched, dissolute; of -loose character, – easy virtue; frail, gay, riggish, incontinent, meretricious, rakish, gallant, dissipated; no better than she should be; on the -town, – streets, – *pavé*, – loose.

adulterous, incestuous, bestial.

962. Libertine.—N. libertine; voluptuary etc. 954*a*; rake, debauchee, loose fish, rip, rake-hell, fast man; *intrigant*, gallant, seducer, fornicator, lecher, satyr, goat, whoremonger, *paillard*, adulterer, gay deceiver, Lothario, Don Juan, Bluebeard.

adulteress, advoutress, courtesan, prostitute, strumpet, tart, hustler, chippy, broad, harlot, whore, punk, *fille de joie*; woman, – of the town; street-walker, Cyprian, miss, piece; frail sisterhood, fallen woman; demirep, wench, trollop, trull, baggage, hussy, drab, bitch, jade, skit, rig, quean, mopsy, slut, minx, harridan; woman -of easy virtue etc. (*unchaste*) 961; wanton, fornicatress; Jezebel, Messalina, Delilah, Thaïs, Phryne, Aspasia, Lais, *lorette*, *cocotte*, *petite dame*, *grisette*; *demimonde*; white slave.

concubine, mistress, fancy woman, kept woman, doxy, *chère amie*, *bona roba*.

pimp; pand-er, -ar; bawd, *conciliatrix*, procuress, mackerel; wittol.

963. Legality.—N. legality; legitima-cy, -teness, legitimization.

legislature; law, code, *corpus juris*, constitution, pandect, charter, act, enactment, statute, rule; canon etc. (*precept*) 697; ordinance, institution, regulation; by-, bye-law, rescript; decree etc. (*order*) 741; *ordonnance*; standing order; *plébiscite* etc. (*choice*) 609.

legal process; form, -ula, -ality; rite; arm of the law; *habeas corpus*.

[Science of law] jurisprudence, nomology; legislation, codification.

equity, common law; *lex* –, *lex nonscripta*, unwritten law; law of nations, international law, *jus gentium*; *jus civile*; civil –, criminal –, canon –, statute –, ecclesiastical- law; *lex mercatoria*.

constitutional-ism, -ity; justice etc. 922.

V. legalize, legitimize; enact, ordain; decree etc. (*order*) 741; pass a law; legislate; codify, formulate; authorize.

Adj. legal, legitimate; according to law; vested, constitutional, chartered, legalized; lawful etc. (*permitted*) 760; statut-able, -ory; legislat-orial, -ive.

Adv. legally etc. *adj.*; in the eye of the law; *de jure*.

964. Illegality. [Absence or violation of law.]—**N.** lawlessness; breach –, violation- of law; disobedience etc. 742; unconformity etc. 83.

arbitrariness etc. *adj.*; antinomy, violence, brute force, despotism, outlawry.

mob –, lynch –, club –, Lydford –, martial –, drumhead- law; *coup d'état*; *le droit du plus fort*; *argumentum baculinum*.

illegality, informality, unlawfulness, illegitimacy, bar sinister.

trover and conversion; smuggling, boot-legging, rum-running, poaching; simony.

speakeasy, speakie, blind pig.

V. offend against –, violate- the law; set the law at defiance, ride rough-shod over, drive a coach and six through a statute; make the law a dead letter, take the law into one's own hands.

smuggle, run, poach.

Adj. illegal; prohibited etc. 761; not allowed, unlawful, illegitimate, illicit, contraband, actionable.

unchartered, unconstitutional; unwarrant-ed, -able; unauthorized; informal, unofficial; in-, extra-judicial.

lawless, arbitrary; despotic, -al; summary, irresponsible; un-answerable, -accountable.

null and void; a dead letter.

Adv. illegally etc. *adj.*; with a high hand, in violation of law.

965. Jurisdiction. [Executive.]—**N.** jurisdiction, judicature, administration of justice, soc; executive, commission of the peace; magistracy etc. (*authority*) 737.

judge etc. 967; tribunal etc. 966; municipality, corporation, bailiwick, shrievalty; lord lieutenant; lord –, mayor, city manager, alderman etc. 745; sheriff, bailie, shrieve, chief –, constable; police, – force; constabulary, bumbledom.

officer; proctor, high –, commissioner; bailiff, tipstaff, bum-bailiff, catchpoll, beadle; police-man, -constable, -sergeant; *sbirro*, *alguazil*, *gendarme*, kavass, *lictor*, macebearer, *huissier*, bedel.

press-gang; exciseman, gauger, custom-house officer, *douanier*.

coroner, edile, aedile, portreeve, paritor; *posse comitatus*.

V. judge, sit in judgment.

Adj. executive, administrative, municipal;

inquisitorial, causidical; judic-atory, -iary, -ial; juridical.

Adv. *coram judice*.

966. Tribunal.—**N.** tribunal, court, board, bench, judicatory, curia; court of -justice, – law, – arbitration; inquisition; guild.

justice –, judgment –, mercy- seat; woolsack; bar, – of justice; dock; forum, hustings, *bureau*, drum-head; jury-, witness-box.

senate-house, town-hall, theater; House of -Lords, – Commons.

assize, eyre; ward-, burgh-mote; superior courts of Westminister; court of -record, – oyer and terminer, – assize, – appeal – error; High court of -Judicature, – Appeal; Judicial Committee of the Privy Council; Star-Chamber; Court of -Chancery, – King's *or* Queen's Bench, – Exchequer, – Common Pleas, – Probate, – Arches, – Admiralty, – Criminal Appeal; Lords Justices' –, Rolls –, Vice Chancellor's –, Stannary –, Divorce –, Palatine –, ecclesiastical –, county –, police- court; sessions; quarter –, petty-sessions; court -leet, – baron, – of pie poudre, – of common council; board of green cloth.

court-martial; drum-head court-martial; *durbar*, divan; Areopagus; *rota*.

Adj. judicial etc. 965; appellate; curial.

967. Judge.—**N.** judge; justi-ce, -ciar, -ciary; chancellor; justice –, judge- of assize; recorder, common serjeant; puisne –, assistant –, county court- judge; conservator –, justice- of the peace, J.P.; court etc. (*tribunal*) 966; grand –, petty –, coroner's- jury; panel, juror, juryman; twelve men in a box; magistrate, police magistrate, stipendiary, the great unpaid, beak; his -worship, – honor, – lordship; deemster, moderator.

Lord Chancellor, – Justice; Master of the Rolls, Vice-Chancellor; Lord Chief -Justice, – Baron; Mr. Justice; Baron, – of the Exchequer.

jurat, assessor; arbi-ter, -trator; umpire; refer-ee, -endary; revising barrister; domesman; censor etc. (*critic*) 480; official –, receiver.

archon, tribune, praetor, *ephor*, syndic, *podestà*, mullah, ulema, mufti, cadi, kadi; Rhadamanthus.

litigant etc. (*accusation*) 938.

V. adjudge etc. (*determine*) 480; try a -case, – prisoner.

Adj. judicial etc. 965.

Phr. 'a Daniel come to judgment.'

968. Lawyer.—**N.** lawyer, jurist, legist, civilian, pundit, publicist, jurisconsult, legal adviser, advocate; barrister, – at law; counsel, -lor; King's *or* Queen's counsel; K.C.; Q.C.; silk gown, leader; junior, – counsel; stuff gown, serjeant-at-law; bencher, tubman; judge etc. 967.

bar, legal profession, gentleman of the long robe; junior –, outer –, inner- bar; Inns of Court; equity draftsman, conveyancer, pleader, special pleader.

solicitor, attorney, proctor; notary, – public; scrivener, cursitor; writer, – to the signet; S.S.C.; limb of the law; pettifogger.

V. practice -at, – within- the bar; plead; call –, to called- -to, – within- the bar; take silk.

Adj. learned in the law; at the bar; forensic.

969. Lawsuit.—**N.** lawsuit, suit, action, cause, petition; litigation; dispute etc. 713.

citation, arraignment, prosecution, impeachment; accusation etc. 938; presentment, true bill, indictment.

apprehension, arrest; committal; imprisonment etc. (*restraint*) 751.

writ, summons, subpoena, *latitat*, *nisi prius*; *habeas corpus*.

pleadings; declaration, bill, claim; *procès-verbal*, bill of right, information, *corpus delicti*; affidavit, state of facts; answer, replication, plea, demurrer, rebutter, rejoinder; surre-butter, -joinder.

suitor, party to a suit; litigant etc. 938; libellant.

hearing, trial; verdict etc. (*judgment*) 480; appeal, – motion; writ of error; *certiorari*.

case, decision, precedent, ruling; decided case, reports.

V. go to –, appeal to the- law; bring to -justice, – trial, – the bar; put on trial, pull up; accuse etc. 938; prefer –, file- a claim etc. *n.*; take the law of, inform against.

serve with a writ, cite, apprehend, arraign, sue, prosecute, bring an action against, indict, impeach, attach, distrain, commit; arrest; summon, -s; give in charge etc. (*restrain*) 751.

empanel a jury, implead, join issue; close the pleadings; set down for hearing.

try, hear a cause; sit in judgment; adjudicate etc. 480.

Adj. litigious etc. (*quarrelsome*) 713; *qui tam*; *coram –, sub- judice*.

Adv. *pendente lite*.

Phr. *adhuc sub judice lis est*.

970. Acquittal. **N.** acquit-tal, -ment; clearance, exculpation, exoneration; discharge etc. (*release*) 750; *quietus*, absolution, compurgation, reprieve, respite; pardon etc. (*forgiveness*) 918.

[Exemption from punishment] impunity, immunity.

V. acquit, exculpate, exonerate, clear; absolve, whitewash, assoil, discharge, release; liberate etc. 750.

reprieve, respite; pardon etc. (*forgive*) 918; let off, – scot free.

Adj. acquitted etc. *v.*; un-condemned, -punished, -chastised; recommended to mercy.

971. Condemnation.—**N.** condemnation, conviction, proscription, damnation; death warrant; penalty etc. 974.

attain-der, -ture, -tment.

V. condemn, convict, cast, bring home to, find guilty, damn, doom, sign the death warrant, sentence, pass sentence on, attaint, confiscate, proscribe, sequestrate; non-suit.

disapprove etc. 932; accuse etc. 938.

stand condemned.

Adj. condem-, dam-natory; condemned etc. *v.*; non-suited etc. (*failure*) 732; self-convicted.

Phr. *mutato nomine de te fabula narratur*.

972. Punishment.—**N.** punishment, punition; chast-isement, -ening; correction, castigation.

discipline, infliction, trial; judgment; penalty etc. 974; retribution; thunderbolt, Nemesis; requital etc. (*reward*) 973; penology; retributive justice.

lash, scaffold etc. (*instrument of punishment*) 975; imprisonment etc. (*restraint*) 751; chain gang; transportation, banishment, expulsion, deportation, exile, involuntary exile, ostracism; penal servitude, hard labor; galleys etc. 975; beating etc. *v.*; flagellation, fustigation, gantlet, *strappado*, *estrapade*, *bastinado*, *argumentum baculinum*, stick law, rap on the knuckles, box on the ear; blow etc. (*impulse*) 276; stripe, cuff, kick, buffet, pummel; slap, – in the face; wipe, douse; *coup de grâce*; torture, rack; picket, -ing; *dragonnade*; capital punishment, extreme penalty; execution; hanging etc. *v.*; de-capitation, -collation; *garrot-te*, *-to*; electrocution, lethal chamber; crucifixion, impalement; martyrdom, *auto-da-fé*; *noyade*; *hara-kiri*, happy despatch.

V. punish; chast-ise, -en; castigate, correct, inflict punishment, administer correction, deal retributive justice.

visit upon, pay; pay – , serve- out; settle with, get even with, get one's own back; do for; make short work of, give a lesson to, strafe, serve one right, make an example of; have a rod in pickle for; give it one.

strike etc. 276; deal a blow to, administer the lash, smite; slap, – the face; smack, cuff, box the ears, spank, thwack, thump, beat, lay on, swinge, buffet; thresh, thrash, pummel, drub, leather, trounce, baste, belabor; lace, – one's jacket; dress, give a -dressing, – down; trim, warm, wipe, tund, cob, bang, strap, comb, lash, lick, larrup, whallop, whop, flog, scourge, whip, birch, cane, give the stick, switch, flagellate, horsewhip, *bastinado*, towel, rub down with an oaken towel, rib roast, dust one's jacket, fustigate, pitch into, lay about one, beat black and blue; beat to a -mummy, – jelly; give a black eye; hit on the head; sandbag.

tar and feather; pelt, stone, lapidate; mast-head, keelhaul.

execute; bring to the -block, – gallows; behead; de-capitate, -collate; guillotine; hang, turn off, gibbet, bowstring, hang, draw and quarter; shoot; decimate; burn; electrocute; break on the wheel, crucify; em-, im-pale; flay; lynch; put to death.

torture; put -on, – to- the rack; picket.

banish, exile; trans-, de-port; expel, ostracize; rusticate; drum out; dismiss, -bar, -bench; strike off the roll, unfrock; post.

suffer, – for, – punishment; be -flogged, – hanged etc.; come to the gallows, dance upon nothing, die in one's shoes, be rightly served.

Adj. punishing etc. *v.*; penal; puni-tory, -tive; inflictive, castigatory; punished etc. *v.*

Int. *à la lanterne!*

973. Reward.—**N.** reward, recompense, remuneration, prize, meed, guerdon, reguerdon; indemni-ty, -fication, price; quittance; compensation; reparation, *ersatz*, assythment, redress; retribution, reckoning, acknowledgment, requital, amends, sop; atonement; consideration, return, *quid pro quo*; salvage, perquisite; vail etc. (*donation*) 784; *douceur*, bribe, bait, baksheesh, tip; hush-, smart-money; black-mail; carcelage; *solatium*.

allowance, salary, stipend, wages; pay, -ment; emolument; tribute; batta, shot, scot; premium, fee, *honorarium*; hire.

crown etc. (*decoration of honor*) 877.

V. re-ward, -compense, -pay, -quite; re-, munerate; compensate; fee, tip, bribe; pay one's footing etc. (*pay*) 807; make amends, indemnify, atone; satisfy, acknowledge.

get for one's pains, reap the fruits of.

Adj. remunerat-ive, -ory; munerary, compensatory, retributive, reparatory.

974. Penalty.—**N.** penalty; retribution etc. (*punishment*) 972; pain, pains and penalties; *peine forte et dure*; penance etc. (*atonement*) 952; the devil to pay.

fine, mulct, amercement; forfeit, -ure; escheat, damages, deodand, sequestration, confiscation, *premunire*.

V. penalize, fine, mulct, amerce, sconce, confiscate; sequest-rate, -er; escheat; estreat, forfeit.

975. Scourge. [Instrument of punishment.]—**N.** scourge, rod, cane, stick; ra-, rat-tan; birch, – rod; rod in pickle; switch, ferule, cudgel, truncheon; rubber hose.

whip, lash, strap, thong, cowhide, knout; cat, – o'-nine-tails, *sjambok*, quirt; rope's end.

pillory, stocks, whipping-post; cuck-, duck-ing stool; brank; triangle, wooden horse, maiden, thumbscrew, boot, rack, wheel, iron heel; treadmill, crank, galleys.

scaffold; block, axe, *guillotine*; stake; cross; gallows, gibbet, Tyburn tree; drop, noose, rope, halter, bowstring; electric chair, lethal chamber.

house of correction etc. (*prison*) 752.

gaol-, jail-er; executioner; hang-, heads-man; Jack Ketch; lyncher.

976. Deity.—**N.** Deity, Divinity; God-head, -ship; Omnipotence, Providence.

[Quality of being divine] divin-eness, -ity.

God, Lord, Jehovah, *Deus*; The -Almighty, – Supreme Being, – First Cause; *Ens Entium*; Author –, Creator- of all things; Author of our being; The -Infinite, – Eternal; The All-powerfull, -wise, -merciful, -holy; The Omni-potent, -scient.

[Attributes and perfections] infinite -power, – wisdom, – goodness, – justice, – truth, – love, – mercy; omni-potence, -science, -presence; unity, immutability, holiness, glory, majesty, sovereignty, infinity, eternity.

The -Trinity, – Holy Trinity, – Trinity in Unity, – Triune God; Three in One and One in Three.

God the Father; The -Maker, – Creator, – Preserver.

[Functions] creation, preservation, divine government; The-ocracy, -archy; providence; ways –, dealings –, dispensations –, visitations- of Providence.

God the Son, Jesus, Christ; The -Messiah, – Anointed, – Savior, – Redeemer, – Mediator,

– Intercessor, – Advocate, – Judge; The Son of - God, – Man, – David; The Only Begotten; The Lamb of God, The Word; Em-, Im-manuel; The - King of Kings and Lord of Lords, – King of Glory, – Prince of Peace, – Good Shepherd, – Way, – Truth, – Life, – Bread of Life, – Light of the World; The -Lord our, – Sun of- Righteousness.

The -Incarnation, – Hypostatic Union, – Word made Flesh.

[Functions] salvation, redemption, atonement, propitiation, mediation, intercession, judgment.

God the Holy Ghost, The Holy Spirit, Paraclete; The -Comforter, – Consoler, – Spirit of Truth, – Dove.

[Functions] inspiration, unction, regeneration, sanctification, consolation.

eon, aeon, special providence, *Deus ex machinâ*; *Avatar*.

V. create, uphold, preserve, govern etc.

atone, redeem, save, propitiate, mediate etc.

predestinate, elect, call, ordain, bless, justify, sanctify, glorify etc.

Adj. almighty, holy, hallowed, sacred, divine, heavenly, celestial; messianic; sacrosanct; all-powerful, -wise, -seeing, -knowing; omnipotent, omniscient; supreme.

super-human, -natural; ghostly, spiritual, hyper-physical, unearthly; the-istic, -ocratic, deistic; anointed.

Adv. *jure divino*, by divine right; *Deo volente*, D.V.

977. Angel. [Beneficent spirits.]—**N.** angel, archangel; heavenly host, choir invisible, host of heaven, sons of God; Michael, Gabriel etc.; seraph, -im; cherub, -im; ministering spirit, morning star; saint, *Madonna*; Our Lady, the Blessed Virgin, the Virgin Mary.

Adj. angelic, seraphic, cherubic.

978. Satan. [Maleficent spirits.]—**N.** Satan, the Devil, Lucifer, Ahrimanes, Belial; Sammael, Zamiel, Beelzebub, the Prince of the Devils; Mephistopheles, his satanic majesty.

the tempter; the evil -one, – spirit; the -author of evil, – wicked one, – old Serpent; the Prince of -darkness, – this world, – the power of the air; the -foul, – arch- fiend; the devil incarnate; the - common enemy, – angel of the bottomless pit; Abaddon, Apollyon, Mammon.

fallen agnels, unclean spirits, devils; the -rulers, – powers- of darkness; inhabitants of Pandemonium; demon etc. 980.

diabolism; devil-ism, -ship, -dom, -ry, -worship; *diablerie*; satanism, manicheism; the cloven foot; black magic etc. 992.

Adj. satanic, diabolic, devilish, infernal, hell-born.

979. Jupiter.—**N.** god, -dess; heathen gods and goddesses; Pantheon; Jupiter, Jove, Zeus, Apollo, Mars, Mercury, Neptune, Vulcan, Bacchus, Pluto, Saturn, Cupid, Eros, Pan; Juno, Ceres, Proserpina, Dina, Minerva, Pallas, Athenae, Venus, Aphrodite, Vesta; The Fates etc. 601.

Allah, Brahma, Vishnu, Siva, Shiva, Krishna, Juggernaut, Buddha; Ra, Isis, Osiris; Belus, Bel, Baal, Asteroth etc.; Thor, Odin; Mumbo Jumbo; good –, tutelary- genius; demiurge, familiar, – spirit; Sibyl; fairy, fay; sylph, -id; Ariel, peri, nymph, nereid, dryad, oread, sea-maid, Banshee, Benshie, Ormuzd; Oberon, Titania, Mab, hamadryad, naiad, mermaid, kelpie, Ondine, nix, nixie, sprite; denizens of the air; pixy etc. (*bad spirit*) 980.

mythology; heathen –, fairy- mythology; Lemprière, folklore.

Adj. fairy-, sylph-like; sylphic.

980. Demon.—**N.** demon, -ry, -ism, -ology; evil genius, fiend, familiar, – spirit, devil; bad –, unclean- spirit; cacodemon, incubus, Frankenstein's monster, succubus and succuba, Titan, Shedim, Mephistopheles, Asmodeus, Moloch, Belial, Ahriman, fury, The Furies etc. 900; harpy; Friar Rush.

vampire, ghoul; af-, ef-freet; afrite; ogre, -ss; gnome, gin, djinn, imp, deev, *lamia*; bo-gie, -gle; nis, kobold, flibbertigibbet, fairy, brownie, pixy, elf, dwarf, urchin, Puck, Robin Goodfellow; lepre-, cluri-chaune; troll, dwerger, sprite, oaf, changeling, bad fairy, nixe, pigwidgeon, Will-o'-the-wisp; Erl King.

[Supernatural appearance] ghost, specter, apparition, genie, spirit, shade, shadow, vision, phantom etc. 443; materialization (*spiritualism*) 992; hob-, goblin; wraith, spook, werwolf, boggart, banshee, *loup-garou*, *lemures*; evil eye.

nisse, necks; mer-man, -maid, -folk; siren, Lorelei; satyr, faun.

Adj. supernatural, weird, uncanny, unearthly, spectral; ghost-ly, -like; elf-in, -like; fiend-ish, -like; impish, demoniacal; haunted.

981. Heaven.—**N.** heaven; kingdom of - heaven, – God; heavenly kingdom; throne , presence- of God; inheritance of the saints in light.

Paradise, Eden, abode of the blessed; Holy City, New Jerusalem; celestial bliss, glory.

[Mythological -heaven] Olympus; [– paradise] Elysium, Elysian fields, Arcadia, bowers of bliss, garden of the Hesperides, Islands of the Blessed; happy hunting-ground; third –, seventh-heaven; Valhalla (Scandinavian); Nirvana (Buddhist).

future state, eternity, eternal life, life after death, eternal home, resurrection, translation; resuscitation etc. 660; apotheosis, deification.

Adj. heavenly, celestial, supernal, unearthly, from on high, paradisiacal, beatific, elysian, Olympian, Arcadian.

982. Hell.—**N.** hell, bottomless pit, place of torment; habitation of fallen angels; Pandemonium, Abaddon, Domdaniel.

hell fire; everlasting -fire, – torment; lake of fire and brimstone; fire that is never quenched, worm that never dies.

purgatory, limbo, gehenna, abyss.

[Mythological hell] Tartarus, Hades, Avernus, Styx, Stygian creek, pit of Acheron, Cocytus,

Phlegethon, Lethe; infernal regions, *inferno*, shades below, realms of Pluto.

Pluto, Rhadamanthus, Erebus, Charon, Cerberus; Tophet.

Adj. hellish, infernal, stygian.

983. Theology. [Religious Knowledge.]—**N.** Theology (natural and revealed); Theo-gony, -sophy; Divinity; Hagio-logy, -graphy; Caucasian mystery; monotheism; religion; religious -persuasion, – sect, – denomination; cult; creed etc. (*belief*) 484; articles –, declaration –, profession –, confession- of faith.

theolog-ue, -ian; divine, schoolman, canonist, monotheist.

Adj. theological, religious; canonical; denominational; sectarian etc. 984.

983a. Orthodoxy.—**N.** orthodoxy; strictness, soundness, religious truth, true faith; truth etc. 494.

Christian-ity, -ism; Catholic-ism, -ity; 'the faith once delivered to the saints;' hyperorthodoxy etc. 984; iconoclasm.

the Holy –, the Orthodox- Church; Catholic –, Universal –, Apostolic –, Established- Church; temple of the Holy Ghost; Church –, body –, members –, disciples –, followers- of Christ; Christian, – community; true believer; canonist etc. (*theologian*) 983; Christendom, collective body of Christians, the Church Militant.

canons etc. (*belief*) 484; thirty-nine articles; Apostles' –, Nicene –, Athanasian- Creed; Church Catechism; textuary.

Adj. orthodox, sound, literal, strict, faithful, catholic, schismless, Christian, evangelical, scriptural, divine, monotheistic; true etc. 494.

984. Heterodoxy. [Sectarianism.]—**N.** heterodoxy; error etc. 495; false doctrine, heresy, schism; schismantic-ism, -alness; recusancy, backsliding, apostasy; atheism etc. (*irreligion*) 989.

bigotry etc. (*obstinacy*) 606; fanaticism, iconoclasm; hyperorthodoxy, precisianism, bibliolatry, hagiolatry, sabbatarianism, puritanism; idolatry etc. 991; superstition etc. (*credulity*) 486; dissent etc. 489.

sectar-ism, -ianism; nonconformity; secularism; syncretism, religious sects; the clash of creeds.

protestant-, advent-, Arian-, Erastian-, Calvin-, quaker-, method-, anabapt-, Pusey-, tractarian-, ritual-, Origen-, Sabellian-, Socinian-, De-, The-, mon-, material-, positiv-, latitudinairan-ism etc.

High –, Low –, Broad –, Free- Church; ultramontanism; monasticism; pap-ism, -istry; papacy; Anglican-, Catholic-, Roman-ism; popery, Scarlet Lady, Church of Rome, Greek Church; Christian Science, The Church of Christ Scientist.

pagan-, heathen-, ethic-ism; mythology; animism; poly-, di-, tri-, pan-theism; dualism; heathendom.

Juda-, Gentil-, Mahometan-, Islam-, Turc-, Brahmin-, Hindoo-, Buddh-, Lama-, Confucian-, Shinto-, Sabian-, Gnostic-. Soofee-, Hylothe-, Mormon-ism.

Theosophy; Spiritualism, Occultism.

heretic, antichrist; pagan, heathen; pai-, pay-nim; *giaour*; gentile; pan-, poly-theist; idolator; misbeliever, apostate, backslider.

bigot etc. (*obstinacy*) 606; fanatic, dervish, abdal, iconoclast.

latitudinarian, limitarian, Deist, Theist, Unitarian; positivist, materialist; agnostic, sceptic etc. 989.

schismatic; sectar-y, -ian, -ist; seceder, separatist, recusant, dissenter; non-conformist, -juror; Huguenot, Protestant; orthodox dissenter, Congregationalist, Independent; Episcopalian, Presbyterian; Lutheran, Calvinist, Quaker, Methodist, Weslayan; Ana-, Baptist; Dunker; Mormon, Latter-day Saint, Irvingite, Sandemanian, Glassite, Erastian; Sub-, Supra-lapsarian; Gentoo, Antinomian, Swedenborgian, Adventist, Plymouth Brother; Theosophist etc.

Catholic, Roman Catholic, Romanist, papist, ultramontane; Old Catholic, tractarian, Anglican, Puseyite, ritualist; Puritan.

Jew, Hebrew, Rabbist; Mahometan, Mohammedan, Mussulman, Moslem, Islamite, Osmanli; Brahm-in, -an; Parsee, Sofi, Soofee; Buddhist; Zoroastrian, Magi, Gymnosophist, fire-worshipper, Sabian, Gnostic, Sadducee, Rosicrucian etc.

Adj. heterodox, heretical; un-orthodox, -scriptural, -canonical; antiscriptural, apocryphal; un-, anti-christian; schismatic, recusant, iconoclastic; sectarian; dis-senting, -sident; secular etc. (*lay*) 997.

pagan; heathen, -ish; ethnic, -al; gentile, painim; pan-, poly-theistic; agnostic, sceptic.

Judaical, Mohammedan, Moslem, Brahminical, Buddhist etc. *n.*; Romish, Protestant etc. *n.*

bigoted etc. (*prejudiced*) 481; (*obstinate*) 606; superstitious etc. (*credulous*) 486; fanatical; idolatrous etc. 991; visionary etc. (*imaginative*) 515.

985. Revelation.—**N.** revelation, inspiration, *afflatus*.

Word, – of God; Scripture; the -Scriptures, – Bible, – Book of Books; Holy -Writ, – Scriptures; inspired writings, Gospel.

Old Testament, Septuagint, Vulgate, Pentateuch; Octateuch; the -Law, – Jewish Law, – Prophets; major –, minor- Prophets; Hagio-grapha, -logy; Hierographa; Apocrypha.

New Testament; Gospels, Evangelists, Acts, Epistles, Apocalypse, Revelations.

Talmud; Mishna, Masorah.

prophet etc. (*seer*) 513; evangelist, apostle, disciple, saint; the –, the Apostolical- fathers; Holy Men of old, inspired -writers, – penmen.

Adj. scriptural, biblical, sacred, prophetic; evangel-ical, -istic; apostolic, -al; inspired, theopneustic, apocalyptic, ecclesiastical, canonical, textuary.

986. Pseudo-Revelation.—**N.** the -Koran, – Alcoran; Ly-king, Shaster, Vedas, Zendavesta, Vedidad, Purana, Edda; Go-, Gau-tama; Book of Mormon.

[False prophets and religious founders] Buddha, Zoroaster, Zerdhusht, Confucius, Mahomet.

[Idols] golden calf etc. 991; Baal, Moloch, Dagon.

987. Piety.—N. piety, religion, theism, faith; religiousness, holiness etc. *adj.*; saintship; religionism; sanctimony etc. (*assumed piety*) 988; reverence etc. (*respect*) 928; humility, veneration, devotion; prostration etc. (*worship*) 990; grace, unction, edification; sancti-ty, -tude; consecration.

spiritual existence, odor of sanctity, beauty of holiness.

theopathy, beatification, adoption, regeneration, conversion, justification, sanctification, salvation, inspiration, bread of life; Body and Blood of Christ.

believer, convert, theist, Christian, devotee, pietist; the -good, – righteous, – just, – believing, – elect; Saint, *Madonna*.

the children of -God, – the kingdom, – light.

V. be -pious etc. *adj.*; have -faith etc. *n.*; believe, receive Christ; revere etc. 928; worship etc. 950; be -converted etc.

convert, edify, sanctify, hallow, keep holy, beatify, regenerate, inspire, consecrate, enshrine.

Adj. pious, religious, devout, devoted, reverent, godly, heavenly minded, humble; pure, – in heart; holy, spiritual, pietistic; saint-ly, -like; seraphic, sacred, solemn.

believing, faithful, Christian, Catholic.

elected, adopted, justified, sanctified, regenerated, inspired, consecrated, converted, unearthly, not of the earth.

988. Impiety.—N. impiety; sin etc. 945; irreverence; profan-eness etc. *adj.*, -ity, -ation; blasphemy, desecration, sacrilege; scoffing etc. *v.*

[Assumed piety] hypocrisy etc. (*falsehood*) 544; pietism, cant, pious fraud; lip-devotion, -service, -reverence; mis-devotion, formalism, austerity; sanctimon-y, -iousness etc. *adj.*; pharisaism, precisianism; sabbat-ism, -arianism; *odium theologicum*, sacerdotalism; bigotry etc. (*obstinacy*) 606, (*prejudice*) 481.

hardening, backsliding, declension, perversion, reprobation apostacy, recusancy.

sinner etc. 949; scoffer, blasphemer; sacrilegist; worldling; hypocrite etc. (*dissembler*) 548; Scribes and Pharisees; Tartufe, Maw-worm.

bigot; saint [ironically]; Pharisee, sabbatarian, formalist, methodist, puritan, pietist, precisian, religionist, devotee, ranter, fanatic, wowser.

the -wicked, – evil, – unjust, – reprobate; son of -men, – Belial, – the wicked one; children of darkness.

V. be -impious etc. *adj.*; profane, desecrate, blaspheme, revile, scoff; swear etc. (*malediction*) 908; commit sacrilege.

snuffle; turn up the whites of the eyes; idolize.

Adj. impious; irreligious etc. 989; desecrating etc. *v.*; profane, irreverent, sacrilegious, blasphemous.

un-hallowed, -sanctified, -regenerate; hardened, perverted, reprobate.

hypocritical etc. (*false*) 544; canting, pietistical, sanctimonious, unctuous, pharisaical, over-righteous, righteous over much.

bigoted, fanatical etc. 481 and 606; priest-ridden.

Adv. under the -mask, – cloak, – pretence, – form, – guise- of religion.

989. Irreligion.—N. irreligion, indevotion; ungodliness etc. *adj.*; laxity, quietism, apathy, indifference, passivity.

scepticism, doubt; un-, dis-belief; incredul-ity, -ousness etc. *adj.*; want of -faith, – belief; pyrrhonism; doubt etc. 485; agnosticism.

atheism, deism; hylotheism; materialism; positivism; nihilism.

infidelity, freethinking, antichristianity, rationalism.

atheist, anti-christian, sceptic, unbeliever, deist, infidel, pyrrhonist; *giaour*, heathen, alien, gentile, Nazarene; *esprit fort*, freethinker, latitudinarian, rationalist; materialist, positivist, nihilist, agnostic.

V. be -irreligious etc. *adj.*; disbelieve, lack faith; doubt, question etc. 485.

dechristianize; serve Mammon, love darkness better than light.

Adj. irreligious; in-, un-devout; devout-, god-, grace-less; un-godly, -holy, -sanctified, -hallowed; atheistic, without God.

sceptical, free-thinking; un-believing, -converted; incredulous, faithless, lacking faith; deistical; un-, anti-christian.

worldly, mundane, earthly, carnal, unspiritual; worldly etc.- minded.

Adv. irreligiously etc. *adj.*

990. Worship.—N. worship, adoration, devotion, aspiration, latria, homage, service, humiliation; kneeling, genuflexion, prostration.

prayer, invocation, supplication, rogation, intercession, orison, holy breathing; petition etc. (*request*) 765; collect, litany, Lord's prayer, paternoster, *Ave Maria*, rosary; bead-roll; latria, dulia, hyperdulia, vigils; revival; cult.

thanksgiving; giving –, returning- thanks; grace, praise, glorification, benediction, doxology, hosanna; h-, allelujah; *Te Deum*, *non nobis Domine*, *nunc dimittis*; paean.

psalm, -ody; hymn, plainsong, chant, chaunt, response, anthem, motet; antiphon, -y.

oblation, sacrifice, incense, libation; burnt –, votive –, thank-offering; offertory, collection.

discipline; self-discipline, -examination, -denial; fasting.

divine service, office, duty; morning prayer; mass, matins, evensong, vespers, compline; holy day etc. (*rites*) 998.

worshipper, congregation, communicant, celebrant.

V. worship, lift up the heart, aspire; revere etc. 928; adore, do service, pay homage; humble oneself, kneel; bow –, bend- the knee; fall -down, – on one's knees; prostrate oneself, bow down and worship, recite the rosary.

pray, invoke, supplicate; put –, offer- up -prayers, – petitions; beseech etc. (*ask*) 765; say one's prayers, tell one's beads.

return –, give- thanks; say grace, bless, praise, laud, glorify, magnify, sing praises; give benediction, lead the choir, intone, chant, sing.

propitiate, offer sacrifice, fast, deny oneself; vow, offer vows, give alms.

work out one's salvation; go to church; attend -service, – mass; communicate etc. (*rite*) 998.

Adj. worshipping etc. *v.*; devout, devotional, reverent, pure, solemn; fervid etc. (*heartfelt*) 821.

Int. h-, allelujah! hosanna! glory be to God! O Lord! pray God that! God -grant, – bless, – save, – forbid! *sursum corda.*

991. Idolatry.—N. idol-atry, -ism; demon-ism, -olatry; idol –, demon –, devil –, fire- worship; zoolatry, fetishism, Mari-, Bibli-, ecclesi-, heliolatry.

deification, apotheosis, canonization; hero worship.

sacrifices, hecatomb, holocaust; human sacrifices, immolation, mactation, infanticide, self-immolation, *suttee*.

idol, golden calf, graven image, fetish, *avatar*, Juggernaut, joss, *lares et penates*; Baal etc. 986.

idolator etc. *n.*

V. worship -idols, – pictures, – relics; put on a pedestal, bow down to, prostrate oneself before, make sacrifice to; deify, canonize, idolize.

Adj. idolatrous.

992. Sorcery.—N. sorcery; superstition; occult -art, – sciences; black –, magic; the black art, necromancy, theurgy, thaumaturgy; demon-ology, -omy, -ship; *diablerie*, bedevilment; witch-craft, -ery; glamor; fetis-hism, -ism; ghost dance; hoodoo, voodoo; Shamanism [Esquimaux], vampirism; conjuration; bewitchery, exorcism, enchantment, incantation, obsession, possession, mysticism, second sight, mesmerism, animal magnetism; od –, odylic- force; electro-biology, *clairvoyance*; spiritualism, spirit-rapping, table-turning; thought reading, telepathy, thought transference, automatic writing, *planchette*, ouija board; crystal gazing; spirit manifestation, materialization, astral body, ectoplasm etc.

divination etc. (*prediction*) 511; sortilege, ordeal, *sortes Virgiliance*; hocus-pocus etc. (*deception*) 545; oracle etc. 513.

V. practice -sorcery etc. *n.*; cast a -horoscope, – nativity; conjure, exorcise, charm, enchant; bewitch, -devil; overlook, look on with the evil eye; entrance, mesmerize, magnetize; fascinate etc. (*influence*) 615; taboo; wave a wand; rub the -ring, – lamp; cast a spell; call up spirits, – from the vasty deep; raise spirits from the dead; raise –, lay- ghosts; command genii.

Adj. magic, -al; mystic, weird, cabalistic, talismanic, phylacteric, incantatory; charmed etc. *v.*

993. Spell.—N. spell, charm, incantation, exorcism, weird, cabala, exsufflation, cantrap, runes, abracadabra, hocus-pocus, open *sesame*, countercharm, Ephesian letters, bell, book and candle, Mumbo-jumbo, evil-eye, fee-faw-fum.

talisman, amulet, periapt, telesm, phylactery, philter, wish-bone, merry-thought, mascot, scarab, swastika; fetish; *agnus Dei*.

wand, caduceus, rod, divining rod, lamp of Aladdin, magic carpet, seven-league boots; magic ring; wishing –, Fortunatus's- cap.

994. Sorcerer.—N. sorcerer, magician; thaumat-, the-urgist; conjuror, necromancer, seer, wizard, witch; fairy etc. 980; *lamia*, hag, warlock, charmer, exorcist, voodoo, mage, diviner, dowser; cunning| –, medicine- ; man, witch doctor; Shaman, figure-flinger, ecstatica, medium, *clairvoyant*, mesmerist, hypnotist; *deus ex machinâ*; astrologer; soothsayer etc. 513.

Katerfelto, Cagliostro, Merlin, Comus, Mesmer, Rosicrucian; Hecate, Circe, Lilith, siren, weird sisters; witch of Endor.

995. Churchdom.—N. church, -dom; ministry, apostleship, priesthood, prelacy, hierarchy, church government, christendom, pale of the church.

clerical-, sacerdotal-, episcopalian-, ultramontan-ism; Theocracy; ecclesiolog-y, -ist; priestcraft, *odium theologicum*.

monach-ism, -y; monasticism, monkhood.

[Ecclesiastical offices and dignities] pontificate, primacy, archbishopric, archiepiscopacy; prelacy; bishop-ric, -dom; episcop-ate, -acy; see, diocese; deanery, stall; canon-ry, -icate; prebend, -aryship; benefice, incumbency, glebe, advowson, living, cure, – of souls; rectorship; vicar-iate, -ship; pastor-ate, -ship; deacon-ry, -ship; -curacy; chaplain, -cy, -ship; cardinal-ate, -ship; abbacy, presbytery.

holy orders, ordination, institution, consecration, induction, reading in, preferment, translation, presentation.

popedom, pàpacy; the -Vatican, – apostolic see, – see of Rome; religious sects etc. 984.

council etc. 696; conclave, college of cardinals, convocation, synod, consistory, chapter, vestry, presbytery; sanhedrim, *congé d'élire*; ecclesiastical courts, consistorial court, court of Arches.

V. call, ordain, induct, prefer, translate, consecrate, present, elect, bestow.

take -orders, – the veil, – vows.

Adj. ecclesi-astical, -ological; clerical, sacerdotal, priestly, prelatical, pastoral, ministerial, capitular, theocratic; hierarchical, archiepiscopal; episcopal, -ian; canonical; mon-astic, -achal; monkish; abbati-al, -cal; pontifical, papal, apostolic; untramontane, priest-ridden.

996. Clergy.—N. clergy, clericals, ministry, priesthood, presbytery, the cloth, the pulpit.

clergyman, divine, ecclesiastic, churchman, priest, presbyter, hierophant, pastor, shepherd, minister, clerk in holy orders; father, – in Christ; *padre*, *abbé*, *curé*; patriarch; reverend; black coat; confessor; sky pilot.

dignitaries of the church; ecclesi-, hier-arch; eminence, reverence, elder, primate, metropolitan, archimandrite, archbishop, bishop, prelate, diocesan, suffragan, dean, subdean, archdeacon, prebendary, canon, rural dean, rector, parson, vicar, perpetual curate, residentiary, beneficiary, incumbent, chaplain, curate, – in charge; deacon, -ess; preacher; lay reader, lecturer; capitular; missionary, propagandist, Jesuit, revivalist, field preacher.

churchwarden, sidesman; clerk, precentor, choir; almoner, *suisse*, verger, beadle, sexton, sacristan; acol-yth, -othyst, -yte; thurifer; chorister, choir boy.

[Roman Catholic priesthood] Pope, *Papa*, Holy

Father, pontiff, high priest, cardinal; ancient –, flamen; confessor, penitentiary; spiritual director.

cenobite, conventual, abbot, prior, monk, friar, lay brother, beadsman, mendicant, pilgrim, palmer; canon-regular, -secular; Jesuit, Franciscan, Friars minor, Minorites; Observant, Capuchin, Dominican, Carmelite; Augustinian; Gilbertine; Austin-, Black-, White-, Grey-, Crossed-, Crutched- Friars; Bonhomme, Carthusian, Benedictine, Cistercian, Trappist, Cluniac, Premonstratensian, Maturine; Templar, Hospitaller.

abb-, prior-, canon-ess; mother superior; *religieuse*, nun, sister, *beguine*, novice, postulant.

[Under the Jewish dispensation] prophet, priest, high priest, Levite; Rabbi, -n; scribe.

[Mohammedan etc.] mullah, ulema, imauam, sheik; so-fi, -phi; mufti, hadji, muezzin, dervish; fakir, -quir; brahmin, gooroo, druid, bonze, santon, abdal, Lama, talapoin, caloyer etc.

V. take orders etc. 995.

Adj. the –, the very –, the Right- Reverend; ordained, in orders, called to the ministry.

997. Laity.—N. laity, flock, fold, congregation, assembly, brethren, people.

temporality, secularization.

layman, civilian; parishioner, catechumen; secularist.

V. secularize.

Adj. secular, lay, laical, civil, temporal, profane.

998. Rite.—N. rite; ceremon-y, -ial; ordinance, observance, function, duty; form, -ulary; solemnity, sacrament; incantation etc. (*spell*) 993; service, psalmody etc. (*worship*) 990; liturgies.

ministration; preach-ing, -ment; predication, sermon, homily, exhortation, lecture, discourse, pastoral.

baptism, christening, chrism; immersion; baptismal regeneration; font; circumcision.

confirmation; imposition –, laying on- of hands; churching, purification, ordination etc. (*churchdom*) 995; excommunication.

Eucharist, Lord's supper, communion; the –, the holy- sacrament; celebration, high celebration; *missa cantata*; offertory; introit; consecration; con-, tran-substantiation; real presence; elements, bread and wine; mass; high –, low –, dry- mass.

matrimony etc. 903; burial etc. 363; visitation of the sick.

seven sacraments, impanation, extreme unction, last rites, *viaticum*, invocation of saints, canonization, transfiguration, auricular confession; fasting; maceration, flagellation, sackcloth and ashes; penance etc. (*atonement*) 952; absolution; telling of beads, reciting the rosary, processional; thurification, incense, holy water, aspersion.

relics, rosary, beads, reliquary, host, cross, rood, crucifix, pax, pix, pyx, *agnus Dei*, censer, thurible, patera, urceole; chalice, patten, Holy Grail, sangrail; seven-branch candle stick, monstrance, sacring bell.

ritual, rubric, canon, ordinal; liturgy, prayer-book, book of common prayer, pietas, euchology, litany, lectionary; missal, breviary, mass-book, bead-roll.

psalter; psalm –, hymn- book; hymn-al, -ology; psalmody.

ritual-, ceremonial-ism; sabbat-ism, -arianism; ritualist, sabbatarian.

holyday, feast, fast; Sabbath, Passover, Pentecost; Advent, Christmas, Noel, Epiphany, Lent, Shrove Tuesday, Ash Wednesday, Maundy Thursday; Passion –, Holy- week; Good Friday, Easter, Ascension Day, Whitsuntide; Trinity Sunday, Corpus Christi; All-Saints' –, – Souls'- Day; Candle-, Lam-, Martin-, Michael-mas; hogmanay; Ramadan, -zan; Bairam etc. etc.

V. perform service, do duty, minister, officiate, baptize, dip, sprinkle; confirm, lay hands on; give –, administer –, take –, receive –, attend –, partake of- the -sacrament, – communion; communicate; celebrate mass; administer –, receive- extreme unction; anele, shrive, absolve, confess; do penance; genuflect; cross oneself, make the sign of the cross.

excommunicate, ban with bell, book and candle.

preach, sermonize, predicate, lecture.

Adj. ritual, -istic; ceremonial, liturgic; baptismal, eucharistical; paschal.

999. Canonicals.—N. canonicals, vestments; robe, gown, Geneva gown, frock, pallium, surplice, cassock, dalmatic, scapulary, cope, scarf, tunicle, chasuble, alb, *alba*, stole; fan-on, -nel; tonsure, cowl, hood; calo-te, -tte; bands; capouch, amice, orarium, ephod; apron, lawn sleeves, pontificals, pall; miter, tiara, triple crown; shovel –, cardinal's- hat; biretta; crosier; pastoral staff; costume etc. 225.

1000. Temple.—N. place of worship; house of -God, – prayer.

temple, cathedral, minister, church, kirk, chapel, meeting-house, bethel, tabernacle, conventicle, *basilica*, fane, holy place, chantry, oratory.

synagogue; mosque; marabout; pantheon; pagoda; joss-house; dagobah, tope; kiosk.

parsonage, rectory, vicarage, manse, deanery, glebe, church house; Vatican; bishop's palace; Lambeth.

altar, shrine, sanctuary, Holy of Holies, *sanctum sanctorum*, sacrarium, -isty; communion –, holy –, Lord's- table; table of the Lord; pyx; baptistery, font; piscina, stoup; aumbry; sedile; reredos; rood-loft, – screen; jube.

chancel, quire, choir, nave, aisle, transept, lady chapel, vestry, crypt, cloisters, porch; triforum, clerestory, churchyard, *golgotha*, calvary, Easter sepulcher; stall, pew, sitting; pulpit, ambo, lectern, reading-desk, confessional, prothesis, credence, baldachin, *baldacchino*; jesse, apse, belfry; chapter-house; presbytery.

monastery, priory, abbey, friary, convent, nunnery, cloister.

Adj. claustral, cloistered; monast-ic, -erial; conventual.

INDEX

The numbers refer to the headings under which the words or phrases occur. When the same word or phrase may be used in various senses, the several headings under which it, or its synonyms, will be found, according to those meanings, are indicated by the words printed in Italics. These words in Italics are not intended to explain the meaning of the word or phrase to which they are annexed, but only to assist in the required reference.

When the word given in the Index is itself the title or heading of a category, the number of reference is printed in blacker type, thus: **abode 189.**

A

D

K

M

T